AF784997

Intermediate Accounting: MANAGEMENT DECISIONS AND FINANCIAL ACCOUNTING REPORTS

Stephen P. Baginski
Kelley School of Business
Indiana University, Bloomington

John M. Hassell
Kelley School of Business
Indiana University, Indianapolis

South-Western College Publishing
Thomson Learning™

Australia • Canada • Denmark • Japan • Mexico • New Zealand • Philippines
Puerto Rico • Singapore • South Africa • Spain • United Kingdom • United States

Intermediate Accounting: Management Decisions and Financial Accounting Reports,
By Stephen P. Baginski and John M. Hassell

Publisher: Dave Shaut
Acquisitions Editor: Rochelle Kronzek
Senior Developmental Editor: Sara Wilson
Marketing Manager: Jennifer Codner
Production Editor: Tamborah E. Moore
Media Technology Editor: Diane von Bakel
Media Production Editor: Lora Craver
Manufacturing Coordinator: Doug Wilke
Internal Design: Michael J. Stratton
Cover Design: Michael J. Stratton
Production House: Litten Editing and Production (LEAP), Inc.
Compositor: GGS Information Services, Inc.
Printer: West Group

COPYRIGHT ©2001 by South-Western College Publishing, a division of Thomson Learning.
The Thomson Learning logo is a registered trademark used herein under license.

All Rights Reserved. No part of this work covered by the copyright hereon may be reproduced or used in any form or by any means—graphic, electronic, or mechanical, including photocopying, recording, taping, or information storage and retrieval systems—without the written permission of the publisher.

Printed in the United States of America
1 2 3 4 5 03 02 01 00

For more information, contact South-Western College Publishing, 5101 Madison Road, Cincinnati, Ohio, 45227, or find us on the Internet at http://www.swcollege.com

For permission to use material from this text or product, contact us by
- **telephone: 1-800-730-2214**
- **fax: 1-800-730-2215**
- **web: http://www.thomsonrights.com**

Library of Congress Cataloging-in-Publication Data
Baginski, Stephen P., 1957–
Intermediate Accounting: Management decisions and financial accounting reports / Stephen P. Baginski, John M. Hassell.
p. cm.
Includes index.
ISBN 0-538-84086-2 (alk. paper)
1. Accounting. I. Hassell, John M. II. Title.
HF5635.B1415 2000
658.15′11—dc21 00-032239

This book is printed on acid-free paper.

About the Authors

Stephen P. Baginski

Steve Baginski is a Professor of Accounting and PricewaterhouseCoopers Fellow at Indiana University's Kelley School of Business, where he teaches MBA Financial Statement Analysis, MBA Managerial Accounting, and Intermediate Financial Accounting. Prior to his Indiana University appointment, Professor Baginski taught at Illinois State University, the University of Illinois, Northeastern University, and Florida State University. During his career, he has taught nearly every offering in both financial and managerial accounting at both the undergraduate and masters levels. In addition, he currently teaches MBA Financial Accounting in the Executive Education Program at Washington University in St. Louis. He has won several teaching awards including the Teaching Excellence Award given annually to the top 12 teachers at Florida State University as determined by alumni, students, and colleagues.

Professor Baginski has published articles in a variety of journals including *The Accounting Review*, *Journal of Accounting Research*, *Contemporary Accounting Research*, *The Journal of Risk and Insurance*, *Quarterly Review of Finance and Economics*, *Review of Quantitative Finance and Accounting*, and *Advances in Accounting*. His research deals primarily with the causes and consequences of voluntary management disclosures of earnings forecasts, but it also examines a variety of issues related to the usefulness of financial accounting reports.

Professor Baginski enjoys playing basketball and golf and is heavily involved in coaching youth sports, including Babe Ruth baseball, girls basketball, and girls softball.

John M. Hassell

John Hassell is Professor of Accounting at Indiana University's Kelley School of Business, Indianapolis. Prior to his Kelley School of Business appointment, Professor Hassell taught at Florida State University, The University of Texas at Arlington, and the University of Utah. Professor Hassell's primary teaching emphasis is financial accounting. During his career, he has taught at the undergraduate, masters, and doctoral levels, and he primarily teaches intermediate accounting.

Professor Hassell has published articles in a wide variety of journals including *The Accounting Review*; *Contemporary Accounting Research*; *Accounting, Organizations and Society*; *European Journal of Operational Research*; *Review of Quantitative Finance and Accounting*; *Journal of Accounting Education*; and *Advances in Accounting*. His research interests deal primarily with the topics of voluntary management disclosures and accounting education issues.

In their free time, Professor Hassell and Barbara, an Associate Professor of Management at the Kelley School of Business, Indianapolis, and his wife of 19 years, enjoy reading, movies, Indiana University and Indianapolis Colts football games, the theater, and daily walks with their two black Labrador Retrievers.

To Our Families

Lynn, Drew, and Kelly

Steve

Barbara, Geoff, and Matt

John

Preface

The past decade has witnessed a great deal of change in the way in which accounting educators instruct business students in the accounting discipline. Less emphasis is placed on the detailed mechanics of accounting, and more emphasis is placed on analytical and interpretive skills. In addition, the relationships between business decisions and accounting and between accounting and investment decisions have taken on increased importance as professional firms broaden the scope of their services and corporations break down traditional job definitions, replacing accountants, finance professionals, and other functional job definitions with "business problem solvers."

Accounting teachers have taken many approaches to retain the rigor of technical accounting, while achieving integration of accounting education with a more general business education. These efforts include custom design of courses beyond principles of accounting for nonaccounting majors, both at the undergraduate and graduate (MBA) levels, and a relatively recent move at some schools to shorten the intermediate accounting sequence (at the undergraduate level) from two semesters to one semester, both for accounting majors and nonmajors. **Our purpose is to assist educators and students by providing a text that will allow an exploration of intermediate accounting topics in a one-semester course. The following sections describe how we achieve this goal.**

Linking Internal and External Decision Makers

As illustrated in the following diagram, financial reporting represents the link between managers' decisions and investor and creditor decisions:

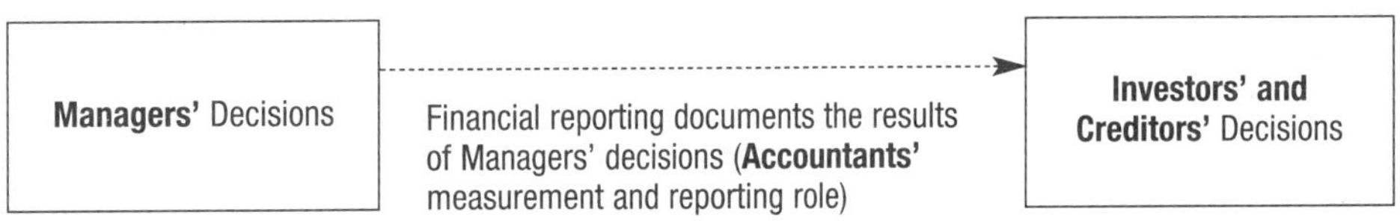

External parties such as investors and creditors are interested in the current and future financial condition of a firm. However, these investors and creditors are separated from management and thus do not observe the day-to-day decisions of managers. **Our presentation helps students understand that accounting is the communication link between managerial decisions and these external parties.** This textbook has been created to support the study of financial reporting from the viewpoint of one or more of the three parties represented in the diagram: managers, accountants, and investors and creditors.

Focusing on Management Decisions that Affect Financial Statements

We have written this text primarily from the point of view of *managers who wish to understand how their decisions are reflected in financial statements.* We take the cash-based financing, investing, and operating decisions made by management and transform them into financial statements through the accountant's measurement and communication process. For example, the following illustrates the financial statement effects of a $100,000 credit sale with $2,000 in cash discounts not taken. The cash discounts not taken are reported as interest revenue.

EXHIBIT 8 Example 9. Baumgart Co. Financial Statements

Statement of Cash Flows

Operating Activities	
Collections from customers	$ 98,000
Interest receipts	2,000
Total cash inflows	$100,000

Balance Sheet

Assets		**Liabilities**	
Current assets:		**Owners' Equity**	
Cash	$100,000 ↑	Retained earnings (through effect	
Inventory	60,000 ↓	on net income)*	$40,000 ↑

Income Statement*

Sales	$98,000
Cost of goods sold	(60,000)
Gross margin	$38,000
Financial revenues, (expenses), gains, and (losses):	
Interest revenue	2,000
Net income	$40,000

Statement of Owners' Equity

Net income*	$40,000 ↑

*Ignores effect of income taxes

See Chapter 9, page 355.

Our presentation is built around management decisions related to three types of activities: financing activities, investing activities, and operating activities. The text starts with an introduction section, Section I (Chapter 1 and Module A), From Decisions to Financial Statements, which reviews basic information from an accounting principles course (more review is provided in Appendices A and B). The remaining sections are organized around the three types of managerial decisions: Section II (Chapters 2–5 and Module B), How *Financing Decisions* Are Reflected in Financial Statements; Section III (Chapters 6–8 and Module C), How *Investment Decisions* Are Reflected in Financial Statements, and Section IV (Chapters 9–12 and Modules D and E), How *Operating Decisions* Are Reflected in Financial Statements.

Focusing on Investor and Creditor Points of View

Students interested in studying financial reporting from the investor and creditor point of view are provided with links between financial statements and underlying business decisions throughout the text. In addition, financial statement analysis modules follow each major section. External parties who wish to understand the effects of managerial decisions of a particular company do not have access to the company's detailed, internal data. However, external parties do have access to publicly available financial statements, which aggregate and report the effects of thousands of managerial decisions. Financial statement analysis tools are used by external parties to help understand and assess the effects of the collective decisions made by managers. The modules introduce ratio analysis, selected pro forma adjustments by analysts, and models relating to valuation and credit extension.

The text has five financial statement analysis modules. The first module (A) provides an overview of financial statement analysis. The next three modules (B, C, and D) discuss how financial statement analysis relates to financing, investing, and operating decisions, respectively. The final module (E) integrates the material in the first four modules, relating the information to specific investor and creditor decision contexts. **These modules (as a group) stand alone from the chapters, and an instructor can choose to omit them without sacrificing continuity.** *It should be emphasized that while this is not a financial statements analysis text, the modules help students understand how financial statements are used by investors and creditors to assess the collective results of managers' decisions.*

For an example of how external user points of view are addressed, Chapter 2 discusses management's debt versus equity choice and the results of the choice on financial statements. Module B analyzes the effects of the choice on specific ratios:

> *Long-term solvency risk* assessment is also affected by capital structure. Consider the following key ratios:
>
> $$\text{Long-term debt to equity} = \text{Long-term debt} \div \text{Shareholders' equity}$$
> $$\text{Long-term debt to total assets} = \text{Long-term debt} \div \text{Total assets}$$
> $$\text{Interest coverage} = \frac{(\text{Income before income taxes} + \text{Interest expense})}{\text{Interest expense}}$$
> $$\text{Operating cash flow to total liabilities} = \text{Operating cash flow} \div \text{Average total liabilities}$$
>
> Clearly, the presence of long-term debt in the capital structure increases the long-term debt to equity and long-term debt to assets ratios. This, in turn, increases the credit analyst's assessment of long-term solvency risk. Higher risk is also indicated by . . .

See Module B, page 193.

Each module provides examples of how analysts can use note information to adjust financial statements:

> . . . The amount reported for 1998, \$3,863,828, represents the tax effects of the cumulative excess of tax depreciation (using an accelerated method) over financial statement depreciation (using straight-line) through time. To find the cumulative excess (instead of the tax effect), we divide \$3,863,828 by the statutory tax rate (35%) to obtain \$11,039,509. This means that, if TCBY had used accelerated depreciation over the years rather than straight-line, then accumulated depreciation, and hence the book values of total assets, would be lower by more than \$11 million.

See Module C, page 325.

Organizing Around Management Decisions: A Unique Approach

Management business decisions lead to accounting measurements and disclosures. Currently, most intermediate accounting texts are organized around a chart of accounts (i.e., cash, receivables, inventory, current liabilities, fixed assets, common stock, etc.) instead of business decisions. The result is a lack of connection between the business decisions that lead to, for example, a repurchase of common stock and the topic of accounting for equity transactions.

Accounting education has been criticized for accounting students' inability to understand what they do in the context of business decisions. **Accordingly, our text is not account-oriented. Instead, the emphasis is on taking cash flow-based management decisions and applying the accountant's measurement and disclosure rules to create financial statements.**

For example, Chapter 6 illustrates a business decision (capital budgeting) and how accountants use accrual financial statements to report the results of that decision through time. The following is a portion of that presentation:

TURNER CORPORATION
Balance Sheets
December 31
(Effects of machinery and patent activities)

	2001	2002	2003	2004	2005
Assets					
Current assets					
Cash	$(677,000)	$(504,000)	$(331,000)	$(158,000)	$245,000
Property, plant and equipment					
Machinery	$800,000	$800,000	$800,000	$800,000	
Less accumulated depreciation	(100,000)	(200,000)	(300,000)	(400,000)	
	$700,000	$600,000	$500,000	$400,000	
Intangible assets					
Patent (less accumulated amortization)	40,000	30,000	20,000	10,000	0
Total assets	$ 63,000	$126,000	$189,000	$252,000	$245,000
Liabilities and Owners' Equity					
Owners' equity					
Retained earnings	$ 63,000	$126,000	$189,000	$252,000	$245,000

See Chapter 6, page 232.

We believe that this business decision focus will be useful to the different student groups interested in learning about intermediate accounting topics. Students, both undergraduate and MBA, who primarily have a **management focus** will study how their decisions are communicated to investors and creditors in financial statements. Students whose primary focus is **finance** will obtain both the understanding of how decisions lead to financial statements and how financial statements can be used in financial analysis. Finally, the approach will provide **accounting** students with (1) a broader understanding of business decisions that generate financial reports, thus aiding their ability to measure the effects of these decisions, (2) technical knowledge about accounting measurement and disclosure, and (3) an understanding of how accounting reports are interpreted by the investors and creditors, thus allowing accounting students to understand how their measurement and reporting decisions affect users.

Demonstrating the Effects of Management Decisions on Several Accounting Periods

A key feature of our text is that it illustrates how a management decision affects financial statements of current and subsequent accounting periods. In other intermediate books, the focus is almost always on the current period only because the material is presented as transaction-based rather than decision-based. **Our examples and end-of-chapter problems provide sets of financial statements that illustrate multi-year effects of decisions.** The following, for example, reflects the multi-year income statement effects of bonds payable:

. . . of the effective interest rate. The accrual financial statements are able to reflect these situations through use of the elements of accrual accounting. The income statement disclosures appear as follows:

EXHIBIT 3 Example 2. Income Statement

WORTHY CO.
Income Statement

	2001	2002	2003	2004	2005	2006
Financial revenues, (expenses), gains, and (losses)						
Interest expense	(107,023)	(109,065)	(111,353)	(113,916)	(116,786)	
Bond issue expense	(2,000)	(2,000)	(2,000)	(2,000)	(2,000)	

See Chapter 3, page 106.

Providing an income statement, balance sheet, and cash flow statement that reflect the full effects of a decision allows students to gain a deeper understanding of what information about business decisions will be communicated over time. A key feature of using examples that reflect the results of a decision over several periods is that it allows us to help the student reconcile the cash flow and accrual accounting models by clearly demonstrating that the two models lead to the same overall results over time but differ with respect to how the two models report the effects of decisions in particular years.

Providing Maximum Flexibility

Disagreement exists currently among accounting educators about how big a role journal entries should have in the accounting education process. While many accounting educators believe that journal entries are necessary for accounting majors, others believe that it is not necessary to use journal entries to teach accounting to nonaccounting majors. Almost all current intermediate texts use the pedagogical technique of simultaneously discussing a transaction and illustrating the journal entry to record it. **In contrast, we first discuss the measurement and disclosure of the effects of management decisions, and then, in a shaded box following each example, we show the journal entries and selected key ledger accounts.**

EXAMPLE 3 Journal Entries

9/1/01 Bond issue:							
Cash		891,857					
Discount on Bonds Payable		108,143					
Bonds Payable			1,000,000				
Bond Issue Costs		10,000					
Cash			10,000				
*Year-end interest accruals**	*12/31/01*		*12/31/02*		*12/31/03*		. . .
Interest Expense	35,674		36,355		37,118		
Discount on Bonds Payable		5,674		6,355		7,118	. . .
Interest Payable		30,000		30,000		30,000	

*Shown for the first three years. The amounts for interest expense and discount on bonds payable equal one-third (4 months/12 months) of the amounts in the effective interest amortization table.

See Chapter 3, page 112.

Separating the discussion of the financial statement effects of management decisions from the illustration of journal entries permits the instructor to tailor the text to the desired audience by either including or excluding coverage of journal entries. Additional flexibility is provided by formatting end-of-chapter problems with a journal entry option so that journal entries may be included or omitted. Therefore, the course can be presented with no emphasis on journal entries or can include the use of journal entries to record accounting information. As illustrated below, students are required to understand the effects of managerial decisions, and providing journal entries is optional.

> b. *Assuming that the purchase gave Sohn significant influence,* describe the financial statement effects of (1) the purchase, (2) Benard's reporting net income, (3) Benard's declaration and payment of dividends, and (4) the December 31, 2001, increase in market value of stock.
>
> **Journal Entry Option:** Prepare the annual 2001 journal entries to reflect these effects.

See Chapter 8, page 312.

Connecting Students with Actual Financial Statements

Traditional intermediate books are transaction-based and typically may include one set of actual financial statements. Frequently, these financial statements are not used throughout the text, but rather, they stand alone. **To focus students on actual financial statements, we use the annual reports of three major companies on an ongoing basis and also provide excerpts from many other company annual reports.**

- Early on, we use the financial statements of TCBY, Inc., to illustrate basic financial statements.

> ***Balance Sheet Elements***
>
> TCBY's 1998 balance sheet lists $94,452,884 of the element "assets" and an equal amount of claims against those assets represented by the sum of two elements, "liabilities" and stockholders' "equity." TCBY did not present a separate subtotal for liabilities, but one can find the total 1998 liabilities of $18,256,730 by summing current liabilities of $11,984,249, long-term debt of $2,952,634, and deferred income taxes of $3,319,847.
>
> Recall that owners' equity represents a residual claim against net assets. If we take $94,452,884 total assets and subtract total liabilities of $18,256,730, we arrive at total stockholders' equity of $76,196,154. If we divide stockholders' resid- . . .

See Chapter 1, page 14.

- At the end of each chapter, we use Southwest Airlines' annual report to illustrate how management decisions discussed in the chapter are reflected in financial statements.

> ***Leasing and Southwest Airlines' Liabilities***
>
> It is evident that leasing has a significant effect on Southwest Airlines' financial statements. On the liability side, capital leases (including current maturities) constituted 20.9% of Southwest's long-term debt in 1998 ($133,190,000 ÷ $637,671,000, see Note 4), and 20.2% in 1997 ($152,324,000 ÷ $752,324,000). Further, using the balance sheet and information in Note 4, capital leases were . . .

See Chapter 4, page 153.

- We use actual footnotes from various companies throughout the text to illustrate financial statement disclosures related to specific decisions.

The following partial footnotes for Hasbro, Inc., and GenCorp, Inc., (slightly modified) illustrate the conversion of convertible debt.

> **Hasbro, Inc., Note (7) Long-Term Debt:**
>
> Substantially all of Hasbro's 6% Convertible Subordinated Notes were converted into 7,636,562 shares of common stock during the year.
>
> **GenCorp, Inc., Note L (In Part): Long-term Debt and Credit Lines**
>
> During the second quarter, the Company called its $115,000,000, 8% Convertible Subordinated Debentures. In the third quarter, substantially all the Debentures were tendered for conversion into GenCorp common stock at a conversion rate of approximately 62.247 shares of common stock per $1,000 principal amount of debentures.

See Chapter 3, page 119.

- Often, we footnote information about the frequency with which particular items appear in annual reports (e.g., how many companies use the LIFO costing method for inventories).

> 6. Of 600 companies surveyed, the 1999 Accounting Trends & Techniques indicates that 319 companies used LIFO for at least some inventories, while 281 did not use LIFO for any inventories. The following companies reported using the different methods (the number is greater than 600 because firms may use different methods for certain inventories): FIFO, 409; LIFO, 319; weighted-average, 176; other, 40. Firms reported using LIFO for all inventories, 30; 50% or more of inventories, 152; 50% or less of inventories, 95; not determinable, 42; total, 319.

See Chapter 9, page 347.

- In each set of end of chapter problems, a comprehensive problem asks the students to use the 1998 annual report of Texas Instruments (found on our Web site, http://baginski.swcollege.com) to answer a series of questions.

http://

> 15. **Texas Instruments.** The Texas Instruments' 1998 financial statements appear at the text Web site (http://baginski.swcollege.com). Review the income statement (income tax provision, discontinued operations, and extraordinary item), balance sheet (deferred income taxes in current asset and noncurrent liability sections), and income taxes note. After reading this information, answer the following questions. (Be sure to use the financial statement amounts, which are in millions of dollars.)
>   a. What are the ending deferred income tax balances on the balance sheet? What are the total *gross* amounts of total deferred income tax assets? Of total deferred income tax liabilities? What is the amount, if any, . . .

See Chapter 11, page 455.

We believe that after taking the course, students will have meaningful exposure to actual financial statements.

Providing Experience with CFA Exam Questions

Many students who use this textbook will be interested in pursuing finance careers, and many students who use this textbook will eventually decide to pursue the CFA designation. **Accordingly, we provide a Chartered Financial Analyst (CFA) Exam section in the problems at the end of each chapter to help students understand how the material covered in the text may be tested on the CFA exam.** This section contains actual CFA exam questions or questions written by the authors that are similar to CFA exam questions.

CFA Exam-Type Problems

15. Because of a court-imposed settlement, a creditor enters into a debt restructuring agreement on an overdue note receivable of $600,000 plus accrued interest of $32,000. The agreement requires the debtor to pay the creditor $400,000 two years from now, plus annual interest of $40,000 (10 percent is the current rate on an investment in this risk classification). At the time of the restructuring, the debtor must recognize a gain of: (CFA adapted, with slight modifications by author)
    a. $0
    b. $152,000
    c. $200,000
    d. $232,000

See Chapter 5, pages 186–187.

The CFA exam is a national exam for financial professionals. Administered by the ©Association for Investment Management and Research (AIMR). The CFA designation is similar to that of CPA for accountants. AIMR is a global nonprofit organization with 87 societies and chapters and more than 80,000 members and candidates: investment analysts, portfolio managers, and other investment decision makers employed by investment firms, banks, broker/dealers, investment company complexes, and insurance companies. The association's mission is to serve investors through its membership by providing global leadership in investment education, sustaining high standards of professional conduct, and administering the CFA Program. For more information about AIMR, contact its Web site (http://www.aimr.org).

http://

The CFA exam is administered once each year in early June. The exam is a three-part exam (Level I, Level II, and Level III), and only one part can be taken during any year. Each part must be passed before the candidate may take the next part. Both the Level I and Level II exams have a section devoted to financial statement analysis, which relies on subject matter normally taught in three courses in an undergraduate accounting curriculum: Intermediate Accounting I, Intermediate Accounting II, and Advanced Accounting. The information in *Management Decisions and Financial Accounting Reports* effectively covers the information contained in Intermediate I and Intermediate II accounting courses.

Providing a Comprehensive Instructor Support Package

- **Instructor's Manual (0-538-84087-0).** This author-created supplement contains guidance, check figures, chapter and module outlines, a guide tying the learning objectives to the assignments, and complete, verified solutions to all assignments.
- **Solutions Transparencies (0-324-02367-7).** Key solutions to problems have been enlarged and reproduced for use for in-class presentations.
- **Test Bank (0-538-84088-9).** Written by Myrtle Clark, University of Kentucky, the test bank contains verified multiple-choice items and short problems for all chapters and modules. The test items are coded for difficulty level and tie to learning objectives.
- **ExamView Testing Software (0-538-87583-6).** This easy-to-use electronic version of the test bank allows for editing of existing items and addition of new ones. Items may be selected in a number of ways and randomized as needed. Requires Windows® 3.1 or higher or Windows® NT 4.0.
- **Web Site (http://baginski.swcollege.com).** At our Web site, you will find a secure instructor resources section that contains PowerPoint® presentation slides for in-class use, the Instructor's Manual, the Texas Instruments 1998 annual report, sample syllabi, check figures, updates as needed, and an e-mail link to the authors.

In addition to the PowerPoint presentation slides and the Texas Instruments 1998 annual report, students will find hotlinks to key locations identified in the text with an icon http:// and interactive quizzes that will assist learning.

Acknowledging Assistance

Many people have contributed helpful ideas and feedback during the development of *Management Decisions and Financial Accounting Reports*. In particular, we thank the following reviewers:

Arijit Aukherji, *University of Minnesota*
Walter W. Austin, *Mercer University*
Clifford D. Brown, *Bentley College*
Myrtle Clark, *University of Kentucky*
Lola W. Dudley, *Eastern Illinois University*
Ken Harper, *DeAnza College*
Jan Heddaeus, *Muskingum Area Technical College*
Becky Jones, *Baylor University*
Charles J. F. Leflar, *University of Arkansas*
Patricia G. Lobingier, *Wake Forest University*
Hong S. Pak, *California State Polytechnic University—Pomona*
Kannan Raghunandan, *University of Massachusetts—Dartmouth*
Barbara Reider, *University of Alaska—Anchorage*
Joe Schramer, *University of St. Thomas*
Wayne H. Shaw, *Southern Methodist University*
Donn Vickrey, *University of San Diego*
John Waters, *Colorado State University*

Many others deserve thanks and recognition for the contributions made to this project. First, we thank all those who prepared ancillary materials. Second, successful completion of this project would not have been possible without the committment to excellence of the editorial, design, and marketing staffs. We especially want to thank Sara Wilson, Rochelle Kronzek, Jennifer Codner, Tamborah Moore, and Malvine Litten for their professional assistance. Finally, we appreciate the rights to provide students with full sets of real-world financial statements conveyed to us by TCBY, Inc., Southwest Airlines, and Texas Instruments.

Steve Baginski and John Hassell

Brief Contents

Contents

Section II

Appendices

I

From Decisions to Financial Statements—A Review of Basic Concepts

Objectives

1 Explain why accounting information is important in financial markets.
2 Identify three kinds of management decisions reflected in the primary financial statements.
3 Explain the role cash flow plays in maximizing investor wealth.
4 Define the fundamental elements of accrual financial statements.
5 Arrange the financial statement elements into the primary accrual-based financial statements.
6 Explain the interrelationships among financial statements.
7 Identify the timing of cash inflows and outflows and their effects on financial statement elements.
8 Explain why financial statements are based on accrual accounting.
9 Describe the basic format of the cash flow statement.
10 Describe the detailed structures used for and the attributes measured in the balance sheet.
11 Describe the detailed structure used for and the attributes used in the income statement.
12 Explain the relationship between the capital maintenance and the transactions approaches to income measurement.
13 Describe the accounting standard-setting environment.

Chapter 1

Management Decisions and Financial Statements

The Role of Accounting Information in Financial Markets

1 Explain why accounting information is important in financial markets.

Access to capital markets is critical in today's corporate environment. Firms require capital to purchase property, plant and equipment, copyrights, patents, franchise rights, and many other items that are needed for production and distribution of products or services. It is rare when an individual or a small group of closely-knit individuals has the financial ability to make these purchases. Therefore, startup enterprises and more established firms look to others for necessary capital.

Fortunately, this demand for capital is met in organized financial markets. In order to obtain cash, firms issue rights to ownership (e.g., common stocks) and promises to repay funds (e.g., bonds). Investors in common stock and creditors holding bonds trade these instruments with other investors and creditors on organized stock and bond exchanges or in private transactions. The end result is that firms obtain necessary capital to fund operations while investors and creditors earn returns on equity and debt investments.

For financial markets to function smoothly, financial information needs to be available. Take the market for common stock as an example. When investors evaluate whether to buy common stock, they identify their potential cash flows from the investment. The cash flows from an investment in common stock are future dividends and the final cash flow received when the stock is sold at the future prevailing market price. Theoretically, at any time, the market price of stock is equal to the present value of all future dividends on the stock.[1] Therefore, the investor views the cash flows from an investment in common stock as a stream

1. This is the general dividend valuation model discussed in most finance textbooks. For example, see Moyer, McGuigan, and Kretlow, *Contemporary Financial Management, 8th ed.* (Cincinnati, Ohio: South-Western College Publishing, 2001).

of future dividends. Finance theory teaches us that in order to determine how much to pay for the stock, investors need two pieces of information about that dividend stream: the expected level of future dividends and the risk of receiving future dividends.[2]

The input for the prediction of the level and risk of future dividends comes from several sources; these sources include the company's past stream of dividends, predictions about the future state of the economy, and predictions about competition in the company's industry. But a key input to the prediction process is the set of information provided by the company's primary financial statements. These statements describe the resources at the company's command (assets) and indicate who has claims against those resources (creditors or owners). The statements also describe how the company's resources have changed over time from earnings and transactions with owners. In short, analysis of these financial statements provides an assessment of the future earnings potential and dividend paying ability of the firm.

It is imperative, then, that operating and financial managers understand how their decisions are reflected in financial statements. Investors and creditors demand information, and financial statements are an important means of providing it. Accountants measure, summarize, and communicate the results of managerial decisions to outside decision makers and thus facilitate the capital allocation process that occurs in financial markets.

Three Kinds of Management Decisions

2 Identify three kinds of management decisions reflected in the primary financial statements.

Financial statements reflect three fundamental kinds of decisions made by managers that result in activities by the company:

- Financing activities
- Investing activities
- Operating activities

***Financing activities* involve raising capital to fund investment and operating activities.** Firms issue common stock, preferred stock, stock options, long-term notes, bonds, and other hybrid securities (e.g., convertible debt) in order to obtain cash. Firms then use the cash to engage in investing activities. ***Investing activities* include the purchase or creation of tangible and intangibles items.** Tangible assets include land, operating plants, rental properties, equipment, and delivery vehicles. Intangible items refer to assets such as copyrights, patents, and franchise rights. Finally, the productive or service capacity created by investment is used to acquire raw materials and other inventory items and to produce and deliver products or services to customers. This final group of ***operating activities* includes the more obvious decisions about when to purchase inventory and how to pay for purchases, whether to make or buy inventory, how to implement credit policy, and how to establish distribution channels.** This kind of activity also includes less obvious but equally important decisions such as employee compensation (e.g., setting levels of executive compensation, deciding whether to establish a pension plan, and selecting appropriate health-care plans).

Each of the three primary activities of the firm has either an immediate or a delayed effect on *each* primary financial statement of the firm. A complete set of financial statements contains at least four financial statements: the income statement (also known as the statement of earnings), the balance sheet (also known as the statement of financial position), the statement of stockholders' equity, and the state-

2. Later in the text (Module E), we consider alternative valuation approaches such as free cash flow discounting and abnormal earnings discounting (i.e., the Edwards/Bell/Ohlson model).

ment of cash flows.[3] The first three financial statements are accrual based, while the fourth is based on cash flows. *The major objective of this chapter is to show how financing, investing, and operating activities affect each of these interrelated financial statements.*

Management Decisions to Maximize Investors' Wealth

3 Explain the role cash flow plays in maximizing investor wealth.

Managers are constantly faced with decisions on how to best acquire and employ resources. In order to make correct decisions, managers need a goal or "an objective function" to maximize. In profit-seeking enterprises, the objective function is owner wealth. Managers weigh alternative courses of action and choose the action that maximizes owner wealth.[4]

Consider a sole proprietorship, where the manager is the owner of the firm. Any action taken by the manager to maximize owner wealth also maximizes the manager's wealth. In today's corporation, however, managers face somewhat of a conflict in choosing the objective function to maximize. Through access to capital markets, management and ownership are separated. As a result, management wealth maximization is not perfectly aligned with owner wealth maximization. Therefore, management incentive structures must be created to ensure that managers make decisions to maximize owner (i.e., shareholder) wealth rather than manager wealth. At this point, we will assume that these incentive structures have been created, so we can proceed with the idea that managers make decisions in order to maximize shareholder wealth. But, in Chapter 12, we discuss this critical topic further in the context of executive compensation.

Owners have the right to receive the value of the assets of the firm after all liabilities have been paid. This right is evidenced by the possession of shares of the firm's common stock. *We assume throughout this text that a firm's shares are held by many owners and that this situation has been achieved by issuing common stock in capital markets.* The concepts that we discuss also apply to sole proprietorships, in which ownership rests with one individual, and partnerships, in which ownership rests with a few individuals.

To maximize the value of investors' wealth, managers should make decisions to maximize the present value of all future dividend cash flows *to investors*. This goal is accomplished if managers choose to invest in projects that maximize the present value of cash flows *to the firm*, because these cash flows can be paid out in dividends or reinvested to create additional future cash flows.

It would appear, then, that the primary financial statements of a firm would communicate directly a firm's current-period cash flows to investors. This is not the case, however. Of the four primary financial statements, only the statement of cash flows directly communicates the cash flows of the firm, listing the cash inflows and outflows for the current period. The other three financial statements are prepared under accrual-basis accounting. This basis seeks to measure and link effort and accomplishment rather than match cash inflows and outflows. ***Accrual-basis accounting* records revenues when they are earned, rather than when cash is received, and records expenses as they are incurred, rather than when cash is paid.** Instead of describing cash inflows and cash outflows, the accrual-based financial statements employ the *elements of accrual accounting* as their building blocks.

3. A fifth statement, a statement of comprehensive income, may be presented separately or as part of the statement of stockholders' equity. Technically, a statement of retained earnings is required rather than a statement of stockholders' equity, but most companies prepare the broader statement of stockholders' equity.

4. In this text, we assume that wealth maximization is the goal of the firm. Of course, other objective functions are possible such as to maximize employment or maximize services provided. Explanations and examples throughout the text are consistent with a wealth maximization goal.

The Elements of Accrual Accounting Financial Statements

4 Define the fundamental elements of accrual financial statements.

The elements of accrual-based financial statements are as follows:[5]

- Assets
- Liabilities
- Equity
- Revenues
- Expenses
- Gains
- Losses
- Investments by owners
- Distributions to owners

Each element is defined in this chapter. The definitions are provided by the Financial Accounting Standards Board's (FASB's) Conceptual Framework Project.[6] When reading the discussion and examples that follow each definition, it is important to concentrate on how each element of accrual accounting differs from the corresponding cash flow concept.

Assets

Definition: ***Assets*** **are probable future economic benefits obtained or controlled by a particular entity as a result of past transactions or events.**

When we think of assets, we often think of cash. But the key term in the asset definition that broadens the definition beyond cash inflows is "probable." Cash received is a *certain* economic benefit. But during the operating cycle of the firm (in which a firm begins and ends with cash), assets are created that have different probabilities of realization. Take, for example, the following simple operating cycle:

Cash ⟶ Inventory ⟶ Accounts Receivable ⟶ Cash

In this operating cycle, a corporation uses cash to acquire inventory. At that point, the probability of receiving economic benefits has changed because the certain benefits of cash have been translated into possibly less certain benefits of holding inventory. The benefits are less probable because additional events the sale of inventory and the collection of accounts receivable—must occur before cash inflows result. Nonetheless, inventory is an asset because its sale and the subsequent collection of the receivable is expected, although possibly not certain.

The next step in the simple operating cycle is a sale of inventory on credit. The company delivers the inventory to the customer, and the customer promises to pay at a future date. Therefore, the company records a sale and an accounts receivable. At this point, the probability of cash collection has risen considerably. Accounts receivable is an asset because it represents probable future economic benefits. Also important for later discussion, the amount of cash to be collected has increased because firms normally sell goods at prices higher than cost.

Another key term in the asset definition is "future." The timing of the cash inflows helps accountants distinguish between those items having future benefits (beyond the current period) and those items having only current period benefits. These latter items are treated as expenses or losses and are discussed in conjunction with the definitions of those two elements.

The definition also describes assets as being "controlled by a particular entity." Thus, a neighboring park at which employees can eat lunch on sunny days and a business-oriented local government, while clearly of benefit to the firm, are not assets of the firm because the firm does not control them.

Finally, the definition states that assets arise from "past transactions or events." In the simple operating cycle example, the asset "inventory" arose from a

5. An additional element, comprehensive income, is not discussed in detail in this chapter. It is explained later in the text.

6. "Elements of Financial Statements," *Statement of Financial Accounting Concepts* No. 6 (Stamford, Conn.: FASB, December 1985), ix–x.

purchase transaction and the asset "accounts receivable" arose from a credit sales transaction.

Liabilities

Definition: ***Liabilities* are probable future sacrifices of economic benefits arising from present obligations of a particular entity to transfer assets or provide services to other entities in the future as a result of past transactions or events.**

Liabilities represent creditors' claims to the assets of an enterprise. Consistent with the asset definition, liabilities are "probable." The "sacrifice of economic benefits" involves either the transfer of assets to other entities or the performance of services. Wages payable is a liability in which an asset, cash, is to be sacrificed in the future. Unearned rent is a liability that is satisfied by providing the renter with the use of the asset being rented. In all cases, liabilities are satisfied by giving the creditor an asset, by giving the creditor some of the services provided by an asset, or by giving the creditor another claim against assets.

A part of the liability definition that has played a major role in recent controversy is the term "present obligation." Examples of controversial liabilities include pensions and postemployment benefits. Taken literally, present obligation means that the firm "now has a duty" to sacrifice economic benefits. For most liabilities, particularly short-term ones, determining when a firm has a duty to perform is quite simple. However, as we shall discuss in later chapters, the measurement of certain long-term liabilities is sufficiently complex in nature that it is difficult to determine whether the obligation is "present" or whether future events determine the liability's measurement.

Equity

Definition: ***Equity* is the residual interest in the assets of an entity that remains after deducting its liabilities. In a business enterprise, the equity is the ownership interest.**

Equity (i.e., ***owners' equity***) **represents a second kind of claim against assets.** Any "residual interest" that remains after fulfilling the first claim against assets (i.e., liabilities) belongs to the owners. Mathematically, equity equals ***net assets*** **(i.e., assets − liabilities)**; therefore, equity is often referred to as net assets.

Revenues

Definition: ***Revenues* are inflows or other enhancements of assets of an entity or settlement of its liabilities (or a combination of both) during a period from delivering or producing goods, rendering services, or other activities that constitute the entity's ongoing major or central operations.**

While assets, liabilities, and owners' equity represent *levels* (amounts), revenues, expenses, gains, losses, investments by owners, and distributions to owners represent *changes in those levels* (amounts). Note that revenues are defined as "inflows of assets" and "settlements of liabilities." When assets increase or liabilities decrease as a result of "delivering or producing goods, rendering services, or other activities that constitute the entity's ongoing major or central operations," revenues are recognized. A cash sale results in the increase of cash. Therefore, sales revenue is recognized. If a company has an obligation to allow a renter to occupy a building for two months and does so for one month, the obligation decreases by one month, and rent revenue is recognized.

Revenues and cash inflows are not the same. A cash sale increases the asset "cash," and sales revenue is recognized. But a credit sale also triggers sales revenue recognition because the asset "accounts receivable" increases. Revenue recognition occurs because revenues are defined as an increase of assets. Cash is only one of many assets that increase as a result of a company's ongoing operations.

Expenses

Definition: ***Expenses*** **are outflows or other using up of assets or incurrences of liabilities during a period from delivering or producing goods, rendering services, or other activities that constitute the entity's ongoing major or central operations.**

Expenses are the opposites of revenues, occurring when assets go down or liabilities go up. For example, when cash is paid for monthly utilities, the asset "cash" decreases and utilities expense is recognized. When a productive asset such as a machine is used up through wear and tear, the asset account "machinery" is decreased and depreciation expense is recognized. When a production supervisor works one week but is not yet paid, the liability "wages payable" is increased and wages expense is recognized.

Just as revenues and cash inflows differ, expenses and cash outflows are not the same. This is because expenses are defined (in part) as decreases of assets. Cash is only one of many assets that decrease as a result of a company's ongoing operations.

Gains (Losses)

Definition: ***Gains (losses)*** **are increases (decreases) in net assets from peripheral or incidental transactions of an entity and from all other transactions and other events and circumstances affecting the entity during a period except those that result from revenues (expenses) or investments by (distributions to) owners.**

The key distinguishing characteristic of gains and losses is that they arise from "peripheral or incidental transactions." Recall that, in contrast, revenues and expenses arise from "the entity's ongoing major or central operations."

Because gains and losses are not central to the firm's operations, they receive less detailed disclosure than revenues and expenses. For example, consider a firm, such as Kinko's Copies, that produces photocopies. The firm earns revenues by charging customers for these copies. The firm incurs expenses for the use of paper and toner, maintenance on machines, utilities, and employee wages. However, if the firm were to sell one of the copy machines at a profit, it would report a gain rather than revenue. The gain is the difference between the increase in the asset cash and a decrease in the asset machine. The "increase in equity (net assets)" is disclosed as a gain. The firm is in the business of producing and selling copies, not selling copy machines. The nature of the business determines what is considered a primary business activity and what is considered a peripheral activity. A firm can have more than one primary business activity.

Investments by or Distributions to Owners

Definition: ***Investments by owners*** **are increases in net assets of a particular enterprise resulting from transfers to it from other entities of something of value to obtain or increase ownership interest (or equity) in it. Assets are most commonly received as investments by owners, but that which is received may also include services or satisfaction or conversion of liabilities of the enterprise.**

Definition: ***Distributions to owners*** **are decreases in net assets of a particular enterprise resulting from transferring assets, rendering services, or incurring liabilities by the enterprise to owners. Distributions to owners decrease ownership interest (or equity) in an enterprise.**

Stockholders are the owners of the firm. Transactions between stockholders and the firm are classified as investments by owners or distributions to owners. Although these transactions can change assets and liabilities, they are not considered revenues, expenses, gains, or losses. They simply *increase or decrease ownership interest (or equity) in an enterprise.* For example, when a firm issues common stock, owners transfer cash to the firm and the firm issues a stock certificate that provides evidence of owners' rights to the net assets of the firm. Net assets have increased by the amount of owners' investments. When a firm pays dividends to its stockholders, cash decreases by the amount of the distribution.

Although most investments and distributions are cash flows, they are not necessarily so. An owner could invest in a corporation by transferring land to the corporation in exchange for stock. A corporation could distribute the stock of another corporation as a dividend rather than cash. These types of transactions are discussed in further detail in later chapters.

Accrual-Based Financial Statements

5 Arrange the financial statement elements into the primary accrual-based financial statements.

The elements of accrual-based financial statements are arranged into the balance sheet, income statement, and statement of owners' equity as follows:

BALANCE SHEET

Resources	**Claims Against Resources**
Assets	Liabilities (primary claim)
	Owners' equity (residual claim)

INCOME STATEMENT

+	Revenues	(primary business activity)
−	Expenses	(primary business activity)
+	Gains	(peripheral business activity)
−	Losses	(peripheral business activity)
=	Net income	

STATEMENT OF OWNERS' EQUITY

	Beginning owners' equity
+	Net income
+	Investments by owners
−	Distributions to owners
=	Ending owners' equity[7]

The balance sheet provides a listing of resources (i.e., assets) and claims against resources (i.e., liabilities and owners' equity) *at a point in time.* In other words, the balance sheet provides information on *levels* or *quantities* of items. The ***balance sheet equation*** **is assets equals liabilities plus owners' equity (A = L + OE).** Because the balance sheet equation is an algebraic equation, it can be transposed to emphasize the nature of owners' equity:

$$\text{Net assets} = \text{Owners' equity } (A - L = OE).$$

7. In later chapters, we add another item to the reconciliation, other comprehensive income.

The income statement and statement of owners' equity provide a listing of the *changes* or *flows* in the resources and claims against resources (i.e., revenues, expenses, gains, losses, investments by owners, and distributions to owners).

Transactions with outside parties that change net resources (i.e., revenues, expenses, gains, and losses) are included on the income statement. *Transactions with owners* that change net resources (i.e., investments by and distributions to owners) are included on the statement of owners' equity.

The Interrelationships among Financial Statements

6 Explain the interrelationships among financial statements.

The relationships among the three accrual-based financial statements for a company with a 12/31 year-end are depicted in Exhibit 1.

The first column shows balance sheet changes during the year. The owners' equity at 1/1 is equal to assets minus liabilities. During the period, assets and liabilities change. If the changes are from nonowner transactions, they are described as revenues, expenses, gains, and losses on the income statement. If the changes in the assets and liabilities are from owner transactions, they are described as distributions to owners and investments by owners on the statement of owners' equity.

The second column shows that revenues, expenses, gains, and losses are combined into a summary measure of the firm's performance called "net income." Net income is attributed to the owners of the firm and, thus, is also shown as an addition in the statement of owners' equity.

The final column describes how owners' equity changed during the period. The entries in the column are classified by whether the increases in equity were from transactions with nonowners (i.e., net income) or from transactions with owners (i.e., distributions and investments). Note that all changes in net assets on the balance sheet flow to the statement of owners' equity. If the change in net assets was from transactions with nonowners, however, the change is described in detail (i.e., revenues, expenses, gains, and losses) on the income statement before being shown in summary as net income on the statement of owners' equity.

EXHIBIT 1 Interrelationships among Financial Statements

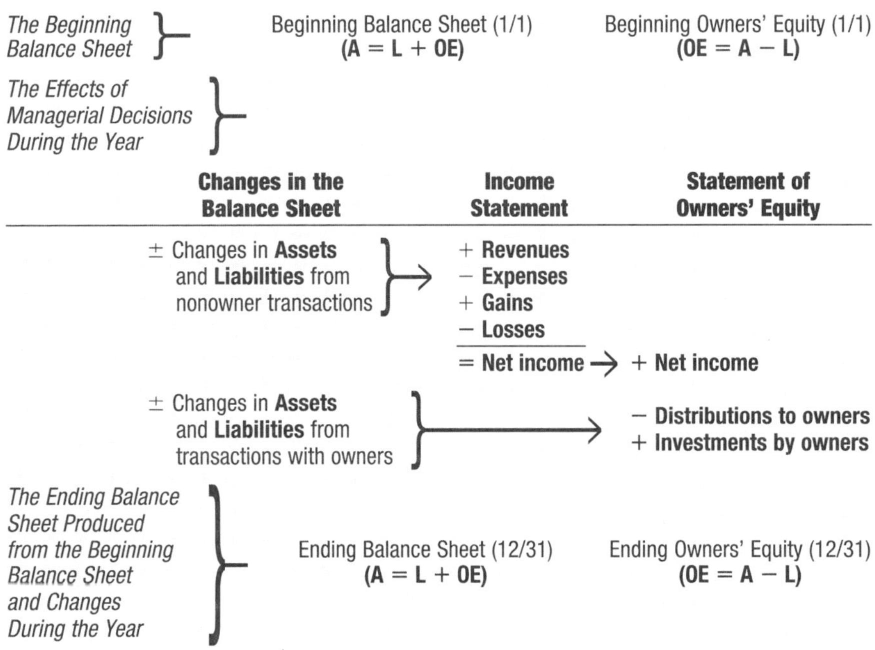

To illustrate the interrelationship of financial statements, consider the situation of a corporation that has raised funds for its operations in two ways, by selling ownership rights (i.e., issuing common stock) and by promising to pay creditors in the bond market (i.e., issuing bonds payable). The shareholders and bondholders each expect a return on their investments; so, the corporation pays cash dividends to shareholders and cash interest to bondholders. The payment of cash for dividends and interest is shown in Exhibit 2 as a decrease in balance sheet assets (Column 1).

EXHIBIT 2 Example of the Interrelationship of Financial Statements

(1) Changes in the Balance Sheet	**(2) Income Statement**	**(3) Statement of Owners' Equity**
Owners' Equity (1/1)		Owners' Equity (1/1)
± Changes in Assets and Liabilities from nonowner transactions **Payment of interest**	+ Revenues **− Expenses** + Gains − Losses	
	= Net income	**+ Net income**
± Changes in Assets and Liabilities from transactions with owners **Payment of dividends**		**− Distributions to owners** + Investments by owners
Owners' Equity (12/31)		**Owners' Equity (12/31)**

A payment of cash for interest is shown as interest expense on the income statement (Column 2). This reduces net income because expenses are subtracted to arrive at income. The net income (that incorporates the interest effect) is also shown as an addition on the statement of owners' equity (Column 3). If the cash is paid to shareholders as dividends, a decrease in assets arising from transactions with owners is recognized. This causes the subtraction for distributions to owners to be shown as a larger amount on the statement of owners' equity (Column 3). Both kinds of cash payments caused owners' equity to decrease because *all net changes in assets and liabilities are also changes in owners' equity.*

Three exceptions exist to the general rule that changes in assets and liabilities from nonowner transactions flow first to the income statement before flowing to the statement of owners' equity. Some assets and liability changes related to (1) pensions, (2) certain investments in marketable equity securities, and (3) foreign subsidiaries skip the income statement and are reported as separate components of owners' equity. We will defer explaining these exceptions until we study decisions related to those areas in Chapters 8 and 12. However, criticism of these exceptions recently prompted the FASB to issue SFAS No. 130, "Reporting Comprehensive Income," to guide the disclosure of these transactions.[8]

Comprehensive income equals net income adjusted for the (net of tax) effects on income of the aforementioned three exceptions. Thus, comprehensive income is a broader concept than net income, but it still does not include asset and liability changes from transactions with owners. Under SFAS No. 130, comprehensive income must be disclosed at the end of the income statement, in a separate statement of comprehensive income, or in the statement of owners' equity. We save our evaluation of the comprehensive income concept until we study the related areas that generate the three exceptions.

8. "Reporting Comprehensive Income," *SFAS No. 130* (Norwalk, Conn.: FASB, 1997).

Cash Flows and Financial Statement Elements

7 Identify the timing of cash inflows and outflows and their effects on financial statement elements.

Throughout this text, we deal with how cash-based decisions are reflected in accrual-based financial statements. In this section, cash inflows and outflows are analyzed in terms of the definitions of the financial statement elements.

Cash Inflows

When a corporation receives cash, it is clear that an asset has increased on the balance sheet. However, other financial statement elements have changed as well. This is because in a normal exchange, *unrelated parties exchange consideration with equal fair market values.* The corporation had to provide something of equal value in order to receive cash. What the corporation gave up can be categorized as follows:

- Another asset that originally cost the corporation an amount *less than* the cash received (e.g., inventory is sold for cash in excess of its cost).
- Another asset that originally cost the corporation an amount *more than* the cash received (e.g., obsolete inventory is sold for cash less than its cost).
- Another asset that originally cost the corporation an amount *equal to* the cash received (this is an unusual case, e.g., a company sold inventory at its cost).
- A service (e.g., a company provided consulting services for cash).
- A promise to deliver a noncash asset or a service at a later date (e.g., a law firm accepted a retainer for future services).
- A promise to repay the cash at a later date (e.g., a company borrowed cash from a bank and signed a note payable).
- An equity claim (e.g., a share of common stock providing an investor/owner with a claim to a proportionate share of the net assets of the corporation is issued for cash).

The first three cases of asset transfer need to be examined under two scenarios. First, the transaction could arise from the ongoing operations of the business. In this scenario, the *increase in the cash asset received* would be a *revenue,* and the *decrease in the asset transferred out* would be an *expense.* A common example of this type of transaction is the sale of inventory. Cash increases, yielding revenue, while inventory decreases, yielding an expense called cost of goods sold.

Second, the transaction could arise from incidental or peripheral transactions. In this scenario, the *change in net assets* would be a *gain* if the cash received was greater than the recorded value of the asset transferred (i.e., net assets increased). The *change in net assets* would be a *loss* if the cash received was less than the recorded value of the asset transferred (i.e., net assets decreased). If the cash received was equal to the recorded value of the asset transferred, there would be *no change* in net assets. A cash sale of a productive asset such as land is an example.

Cash receipt in exchange for services rendered is a *revenue.* Receiving cash for legal services rendered is an example. But if the cash is received in exchange for a promise to deliver an asset or service, a *liability* is created instead of a revenue because the revenue must still be earned. The requirements for revenue recognition are realization (i.e., cash or near-cash asset received) *and* an exchange of assets or services. Until that time in which delivery of assets or services occurs, an obligation to deliver exists. The liability is often described as ***deferred*** (or ***unearned***) ***revenue.*** **It represents the value of assets received in advance of earning revenue.** When the revenue is earned, unearned revenue is decreased and revenue is recorded. A good example of this type of transaction is collecting rent before the premises are occupied. The liability unearned rent is recorded.

Finally, cash received upon issuing an equity claim (e.g., common stock) is an *investment by an owner.* Given that this is a transaction with an owner, the income statement elements are not affected.

In summary, cash inflows create one of the following:

- Revenues
- Gains or losses (cash inflow compared to resource outflow)[9]
- Liabilities
- Investments by owners (increase in owners' equity)

Cash Outflows

When a corporation disburses cash, an asset decreases on the balance sheet. But the corporation receives something of equal value, which can be categorized as follows:

- Future economic benefits
- Economic benefits that are used up in the current period
- The forgiveness of a liability
- The reduction of an equity claim

Future economic benefits are *assets*. Because they will eventually be recognized as expenses when the assets are used up in the future, they are often called **deferred** (or **prepaid**) **expenses**. Thus, ***deferred (prepaid) expenses*** **represent the value of assets given up that will be matched as expenses against revenues earned in future periods.** Purchasing a two-year insurance policy near year-end is an example. Because the benefits of insurance coverage will occur for the next two years, the asset "prepaid insurance" is created. ***Capitalization*** **is the act of increasing an asset account to recognize probable future economic benefits of a cash outflow.**

Economic benefits that are related to the current period are also assets. However, because they are immediately used up in the current period, they are recorded as *expenses*. For example, if a plant manager is paid a salary for the current month's work, no future benefit is received (the benefit is all received in the current period) and salary expense is recorded.

The last two situations arise from financing transactions with creditors and owners. Regarding financing transactions with creditors, if, for example, a company has a note payable with a bank, paying principal back to a lender reduces a *liability*. No effect on income occurs when both cash and the liability are reduced because net assets have not changed. As an example of a transaction with an owner, consider a dividend, the most common distribution to owners. The reduction of an equity claim by disbursing cash is a *distribution to owner*. Again, no income effect is recorded because it is a transaction with an owner.

In summary, cash outflows create one of the following:

- An asset
- An expense
- The reduction of a liability
- A distribution to owners (the reduction of owners' equity)

Future Cash Flows

The effects of current cash flows on the financial statement elements were illustrated above. It was shown that cash flows can occur *at the same time* as revenues are earned or expenses are incurred. Or cash flows could also *precede* revenue recognition or expense incurrence, in which case deferred revenues (i.e., liabilities) or deferred expenses (i.e., assets) would be recognized.

A third possibility—cash flows that *occur after* revenue recognition or expense incurrence—is now examined. Whereas cash flows preceding revenue recognition or expense incurrence are called deferred revenues or expenses, **revenues and**

9. When cash inflow equals the amount of the asset given up, nonasset elements are not affected.

expenses preceding cash flow are referred to as *accrued revenues* and *accrued expenses*.

For example, if a tenant is allowed to stay in a building for one month before rent is collected, the landlord has clearly earned rent revenue before receiving it. This situation increases an *asset* "rent receivable" because a probable future economic benefit now exists. As a result, rent revenue is recorded. Because cash flow has not yet occurred, this is an accrued revenue. Similarly, consider maintenance personnel who are owed one week's wages at the end of the month because payday does not occur until the week after month-end. Since the disbursement of wages is probable, wages payable (a *liability*) is increased and wages expense is recorded. Wages expense is an accrued expense because cash flow has not yet occurred.

Summary of Financial Statement Elements and Cash Flows

The relationships between asset and liability changes and revenue and expense recognitions are summarized in series of timelines presented in Exhibits 3, 4, and 5.

EXHIBIT 3 Deferrals: Cash Flows Preceding Revenue and Expense Recognition

Example: Rent revenue is received in advance.

Now	**Later**
Cash inflow	Revenue earned
Liability (deferred revenue) created	Liability removed; revenue recognized

Example: Insurance is prepaid.

Now	**Later**
Cash outflow	Expense incurred
Asset (deferred expense) created	Asset removed; expense recognized

EXHIBIT 4 Accruals: Revenue and Expense Recognition Preceding Cash Flows

Example: Interest is earned before payment is received.

Now	**Later**
Revenue earned	Cash inflow
Asset (accrued revenue) created; revenue recognized	Asset removed

Example: Wages are earned by employees before being paid.

Now	**Later**
Expense incurred	Cash outflow
Liability (accrued expense) created; expense recognized	Liability removed

EXHIBIT 5 Simultaneous Cash Flows and Revenue and Expense Recognition

Example: Cash sales are made.

Now
Cash inflow; revenue earned
Revenue recognized

Example: The current month's utility bill is paid at the end of the month.

Now
Cash outflow; expense incurred
Expense recognized

The Accrual Elements in Actual Financial Statements: TCBY Enterprises, Inc.

The 1998 annual report of TCBY Enterprises, Inc., is presented in Appendix D at the end of the text. TCBY's annual report presents comparative balance sheets for the years ended November 29, 1998, and November 30, 1997, and comparative income statements for 1998, 1997, and 1996. TCBY's statement of stockholders' equity shows changes in equity from December 1, 1995, to the end of fiscal year, November 29, 1998. In this section, we refer to those financial statements. As we describe how the financial statement elements are reflected in TCBY's financial statements, turn to the financial statements and cross-reference the items and amounts in the text to those in the financial statements.

Balance Sheet Elements

TCBY's 1998 balance sheet lists $94,452,884 of the element "assets" and an equal amount of claims against those assets represented by the sum of two elements, "liabilities" and stockholders' "equity." TCBY did not present a separate subtotal for liabilities, but one can find the total 1998 liabilities of $18,256,730 by summing current liabilities of $11,984,249, long-term debt of $2,952,634, and deferred income taxes of $3,319,847.

Recall that owners' equity represents a residual claim against net assets. If we take $94,452,884 total assets and subtract total liabilities of $18,256,730, we arrive at total stockholders' equity of $76,196,154. If we divide stockholders' residual claims by the 22,919,069 shares of common stock outstanding on November 29, 1998 (27,759,021 shares issued minus 4,839,952 shares held as treasury stock), we obtain an equity claim per share of approximately $3.32 per share. If one of TCBY's 4,467 shareholders[10] of record at November 29, 1998, were to sell a share of stock, the shareholder would likely receive more than $3.32. In fact, TCBY's common stock traded between $5.31 and $7.75 during the fourth quarter of fiscal 1998. As we will discuss throughout this text, the balance sheet elements are measured using GAAP rules that often deviate from current market values in favor of historical measures. It is apparent from TCBY's stock price during October–December 1998 that investors on the New York Stock Exchange believed that the fair value of TCBY Enterprises was greater than the $76,196,154 amount ($94,452,884 assets − $18,256,730 liabilities) reported in the balance sheet for net assets.

Income Statement Elements

TCBY uses the income statement elements (revenues, expenses, gains, and losses) to compute net income in the comparative income statements for 1996 through 1998. Examples of 1998 "revenues" are sales of $93,865,413 and total franchising revenues of $13,113,863, which reflects TCBY's share of the profits of stores owned by local entrepreneurs. Examples of "expenses" include the cost of sales ($64,098,811) and selling, general, and administrative expenses ($30,393,591). The "other income" of $2,293,024 is likely a net "gain" from peripheral or incidental transactions. TCBY also reports interest expense from borrowing, interest revenue from lending, and more than $5 million in income tax expense. The revenues, expenses, gains, and losses are totaled to yield $10,195,612 in 1998 net income.

Statement of Stockholders' Equity Elements

The statement of stockholders' equity summarizes all changes in assets and liabilities from transactions with owners ("investments by owners" and "distributions to

10. The number of shareholders was obtained from the "Corporate Information" section at the end of TCBY's annual report.

owners") and transactions with outside parties ("net income"). TCBY had several transactions with owners during the three-year period. In fiscal years 1996–1998, TCBY made distributions to owners in two forms. First, cash dividends of $0.20 per share were paid in each year. Second, TCBY repurchased previously issued shares from stockholders ("treasury stock") in each year.

The shareholders' equity statement also reports investments by owners. In 1997 and 1998, employees exercised stock options to purchase stock. When the options were exercised, TCBY collected the option price from the owners. The transfer of cash to TCBY increased assets and the owners' claims against the assets. Finally, net income is shown as an addition to stockholders' equity in each year.

In a pure cash-basis model, TCBY's balance sheet would include only cash on the asset side and the combination of long-term financing used on the liabilities and equity side. But an accrual-based model measures assets other than cash and additional operating liabilities as well. In the next two sections, TCBY's financial statements are used to illustrate the accountant's use of deferrals and accruals.

Examples of Deferrals (Cash Flow Precedes Revenue/Expense Recognition)

A good example of a deferred expense is TCBY's "Inventory" balance of $12,554,875 reported in the November 29, 1998, balance sheet. Cash outflow occurred to acquire the inventory. However, expense recognition is delayed (i.e., deferred) until the inventory leaves the company through sale. Similarly, TCBY reports $46,637,567 in "Furniture, vehicles, and equipment" in the Property, Plant, and Equipment section of the balance sheet. Again, cash flow occurred to acquire the operational assets, but expense recognition is matched to the revenues generated in future periods by recognizing depreciation expense.

Although TCBY did not report any deferred revenue as a separate item on the balance sheet, its willingness to do so is indicated by the following footnote description of its accounting policy with respect to franchise revenues:

> "Franchising revenues consist of initial franchise and license fees and royalty income. Initial franchise and license fees are recognized as revenue when the Company has substantially completed its obligations under the franchise or license agreement. Royalty income is earned on sales by franchisees and is recognized as revenue when the related sales are made." (1998 TCBY annual report, p. 30)

In adherence to this policy, TCBY would record initial cash flows under franchising agreements as deferred revenue if it had not completed its obligations under the franchise or license agreement. That is, revenue must be earned before it is reported as revenue.

Examples of Accruals (Revenue/Expense Recognition Precedes Cash Flow)

The preceding revenue recognition also provides an example of "accrued revenue." Royalty income is recognized as sales are made, not as franchisees pay cash to TCBY. Note that one of the largest current assets reported in TCBY's balance sheet is $10,078,733 of trade accounts receivable. These receivables are the uncollected balance of accrued revenues. Note also that the largest current liability is "accrued expenses" in the amount of $6,682,371. These liabilities represent expenses that have been recognized even though cash has not been paid.

Why Financial Statements Are Based on Accrual Accounting

8 Explain why financial statements are based on accrual accounting.

The diagrams in the section "Summary of Financial Statement Elements and Cash Flows" show that the difference between net cash inflows (cash inflows minus cash outflows) and accrual accounting net income (recognized revenues minus recognized expenses) is related to timing. By the time each diagram's time line is completed, cash flow equals revenue or expense recognition.

Why, then, do accountants adopt the fairly complicated accrual model to document the effects of management decisions rather than simply reporting cash flows? By definition, over the life of the firm, net cash inflows from all transactions other than investments by owners and distributions to owners must equal accrual net income. One reason is that simply reporting cash flows documents *past cash flows*. Recall that finance valuation theory holds that investors and creditors who provide capital to the firm are interested in *future cash flows* from dividends and interest. These future cash flows to investors and creditors are created by the firm's ability to generate *cash*. Accountants believe that the accrual-based financial reporting model provides better information about future cash flows than a cash-based financial reporting model.

Accounting policy-making bodies support the use of the accrual model rather than the cash flow model for income determination. The FASB outlined the following three objectives of financial reporting by business enterprises:[11]

1. To provide information that is useful to present and potential investors and creditors and other users in making rational investment, credit, and similar decisions. The information should be comprehensible to those who have a reasonable understanding of business and economic activities and are willing to study the information with reasonable diligence.
2. To provide information to help present and potential investors and creditors and other users in assessing the amounts, timing, and uncertainty of prospective cash receipts from dividends or interest and the proceeds from the sale, redemption, or maturity of securities or loans. Since the cash flows of investors and creditors are related to enterprise cash flow, financial reporting should provide information to help investors, creditors, and others assess the amounts, timing, and uncertainty of prospective net cash inflows to the related enterprise.
3. To provide information about the economic resources of an enterprise, the claims to those resources (obligations of the enterprise to transfer resources to other entities and owners' equity), and the effects of transactions, events, and circumstances that change its resources and claims to those resources.

The third objective appears to be satisfied by the three primary accrual-based financial statements. Information about "economic resources" and "claims to those resources" is provided by asset, liability, and equity disclosures on the balance sheet. Information about "changes in resources and claims to those resources" is provided by revenue, expense, loss, and gain disclosures on the income statement and by investments by owners and distribution to owners disclosures on the statement of owners' equity.

The second objective is served to some extent by the statement of cash flows that lists the firm's cash inflows and outflows for a period. However, it is clear from the following excerpt that the FASB finds accrual information to be more useful than cash flow information in providing present and potential investors and creditors and other users with help in assessing the amounts, timing, and uncertainty of prospective cash receipts:

11. *SFAC No. 1:* viii.

> Financial statements that show only cash receipts and payments during a short period, such as a year, cannot adequately indicate whether or not an enterprise's performance is successful. Information about enterprise earnings and its components measured by accrual accounting generally provides a better indication of enterprise performance than information about current cash receipts and payments.[12]

The Cash Flow Statement

9 Describe the basic format of the cash flow statement.

Up to this point, we have concentrated on the relationship between cash flows and accrual accounting elements. The balance sheet, income statement, and statement of owners' equity are created by using the accrual accounting elements as building blocks. However, the FASB requires that information about cash flows be presented in a set of financial statements. The basic outline of the statement of cash flows is shown in Exhibit 6.

EXHIBIT 6 Basic Outline of the Statement of Cash Flows

STATEMENT OF CASH FLOWS		
Operating Activities		
Cash inflows*	$XXX	
Cash outflows*	(XX)	
Net cash flow from operating activities		$XXX
Investing Activities		
Cash inflows	$XXX	
Cash outflows	(XX)	
Net cash flow from investing activities		XXX
Financing Activities		
Cash inflows	$XXX	
Cash outflows	(XX)	
Net cash flow from financing activities		XXX
Net change in cash		$XXX

*This format reflects the "direct approach."

The statement of cash flows is organized around the three decisions/activities of the firm that we previously identified in this chapter: operating activities, investing activities, and financing activities. Material cash inflows and outflows are listed under each activity. The operating activities classification is closely linked to accrual accounting net income. When we study the statement of cash flows more closely in later chapters, we will discuss an alternative structure for the operating activities section of the statement that reconciles accrual accounting net income to operating cash flows (the so-called "indirect approach"). TCBY's statement of cash flows uses the indirect approach. For the majority of our text discussion, we use the "direct approach" for the presentation of the operating cash flow sections. Later in the text, we show both direct and indirect approaches in comprehensive examples.

Refer to TCBY's 1998 statement of cash flows. Note that $9,460,072 was generated by 1998 operating activities. Across the three years presented, operating cash flows are positive, although declining, each year. In 1998, $3,371,987 was provided by investing activities, primarily from sales of property and equipment. Cash is generated by investing activities each year. In 1998, $15,601,609 was used in financing activities. TCBY paid back the cash borrowed from long-term creditors in each year (principal payments on long-term debt) and sent cash to shareholders in

12. *SFAC No. 1,* pars. 43 and 44.

two ways: by issuing dividends and engaging in large treasury stock repurchases each year. In summary, a great deal of information about the past *cash flow* results of managers' decisions is provided in the statement of cash flows.

A Closer Look at the Balance Sheet

10 Describe the detailed structures used for and the attributes measured in the balance sheet.

As shown in Exhibit 7, the balance sheet reflects the fundamental accounting equation: Assets = Liabilities + Owners' equity (A = L + OE).

EXHIBIT 7 The Balance Sheet

BALANCE SHEET

Assets		**Liabilities**		
Current assets	$XXX	Current liabilities	$XXX	
Investments and funds	XXX	Long-term liabilities	XXX	$XXX
Property, plant, and equipment	XXX			
Intangible assets	XXX	**Owners' Equity**		
Other assets	XXX	Contributed capital	$XXX	
		Retained earnings	XXX	XXX
Total assets	$XXX	Total liabilities and owners' equity		$XXX

Assets

Assets are classified on the balance sheet in several ways. No grand theory underlies these particular classifications. Traditional categories have arisen over time to reflect differences in the characteristics of assets. The characteristics are *liquidity* and, to a lesser extent, *intended asset use*. ***Liquidity*** **refers to how long it will take the company to convert the asset into cash.** In other words, it indicates how close an asset is to realizing its economic benefits.

An asset is classified as a *current asset* if it will be realized (i.e., converted to cash) within one year or within one operating cycle, whichever is longer. The *operating cycle* is the length of time that it takes a firm to begin with cash and end with cash. The cycle usually involves cash payments for acquiring inventory or producing inventory (materials, labor, and overhead), sale, and finally, cash collection. In most industries, the length of the operating cycle is less than one year. However, we will note in our discussion of operating decisions in a later chapter that, in industries such as construction, the operating cycle may exceed one year. Current assets include items such as cash, items equivalent to cash (e.g., checking and savings accounts), accounts receivable, short-term investments, inventory, and short-term prepayments that are expected to benefit the firm for less than one year. These items are listed within the current asset classification in the order of their liquidity, from most liquid to least liquid (e.g., cash, followed by accounts receivable, followed by inventory, etc.). Almost all current asset transactions are related to operating activities of the firm.

An asset is classified as a *noncurrent asset* if it will be realized (i.e., converted to cash) after one year or beyond one operating cycle, whichever is longer. Traditional noncurrent asset categories are investments and funds; property, plant and equipment; intangible assets; and other assets. Noncurrent assets follow the presentation of assets, and the noncurrent asset categories are listed in decreasing order of liquidity. Transactions within noncurrent asset categories are almost always related to investing activities of the firm.

Investments and funds is a noncurrent asset classification that includes cash and securities that do not mature within the next year and/or are not intended by management to be sold within the coming year. Examples are stock investments in other companies, bond investments, funds held for the retirement of bonds, funds held for the acquisition of plant and equipment, and cash that legally may not be disbursed within the coming year.[13] Assets in this classification have different intended uses. Investment and fund assets typically are the most liquid of the noncurrent assets.

Property, plant, and equipment (often called "operational assets") includes the long-lived assets that make up the company's *capacity* to produce, sell, and distribute a product. Corporations report land, buildings, machinery, and delivery vehicles in this category. Companies in the extractive industries report additional assets peculiar to their industries, such as timber tracts, oil and gas reserves, or mineral deposits. Although items in the property, plant, and equipment classification could be converted into cash through sale, management intends the assets to be used in the operating cycle to create products or services that are cash-producing. Because this intent places the asset's use early in the operating cycle, the assets are less liquid than current assets or investments and funds.

Intangible assets is a classification similar to property, plant, and equipment in that it represents significant expenditures to create long-term capacity. However, intangible assets lack physical substance. Examples are goodwill, patents, licenses, and trademarks. The difficulty in properly measuring the economic benefits of intangible assets warrants their placement in another category separate from property, plant, and equipment.

Other assets represents a catchall category. As we will note throughout this text, not all assets are easily classified into one of the four preceding categories. One particular asset often classified as other assets is a long-term deferred charge. The exact nature of deferred charges is discussed later in the text within the context of the decisions that create them.

In summary, **in a *classified balance sheet* assets are arranged on the balance sheet in order of liquidity and, to some extent, by the intended use of the asset.** A classified balance sheet is useful to investors and creditors in helping them to assess a company's creditworthiness. Liquid assets are more readily available to meet current obligations of the firm. As mentioned earlier, the FASB indicates that a primary objective of financial reporting is to provide information useful in assessing the nature and timing of cash flows.

Liabilities

The liability portion of the balance sheet contains a single breakdown between current and noncurrent (i.e., long-term) liabilities. Once again, timing is the determining factor. **If a liability is expected to be liquidated within the current year or operating cycle (normally by using current assets), then it is classified as a *current liability*.** Otherwise, it is classified as long-term. Examples of current liabilities include accounts payable, property taxes payable, interest payable, income taxes payable, and currently maturing portions of long-term debt. Examples of long-term liabilities include notes payable, bonds payable, lease obligations, and pension obligations. The amount of total liabilities is a quantitative measure of the claims of creditors against corporate assets that arise from transactions with the corporation. Almost all current liability transactions are related to operating activities of the firm, and almost all noncurrent liability transactions are related to financing activities of the firm.

Current assets minus current liabilities yields *working capital*. Current assets divided by current liabilities yields the *working capital (current) ratio*. *These measures are used by current and potential creditors to assess the debt-paying ability of the company.* For the potential creditor, a great deal is learned about the

13. Legally restricted cash often takes the form of compensating balances, which are required deposits at a lending institution.

liquidity of the firm by comparing the behavior of these measures over time and to other firms in the same industry. For current creditors, these measures serve as a monitoring device. Working capital requirements are an important part of the debt covenants and restrictions that determine whether a corporation is in default on an outstanding debt issue.

Owners' Equity

The owners' equity section is divided into contributed capital and retained earnings (earned capital). ***Contributed capital* is equal to the resources (assets) contributed to the firm by its owners.** It includes the proceeds from issuance of common stock, preferred stock, options, and warrants. ***Retained earnings* is equal to the amount of assets that have been accumulated over time through operational activities (as measured by net income)** but not yet distributed to owners. Because owners' equity is positive only when assets are greater than liabilities, it is an indicator of solvency.

Both total liabilities and total owners' equity are measures of claims against corporate assets. The relationship (mix) between total liabilities and total equity is determined by firm management, and financial analysts often scrutinize this relationship closely. For example, the debt-to-equity ratio, a comparison of long-term liabilities to owners' equity, provides an important measure of a firm's *financial flexibility*. Also, the debt-to-equity ratio has been tied to the firm's systematic risk and, hence, to the return that investors require on an investment in the firm's common stock.[14]

Attributes Measured in the Balance Sheet

Accountants measure each financial statement element in terms of money that is assumed to be constant in value. If every transaction involved the exchange of cash, the elements of financial statements would be simple to measure. For example, if you obtained a boat by giving up $5,000 in cash, it would be reasonable to assign a $5,000 valuation to the boat. However, if you gave up a 1967 Ford Mustang to acquire the boat, the valuation of the boat would not be so clear. Accountants face this valuation problem when they attempt to assign values to the balance sheet elements.

The FASB has identified five attributes measurable in terms of dollars. All financial statement elements reflect one of these attributes. We will learn which particular attribute is used for individual financial statement elements in later chapters. At this point, it is important to understand what alternatives are available for asset measurement, rather than to learn exactly when each alternative is used. The attributes that are currently reflected in the balance sheet are:

1. historical cost (or historical exchange price)
2. net realizable value (or exit value)
3. current replacement cost (or current cost)
4. market value
5. present value

In order to understand these concepts, it is useful to look at a picture of the firm and the markets that a firm faces. The following diagram illustrates three of the five attributes and shows a firm that obtains labor and capital in input markets and sells products or delivers services in output markets:[15]

14. Other balance sheet links to risk assessment are discussed in Module A.
15. It stands to reason that one entity's output market is another entity's input market. To understand this illustration, the reader should concentrate on a single firm.

Input Markets	→	**Firm**	→	**Output Markets**
Historical Cost Replacement Cost				Net Realizable Value

Example: Potential Attribute Measures of Machinery in Alternative Markets ***Historical cost*** **represents the original transaction amount in dollars.** It is an attribute measured in the *input* market. For example, assume that a machine cost $60,000 on January 1, 2001. At the balance sheet date, December 31, 2001, the attribute "historical cost" would be measured as $60,000. ***Replacement cost*** **represents the amount that it would currently take to acquire an asset with the same productive characteristics.** It is also an attribute measured in the *input* market. In our example, replacement cost on December 31, 2001, would be equal to what it would take to buy a one-year-old machine with the same productive capabilities. ***Net realizable value*** **equals the amount that would be received upon selling the item in the normal course of business.** It is an attribute measured in *output* markets. In our example, net realizable value would be equal to what the corporation would receive upon selling the machine.

The relationship between input and output attributes depends upon the type of item being measured. In the case of inventory, we normally expect net realizable value to be higher than historical and replacement costs because a firm "buys low and sells high" in the normal course of business. Of course, this might not be the case for damaged or obsolete inventory or for inventory for which prices may drop rapidly (e.g., computer chips). For fixed assets, we normally expect that replacement costs are higher than net realizable value. This is readily illustrated by our machinery purchase example. Normally, we expect to pay more for a machine (input market) than we could obtain from selling the machine (output market). Lack of access to distribution channels, lack of a service and parts department, and certainly many other disadvantages make recouping original purchase price through resale difficult.

The other two measurement attributes, market value and present value, are more general concepts present in both input and output markets and usually coincide, or help determine, the other attributes. ***Market value*** **is the arm's-length bargained, current exchange price between two unrelated parties.** The definition of market value depends upon the context in which it is used. For example, market value equals historical cost at the date of acquisition. Alternatively, as we will see in a later discussion of inventory valuation, accounting standard setters use the term "market value" to refer to replacement cost. Market value has also been used to describe an attribute of the output market. For example, it is common for accountants and standard setters to refer to the realizable value of marketable debt and equity securities as "market value" (i.e., the securities are marked-to-market). ***Present value*** **is most often used to describe discounted cash flow.** Theoretically, the value placed on an element in either input or output markets is a function of all future cash flows received or paid discounted to the present date using a rate of return commensurate with the risk of cash flow realization.[16] Present value techniques can be used to establish the market value of any asset or liability because both elements ultimately involve the receipt or disbursement of cash (or products or services that have a cash-equivalent price). Present value computations are most often used for financial assets and liabilities (e.g., bonds and notes).

Summary Balance sheet financial statement elements usually possess several measurement attributes (e.g., inventory has both a replacement cost, which is measured as a purchase price, and a net realizable value, which is measured as a sales price). However, normally the financial statements report only one measurement attribute

16. If you need to learn or brush up on the time value of money concepts, see Appendix B, which includes a short tutorial and practice problems on the topic.

for each balance sheet classification (e.g., accounts receivable at net realizable value and bonds payable at present value). Usually, the choice of measurement attribute is prescribed by standard setters. If standard setters want multiple attributes to be presented, generally, one attribute will be reflected in the financial statements while other attributes will be reported in footnotes to the financial statements. *Why standard setters have chosen particular attributes and how their choice influences the financial statements through operating, investing, and financing decisions are major themes of this book.*

A Closer Look at the Income Statement

11 Describe the detailed structure used for and the attributes used in the income statement.

Most firms that sell products use some variation of a multiple-step income statement.[17] Exhibit 8 illustrates a multiple-step income statement. By definition, all items appearing on the income statement must be ***material*, which means they are large enough to make a difference in the decisions of investors and creditors.**

Although numerous classifications are used on the income statement, only four financial statement elements are present: revenues, expenses, gains, and losses. The classifications describe the functional source of the elements within the corporation, and in doing so, they signal the regularity of the item to some extent. The first distinguishable section of the income statement, which shows the computation of gross margin (profit), is depicted below.

Sales revenue	$XXX
Less: Cost of goods sold	XXX
Gross margin (profit)	$XXX

This section shows the **revenues from sales activities less the costs of purchasing or producing the inventory that was sold, which equals *gross margin*** (or ***gross profit***). If the corporation were a service firm, this section would be replaced by a single disclosure of "service revenue." A service firm does not report cost of goods sold. It is important to note that *income statements describe a single period,* such as a quarter or a year. Therefore, the revenues or expenses listed may not be indicative of "normal" or long-run average revenues or expenses.

EXHIBIT 8 Multiple-Step Income Statement

Income Statement (Multiple-Step)

Sales revenue		$XXX
Less: Cost of goods sold		XXX
Gross margin (profit)		$XXX
Less: Operating expenses		
General and administrative expenses	$XXX	
Selling expenses	XXX	XXX
Operating income		$XXX
Financial revenues and expenses, gains and losses		XXX
Income before income taxes (pretax income)		$XXX
Income tax expense		XXX
Income from continuing operations		$XXX
Discontinued operations (net of tax)		XXX
Extraordinary items (net of tax)		XXX
Cumulative effect of a change in accounting principle (net of tax)		XXX
Net income		$XXX
Earnings per share		$XXX

17. In a single-step format, all expenses are subtracted from all revenues in one step to report net income.

Gross margin divided by sales revenue yields the *gross margin (profit) percentage.* This percentage is an important summary statistic that is tracked by managers, investors, and creditors over time and compared to gross margin percentages of competitor firms. Decreasing gross margins may signal that costs are increasing faster than the firm's ability to pass those costs on to customers, a condition that raises questions about future profitability.

Cost of goods sold is not the only expense necessary to generate sales revenue. The corporation has administrative functions including accounting, legal work, corporate-level management, and selling functions such as advertising, sales, and shipping. Thus, to more fully describe operating income, the income statement is expanded to include operating expenses, as shown below.

Sales revenue		$XXX
Less: Cost of goods sold		XXX
Gross margin (profit)		$XXX
Less: Operating expenses		
General and administrative expenses	$XXX	
Selling expenses	XXX	XXX
Operating income		$XXX

The preceding operating section lists revenues and expenses from the primary ongoing activities of the firm. The next disclosure on the income statement is a listing of revenues and expenses from changes in financial assets and liabilities. It also lists gains and losses from incidental or peripheral transactions, as shown here.

Operating income	$XXX
Financial revenues and expenses, gains and losses[18]	XXX
Income before income taxes (pretax income)	$XXX

Borrowing and investing activities yield financial expenses and revenues. These activities are necessary recurring events in a firm's life. However, unless the firm is a financial institution, these activities are not a primary source of earnings. Instead, they represent the results of cash management activities. Examples of items appearing in this classification are dividend revenue, interest revenue from investments, and interest expense on borrowings.

Transactions relating to the sale of operational assets yield gains and losses, which are, by definition, peripheral or incidental. Examples are gains and losses on the sale or disposal of plant or machinery and gains and losses on sales of long-term investments in equity or debt securities. Financial revenues and expenses and gains and losses are subtracted from operating income to obtain income before income taxes.

Income tax expense is subtracted from income before income taxes (pretax income) to arrive at *income from continuing operations:*

Income before income taxes (pretax income)	$XXX
Income tax expense	XXX
Income from continuing operations	$XXX

Income from continuing operations is a major subtotal on the income statement. Three items appearing after this amount receive special net-of-tax treatment: discontinued operations, extraordinary items, and cumulative effects of changes in certain accounting principles.[19]

18. In many financial statements, this caption is "other revenues and expenses, gains and losses."
19. Although not a rule as of the writing of this text, the Financial Accounting Standards Board is considering an additional item for the special net-of-tax treatment, amortization of goodwill acquired in an acquisition. We discuss the proposed rule in Chapter 8.

Income from continuing operations	$XXX
Discontinued operations (net of tax)	XXX
Extraordinary items (net of tax)	XXX
Cumulative effect of a change in accounting principle (net of tax)	XXX
Net income	$XXX
Earnings per share	$XXX

The category ***discontinued operations*** **aggregates revenues, expenses, gains, and losses from operation and disposal of a segment of the business.** The rules for measuring discontinued operations are extremely complex. Because discontinuing a segment of the business is simultaneously an operating, investing, and possibly, financing activity, we hold off on examining the specific rules until Chapter 10.

Extraordinary items **are events that are both unusual in nature and infrequent in occurrence.** Taking the environment in which the business operates into account, the event must be a rarely occurring event that is only tangentially related to the regular operations of the firm. As a result, very few items are considered extraordinary. For example, a major loss of Florida orange crops due to frost damage would not be considered extraordinary because the event is not rare. Similarly, a material loss from a write-down of obsolete inventory would fail to meet the "unusual in nature" criterion. Most extraordinary items arise from catastrophic casualty losses that are completely unexpected or political actions such as asset expropriations. Additionally, the FASB periodically mandates that a particular transaction, which may not be unusual and infrequent, be presented as an extraordinary item (e.g., early extinguishment of debt).

Cumulative effects of changes in accounting principles **are disclosures of the effects on prior periods' revenues and expenses of changes in the way assets and liabilities are measured because a company changes the accounting principle it uses** (e.g., from accelerated depreciation to straight-line depreciation). Again, the complexity of this topic (and the motivations of those who undertake changes in accounting principles) warrants coverage in Chapter 10. At this point in your study, do not concern yourself with the measurement of these three special items, but instead, keep the following facts in mind:

1. Accountants include these three items in net income of the period.
2. Accountants separate the special items from other, more regular items by listing the special items below income from continuing operations and presenting them net of tax.

The disclosure of special items below income from continuing operations signals to investors that further analysis is needed to determine the impact of these items on future profitability. The inclusion of these special items in income is a manifestation of GAAP's adherence to the *all-inclusive income approach* rather than the *current operating performance approach* for measuring income. The current operating performance approach would include only regular, recurring revenues and expenses in net income of the period. The idea behind this is that assessment of the profit-generating potential of the firm is enhanced by exclusion of most gains and losses and discontinued operations, extraordinary items, and cumulative effects of accounting changes.

The all-inclusive approach treats all changes in net assets (assets minus liabilities) that are not capital transactions with owners as affecting net income. Accountants who favor the all-inclusive approach believe that exclusion of gains and losses and special items from income can distort the assessment of longer-run profitability. Current practice favors the all-inclusive concept, with gains, losses, and special items reported as affecting net income. A side issue in the current operating performance versus all-inclusive debate is the determination of which items to exclude under the current operating approach. Certainly, a great deal of management discretion and judgement would be necessary to classify items as regular or irregular. The accounting information quality of reliability would likely be violated.

Finally, earnings per share (EPS) is shown on the face of the income statement. This summary statistic is used to standardize net income so that it can be compared across time and across companies. We discuss the computation of EPS in Chapter 10.

Transitory versus Permanent Earnings

One of the most useful aspects of the income statement is its transformation of the results of operations into a single number: net income, or "net earnings." The level of corporate earnings frequently is an input into the determination of equity security (i.e., stock) price. The usefulness of earnings in determining security prices is one of the first and most often corroborated findings in empirical accounting research. Also, as a practical matter, the amount of effort spent by managers and financial analysts in forecasting earnings is a sound basis for an argument for the importance of earnings in security valuation.

Investors place a greater weight on permanent earnings as opposed to transitory earnings when valuing the firm. To some extent, the current standard income statement helps separate transitory and permanent components. In the income statement presented previously in the chapter, special "bottom of the income statement" treatment is provided for discontinued operations, extraordinary items, and accounting changes. These items are transitory in nature. Also in the income statement, peripheral gains and losses are identified separately from operating revenues and expenses.

Capital Maintenance Approach to Income Measurement

12 Explain the relationship between the capital maintenance and the transactions approaches to income measurement.

The concept underlying the computation of net income is that of capital maintenance. Capital maintenance is based upon economic theory. In this context, capital is defined as being equal to net assets, which, by the accounting equation's construction, is also equal to owners' equity. The ***capital maintenance approach* measures income during an accounting period as the amount of increase in net assets, after adjusting for any investments by owners and distributions to owners.** If the firm is better off at the end of the period (i.e., net assets have increased), then the firm has generated income. If the firm is worse off, then the firm has incurred a loss.

Financial Capital Maintenance

Under the financial capital maintenance approach, the amount of net assets is computed in monetary units. To illustrate the computation of net income under a financial capital maintenance approach, consider the following example problem.

Example 1. Williams Enterprises began the year with assets of $600,000 and liabilities of $200,000. At the end of the year, assets were $900,000 and liabilities were $300,000. Williams issued $100,000 of common stock and paid $25,000 of dividends during the year. What was net income for the period?

Solution. The capital maintenance approach compares beginning and ending owners' equity:

Owners' equity (beginning)	
equals Beginning net assets	= Assets (beginning) − Liabilities (beginning)
	= $600,000 − $200,000
	= $400,000
Owners' equity (ending)	
equals Ending net assets	= Assets (ending) − Liabilities (ending)
	= $900,000 − $300,000
	= $600,000
Increase in owners' equity	= $600,000 − 400,000
	= $200,000

The $200,000 would represent net income for the period if no transactions with owners occurred during the period. That is, under the classical economic definition of income, the firm could consume the $200,000 and be as well off at the end of the period as it was at the beginning (i.e., if the company consumed $200,000 in net assets, ending owners' equity would equal $400,000, the amount of beginning owners' equity). However, in this example, the company engaged in transactions with owners: $100,000 of the $200,000 is an increase in assets that came from investments by owners through common stock issuance, and there was an additional $25,000 increase in equity before assets were distributed to owners in the form of dividends. To arrive at changes in owners' equity arising from net income, these owner transactions must be "adjusted out" as follows:

Net income = Increase in owners' equity + Distribution to owners − Investments by owners
= $200,000 + $25,000 − $100,000
= $125,000[20]

Financial Capital Maintenance and the Transactions Approach

It turns out that investors, creditors, and other interested parties want more information about net income than simply the amount of net income during the period. Information users want detail about what events caused the net income (or loss). Accountants meet this information need by using the transactions approach. **Under the *transactions approach,* the accounting system classifies each change in net assets during the period as being either (1) an investment by owners or distribution to owners or (2) a transaction that affects net income.**[21] Individual transactions and events are recorded as individual changes in financial statement elements. An income statement summarizes and lists revenues, expenses, gains, and losses, and net income is the sum of these items. *The transactions approach also uses the financial capital maintenance concept to measure income.*

Physical Capital Maintenance Contrasted with Financial Capital Maintenance

In the preceding example, Williams Co. had $125,000 in net income after maintaining $400,000 in financial capital. **Under a *financial capital maintenance* approach net income is the increase in the total dollar amount of net assets during the period, after adjustments for capital investments by owners and distribution to owners.** Economists, however, generally view income as what is left after maintaining real or physical capital rather than financial capital. ***Physical capital* is a measure of the capacity of a firm to produce goods and services.** Therefore, **under the *physical capital maintenance* approach, net income is a measure of the increased physical capacity during the period to produce goods and services, after adjusting for contributions by owners and distributions to owners.**

To illustrate the physical capital maintenance approach to income computation and to contrast it with the financial capital maintenance approach, consider the following example.

Example 2. Pirate Co. has a single item of inventory at the beginning of the period. The inventory has a historical cost of $10. Pirate sells the inventory near

20. To reconcile owners' equity, start with $400,000 of owners' equity, add $100,000 for the stock proceeds, add $125,000 of net income, and subtract $25,000 dividend payment. This yields ending owners' equity of $600,000.

21. There are a few instances in which asset and liability changes from transactions other than with owners are not included in income of the period. As discussed in this chapter, the FASB has issued a standard requiring disclosure of *comprehensive income,* which is a broader concept that adjusts net income to reflect all net asset changes. The presence of accumulated other comprehensive items, a topic discussed later in the text, means that GAAP reflects a modified all-inclusive approach rather than a pure all-inclusive approach.

the end of the period for $15 cash. Due to a restriction in input market supply, the inventory costs Pirate $11 to replace at year-end. Compute Pirate's net income using the capital maintenance approach assuming the capital to be maintained is (a) financial capital or (b) real or physical capital.

Solution. Letting CGS = Cost of goods sold and NI = Net income:

Type of Maintenance	Beginning Net Assets	Income Statement		Ending Net Assets
Financial	$10	Sales	$ 15	$15
		CGS	(10)	
		NI	$ 5	
Physical	$10	Sales	$ 15	$15
		CGS	(11)	
		NI	$ 4	

Under either type of capital maintenance assumption, Pirate begins with $10 of net assets (held as inventory) and, due to the sale for $15, ends with $15 of net assets (held as cash). The difference in the two assumptions lies in the calculation of net income. The financial capital maintenance concept matches $10 inventory historical cost with the $15 revenue to generate $5 in net income. The physical capital maintenance concept matches the $11 replacement cost of the inventory with the $15 revenue in order to generate $4 in net income.

The difference in the financial and physical capital maintenance approaches can have a profound effect on dividend policy. For example, assume that Pirate Co.'s goal for the period is to pay out all net income in dividends. If Pirate Co. were to behave as if financial capital maintenance yielded an appropriate measure of income, it could pay a dividend of $5. Would Pirate be as well off at the end of the period as it was at the beginning? After distributing the $5 dividend, Pirate would still have $10 of financial capital. Pirate is as well off at the end of the period as at the beginning because it has the same amount of financial capital at the end of the period as at the beginning.

Under the physical capital maintenance approach, Pirate could pay out dividends of only $4, because inventory now costs $11. Unless Pirate keeps $11, it cannot maintain real or physical capital. Physical capital could be maintained only by using the $11 to replace inventory. Over time, if a company fails to maintain physical capital, and hence, the ability to produce the current level of goods and services, operations will suffer.

Under current GAAP, the income statement reflects a financial capital maintenance approach to income measurement. Standard setters have decided that reliably measured replacement cost, a necessary condition for the physical capital maintenance approach, is difficult (and costly) to obtain. Because managers make frequent decisions regarding the level of investments in productive assets and inventory, and annually determine the level of dividends, it is necessary that they recognize the potential limitations of financial capital maintenance in providing a measure of consumable income, especially if the industry in which they work has rapidly increasing input costs.

Regulation of Accounting Standard Setting

13 Describe the accounting standard-setting environment.

Accountants employ a set of rules and judgements to produce financial statements. At times, it appears as if accountants' rules are not consistent across decisions. Furthermore, it often appears as if the rules do not come from a single overriding theory. This can be disconcerting to a manager who makes cash-flow-oriented decisions because the cash flow event is relatively easy to observe and measure. The following sections provide an overview of accounting standard setting and its regulation in the hope that you will better understand why the accountant's measurement and reporting rules "are as they are." In addition, opportunities for management, accountant, and investor and creditor input into the rule-making process are identified.

Current Standard-Setting Bodies

The two organizations that have the greatest effect on accounting standard setting are the Securities and Exchange Commission, a public sector organization, and the Financial Accounting Standards Board, a private sector organization. The Securities and Exchange Commission has statutory authority from the U.S. Congress to set accounting standards but has delegated most of the standard-setting authority to the Financial Accounting Standards Board.

Private Sector For the most part, accounting standard setting has been a private-sector phenomenon since 1939, under the direction of a progression of three private rule-making bodies The current organization is the ***Financial Accounting Standards Board (FASB)***,[22] which consists of seven full-time, paid members serving renewable five-year terms. The members, while generally accountants or other financial experts, are not necessarily certified public accountants (CPAs). The members are required to sever ties with their previous employers.

FASB membership is designed to provide broad representation and independence. In addition, a key characteristic of FASB operations is the due process by which standards are set. Basically, this process involves the following steps (in the order provided):

1. The topic is placed on FASB agenda.
2. The topic is studied by a task force of experts and by FASB technical staff.
3. A *discussion memorandum* is issued.
4. A public hearing is held.
5. The FASB deliberates on issues.
6. An *exposure draft* is released.
7. A public response period occurs.
8. The FASB reevaluates position and revises draft.
9. The standard is issued if at least five of seven FASB members vote to do so.

The items in italics represent publicly released documents to which the public may respond. After each document is issued, a period of time is provided for comment. The FASB is particularly interested in implementation problems that their proposed standards may cause. An implicit constraint in standard setting is that the benefits of the standard exceed costs of implementation. It is in this regard that corporations can provide counsel to the FASB.

http://

The FASB's home page on the World Wide Web contains summaries of all FASB statements, agendas, and document ordering information. Link to the FASB information from our Web site (http://baginski@swcollege.com).

Public Sector The ***Securities and Exchange Commission (SEC)* is the public sector organization that has statutory authority to regulate accounting standards.** The SEC was created to enforce the Securities Acts of 1933 and 1934. These Acts arose amid economic depression and the collapse of the securities market.

Essentially, the SEC requires registrants to follow ***generally accepted accounting principles (GAAP)*** that have been established by the private sector. In addition, the SEC stimulates FASB activity, consults with the FASB, and takes regular advantage of opportunities for public comment provided by the FASB's due process.

22. Actually, the FASB is the operating unit in a group of three bodies. The other two are the Financial Accounting Standards Advisory Council and the Financial Accounting Foundation. The former is a consulting group to the FASB. The latter selects members of the FASB, selects members of the consulting branch, and funds and oversees activities of the group.

The SEC imposes additional reporting requirements on firms under its jurisdiction (i.e., firms issuing securities pursuant to the 1933 and 1934 Acts). The primary ongoing reporting requirements are the issuance of an annual report form (Form 10-K) and an interim report form for each of the first three quarters of the firm's fiscal year (Form 10-Q). The format of these reports differs somewhat from that of publicly available, GAAP-based financial statements. The specific differences may be investigated by downloading forms from the SEC via the EDGAR system. EDGAR is an electronic system by which users can access reports (such as the 10-K and 10-Q) filed by registrant companies.

http://

Two Web sites can be very helpful in accessing financial information. The EDGAR system is available at the SEC site. Many well-formatted, easy-to-use annual financial reports are available through PricewaterhouseCoopers at a site called EdgarScan. Access both sites at http://baginski@swcollege.com.

GAAP: More Than Just FASB Standards

A company in search of capital must either issue equity securities or borrow and issue debt securities. It is highly likely (and very often required by regulation) that audited financial statements will have to be presented in order to access capital markets. A CPA must sign an opinion that accompanies these statements. In that opinion, the CPA certifies that the financial statements are prepared in accordance with GAAP.

Because nonaccountants have an opportunity to influence standard setting through the FASB's due process, it is important that the nonaccountant be armed with a greater appreciation of exactly what GAAP is and what it is not. **GAAP is comprised of rules, procedures, and historical precedents that are used to prepare U.S. financial statements.** Even though the FASB is the current source of the most significant rule changes, GAAP is more than just FASB Standards. GAAP also consists of standards issued by predecessor organizations to the FASB, authoritative pronouncements from other sources such as the American Institute of CPAs (AICPA), and procedures that over time have become generally accepted through prolonged use. GAAP does not consist of a set of rules that is internally consistent with a single theoretical model.

It takes the FASB a great deal of time to deliberate and issue a standard. To deal with emerging problems on a timely basis, the FASB uses the ***Emerging Issues Task Force (EITF)***. The EITF membership composition is particularly important for understanding the role of this body in the standard-setting process. The 17-member task force has one member of the FASB, one member of the SEC, four corporate members, and 11 members from CPA firms. The charge of the EITF is to reach consensus (15 of 17 members) on quickly emerging, high-profile accounting issues that are likely to have material effects on financial statements.

The trade-off between the EITF recommendations and the FASB Standards is a trade-off between speed and due process. The trade-off appears to be acceptable to the SEC, which views the EITF recommendations as adherent to GAAP. The EITF's early success has raised the possibility of a two-pronged FASB approach to future standard setting, with the EITF resolving the important issues as they can, and the FASB's normal standard-setting process applied to controversial issues for which consensus is difficult to obtain.

The Future of Standard Setting

The accounting profession faces an interesting struggle in the years that lie ahead. In recent years, public confidence in financial reports has been shaken. Savings and loan institutions have failed. Fraud and white-collar crime related to financial reporting has increased substantially. Bankruptcies abound. Large and prestigious CPA firms have been sued for enormous amounts. Congressional hearings have questioned the effectiveness of both the FASB and the SEC.

The accounting profession is likely to rely on a three-tiered approach to address this crisis. First, traditional limitations of financial statements will be removed. Examples are recent standards that require debt and equity securities to be reported at market values rather than historical costs. Second, the profession will educate the public about the limitations of financial statements that cannot be removed. This is a survival tactic. In the presence of financial disaster, the public accounting firms often find that they are the remaining "deep pocket" in an increasingly litigious society. Accountants, however, cannot be held responsible for every financial disaster or act of fraud. Third, the profession is likely to engage in the compromise of continued expansion of notes to the financial statements. Moving information not deemed worthy of recognition in the body of the financial statements to the notes section permits standardization of financial statement information.

The Political Process

The stakes are high in the standard-setting process. Firms realize the importance of accounting reports in raising capital. Politicians recognize the link between financial information, social goals, and wealth. Public accounting firms understand the relationship between alternative measurement rules and the probability of being sued. As a result, these parties lobby to influence accounting standards. Often, their arguments are related to theoretical considerations such as relevance and reliability. But, in other instances, they attempt to influence standard setters by identifying the *economic consequences* of a given standard. ***Economic consequences*** **refer to a given party's misfortune to bear some harm as a result of a given accounting rule, or to a comparative advantage for one party over another created by an accounting rule.**

The economic consequences argument bears some relation to the qualities of accounting information. Information should be provided only if the benefits of the information exceed the costs of providing it. While most people would think of these costs as primarily record-keeping and report preparation costs, the economic consequences argument extends the cost definition. A potentially fruitful economic consequences strategy would be to argue relevance and reliability deficiencies of some proposed standard (i.e., few benefits) while pointing out inexcusably large costs if the standard is implemented.

An Example, Executive Stock Compensation During the early 1990s, the FASB struggled to issue a new standard on executive compensation. Stock options are widely used by startup enterprises to attract and compensate managerial talent, as well as mature companies in an effort to tie executive compensation to stock prices. Clearly, stock options are issued to motivate and compensate individuals. Prior GAAP allowed firms to issue large numbers of stock options without recording any compensation expense. The FASB believed that stock options were awarded to compensate employees; therefore, the value of the options should be charged to expense, which would reduce net income. The FASB proposed this accounting in an Exposure Draft.

The corporate community vehemently objected to the proposal to expense the cost of stock options and fiercely fought the proposed standards. Opponents of the proposed accounting largely used economic consequences and cost/benefit arguments. For example, startup businesses (particularly high-technology businesses) reasoned that if they had to expense stock options, their ability to raise equity capital would be affected, perhaps even eliminated. In response to the political furor generated by the proposed accounting, the FASB backed off the requirement that the value of the options must be expensed. Instead, the FASB allowed companies to use one of two methods. Companies could use the new "fair value" method and measure the value of the options at issuance and record an expense. Alternatively, companies could continue to use the popular "intrinsic value" method, which in most cases required no expense to be recorded. However, if the intrinsic value method were used, the company would be required to report in a financial statement footnote what net income and earnings per share would have been if the value of the options had been expensed. This footnote disclosure promotes comparability across firms, with all firms either recording the expense or disclosing an expense.

Exhibit 9 (pages 32–33) presents a comment letter from a large international public accounting firm, BDO Seidman, in response to the FASB Exposure Draft detailing the proposed accounting for executive stock compensation plans. In the comment letter, you will see references to "economic consequences" and accounting information quality issues such as "reliability." This letter is representative of the hundreds of letters that the FASB may receive on a controversial accounting issue. Even though you may not (at this point) understand the technical issues discussed in the letter, take some time to read the letter and discover how this interested party argues its point. You will also obtain a feel for the importance of standard setting to the business community.

Theory versus Politics: Which Consideration Emerges Victorious? Maintaining neutrality and surviving in the political arena is a serious FASB concern. The FASB and EITF memberships are broad-based. Further, due process, which involves negotiation to some extent, is a characteristic of standard setting. Theoretical concerns should dominate accounting standard setting. However, ignoring political ramifications could lead to the FASB's demise, which could force standard setting to move from the private sector to the public sector. In the United States, this would be a purely political process. The desirability of such an outcome depends on one's political views.

Review of Southwest Airlines Co.'s Financial Information

The focus of the text is on how managerial decisions are reflected in financial statements. To provide concrete examples of how various decisions affect financial statements, we use the financial statements of Southwest Airlines throughout the text to illustrate the effects on items discussed in a chapter. Additionally, in the end-of-chapter problems, we use the financial statements of Texas Instruments, which appear on our Web site (http://baginski@swcollege.com). Therefore, after completing the text, you will have broad, in-depth exposure to the financial statements of two different companies, a major service provider and a major manufacturing company. Both of these firms are leaders in their industries.

The complete 1998 financial statements of Southwest Airlines Co. as well as the MD&A section of the annual report appear in Appendix C at the end of this text. Review Southwest Airlines' balance sheet and income statement at this time. For both financial statements, note that comparative information is presented. For the balance sheet, 1997's results are presented for comparison. For the income statement, comparative results for 1997 and 1996 are presented. After you review the balance sheet and income statement, continue reading in this section. As we discuss the detail, make sure you cross-reference the amounts to the appropriate Southwest Airlines financial statement. The purpose of this section is for you to become familiar with the balance sheet and income statement formats and the types of items that appear on the financial statements.

EXHIBIT 9 Example of Comment Letter

BDO Seidman
Accountants and Consultants

15 Columbus Circle
New York, New York 10023-7711
Telephone: (212) 765-7500
Fax: (212) 765-4648

December 31, 1993

Mr. Timothy S. Lucas
Director of Research and Technical Activities
Financial Accounting Standards Board
401 Merritt 7
P.O. Box 5116
Norwalk, Connecticut 06856-5116

Re: Proposed Statement of Financial Accounting Standards
Accounting for Stock-based Compensation
File Reference No. 127-C

Dear Mr. Lucas:

We welcome this opportunity to express our views on the Board's Exposure Draft.

We agree that even "at the money" stock-based awards are valuable to recipients and that there is a strong conceptual argument to record this value when such awards are made. In addition, we commend the Board for clearly describing its proposal to achieve that objective and to reduce the inconsistencies in accounting for fixed and variable plans under APB Opinion 25. However, we have serious concerns that the values obtained by applying the provisions of the Exposure Draft are insufficiently reliable and the methodology is overly complex. When these concerns are considered together with the user community's general opposition to the proposed new accounting rules in this area, it seems to us that the cost-benefit criterion needed to support adoption of the ED is not achieved, particularly for non-public entities. Therefore, we are unable to support the Board's proposal.

While we oppose adoption of the ED, we do so within the framework of the private sector standards-setting process. In that regard, we strongly oppose any legislative initiatives to mandate a particular accounting treatment. Removal of the standards-setting process from the private sector would create a politicized environment within which special interests could erode the neutrality so important to financial statement credibility. It would be unfortunate, therefore, if we were to start on such a legislative path as a result of a proposal that (1) is opposed by so many segments of the Board's constituency, (2) has not been identified by users as a high priority concern in relation to other, more pressing, issues to be considered by the Board, (3) has no effect on cash flows or total equity (except for what we believe to be a questionable increase in equity at the date prepaid stock compensation is initially recorded), and (4) is in an area where significant relevant information is already required by SEC proxy rules.

Our views in support of our position address the following concerns, which are described in subsequent sections of this letter:

- Reliability of information
- Implementation costs
- Applicability to privately-held companies
- Disclosures in lieu of recognition
- Economic consequences
- Broad-based plans
- Changes in estimates
- Prepaid compensation
- Other comments

Reliability of information

We do not believe the values derived from application of the option pricing models contemplated by the Board are a sufficiently reliable representation of fair value to justify their recognition in the financial statements.

According to Concepts Statement 2, "[r]elevance and reliability are the two primary qualities that make financial information useful for decision making . . .. Reliability rests upon the extent to which the accounting description or measurement is verifiable . . .. [V]erifiability means . . . that several measurers are likely to obtain the same measure."

It is doubtful that different measurers could arrive at the same (or even a similar) measure of fair value of nontraded stock options using various pricing models due to the significant judgment inherent in determining certain variables used in these models (e.g., volatility, dividend yield, performance levels). Moreover, while verifiability in accounting ordinarily assumes a future event will corroborate the amount of an asset or liability whose value has been estimated (e.g., loan loss reserves, pension liabilities, realizable value of discontinued operations), such is not the case with untraded stock-based awards, whose value is based on management's best estimates. While the pricing models described in the ED are intended to provide a practical surrogate for fair value, they are designed to be used for short-term tradeable options. Accordingly, their application to longer-term, nontraded options with significant risks of forfeiture is questionable.

The first sentence of the definition of fair value, as included in the Glossary to the ED, states that fair value is "[t]he amount at which a financial instrument could be exchanged in a current transaction between willing parties . . .." This is the usual concept of fair value contemplated by other aspects of the professional literature. However, we doubt that option values derived from applying option pricing models, particularly for companies with volatile securities, would approximate what a willing buyer would pay for those options. In fact, such derived values could significantly overstate an option's value. Moreover, such models do not reflect macro-economic factors that could significantly affect value, such as government regulation, international trade flows, and economic cycles.

We are particularly concerned about certain of the more dynamic assumptions used to estimate fair value: expected volatility, expected dividend yield and expected option term, all of which are extremely subjective. Slight changes in any of these elements could dramatically change the estimate of fair value, even for companies with similar characteristics. Although we would not support a cookbook approach to simplifying the fair value exercise (e.g., using the minimum value method for all companies), we believe that use of the minimum value method would be more sensible for certain publicly-held companies whose shares trade infrequently.

Implementation costs

The ED states that new computer software "reduces the application of . . . models to a fill-in-the-blank exercise." Although the mechanical exercise of inputting numbers is simple enough, it assumes availability of appropriate input data. It is here that the implementation costs become a real issue.

Determining the variables of the pricing model will often require significant time and effort and might require retention of valuation specialists for certain of the more unusual types of grants. The attachment to the Board Chairman's August 3, 1993 letter to Senator Joseph Lieberman states that "Compensation Committees routinely use option-pricing methods in the design and administration of compensation packages . . .. Option traders in financial markets and companies that use strategies to hedge certain risks often employ methods similar to the option pricing models described in the Board's Exposure Draft." These statements are certainly valid. However, they ignore many smaller publicly-held companies as well as non-public companies, which are not familiar with such techniques. Therefore, we believe the preparers' learning curves are greater than that which seems to be perceived by the Board.

Another important cost consideration is the possibly extensive calculations needed to adjust the estimates used to determine fair value (e.g., term, forfeitures, performance). As we indicate in a subsequent section of this letter, we disagree with the need for this reassessment.

Applicability to privately-held companies

In recent years, there has been widespread publicity surrounding significant stock compensation arrangements for certain executives of publicly-held companies. Of course, the compensation receiving so much attention resulted not from concerns about initial valuation of options at the grant date, but rather from the excess of the market value over the option price at the exercise date. This excess is not addressed by the proposed accounting rules, although it is covered by the SEC proxy rules, and we would oppose exercise date measurement for conceptual reasons.

It seems to us that these kinds of user concerns, as well as concerns to eliminate the perceived inconsistencies in APB Opinion 25 have focused substantially on publicly-held companies. Unfortunately, though, the proposal also has swept in privately-held companies, for which stock compensation has not been a significant concern and which can least afford the cost of implementing the proposed rules. Ordinarily, we prefer the same measurement principles for all companies. However, if the Board adopts its proposed rules, we believe it is essential to exempt privately-held companies.

Privately-held companies should not be burdened with the cost of complying with rules that are only nominally useful, at best, to users of their financial statements. We believe that lenders, who are the primary external users of privately-held companies' financial statements, place their emphasis on a company's ability to generate cash flows to repay loans and on tangible assets. Because the financial statement impact of the proposed stock compensation rules has no effect on cash flows or tangible assets, such information is not relevant to lenders.

If the Board concludes that measurement differences are inappropriate, it should not require any category of company to recognize compensation under the proposal. Instead, as discussed in the next section of this letter, it could require only publicly-held companies to disclose in the footnotes information similar to that recommended in Appendix E to the ED, while exempting privately-held companies.

Disclosures in lieu of recognition

As an alternative to changing the accounting for stock-based compensation, we would support retention of the current accounting rules and, for publicly-held companies, disclosures similar to those contained in Appendix E of the ED. Because those disclosures were proposed by a broad spectrum of the Board's main user constituencies, and because the information called for is objective, we believe that the test of reliability of the information will be met.

However, we would oppose application of those proposed disclosures to privately-held companies because we believe it would not be relevant to the primary external users of their financial statements for the reasons expressed previously in this letter and would be costly to implement.

Economic consequences

Much has been publicized about the severe adverse effects the proposal would have on emerging growth companies whose share prices are highly volatile. It has been argued that such companies would be forced either to (1) absorb significant charges to earnings for the value of stock-based compensation, thereby reducing their share values and their ability to raise capital or (2) forego stock compensation and thereby fail to recruit the best personnel. Indeed, such arguments are instrumental in legislative efforts to block adoption of the ED.

While these arguments are compelling, we do not believe it is appropriate for economic consequences to dictate accounting treatment. On the contrary, accounting should neutrally reflect the substance of economic transactions. If there is a reliable, relevant economic event, it should be accounted for according to its substance. However, as previously stated, we do not believe the reliability threshold has been achieved with respect to the Board's proposal.

Broad-based plans

We believe that stock option and stock purchase plans that meet the criteria of paragraph 7 of APB Opinion 25 should continue to be treated as noncompensatory. Such plans are fundamentally a cost-effective method to raise capital and a way to instill in employees an "ownership" attitude, rather than as a means of compensation, and should be accounted for accordingly.

Changes in estimates

Under the proposal, issuance of stock-based compensation (except where settlement may be in cash) results in a credit to equity, not to a liability account. Nevertheless, the Board concluded that SFAS 5 should be applied to assess the probability of achieving performance goals. We do not understand this conclusion because SFAS 5 deals with the probability of an asset impairment or incurrence of a liability. Therefore, it appears that SFAS 5 is not the logical reference for this periodic re-estimation process.

In our view, if issuance of stock-based compensation does not create a liability, any change to the original estimate should not be recognized in the financial statements. While subsequent adjustments to market in performance-based plans are recorded under APB 25, market fluctuations after the grant date are prohibited under the proposal. The reason for using the grant date to measure fair value is because that is when the employer and employee agree to the terms of the award (i.e., an exchange of services for a stock-based award has taken place.)

While we agree with the "mark to market" prohibition, we believe it should extend to other changes in estimates after the grant date. Because the variables comprising fair value are inherent in the initial exchange, any changes in them reflect subsequent developments that were not contemplated when the original exchange was made. In fact, one such possible change—in the estimated exercise period—calls into question the logic of subsequent adjustments. In that regard, we agree that a longer exercise period adds value to stock options. However, the fact that options are exercised later than originally estimated at the grant date might be attributable to a declining stock price. Nevertheless, the ED would require an increase in the fair value of the stock award to reflect the longer exercise period, while ignoring the lower share value. As previously stated, we believe neither of these changes should affect the original recorded cost of the award.

Prepaid compensation

The Board makes a strong case for classifying as an asset the prepaid compensation resulting from issuance of stock-based compensation. However, we are concerned that the uncertainties implicit in valuing the compensation also cloud the amount of probable future economic benefits obtained or controlled by the entity. It also troubles us that companies can create an immediate increase in equity simply because they have issued stock options or other equity instruments in exchange for future services. In that regard, the Board Chairman's August 3, 1993 letter to Senator Lieberman rightfully concludes that the collapse of the thrift industry "demonstrated the consequences of abandoning neutrality" because RAP "obscured problems in troubled institutions." It is anomalous, therefore, that under the ED, equity would generally be increased without a substantive economic improvement in an entity's resources, which could mask an otherwise eroding financial position.

In addition, classifying prepaid stock-based compensation as an asset appears to conflict with EITF Issue 85-1, which requires notes receivable from sales of stock to be deducted from stockholders' equity, except in very limited circumstances. It seems to us that if a note receivable, which may be more objectively valued than prepaid stock-based compensation, is required to reduce equity, the treatment of prepaid stock-based compensation should be consistent. If, however, the proposed provision regarding prepaid stock-based compensation is adopted, the conclusion in EITF Issue 85-1 should be changed.

Other comments

- *Pro-forma disclosures*

  We oppose the ED requirement to disclose the pro forma impact of the new rules on net income and earnings per share three years before the recognition requirements would take effect. While we agree with the reasons expressed by the Board for delaying the recognition provisions, we are concerned that the same problems that befall preparers and users in familiarizing themselves with valuation methodology and financial statement effects, as described in paragraphs 186 and 187, will also exist in preparing and using the pro forma information. For example, it is difficult to imagine that the users of financial statements of an emerging growth company would not be as concerned with footnote disclosure of a substantial charge to earnings resulting from compliance with the new standard as they would be if the charges were recognized directly in the financial statements.

- *Definition of a public entity*

  The definition of public entity in footnote 7 includes "a subsidiary, corporate joint venture, or other entity controlled by an entity covered by (a) or (b)" in that footnote. It is not clear to us why such entities are required to include expected stock price volatility in a pricing model because, like non-public entities, their shares apparently have no trading history on which to base an estimate of expected volatility.

- *Transition*

  According to paragraph 33, "[i]f applied early, the recognition provisions may be applied . . . to all awards that are not already vested at that date." It is unclear whether this provision is to be applied prospectively or on a "catch-up" basis.

- *Amendment to APB Opinion 29*

  Paragraph 267 of the ED states that APB Opinion 29 would be amended to indicate that the new standard "addresses the accounting for the acquisition of employee services for stock or stock-based instruments." However, the new standard also addresses stock-based payments to other suppliers of goods or services.

• • •

We would be pleased to discuss our views with members of the Board or its staff. Please contact us if you have any questions concerning our comments.

Very truly yours,

BDO Seidman

BDO Seidman

Material discussed is meant to provide general information, and should not be acted on without obtaining professional advice appropriately tailored to your individual needs.

http://

You can access the current-year financial statements of Southwest Airlines through our Web site (http://baginski@swcollege.com).

Balance Sheet

Southwest's balance sheet is in the report form and is a classified balance sheet (current and noncurrent status is shown). The amounts are reported in thousands of dollars, except per-share amounts. The asset section of the balance sheet contains three subsections: current assets, property and equipment, and other assets. For 1998 and 1997, respectively, current assets were $574,155,000 and $806,416,000, which represent 12.2% ($574,155,000 ÷ $4,715,996,000) and 19.0% ($806,416,000 ÷ $4,246,160,000) of total assets, respectively. The primary current asset is cash and cash equivalents (over $378 million in 1998 and over $623 million in 1997). Current assets decreased from 1997 to 1998 in both absolute and percentage terms.

Because the airline industry is capital intensive, it not surprising that the property and equipment category accounts for the bulk of assets, with total property and equipment of about $4.14 billion in 1998 ($4,137,610,000 equals 87.7% of total assets) and $3,435,693,000 (80.9% of total assets) in 1997. The bulk of property and equipment is flight equipment. Other assets are less than 0.1% of total assets.

Liabilities are separated into current and noncurrent sections. For 1998 and 1997, current liabilities are $850,653,000 (18.0% of total liabilities and stockholders' equity, $850,653,000 ÷ $4,715,996,000) and $868,513,000 (20.5% of total liabilities and stockholders' equity, $868,513,000 ÷ $4,246,160,000). A separate total is not provided for noncurrent liabilities; therefore, we must compute the total. For 1998 and 1997, noncurrent liabilities (long-term debt, deferred income taxes, deferred gains, and other deferred liabilities) equal $1,467,425,000 and $1,368,629,000, respectively. The primary noncurrent liabilities are long-term debt and deferred income taxes (we will cover deferred income taxes in a later chapter).

Adding current and noncurrent liabilities together results in total liabilities of $2,318,078,000 and $2,237,142,000 in 1998 and 1997, respectively. The ratio of total liabilities to stockholders' equity can be computed as a relative measure of how assets are being financed. The total liabilities to equity ratio is 0.97 in 1998 ($2,318,078,000 ÷ $2,397,918,000) and 1.11 in 1997 ($2,237,142,000 ÷ $2,009,018,000), which means that total obligations to creditors decreased from 1997 to 1998 relative to stockholders' equity.

Stockholders' equity contains common stock and capital in excess of par (which sum to contributed capital), retained earnings, and treasury stock. Southwest Airlines issued only common stock; no preferred stock has been authorized. Southwest Airlines had much more common stock issued at December 31, 1998, than at December 31, 1997 (335,904,306 shares versus 221,207,083 shares).

Income Statement

Note that as a service company, Southwest Airlines uses a multiple-step income statement but does not report gross margin (profit) separately. The income statement indicates that net income increased from $207,337,000 in 1996 to $317,772,000 in 1997, and then to $433,431,000 in 1998. Income (earnings) per share also increased substantially (from $0.61 diluted in 1996 to $1.23 diluted in 1998). Southwest separates revenues into three components (passenger, freight, and other) with passenger revenue equal to 95.2% of the total 1998 revenues ($3,963,781,000 ÷ $4,163,980,000). Total operating expenses of $3,480,369,000 in 1998 is comprised of eight items. Salaries, wages, and benefits is the largest operating expense item, accounting for 36.9% of total operating expenses in 1998 ($1,285,942,000 ÷ $3,480,369,000). The next largest operating expense item is other operating expenses, followed by fuel and oil.

The other expenses (income) category includes four items: interest expense, capitalized interest, interest income, and nonoperating gains (losses), net. Total other expenses (income) reflect expenses in 1996 and 1997 and income in 1998. The item "provision for income taxes" represents income tax expense.

Management's Discussion and Analysis (MD&A)

Reviewing the balance sheet and income statement allow the reader to glean much information about a company. To assist readers in understanding the financial statements, a company is required to provide a management discussion and analysis (MD&A). Turn now to Southwest Airlines' MD&A and read the RESULTS OF OPERATIONS section. This section will provide you much more information about the 1998 and 1997 results. In the airline industry, two standardized measures have evolved to help understand performance. On the revenue side, companies report revenue passenger miles (RPMs) flown. Total RPMs are the total miles flown by revenue-paying passengers. In 1998, Southwest Airlines' RPMs were up 10.8% over 1997. A second standardized measure is available seat miles (ASM), which is a measure of capacity. Note in the MD&A section that operating expenses are presented on an ASM basis. For example, 1998 salaries, wages, and benefits were 2.35 cents per ASM, a slight increase from 2.26 cents per ASM in 1997. Total operating expenses per ASM were down to 7.32 cents in 1998 from 7.40 cents in 1997. Financial analysts closely track RPMs, revenue per RPM, ASMs, and expenses per ASM. The goal in this chapter is to provide you with an understanding of why the MD&A is provided in annual reports and how it can provide useful, interpretive information to readers. As we continue in the text, we return to the Southwest financial statements and MD&A to take a closer look at many items.

Chapter Summary

Managers are continually called upon to make operating, investing, and financing decisions. The effects of these decisions are measured by accountants and reported in financial statements. We assume that the goal of a firm's management is to maximize the value of the firm. While value, from the investor and creditor's point of view, is determined by the cash flows that they receive from holding claims against the firm's assets, investors and creditors still use accrual-based financial statements to assess value. These accrual-based statements—the income statement, balance sheet, and statement of shareholders' equity—are interrelated arrangements of accrual elements, which are the assets, liabilities, owners' equity, revenues, expenses, gains, losses, investments by owners, and distributions to owners. Assets describe the resources available to the firm, while liabilities and owners' equity describe the claims against those assets. Revenues, expenses, gains, losses, investments by owners, and distributions to owners describe the changes in assets, liabilities, and owners' equities.

Over the life of a firm, cash flows and accrual-based financial statement elements are equivalent. But, in the short run, cash flows may precede, coincide with, or follow accrual accounting recognition. When cash flow timing differs from expense and revenue recognition, either deferrals or accruals are recognized as assets and liabilities.

Different measurement attributes are used in the financial reporting process: historical cost, net realizable value, current replacement cost, market value, or present value. The balance sheet presents the amounts of asset and liabilities at the beginning and end of the year. The annual changes in these balance sheet elements that are related to earnings are shown on the income statement.

The concept of capital maintenance underlies financial reporting. Current GAAP reflects a *financial* capital maintenance model rather than a *physical* capital maintenance model. GAAP uses the transactions approach to income measurement rather than the simple capital maintenance approach. In the transactions approach, the effect of each transaction on net income is recorded. Under a simple capital maintenance approach, the effect of specific transactions is of no interest, and net income is computed simply with reference to beginning and ending net asset values, adjusted for contributions by and distributions to owners. An income statement prepared in accordance with GAAP aggregates the effects of similar transactions during the period into certain categories (e.g., sales, cost of goods sold, general and administrative expenses). In computing the value of a company's stock, financial analysts would make adjustments for income statement items that are transitory (i.e., not permanent). Accountants use the income statement, to some extent, as a means of conveying the source and likely permanence of earnings components.

During the rest of the text, we proceed on a journey to discover what particular measurement attributes are used for different financial statement elements. The focus is on how accountants reflect managerial decisions in the financial statements. Accountants are constrained by rules promulgated by the SEC and FASB. However, the political process used in standard setting allows many opportunities for managers (and accountants) to influence the financial reporting process.

Key Terms

accrual-basis accounting 4
accrued expenses 13
accrued revenues 13
assets 5
balance sheet equation 8
capital maintenance approach 25
capitalization 12
classified balance sheet 19
contributed capital 20
cumulative effect of changes in accounting principles 24
current asset 18
current liability 19
current ratio 19
deferred expenses 12
deferred revenue 11
discontinued operations 24
distributions to owners 8
economic consequences 30
Emerging Issues Task Force (EITF) 29
equity 6
expenses 7
extraordinary items 24
Financial Accounting Standards Board (FASB) 28
financial capital maintenance 26
financing activities 3
gains 7
generally accepted accounting principles (GAAP) 28
gross margin 22
gross margin percentage 23
gross profit 22
gross profit percentage 23
historical cost 21
investing activities 3
investments by owners 7
liabilities 6
liquidity 18
losses 7
material 22
market value 21
net assets 6
net realizable value 21
noncurrent asset 18
operating activities 3
operating cycle 18
owners' equity 6
physical capital 26
physical capital maintenance 26
prepaid expenses 12
present value 21
replacement cost 21
retained earnings 20
revenues 6
Securities and Exchange Commission (SEC) 28
transactions approach 26
unearned revenue 11
working capital 19
working capital ratio 19

Questions

Q1. **Stock Valuation.** What are the two pieces of information that common stock investors need to value common stock? How can financial statements be used to assist investor stock valuation?

Q2. **Types of Managerial Decisions.** What are the three fundamental types of decisions managers make that lead to activities within the firm? Give three examples of each.

Q3. **Managers' Objective.** What is the objective function that managers attempt to maximize when making decisions? What potential conflict exists that could cause a manager to deviate from this objective function?

Q4. **Financial Statements.** What are the four primary financial statements?

Q5. **Financial Statement Elements—Assets.** Using the definitions of the financial statement elements provided in the text, explain why the following situations would *not* lead to the recognition of assets of Cub Food Co.:

a. Cub Food Co. sued Wrigley Co. for patent infringement. Cub Food's attorney believes that there is some chance that Cub will win the suit.
b. A large number of city officials favor Cub's management. As a result, Cub will have little problem securing prime land and obtaining building permits for new stores. This will definitely provide future economic benefit for Cub.
c. Cub possesses inventory that it will sell for a higher price, on credit, next period. Since a contract has been signed specifying that the transaction will occur early next period, Cub would like to record the asset accounts receivable at the higher price in the current period.
d. Cub paid its district manager a monthly salary.

Q6. **Financial Statement Elements—Liabilities.** Using the definitions of the financial statement elements provided in the text, explain why the following situation would *not* be considered a liability of Met, Inc.:

Met, Inc. purchased another corporation, Gooden Co., from Gooden Co.'s shareholders. The shareholders were reluctant to sell this year because they believed that Gooden would have unusually high profits next year. To entice the shareholders to sell, Met agreed to pay shareholders 70% of any earnings that the new Gooden Subsidiary would earn next year over and above Gooden's prior record earnings set several years ago.

Q7. **Financial Statement Elements.** For each of the following changes in balance sheet elements, indicate the income statement element (i.e., revenue or expense) affected: (Note: Multiple answers are possible. Assume that the change listed is the *only* change in a balance sheet element.)
a. Liabilities reduced in the ordinary course of business.
b. Assets reduced in the ordinary course of business.
c. Liabilities increased in the ordinary course of business.
d. Assets increased in the ordinary course of business.

Q8. **Financial Statement Elements—Income Statement.** What is the primary distinction between revenues/expenses and gains/losses?

Q9. **Financial Statement Elements.** Name the two changes in balance sheet elements that are not reported on the income statement.

Q10. **Balance Sheet—Liquidity.** Define the balance sheet concept of liquidity. How is liquidity reflected on the balance sheet?

Q11. **Operating Cycle.** What do we mean by a firm's "operating cycle"?

Q12. **Balance Sheet—Current versus Noncurrent.** In general, how does the accountant determine whether an item is current or noncurrent?

Q13. **Balance Sheet Classifications.** Which balance sheet classification describes specific assets that make up the company's capacity to operate?

Q14. **Balance Sheet Classification—Tangible versus Intangible Assets.** What are three characteristics that distinguish intangible assets from tangible assets?

Q15. **Balance Sheet—Working Capital.** Define working capital and working capital ratio. How might these measures be evaluated and what might they reveal?

Q16. **Balance Sheet—Financial Flexibility.** What two balance sheet elements are most often compared to assess a firm's financial flexibility?

Q17. **Balance Sheet Attributes.** At what time are historical cost and market value equal?

Q18. **Present Value.** When we compute present value, what are we doing in economic terms?

Q19. **Income Statement Classification.** Income from continuing operations is a major subtotal on the income statement. Indicate whether the following items are disclosed above or below this subtotal:
- discontinued operations
- operating expenses
- extraordinary items
- gains and losses not meeting extraordinary item definition

Q20. **Capital Maintenance.** How is net income defined under the capital maintenance approach?

Q21. **Financial versus Physical Capital Maintenance.** Explain the difference between physical and financial capital maintenance. Give an example. Do GAAP financial statements reflect a financial or physical capital maintenance approach?

Q22. **Capital Maintenance and the Transactions Approach to Income Measurement.** Is the transactions approach to income measurement that is reflected in GAAP income statements consistent or inconsistent with the concept of the capital maintenance approach to income measurement?

Q23. **Permanent versus Transitory Earnings.** What is meant by the statement that "permanent earnings have a more pronounced effect on security prices than transitory earnings"?

Q24. **Accounting Rule-Making Organization.** What is the name of the current private accounting rule-making organization?

Q25. **Due Process.** How is due process used in the private standard-setting process?

Q26. **SEC.** How does the Securities and Exchange Commission influence standard setting?

Q27. **GAAP.** Define GAAP.

Q28. **Emerging Issues Task Force (EITF).** What is the Emerging Issues Task Force (EITF), and how does its composition and role differ from that of the FASB?

Q29. **Economic Consequences.** What does the term economic consequences mean? How can economic consequences be used in making an argument against an accounting standard?

Q30. **Comment Letter.** Refer to text Exhibit 9, the comment letter from BDO Seidman to the FASB. The firm of BDO Seidman opposed the implementation of the stock-based compensation accounting prescribed in the exposure draft. Summarize BDO Seidman's concerns regarding the reliability of the prescribed information. What implementation costs did BDO Seidman identify? BDO Seidman opposes the applicability of the proposed accounting standards to private companies. Why would private companies with nonpublicly traded securities prepare GAAP-based financial statements? What primary argument(s) does BDO Seidman make in its opposition to requiring private companies to implement the proposed accounting standard? Summarize BDO Seidman's economic consequences arguments.

Q31. **Accrual Accounting.** GAAP-based financial statements, except the statement of cash flows, are based upon accrual accounting rather than cash-based accounting. Briefly describe how the accrual accounting process records revenues and expenses. Why does GAAP use accrual accounting rather than cash flows for the balance sheet and income statement?

Q32. **Statement of Cash Flows.** In the statement of cash flows, activities are separated into what three major areas?

Short Problems

1. **Financial Statement Preparation.** Draw sketches of the balance sheet (account form), income statement, and statement of owners' equity, arranging the elements of financial statements within each statement (i.e., prepare financial statements without numbers). Draw a sketch of the statement of cash flows, identifying the categories of cash flow.

2. **Financial Statement Elements.** Listed below are items that a corporation gave up in order to receive cash.
   a. Another asset that originally cost the corporation an amount *less than* the cash received. (The transaction was not in the primary course of business.)
   b. Another asset that originally cost the corporation an amount *more than* the cash received. (The transaction was not in the primary course of business.)
   c. Another asset that originally cost the corporation an amount *equal to* the cash received.
   d. A service.
   e. A promise to deliver a noncash asset or a service at a later date.
   f. A promise to repay cash at a later date to a bank.
   g. An equity claim (e.g., a share of common stock that provides an investor/owner with a claim to a proportionate share of the net assets of the corporation).

   For each item, describe the effect on the elements of each financial statement using the format shown. Indicate "NE" for no effect. The first transaction has been completed for you.

Change in Balance Sheet	Effect on Income Statement	Effect on Owners' Equity
Increase in assets (cash)		
Decrease in assets	Increase in income through a gain	Increase in net income

3. **Financial Statement Elements.** Listed below are items that a corporation received upon disbursing cash.
   a. Future economic benefits
   b. Economic benefits that are used up in the current period
   c. The forgiveness of a liability
   d. The reduction of an equity claim

   For each item, describe the effect on the elements of each financial statement using the same format as in Problem 2.

4. **Revenue Recognition.** Prepare two time lines, one to illustrate a deferred revenue and one to illustrate an accrued revenue. Label the time lines to indicate when the cash inflow occurs and when the revenue is earned. Also label how the financial statement elements are changed at each of the two points on each time line.

5. **Expense Recognition.** Prepare two time lines, one to illustrate a deferred expense and one to illustrate an accrued expense. Label the time lines to indicate when the cash outflow occurs and when the expense is incurred. Also label how the financial statement elements are changed at each of the two points on each time line.

6. **Balance Sheet Preparation.** Prepare a balance sheet in good summary form using the following information (which is presented in alphabetical order) for McConnell Co. for the year ended December 31, 2001.

Account	Amount (in thousands)
Contributed capital	$450,000
Current assets	80,000
Current liabilities	75,000
Intangible assets	130,000
Investments and funds (noncurrent)	110,000
Long-term liabilities	150,000
Other assets	80,000
Property, plant, and equipment	550,000
Retained earnings	275,000

7. **Balance Sheet Preparation.** Prepare a balance sheet with categories and account titles but without dollar amounts for the XYZ Co., omitting any dollar amounts. Use five categories within the asset elements, and two each within the liability and owners' equity elements. Use broad categories rather than any individual account titles. Make sure to correctly order the classifications as they would be presented in the balance sheet. Use the following format.

XYZ CO.
Balance Sheet
December 31, 20XX

Assets	Liabilities
______	______
______	______
______	Owners' Equity
______	______
______	______

8. **Balance Sheet Measurement Attributes.** Several financial statement measurement attributes are present in the balance sheet. Match the attribute below with the phrase that best describes it.

Attribute	Phrase
Historical cost	amount received upon asset liquidation
Net realizable value	discounted cash flow
Replacement cost	generic term for current input or output price
Market value	amount needed to acquire asset with same capabilities
Present value	original cost to acquire

9. **Income Statement Preparation.** Prepare an income statement in good form using the following information (which is presented in alphabetical order) for McConnell Co. for the year ended December 31, 2001. Use positive numbers for income/gain amounts and negative numbers for expense/loss amounts. McConnell had 100,000 shares of common stock outstanding during 2001.

Account	Amount Income/gain (Expense/loss)
Cost of goods sold	$ 500,000
Cumulative effect of accounting change (net of tax of $40,000)	60,000
Discontinued operations (net of tax of $20,000)	(30,000)
Extraordinary item (net of tax of $32,000)	48,000
Financial revenues and expenses, gains and losses	(10,000)
General and administrative expenses	200,000
Income tax expense (on items other than shown net of tax)	56,000
Sales revenue	1,000,000
Selling expenses	150,000

10. **Income Statement Preparation.** Prepare an income statement for the XYZ Co., omitting any dollar amounts. Use the income statement classifications used in the text. Use the following format.

XYZ CO.
Income Statement
For the Year Ended December 31, 20XX

11. **Net Income—Capital Maintenance.** Given the following information, compute Bailey Company's net income:

Liabilities, January 1, 2001	$175,000
Liabilities, December 31, 2001	180,000
Assets, January 1, 2001	400,000
Assets, December 31, 2001	420,000
Stock issues in 2001	50,000
Dividends in 2001	5,000

Analytical and Comprehensive Problems

http://

12. **Texas Instruments Balance Sheet and Income Statement.** Each chapter in the text includes at least one end-of-chapter problem that uses the 1998 Texas Instruments (TI) financial statements. The TI financials will be used to illustrate the chapter material. In this chapter, we concentrated on the balance sheet and income statement. So that you will become more familiar with these financial statements, answer the following questions about TI. For most of the questions, you will simply have to find the appropriate number in the financial statements and write it down. **Before starting this problem, access the TI balance sheets and income statements at our Web site** (http://baginski.swcollege.com).
    a. Balance sheet liquidity: For 1998 and 1997, what are the amounts of total current assets, total current liabilities, working capital, and the working capital ratio? Did liquidity increase or decrease in 1998 over 1997? What is the largest current asset, and what is its percentage relationship to total current assets?
    b. Assets: What are the amounts of total assets in 1998 and 1997? TI uses the following asset categories: current assets, property, plant and equipment, investments, deferred income taxes, and other assets. Did the amounts associated with each noncurrent asset category increase or decrease in 1998? Which two categories had the biggest change?
    c. Liabilities and stockholders' equity: For 1998 and 1997, what are the amounts for total liabilities, and what are the categories of liabilities presented? Did the liability amounts increase or decrease in 1998? What is the largest liability? For 1998 and 1997, what are the amounts for total stockholders' equity? What amounts of the total assets of the firm are financed by creditors and owners? What percentages of total assets were financed by creditors and by owners?
    d. Income statement: TI does not report gross margin (profit) separately, but it does provide the detail to compute gross margin. For 1998 and 1997, compute gross margin and the gross margin percentage (gross margin/net revenues). What transitory items are highlighted in TI's 1997 income statement? Net income is $407 million and $1,805 million in 1998 and 1997, respectively. What amount is reported for earnings per share?

13. **Financial Statement Elements.** Presented below are descriptions of several events, conditions, and transactions of Firehouse Industries. For each situation (1) identify elements that emerge from the transaction, (2) identify the financial statements to which the ele-

ments belong (balance sheet, income statement, statement of shareholders' equity), and (3) identify where on the year-end statements each element should be reported. For requirement 3, use the following subclassifications:

Financial Statement	Subclassifications
Balance Sheet	Current assets; Investments and funds; Property, plant and equipment; Intangible assets; Current liabilities; Long-term liabilities; Contributed capital; Retained earnings
Income Statement	Part of Operating income, after Operating income but before Income from continuing operations, after Income from continuing operations
Shareholders' Equity	Investment by owner, Distribution to owner (Note: Any transaction that affects shareholders' equity also affects the shareholders' equity section of the balance sheet.)

If you believe that the element's classification depends on other information, identify the other information and state how it would help determine your classification. For example, assume that at year-end, Firehouse had earned interest for which payment had not been received. Use the following format in your answer.

Item	(1) Financial Statement Element	(2) Financial Statement	(3) Placement on Financial Statement
	Asset (interest receivable)	Balance sheet	Current assets
	Revenue (interest revenue)	Income statement	After operating income

a. On January 1, 2001, Firehouse raised capital from operations by issuing several million shares of common stock. During 2001, Firehouse paid dividends to stock investors and repurchased some of the shares and retired them.
b. Firehouse floated a $100,000,000 long-term bond issue on the last day of the year.
c. During 2001, Firehouse sold merchandise for cash on credit (accounts receivable).
d. Several obligations to suppliers for inventory and to employees for wages had not been paid by year-end.
e. On June 1, 2001, Firehouse acquired, from Davis Properties, land and a building to use as a retail store site. Firehouse signed a note payable, promising to pay Davis in 40 equal annual payments, due on May 31 of each year. During 2001, Firehouse used the building although part of the building was destroyed by fire on November 11. The fire loss was uninsured.
f. An employee was injured in the fire and sued Firehouse on December 3. Although the suit has not been decided, Firehouse is clearly at fault and expects to have to pay the full amount of the judgement early next year.
g. Firehouse decided to set aside funds each year to retire the bond issue when it became due. The first deposit was made on July 11.
h. A material amount of fabric inventory was permanently stained by the growth of an unusual fungus at Firehouse's warehouse. This event, which had never occurred before, caused a large loss. The inventory had to be destroyed. The fungus was judged to be a one-time event, and Firehouse appropriately decided to treat it as an extraordinary item.

14. **Balance Sheet Measurement Attributes.** Haselcorn Foundries has a machine that melts scraps of heavy metals and forms the metal into sinkers that are used extensively in the commercial fishing industry. Haselcorn has owned the machine for about half of its expected 20-year useful life.
    a. Identify four different measurement attributes that could be used for this machine for purposes of balance sheet disclosure.
    b. How would you measure each attribute? Be specific. Don't just recall the general process of measurement.
    c. Which measurement attribute do you believe is the most appropriate to present on the balance sheet if Haselcorn continues to use the machine to produce sinkers? Which measurement attribute is used in GAAP balance sheets?

15. **Financial Statement Transaction Classification.** The President of NotSoSure Enterprises is confused over how to report losses from rearranging the production facilities. It took time (i.e., salary and wages) to accomplish the task, and one machine was inadvertently destroyed in the process. Four potential financial statement presentations for the cost of the destroyed asset are shown below. Briefly comment about the appropriateness of each possible presentation, and indicate which alternative is the best.
    - Balance Sheet: Report cost in Property, plant, and equipment
    - Income Statement: Report time costs in general and administrative expenses and machine write-off in other expenses, revenues, gains and losses
    - Income Statement: Extraordinary item
    - Statement of Owners' Equity: Reduction of retained earnings

16. **Capital Maintenance—Compute Missing Amount.** A flash flood in 2001 destroyed the long-term liabilities records of Soggy, Inc. In a desperate attempt to prepare the December 31, 2001, financial statements, you are able to obtain the following information that survived the disaster:

December 31, 2001 Account classification	Amount
Intangible assets	$ 200,000
Current liabilities	50,000
Current assets	300,000
Retained earnings	2,000,000
Property, plant, and equipment	3,000,000
Long-term investments and funds	200,000

You are also aware of the following additional information:

• Total liabilities, January 1, 2001	$ 600,000
• Stock issued during 2001	400,000
• Net loss for 2001	180,000
• Dividends paid in 2001	20,000
• Total assets, January 1, 2001	3,400,000

Compute long-term liabilities at December 31, 2001.

17. **Income Statement Preparation.** Listed below are the amounts from The Sherwin-Williams Company's 1998 statement of consolidated income. Use the amounts to prepare a 1998 income statement, in good form, using the multiple-step format. Your income statement may not match exactly the one that Sherwin-Williams actually reported because you may make different classification choices.

Income Statement Item (alphabetical order)	Amount*
Revenue and income items:	
Interest and net investment income	$ 6,482
Net sales	4,934,430
Expense and loss items:	
Cost of goods sold	2,804,459
Income taxes	167,239
Interest expense	71,971
Other expenses	26,046
Selling, general and administrative expenses	1,598,333
Earnings per share:	
Basic	$1.58
Diluted	1.57

*Amounts in thousands, except per-share amounts

CFA Exam-Type Problems

18. Compared with firms that expense costs, firms that capitalize costs can be expected to report: (CFA adapted)
    a. higher asset levels and lower equity levels.
    b. lower asset levels and lower equity levels.

c. higher asset levels and higher equity levels.
d. lower asset levels and higher equity levels.

19. For a material item to be classified as an extraordinary item on the income statement, it must be: (CFA adapted)
    a. estimated and probable.
    b. current and unusual in frequency.
    c. probable and infrequent in nature.
    d. unusual in nature and infrequent in occurrence.
20. For accounting purposes, which one of the following is *not* an essential characteristic of an asset? (CFA adapted)
    a. Its value is known with certainty.
    b. It embodies a probable future economic benefit.
    c. The enterprise can obtain the benefit and can limit others' access to it.
    d. The event giving the enterprise the claim to the benefit has already occurred.
21. Purvis Corp. wants to increase its current ratio from the present level of 1.5 when it closes its books next week. Which one of the following actions will have the desired effect? (CFA adapted)
    a. Payment of current payables from cash
    b. Sale of current marketable securities for cash
    c. Write-down of impaired assets
    d. Delay of the next payroll

Objectives

1. Explain the link between internal decisions and external decision making provided by financial statements.
2. Calculate selected financial ratios and use them to assess profitability.
3. Calculate selected financial ratios and use them to assess risk.
4. Interpret ratios in the context of a firm's business strategy.
5. Explain the meaning of accounting quality and how it relates to external decision makers' use of financial statements.

Module A

Financial Statements and External Decision Making

1 Explain the link between internal decisions and external decision making provided by financial statements.

Chapter 1 provides an introduction to how management decisions are reflected in financial statements. The three primary accrual financial statements (income statement, balance sheet, and statement of owners' equity) and the statement of cash flows aggregate the outcomes of many management decisions. External decision makers combine an examination of these financial statements with knowledge of a firm's industry conditions and competitive strategies to form opinions about a firm's future prospects.

Financial statement analysis is the process of understanding the *profitability* and *risk* of the firm. Different external decision makers have varying objectives in such an analysis. Short-term lenders (e.g., banks and trade creditors) have immediate liquidity as their primary concern. Long-term creditors are less interested in immediate liquidity, but are more concerned with the solvency of the firm, the strength of its long-term asset position, and its current, intermediate, and long-term profitability. Equity investors are interested in the level and variability of the residual cash flows after satisfying debt claims. Labor unions, such as those formed by professional athletes, pay attention to the owners' long-term profitability. Government regulators are worried about the excess profitability in certain high-profile industries (e.g., oil and gas and pharmaceuticals) and the solvency of key firms whose financial health affect economic growth (e.g., General Motors) or national defense (e.g., Lockheed).

In this module, we develop a general structure for financial statement analysis that should be useful for each kind of external decision maker. Management decisions discussed throughout the text are reflected in the financial statements and directly affect financial ratios and other financial measures that are described in this module. This module includes the following:

- Ratio analysis of profitability
- Ratio analysis of risk

- Ratio interpretation in the context of a firm's business strategy
- Introduction to the analysis of "accounting quality"

The first three topics are entirely developed in this module. Accounting quality is also introduced, but specific examples of its application appear later in Modules B, C, and D. Throughout Module A, we use the 1998 TCBY annual report (Appendix D) to illustrate the financial statement analysis concepts presented.

Ratio Analysis of Profitability

2 Calculate selected financial ratios and use them to assess profitability.

Several parties provide the financing that supports a firm's investing and operating activities. These parties may differently assess a firm's profitability. For example, a bondholder may believe that a firm is profitable if it generates enough profits to ensure a return of debt capital invested and to provide interest revenue. For a common shareholder, the residual increase in capital per dollar of equity capital invested may be the most important measure of profitability.

The Firm's (All Capital Providers) View of Profitability

We begin our analysis of profitability by presenting the return on assets (ROA) ratio as a measure of how profitable a company is *regardless of how the company's assets are financed.* In terms of the three types of firm activities—operating, investing, and financing—***Return on assets (ROA)*** **measures the net profitability of operating activities per dollar of average investment.**[1] ROA is computed as:

ROA = [Net Income + Interest expense, net of income taxes] ÷ Average total assets

$$\text{ROA} = [\text{Net income} + \text{Interest expense } (1 - t)] \div \text{Average total assets}$$

where t equals the marginal (or statutory) tax rate

Interest expense is added back because it is the only capital charge that is subtracted in the calculation of net income. Adding back this after-tax charge transforms the numerator into a measure of the increase in net assets *before* financing. We do not add back dividends to common or preferred shareholders because dividends are not deducted in arriving at net income.

In Chapter 1, we introduced the financial statements of TCBY Enterprises. To compute TCBY's 1998 ROA, we need net income, interest expense, average total assets, and the marginal income tax rate. Net income of $10,195,612 and interest expense of $545,664 are found on the income statement. Firms commonly disclose interest expense in a footnote; the disclosure of interest expense on the income statement is a less common practice. Total assets is found on the balance sheet. Average total assets is computed as $96,858,640 [(1998 total assets $94,452,884 + 1997 total assets $99,264,396) ÷ 2]. *For convenience, we use a statutory tax rate of 35% throughout this module.* TCBY's 1998 ROA is:

$$\text{ROA (1998)} = [\$10{,}195{,}612 + \$545{,}664\,(1 - 0.35)] \div \$96{,}858{,}640 = 10.89\%$$

To understand TCBY's performance, a financial analyst will track TCBY's ROA through time, compare it to expected ROA given the risk level of a firm, and compare it to average industry ROA as well as the ROA of key industry competitors. As an example of the latter kind of analysis, *Ward*'s classifies TCBY in Standard Industrial Classification (SIC) Code 5812, "Eating Places (Fast Foods)."[2] *Robert*

1. Although net income primarily reflects operating decisions, it is also affected by investing and financing decisions.
2. *Ward's Business Directory of U.S. Private and Public Companies* (International Thomson Publishing Co., 1999). SIC codes are used to categorize groups of firms providing similar products or services into a predetermined set of standard classifications.

Morris and Associates reports the following industry ROA figures for SIC #5812 for the fiscal year ending March 31, 1998:[3]

Upper quartile	20.9%
Median	8.8%
Lower quartile	1.4%

At first glance, it appears that TCBY's 1998 ROA of 10.89% was slightly above the industry median but substantially below the upper quartile. However, one problem that precludes direct comparison is that TCBY's 1998 fiscal year-end is November 29, while the industry ratios are computed for a March 31 fiscal year-end. An analyst has several choices in dealing with this timing problem. First, a November 29 fiscal year-end implies a February 28 first quarter-end, which is only one month from the quoted March 31 year-end amounts. The analyst could combine TCBY's annual financial statements with interim reports to simulate a February 28 year-end. However, this approach can cause some problems; aside from being unaudited, interim reports are not as detailed, involve more accountant's estimation, and do not include fourth-quarter adjustments from estimated to actual amounts that arise from the annual audit. A second choice would be for the analyst to construct ratios for the April 1, 1998, to March 31, 1999, period (or wait for them to be accumulated and published), viewing this time frame as a more appropriate comparison because it includes the same summer time-period as TCBY's November 29, 1998, annual report. A third approach would be to use the weighted averages of the two March 31 year-end periods. For our purposes, we use the March 31, 1998, industry ratios.

Another major problem that arises in comparing a ratio for a particular company with published industry statistics is the definition of ratios. For example, Robert Morris defines ROA in *before-tax* terms and does not adjust for interest expense:

$$\text{ROA (Robert Morris definition)} = \text{Income before taxes} \div \text{Total assets}$$

By recomputing TCBY's 1998 ROA in before-tax terms, we get 15.95%, an amount that is much higher than the industry median of 8.8% but still below the industry upper quartile of 20.9%.

$$\text{ROA (Robert Morris definition)} = \$15{,}447{,}896 \div \$96{,}858{,}640 = 15.95\%$$

Which is the correct ROA computation? We believe that our computation is more theoretically correct, but no particular ratio computation is *most* correct in an absolute sense. The major point to remember in ratio analysis is the old adage "compare apples to apples, not apples to oranges." For ratio comparisons, make sure that the ratios were computed according to the same definitions. *Throughout the text we use our definition of ROA, unless otherwise indicated.*

In the ROA numerator, the dollar amount represents the amount that is available for distribution to preferred and common shareholders through dividend payments, and to debt holders through interest payments. Therefore, although the level of ROA may affect the amount of dividends paid to common stockholders, it does not determine the amount of preferred dividends or the amount of interest expense. These are fixed charges, set by contract to equal a stated rate. Common equity shareholders and creditors pay close attention to the level of and variability in ROA.

3. *Robert Morris and Associates Annual Statement Studies* (Robert Morris and Associates, 1998–1999).

The Common Equity Holders' View of Profitability

The common equity holder's unique view of profitability motivates an alternative, related profitability measure, the ***return on common equity (ROCE)***. ROCE is expressed as follows:

$$\text{ROCE} = \text{ROA} \times \text{Common earnings leverage ratio} \times \text{Capital structure leverage ratio}$$

where

$$\text{ROA} = [\text{Net income} + \text{Interest expense } (1 - t)] \div \text{Average total assets}$$

$$\textit{Common earnings leverage ratio} = \frac{\text{Net income} - \text{Preferred stock dividends}}{\text{Net income} + (1 - t)\text{ Interest expense}}$$

$$\textit{Capital structure leverage ratio} = \text{Average total assets} \div \text{Average common stockholders' equity}$$

The denominator in ROA cancels with the numerator in the capital structure leverage ratio, and the numerator in ROA cancels with the denominator in the common earnings leverage ratio. These steps reduce the ROCE formula to:

$$\textbf{ROCE} = \frac{\textbf{Net income} - \textbf{Preferred stock dividends}}{\textbf{Average common stockholders' equity}}$$

The first component of the expanded ROCE definition is ROA, the contribution to ROCE that occurs primarily from operating and some investing activities. The remaining terms, common earnings leverage ratio and capital structure leverage ratio, **jointly determine the effect on ROCE of financing activities.** Thus, ROCE is directly linked to all three activities of corporations: operating, investing, and financing. For a given ROA, the ROCE is higher when the two leverage components are higher. Common earnings leverage ratio and capital structure leverage ratio capture the negative and positive effects of using interest bearing financing, respectively.

We provide a very specific formulation for ROCE. Frequently in the popular press, the term *return on equity (ROE)* is used. Very often, ROE is defined as we define ROCE. However, ROE might simply be defined as net income divided by average total stockholders' equity. Once again, when considering ratios provided by other parties, make sure you know exactly how the ratio is defined.

Common Earnings Leverage Ratio The common earnings leverage ratio uses preferred dividends and interest expense, net of tax, to adjust net income in the numerator and denominator. ***Common earnings leverage ratio* captures the *negative* effects of capital structure on ROCE.**

$$\textbf{Common earnings leverage ratio} = \frac{\textbf{Net income} - \textbf{Preferred dividends}}{\textbf{Net income} + (1 - t)\textbf{ Interest expense}}$$

To understand the common earnings leverage ratio, we will separately discuss the effect of preferred dividends and interest expense. First, consider the effect of debt. Assume that a company has no preferred shareholders. The common earnings leverage ratio numerator would be net income, and the denominator would be net income plus after-tax interest expense. If the company uses no interest-bearing debt, then the common earnings leverage ratio is equal to one. However, as interest-bearing debt is added to the capital structure (i.e., interest expense is incurred), the denominator increases causing the common earnings leverage ratio to become less than one. In the ROCE formula, this causes ROA to be multiplied by a number less than one, which decreases ROCE. Second, consider the effect of preferred stock. If preferred stock is present in the capital structure but debt is not, then preferred stock dividends are subtracted from the numerator with no effect on the denominator, which again results in a common earnings leverage ratio of less than one. This also lowers ROCE because ROA is multiplied by a ratio of less than one to arrive at ROCE.

Capital Structure Leverage Ratio The *positive* effect of leverage on ROCE is captured by the *capital structure leverage ratio*:

$$\text{Capital structure leverage ratio} = \frac{\text{Average total assets}}{\text{Average common stockholders' equity}}$$

The positive effect is realized by the firm earning a return on assets that common shareholders did not have to finance. Note that the numerator of the capital structure leverage ratio is average total assets, which are financed by three sources: debt, preferred equity, and common equity. However, the denominator of the capital structure leverage ratio is average common stockholders' equity, which equals the portion of assets financed by common equity. As the company uses more preferred equity and debt financing to acquire assets, the numerator increases but the denominator stays the same. Therefore, the ratio increases, leading to an increase in ROCE.

TCBY's ROCE

We can compute 1998 ROCE from TCBY's financial statements by subtracting preferred dividends (normally disclosed in the statement of owners' equity) from net income ($10,195,612). Preferred dividends do not appear in TCBY's 1998 statement of owners' equity. The absence of preferred dividends in the statement of owners' equity is confirmed on the balance sheet—TCBY reports preferred stock authorized, but none outstanding. Average common stockholders' equity is computed by averaging the beginning and year-end stockholders' equity excluding preferred stock. From TCBY's balance sheet, average common stockholders' equity is $76,810,838 [(1998 common stockholders' equity $76,196,154 + 1997 common stockholders' equity $77,425,522) ÷ 2]. TCBY's 1998 ROCE computed using the reduced ROCE formula is:

$$\text{ROCE} = (\text{Net income} - \text{Preferred stock dividends}) \div \text{Average common stockholders' equity}$$
$$\text{ROCE} = (\$10{,}195{,}612 - 0) \div \$76{,}810{,}838 = 13.27\%$$

Alternatively, ROCE may also be computed in terms of the three components of ROA as follows:

$$\text{ROCE} = \text{ROA} \times \text{Common earnings leverage ratio} \times \text{Capital structure leverage ratio}$$
$$\text{ROCE} = 10.89\% \times 0.966 \times 1.261 = 13.27\%$$

where

ROA = 10.89%, as previously calculated

$$\text{Common earnings leverage ratio} = \frac{\text{Net income} - \text{Preferred dividends}}{\text{Net income} + (1 - t)\text{ Interest expense}}$$
$$= \frac{\$10{,}195{,}612 - 0}{\$10{,}195{,}612 + (1 - 0.35)\ \$545{,}664} = 0.966$$

$$\text{Capital structure leverage ratio} = \frac{\text{Average total assets}}{\text{Average common stockholders' equity}}$$
$$= \frac{\$96{,}858{,}640}{\$76{,}810{,}838} = 1.261$$

The components of ROCE reflect that the capital structure has a slightly negative effect in the computation of ROCE (the common earnings leverage ratio is 0.966, slightly less than 1.0) and a slightly positive effect (the capital structure leverage ratio is 1.261, which is greater than 1.0).

To compare TCBY's ROCE with publicly available information about its competitors, we again use the data from Robert Morris. Consistent with its ROA definition, Robert Morris defines ROCE on a before-tax basis. In addition, Robert Morris subtracts intangible assets from common shareholders' equity to establish a return on "tangible net worth." Industry data from Robert Morris for return on tangible net worth is as follows:

Upper quartile	85.3%
Median	34.2%
Lower quartile	11.2%

In order to compare TCBY to the given industry data, we redefine the ROCE numerator to a before-tax basis and deduct intangible assets ($4,250,684 in 1998 and $4,326,193 in 1997, which are found on the balance sheet) in determining tangible net worth (or average tangible common equity). The adjustments yield a 1998 TCBY ROCE of 21.3%, calculated as follows:

$$\text{ROCE (Robert Morris definition)} = \frac{\text{Income before income taxes}}{\text{Average tangible common stockholders' equity}}$$

$$\text{ROCE (Robert Morris definition)} = \frac{\$15,447,896}{[(76,196,154 + \$77,425,522) \div 2] - [(\$4,250,684 + \$4,326,193) \div 2]}$$

$$= \frac{\$15,447,896}{\$72,522,399} = 21.30\%$$

The 21.3% ROCE is substantially below the industry median ROCE of 34.2%. This occurs because TCBY' capital structure ratio of 1.261 is far below the industry average of approximately 3.55 (source: Robert Morris). As a result, TCBY's above-median ROA performance does not translate to an above-median ROCE performance.

The effect of management's capital structure decisions is evident in the ROCE formulation. ROCE is maximized when leverage is optimally employed. When ROCE is viewed in isolation, it appears that leverage should be maximized. However, in typical earnings-based valuation formulas, ROCE is discounted by risk measures. Increased leverage results in increased risk, which leads to an increased interest rate at which future dividends (in a dividend-based valuation model) or permanent earnings (in an earnings-based valuation model) are discounted.

ROA and Management's Operating and Investing Decisions

The contribution of management's operating and investing decisions to ROCE can be evaluated by breaking ROA down into the ratios for net profit margin and asset turnover:

$$\text{ROA} = \text{Net profit margin ratio} \times \text{Asset turnover ratio}$$

where

$$\text{Net profit margin ratio} = [\text{Net income} + (1 - t)\ \text{Interest expense}] \div \text{Sales}$$

and

$$\text{Asset turnover ratio} = \text{Sales} \div \text{Average total assets}$$

Net Profit Margin Ratio The *net profit margin ratio* **is the ratio of prefinancing income per dollar of sales.** Net profit margin ratio is increased by management's efforts to increase sales revenue and control costs. *Thus, operating decisions are primarily responsible for the net profit margin ratio.* The net profit margin ratio may be further broken down into the ratio of gross margin (Sales − Cost of goods sold) to sales and into ratios of individual expenses to sales:

Gross margin ratio **= Gross margin ÷ Sales**
Individual expense ratio **= Each individual expense ÷ Sales**

Asset Turnover Ratio The *asset turnover ratio* **measures the ratio of sales (an operating activity) per dollar of average investment in net assets (primarily investing activities).** ROA can be increased even in the presence of low net profit margins by "selling" total assets several times. Grocery stores are a perfect example of low net profit margins and high asset turnover. There are three activity ratios that explain the majority of asset turnover: accounts receivable turnover, inventory turnover, and fixed asset turnover:

Accounts receivable turnover ratio **= Sales ÷ Average accounts receivable**

This ratio reflects the effects of management operating decisions that affected sales, as well as operating decisions about managing accounts receivable. This ratio is frequently used to calculate the ***average number of days receivables outstanding ratio***, which is calculated by dividing 365 by the accounts receivable turnover ratio.

Inventory turnover ratio **= Cost of goods sold ÷ Average inventory**

This ratio reflects the effects of management operating decisions that affected the cost of goods sold and the cost levels of inventories.[4]

Fixed asset turnover ratio **= Sales ÷ Average property, plant, and equipment**

This ratio reflects the effects of management operating decisions regarding sales, and investing decisions pertaining to property, plant, and equipment.

Decomposing TCBY's ROA To compute TCBY's 1998 ratios for net profit margin and asset turnover, we use the previously identified amounts for net income, interest expense, the income tax rate, and average total assets, as well as 1998 net sales ($93,865,413 in the income statement). TCBY's 1998 net profit margin ratio and asset turnover ratio are computed as:

$$\text{Net profit margin ratio} = [\text{Net income} + (1 - t)\ \text{Interest expense}] \div \text{Sales}$$
$$= [\$10{,}195{,}612 + (1 - 0.35)\$545{,}664] \div \$93{,}865{,}413 = 11.24\%$$

$$\text{Asset turnover ratio} = \text{Sales} \div \text{Average total assets}$$
$$= \$93{,}865{,}413 \div \$96{,}858{,}640 = 0.969$$

These ratios may be combined to compute TCBY's previously calculated 10.89% ROA.

$$\text{ROA} = \text{Net profit margin ratio} \times \text{Asset turnover ratio}$$
$$10.89\% = 11.24\% \times 0.969$$

4. The inventory turnover ratio is also often expressed in terms of number of days by dividing 365 by the ratio.

In relation to the industry, TCBY's 1998 net profit margin of 11.24% on an after-tax basis is very high. (Robert Morris and Associates reports a median of 3.9% on a *before*-tax basis for the April 1, 1997, to March 31, 1998, period.) Further, TCBY's asset turnover ratio of 0.969 is low relative to the industry median of 3.1 for the same period.[5]

To compute TCBY's accounts receivable, inventory, and fixed asset turnover ratios, we need additional information from the financial statements: average trade accounts receivable, average inventory, and average fixed assets from the balance sheet; and cost of goods sold from the income statement. Average trade accounts receivable is $9,414,470 ($10,078,733 and $8,750,207 are the 1998 and 1997 trade accounts receivable, respectively); average inventory is $11,617,053 (1998 and 1997 inventory, $12,554,875 and $10,679,231, respectively); average fixed assets is $38,166,698 (1998 and 1997 property, plant, and equipment of $35,992,113 and $40,341,282, respectively). The 1998 cost of goods sold is $64,098,811.

Accounts receivable turnover ratio = $93,865,413 ÷ 9,414,470 = 9.97

Inventory turnover ratio = $64,098,811 ÷ $11,617,053 = 5.52

Fixed asset turnover ratio = $93,865,413 ÷ $38,166,698 = 2.46

These turnover ratios are examined through time. Generally, increases in turnover ratios are good news because the turnovers are multiplied by profit margins to generate ROA.

Profitability can be better understood by examining TCBY's gross margin ratio and the ratios of expenses to sales. To track these amounts over time, we compute the gross margin and selling, general, and administrative expense ratios for 1998, 1997, and 1996.

	1998	1997	1996
Sales	$93,865,413	$90,577,654	$82,964,258
Gross margin	$29,766,602	$30,179,188	$29,416,013
Gross margin ratio* (Gross margin/Sales)	31.7%	33.3%	35.5%
Selling, general, and administrative expense	$30,393,591	$30,974,594	$32,601,401
Selling, general, and administrative expense ratio (SG&A expense/Sales)**	32.4%	34.2%	39.3%

*Referred to in Chapter 1 as gross margin percentage. Also called ***gross profit ratio*** (or percentage).
**An alternative definition is SG&A expense/Total revenue, where total revenue = (Sales + Interest income + Other income).

Two observations are noteworthy. First, TCBY's gross margin ratios fell between 1996 and 1998, probably due to the effect of increased competition on prices. But, it appears that an offsetting reduction in selling, general, and administrative expenses was achieved as well; selling, general, and administrative expenses declined as a percent of net sales between 1996 and 1998, thus preserving a high ROA. Second, these figures suggest that an analyst might need to compare TCBY ratios to industry averages for "Eating Places–Fast Foods" with great care. Industry medians for the gross margin ratio and the selling, general, and administrative expense ratio are 61.2% and 55.8%, respectively. The substantial difference between the ratios for TCBY and the industry average suggests that the analyst might wish to compare other firms with TCBY on several dimensions. These dimensions include but are not limited to:

5. The asset, accounts receivable, and fixed asset turnover ratios include sales but do not include TCBY's franchise revenues in the numerator. TCBY reports franchise revenues separately after gross profit. Inclusion of franchise revenues in the numerator would increase the average ratio significantly, but not enough to bring the ratios near industry averages. For example, the asset turnover ratio would increase to 1.10 if franchise revenues were included in sales.

- *Distribution channel:* TCBY's 1998 sales distribution includes 50% to food service distributors and 31% to the retail grocery trade. Possibly other firms in the industry are not engaged in as much wholesaler activity.
- *Asset structure:* TCBY has a much larger investment activity than the industry, holding higher short-term marketable securities and notes receivable from financing franchise operations. Investment income is also quite high relative to the industry.

A High Profile Measure of Profitability: Earnings Per Share

Financial press discussions of current results and future prospects often focus on another measure of profitability, earnings per share (EPS), which is the most often quoted performance statistic about a firm. This measure is so important that it is presented on the income statement under generally accepted accounting principles. EPS standardizes net earnings, a measure of the company's performance, on a per share of common stock basis. EPS is useful in comparing performance over time and across firms. We discuss the computation of EPS in Chapter 10. For 1998, TCBY's EPS = $0.44; TCBY's EPS increased over the 1996–1998 period from $0.26 to $0.44.

Expressing earnings on a per share basis is useful because common stock prices are quoted on a per share basis. Also, financial analysts and managers present forecasts that are most often expressed in terms of EPS. Investors and analysts construct *price to earnings (PE) ratios* to relate the two per share measures.

***Price/Earnings Ratio (PE Ratio)* = Stock price per share ÷ EPS**

Despite the high profile of EPS, it is not the best measure of profitability. Although it is a ratio, it ignores the level of investment required to generate earnings, and thus, is influenced by the size of the firm and the number of shares offered and outstanding. For this reason, PE ratios are computed in many valuation contexts in order to relate earnings to capital market investment. TCBY's 1998 share price averaged $6.53 in the fourth quarter (from the corporate information section of the annual report), and its EPS was $0.44 (from the income statement). Therefore, TCBY's 1998 PE ratio is approximately 14.8 ($6.53/$0.44).

Ratio Analysis of Risk

3 Calculate selected financial ratios and use them to assess risk.

The sources of risk are numerous; they are also often necessary to generate an above average ROCE. For example, consider the risk exposure of a firm that launches a venture to produce a computer component in a foreign country. What are a creditor's risks of receiving interest payments and maturity value if a loan is made to the company? To answer this and related questions, we examine firm risks, industry risks, and general economic risks.

Firm Risks

A major source of risk for this venture is the risk of strategic management error. Managers must identify and implement a viable strategy to produce and market the computer component. Is it best for the firm to compete on price or differentiate the quality of the component? What are the key economic assets (often referred to as "core competencies") that must be in place to achieve and sustain the strategy? How will the assets be used and replaced? The answers to each of these questions require imperfect projections, and thus, introduce risk of strategic error.

Industry Risks

The manufacture of computer components requires raw materials and a trained, cooperative work force. Disruption in the supply of either materials or labor is possible. Output market risks are also present. As well, an increase in component production by competitors and technological change could threaten profits.

General Economic Risks

Changes in the demand for the component can occur from general economic conditions. Recession and/or inflation might reduce disposable income, and as a result, decrease the demand for consumer durables and the components needed to assemble them. Input costs might also change unexpectedly due to inflation and interest rate changes. In our example, home country political changes might have little effect, but foreign government changes could cause dramatic fluctuations in host country economic conditions. Resulting fluctuations in the exchange rate or difficulty in transferring funds pose significant risks of not having the cash available to meet contractual debt obligations.

The primary financial statements generally do not accurately reflect these future-oriented risks. However, ratios constructed from current financial conditions can give some indication of the financial health of the company. The analyst can sense how a company could respond to the downsides posed by firm, industry, and general economic risks. Generally, bankruptcy or less severe disruptions in operations can be avoided by raising cash internally or externally. The analysis of short-term liquidity risk answers the question of how quickly cash can be raised internally; the analysis of long-term solvency risk addresses the firm's ability to raise cash in external markets at a reasonable cost.

Short-Term Liquidity Risk

Comprehending short-term liquidity involves the understanding of how a firm conducts operating activities. The firm's operating cycle is the process of using cash to acquire inventory or the factors of production (materials, labor, etc.), generating receivables from sales, and collecting cash from customers. The primary ratios used to understand short-term liquidity risk involve comparisons between two sections of the balance sheet: current assets and current liabilities. The current assets section lists accounts in order of liquidity. The current liabilities section discloses the obligations that are to be satisfied by using current assets.

The ***current ratio*** shows the relation between current assets and current liabilities:

Current ratio = Current assets ÷ Current liabilities

Most firms carry current ratios between 1.0 and 2.0. Ratios below 1.0 suggest insufficient current assets to satisfy current liabilities.[6]

Several problems occur when using the current ratio as the sole evaluative tool for short-term liquidity risk. First, current liabilities are dominated by contractual promises to pay cash in fixed amounts.[7] However, current assets may include a large portion of inventory that is reported on the balance sheet at historical cost but is likely to sell at an amount that is significantly higher. For this reason, the

6. Alternatively, from a profitability perspective, a high current ratio might indicate overinvestment in working capital (e.g., inventory is too high).

7. Exceptions would include promises to deliver services (such as unearned rent) and promises to deliver goods (such as unearned subscriptions).

analyst should interpret the current ratio with regard to the proportion of inventory in the numerator and the gross profit margin that the company earns on inventory sales. Second, a general economic downturn may cause companies to contract production, pay liabilities, and render the denominator so small that the current ratio becomes inflated. A subsequent economic expansion can then result in a reduced current ratio. Third, the current ratio basically ignores variations in cash realization timing among the various current assets in the numerator. For this reason, a second ratio, the *quick ratio,* is often calculated as a measure of short-term liquidity risk:

Quick ratio **= Quick assets ÷ Current liabilities**

Quick ratio = **(Cash + Marketable securities + Receivables) ÷ Current liabilities**

The quick ratio removes inventories and prepaid items from the current ratio numerator, leaving only the items that are highly liquid. Marketable securities can be sold quickly, and accounts receivable are generally collected within a 30 to 60 day period. Inventories, however, might take a long time to sell, especially in a recessionary period. Cash, marketable securities, and receivables tend to equal an average of approximately 50% of current liabilities.

Current assets provide an estimate of amounts to be realized in the next operating cycle (i.e., operating cash inflow), and current liabilities provide (with a higher degree of certainty) the amounts to be paid in the upcoming operating cycle (i.e., operating cash outflow). The speed at which current assets become cash inflows and current liabilities become cash outflows is critical to internal cash flow generating ability. To understand the speed of operating cash sources and uses, *activity ratios* are defined as follows:

Key ratios using assets that generate working capital (defined previously):

Accounts receivable turnover ratio = Sales ÷ Average accounts receivable

Inventory turnover ratio = Cost of goods sold ÷ Average inventory

Key ratio using liabilities that decrease working capital:

Accounts payable turnover ratio **= Purchases[8] ÷ Average accounts payable**

Dividing 365 by the ratios provides the activity in terms of number of days.

Each ratio described in this section is derived from accrual accounting elements. The cash flow effects of management decisions are reflected in the statement of cash flows. Recall that the cash flow statement separates all cash flows into those from operating, investing, and financing activities. Cash flow from operations shows how much cash was available for investing and financing activities after adjustment for changes in working capital assets (such as accounts receivable and inventory) and working capital liabilities (i.e., current liabilities). The *cash flow from operations to current liabilities ratio* is computed as follows:

$$\textit{Cash flow from operations to current liabilities ratio} = \frac{\textbf{Cash flow from operations}}{\textbf{Average current liabilities}}$$

Because the numerator is a net cash inflow after paying current liabilities, this ratio can be interpreted as a safety net. **It represents excess cash inflow that could be used to grow through additional capital investment, or to reduce financing.** In finance literature, this ratio is frequently labeled as **cash flow from operations ratio,** with the conventional understanding that average current liabilities is the denominator.

8. Purchases is often not disclosed in the income statement; it is equal to Cost of goods + Ending inventory − Beginning inventory.

Long-Term Solvency Risk

The ability to raise cash externally through debt financing is ultimately determined by a company's demonstrated ability to service current debt requirements. Debt servicing ability is a function of the amount of debt in the financial statements. Analysts compute several different *debt ratios;* the two most common are *long-term debt to equity ratio* and *long-term debt to total assets ratio.*

Long-term debt to equity ratio = Long-term debt ÷ Shareholders' equity

This ratio can be computed with either the book value of shareholders' equity or the market value of shareholders' equity (Number of shares outstanding × Market price per share) in the denominator.

Long-term debt to total assets ratio = Long-term debt ÷ Total assets

Frequently, the popular financial press will report the *debt-to-equity ratio.* Unless the ratio is clearly defined, it may be difficult to know exactly what is being communicated. Normally, debt would mean total debt, but it could also be defined as long-term debt or any combination of various debt amounts.

In addition, a firm's level of profitability relative to interest cost demonstrates the ability to service the debt. For this reason, analysts compute an ***interest coverage ratio*** **to measure the number of times that income before interest and tax expense covers interest expense:**

$$\textbf{Interest coverage ratio} = \frac{\textbf{Income before income taxes + Interest expense}}{\textbf{Interest expense}}$$

Frequently, this ratio is labeled as ***times interest earned.***

A cash flow version of this ratio using cash flow from operations before taxes and interest payments divided by cash interest payments also can be computed. The rationale for the cash flow version is that risk is probably more highly related to missing interest payments than to having net income that is insufficient to cover accrual based interest expense.

Finally, the long-term asset position of the firm is important for long-term creditors. In order for a firm to meet its needs and grow, long-term debt must be repaid and long-term assets need to be replaced and increased. The sufficiency of a firm's operating cash flow in this regard is indicated by two ratios: *operating cash flow to total liabilities* and *operating cash flow to capital expenditures.*

Operating cash flow to total liabilities ratio = Operating cash flow ÷ Average total liabilities

Operating cash flow to capital expenditures ratio = Operating cash flow ÷ Capital expenditures

TCBY's Risk Ratio Computations

We compute some 1998 measures of risk for TCBY in this section. Before continuing, refer to the TCBY financial statements and to the ratio definitions previously presented in the module and compute the following ratios: current, quick, cash flow from operations to current liabilities, long-term debt to equity, long-term debt to total assets, interest coverage, operating cash flow to total liabilities, and operating cash flow to capital expenditures. After completing these computations, continue with this section and compare your computations with those given.

TCBY's 1998 ratios are as follows.

Current ratio = $46,833,211 ÷ $11,984,249 = 3.91

Traditionally, the current ratio is expressed as 3.91 to 1.

Quick ratio = \$31,383,168* ÷ \$11,984,249 = 2.62 (or 2.62 to 1)

*Quick assets = Cash and cash equivalents (\$16,924,143) + Short-term investments (\$2,967,135) + Receivables (\$11,334,939) + Refundable income taxes (\$156,951) = \$31,383,168

Cash flow from operations to current liabilities ratio = \$9,460,072 ÷ \$11,839,129* = 0.799

*Average current liabilities = [1998 current liabilities (\$11,984,249) + 1997 current liabilities (\$11,694,008)] ÷ 2 = \$11,839,129

Long-term debt to equity ratio = \$2,952,634 ÷ \$76,196,154 = 0.039

Note that the numerator used in the ratio is the one reported as long-term debt on the balance sheet. If the numerator is defined as all noncurrent liabilities, then the ratio would be (\$2,952,634 long-term debt + \$3,319,847 deferred income taxes) ÷ \$76,196,154 = 0.082.

Long-term debt to total assets ratio = \$2,952,634 ÷ \$94,452,884 = 0.031

Interest coverage ratio = (\$15,447,896 + \$545,664) ÷ \$545,664 = 29.31

Therefore, TCBY earned more than 29 times the fixed interest cost during 1998.

Operating cash flow to total liabilities = \$9,460,072 ÷ \$20,047,802 = 0.472

Operating cash flow to capital expenditures = \$9,460,072 ÷ \$1,982,769 = 4.77

Although comparisons for the industry or competing firms are not presented in this section, the current and quick ratios are quite high, indicating a low risk of short-term liquidity problems. In addition, the cash flow to current liabilities ratio is much higher than would be expected for a healthy firm. The long-term debt to equity ratio of 3.9% and the long-term debt to assets ratio of 3.1% are very low, indicating low default risk; the operating cash flows to total liabilities is also what would be expected for a low risk company. The interest coverage ratio of 29.31 shows that TCBY can easily cover its interest obligations. Finally, the operating cash flow to capital expenditures ratio is very high, indicating sufficient cash flow to support any needed plant expansion.

http://

Many firms put their financial statements online. Choose a firm in which you are interested. Try to find a set of recent financial statements on that company's homepage. (Most major companies provide their financial statements on their Web sites.) When you find the financial statements, calculate the company's ROA and ROCE. If you have problems finding a site, visit our Web site (http://baginski@swcollege.com) for links to a few selected sites. Happy Surfing!

Ratios and a Firm's Business Strategy

4 Interpret ratios in the context of a firm's business strategy.

Financial ratios must be interpreted within the context of industry conditions and the firm's competitive strategy. Basically, the analyst must attempt to answer the following questions:

- Why are the ratios at their current levels?
- Will the ratios continue at this level? If not, how will they change?

The first question deals with explanation of past events. It is important to understand the business conditions that lead to a given set of ratios. The second question deals with prediction. An understanding of industry conditions and how a firm plans to compete facilitates predictions such as ROCE sustainability (valuation context), variability in ROA, and cash flow generating ability (credit extension context). In order to explain and predict ratios, several conditions must be analyzed:

Industry conditions:

- Industry growth rate
- Firm concentration
- Product differentiation
- Scale economies

- Cyclicality and exit barriers
- Legal barriers to entry
- Relative bargaining power of buyers and suppliers
- Access to distribution channels

Firm competitive strategy:

- Cost leadership versus product differentiation
- Demonstration of acquisition of unique core competencies and value chain

Although single firm GAAP financial statements provide little information about industry conditions and competitive strategy, the firm's annual report will provide some of this information. Most financial analysts access a large amount of information from a wide variety of sources to undertake analysis of industry conditions and the firm's competitive strategy.

Industry Conditions

With all else held equal, a high *industry growth rate* suggests higher current and future profit margins. Lower growth rates provoke price wars with resulting lower gross margins, or attempts at product differentiation with incurrence of higher advertising expense to support higher gross margins.

Firm concentration determines the latitude to set prices. Single firm industries generally produce higher prices and higher profit margins. The opposite is true for a fragmented industry. The sustainability of profits, while generally higher in the single or "few firms" industry, depends on several additional factors (described below).

The potential for *product differentiation* on quality (e.g., brand name replacement auto parts) generally leads to higher current and future profit margins. In contrast, a product viewed as a commodity most often results in lower profit margins because product differentiation opportunities do not exist and it costs consumers very little to switch to alternative products.

Certain firms (e.g., airlines) need large capital investments to operate. The resulting fixed charges from these investments make generating a high sales volume a critical objective. Firms involved in transacting on these *scale economies* must often reduce prices (and hence, profit margins) to gain market share. Once market share is gained, however, scale economies serve as a barrier to other entries into the industry. New entrants must either take a high risk by engaging in the huge initial investment to match the incumbent firms' size, or they must suffer low profit margins until they can gain sufficient market share.

While scale-based entry barriers suggest sustainability of higher profit margins (and, on the negative side, lower asset turnovers), the analyst must interpret size advantages in the context of **fluctuations in industry sales value caused by the business cycle** (***cyclicality***). During periods of economic downturn, size also creates excess capacity and resulting price reductions to use excess capacity. If productive assets are specialized (as in the airline industry), size also creates ***exit barriers*** **in that large-scale operations are difficult to sell.**

Licenses and patents restrict competition and lead to higher profit margins. But, these *legal barriers* also have downsides. Licenses usually result in regulatory scrutiny, and patents expire. Successful relations with regulators signal sustainability of current margins. The time remaining until patent expiration is an important variable in predicting new entrants into a product line and the resulting dampening effect of competition on profit margin.

Finally, certain buyers have a great deal of *bargaining power* relative to suppliers. Buyers gain the advantage over suppliers for several reasons. The supplier may have a commodity product (for which product differentiation is not possible), and thus, must supply the product at the lowest price. The buyer might also demand such a large portion of the supplier's sales that the supplier must cater to the buyer's preferences. As well, the buyer's cost of switching to another supplier might be low. In addition, the component might be a significant portion of the buyer's cost, which translates into price pressure on the seller, especially if the buyer competes with a low cost strategy. Finally, alternative buyers may not be able to enter the market because of a *lack of access to distribution channels*. The scale of the entrant might be too low to justify increased distribution capacity in the industry.

Competitive Strategy

A key to predicting future profitability is the analyst's understanding of the corporation's competitive strategy. Strategy theorists argue that sustainable profit comes from identifying **a unique and not easily imitated sequence of events that creates value (*value chain*)**, and from acquisition of ***core competencies*, which are the key economic assets that allow delivery of goods and services in the value chain.** The structure and activities of the firm (and hence, its balance sheet and income statement) should be consistent with corporate strategy. If it is not, the commitment to the strategy is questionable, and there is little likelihood that successful strategy implementation will occur.

TCBY Enterprises' Business Strategy

TCBY faces a highly competitive industry. The barriers to entry into the ice cream and yogurt business are few. As a snack food, TCBY must compete with all restaurants for the consumer dollar. Price pressure is a constant problem. Further, the cost of its most significant raw material, milk, rose in the 1990s.

TCBY appears to follow a product differentiation strategy, emphasizing the extremely high quality of its product. To gain and keep market share and to build consumer recognition of the product (thus creating a brand name barrier to entry), TCBY has emphasized new product development and placement (TCBY Treats) and international franchise growth. It has also created more nontraditional stores in airports, convenience stores, stadiums, and on university campuses, including co-branding with Subway and other partners.

These strategic actions are reflected in the financial statements. Over the 1996–1998 three-year period, TCBY experienced decreased gross margins, a reflection of competition, increased wholesaling activities, and increased raw materials prices. Franchise revenues flattened (with fewer traditional stores), while yogurt sales increased.

The nontraditional store strategy started around 1994. Although there were concerns that nontraditional stores would compete somewhat with established franchises, the belief was that increased brand recognition should increase sales for most stores. Declining sales throughout the early 1990s followed by large sales increases in 1994 was a positive sign that the strategy worked. The strategy continues through 1998 as a result.

Accounting Quality

5 Explain the meaning of accounting quality and how it relates to external decision makers' use of financial statements.

In the calculation of TCBY's financial ratios, we used the numbers available in the financial statements and made no adjustments to reported figures. TCBY's financial statements are prepared in accordance with GAAP, as witnessed by the signed auditor's report. However, in the assessment of current profitability and risk (and whether current profitability is sustainable), GAAP allows variation in accounting measurement rules. This condition often weakens the link between GAAP numbers and the assessment of profitability and risk.

We define *accounting quality* broadly to include general characteristics of information that enable analysts to assess and predict sustainability of current financial characteristics. Accounting quality comes from several sources:

- Truthful reporting (lack of earnings manipulation)
- Persistence of earnings
- Adequate disclosure
- Conservative use of assumptions in applying GAAP

We illustrate the concept of accounting quality with TCBY's financial statements. Truthful reporting involves choosing accounting techniques and estimates that are consistent with business strategy, and avoiding changes in those techniques and estimates that would distort the profitability and risk picture. For example, in its 1994 financial statements (not reproduced in this text), TCBY capitalized and amortized distribution allowances over a three-year period. If TCBY lost a customer, then the distribution allowances were written off as a loss. If the allowances were made to acquire shelf space for a three-year period (or if a three-year period appears appropriate to TCBY as a period to build customer loyalty), then it chose an accounting technique and an estimate that corresponds to business strategy, and thereby achieved truthful reporting of such allowances. Changing an amortization period estimate without a legitimate business reason (i.e., simply to change amortization expense) would be earnings manipulation.

Even though TCBY follows GAAP, not all components of its earnings are relevant for profitability and risk assessment; as well, some items that do not affect the financial statements might be relevant for profitability and risk assessment. For example, nearly $2.3 million "other income" is reported in 1998. The annual report does not provide complete information on the nature of this item, and thus, it is difficult to estimate the probability that it will occur again. However, its location in the income statement (i.e., not shown as a regular operating item) and the fact that other income in previous periods was much less (e.g., $148,029 in 1997) leads one to believe that it is not indicative of future profitability (i.e., it will not persist).

TCBY's Note #4 to the financial statements does not disclose that long-term debt includes any capitalized lease obligations.[9] Note #7 indicates that more than $10,000,000 of cash outflows must be paid in future years for operating leases. Many analysts would make an adjustment to TCBY's balance sheet, capitalizing the operating lease payments and adding their present value to long-term debt when computing debt-to-equity ratios. (We illustrate this process in Module B.) Similarly, deferred taxes of $3,319,847 are shown for 1998. Some analysts would argue that deferred taxes should be reclassified as owners' equity for a growing company like TCBY. (We cover lease capitalization and deferred taxes in later chapters.) The point is that GAAP does not always provide all necessary information for profit and risk assessment in the face of the financial statements.

Analysts need additional information in order to remeasure some of the financial statement elements. Several examples of adequate disclosure can be found in TCBY's financial statements. The accounting policies note (Note #1) provides numbers of business locations and the basis for all accounting measurements. The other notes provide detailed information to help the analyst understand the balances in the accounts. The analyst could, for example, capitalize lease payments using the information in Note #7. TCBY's financial statements do not reflect any accounting changes, although Note #1 reports that three new FASB standards (*SFAS No. 130*, *SFAS No. 131*, and *SFAS No. 133*) will have no material effect on the financial statements.

The level of detail in certain classifications is lacking. For example, the classification of selling, general, and administrative expenses does not provide the individual items separately. This lack of detail might make it difficult to assess the effects of items such as advertising programs.

We will study accounting quality in greater detail in future chapters as we study each individual corporate activity. We will pay particular attention to the kinds of

9. In past years, TCBY has used this note to indicate if such obligations are present.

adjustments to financial statement data that are made by financial analysts. Also, for analysts who prefer a cash flow approach to statement analysis (there are many!), we will examine how the statement of cash flows aids in the assessment of accounting quality.

Module Summary

This text concentrates on how the results of management operating, investing, and financing activities are reflected in financial statements. This particular module changed the frame of reference to examine how external parties can use financial statements for financial analysis. External parties are required to make decisions that include extending credit, purchasing common shares, and developing strategic relationships. Financial statement analysis provides a major source of input into these decisions. Ratio analysis involves understanding profitability and risk. Ratios must be interpreted, however, within the context of a firm's business strategies and accounting quality.

As you continue throughout the text, we return to financial statement analysis in various modules after each major section. In these modules, we expand the process of financial statement analysis to incorporate new material presented in each section. After completing this module (and other modules), you should better appreciate how financial analysts and other interested parties can use quantitative techniques to better understand a particular firm and compare it to other firms.

Appendix—Ratio Definitions

This appendix contains the formulas for the ratios introduced in Module A.

- **Accounts payable turnover ratio** = Purchases ÷ Average accounts payable.
- **Accounts receivable turnover ratio** = Sales ÷ Average accounts receivable. See the related ratio *average number of days receivables outstanding.*
- **Asset turnover ratio** = Sales ÷ Average total assets.
- **Average number of days receivables outstanding ratio** = 365 ÷ Accounts receivable turnover ratio.
- **Capital structure leverage ratio** = Average total assets ÷ Average common stockholders' equity.
- **Cash flow from operations to current liabilities ratio** = Cash flow from operations ÷ Average current liabilities. This ratio is frequently labeled as the *cash flow from operations ratio*, with the denominator conventionally defined as *average current liabilities.*
- **Common earnings leverage ratio** = (Net income − Preferred stock dividends) ÷ [Net income + (1 − t)Interest expense].
- **Current ratio** = Current assets ÷ Current liabilities.
- **Fixed asset turnover ratio** = Sales ÷ Average property, plant, and equipment.
- **Gross margin ratio** (or *gross profit ratio*) = Gross margin ÷ Sales.
- **Individual expense ratio** = Each individual expense ÷ Sales.
- **Interest coverage ratio** = (Income before income taxes + Interest expense) ÷ Interest expense. This ratio is frequently labeled as *times interest earned.*
- **Inventory turnover ratio** = Cost of goods sold ÷ Average inventory.
- **Long-term debt to equity ratio** = Long-term debt ÷ Shareholders' equity. Shareholders' equity can be defined either as the *book value of shareholders' equity* or the *market value of shareholders' equity.*
- **Long-term debt to total assets ratio** = Long-term debt ÷ Total assets.
- **Net profit margin ratio** (sometimes called *net profit margin*) = [Net income + (1 − t)Interest expense] ÷ Sales.
- **Operating cash flow to capital expenditures ratio** = Operating cash flow ÷ Capital expenditures.
- **Operating cash flow to total liabilities ratio** = Operating cash flow ÷ Average total liabilities.

- **Price/Earnings Ratio** (PE Ratio) = Stock price per share ÷ EPS.
- **Quick ratio** = Quick assets ÷ Current liabilities = (Cash and cash equivalents + Marketable securities + Receivables) ÷ Current liabilities.
- **Return on Assets** (ROA) = (Net income + Interest expense, net of income taxes) ÷ Average total assets. Alternatively, *ROA* = Net profit margin ratio × Asset turnover ratio.
- **Return on Common Equity** (ROCE) = ROA × Common earnings leverage ratio × Capital structure leverage ratio. In the reduced form, *ROCE* = (Net income − Preferred stock dividends) ÷ Average common stockholders' equity.
- **Times interest earned** (see *Interest coverage ratio*) = (Income before income taxes + Interest expense) ÷ Interest expense.

Key Terms

Questions

Q1. **Focus of Creditors When Analyzing Financial Statements.** When lenders or potential creditors review financial statements, what is the primary focus of creditors with a short-term focus? Those with a long-term focus?

Q2. **Purpose of Ratios.** Financial analysts use ratio analysis to help understand the firm. Module A introduced many common ratios. Why does a financial analyst construct a ratio (i.e., what is the purpose of constructing a ratio)?

Q3. **Profitability Ratios.** In the text, we discussed two overall profitability ratios, one from the "all capital providers point of view" and one from the "common equity holders' point of view." What are the two ratios? Which ratio relates to each of the different points of view?

Q4. **ROA.** Provide the ratio definition of ROA. Net profit margin ratio and asset turnover ratio are the two components of ROA. Provide these definitions. Briefly explain what information is conveyed by the ratios.

Q5. **ROCE.** Provide the ratio definition of ROCE. ROA, common earnings leverage ratio, and capital structure leverage ratio are the three components of ROCE. Provide these definitions. Briefly explain what information is conveyed by the ratios.

Q6. **Ratios Related to Short-Term Liquidity Risk.** List and define the ratios for the following items that are used to assess short-term liquidity risk: current ratio, quick ratio, accounts receivable turnover ratio (and the related number of days of receivables), accounts payable turnover ratio, inventory turnover ratio, and cash flow from operations to current liabilities ratio. Try to write the definitions from memory or guess at the definition before turning to the text to find the formula.

Q7. **Ratios Related to Long-Term Solvency Risk.** List and define the ratios for the following items that are used to assess long-term solvency risk: long-term debt to equity ratio, long-term debt to total assets ratio, interest coverage ratio, operating cash flow to total liabilities ratio, and operating cash flow to total capital expenditures ratio. Try to write the definitions from memory or guess at the definition before turning to the text to find the formula.

Q8. **Ratios and the Firm's Business Strategy.** An analyst who uses ratios is attempting to understand the firm's business strategy. The firm's business strategy is affected by industry conditions and the firm's approach to dealing with competition (competitive strategy). List some of the factors used to analyze industry conditions and the firm's competitive strategy.

Q9. **Accounting Quality.** Financial analysts are interested in the quality of the amounts presented in financial statements. What is accounting quality?

Problems

1. **Compute Ratios for Southwest Airlines.** The complete 1998 GAAP financial statements for Southwest Airlines Co. are presented in Appendix C. Use these statements to calculate the ratios introduced in this module as follows:
   a. **Return on Assets (ROA) and Related Ratios.** Compute Southwest Airlines' 1998 ROA using the overall ratio definition introduced in the text. Next, compute ROA a second time using the net profit margin ratio and asset turnover ratio components. Finally, compute Southwest Airlines' 1998 ratios for accounts receivable turnover, inventory turnover, fixed asset turnover, and gross margin. Southwest Airlines breaks down operating expenses into several categories on the income statement. Compute the total operating expense ratio (Total operating expenses ÷ Total operating revenue) and the salaries, wages, and benefits expense ratio (Salaries, wages, and benefits expense ÷ Total operating revenue). Use an effective tax rate of 40%. *Note: Because Southwest Airlines is a service company, some of these ratios are inappropriate. Indicate which of the ratios generally would not be computed for service companies.*
   b. **Return on Common Equity (ROCE).** Compute Southwest Airlines' 1998 ROCE using the reduced form of the ratio introduced in the module. Next, compute ROCE a second time using its ROA, common earnings leverage ratio, and capital structure leverage ratio components.
   c. **Price/Earnings (PE) Ratio.** Southwest Airlines' 1998 high stock price was $23.75 per share; its low stock price was $15.31. Using 1998 EPS as your frame of reference, what was the range of PE ratios at which the stock sold during the year?
   d. **Short-Term Liquidity Ratios.** Compute Southwest Airlines' 1998 current ratio, quick ratio, and accounts payable turnover ratio. *Indicate which of the ratios generally would not be computed for service companies.*
   e. **Long-Term Solvency Ratios.** Compute Southwest Airlines' 1998 ratios for long-term debt to equity, long-term debt to total assets, interest coverage, operating cash flow to total liabilities, and operating cash flow to capital expenditures. For long-term debt, use only the long-term debt category instead of total noncurrent liabilities.

http://

2. **Compute Ratios for Texas Instruments.** The complete 1998 GAAP financial statements for Texas Instruments are presented at our Web site (http://baginski.swcollege.com). Use these statements to calculate the following ratios. *Note: The financial statements report amounts in millions, except per share amounts.*
   a. **Return on Assets (ROA) and Related Ratios.** Compute Texas Instruments' 1998 ROA using the overall ratio definition introduced in the text. Next, compute ROA a second time using the net profit margin ratio and asset turnover ratio components. Finally, compute Texas Instruments' 1998 ratios for accounts receivable turnover, inventory turnover, fixed asset turnover, and gross margin. Texas Instruments breaks down operating expenses into only three categories on the income statement. Compute the total operating costs and expenses ratio (Total operating costs and expenses ÷ Net revenues) and the marketing, general, and administrative expense ratio (Marketing, general, and administrative expense ÷ Total operating revenue). On the income statement, Texas Instruments has the category *interest on loans*. Use that category as interest expense. Use an effective tax rate of 33.33%.
   b. **Return on Common Equity (ROCE).** Compute Texas Instruments' 1998 ROCE using the reduced form of the ratio introduced in the module. Next, compute ROCE a second time using the ROA, common earnings leverage ratio, and capital structure leverage ratio components.
   c. **Price/Earnings (PE) Ratio.** Texas Instruments' 1998 high stock price was $90.44 per share; its low stock price was $40.25. Using 1998 EPS as your frame of reference, what was the range of PE ratios at which the stock sold during the year?
   d. **Short-Term Liquidity Ratios.** Compute Texas Instruments' 1998 current ratio, quick ratio, accounts receivable turnover ratio, inventory turnover ratio, and accounts payable turnover ratio.
   e. **Long-Term Solvency Ratios.** Compute Texas Instruments' 1998 ratios for long-term debt to equity, long-term debt to total assets, interest coverage, operating cash flow to total liabilities, and operating cash flow to capital expenditures. For long-term debt, use the long-term debt amount from TI's balance sheet—do not use total noncurrent liabilities.

http://

3. Pick a company about which you are interested in learning more. Obtain the financial statements for the latest year either by going to the company's Web site or accessing SEC's Edgar site or PricewaterhouseCoopers' EdgarScan site, which are accessible at our Web site (http://baginski.swcollege.com). For that company, calculate as many of the Module A ratios as possible. Note that you may not have sufficient information to compute all ratios, and you may have to use some numbers that do not exactly meet the module definitions. Treat this assignment as an opportunity to learn more about a company. A financial analyst who performed this task would also probably compute the same ratios for other firms in the industry in order to compare the company of interest to its competitors.

CFA Exam-Type Problems

4. A corporation wants to increase its current ratio from the present level of 1.5 before its fiscal year-end. The action providing the desired effect is: (CFA adapted)
   a. delaying the next payroll.
   b. writing down impaired assets.
   c. paying current payables from cash.
   d. selling current marketable securities for cash at their book value.
5. Some ratios are primarily used to assess profitability and some primarily to assess risk. Which of the following is primarily used to assess profitability? (author constructed)
   a. current ratio
   b. interest coverage ratio
   c. return of assets (ROA)
   d. debt to equity ratio
6. Which of the following is not a source of "accounting quality"? (author constructed)
   a. persistence in earnings
   b. using conservative assumptions in applying GAAP
   c. adequate disclosure
   d. earnings manipulation to meet current-year targets
7. Refer to Table 1 below. Calculate the ratios listed below for Disney as of September 30, 1993 (use ending balance sheet amounts). Briefly explain the use of each ratio in evaluating a company's operations. (CFA adapted, with slight modification by author)
   a. Average number of days receivables outstanding
   b. Cash flow from operations
   c. Debt to capital (with equity at market)
   d. Times interest earned (interest coverage)

TABLE 1

THE WALT DISNEY COMPANY
Selected Financial Statement and Other Data
Years Ending September 30
($ millions, except per share data)

	1993	**1992**
Income Statement		
Revenue	8,529	4,594
Operating expenses	(6,805)	(3,365)
Operating income	1,724	1,229
General and administrative expenses	(163)	(119)
Interest expense	(158)	(24)
Investment and interest income	186	67
Income (loss) from Euro Disney	(515)	0
Pretax income	1,074	1,153
Taxes	(403)	(450)
Net income	671	703
Earnings per share	$1.23	$1.27
Dividends per share	$0.23	$0.11

(continued)

TABLE 1 (concluded)

	1993	1992
Balance Sheet		
Cash	363	381
Receivables	1,390	224
Inventories	609	909
Other	1,889	662
Current assets	4,251	2,176
Property, plant and equipment, net	5,228	3,397
Other assets	2,272	1,084
Total assets	11,751	6,657
Current liabilities	2,821	1,262
Borrowings	2,386	861
Other liabilities	1,514	1,490
Stockholders' equity	5,030	3,044
Total liabilities and stockholders' equity	11,751	6,657
Cash Flow from Operations		
Net income	671	703
Depreciation	364	272
Goodwill	0	0
Other	1,110	300
Total	2,145	1,275
Other Data		
Common shares outstanding (millions)	544	552
Closing price common stock per share	$37.75	$30.22

II

How Financing Decisions Are Reflected in Financial Statements

Objectives

1 Identify characteristics that distinguish debt from equity.
2 Describe the characteristics of hybrid securities.
3 Describe the determinants of capital structure.
4 Account for the various forms of equity issues.
5 Account for the various forms of dividend distributions.
6 Explain how external decision makers view owners' equity.

Chapter 2

Financing Decisions (Introduction and Equity Decisions)

Businesses need to obtain cash in order to engage in operations. Accordingly, we devote the next four chapters of this text to explain how a firm procures cash through financing activities. In this chapter, we introduce and provide an overview of the financing decision, and then we discuss equity financing. In Chapter 3, debt financing is addressed. In Chapter 4, a particular form of debt financing, leasing, is examined. Finally, in Chapter 5, we discuss the issues surrounding the decision of whether to reduce outstanding equity and debt financing and how to do so.

Financing Decisions—Introduction[1]

Firms must raise capital for investment and operating activities. Transacting in capital markets involves issuing securities (i.e., stocks and bonds) or promissory notes in exchange for cash or other assets. Investors holding the securities or notes have a claim against the assets that they provide to the corporation. The corporation repays the funds to investors from earnings produced by the invested capital.

The contractual nature of investors' claims to corporate assets determines their classification as debt or equity instruments. Initially, we consider the distinguishing characteristics between debt and equity securities. Then we consider securities that combine the debt and equity features. Finally, we discuss how firms determine capital structure.

1. In this introductory section, we review basic material usually covered in a corporate finance course in order to set the stage for the discussion of equity decisions (later in this chapter) and debt finance decisions (in Chapter 3). You might want to refer to a financial management text for additional assistance. For example, see Moyer, McGuigan, and Kretlow, *Contemporary Financial Management, 8th Edition* (Cincinnati, Ohio: South-Western College Publishing, 2001).

Contractual Characteristics that Distinguish Debt from Equity

1 Identify characteristics that distinguish debt from equity.

Debt is usually distinguished from equity in several ways:

- The rights of claim holders to assets upon corporate dissolution
- Voting rights
- The nature of periodic cash flows paid to claim holder
- The nature of final, liquidating payment

Claims of Debt Holders in a Corporate Dissolution Debt is senior to equity in corporate dissolution. That is, bond and note holders are paid off before stockholders. Often, debt holders have secured claims against specific assets (e.g., inventory, receivables, property and equipment) that serve as collateral. Appropriately, accountants generally view owners' equity as the *residual interest* in the firm, a view consistent with common shareholders receiving assets that remain after the creditors' claims are satisfied.

Voting Privileges Equity holders (i.e., common stockholders) normally have voting rights, while debt ownership does not convey voting privileges. While, at first glance, this appears to suggest total control of the firm by common shareholders, creditors maintain some control through prespecified covenants and restrictions on management behavior executed at the time debt is issued. For example, debt covenants frequently restrict (1) the amount of dividends that can be paid, (2) the ability of the firm to issue new equity, and (3) the ability of the firm to issue additional debt.

Claims to Future Cash Flows In the case of debt, periodic cash flows (i.e., interest payments) are specified contractually as to amount and timing, and principal is repaid at a specified time. As time passes, accountants accrue the interest obligations of the firm and report them as interest payable in the balance sheet. Alternatively, equity instruments offer no guarantee of the existence or timing of periodic cash flows (i.e., dividends). Dividend payments are at the discretion of management, although firms that issue dividends generally like to maintain a record of continually declaring dividends. In some cases, dividends on preferred stock may become obligations of a firm if the designated preference is not paid in a particular year.

The Final, Liquidating Payment The final liquidating payment of debt principal is also specified in amount and timing by contract. Equity securities normally have no maturity date. Secondary markets exist for both debt and equity, however. Transacting in secondary markets allows the holders of debt or equity securities to sell their investments.

Hybrid Securities

2 Describe the characteristics of hybrid securities.

Corporations also issue securities that combine elements of debt and equity. These hybrid securities exist because the security market demands them. For example, an investor may wish initially to loan funds to a firm while reserving the option to become a shareholder at a later date. Corporations can respond to this type of investor demand by issuing debt with equity conversion features. However, hybrid securities cause classification and interpretation problems because it is often unclear whether they are debt or equity instruments. We discuss four hybrid securities: preferred stock, convertible preferred stock, convertible debt, and bonds issued with detachable stock warrants.

Typical Preferred Stock ***Preferred stock* is an equity security that typically has debt-like features.** Preferred stockholders exercise the following rights, though they do not vote:

- They receive dividends before common shareholders can receive dividends.
- They receive dividends at a prespecified stated rate.
- They receive dividends in a given year only if they are declared.
- They receive dividends not issued in prior years (i.e., *dividends in arrears*) before common shareholders can receive dividends if the preferred stock is *cumulative.*
- They can receive dividends in excess of the prespecified amount if the stock is *participating.*
- They have rights to assets in dissolution before common shareholders, but only after claims of debt holders are satisfied.

Preferred stock has a dividend preference each period. **If the preferred stock is cumulative, i.e., *cumulative preferred stock*, any year's dividend preference that is not declared becomes a dividend in arrears, and it is carried over to subsequent periods.** Generally, preferred stock is cumulative. ***Dividends in arrears* are dividends not declared in a previous period on cumulative preferred stock.** Dividends in arrears must be paid before any other dividends can be paid in the current period. ***Participating preferred stock* is preferred stock that is entitled to a bigger dividend than nonparticipating preferred stock. The participating feature allows preferred stockholders to receive a dividend above the stated preference, if declared by the board of directors.** Generally, preferred stock is not participating.[2]

A review of the preceding list makes it apparent that the classification of preferred stock as debt or equity is not clear. The lack of voting privileges is a debt-like characteristic. Also, the prespecified stated dividend rate seems to be very much like interest on debt. However, the fact that dividends to preferred stockholders must be declared before they are paid is clearly different from interest, which becomes a legal liability as time passes. This makes preferred stock more like equity than debt. But because the preferred stock normally is cumulative, any missed dividend payments must be paid before common shareholders receive dividends, and cumulative preferred dividends resemble interest payments. If the preferred stock is participating, allowing the preferred shareholders to receive dividends in excess of the prespecified rate, the stock seems to be an equity instrument. The "in between" nature of preferred stock is further evidenced by the fact that, in dissolution, preferred shareholders' claims against assets follow creditors but precede common shareholders. Historically, accountants have treated preferred stock as an equity instrument, with dividends being recorded as a direct charge to retained earnings (as a distribution to owners) rather than as interest expense. *To repeat for emphasis, dividends (on preferred stock and common stock) are treated as distributions to owners, and they are not reflected on the income statement; therefore, they do not affect net income.*

Convertible Preferred Stock ***Convertible preferred stock* is similar to preferred stock, except that the holder has the option to exchange the convertible preferred stock for common stock under some previously agreed-upon exchange ratio.** For example, a holder of 1,000 shares of $100 par, 7% convertible preferred stock may have the right to exchange each share of convertible preferred for five shares of $10 par common stock. Corporations issue convertible preferred instead of nonconvertible preferred for various reasons. First, compared to nonconvertible preferred, convertible preferred carries a slightly lower dividend rate (i.e., it sells for slightly more). The purchaser is paying an additional amount for the option to convert the preferred stock into common. Second, at certain times during the business cycle, corporations may find it difficult to sell any type of security. By offering convertible preferred stock, a corporation may be able to sell stock that would

2. American Institute of Certified Public Accountants, *1999 Accounting Trends & Techniques,* 52nd edition (New York) reports that of 600 companies surveyed, 102 had one or more classes of preferred stock outstanding and 498 firms had issued no preferred stock.

otherwise be unmarketable. For accounting purposes, convertible preferred is treated as equity.[3]

Convertible Debt ***Convertible debt*** **may, at the creditor's option, be converted into common shares at a prespecified exchange rate.** When purchasing the debt, the creditor is really purchasing two things: (1) debt with a stated interest rate and maturity date and (2) an option to exchange the debt for equity. However, the debt and option features do not trade separately on secondary markets. While holding the convertible debt, the creditor receives interest payments, a feature of debt. Also, the bondholder has the ability to exchange the debt for equity, an equity-like feature. Accountants have historically recorded convertible debt as a debt instrument, recording interest expense. The option to exchange the debt for equity is not valued and recorded.[4]

Bonds Issued with Detachable Warrants Bonds issued with detachable warrants provide a good example of where debt and equity features can be separated. Typically, after issuance, bonds and detachable warrants are traded separately in secondary markets. When purchasing bonds with detachable warrants, an investor is buying a debt instrument (the bond) and the option to acquire equity (the stock warrants). Because the debt and equity features trade separately after issuance, accountants allocate the purchase price of the bond with detachable warrants between the bond and the stock warrants on the basis of the two instruments' relative fair market values. As a simple example, assume that bonds with a face value of $1,000,000 plus detachable warrants are issued for $975,000. Assume that immediately after issue, the bonds trade for $900,000 and the warrants for $100,000. Accountants would allocate 90% ($900,000 value of the bonds ÷ $1,000,000 value of bonds plus warrants) of the $975,000 value received to the bonds ($975,000 × 90% = $877,500) and 10% to the warrants ($975,000 × 10% = $97,500).

Theoretical and Practical Determinants of Capital Structure

3 Describe the determinants of capital structure.

In choosing between debt and equity financing, standard finance theory holds that managers should attempt to maximize a firm's value. One of the most important topics in financial theory has been the determination of an optimal capital structure.[5] Since the late 1950s, theoreticians have analyzed the role of debt financing on the value of the firm prompting a search for a theoretical specification of optimal capital structure.[6]

The capital structure debate has greatly increased our understanding of the financing decision. The debate has identified several key determinants of the optimal capital structure:

3. The 1999 edition of *Accounting Trends & Techniques* reported that of 600 companies surveyed, 37 instances of preferred stock conversions were reported.
4. The 1999 edition of *Accounting Trends & Techniques* reported that of 600 companies surveyed, 19 had debt conversions or extinguishments.
5. Optimal capital structure is the "mix of debt, preferred stock, and common equity that *minimizes* the *weighted cost* to the firm *of* its employed *capital.*" Moyer, McGuigan, and Kretlow *Contemporary Financial Management, 8th Edition* (Cincinnati, Ohio: South-Western College Publishing, 2001). Alternatively, optimal capital structure is the debt-to-equity ratio or debt-to-value ratio at which the value of the firm is maximized. See Moyer et al.'s Chapter 12 for a discussion of optimal capital structure.
6. Modigliani and Miller's seminal work discussed propositions about the value of the firm. See "The Cost of Capital, Corporation Finance and the Theory of Investment," *American Economic Review* (June 1958): 261–297.

- Tax savings of debt
- Costs of financial distress
- Agency costs
- Superior management information
- Underwriting costs
- Perceived importance of control

Tax Savings of Debt Interest payments to bondholders and other creditors are tax deductible. Dividend payments to stock investors are not. As a result, using debt financing has a tax advantage in that a lower net cost is associated with providing a return to investors. In fact, all else being equal, it has been shown that 100% debt financing may be optimal for a normal range of corporate tax rates. The issue becomes a little clouded if one acknowledges the existence of individual tax rates. But analyses incorporating both corporate and individual taxes still yield a tax advantage to the use of corporate debt.

Costs of Financial Distress As corporations add more debt, they also increase interest payments. As noted previously, a distinguishing feature of debt is that these periodic payments are fixed. Equity financing payments (i.e., dividends on common stock) are not fixed. Debt financing imposes a significant cost upon the firm in the presence of decreased earnings. Interest payments on the debt financing must be paid regardless of the level of company earnings. The combination of decreased earnings and required interest payments increases the likelihood that a firm will enter a state of financial distress. Using equity rather than debt financing would permit reducing dividends and thus lessen the damaging cash flow consequences of short-term to intermediate-term depressions in earnings.

The specific costs of financial distress are numerous. They include the more obvious costs of attorneys' fees, court costs, and disruptions in operations. But they also include the less apparent costs associated with damage to reputation. Most customers do not want to deal with financially unstable corporations. Further, managerial reputation is tainted through association with a financially distressed firm. The managerial reputation effect, in combination with managerial discretion, presents potentially significant hidden costs. If managers realize financial distress is imminent, they may have time to alter investment and operating decisions in favor of short-run cash flow over the long-run success of the firm. Of particular concern, however, is the possibility that managers would liquidate a portion of an investment that yields positive net present value in an attempt to satisfy interest obligations.

Agency Costs As noted in Chapter 1, the separation of ownership and management introduces the possibility that the decisions managers make to maximize their wealth may not necessarily maximize owners' wealth. Understandably, **owners take measures to ensure that managers make decisions that do maximize owner wealth, which leads to costs known as *agency costs*.** These costs include monitoring costs by independent auditors and the use of costly managerial evaluation and compensation schemes. The potential for owner/manager conflicts exists even if the firm is financed entirely with equity. However, additional agency costs are imposed when debt is present in the capital structure. These costs arise because managers can alter the risk characteristics of the firm *after* debt is issued. A subsequent increase in the riskiness of the firm increases the required return on investment. Because the interest rate paid to original debt holders is fixed, the value of the debt falls and original debt holders suffer.

Changes in the risk of the firm occur when managers alter business risk or financial risk. Alterations of business risk are brought about when asset composition is changed. For example, a manager can replace assets yielding variable charges against income (e.g., labor) with assets yielding fixed charges against income (e.g., machinery). Business risk is increased with the increase in fixed charges.

Financial risk alteration occurs when additional debt is issued. The first layer of debt bears an interest rate that is determined by the relation of debt to equity at that point in time. Subsequent layers of debt bear interest rates that are a function of total debt relative to equity. More debt makes financial risk higher, and hence, the value of all debt falls.

Because of this situation, bondholders will seek to monitor and enforce ***debt covenants and restrictions,*** **which are contracts between bondholders and management that limit management actions.** One cost associated with these contracts is the adverse effects on a firm's value. For example, if a restriction requires a certain ratio of cash to current liabilities, then management may have to pass up a positive net present value project in order to avoid violating the covenants. A second cost is monitoring. Independent accountants will increase fees to broaden the scope of their audits to include examining whether the debt covenants have been violated. A third potential cost is higher interest rates on debt as an alternative to strong covenants and restrictions.

Superior Management Information Managers generally possess information about the firm that is superior to information outsiders have. Because equity returns depend on this information, investors are at an information disadvantage when dealing with managers in an equity issue. Interest payments do not depend on private information.

Of primary concern to new shareholders is the existence of private bad news that is not revealed until after a new share issue. Revelation of the bad news prior to the new stock issue would cause prices to fall, avoiding losses to new shareholders from purchasing the stock at an inflated price. Existing shareholders would also lose, but they would have lost regardless of the new stock issue. Their primary concern is that management would suppress good news prior to a share issue. In this case, more shares must be issued at artificially low prices in order to raise the required capital. Future earnings per share are diluted by the unnecessary increment in outstanding shares.

Investors realize that managers possess superior information and assign a positive probability to suffering capital losses in transactions with managers. As an insurance policy against losses occurring, investors are willing to pay less for stock issues.

Underwriting Costs The costs of issuing common stock are higher relative to issuing debt. Because many of the flotation costs for equity issues are fixed, the cost per dollar of stock issued rises dramatically for small issues. The costs for initial public offerings (IPOs) are particularly severe. A great deal of financial disclosure is required by regulators. Due to the high degree of private management information present in IPOs, the offerings are often underpriced to compensate the uninformed investor for dealing with the informed manager. An extreme example of the underpricing of IPOs in the 1990s was the IPO of Netscape on August 9, 1995. Underwriters initially set the IPO tentative price at $14 per share. After the shares were oversubscribed, underwriters set the IPO price to $28 per share. When these shares began trading on August 9, 1995, the price opened at $71 per share. Because the market opened at $71, it seems that the shares were initially underpriced by $43 per share.

Perceived Importance of Control The issuance of new common shares dilutes control by existing shareholders. To the extent that current managers fear this loss of control, a cost of equity is imposed. This cost can be mitigated by the preemptive rights feature of stock ownership, which allows current shareholders to maintain their ownership percentages when new issues occur. This, of course, assumes that current shareholders have sufficient cash to maintain their ownership percentage.

Financing Decisions—Equity Issues

4 Account for the various forms of equity issues.

The decision to raise funds by issuing stock is a financing activity. Three different kinds of cash flows result from stock transactions:

1. Cash received at issue date (sales price).
2. Transaction costs paid at issue date (often deducted by underwriter before remitting issue proceeds to company).
3. Periodic cash dividend payments to investors.

Cash-Based Equity Transactions

The financial statement treatment of typical cash-based equity transactions is illustrated by the following example:

Example 1. During 2001, Bradshaw Properties authorized the issuance of 100,000 shares of $2 par value common stock. Bradshaw issued 70,000 shares at a price of $7 per share and incurred underwriter fees, legal costs, printing costs, and registration fees totaling $12,000. The company declared and paid a $1 dividend per share during the year.

Solution. The total proceeds of the issue are $478,000, which represent the $490,000 selling price (70,000 shares @ $7) less the $12,000 issue costs. As shown in Exhibit 1, Bradshaw reports the net proceeds as a cash inflow from financing activities on the accompanying statement of cash flows. The dividend payment of $70,000 (70,000 shares @ $1) is shown as a cash outflow from financing activities.

EXHIBIT 1 Impact of Cash-Based Equity Transactions on the Statement of Cash Flows

BRADSHAW PROPERTIES
Statement of Cash Flows
For the Year Ended December 31, 2001
(in thousands)

Operating Activities		
Cash inflows	$XXX	
Cash outflows	(XX)	$XXX
Investing Activities		
Cash inflows	$XXX	
Cash outflows	(XX)	XXX
Financing Activities		
Cash inflows (**Net proceeds from stock issue**)	**$478**	
Cash outflows (**Cash dividends paid**)	**(70)**	**408**
Net change in cash		$XXX

Exhibit 2 displays the simultaneous effects of each transaction on the accrual-based financial statements. The top half of the exhibit (balance sheet) shows *resources and claims against resources.* The bottom half of the exhibit (income statement and statement of owners' equity) shows *changes in those resources and claims against resources.*

EXHIBIT 2 Impact of Cash-Based Equity Transactions on Accrual-Based Financial Statements

BRADSHAW PROPERTIES
Balance Sheet
December 31, 2001
(in thousands)

Assets		**Liabilities**			
Current assets		Current liabilities		$XXX	
Cash (share issue)	**$478 ↑**	Long-term liabilities		XXX	$XXX
Cash (dividend)	**70 ↓**				
Investments and funds	XXX	**Owners' Equity**			
Property, plant, and equipment	XXX	Contributed capital			
Intangible assets	XXX	**Common stock (par)**		**$140 ↑**	
Other assets	XXX	**Additional paid-in capital**		**338 ↑**	**478 ↑**
		Retained earnings			**70 ↓**
		Total owners' equity			$XXX
Total assets	$XXX	Total liabilities and owners' equity			$XXX

BRADSHAW PROPERTIES
Income Statement
For the Year Ended December 31, 2001
(in thousands)

Sales revenue	$XXX
Less: Cost of goods sold	(XXX)
Gross margin	XXX
Less: Operating expenses	(XXX)
Operating income	XXX
Financial revenues (expenses), gains (losses)	XXX
Pretax income	XXX
Less: Income tax expense	(XXX)
Net income	$XXX

Note: The transactions do not affect the income statement.

BRADSHAW PROPERTIES
Statement of Owners' Equity
For the Year Ended December 31, 2001
(in thousands)

Beginning owners' equity	$XXX
Add: Net income	XXX
Investments by owners (**common stock issue**)	**478**
Deduct: Distributions to owners (**dividends**)	**(70)**
Ending owners' equity	$XXX

EXAMPLE 1 Journal Entries

Cash	478,000	
Common Stock		140,000
Additional Paid-In Capital		338,000
Issue of common stock		
Dividends*	70,000	
Cash		70,000
Payment of dividends		

*Many companies use a "Dividends" account that is closed directly to Retained Earnings through the closing process. Alternatively, the account "Retained Earnings" may be debited in the journal entry.

On the balance sheet, Bradshaw reports the $478,000 net proceeds as an increase in assets and a corresponding increase in owners' equity. The increase in owners' equity is divided between the $140,000 par value of the shares (70,000 @ $2) and the $338,000 in excess of par ($478,000 − 140,000).[7] If no par value were stated, a single capital stock account would be used for the entire proceeds. The $70,000 dividend is reported as a decrease in both assets (cash) and owners'

7. Par value is *designated* by the corporation. It has no economic meaning. In some states, par value may be related to "legal capital." Issues of shares below par value may be illegal or may subject shareholders to future contributions to the corporation.

equity (retained earnings). The share issue also is reported on the statement of shareholders' equity as an investment by owners, while the dividend is reported as a distribution to owners.

It is important to note that the income statement is not affected by equity transactions. Although resources change, they result from transactions with owners. This is a perfect example of why, in Chapter 1, we adjusted for investments by owners and distributions to owners when we used the capital maintenance approach to income measurement. There were increases and decreases in owners' equity on the balance sheet, but no change in net income.

In recording transactions with owners, a *general rule* is as follows: *Equity transactions do not affect net income.* This rule means that net income is unchanged when corporations and their owners engage in transactions classified as equity transactions. Rather, the transactions are reflected as capital transactions in the statement of owners' equity as "investments by owners" and "distributions to owners." Note that in the previous Bradshaw Properties example, the issuance of common stock does not affect income and neither does the payment of dividends (dividends are treated as a distribution to owners rather than an expense). *One of the more common mistakes made by students is to treat a dividend as an expense; a dividend is not an expense, it is a distribution to owners.*

Noncash Contributions by Investors

Not all equity transactions are as simple as the one illustrated above. At the date of original issue, corporations may issue equity instruments that are not common stock. Also, owners (i.e., investors) may contribute items other than cash to the corporation. The following diagram depicts the potential complexities of the transaction:

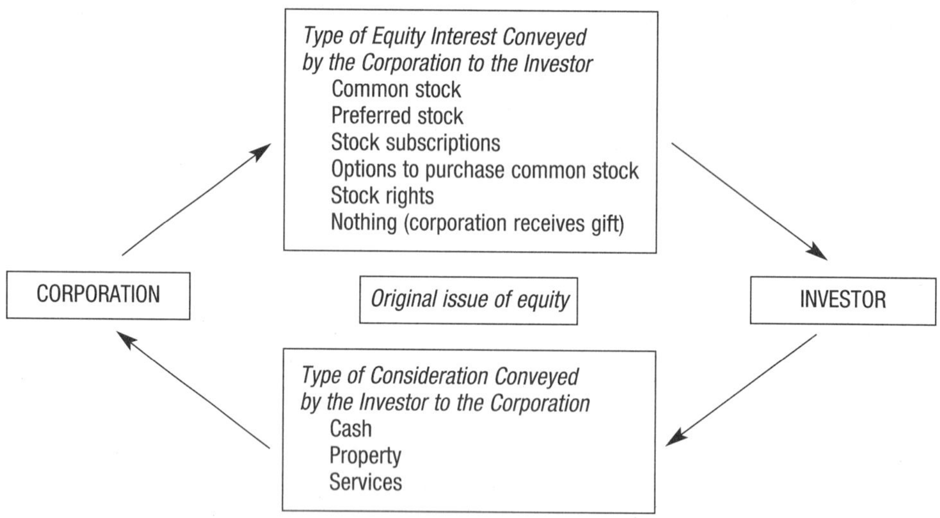

The diagram shows that, instead of transferring cash, the investor could transfer property to the corporation or perform services for the corporation in return for an equity interest. Instead of issuing common stock, the corporation could issue other types of equity interests: preferred stock, stock subscriptions, options to purchase common stock, or stock rights to the investor. The diagram also illustrates the transfer of consideration as a gift from the investor, which would result in no equity interest being conveyed to the investor. In the previous Bradshaw Properties example, Bradshaw issued stock in return for cash. We consider the accounting for each of the other situations in turn in subsequent examples.

Although most stock issues result in cash proceeds, stock may also be issued in exchange for expected future benefits other than cash (i.e., noncash assets) and for benefits used up this period (i.e., expenses). Examples of noncash assets that could be received in a stock issue are long-term investments in other companies and property, plant, & equipment. Examples of stock issues to acquire current-period benefits include legal services and executive compensation.

A second general rule is to record equity issued at the fair market value (FMV) of what the corporation receives in return. In the previous Bradshaw example, the amount to record as equity is clear because the FMV of cash is certain. But the FMV of noncash assets or services may be less determinable. *As long as the FMV of one side of the exchange is determinable, the FMV of the other side of the transaction is implied.* Accountants assume that unrelated parties engage in exchanges of equal FMVs. *This equality leads to the more general rule in accounting to record a transaction at either the FMV of what is given up or the FMV of what is received, whichever is more determinable.* This is an important general rule to remember.

Investor Provides Property To illustrate the situation where stock is issued for property rather than cash, consider the following example:

Example 2. An investor transfers an office building to Jackson Investment in return for common stock. The office building cost the investor $500,000 several years ago but now has a FMV of $800,000. Jackson Investment issues 100,000 shares of $1 par value common stock in exchange for the building.

Solution. The effects on the financial statements are shown in Exhibit 3.

EXHIBIT 3 Impact of Property Contribution by Investor on the Financial Statements

JACKSON INVESTMENT
Balance Sheet

Assets		**Owners' Equity**	
Property, plant, and equipment		Contributed capital	
Office building	**$800,000 ↑**	**Common stock (par)**	**$100,000 ↑**
		Additional paid-in capital	**700,000 ↑**

Income Statement	**Statement of Owners' Equity**	
No effect	Investments by owners	
	Common stock issue	**$800,000**

EXAMPLE 2 Journal Entries

Office Building	800,000	
Common Stock		100,000
Additional Paid-In Capital		700,000

The increases in equity and assets are recorded at $800,000, the FMV received by Jackson Investment. If the FMV received is not determinable, Jackson can use the FMV of what has been given as a basis for recording the transaction. If in the preceding example, the FMV of the building was unknown but the common stock (regularly traded in organized markets) was selling at $7.50 per share, the office building would be reported at $750,000 (100,000 shares @ $7.50), the common stock at $100,000 (100,000 shares @ $1.00 par), and the additional paid-in capital at $650,000 (100,000 shares @ $6.50). Note that the general rule for recording equity transactions is followed. Assets increase, owners' equity increases (contributed capital), and net income is not affected.

Investor Provides Services In the preceding example, Jackson Investment received future economic benefits in the form of an office building. Stock issues could also occur in exchange for current-period benefits (i.e., expenses), as illustrated in Example 3.

Example 3. Assume that in one transaction Taylor Co. received legal services from a local law firm. The services benefited the current period only, and Taylor records a liability and an offsetting expense. Because Taylor is short of cash, the law firm agrees to accept Taylor's common stock instead of cash. Therefore, in a second transaction Taylor issues 1,000 shares of $1 par common stock that is currently selling for $4 per share.

Solution. Exhibit 4 shows the effects of the two transactions on Taylor's financial statements after the stock is issued, ignoring income taxes.

EXHIBIT 4 Impact of Service Contribution by Investor on the Financial Statements

TAYLOR CO.
Balance Sheet

Assets	Liabilities	
No effect	**Owners' Equity**	
	Contributed capital	
	Common stock (par)	**1,000 ↑**
	Additional paid-in capital	**3,000 ↑**
	Retained earnings (through effect on net income)	**4,000 ↓**

Income Statement*

Operating expenses	
Legal expense	**4,000**

*Ignores income tax effects

Statement of Owners' Equity

Investments by owners	
Common stock issue	**4,000**
Net income (effect of legal expenses)	**(4,000)**

EXAMPLE 3 Journal Entries

Legal Expense	4,000	
Legal Fees Payable		4,000
Legal Fees Payable	4,000	
Common Stock		1,000
Additional Paid-In Capital		3,000

For the entire year, the net effects of the two transactions are that assets are unaffected, no liability exists at year-end, but accounts *within* owners' equity change. Contributed capital increases by $4,000, with a split between increases in common stock and additional paid-in capital, and retained earnings decreases. Retained earnings decreases because, on the income statement, the $4,000 legal expense increases operating expenses. As a result, net income is lower. Because net income increases (and net losses decrease) retained earnings, retained earnings decreases by $4,000. Thus, the net effect on the balance sheet of the two transactions is *no change* in total owners' equity, although the components of owners' equity (contributed capital increases and retained earnings decreases) do change. The lack of effect on total equity is illustrated by disclosures on the statement of owners' equity. The owners' equity statement shows a $4,000 investment by owners, but an exactly offsetting, simultaneously smaller net income (ignoring income taxes).

This accounting seemingly violates the general rule of transactions with owners because an expense is recorded and net income is affected. Actually, the issue of common stock in the Taylor Co. example did not cause the legal expense. The work was performed causing a "fee payable" (liability). An increase in liability resulting in only current-period benefits is, by definition, an expense. The liability was satisfied through the law firm deciding to become an owner of the corporation by accepting common stock.[8]

Another issue related to exchanges of stock for goods or services is how to report these transactions on the statement of cash flows. In the Jackson Investment example, a building is exchanged for common stock. Clearly, this is a material financing activity (issue of stock) *and* a material investing activity (acquisition of building). However, no cash flows are involved. This transaction could have been accomplished in two stages, with cash flow occurring in both stages. The stock could have been issued causing a cash inflow. Then, the cash could have been used to purchase the building. Because another objective of the cash flow statement is to report significant operating, investing, and financing activities, GAAP requires that a separate schedule accompany the statement of cash flows that summarizes simultaneous investing and financing activities that did not affect cash.

Corporate Issuance of Preferred Stock

Corporations often issue preferred stock instead of common stock. Issuing preferred stock involves a trade-off between maintaining corporate control (preferred stock does not have voting rights) and creating a class of shareholders with preference in all asset distributions, including dividends. The initial issue of preferred stock is no different than the issue of common stock. Preferred stock (at par) is normally reported before common stock in the owners' equity section. While it is permissible to use separate accounts, frequently any additional paid-in capital on preferred stock usually is listed with additional paid-in capital amounts on common stock so that only one amount appears for additional paid-in capital. In Exhibit 5, the partial shareholders' equity section from Dollar General Corporation's 1999 annual report illustrates how common stock, preferred stock, and additional paid-in capital are reported in financial statements.

EXHIBIT 5 Preferred Stock Presentation by the Dollar General Corporation

DOLLAR GENERAL CORPORATION
Partial Shareholders' Equity Section of Balance Sheet
January 29, 1999 and January 30, 1998
(Dollars in thousands)

Shareholders' Equity	**1999**	**1998**
Preferred stock, stated value $0.50 per share:		
Shares authorized: 1998—10,000,000; 1997—5,000,000		
Issued: 1998—1,716,000; 1997—1,716,000	858	858
Common stock, par value $0.50 per share:		
Shares authorized: 1998—500,000,000; 1997—200,000,000		
Issued: 1998—210,242,000; 1997—167,052,000	105,121	83,526
Additional paid-in capital	418,039	379,954
Retained earnings	402,270	320,085

Corporate Issuance of Stock Subscriptions

In order to market shares in initial (and, less often, seasoned) public offerings, firms sometimes enter into agreements whereby the company agrees to issue shares in the future while a potential buyer agrees to pay for the shares in the future (frequently,

8. A crucial element in fairly presenting the transaction in the financial statements is that the legal services be appropriately valued. This transaction has the appearance of not being arm's length. Therefore, outside parties such as auditors and financial analysts would want to ensure that the legal services were appropriately valued.

a down payment is required). The transaction, called a stock subscription agreement, is diagramed as follows:

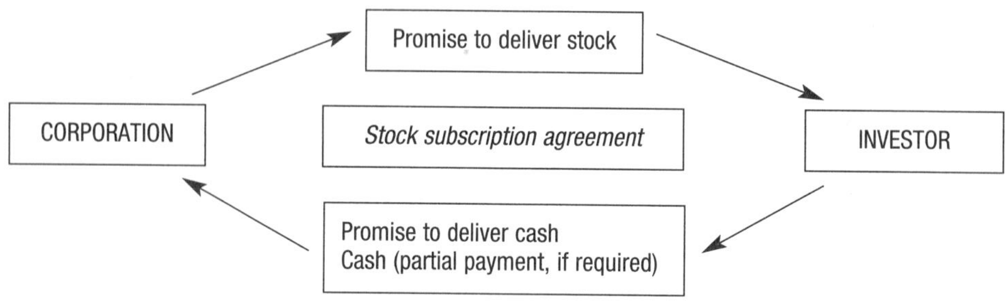

A ***stock subscription agreement*** **is an agreement for which one party agrees to purchase stock at a future date at an agreed price, and a company agrees to issue the stock at a future date at an agreed price.**

A consensus of opinion does not exist on how a subscription agreement should be reported in the financial statements. Two issues drive the controversy. First, although promises are usually associated with liabilities, recall that liabilities are probable future sacrifices of economic resources (i.e., assets). The corporation's own stock is not an asset. Therefore, the promise to deliver stock is not a liability. But is it equity? Second, recording financial statement elements normally involves a transaction or event in which something is exchanged. In a stock subscription, the only things exchanged are promises by both parties. **When neither party has performed in a transaction, the contract is referred to as an *executory contract*.** Accountants generally do not record executory contracts.

One logical way to account for this contract is to increase both assets (cash) and equity by an amount equal to the partial payment for the subscribed stock. Consider the following example:

Example 4. The Baumgart Corp. issues subscriptions for 3,000 shares of $1 par value common stock at $10 per share, and a 20% downpayment is required. We illustrate financial statement effects under two assumptions about the collectibility of the remaining 80%:

A. A major uncertainty exists regarding collectibility.
B. Such uncertainty does not exist.

Solution to Assumption A. As shown in Exhibit 6, if such a major uncertainty exists, no liability is recorded and no asset is recorded for the unpaid portion of the subscription receivable.

EXHIBIT 6 Stock Subscription—Major Uncertainty About Collectibility

BAUMGART CORP.
Balance Sheet

Assets		**Liabilities**	
Current assets			
Cash	**$6,000 ↑**	**Owners' Equity**	
		Contributed capital	
		Common stock subscribed	**$ 3,000 ↑**
		Additional paid-in capital	**27,000 ↑**
		Stock subscriptions receivable	**(24,000) ↑**

Income Statement	
No effect	

Statement of Owners' Equity	
Investments by owners	
Common stock issue subscribed	**$6,000**

EXAMPLE 4 Journal Entry under Assumption A

Cash	6,000	
Stock Subscriptions Receivable	24,000	
Common Stock Subscribed		3,000
Additional Paid-In Capital		27,000

The $6,000 cash receipt (3,000 shares @ $10 per share × 20%) is recorded as an increase in assets, and it equals the net increase in owners' equity. If accountants follow this approach for recording subscriptions, a temporary, special account—"common stock subscribed"—increases by the shares' par value (3,000 shares @ $1). This account is eventually reduced and replaced by the account "common stock" when the shares are issued. Additional paid-in capital increases by the excess of the issue price ($10) over the par value ($1) for all shares, whether issued or not ([$10 − $1] × 3,000 shares = $27,000). The unpaid portion of the subscription price (3,000 shares @ $10 per share × 80%) is shown as a contra equity account, "stock subscriptions receivable."

Solution to Assumption B. An alternative method of recording this contract is allowable if the collection of the stock subscription receivable is reasonably certain and rights for common stock ownership are conveyed by the subscription.[9] This method treats the subscription receivable as an asset. Exhibit 7 shows the alternative accounting for the same transaction.

EXHIBIT 7 Stock Subscription—No Uncertainty About Collectibility

BAUMGART CORP.
Balance Sheet

Assets		Liabilities	
Current assets		**Owners' Equity**	
Cash	**$ 6,000 ↑**	Contributed capital	
Subscriptions receivable	**24,000 ↑**	**Common stock subscribed**	**$ 3,000 ↑**
		Additional paid-in capital	**27,000 ↑**

Income Statement
No effect

Statement of Owners' Equity	
Investments by owners	
Common stock issue subscribed	**$30,000**

Assets and equity both increase by $30,000. The treatment of stock subscriptions receivable as an asset (rather than as a contra equity account) is warranted if the collection of the receivable is reasonably assured. This treatment is less conservative than the first alternative that treats subscriptions receivable as a contra equity account because under this alternative an asset is recorded.[10]

The SEC requires the reporting of subscriptions receivable as contra equity, unless the subscription is collected after year-end and before the financial statements are issued, in which case the subscription receivable could be reported as an asset at year-end.[11]

If the stock buyer does not keep the promise to deliver cash, then the subscription is in default. "Defaulted stock subscriptions" is a complex topic governed by

9. Some state laws specify such rights. In fact, state laws have their most profound effect on equity accounting relative to other areas of accounting.

10. In Example 4, the journal entry under Assumption B would be the same as that under Assumption A.

11. The 1999 *Accounting Trends & Techniques* shows that 14 of 600 companies surveyed had subscriptions receivable reported in stockholders' equity as a contra equity amount.

contract, corporate discretion, and state law. As a general summary, if an investor defaults on a subscription, and the down payment is returned by the corporation, assets and contributed capital must be reduced by like amounts. If the corporation keeps the down payment, then the subscriptions receivable and a like amount of capital is removed. In no instance is a gain or loss recorded. The amount of down payment is permanent contributed capital if it is kept by the corporation.

Corporate Issuance of Stock Options

The original issue of stock options involves an increase in assets (cash) and equity (contributed capital from stock options) for the amount of the issue price. Stock options allow investors to acquire stock by exchanging an option and an amount of cash equal to the option price. We discuss accounting for options in Chapter 3, in conjunction with the accounting for bonds issued with detachable warrants, and in Chapter 12, in combination with executive compensation.

Corporate Issuance of Rights

Common shareholders normally possess a preemptive right, which enables current shareholders to maintain a proportional ownership in the corporation if additional stock is issued. When a corporation issues stock rights, it receives nothing from investors in return. The issuance of rights is simply a formal recognition of a right that already existed. The issuance of stock rights has no effect on financial statements. When investors exercise their stock rights, the resulting issuance of common stock is reported as an issue of stock for cash.

Another type of stock right, "stock purchase rights," is sometimes issued by a company as a takeover defense. A ***stock purchase right*** **allows current shareholders to purchase an additional number of shares in the event that an outside party either acquires or attempts to acquire a substantial equity stake in the company.** The aim of the company is to have a mechanism in place to issue more shares quickly so as to make any takeover prohibitively expensive.[12]

Corporate Issuance of Nothing in Exchange for Assets (Donations)

On occasion, individuals or governments donate assets to a corporation. Although the corporation issues nothing in return to new shareholders, existing shareholders have greater equity because of the donation. The basis for recording a donation is the FMV of the donated asset.

Example 5. Bombay, Inc., received a $900,000 parcel of land as a donation from an owner (or from a governmental unit).

Solution. Exhibit 8 shows the effects of the transaction on Bombay's financial statements.

EXHIBIT 8 Impact of Donation on Financial Statements

BOMBAY, INC.
Balance Sheet

Assets		**Liabilities**	
Property, plant, and equipment		**Owners' Equity**	
Land	**900,000 ↑**	Contributed capital	
		Donated capital	**900,000 ↑**

(continued)

12. The 1999 *Accounting Trends & Techniques* shows that for the 600 companies surveyed, 42 companies issued stock purchase rights in the most recent year.

EXHIBIT 8 (concluded)

Income Statement	Statement of Owners' Equity	
No effect	Investments by owners	
	Donated capital	**900,000**

EXAMPLE 5 Journal Entry

Land	900,000	
Donated Capital (Owners' Equity)		900,000

GAAP (SFAS No. 116) requires that not-for-profit entities treat donations as revenue. However, if a donation is made to a for-profit enterprise by an owner or governmental unit, it is appropriate to treat the donation as contributed capital. If a donation is made to a for-profit enterprise by a nongovernmental unit, the donation is recorded as revenue.

Dividends

5 Account for the various forms of dividend distributions.

To equity investors, the receipt of a dividend is the realization of their predicted future cash flows. Recall that these cash flows form the basis for the market value of the firm's stock. Thus, a firm views the declaration of dividends as an important financing activity.

In order to understand how the securities market views a dividend declaration, it is important to realize that declaration is not a value-producing act. Operating activities produce value by generating net assets (assets − liabilities), which in turn increase net income. A dividend distribution simply distributes to owners what they already own, namely, the net assets created by operations.

For example, assume that Martin Co. begins operations on January 1, 2001, by selling 100 shares of no-par common stock for $1, equally to 100 shareholders. After the issue, Martin has $100 of assets (cash), no liabilities, and $100 of equity (common stock). Each shareholder now has a $1 claim against assets ($100 equity/100 shareholders). If Martin subsequently increases its net assets by $50 (net income) due to operating the firm, each shareholder would have a $1.50 claim against assets ($150 equity/100 shareholders). Martin could declare a $0.50 per share dividend ($50 net income/100 shares) and still maintain financial capital at the beginning-of-the-period amount of $100. If Martin does not declare and pay the dividend, any of the shareholders could receive an amount equal to the dividend plus their original investment by selling their shares at $1.50.

The valuation implications of earnings and dividends lie in whether they are unexpected and whether the unexpected amount is permanent or transitory. One interesting question about dividend declarations that has attracted accounting and finance researchers is what happens to security prices if firms declare an unexpectedly higher or lower dividend. We know that dividends are no more than a distribution to owners of assets already earned. Theoretically, changes in payout rates and dividend amounts should have no effect on stock prices, per se. But, researchers have long believed that firms *signal something about the future* when they change dividend amounts. For example, investors observing a firm unexpectedly increasing dividends could infer that the corporation believes that higher future permanent earnings will be generated to support the continuation of the new level of dividends, since firms are reluctant to ever reduce dividends. This situation would translate into higher market prices for the firm's shares. Although not conclusive, empirical research has found evidence that supports the belief that dividends are a signaling mechanism for managers anticipating changes in permanent earnings.

Dividends can take varying forms, as the following diagram illustrates:

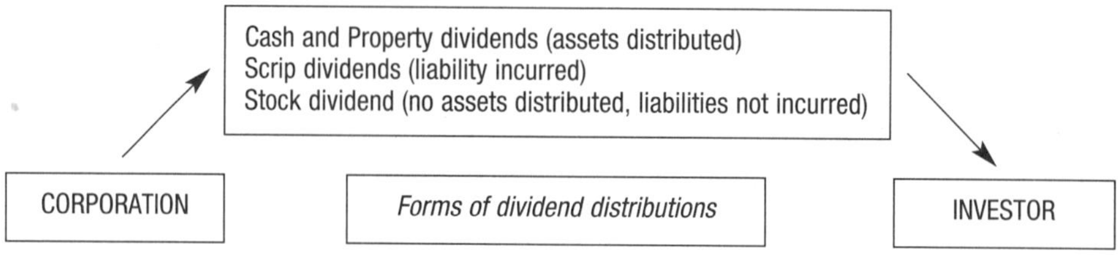

Of these dividend options, cash is most often used. However, corporations can issue interest-bearing promises to pay dividends (scrip dividends), investments in other corporations (property dividends), and additional shares of the corporation's own stock (stock dividends).[13]

In the following sections, we consider the financial statement presentation of the various kinds of dividends. But before elaborating on the complexities of dividends, it is necessary to discuss three important dates common to all forms of dividends: date of declaration, date of record, and date of payment (or distribution). **On the *date of declaration* the firm incurs a legal liability to distribute the dividend to owners of the stock on a specific future date, which is the *date of record*.** Finally, on the ***date of payment*, the dividend distribution occurs.** Typically, these three dates are several weeks apart.[14]

For cash, scrip, and property dividends, *owners' equity is reduced on the date of declaration and a liability is recorded.* The decrease in net assets results from transactions with owners. The date of record has no impact on the corporation's accounting. No change in equity occurs on the date of payment because both assets (cash or property) and liabilities (dividends payable) decrease (i.e., there is no change in *net* assets).

Cash Dividends

Cash dividends are, by far, the most common form of dividend.

Example 6. Black Cat, Inc., declares a dividend of $100,000 on common stock. Show the financial statement effects assuming two different situations: (1) the dividend is declared but not paid by year-end (Exhibit 9), and (2) the dividend is declared and paid by year-end (Exhibit 10).

Solution.

EXHIBIT 9 Dividend Declared but Not Yet Paid by Year-End

BLACK CAT, INC.
Balance Sheet

Assets	**Liabilities**	
Current assets	Current liabilities	
No effect	**Dividends payable**	**100,000 ↑**
	Owners' Equity	
	Retained earnings	**100,000 ↓**

(continued)

13. The 1999 *Accounting Trends & Techniques* shows that of 600 companies surveyed, there were 435 instances of the payment of cash dividends to common shareholders, 83 instances of cash dividend payments to preferred shareholders, 9 instances of the issuance of stock dividends, and 10 instances of the issuance of property (in kind) dividends.

14. Organized stock exchanges routinely require four business days prior to the date of record to document ownership changes. The *ex-dividend date* begins that four-day period. Individuals who purchase the stock after the ex-dividend date and before the date of record are not entitled to receive the dividend.

EXHIBIT 9 (concluded)

Income Statement		**Statement of Owners' Equity**	
No effect		Distributions to owners	
		Cash dividends declared	**(100,000)**

EXHIBIT 10 Dividend Declared and Paid by Year-End

BLACK CAT, INC.
Balance Sheet

Assets		**Liabilities**	
Current assets		Current liabilities	
Cash	**100,000 ↓**	**No ending balance**	
		Owners' Equity	
		Retained earnings	**100,000 ↓**

Income Statement		**Statement of Owners' Equity**	
No effect		Distributions to owners	
		Cash dividends declared	**(100,000)**

EXAMPLE 6 Journal Entries

Dividends	100,000	
Dividends Payable		100,000
Declaration of dividends.		
Dividends Payable	100,000	
Cash		100,000
Payment of dividends (either in subsequent year, Situation 1, or current year, Situation 2).		

If dividends are declared but not paid by year-end, a liability for dividends payable is recorded in the current liabilities section of the balance sheet. If the dividend is declared and paid in the same year, no liability exists and cash is $100,000 lower. Cash dividends are direct reductions of retained earnings, regardless of whether they have been paid by year-end. Although not shown above, the statement of cash flows would report an outflow of cash from financing activities *only if* the dividends had been paid by year-end. *From this point forward, we will assume that the dividends are declared and paid in the same period.*

Scrip Dividends

Due to the potential signaling aspects of increasing, decreasing, or omitting dividends, corporations like to declare and distribute dividends on regularly expected dates. On rare occasions, a short-term expected cash shortage may necessitate a delay in the payment date. In such a situation, **corporations may issue interest-bearing promises to pay dividends as of a certain future date. These promises are called *scrip dividends*.**

Example 7. Glower Products normally declares annual dividends on June 1, payable on July 1. Instead of following the normal process, Glower declares a $400,000, 12% scrip dividend on June 1 with payment delayed from July 1 to August 1 and interest payable from July 1 to August 1.

Solution. The effects on the financial statements through August 1, ignoring income tax effects, are shown in Exhibit 11.

EXHIBIT 11 Scrip Dividend Declared and Paid

GLOWER PRODUCTS
Balance Sheet

Assets		**Liabilities**	
Current assets			
Cash	**404,000 ↓**	**Owners' Equity**	
		Retained earnings	**404,000 ↓**

Income Statement*	
Financial revenues and (expenses), gains and (losses)	
Interest expense	**(4,000)**

*Ignores income tax effects

Statement of Owners' Equity	
Distributions to owners	
Cash dividends declared	**(400,000)**
Net income (effect of scrip dividend)	**(4,000)**

EXAMPLE 7 Journal Entries

Dividends	400,000	
Dividends Payable		400,000
Declaration of scrip dividend (June 1).		
Dividends Payable	400,000	
Interest Expense	4,000	
Cash		404,000
Payment of dividend and associated interest (August 1).		

A total of \$404,000 is paid on August 1, with \$4,000 (\$400,000 × 12% × 1/12) of the total representing interest expense reported on the income statement. Retained earnings decreases \$404,000. The statement of owners' equity shows the two effects of scrip dividends that combine to reduce retained earnings. The direct effect on retained earnings (equity) is a \$400,000 dividend. The indirect effect occurs when the \$4,000 interest expense reduces net income, which is a determinant of owners' equity. Note that the general rules apply: The dividend was recorded at FMV (\$400,000), and the dividend did not affect net income, although the interest paid on the scrip dividend did affect net income.

The statement of cash flows would also reflect two different activities creating cash outflows. The financing activities section would report a cash outflow of \$400,000 for dividends paid. The \$4,000 cash interest payment would be reported as a cash outflow from operating activities.

Property Dividends

Property dividends are distributions of noncash assets or services to owners. These dividends most often take the form of distributing shares of another corporation's stock due to their ease of divisibility among shareholders. The general rule of equity transactions applies—transfer at FMV. If the property is recorded in a company's records at an amount different from its FMV, the asset should first be written up to its FMV and a gain or loss recognized. Then, the property dividend is recorded at the property's FMV.

Example 8. Shares of XYZ (a long-term investment) are to be distributed by ABC Co. as a property dividend. The XYZ shares have an original cost of \$100,000 and a FMV of \$150,000 at the declaration date. Accounting for long-term investments in common stocks is discussed in Chapter 8. For now, assume that the long-term investments are recorded at FMV (i.e., the shares are marked to market).

Solution. The balance sheet in Exhibit 12 shows the simultaneous decline in assets and owners' equity caused by the property dividend distribution. The statement of owners' equity also reflects the effect on retained earnings.

EXHIBIT 12 Declaration and Payment of a Property Dividend

ABC CO.
Balance Sheet

Assets		**Liabilities**	
Investments and funds		**Owners' Equity**	
Investment in XYZ	**150,000 ↓**	**Retained earnings**	**150,000 ↓**

Income Statement	**Statement of Owners' Equity**	
No effect	Distributions to owners	
	Property dividend	**(150,000)**

EXAMPLE 8 Journal Entries

Dividends	150,000	
Investment in XYZ Stock		150,000

Stock Dividends and Stock Splits

A final kind of dividend occurs when **a corporation distributes shares of its own stock to investors.** For accounting purposes, three kinds of ***stock dividend*** distributions may occur:

- Small stock dividends (distributions of < 20%)
- Midrange stock dividends (distributions of 20%–25%)
- Large stock dividends (distributions of > 25%)

A fourth type of stock distribution, a stock split, is discussed later in this chapter.

A stock dividend does not involve a transfer of assets to investors. Thus, unlike other dividends, *stock dividends result in no change to total owners' equity.* Also, because no change occurs in the assets of the corporation and proportional ownership is retained, investor wealth is unchanged by stock dividends, per se. Once again, however, the signaling implications of these activities may change investor wealth.[15]

Even though there are no economic differences among small, midrange, and large stock dividends, the accounting may be different. The effects on retained earnings and contributed capital are determined by accounting rules (ARB No. 43) and state legal requirements.[16]

Small Stock Dividends GAAP (ARB No. 43) requires a transfer of the fair market value of shares issued in a small stock dividend from retained earnings to contributed capital.

15. Empirical accounting and finance research has demonstrated that abnormal returns are associated with stock distributions. Therefore, normally stockholder wealth does change in response to a stock distribution.

16. Legal requirements broadly depend upon whether the state of incorporation follows the concept of legal capital. See R.O. Kummert, "State Statutory Restriction on Financial Distributions by Corporations to Shareholders," *Washington Law Review* 59 (April 1994): 185–287.

Example 9. Consider the stockholders' equity section of Bastille Co.:

Common stock ($10 par, 50,000 shares issued and outstanding)	$ 500,000
Additional paid-in capital on common stock	600,000
Retained earnings	2,300,000
Total stockholders' equity	$3,400,000

Assume that Bastille issues a 10% stock dividend when shares are selling at $15.

Solution (10% Small Stock Dividend—FMV). Dividends of less than 20% are considered by accounting standard setters to be "small." The amount shifted from retained earnings to contributed capital is at the $75,000 market value of the new shares (50,000 shares × 10% dividend × $15 market price per share). The effect of the 10% dividend on the financial statements is shown in Exhibit 13.

EXHIBIT 13 Impact of a Small Stock Dividend on Financial Statements

BASTILLE CO.
Balance Sheet

Assets	Liabilities	
No effect	No effect	
	Owners' Equity	
	Contributed capital	
	Common stock ($10 par)	**$50,000 ↑**
	Additional paid-in capital	**25,000 ↑**
	Retained earnings	**75,000 ↓**

Income Statement	Statement of Owners' Equity	
No effect	Contributed capital	
	10% stock dividend	**75,000**
	Retained earnings	
	10% stock dividend	**(75,000)**

EXAMPLE 9 Journal Entry

Retained Earnings*	75,000	
Common Stock		50,000
Additional Paid-In Capital		25,000

* Alternatively, use the temporary account "Dividends," which is closed directly to Retained Earnings at year-end.

The following is an example of the disclosure of a small stock dividend:

Small Stock Dividend Disclosure—Republic Group, Incorporated

On January 28, 1997, the Company declared a 10% stock dividend on the Company's common stock, which was paid on March 14, 1997 to stockholders of record on February 28, 1997. The dividend was charged to retained earnings in the amount of $16.2 million, which was based on the fair value of the Company's common stock.

Midrange Stock Dividends Accounting standard setters describe a transitional range from small to large dividends (20%–25%), which we refer to as "midrange." To illustrate a midrange stock dividend, we change an assumption in Example 9:

Example 9a (example 9 continued). Assume that instead of issuing a 10% small stock dividend, Bastille issued a 25% midrange stock dividend.

Solution (25% Midrange Stock Dividend—Par Value Transferred from Paid-In Capital). GAAP is ambiguous with respect to these dividends, and the accounting treatment is frequently determined by state laws in which the corporation is incorporated. Zucca and Kirch (1996) report an investigation of a random sample of 388 midrange stock distributions (both stock dividends and stock splits) between 1980 and 1990.[17] Of the 388 announcements, 64 were of midrange stock dividends, for which the following accounting treatments occurred: 46 transferred amounts from paid-in capital to stated capital (note that both are part of total contributed capital), 15 transferred amounts from retained earnings to stated capital (most at the par value of the shares, but a small number at the fair market value of the shares), and 3 restated the par values so that no amount was transferred to stated capital. In our example, a 25% dividend would mean that Bastille would issue 12,500 shares of common stock. If Bastille recorded the transaction based upon the par value of the shares issued as a transfer from paid-in capital to common stock (stated capital), the most common approach cited by Zucca and Kirch, then the effect of the 25% stock dividend would be as follows (50,000 shares × 25% dividend = 12,500 shares, and 12,500 shares × $10 par value = $125,000). This is shown in Exhibit 14.

EXHIBIT 14 Impact of a Midrange Stock Dividend on Financial Statements—Transfer from Additional Paid-In-Capital

BASTILLE CO.
Balance Sheet

Assets		Liabilities	
No effect		No effect	
		Owners' Equity	
		Contributed capital	
		Common stock ($10 par)	**$125,000 ↑**
		Additional paid-in capital	**125,000 ↓**
		Retained earnings	**No effect**

Income Statement	Statement of Owners' Equity	
No effect	Capital stock	
	25% stock dividend	**125,000**
	Additional paid-in capital	
	25% stock dividend	**(125,000)**
	Retained earnings	
	25% stock dividend	**No effect**

EXAMPLE 9a Journal Entry

Additional Paid-In Capital	125,000	
Common Stock		125,000
If par value transferred within contributed capital accounts.		

Solution (25% Midrange Stock Dividend—Par Value Transferred from Retained Earnings). If the 25% stock dividend were recorded as a restatement of the par value of the shares, then the amount of total common stock would not change. If Bastille recorded the transaction as a transfer at par value from retained

17. Linda J. Zucca and David P. Kirch, A Gap in GAAP: Accounting for Midrange Stock Distributions, *Accounting Horizons* (June 1996): 100–112.

earnings to common stock (stated capital), then the effect of the 25% stock dividend is as follows (50,000 shares × 25% dividend = 12,500 shares, and 12,500 shares × $10 par value = $125,000). Exhibit 15 illustrates the effects of this transaction.

EXHIBIT 15 Impact of a Midrange Stock Dividend on Financial Statements—Transfer from Retained Earnings

BASTILLE CO. (EXAMPLE 9A)
Balance Sheet

Assets		Liabilities	
No effect		No effect	
		Owners' Equity	
		Contributed capital	
		Common stock ($10 par)	**125,000 ↑**
		Additional paid-in capital	**No effect**
		Retained earnings	**125,000 ↓**

Income Statement

No effect

Statement of Owners' Equity

Capital stock	
25% stock dividend	**125,000**
Contributed capital	
25% stock dividend	**No effect**
Retained earnings	
25% stock dividend	**(125,000)**

EXAMPLE 9a Journal Entry

Retained Earnings	125,000	
Common Stock		125,000
If par value transferred from retained earnings to contributed capital.		

Large Stock Dividends and Stock Splits Large stock dividends are those greater than 25%. Large distributions of ≥ 100% are often in the form of a stock split. Assuming the facts in Example 9, suppose that Bastille wanted to double the number of shares outstanding in order to halve the price of its stock. Bastille could issue either a 100% stock dividend or a 2-for-1 stock split. As with midrange stock dividends, accounting for a large stock dividend depends upon GAAP and appropriate state law. Most of the time, this will mean that the par value of the shares is transferred to common stock from either retained earnings or additional paid-in capital.

Example 9b (example 9 continued to illustrate a *100% Stock Dividend*). Assume that instead of issuing a 10% small stock dividend, Bastille issued a 100% large stock dividend.

Solution (100% Large Stock Dividend—Par Value Transferred from Retained Earnings). The 100% dividend means that Bastille would issue an additional 50,000 shares of common stock. If the stock dividend were recorded as a transfer of the par value from retained earnings to common stock (the preferred treatment under ARB No. 43), then the financial statement effect is to transfer $500,000 (50,000 shares @ $10) from retained earnings to contributed capital. This transfer is illustrated in Exhibit 16.

EXHIBIT 16 Large Stock Dividend—Par Value Transferred from Retained Earnings

BASTILLE CO. (EXAMPLE 9B)
Balance Sheet

Assets		**Liabilities**	
No effect		No effect	
		Owners' Equity	
		Contributed capital	
		Common stock ($10 par)	**500,000 ↑**
		Retained earnings	**500,000 ↓**

Income Statement	**Statement of Owners' Equity**	
No effect	Contributed capital	
	100% stock dividend	**500,000**
	Retained earnings	
	100% stock dividend	**(500,000)**

EXAMPLE 9b Journal Entry (100% Stock Split)

Retained Earnings	500,000	
Common Stock		500,000
If par value transferred from retained earnings to contributed capital.		

Similar to the midrange distribution illustrated previously, if the 100% stock dividend were recorded as a transfer from paid-in capital, then total contributed capital would not change, but $500,000 would be transferred from additional paid-in capital to common stock.[18]

The following is a large stock dividend disclosure:

Large Stock Dividend Disclosure—Compaq Computer Corporation.

On July 28, 1997 and January 20, 1998, Compaq effected a five-for-two and a two-for-one stock split, respectively, both in the form of a stock dividend.

Example 9c (example 9b continued to illustrate a *2-for-1 Stock Split*). In Example 9b, Bastille issued a 100% stock dividend. Assume instead that Bastille issued a 2-for-1 stock split.

Solution. In a stock split, GAAP does not require an amount to be shifted from retained earnings to contributed capital, but state laws may allow an amount to be shifted from either retained earnings or additional paid-in capital to common stock. Accounting rules indicate that the par value of individual shares is to be adjusted such that the total par value after the stock split is the same as the total par value before the split. Therefore, if Bastille Co. were to declare a 2-for-1 split on its 50,000 shares of $10 par value stock, it would issue an additional 50,000 shares and reduce par value to $5 par value on all 100,000 shares. This accounting is illustrated as follows in Exhibit 17.

18. If par value was transferred within contributed capital accounts, the journal entry would be:
Additional Paid-In Capital 500,000
Common Stock. 500,000

EXHIBIT 17 Impact of 2-for-1 Stock Split on Financial Statements

BASTILLE CO. (EXAMPLE 9C)
Balance Sheet

Assets	**Liabilities**	
No effect	**No effect**	
	Owners' Equity	
	Contributed capital	
	Common stock ($5 par)	**No change**
	Retained earnings	**No change**

Income Statement	**Statement of Owners' Equity**	
No effect	Contributed capital	
	2-for-1 stock split	**No effect**
	Retained earnings	
	2-for-1 stock split	**No effect**

Alternatively, the accounting could transfer the par value of the shares either from retained earnings or paid-in capital. Examples of these accounting treatments were shown in previous sections. The AICPA's 1999 *Accounting Trends & Techniques* documents that all three accounting possibilities have been used.[19]

General Rules to Follow Accounting for stock dividends and stock splits can differ depending upon state laws. However, we formulate general rules to follow in absence of specific facts. Record *small stock dividends* (<20%) at the fair market value of the shares issued by transferring the appropriate amount from retained earnings to contributed capital accounts (common stock and additional paid-in capital). Record *midrange stock dividends* and *large stock dividends* at the par value of the shares issued by transferring the appropriate amount from retained earnings to the common stock account. Record *stock splits* with a memo journal entry (no accounts are affected).

http://

Learn more about the institutions that provide organized markets for equity financing. Pay a cyber-visit to a national exchange in New York, a regional exchange in Arizona, and a foreign exchange in Australia. Access these sites through our Web site (http://baginski@swcollege.com).

The External Decision Makers' Perspective

6 Explain how external decision makers view owners' equity.

To external decision makers, owners' equity represents the dollar amount of their claims to the net assets (assets minus liabilities) of the company. **If we divide common shareholders' equity (contributed capital plus retained earnings) by the number of common shares outstanding, we obtain a measure called *book value per share*.** The economic meaning of this number to external decision makers is not clear because owners' equity is the difference between assets and liabilities, each measured using different attributes (e.g., historical cost, present value, market value, net realizable value, etc.). Further, book value per share is influenced by both the accounting policies of a company and the kinds of operations in which the company engages. For example, if a company is conservative in its accounting, assets are written off and liabilities are recognized more quickly, and the result is a lower

19. The AICPA's 1999 *Accounting Trends & Techniques* reports that of 600 companies surveyed, 83 issued stock splits: less than 3 for 2 (4 instances), 3 for 2 (12 instances), 2 for 1 (60 instances), and greater than 2 for 1 (7 instances). Of the 83 splits, 30 were charged to additional paid-in capital, 19 to retained earnings, and 34 did not change stockholders' equity accounts.

book value per share. Also, if a company's operations include a great deal of research and development (expensed immediately by FASB rule), then the unrecorded economic assets created by R&D cause book value per share to be lower.

Equity securities markets provide a market price per share of common stock that is created by the interaction of supply and demand for the shares. This market price is the dollar amount that a common shareholder would actually receive from giving up a share of owners' equity. Many external decision makers relate the book value per share of common equity to the market price per share through construction of the market-to-book ratio:

***Market-to-book ratio* = Market price per share / Book value per share**

Market-to-book ratios greater than one are the most common. The number of times that market price is greater than book value (i.e., the "multiple") stems from several factors:

1. the conservatism of accounting principles,
2. the extent to which the economic value of the assets in place exceed their book values as determined by accounting rules, and
3. future growth opportunities that have not been reflected in accounting measurements.

Items 1 and 2 reflect information about the firm that can be incorporated quickly into common stock prices. The accounting measurement rules for owners' equity depend on measurement rules for assets and liabilities. These rules tend to require either that transactions have taken place or that unresolved future events can reliably be estimated. Therefore, owners' equity tends to reflect a firm's market value with a delay.

Book value per share is still a useful number for external decision makers. As we noted in Module A, important financial ratios (e.g., return on common equity) employ book-value-per-share measures. We will see in Module E that it is also possible to use book value per share in valuing the firm.

Southwest Airlines' Equity Financing Decisions

Several portions of Southwest Airlines' financial statements pertain to equity financing decisions. Before continuing in this section, please review the following sections of Southwest Airlines' 1998 annual report information (the annual report is reproduced in Appendix C at the end of this text): (1) management's discussion and analysis (MD&A)—Liquidity and Capital Resources subsection, (2) consolidated balance sheet—stockholders' equity section (and related accompanying Notes 7 and 8—notes to the financial statements), (3) consolidated statement of stockholders' equity, and (4) consolidated statement of cash flows—Financing Activities section. The purpose of this section is to help you become comfortable referring to actual financial statements and to help you develop an understanding of how pertinent information about a particular topic may be spread throughout the financial statements.

The consolidated balance sheets indicate that Southwest had 850,000,000 shares authorized, and 335,904,306 and 221,207,083 shares issued at December 31, 1998 and 1997, respectively. The consolidated statement of stockholders' equity reconciles the change in the shares outstanding during 1998. The statement of stockholders' equity and Note 7 indicate that 111,894,315 shares were issued on August 20, 1998, in a 3-for-2 stock split, and 73,577,983 shares were issued in a 3-for-2 stock split on November 26, 1997. During 1998, Note 7 and the statement of cash flows indicate that 4,885,763 shares were repurchased as treasury stock during 1998 in a $100 million acquisition. The balance sheet shows that 3,601,121 of these treasury shares were still on hand at December 31, 1998; therefore, South west had 332,303,185 shares outstanding (335,904,306 shares issued − 3,601,121 treasury shares).

The statement of stockholders' equity reveals that 2,803,000 shares were issued upon exercise of executive stock options in 1998 and approximately 2,517,000 shares in 1997. The statement of cash flows indicates that Southwest received $44,272,000 (1998) and $40,335,000 (1997) from employees purchasing stock under employee stock plans. Southwest's stock option plan is described in Note 8, and this topic is covered subsequently in the text in Chapter 12.

Using the statement of cash flows and the statement of stockholders' equity, it is apparent that Southwest does not declare and pay all dividends in the same year. The statement of stockholders' equity shows that $10,387,000 ($0.0283 per share) and $7,207,000 ($0.0221 per share) were charged to retained earnings in 1998 and 1997, respectively, while the statement of cash flows shows that Southwest paid dividends of $9,284,000 and $6,593,000 in 1998 and 1997, respectively.

Note 7 is interesting because it describes a "poison pill" provision that companies use to discourage hostile takeovers. Each outstanding share of Southwest common stock has one *stock purchase right,* exercisable at $7.41 per right, that is usable only in a proposed takeover. Current shareholders can effectively double the number of shares outstanding, thereby increasing the takeover cost to the hostile firm. If the purchase right's exercise price is considerably below the market price at the time of a proposed hostile takeover, then the current shareholders can profit handsomely. Note 7 reveals that of the 850,000,000 shares authorized, 69,453,206 shares are reserved pursuant to employee stock benefit plans (discussed in Note 8) and 405,357,512 shares are reserved for stock purchase rights pursuant to the Common Stock Rights Agreement.

Chapter Summary

No great controversies exist in the accounting for equity financing. This is probably because the majority of significant transactions involve cash. When cash is present in a transaction, the FMV of the transaction is clearly determinable. The general rule of accounting for equity financing is that transactions are recorded at FMV.

Also, equity transactions involve exchanges of net assets and claims to net assets. Accordingly, gains and losses are not recorded on equity transactions. Equity issues increase the contributed capital component of owners' equity. Dividend declaration decreases the retained earnings component of owners' equity.

Other transactions affect the owners' equity section of the balance sheet. We discuss these transactions in future chapters in the context of the decision that creates them, as follows:

- The decision to reduce financing (Chapter 5).
- Holding long-term marketable equity securities (Chapter 8).
- Maintaining a pension plan (Chapter 12).
- Employee compensation using stock options and stock appreciation rights (Chapter 12).

In summary, corporations record the issuance of equity securities at either the FMV of what has been received, whether it be cash, property, or services, or the FMV of the equity securities, whichever is more determinable. Contributed capital is segregated between par value and amounts contributed in excess of par. The statement of owners' equity reports the changes in the equity accounts during the period.

The search for the optimal capital structure involves trade-offs between the costs and benefits of the various financing options. The perceptions of investors and rating agencies about the impact of the firm's capital structure on value shape future capital structure decisions. Financial statements play an important role in assessing the effects of capital structure on the debt paying and dividend generating abilities of the firm.

Key Terms

Questions

Q1. **Debt Versus Equity Securities.** What are the primary characteristics that distinguish debt from equity securities?

Q2. **Hybrid Securities.** What is a hybrid security? What are the four hybrid securities identified in the text and what makes them hybrid?

Q3. **Optimal Capital Structure.** What is the definition of optimal capital structure?

Q4. **Determinants of Capital Structure.** What are the key determinants of capital structure discussed in the text?

Q5. **Cash Flows and Stock Transactions.** What are three different kinds of cash flows resulting from stock transactions that are experienced by the issuing corporation?

Q6. **Cash Flows and Stock-Related Transactions.** In what section of the statement of cash flows are a stock issue, a cash dividend, and a stock dividend reported?

Q7. **Par value.** What is par value and how is it determined?

Q8. **Equity Instruments.** Identify five equity instruments that corporations may issue to investors in an equity transaction.

Q9. **Exchange for Equity Claims.** Identify three types of consideration that investors can convey to the corporation in exchange for an equity claim.

Q10. **Equity Transactions.** What is the basis for recording equity transactions when cash, property, or services are received by the issuing corporation in exchange for the equity interest (i.e., at what value is the transaction recorded when equity securities are issued)?

Q11. **Common Stock Issuance.** When common stock is issued in exchange for services that benefit only the current period, owners' equity is both increased and decreased by the same amount. Identify the components of owners' equity that are affected, and explain why they change.

Q12. **Building Acquired for Common Stock.** If a corporation acquires a building in a cash transaction, the statement of cash flows reports the transaction as a cash outflow from investing activities. What kind of cash flow reporting occurs if the same building is acquired directly by issuing common stock?

Q13. **Stock Subscriptions.** Describe the two possible treatments of the account "stock subscriptions receivable" that arise in a stock subscription arrangement.

Q14. **Executory Contract.** What is an executory contract?

Q15. **Contra Equity Account.** What is a contra equity account?

Q16. **Stock Subscription.** If a stock subscription is defaulted and the corporation keeps the down payment, is a "gain on defaulted subscriptions" recognized?

Q17. **Stock Rights Issued.** What is the effect on the financial statements of the issuance of stock rights? Why?

Q18. **Donated Land.** Mercer Corp. received a $500,000 parcel of land as a donation from the Megabyte Township. Mercer's president wants to value the land at $0 in the financial statements because Mercer gave up nothing to receive the land. What general rule would the $0 valuation violate? How should the land be recorded in the financial statements?

Q19. **Cash Dividend Declared.** Strawberry Fields Enterprises declared a $4 per share cash dividend for the 23rd consecutive quarter. What is the probable effect of the declaration on security prices? Why?

Q20. **Dividend Declaration.** What is a potential signaling aspect of dividend declaration?

Q21. **Dividends.** Identify four possible kinds of dividends.

Q22. **Dividends.** At which date is the dividends payable liability established?

Q23. **Scrip Dividends.** What are scrip dividends, and why might they be declared?

Q24. **Property Dividend.** At a conceptual level, how are property dividends similar to cash dividends? As a practical matter, how does property dividend measurement differ?

Q25. **Stock Distributions, Cash Not Received.** It is not uncommon for a corporation to issue stock to its owners proportionate to the shareholders' existing ownership positions and receive nothing in return from the shareholders. Identify the four classifications accountants use to distinguish distributions of stock in lieu of cash. What is the change in investor wealth from these four distributions?

Q26. **Stock Distributions.** Which stock distribution causes a reduction in owners' equity equal to the par value of the new shares that are distributed? Which stock distribution causes a reduction in owners' equity equal to the fair market value of the new shares that are distributed? Which stock distribution causes no change in owners' equity?

Short Problems

Problems 1–10 require you to indicate the financial statement effects of equity financing transactions (ignore income tax effects). Use the following format that was used in the text to present your answers. Make sure that, within each major classification, you indicate the subclassification under which the account will appear. On the balance sheet, use arrows to indicate whether the account will be higher (↑) or lower (↓) and the amount of the effect on the account. To illustrate how the format is used, we include the answer to Problem 1.

Journal Entry Option: Students who are interested in how the transactions would be recorded in the accounting system should also make journal entries for each situation.

Balance Sheet

Assets	**Liabilities**
	Owners' Equity

Income Statement	**Statement of Owners' Equity**

1. **Effects of Equity Transactions.** Fruit and Nut Enterprises issued 65,000 shares of $1 par value common stock. The shares sold for $4 per share. The underwriter remitted proceeds to Fruit and Nut after deducting $11,500 in issue costs. In a separate transaction, Fruit and Nut issued 2,000 shares of 6%, $100 par value preferred stock for $115 per share. The issue costs were $3,000 on this separate issue.

   Answer.
   Common Stock
   Sales price = 65,000 shares × $4 = $260,000
   Net proceeds = $260,000 − $11,500 = $248,500
   Par value of shares issued = 65,000 shares × $1 = $65,000
   Paid-in capital in excess of par = $248,500 − $65,000 = $183,500
   Preferred Stock
   Sales price = 2,000 shares × $115 = $230,000
   Net proceeds = $230,000 − $3,000 = $227,000
   Par value of shares issued = 2,000 shares × $100 = $200,000
   Paid-in-capital in excess of par = $227,000 − $200,000 = $27,000
   Total proceeds = $248,500 + $227,000 = $475,500.
   Total additional paid-in capital in excess of par = $183,500 + $27,000 = $210,500

   FRUIT AND NUT ENTERPRISES
   Balance Sheet

Assets		**Liabilities**	
Cash	475,500 ↑	No effect	
		Owners' Equity	
		Contributed capital	
		Common stock	**65,000 ↑**
		Preferred stock	**200,000 ↑**
		Additional paid-in capital	**210,500 ↑**
		Total	**475,500 ↑**

Income Statement	**Statement of Owners' Equity**	
No effect	Issued common stock	248,500
	Issued preferred stock	227,000

2. **Effects of Equity Transactions.** As part of the Makepeace Properties incorporation agreement, a consultant was retained at an agreed-upon fee of $80,000 to provide a marketing plan for the first year. The plan benefited the first year only. The consultant felt that Makepeace had an excellent opportunity for success. So, the consultant waived the normal $80,000 consulting fee in exchange for 1,000 shares of Makepeace's no-par common stock.

3. **Effects of Equity Transactions.** Honest Vegetable Co. acquired a tract of undeveloped land in exchange for 9,000 shares of $1 par value common stock. The land's market value

was not easily determinable, but the common stock sold on the New York Stock Exchange for $21 per share on the date of the transaction.

4. **Effects of Equity Transactions.** Neill Co. engages in an initial public offering (IPO) of 2,000,000 shares of its $1 par value common stock. Investors may subscribe to the issue at a price of $4. A down payment equal to 50% of the price of the stock is required at the subscriptions date. The remainder is due when Neill Co. delivers the stock.
   a. Assume that the collection of the receivable is reasonably certain and Neill's state of incorporation extends voting privileges to common stock subscribers.
   b. Assume that collection of the receivable is not reasonably certain.

5. **Effects of Equity Transactions.** Corn-from-the-Farm, Inc., currently has 1 million shares of $2 par value common stock outstanding that originally sold for $6 per share in a previous year. Due to superior past profits and future profit potential, the shares are currently selling for $51 per share. Corn-from-the-Farm wishes to raise additional capital by issuing 10% more shares to the market. In recognition of preemptive rights, Corn-from-the-Farm issues 100,000 rights to existing shareholders. Each right plus $50 can be used to purchase one new share in the upcoming seasoned offering.

6. **Effects of Equity Transactions.** LotsofJobs Manufacturing was enticed by the local city council to open a plant in Drawbridge, Arkansas, in the current period. The city donated to the corporation a tract of land suitable for a plant site as an enticement. The land was valued at $375,000.

7. **Effects of Equity Transactions—Cash Dividend.** The following is the owners' equity section of Billboard Co. at November 1, 2001:

Common stock ($1 par value, 300,000 shares authorized; 200,000 issued and outstanding)	$ 200,000
Additional paid-in capital on common stock	900,000
Retained earnings	1,600,000

   On November 1, 2001, Billboard declares a $0.40/share dividend payable on January 9, 2002 to shareholders of record at December 31, 2001.

8. **Effects of Equity Transactions—Scrip Dividend.** Robber Bakery regularly pays a dividend on March 1. Due to a cash shortage, this year's dividend payment is delayed to May 1. Robber accomplishes this delay by issuing a $420,000 scrip dividend on March 1, bearing a 10% interest rate.

9. **Effects of Equity Transactions—Property Dividend.** Soup Distributors declares a dividend on December 1, 2000, payable on January 7, 2001, to shareholders of record on December 20, 2000. The dividend payment is in shares of an investment in Noodle Co. that Soup is holding as a short-term investment. As of December 1, 2000, the investment in Noodle Co. had a fair market value of $65,800. The original cost of the investment was $70,000; however, the Noodle Co. stock had been marked to market and is recorded at $68,500.

10. **Effects of Equity Transactions—Stock Dividends and Stock Split.** The following is the owners' equity section of Wood Doors, Inc., just before declaration of a stock distribution:

Common stock ($3 par value, 30,000 shares issued and outstanding)	$ 90,000
Additional paid-in capital on common stock	1,800,000
Retained earnings	3,500,000

   Wood Doors has a small number of stockholders; therefore, it declared and distributed the stock distribution on the same day. The market price of the common stock is $15 on the date of declaration.
   a. Assume that the stock distribution was a 10% stock dividend and that the fair market value of shares issued was transferred from retained earnings to contributed capital.
   b. Assume that the stock distribution was a 100% stock dividend and that the par value of the shares was transferred from retained earnings to contributed capital.
   c. Assume that Wood Doors' stock distribution was a 3-for-1 stock split, with the par value of the shares adjusted to reflect the split.

Analytical and Comprehensive Problems

11. **Effects of Various Transactions on Owners' Equity.** Using the following key, identify the effects of the following transactions or conditions on the various components of owners' equity: I = increases; D = decreases; NE = no effect.

	Contributed Capital			Retained Earnings	
Transaction	**Common Stock**	**Additional Paid-In Capital**	**Other Contributed Capital**	**Direct Effect**	**Indirect Effect (Through Net Income)**
a. Common Stock Issue					
For cash					
For property					
For expenses					
b. Existence of Stock Issue Costs					
c. Combined Effect of Taking Stock Subscriptions and Issuing Stock					
Contra Equity Treatment					
Asset Treatment					
d. Issue Stock Rights					
e. Donation to Corporation by Owners					
f. Cash Dividend Declared					
g. Payment of Previously Declared Cash Dividend					
h. Scrip Dividend Declared					
i. Previously Declared Scrip Dividend and Interest Paid					
j. Property Dividend Declared (property recorded at fair value)					
k. Previously Declared Property Dividend Distributed					
l. Large Stock Dividend Issued, par value transferred from retained earnings					
m. Small Stock Dividend Issued, fair value transferred from retained earnings					
n. Midrange Stock Dividend Issued, par value transferred from retained earnings					
o. Midrange Stock Dividend Issued, par value transferred from additional paid-in capital					
p. Stock Split Announced and Issued					

12. **Stockholders' Equity.** Poolhouse Products incorporated at the beginning of 2001. Poolhouse issued 100,000 shares of no-par common stock on January 1, 2001, for \$10 per share. On that date, Poolhouse's beginning balance in retained earnings was \$750,000, its beginning balance in common stock was \$1,000,000, and no other stockholders' equity accounts existed. For the year ended December 31, 2001, Poolhouse reported net income of \$90,000. Poolhouse paid 40% of its 2001 net income in cash dividends on December 31, 2001.
    a. What was the effect of the dividend on Poolhouse's balance sheet, income statement, and statement of stockholders' equity?
    b. Compute equity per share (total stockholders' equity divided by number of common shares outstanding) at December 31, 2001.
    c. On December 31, 2001 (after the dividend was paid), Poolhouse's common stock traded frequently, with an ending fair market value at \$20.75 per share. Give some reasons as to why this amount differs from the amount computed in (b).

13. **Earnings per Share.** We will learn in a later chapter that earnings for the period is divided by common shares outstanding to arrive at earnings per common share. Recall that dividends are not an expense that reduce earnings, but instead, they are recorded as a direct reduction of retained earnings (owners' equity). Some theorists argue that there should be some charge against earnings to reflect the cost of equity financing.
    a. What do you think "earnings per common share" means to an investor?
    b. If a cost for equity financing were subtracted to arrive at net income (i.e., dividends were shown as an expense), what would be the new interpretation of "earnings per common share"? Why?

14. **Effects of Transactions on Retained Earnings.** MacBeth Enterprises had $455,000 in retained earnings at December 31, 2000. Prepare a schedule to compute retained earnings at December 31, 2001, using the information provided below. For each of the six situations below, identify the items that would affect retained earnings indirectly through their effect on net income. Ignore income tax effects. MacBeth's contributed capital at December 31, 2000, was as follows:

Preferred stock (8%, $100 par, 7,000 shares issued and outstanding)	$ 700,000
Common stock ($1 par, 30,000 shares issued and outstanding)	30,000
Additional paid-in capital on preferred stock	42,000
Additional paid-in capital on common stock	240,000
Total	$1,012,000

a. Before considering the transactions described below, MacBeth reported $621,000 of revenues and gains and $390,000 of expenses and losses for 2001.
b. On April 1, 2001, MacBeth declared and distributed a 15,000-share common stock dividend. (Assume that the transfer from retained earnings occurs at par in this large distribution.)
c. On July 1, 2001, MacBeth declared and distributed a property dividend to common shareholders. The property was inventory originally costing $27,000, and it is recorded in the financial records at $27,000. The market value of the inventory was $30,000 at the date of declaration.
d. On August 1, 2001, MacBeth declared and paid its annual $56,000 dividend to preferred shareholders.
e. On September 1, 2001, MacBeth acquired a piece of property by issuing 2,000 shares of preferred stock. The preferred traded for $109 per share on that date. The market value of the property was $250,000.
f. On November 1, 2001, MacBeth declared a $0.45-per-share cash dividend on common stock. The date of record is December 29, 2001, and the date of payment is January 4, 2002.

15. **Dividends.** Wally Co. pays regular quarterly cash dividends on its 3,000,000 common shares outstanding. The per-share amount of the dividend has always been $2. Due to a cash shortage at the end of 2000, Wally declares a dividend on December 20, 2000, payable in February 2001. The dividend allows the investor to choose between the regular cash dividend and one week's stay (per one hundred shares owned) at any of Wally's resorts. Wally estimates that holders of approximately 20% of the shares will choose the vacation instead of cash. Half of those investors will choose to take the vacation when hotel rooms are renting at $150 a day, while the other half will choose to take the vacation when rooms are renting at $115 a day. Wally estimates that its incremental cost of providing the rooms is equal to $200 a week, regardless of the time of year.
a. How would you account for this dividend?
b. What is the effect of the December 20, 2000, dividend on Wally's financial statements?

16. **Texas Instruments' Financing Decisions.** Several portions of Texas Instruments' financial statements pertain to equity financing decisions. Before continuing in this problem, please review the following sections of Texas Instruments' 1998 annual report information available at our Web site (http://baginski.swcollege.com): (1) consolidated balance sheet—stockholders' equity section (and related accompanying notes to the financial statements—stockholders' equity, and stock options), (2) consolidated statement of stockholders' equity, and (3) consolidated statement of cash flows—Financing Activities section. You may not currently understand the entire stock option footnote, but it does give some basic information that you are familiar with. This information includes the number of shares issued during the year because stock options were exercised, the number of shares reserved for issuance because of stock option plans, and information related to treasury stock purchases. Rather than asking you to read the entire MD&A section, we have included parts of the MD&A below that pertain to equity financing.

Portions of Texas Instruments' MD&A

During 1998, TI repurchased approximately 4.5 million shares of common stock, at a cost of $294 million, as part of its previously stated intent to neutralize the potential dilutive effect of shares to be issued under employee stock options.

As previously announced, the timing of TI dividend declarations in 1998 was moved, effective March 1998, from the third month of a quarter to the first month of the following quarter. As a result of this one-time lag, 1998 contains three, rather than four, dividend declarations.

TI common stock is listed on the New York Stock Exchange and traded principally in that market. The table below shows the high and low prices of TI common stock on the composite tape as reported by *The Wall Street Journal* and the dividends paid per common share for each quarter during the past two years.

		Quarter			
		1st	**2nd**	**3rd**	**4th**
Stock Prices:					
1998	High	$62.75	$67.00	$63.69	$90.44
	Low	40.25	46.88	46.06	45.38
1997	High	43.63	48.19	71.00	71.25
	Low	31.06	36.81	42.13	39.63
Dividends Paid:					
1998		$0.085	$0.085	$0.085	$0.085
1997		$0.085	$0.085	$0.085	$0.085

Required The purpose of this problem is to familiarize you with actual financial statements and to help you develop an understanding of how pertinent information about a particular topic may be spread throughout the financial statements. Answer the following questions.

a. Does TI have common and preferred stock? If so, how many shares of common and preferred are authorized, issued, and outstanding at December 31, 1998?
b. Using the statement of stockholders' equity and appropriate related footnotes, reconcile the number of common shares outstanding from January 1, 1997, to December 31, 1998, listing the causes of the changes. Prepare the same reconciliation for preferred stock.
c. What was the amount per share and total amount of dividends declared during 1998 and 1997? What was the amount of dividends paid during 1998 and 1997?
d. At December 31, 1998, how many shares of TI common are reserved for possible issuance because of stock option plans?

CFA Exam-Type Problems

17. Cavalier Corporation issues a 5% stock dividend when the market value of a share exceeds par value. The effect on common stock and total shareholders' capital items on the balance sheet will be: (CFA adapted)
    a. decrease common stock, decrease total shareholders' capital
    b. no change in common stock, no change in total shareholders' capital
    c. increase common stock, no change in total shareholders' capital
    d. increase common stock, increase total shareholders' capital

    Note: This same question was asked on the 1990 CFA exam. (CFA adapted)

18. On December 31, 2000, the shareholders' equity section of Batman Corporation was as follows:

Common stock, $5 par value, 1,000,000 shares authorized; 25,000 shares issued and outstanding	$125,000
Additional paid-in capital	60,000
Retained earnings	87,000
Total shareholders' equity	$272,000

On June 30, 2001, the board of directors declared a 5% stock dividend. The fair market value of the stock on June 30 was $9 per share. For the year ending December 31, 2001, Batman Corporation reported a net loss of $13,000. What amount should Batman report as retained earnings as of January 1, 2002? (CFA modified)
a. $51,500
b. $62,750
c. $68,375
d. $75,750

19. Which of the following *does not result in a change in total stockholders' equity?* (Author constructed)
a. Cash dividend
b. Property dividend
c. Scrip dividend
d. Stock dividend

20. Which of the following privileges/preferences do preferred stockholders normally give up compared to common stockholders? (Author constructed)
a. Voting privileges
b. Preference in liquidation
c. Preference when dividends are declared by a company's board of directors
d. Preferences to dividends in arrears

21. In the discussion of optimal capital structure (i.e., how to allocate asset financing between debt—liabilities—and equity), all of the following are important determinants of optimal capital structure except? (Author constructed)
a. Tax savings related to debt
b. Whether the long-term debt is structured as unsecured notes or unsecured bonds
c. Agency costs (e.g., monitoring costs)
d. Costs related to financial distress

22. Which of the following items has an effect on the income statement? (Author constructed)
a. Stock dividend
b. Cash dividend declaration
c. Property dividend, where fair market value of the property is greater than its book value
d. Stock split

23. On December 31, Andrews Co. had the following information available: total assets = $8,000,000; total liabilities = $3,000,000; total stockholders' equity = $5,000,000; and 1,000,000 common shares were outstanding. Andrews' book value per share at December 31 is: (Author constructed)
a. $8.00
b. $5.00
c. $3.00
d. $2.00

Objectives

1 Describe the characteristics that distinguish different kinds of debt instruments.

2 Explain the difference between cash interest and effective interest, and identify the determinants of effective interest.

3 Describe the process for issuing debt securities.

4 Explain the accounting for bonds payable over the life of the bond.

5 Describe how financial statements articulate in the long-term debt area.

6 Explain the accounting for notes payable over the life of the note.

7 Explain the accounting for hybrid securities.

8 Describe the debt characteristics of preferred stock.

9 Analyze the effects of leverage on cash flow and income variability.

Chapter 3

Financing Decisions—Debt

This chapter discusses how firms raise capital by issuing debt. Debt claims against assets do not diminish current shareholder control by conveying voting privileges to new shareholders. Debt claims, in general, also do not participate in the potential profits of the firm. The trade-off, however, is that these claims have first preference in asset distribution, create obligations to deliver periodic interest payments, and must be paid back. In Chapter 4, we investigate another type of debt financing—leasing. In Chapter 5, we discuss the decisions involved in reducing outstanding debt.

Characteristics of Debt Securities

1 Describe the characteristics that distinguish different kinds of debt instruments.

The various types of debt securities are limited only by the creativity of debtors and creditors. To better understand the diversity present in debt securities, we consider the following characteristics:

- Security
- Maturity
- Convertibility
- Interest payment characteristics

Security

Creditors' claims against assets may be general, or they may be more specific as agreed on by the parties involved. A ***debenture bond*** **is an example of a general debt claim secured by all of a firm's assets.** The creditor relies on the general credit worthiness of the firm as a guarantee of future payment. Evidence of general credit worthiness may be obtained by analyzing the firm's financial statements, or by relying on companies that rate the bond as to riskiness (e.g., Moody's). Bond ratings range from "investment grade" (the least risky bonds with the lowest returns) to "junk bonds" (the most risky bonds with the highest returns).

Other types of debt claims are secured by specific assets. ***Collateral trust bonds*** are **bonds secured by investments in lower risk securities that are held in trust.** *Mortgage bonds* are **secured by real estate.** ***Equipment notes*** are **secured by the equipment purchased with the proceeds.** Other kinds of notes payable may also be secured by specific assets. An example would be a note payable secured by assigned accounts receivable. *Full disclosure of the security for a bond or note is required in financial statements.*

Maturity

Unlike equity securities, debt securities require a final payment of maturity value to investors. Bonds and notes have varying maturity dates depending on the wishes of the borrower and lender. While notes typically have a single maturity date, the long-term nature of bonds necessitates some flexibility in maturity provisions. **A bond with a single maturity date** is referred to as a ***term bond.*** If **a bond has several maturity dates (i.e., installments),** it is a ***serial bond.*** If **the corporation has the discretion to set the maturity date after the bonds are issued by requiring investors to return the bonds to the corporation,** the bond is referred to as a ***callable bond.***

The *maturity dates of bonds and notes* (including any call provisions) must be disclosed in the financial statements. Recall that one of the objectives of financial reporting is to provide information on the *timing of cash flows.*

Convertibility

Corporations sometimes wish to issue debt when investors demand equity. Debt issued with equity privileges arises in response to this conflict. Bonds may be *convertible into shares of stock* upon tender of the bond back to the corporation. Bonds may also be issued with ***detachable warrants*** that **give investors the right to become owners by exercising the options to purchase stock conveyed by the warrants.**

The *conversion privileges of debt* must be disclosed in the financial statements for two reasons. First, investors and creditors are very interested in debt/equity ratios. Conversion could move amounts from the numerator (debt) to the denominator (equity), thus reducing financial risk. Second, there is a potential dilution of earnings per common share if conversion were to occur.

Interest Payment Characteristics

The interest payment provisions of debt are a result of negotiations between borrowers and lenders. The lender views the debt agreement as the receipt of a contractually fixed cash flow at specified intervals. The level of the cash flows is determined by the *timing* of the flows and the *risks* associated with entering a contract with fixed cash flows. The following diagram illustrates how timing and risk affect the determination of the level of cash flows:

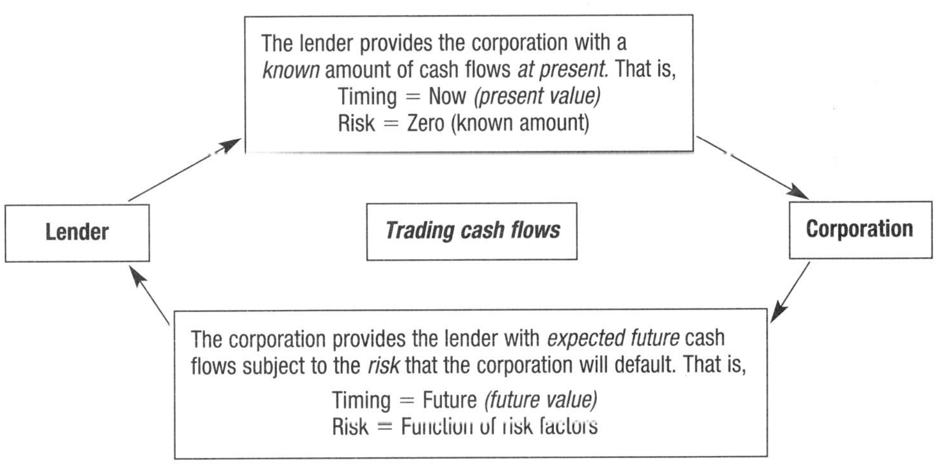

The diagram shows the lender trading a known amount at present for expected future cash flows subject to a risk of realization. The lender's problem of setting the level of future cash flows can be expressed by the present value formulation:

$$\text{Present value} = \sum_{n=1}^{t} \frac{\text{Cash interest}}{(1+i)^n} + \frac{\text{Maturity value}}{(1+i)^n}$$

Based on *when* the parties negotiate the occurrence of cash interest and maturity value (i.e., determination of n) and the lender's required rate of return on the transaction (i.e., determination of i), the equation can be solved. There are two practical means by which this occurs. If the lender knows the present value of the consideration that will be provided, then the levels of future cash flows can be determined. Alternatively, if the levels of the future cash flows (cash interest and maturity value) are known, then the present value can be determined.

The different cash flow patterns that can be established by this equation are unlimited. As a practical matter, however, the maturity value is most often equal to the face amount of the note or bond, and the manipulated number in the equation is cash interest. For example, when bonds are issued, the issuer sets the terms of the note or bond (the maturity value, maturity date, and stated or coupon interest rate) and the price of the bond is determined in the market place by supply and demand considerations. The resulting bond price implies an effective (market) interest rate that differs from the stated interest rate. This leads to a very important distinction between cash interest and effective interest.

Cash Interest Versus Effective Interest

2 Explain the difference between cash interest and effective interest, and identify the determinants of effective interest.

Cash interest is determined by the ***coupon rate*** or ***stated rate*** of interest times the face value of the debt. The coupon rate is **the rate agreed upon by borrower and lender and included in the debt agreement.** Cash interest may be negotiated in a note or private bond placement or simply presented to potential buyers in a public bond issuance. Cash interest may or may not be a function of the risk characteristics of the transaction.

Effective interest, also known as the ***yield***, ***yield-to-maturity***, or ***rate of return***, **is the economic return on the transaction to creditors and the economic cost to debtors;** it is a function of the risk characteristics of the transaction. A good illustration of the difference between cash interest and effective interest is the *deep discount bond*. The most deeply discounted bonds, known as "zeros," have a coupon or stated rate of zero. However, it is clear that a non-interest-bearing bond or note has a *nonzero* effective rate of interest. The existence of a nonzero effective yield is evidenced by the fact that the bonds are issued (as the name implies) at a deep discount (i.e., an amount far less than face value). Investors transfer less current cash flow for the expected greater future cash flow. The difference between current and future cash flow is interest expense.

Example 1. Smith Co. borrowed $70,000 on January 1, 2001, from Jones Finance Co. The following terms were negotiated: matures on December 31, 2003, zero stated interest rate, maturity value equals $100,000. Compute both the cash interest and effective interest.

Solution. Smith Co. pays back more ($100,000 in principal and $0 in interest) than was borrowed ($70,000). Interest expense is defined as the excess of the amount repaid over the amount borrowed. Therefore, the additional $30,000 ($100,000 − $70,000) is interest expense. Cash interest equals $0, and effective interest expense equals $30,000.

Many factors determine the effective interest rate:

- Economywide conditions
  - Investment opportunity
  - Inflation
  - Currency exchange rates
- Firm-specific risk factors
  - Business risk
  - Financial risk

A portion of the effective interest rate contains compensation for the lender's "tying up" of funds. While the funds are on loan, the *alternative lending opportunities* can change. Also, *inflation* could occur, causing future dollars to have less purchasing power. Finally, if the loan is denominated in a foreign currency, relative changes in economic conditions across countries could result in an *unfavorable transformation of foreign currency* into the dollar.

In addition, firm-specific factors explain differences in effective interest rates. The risk of receiving cash flows is determined by business risk and financial risk. ***Business risk*** is primarily determined by the risk of generating sales or service revenues to service the debt (*revenue risk*) and the asset composition of the firm (*operating risk*).

To some extent, business risk is beyond the control of the firm. For example, general economic swings and unpredictable competitor actions lead to an increase in revenue risk. But, to some extent, the risk is controllable. For example, although we will see in a later chapter that the presence of fixed operating costs increases operating risk, managers often have the choice of mechanization (yielding higher fixed operating costs from depreciation) or using more labor (a variable cost).

As discussed in Chapter 2, ***financial risk*** is also a fixed-charge phenomenon related to the presence of debt financing. Higher debt levels result in fixed cash interest outflows. These payments must occur regardless of the cash flow position of the firm. Financial risk is one of the strongest influences on the effective interest rate.

Issuing Debt Securities

3 Describe the process for issuing debt securities.

Debt security issuance is evidenced by **documentation agreed upon by borrower and lender referred to as the *bond indenture* or *note agreement*.** This documentation specifies:

- Promises to pay maturity amounts at specified dates
- Promises to pay specified amounts of cash interest at specified dates
- Call provisions
- Descriptions of property pledged as security
- Covenants and restrictions

The *covenants* and *restrictions* are written for the protection of creditors. Because managers can make decisions subsequent to a debt issue that alter business and financial risks, covenants and restrictions specify sinking fund requirements and restrictions on working capital, dividend payments, and the assumption of new debt, as well as other restrictions. As discussed in Chapter 2, these restrictions impose costs on the firm by limiting management action and creating monitoring costs.

Debt is issued through *private placement* with several willing lenders or through *open market transactions* with a variety of investors. Open market issue requires the use of an ***underwriter*** (or *investment banker*) who **guarantees an issue price** (*firm underwriting*) **or promises to obtain the best price possible for the issue** (*best efforts underwriting*).

Debt can be issued in the form of bonds payable or notes payable. Bonds are issued almost exclusively for cash consideration. Notes are issued for cash consideration, but may also be issued for noncash consideration as well. We will split the remainder of the chapter between bonds and notes.

Bonds Payable

4 Explain the accounting for bonds payable over the life of the bond.

Four different kinds of cash flows result from bonds payable transactions:

- Cash received at issue date (sales price)
- Transaction costs paid at issue date (often deducted by underwriter before remitting issue proceeds to company)
- Periodic cash interest payments to investors
- Cash paid to retire the issue at maturity[1]

To illustrate the reporting of these cash flows and the presentation of the elements of accrual accounting financial statements, we first present a simple example and then a more complex one.

A Simple Bonds Payable Example

Example 2. On January 1, 2001, Worthy Co. issued $1,000,000 in bonds payable. The bonds are dated January 1, 2001, mature in five years (January 1, 2006), and pay 9% interest every year on December 31. The issue sold for $891,857 (rounded to the nearest dollar). The underwriter deducted $10,000 in fees and remitted the proceeds to Worthy. Worthy has a December 31 year-end.

Solution. The cash flows from this bond are as follows:

Cash inflow at issue:	
Selling price of the bonds	$ 891,857
Underwriter fees	(10,000)
Net proceeds	$ 881,857
Annual cash outflows (interest payments):	
Face amount of issue	$1,000,000
Coupon or stated interest rate	× 9%
Annual cash interest payment	$ 90,000
Total interest payments	$90,000 × 5 = $450,000
Cash outflow at retirement date	$1,000,000

By paying less than $1,000,000 for the bonds, the market signals that the expectation for return on these bonds is greater than the 9% stated rate. That is, this investment is sufficiently risky, such that a yield or effective rate of interest on this type of investment is higher than 9%. To solve for the market's effective rate of return based upon the bonds' sales price, the following formula is used:

$$\text{Present value} = \sum_{n=1}^{t} \frac{\text{Cash interest}}{(1+i)^n} + \frac{\text{Maturity value}}{(1+i)^n}$$

$$\$891{,}857 = \sum_{n=1}^{5} \frac{\$90{,}000}{(1+i)^5} + \frac{\$1{,}000{,}000}{(1+i)^5}$$

Solving for i results in a yield of 12%.[2] Investors ***discounted*** the bond so that they receive their 12% return in two ways—through both annual interest and the receipt of a $1,000,000 maturity value that exceeds their original $891,857 investment. This phenomenon can be best understood by constructing an effective interest amortization table:

1. Cash could be paid to retire the bond early. We discuss early debt retirement, debt restructuring, and equity retirements in Chapter 5.

2. Using a financial calculator to solve for i involves setting n (number of annual interest payments) = 5, payment (annual cash interest payment) = $90,000, present value (sales price) = $891,857, and future value = $1,000,000.

EXHIBIT 1 Example 2. Effective Interest Amortization Table

Date	9% Cash Interest	12% Effective Interest Expense*	Discount Amortization	Book Value of Debt
01/01/01				$ 891,857
12/31/01	$ 90,000	$107,023	$ 17,023	908,880
12/31/02	90,000	109,065	19,065	927,945
12/31/03	90,000	111,353	21,353	949,298
12/31/04	90,000	113,916	23,916	973,214
12/31/05	90,000	116,786	26,786	1,000,000
	$450,000	**$558,143**	**$108,143**	

*Book value of debt at beginning of the interest period × 12% effective interest rate

GAAP requires the ***effective interest method*** to compute interest expense and discount (or premium) amortization. For each date, an effective interest amortization table shows the book value of debt (i.e., *present value of the remaining cash flows at the historical effective interest rate*); the effective interest expense that accrues on the debt; the cash flow that reduces the debt; and the comparison of effective interest-driven debt increases and cash paid to decrease the debt (i.e., amortization). The cash interest column is calculated by multiplying the constant face value of the debt by the constant stated or coupon interest rate of 9%. The effective interest column is computed by multiplying the beginning of the period book value of debt (previous row) by the constant 12% effective interest rate earned by the market.

The beginning book value represents what has been lent to the firm for that period. In the first period, the market (i.e., the group of creditors who purchased the debt) requires a 12% return on its $891,857 initial investment, $107,023 of effective interest expense. However, the firm pays only $90,000 in cash interest to creditors. Thus, the difference between the effective interest expense and cash interest paid (shown as $17,023 in the amortization column) increases the book value of the debt. Note that the amount of effective interest increases in each period. This occurs because the amount borrowed increases each period, and the firm incurs a constant 12% interest on the debt. The annual increase in the debt is paid off as part of the $1,000,000 maturity payment.

In summary, the effective interest method computes interest expense and discount (or premium) amortization for a given period as follows:

$$\text{Beginning book value} \times \text{Effective interest rate} = \begin{array}{c}\text{Interest expense}\\ \text{(i.e., } \textit{effective interest}\text{)}\end{array}$$

$$\begin{array}{c}\text{Interest expense}\\ \text{(i.e., } \textit{effective interest}\text{)}\end{array} - \begin{array}{c}\text{Interest paid (or payable)}\\ \text{(i.e., } \textit{cash interest}\text{)}\end{array} = \text{Discount/premium amortization}$$

Another way to look at this situation is to compare the total cash inflows and outflows over the life of the debt:

Total cash outflows:		
Maturity payment	$1,000,000	
Interest payments (5 × $90,000)	450,000	$1,450,000
Total cash inflows:		
Bond selling price		891,857[3]
Effective interest expense		$ 558,143

Recall that decreases in assets cause expense recognition. The asset "cash" decreases by $558,143 over the life of the issue (inflows of $891,857 and outflows

3. Note that we use the sales price of the bonds ($891,857) rather than the net proceeds received ($881,857). We discuss this reasoning later in the chapter.

of $1,000,000 in principal repayment plus $450,000 in cash interest). Thus, $558,143 in interest expense is recognized over the life of the issue.

Financial Reporting

The goals of the financial reporting for bonds are to reflect the cash flows for each period and the levels and changes in the accrual accounting elements over the life of the issue. First, the statement of cash flows reports the net proceeds at issue (price less underwriter fees), interest payments, and the maturity payment as follows:

EXHIBIT 2 Example 2. Statement of Cash Flows*

WORTHY CO.
Statement of Cash Flows

	2001	2002	2003	2004	2005	2006
Operating Activities						
Interest payments	(90,000)	(90,000)	(90,000)	(90,000)	(90,000)	
Financing Activities						
Bond issue proceeds	891,857					
Transactions costs	(10,000)					
Bond retirement						(1,000,000)
Net change in cash	791,857	(90,000)	(90,000)	(90,000)	(90,000)	(1,000,000)

*Cash outflows in parentheses

The statement of cash flows shows the initial increase in debt and the cash interest payments. Under GAAP, cash flows for principal amounts of debt are reported as financing activities, while cash flows for interest are reported as operating activities. The cash flow statement does not, however, show the periodic increases in debt resulting from the firm paying less interest than the market desires. It also does not indicate the true interest cost of the debt, which is a function of the effective interest rate. The accrual financial statements are able to reflect these situations through use of the elements of accrual accounting. The income statement disclosures appear as follows:

EXHIBIT 3 Example 2. Income Statement

WORTHY CO.
Income Statement

	2001	2002	2003	2004	2005	2006
Financial revenues, (expenses), gains, and (losses)						
Interest expense	(107,023)	(109,065)	(111,353)	(113,916)	(116,786)	
Bond issue expense	(2,000)	(2,000)	(2,000)	(2,000)	(2,000)	

Note that the interest expense amounts are those previously calculated in the effective interest amortization table. Effective interest represents the cost of borrowing the beginning book value of the debt and holding the debt for one-year periods. Interest expense is the increase in the bonds payable liability from the passage of time. Interest expense is different from the yearly cash flow. Note that while the statement of cash flows indicates a $90,000 interest payment for each year, the income statement shows a larger amount of yearly interest expense. This difference is the recognition of the fact that the corporation must pay back more in maturity value than it initially borrowed.

Current GAAP requires that the $10,000 bond issue costs be capitalized and amortized over the life of the bond. In this example, $2,000 ($10,000 ÷ 5) is expensed each year. Transaction costs reduce the net proceeds to the issuer and theoretically should be treated as an adjustment to the yield. Therefore, current GAAP is not theoretically correct. In *Statement of Financial Accounting Concepts No. 3*, the FASB acknowledged this theoretical deficiency.[4]

On the balance sheet, Worthy Co. shows cash and unamortized bond issue costs as assets, and bonds payable as a liability. We ignore the income tax effects in this presentation. The owners' equity section reflects the income statement effects of interest expense and bond issue expense in retained earnings:

EXHIBIT 4 Example 2. Balance Sheet December 31

WORTHY CO.
Balance Sheet

	2001	2002	2003	2004	2005	2006
Assets						
Current assets						
Cash (net cumulative effect of bond transaction only)	791,857	701,857	611,857	521,857	431,857	(568,143)
Other assets						
Bond issue costs	8,000	6,000	4,000	2,000	0	0
Liabilities						
Current liabilities						
Bonds payable					1,000,000	0
Long-term liabilities						
Bonds payable	1,000,000	1,000,000	1,000,000	1,000,000		
Less discount	(91,120)	(72,055)	(50,702)	(26,786)		
	908,880	927,945	949,298	973,214		
Owners' Equity						
Retained earnings (through cumulative effect on net income, ignoring income taxes)	(109,023)	(220,088)	(333,441)	(449,357)	(568,143)	(568,143)

The current asset "cash" at December 31, 2001, represents the net proceeds from the issue ($881,857) less one $90,000 interest payment. The annual interest payment reduces cash by $90,000 in each successive year through December 31, 2005. On January 1, 2006, the bond is retired by paying $1,000,000 in cash, lowering the cumulative effect of the bond's transactions on the cash balance to a negative $568,143. Hopefully, the corporation has used the cash acquired in 2001 to engage in investing and operating activities that produce additional cash inflows over the amounts repaid in principal and interest, leaving a positive cash balance at December 31, 2006. However, it is useful to concentrate on the bond payable effect on cash in isolation. The cumulative net cash outflow from the bond transaction of $568,143 represents the total cost of the debt issue over the five-year period,

4. If the transaction costs had been treated as an adjustment to the yield, then Worthy's effective interest rate would have been 12.30% (present value factors are n = 5; payment = $90,000; present value = $881,857; and future value = $1,000,000, with the present value amount being lowered from $891,857 in the previous example to $881,857 to reflect the transaction costs).

which equals the effective interest cost of $558,143 (see amortization table) plus the bond issue cost of $10,000.

Within the other assets classification, the account "bond issue costs" is reported at *unamortized historical cost.* The first year's amount is equal to the initial cost of $10,000 less $2,000 from straight-line amortization in 2001. It is not clear why bond issue costs should be an asset, although current financial statements report it as such; no probable future economic benefits are associated with bond issue costs. As discussed previously, the FASB has acknowledged that bond issue cost accounting is not theoretically correct, but it has yet to change GAAP with respect to bond issue costs.

In the liability section, bonds payable are reported at the *present value of future cash flows* using the *historical effective rate of interest at the issue date.* This is accomplished by showing the face amount of the bonds less a discount amount (or plus a premium in the cases when bonds are issued at a premium), yielding a book value. Note that because the effective interest amortization table reports the book values of the debt at each year-end, it is not necessary to recompute present value at each balance sheet date. But, it could be done. Consider the December 31, 2004, book value of bonds payable of $973,214. This amount can be computed independently by discounting the sum of the one remaining interest payment of $90,000 and the $1,000,000 maturity payment at the effective interest rate of 12%:

$$\text{Present value} = (\$90{,}000 + 1{,}000{,}000) / 1.12 = \$973{,}214$$

At December 31, 2005, the $1,000,000 maturity value must be reclassified as a current liability because funds will be disbursed within one year of the balance sheet date (actually, the next day). This reclassification is important because investors and creditors evaluate the financial flexibility of the firm by constructing ratios from balance sheet disclosures. A reclassification of a large bond issue from long-term to current may have a material adverse impact on working capital (current assets minus current liabilities) and the current ratio (current assets divided by current liabilities). In practice, this potential adverse impact is alleviated in two ways. First, a firm may set up a bond sinking fund (either because of debt covenants or as part of the firm's cash management policy) to be used to repay the debt. The matching of the bond sinking fund and debt classifications causes working capital to be unaffected.[5]

Another method of avoiding the reclassification of long-term debt to a current liability is to enter into a refinancing agreement. If management both *intends to refinance the debt* before cash is disbursed to retire it and the corporation *demonstrates the ability to refinance the debt,* then GAAP allows the obligation to remain in the long-term classification at the balance sheet date. Auditors will investigate whether the ability to refinance is present by searching for a refinancing agreement with a lender or evidence that actual refinancing has taken place before the financial statements are issued.[6]

This example problem illustrates the artificiality introduced by the accounting conventions used to classify assets and liabilities as current and noncurrent. At December 31, 2004, the bond is due in one year and one day. Therefore, since it is not due within one year, it is classified as noncurrent, and any impact on the current ratio and working capital is avoided. Yet, if the balance sheet were prepared one day later (January 1, 2005), the bond would be shown as current because it would be due in one year. Consequently, a financial analyst reviewing the finan-

5. *FASB No. 47* requires note disclosure of sinking fund and bond retirement payments for each of the next five years after the balance sheet date.

6. Balance sheet classification intricacies of long-term debt are addressed in *FASB Statements of Financial Accounting Standards No.* 6, "Balance Sheet Classification of Short-Term Obligations Expected to Be Refinanced" (Stamford, Conn.: FASB 1975); *No. 47*, "Disclosure of Long-Term Obligations" (1981); and *No. 129*, "Disclosure of Information About Capital Structure" (1997).

cial statements of a company should determine whether any noncurrent items are about to be (or should be) reclassified as current.

5 Describe how financial statements articulate in the long-term debt area.

Finally, if you total the assets and subtract the liabilities, you will note that in order to maintain the fundamental accounting equation (assets equals liabilities plus owners' equity), a component of owners' equity must decrease. Retained earnings decreases each period because it accumulates the decreases in net income shown on the income statement. For example, by December 31, 2003, retained earnings is a negative $333,441 in order to make the balance sheet equation hold. If you total bond interest expense and bond issue expense for 2001, 2002, and 2003 on the income statement, you will get the same number. This is an excellent illustration of the fact that changes in assets and liabilities from nonowner transactions are reflected in the balance sheet and the income statement.

EXAMPLE 2 Journal Entries

1/1/01 Bond issue:

Cash	891,857	
Discount on Bonds Payable	108,143	
Bonds Payable		1,000,000
Bond Issue Costs	10,000	
Cash		10,000

*Interest payment dates**	*12/31/01*		*12/31/02*		*12/31/03*		. . .
Interest Expense	107,023		109,065		111,353		
Discount on Bonds Payable		17,023		19,065		21,353	
Cash		90,000		90,000		90,000	
Bond Issue Expense	2,000		2,000		2,000		
Bond Issue Costs		2,000		2,000		2,000	

*Shown for the first three years. Journal entries for 2004 and 2005 would be in similar form and would use the amounts shown in the effective interest amortization table.

1/1/06 Maturity payment:

Bonds Payable	1,000,000	
Cash		1,000,000

Selected Ledger Accounts

Bonds Payable

		1/1/01	1,000,000
⋮			⋮
1/1/06	1,000,000		
		1/1/06 Bal.	0

Discount on Bonds Payable

1/1/01	108,143		
		12/31/01	17,023
12/31/01 Bal.	91,120		
		12/31/02	19,065
12/31/02 Bal.	72,055		
		12/31/03	21,353
12/31/03 Bal.	50,702		
	⋮		⋮
1/1/06 Bal.	0		

A More Complex Bonds Payable Example

The computations for bonds payable can become complex if the bond amortization periods do not match the corporation's reporting period.

Example 3. On September 1, 2001, Worthy Co. issued $1,000,000 in bonds payable. The bonds are dated September 1, 2001, mature in five years (September 1, 2006), and pay 9% interest every year on September 1. The issue sold for $891,857. The underwriter deducted $10,000 in fees and remitted the proceeds to Worthy. Worthy has a December 31 year-end.

Solution. In this example, only the issue date has changed from the previous example problem. The cash flows from this bond are identical to the previous example but are timed in a slightly different manner. The effective interest amortization table reflects the date changes, but the computations of interest and book value are unaffected:

EXHIBIT 5 Example 3. Effective Interest Amortization Table

Date	9% Cash Interest	12% Effective Interest Expense	Discount Amortization	Book Value of Debt
9/1/01				$ 891,857
9/1/02	$ 90,000	$107,023	$ 17,023	908,880
9/1/03	90,000	109,065	19,065	927,945
9/1/04	90,000	111,353	21,353	949,298
9/1/05	90,000	113,916	23,916	973,214
9/1/06	90,000	116,786	26,786	1,000,000
	$450,000	**$558,143**	**$108,143**	

The statement of cash flows appears as follows:

EXHIBIT 6 Example 3. Statement of Cash Flows*

WORTHY CO.
Statement of Cash Flows

	2001	2002	2003	2004	2005	2006
Operating Activities						
Interest payments	0	(90,000)	(90,000)	(90,000)	(90,000)	(90,000)
Financing Activities						
Bond issue proceeds	891,857					
Bond issue costs	(10,000)					
Bond retirement						(1,000,000)

*Cash outflows in parentheses

Compared to the simple example, the only change in the cash flow statement is the delay of interest payments to September 1 of each year, beginning September 1, 2002.

The change of the issue date from January 1, 2001, to September 1, 2001, complicates the income statement disclosure, which appears as follows:

EXHIBIT 7 Example 3. Income Statement

WORTHY CO.
Income Statement

	2001	2002	2003	2004	2005	2006
Financial revenues, (expenses), gains, and (losses)						
Interest expense	(35,674)	(107,704)	(109,828)	(112,207)	(114,873)	(77,857)
Bond issue expense	(667)	(2,000)	(2,000)	(2,000)	(2,000)	(1,333)

Interest expense for each calendar year is obtained by weighting the 12% effective interest (shown in the amortization table) by the number of months the bond was outstanding:

EXHIBIT 8 Example 3. Interest Expense Calculation (Partial)

Calendar Year	Interest Expense from Amortization Table	Time Outstanding During Year		Calendar-Year Interest Expense
2001	Year 1: $107,023	4 months (9/1/01–12/31/01) ÷ 12 months		$ 35,674
2002	Year 1: $107,023	8 months (1/1/02–9/1/02) ÷ 12 months	$71,349	
	Year 2: $109,065	4 months (9/1/02–12/31/02) ÷ 12 months	$36,355	$107,704
2003	Year 2: $109,065	8 months (1/1/03–9/1/03) ÷ 12 months	$72,710	
	Year 3: $111,353	4 months (9/1/03–12/31/03) ÷ 12 months	$37,118	$109,828

The effective interest in the first row of the amortization table ($107,023) covers the period September 1, 2001, to September 1, 2002. Thus, we take only four months of the amount for the calendar period September 1, 2001, to December 31, 2001. The next eight months represent the first eight months of 2002 and are appropriately included in the 2002 interest expense calculation along with the first four months of the second entry in the amortization table ($109,065). The process continues until the last eight months' interest is reported for the last time period that the bond is outstanding, January 1, 2006, to September 1, 2006. The 2006 interest expense reported on the income statement is obtained by multiplying the effective interest from the last row in the amortization table ($116,786) by 8 months/12 months.

Bond issue expense for 2001 is calculated using the straight-line method, $10,000 divided by 5 years equals $2,000 per year. Since the bonds were outstanding for only four months in 2001 (September 1, 2001–December 31, 2001) and for only eight months in 2006 (January 1, 2006–September 1, 2006), the $2,000 is weighted by 4/12 and 8/12 in arriving at bond issue expense for 2001 and 2006, respectively.

The primary balance sheet difference caused by the mid-year issue is the disclosure of a short-term liability (interest payable) of $30,000 at the end of each year that the bond is outstanding.

EXHIBIT 9 Example 3. Balance Sheet December 31

WORTHY CO.
Balance Sheet

	2001	2002	2003	2004	2005	2006
Assets						
Current assets						
Cash (net cumulative cash effect of bond transaction only)	881,857	791,857	701,857	611,857	521,857	(568,143)
Other assets						
Bond issue costs	9,333	7,333	5,333	3,333	1,333	0
Liabilities						
Current liabilities						
Interest payable	30,000	30,000	30,000	30,000	30,000	0
Bonds payable					1,000,000	0
Less discount					(17,857)	
					982,143	
Long-term liabilities						
Bonds payable	1,000,000	1,000,000	1,000,000	1,000,000		
Less discount	(102,469)	(84,765)	(64,937)	(42,730)		
	897,531	915,235	935,063	957,270		
Owners' Equity						
Retained earnings (through cumulative effect on net income)	(36,341)	(146,045)	(257,873)	(372,080)	(488,953)	(568,143)

In Example 2, the interest that accrued for 2001 was paid on December 31, 2001. So, no liability for interest payable was reported at December 31, 2001. In Example 3, interest is paid each September 1. Four months of interest accrue (September 1 to December 31) but are unpaid as of year-end. This is a good example of an accrued liability, which, as you may recall from Chapter 1, occurs when the accrual element "liabilities" increases *prior* to cash flow occurring. The amount of the accrued liability ($90,000 × 4/12 = $30,000) appears each year.

Bonds payable are reported at the *present value of future cash flows* using the effective rate of interest at the issue date. These amounts are obtained from the amortization table, which provides a book value at September 1 for each year. The book value must be moved from September 1 to December 31 by adding four months amortization at the end of each year. The first three years are shown below.

Book Value at 9/1 from Table*	+	Amortization for Portion of Year	=	Book Value at 12/31
2001: $891,857	+	$17,023 × (4 months/12 months)	=	$897,531
2002: $908,880	+	$19,065 × (4 months/12 months)	=	$915,235
2003: $927,945	+	$21,353 × (4 months/12 months)	=	$935,063

*See Exhibit 5.

As always, retained earnings accumulates the income statement effects across years. For example, the $146,045 negative balance in retained earnings as of December 31, 2002, can be reconciled by totaling the 2001 and 2002 income statement expenses ($35,674 + $667 + $107,704 + $2,000). An alternative way to see how the balance sheet and income statements articulate is to remember that the changes in net assets between any two dates should give net income for the period (capital maintenance approach to computing income). Consider the change in assets and liabilities between December 31, 2004, and December 31, 2005, as an example:

Increase (decrease) in net assets = (Net assets 12/31/05 − Net assets 12/31/04)
Increase (decrease) in net assets = ($521,857 + $1,333 − $30,000 − $982,143)
− ($611,857 + $3,333 − $30,000 − $957,270)
Increase (decrease) in net assets = ($488,953) − ($372,080) = ($116,873)

A quicker way to obtain the same result is simply to note the decrease in owners' equity from 2004 to 2005: $488,953 (12/31/05) − $372,080 (12/31/04) = $116,873. The increase is negative, indicating a net asset decrease of $116,873, which is exactly equal to the decrease in net income for 2005 from interest expense and bond issue expense.

EXAMPLE 3 Journal Entries

9/1/01 Bond issue:							
Cash	891,857						
Discount on Bonds Payable	108,143						
Bonds Payable			1,000,000				
Bond Issue Costs	10,000						
Cash			10,000				
*Year-end interest accruals**	*12/31/01*		*12/31/02*		*12/31/03*		. . .
Interest Expense	35,674		36,355		37,118		
Discount on Bonds Payable		5,674		6,355		7,118	. . .
Interest Payable		30,000		30,000		30,000	

*Shown for the first three years. The amounts for interest expense and discount on bonds payable equal one-third (4 months/12 months) of the amounts in the effective interest amortization table.

continued

EXAMPLE 3 (concluded)

*Interest payment dates***	*9/1/02*		*12/31/02*		*12/31/03*		. . .
Interest Payable	30,000		30,000		30,000		
Interest Expense	71,349		72,710		74,235		
Discount on Bonds Payable		11,349		12,710		14,235	. . .
Cash		90,000		90,000		90,000	
Bond Issue Expense	667		2,000		2,000		
Bond Issue Costs		667		2,000		2,000	

**Shown for the first three years. The amounts for interest expense and discount on bonds payable equal two-thirds (8 months/12 months) of the amounts in the effective interest amortization table.

9/1/06 Maturity payment:		
Bonds Payable	1,000,000	
Cash		1,000,000

Issuance Between Interest Payment Dates

A final complexity of accounting for bonds payable occurs because bonds are rarely issued on the date on which they are dated.

Example 4. Mailman Enterprises planned to issue 100, $1,000, 6% bonds on January 1, 2001, the date the bonds are dated. However, the bonds are issued at face value on February 1, 2001. The bonds pay interest annually on January 1.

Solution. Mailman receives the $100,000 issue price on February 1, 2001, and is obligated to pay investors $6,000 interest each January 1. However, because the bonds are not issued until February 1, 2001, Mailman owes only eleven months of interest to investors on January 1, 2002. Keeping track of the interest owed would become increasingly difficult if the bonds were issued on a series of dates in early 2001; Mailman would have to record when each individual investor purchased the bonds so that the correct amount of interest would be paid on January 1, 2002, to each investor.

A simpler system is to require each investor to purchase the "missed" interest plus the bond from Mailman and then have Mailman pay the full twelve-months interest at January 1 to each investor. Because Mailman issued all the bonds on February 1, 2001, Mailman would receive the purchase price of $100,000 plus accrued interest of $500 ($100,000 × 6% × 1 month/12 months) and would pay the full $6,000 of interest on January 1, 2002. Interest expense for 2001 would be based on the eleven months that the bond was outstanding ($100,000 × 6% × 11 months/12 months = $5,500).

EXAMPLE 4 Journal Entries

At issue on 2/1/01:		
Cash	100,500	
Bonds Payable		100,000
Interest Payable		500
At 12/31/01 year-end accrual:		
Interest Expense	5,500	
Interest Payable		5,500
On 1/1/02 interest payment date:		
Interest Payable	6,000	
Cash		6,000

Summary of Accounting for Bonds Payable

Bonds payable are disclosed on the balance sheet at the present value of future cash flows using the effective rate of interest at the date of bond issue. The market's effective rate of interest can change during the life of the bond. In a valuation context, increases (decreases) in the market's required rate of return on the bond decrease (increase) the *market value* of the bond. However, these changes in *market value* are not reflected in the financial statements of the borrower. The predominant view of standard setters has traditionally been that estimated market value, while relevant, is generally unreliable and, thus, unworthy of presentation in the financial statements. However, recent pronouncements of the FASB have increased disclosure in the area of bonds and other financial instruments. *SFAS No. 107*, "Disclosures about Fair Value of Financial Instruments," requires note disclosure of the market value of all financial instruments for which market value measurement is practical. For actively traded bonds payable, market value quotes are available. For less actively traded bonds, the company will have to estimate an appropriate current effective rate of interest and compute the present value of the bond at that rate of interest. This estimated market value is disclosed in the notes to the financial statements.

The income statement effects of bonds payable are determined by the effective interest method. The effective interest method recognizes the constant rate of interest incurred by the borrower over the life of the bond on an often-changing amount borrowed. The carrying value of the bond changes because differences between the stated interest rate and the effective interest rate on a bond result in the borrower paying more (or less) cash interest than is accrued as interest expense. The difference between effective interest expense and cash interest paid causes a change (i.e., amortization) in the bond's book value.

Notes Payable

6 Explain the accounting for notes payable over the life of the note.

Accounting for the issue of notes payable mirrors bonds payable accounting. A minor difference is that issue costs are relatively small. Also, whereas bonds are usually issued at a premium or discount, notes are normally not. A major difference results from the type of transaction that creates a note payable. While bonds are primarily issued for cash, notes can be issued for cash as well as noncash consideration:

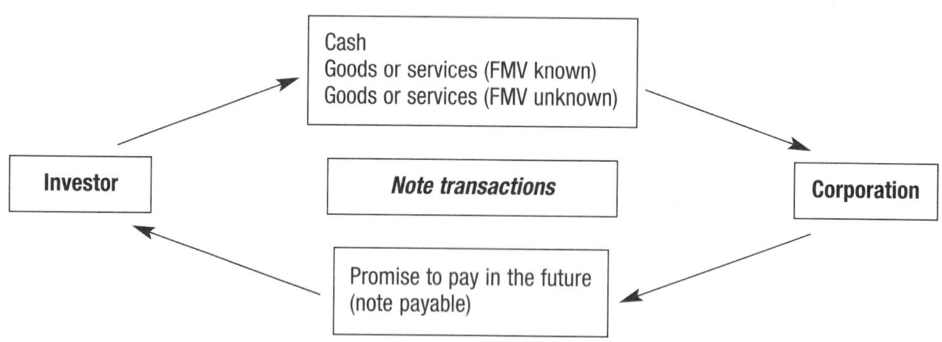

Notes Issued for Cash

When a corporation accepts cash in exchange for a note, the same accounting as shown for bonds payable is performed. The note bears a stated interest rate, but the note is valued at present value using the effective interest rate that the investor requires on a risky investment. The effective interest rate is easily calculated in this type of transaction because *cash is the best measure of present value.*

Notes Issued for Noncash Consideration

Two different general situations occur in noncash exchanges. If goods or services with a known cash exchange price (i.e., fair market value) are received in exchange for the note, then the effective rate is easily calculated because *goods or services with a known cash exchange price are good measures of present value.*

In contrast, it is more difficult to account for notes payable when it is exchanged for unique goods or services. Unique goods and services often have no readily determinable cash exchange price. In this case, the market value of the note (and hence, the goods or services) must be determined directly by examination of the note's characteristics to calculate the value of the items exchanged. Because the cash flow characteristics of the note (i.e., interest payments, maturity value, and cash flow dates) are known, the present value of the note is determined by choosing an appropriate effective interest rate. As previously noted, the risk of realizing cash flows is the determining factor for the effective interest rate. As a practical matter, the accountant would examine similar notes by similar makers to estimate the interest rate that would have been negotiated in an "arm's length" cash for note exchange. Once the effective interest rate is estimated, the present value of the note is computed, and the accounting disclosure is the same as that illustrated for bonds payable.

It is important to understand the nature of the judgement call that will have to be made in choosing the appropriate effective interest rate. All other things being equal, incremental borrowing increases financial risk. Therefore, each incremental borrowing is likely to bear a slightly higher interest rate to reflect the increased financial risk. Also, if plant or equipment is received in exchange for the note, the operating risk of the firm is altered. Consequently, it is important to consider both the increased financial risk and the operating risk when estimating the appropriate effective interest rate to use in a transaction when the fair value of the goods and services received for the note is difficult or impossible to determine.

Note and Bond Disclosure

To illustrate actual long-term debt presentation, the following information was presented in Ecolab, Inc.'s, 1998 annual report.

EXHIBIT 10 Notes Payable and Bonds Payable Information—Ecolab, Inc.

December 31 ($ thousands)	1998	1997
Partial balance sheet information		
Current liabilities—short term debt	67,991	48,884
Long-term debt	227,041	259,384
Note 3		
Short-term debt		
Notes payable	52,441	33,440
Long-term debt, current maturities	15,550	15,444
Total	67,991	48,884
Long-term debt		
7.19% senior notes, due 2006	75,000	75,000
9.68% senior notes, due 1995–2001	42,857	57,143
6.00% medium-term notes, due 2001	62,761	—
Multicurrency credit agreement, due 2002	44,000	116,450
Other	17,973	26,235
	242,591	274,828
Long-term debt, current maturities	(15,550)	(15,444)
Total	227,041	259,384
Statement of cash flows: Financing activities		
Notes payable	24,820	9,280
Long-term debt borrowings	117,740	117,000
Long-term debt repayments	(151,143)	(15,210)

In the Ecolab, Inc., financial statements, the balance sheet presented two summarized amounts related to debt securities: short-term debt (current liabilities) and long-term debt (noncurrent liabilities). The detail of the summary amounts appears in Note 3. The statement of cash flows provides information about the cash inflows and outflows related to long-term and short-term borrowings.[7]

Hybrid Securities

7 Explain the accounting for hybrid securities.

In this section, we consider three financing instruments that possess both debt and equity characteristics: convertible debt, debt issued with detachable warrants, and preferred stock. The proper classification of these securities is important because the ratio of debt to equity is a measure of financial risk. Chapter 2 outlines certain characteristics that determine whether a security is classified as debt or equity, and it discusses other hybrid securities.

Convertible Bonds

Convertible bonds are financial instruments that are initially in the form of a bond, but the investor may tender the bonds to the corporation in exchange for equity securities at a stipulated conversion rate (e.g., each $1,000 bond is exchangeable for 30 shares of $10 par common stock).[8] In essence, the buyer of a convertible bond acquires a portfolio of two securities: a nonconvertible bond (carrying the stated interest rate) and an option to purchase common stock by exchanging the bond. An advantage for the issuing corporation is that convertible debt has a lower interest rate (frequently 300 to 600 basis points) than nonconvertible debt of the same terms.[9] At issuance, the conversion rate is set at a premium over the current stock price (frequently, the premium is 15%–30% of the stock's market value).

It is important to realize that corporations structure convertible bonds in response to investor demand for a security that initially yields a fixed return, has first claim against assets in dissolution, and has no voting privileges. However, at the investor's option, it is possible for the security to yield a variable return, have a residual claim against assets, and convey voting privileges. While acknowledging the presence of both debt and equity characteristics, accounting standard setters have chosen to base the accounting for convertible debt on the *inseparability of the debt and equity features*. Because the corporation has *either* debt or equity outstanding (but never both at the same time), convertible debt is initially treated as a debt security, and only as an equity security if conversion takes place. Therefore, until conversion, accounting for convertible bonds is the same as for nonconvertible bonds.

To illustrate how these hybrid securities are reported, consider the following example:

Example 5. Scott Inc. issued 100, $1,000 bonds on January 1, 2001. The bonds mature on December 31, 2006, and pay 8% interest annually each December 31. Each $1,000 bond is convertible into 50 shares of Scott's $1 par value common stock. The stock's market value at January 1, 2001, was $17 per share. The bonds

7. For the 600 companies surveyed, the *1999 Accounting Trends and Techniques* shows the following number of companies that had various long-term debt securities outstanding: **unsecured securities**—*notes*, 430, *debentures*, 162, *loans*, 78, *commercial paper*, 83; **collateralized securities**—*capital leases*, 298, *mortgages*, 53, *notes or loans*, 84; **convertible securities**—*debentures*, 30, and *notes*, 18.

8. The conversion of most convertible bonds does not require a cash payment by the owner of the bonds (i.e, the bonds are exchangeable for common stock with no additional cash payment).

9. One percent equals 100 basis points. Therefore, convertible debt typically has a 3 to 6% lower interest rate.

sold for $104,100. On January 1, 2001, Scott had other bonds currently outstanding due on December 31, 2006, that pay 9% interest. These other bonds, originally issued at face value, were trading at face value on January 1, 2001. On December 31, 2002 (after interest was paid), investors converted the 8% convertible bonds into common stock.

Solution. Scott Inc. records the bond issue at a premium because the $104,100 issue price exceeds the $100,000 maturity amount. The bond selling price reflects a 22.5% common stock premium over the current stock price.

Price per $1,000 bond (each bond convertible into 50 shares of common stock)	$1,041
Price per share ($1,041 ÷ 50)	$20.82
Current market price	$17.00
Pricing premium at issuance	$3.82 (22.5%)

The income statement reflects interest expense using the effective interest method. We would expect the effective interest rate to be less than the stated rate of 8% because the market paid a premium for the bonds. Using a financial calculator to compute the effective rate yields a 7% effective interest rate (present value = $104,100; future value = $100,000; payment (ordinary annuity) equals $100,000 × 8% = $8,000; number of periods = 5; i = ? = 7%). Scott's other bonds, due December 31, 2006, have a current yield of 9% (stated rate of 9% and the bonds are trading at face value). Therefore, by offering the conversion feature Scott received an interest rate reduction of 200 basis points (i.e., 2%) over the current 9% interest rate of its nonconvertible bonds.

The statement of cash flows reports the cash inflow from issue of the bond and the cash outflows for interest in 2001 and 2002:

EXHIBIT 11 Example 5. Statement of Cash Flows*

SCOTT INC.
Statement of Cash Flows

	2001	2002
Operating Activities		
Interest payments	(8,000)	(8,000)
Financing Activities		
Issue bonds payable	104,100	

*Cash outflows in parentheses

The income statement reports the effective interest expense of $7,287 in 2001 ($104,100 × 7%). Because $8,000 of cash interest is paid, the book value of the bond decreases by $713 by the end of 2001 ($8,000 interest paid less $7,287 accrued interest expense). Thus, the interest expense for 2002 is computed as the $103,387 book value at January 1, 2002 ($104,100 − $713), times the 7% effective rate to obtain $7,237:

EXHIBIT 12 Example 5. Income Statement

SCOTT INC.
Income Statement

	2001	2002
Financial revenues, (expenses), gains, and (losses)		
Interest expense	(7,287)	(7,237)

The problem indicates that conversion took place at December 31, 2002. The following partial amortization schedule shows the book value of the bond at that date:

EXHIBIT 13 Example 5. Effective Interest Amortization Table (Partial)

Date	8% Cash Interest	7% Effective Interest Expense	Premium Amortization	Book Value of Debt
01/01/01				104,100
12/31/01	8,000	7,287	713	103,387
12/31/02	8,000	7,237	763	102,624

Accountants record the conversion using the *book value method*. The concept underlying this method is that the conversion represents the completion of a transaction involving the issue of equity for cash—the outstanding debt was simply an intermediate step in the process. Thus, the bond book value at the date of conversion ($102,624) is transferred to equity accounts as follows:

Shares issued: $100,000 bonds ÷ $1,000 per bond = 100 bonds
100 bonds × 50 shares per bond = 5,000 shares issued
Assigned to common stock: 5,000 shares × $1 par value = $5,000
Assigned to additional paid-in capital: $102,624 − $5,000 = $97,624

No gains or losses are recognized in the income statement under the book value method, which is consistent with the general rule of no gains and losses on equity transactions identified in Chapter 2.

The balance sheet reports the existence of a bond payable at December 31, 2001, and since the conversion occurred on December 31, 2002, common equity is reported at December 31, 2002. The retained earnings account accumulates the income statement effects of interest expense.

EXHIBIT 14 Example 5. Balance Sheet

SCOTT INC.
Partial Balance Sheet

	2001	2002
Assets		
Current assets		
Cash (net cumulative effect of bond transaction only)	96,100*	88,100**
Liabilities		
Long-term liabilities		
Bonds payable	100,000	
Add premium on bonds payable	3,387	
	103,387	
Owners' Equity		
Contributed capital (reflects only effects of conversion of convertible bonds to common stock)		
Common stock (at par)		5,000
Additional paid-in capital		97,624
Retained earnings (Cumulative effect of bond only; income taxes ignored)	(7,287)	(14,524)

*$104,100 − $8,000 interest payment = $96,100
**$96,100 − $8,000 interest payment = $88,100

In summary, current GAAP recognizes the equity feature of the bond only after conversion has taken place. Re-examining the original information calls such treatment into question. The existence of Scott's other 9% bonds, issued and currently trading at face value, indicates that the securities market requires at least a 9% return on investment in Scott bonds. (The correspondence of the market and face values implies equality of the effective and stated interest rates.) In fact, it is more likely that the market would require a return on the newly issued bonds that is greater than 9% given that the incremental nature of the new issue will increase financial risk. Why, then, did the market pay a premium for an issue paying only 8%? Clearly, the equity feature has value. An estimate of this value could be obtained by discounting the bond's cash flows at 9% estimated effective interest to yield a present value of \$96,110 at January 1, 2001 [using a financial calculator to solve for present value, $i = 9\%$; future value = \$100,000; payment (ordinary annuity) equals \$100,000 × 8% = \$8,000; present value = ? = \$96,110]. Therefore, the implied value of the equity feature is \$7,990 (\$104,100 − \$96,110).

EXAMPLE 5 Journal Entries

1/1/01 Issue of convertible bond:		
Cash	104,100	
Bonds Payable		100,000
Premium on Bonds Payable		4,100
12/31/01 Interest payment:		
Interest Expense	7,287	
Premium on Bonds Payable	713	
Cash		8,000
12/31/02 Interest payment:		
Interest Expense	7,237	
Premium on Bonds Payable	763	
Cash		8,000
12/31/02 Conversion:		
Bonds Payable	100,000	
Premium on Bonds Payable	2,624	
Common Stock		5,000
Additional Paid-In Capital		97,624

The following partial footnotes for Hasbro, Inc., and GenCorp, Inc., (slightly modified) illustrate the conversion of convertible debt.

Hasbro, Inc., Note (7) Long-Term Debt:

Substantially all of Hasbro's 6% Convertible Subordinated Notes were converted into 7,636,562 shares of common stock during the year.

GenCorp, Inc., Note L (In Part): Long-term Debt and Credit Lines

During the second quarter, the Company called its \$115,000,000, 8% Convertible Subordinated Debentures. In the third quarter, substantially all the Debentures were tendered for conversion into GenCorp common stock at a conversion rate of approximately 62.247 shares of common stock per \$1,000 principal amount of debentures.

Bonds Issued with Detachable Warrants

Another financing alternative is to issue bonds with detachable stock warrants. The following example is a revised version of Example 5 so that you can compare and contrast the accounting for convertible bonds with that for bonds issued with detachable warrants. The conversion feature has been removed, and warrants have been attached to the bond issue.

Example 6. Scott Inc. issued 100, $1,000 bonds on January 1, 2001. The bonds mature on December 31, 2006, and pay 8% interest annually each December 31. Each $1,000 bond contains 50 detachable warrants. Each warrant may be redeemed with $16 per share to acquire one share of Scott's $1 par value common stock. The stock's market value at January 1, 2001, was $17 per share. The bonds sold for $104,100. Immediately after the issue, several investors detached the warrants and began trading them on an organized exchange at $1.60 per warrant. On December 31, 2002, investors converted 2,000 of the warrants into common stock.

Solution. For bonds issued with detachable warrants, the debt and equity features are clearly separable. As a result, the issue price is allocated based on the relative fair values of the two financial instruments. In most cases, a reliable market value quickly emerges for either the debt or equity feature (or both), and the remainder of the issue price is allocated to the other feature. In the case of Scott Inc., the value of the warrants has been determined by trading on an organized exchange.[10]

The allocation proceeds as follows:

Total issue price	$104,100
Allocation to equity:	
100 bonds × 50 warrants × $1.60 per warrant	(8,000)
Allocation to debt	$ 96,100

The statement of cash flows for the nonconvertible portion of the bond is the same as in the previous example. However, the statement of cash flows would also reflect the conversion of 2,000 warrants on December 31, 2002 (2,000 warrants × $16 per warrant = $32,000).

EXHIBIT 15 Example 6. Statement of Cash Flows*

SCOTT INC.
Statement of Cash Flows

	2001	2002
Operating Activities		
Interest payments	(8,000)	(8,000)
Financing Activities		
Issue bonds payable and detachable warrants	104,100	
Proceeds from conversion of warrants		32,000

*Cash outflows in parentheses

The income statement reports the effective interest expense based on a beginning book value of $96,100 at January 1, 2001, and an implied effective interest rate of 9%, with $8,649 reported in 2001 ($96,100 × 9%).[11] Because $8,000 of cash interest was paid, the book value of the bond increases by $649 by the end of 2001 ($8,649 interest accrued less $8,000 interest paid). Thus, the interest expense for 2002 is computed by multiplying the $96,749 book value at January 2, 2002 ($96,100 + $649), by the 9% effective rate to obtain $8,707.

10. Bond trading is often "thin," with market values not as readily determinable.
11. To obtain the 9% effective rate using a financial calculator, set $n = 5$; present value = $96,100; future value = $100,000; payment (ordinary annuity) = $8,000; and then solve for the interest rate.

EXHIBIT 16 Example 6. Income Statement

SCOTT INC. Income Statement	2001	2002
Financial revenues, (expenses), gains, and (losses)		
Interest expense	(8,649)	(8,707)

The balance sheets for 2001 and 2002 are as follows.

EXHIBIT 17 Example 6. Balance Sheet

SCOTT INC. Balance Sheet	2001	2002
Assets		
Current assets		
Cash (Net cumulative effect of bond transaction and warrant conversion only)	96,100	120,100
Liabilities		
Long-term liabilities		
Bonds payable	100,000	100,000
Deduct discount on bonds payable	3,251	2,544
	96,749	97,456
Owners' Equity		
Contributed capital		
Common stock (at par)		2,000
Additional paid-in capital—common stock		33,200
Additional paid-in capital—stock warrants	8,000	4,800
Retained earnings (Cumulative effect of bond only; income taxes ignored)	(8,649)	(17,356)

The balance sheet reports the existence of a bond payable and additional paid-in capital—stock warrants of $8,000 at December 31, 2001.[12] At December 31, 2002, 2,000 of the 5,000 warrants outstanding (40%) and $16 per warrant are tendered to the corporation in exchange for 2,000 shares of common stock. According to GAAP, the common stock issued must be valued at the amount of cash received upon conversion ($16 per share) plus the book value of the warrants converted ($1.60 per warrant). Therefore, the common stock is recorded at $17.60 per share.

Book value of warrants converted: 2,000 × $1.60 (or 40% × $8,000 book value)	$ 3,200
Cash received in warrant conversion: 2,000 shares × $16 per share	32,000
Total book value allocated to common stock	$35,200

The valuation of the common stock is separated into common stock (at par value of $1 per share) and paid-in capital (at $17.60 − $1.00 = $16.60 per share).

Par value: 2,000 shares × $1	$ 2,000
Additional paid-in capital (2,000 shares at $16.60)	33,200
	$35,200

12. The equality of the $8,000 allocated to the warrants and the $8,000 annual interest payment is merely a coincidence.

Note that the $35,200 assigned to the common stock is equal to the fair value received by the corporation in exchange for common equity—$3,200 cash when the warrants were originally issued and $32,000 cash when the warrants were exercised. Although the warrants may have increased in value between January 1, 2001, and December 31, 2002, the increase does not accrue to the corporation as an increase in net assets. Following the general rule, the issue of common equity is recorded at the fair market value of what the corporation has received, $35,200. As always, the $35,200 increase in equity is split between par value and additional paid-in capital on common stock. Further, $4,800 remains as additional paid-in capital from the 60% of the warrants still outstanding.

EXAMPLE 6 Journal Entries

1/1/01 Issue of bond with detachable warrants:		
Cash	104,100	
Discount on Bonds Payable	3,900	
Bonds Payable		100,000
Additional Paid-In Capital—Stock Warrants		8,000
12/31/01 Interest payment:		
Interest Expense	8,649	
Discount on Bonds Payable		649
Cash		8,000
12/31/02 Interest payment:		
Interest Expense	8,707	
Discount on Bonds Payable		707
Cash		8,000
12/31/02 Conversion:		
Cash	32,000	
Additional Paid-In Capital—Stock Warrants	3,200	
Common Stock		2,000
Additional Paid-In Capital—Common Stock		33,200

Preferred Stock

8 Describe the debt characteristics of preferred stock.

As discussed in Chapter 2, preferred stock is considered an equity instrument. Its issue increases contributed capital in the same way as the issue of common stock. However, preferred stock has debt-like characteristics. Because both dividends and interest payments involve cash outflows, retained earnings is similarly reduced when these occur. However, because preferred stock is an equity instrument, dividends on preferred stock do *not* appear on the income statement, but instead, are reported on the statement of owners' equity as a distribution to owners.

Two "debt-like" dividend characteristics of most preferred stock issues are the *stated dividend rate* and the *cumulative feature.* The dividend rate is stated as a percentage of par value. Preferred dividends must be declared and paid at this stated rate before common stock dividends are declared and paid. If a corporation is short on assets to be disbursed as dividends, then it does not have to declare either preferred or common dividends. But if the preferred stock has the cumulative feature, **the passed dividend** is referred to as a ***dividend in arrears.*** Dividends in arrears must be satisfied in subsequent years *before* any common dividends are declared and paid. The amount of dividends in arrears is not a liability because, technically, it never has to be paid. However, because it is important for common shareholders to know the existence of such arrearages, *disclosure of the amount in arrears in the notes to financial statements is required.*

The Effects of Leverage on Cash Flow and Income Variability

9 Analyze the effects of leverage on cash flow and income variability.

Now that we have studied equity, debt, and hybrid securities, a comparative analysis of the effects of financing is in order. Investors are interested in two characteristics of an investment—risk and return. The risk of the firm is a function of the timing and amount of cash flows generated by that firm. To illustrate the effects of alternative financing arrangements on risk and return, consider the following case of Mythical Co.

Example 7. Mythical Co. makes all sales on a cash basis and pays for all expenses in cash. Assume that all expenses except interest are variable so that we can disregard the effects on risk of fixed charges other than interest. Mythical incurs expenses before interest at the rate of 70% of sales revenue. Assume the following seven-year sales projections (in millions): $40, $120, $110, $140, $90, $40, and $160. Ignore income tax effects. Mythical needs $100 million in financing to generate projected sales. *What will be the expected level and risk of income and cash flows under the three alternative financing arrangements presented below?* (Estimates of level and risk are provided by the mean and variance of the distribution.)

Financing Options

1. Issue $100 million of common stock. Pay dividends at the rate of 40% of income.
2. Issue $100 million of 12% preferred stock.
3. Issue $100 million of 12% bonds payable.

In all three financing options, the mean expected net income is $18 million for debt financing and $30 million for equity financing. After paying dividends (options 1 and 2), the mean net cash flow is $18 million for each alternative.

Solution. The following schedules show net income and cash flow for each year under each of the three financing options. Note that dividends on common and preferred stock are not subtracted in determining net income because they are distributions to owners. Also, because all sales and expenses are in cash, net income represents net cash flows before dividends. The common and preferred dividends are subtracted to arrive at net cash flow.

EXHIBIT 18 Schedules of Net Income and Net Cash Flow for Mythical Co.

Common stock issue:								**Mean**	**Variance**
Sales	40	120	110	140	90	40	160		
Expenses @ 70%	(28)	(84)	(77)	(98)	(63)	(28)	(112)		
Income before financing	12	36	33	42	27	12	48		
Interest expense	(0)	(0)	(0)	(0)	(0)	(0)	(0)		
Net income	**12**	**36**	**33**	**42**	**27**	**12**	**48**	**30**	**167.14**
Dividends @ 40%	(4.8)	(14.4)	(13.2)	(16.8)	(10.8)	(4.8)	(19.2)		
Net cash flow	**7.2**	**21.6**	**19.8**	**25.2**	**16.2**	**7.2**	**28.8**	**18**	**60.17**

Preferred stock issue:								**Mean**	**Variance**
Sales	40	120	110	140	90	40	160		
Expenses @ 70%	(28)	(84)	(77)	(98)	(63)	(28)	(112)		
Income before financing	12	36	33	42	27	12	48		
Interest expense	(0)	(0)	(0)	(0)	(0)	(0)	(0)		
Net income	**12**	**36**	**33**	**42**	**27**	**12**	**48**	**30**	**167.14**
Dividends (100 × 12%)	(12)	(12)	(12)	(12)	(12)	(12)	(12)		
Net cash flow	**0**	**24**	**21**	**30**	**15**	**0**	**36**	**18**	**167.14**

(continued)

EXHIBIT 18 (concluded)

Bond issue:

								Mean	Variance
Sales	40	120	110	140	90	40	160		
Expenses @ 70%	(28)	(84)	(77)	(98)	(63)	(28)	(112)		
Income before financing	12	36	33	42	27	12	48		
Interest expense	(12)	(12)	(12)	(12)	(12)	(12)	(12)		
Net income	**0**	**24**	**21**	**30**	**15**	**0**	**36**	**18**	**167.14**
Dividends	(0)	(0)	(0)	(0)	(0)	(0)	(0)		
Net cash flow	**0**	**24**	**21**	**30**	**15**	**0**	**36**	**18**	**167.14**

The variability of net income is equal across all alternatives (167.14).[13] But, the mean net income is lowest for the debt financing. That is, for a given level of net income, debt financing is riskier.

The mean net cash flow is equal across alternatives. But, the variability is lower for the common equity financing. The preferred stock and debt financing involve a fixed cash outflow in each period. If common equity is used, the amount of the dividend can be set at a percentage of net income, thus reducing the variability of cash flows.

In summary, common stock financing is less risky than bond financing whether the net income or net cash flow series is examined. The apparent riskiness of preferred stock financing depends on whether net income or net cash flow is being considered. If the net income series is examined, preferred financing is indistinguishable from common financing. This occurs because both types of financing have no effect on net income. However, if the net cash flow series is examined, common stock financing has the lower variance, which makes it less risky.

http://

Financial statement data for many companies is available to download at both their home page and the EDGAR site maintained by the SEC. Access the EDGAR site through our Web site (http://baginski@swcollege.com) and obtain financial statement data for Kmart and Sears. Examine the long-term liabilities sections of these two companies. Which company finances most of its assets with long-term debt?

The External Decision Makers' View of Debt

External decision makers view the amount of debt shown in a company's balance sheet in both positive and negative ways. The primary positive implication is that debt is generally cheaper than equity financing, and thus, a means of leveraging returns to common shareholders. On the negative side, not only does too much debt increase the risk of bankruptcy and debt covenant default, but it also hampers the ability to raise future capital should profitable projects come along.

The variability of income and cash flows is increased in the presence of debt financing. The use of non-interest-bearing debt is not a way to dampen the variability because interest expense is computed using the effective interest method. Therefore, fixed charges against income for interest expense occur each period regardless of whether cash interest is paid.

Finally, investors use information in annual reports about debt maturity dates to assess whether financial management practices are sound. The timing of large debt maturations must be met by sufficient cash accumulations or the company must be sufficiently flexible to refund old debt with new debt.

13. Variance equals the sum of the squared deviations of each observation in the series from the mean, divided by the number of observations.

Southwest Airlines' Debt Financing

Several portions of Southwest Airlines' financial statements pertain to debt financing decisions. Before continuing this section, please review the following sections of Southwest Airlines' 1998 annual report information (Appendix C): (1) from Management's Discussion and Analysis (MD&A), the Liquidity and Capital Resources and Liquidity Risk sections; (2) from the Balance Sheet, the liabilities section; (3) from the Statement of Cash Flows, the financing activities section; and (4) from footnote 4, Long-Term Debt.

The Liquidity and Capital Resources section indicates that in 1998 Southwest redeemed \$100 million in notes (the statement of cash flows shows payments for long-term debt and capital lease obligations of \$118.859 million). Southwest had a \$475 million revolving credit line at December 31, 1998 (terms of the credit line are discussed in footnote 4, Long-Term Debt). As of December 31, 1998, the credit line had not been drawn. Southwest had outstanding shelf registrations for the issuance of \$318.8 million in public debt securities. This information is useful in predicting cash flows because the discussion indicates that Southwest intended to issue the debt securities in 1999 and 2000 to finance aircraft purchases. The statement of cash flows indicates that Southwest did not issue any long-term debt in 1998 (but it did in 1997).

Southwest's balance sheet indicates that at December 31, 1998, the company had long-term debt of \$623,309,000 net of \$11,996,000 in current maturities (those maturing within 12 months). The \$623,309,000 represented 26.9% (\$623,309,000 ÷ \$2,318,078,000) of Southwest's total liabilities, and 13.2% (\$623,309,000 ÷ \$4,715,996,000) of total liabilities and stockholders' equity. Footnote 4, Long-Term Debt, separates the long-term debt amount into its components. Of the total net long-term debt at December 31, 1998, \$637,671,000 was principal, \$2,366,000 was discount, and \$11,996,000 was current (due within 12 months). The long-term debt includes \$133,190,000 in capital lease obligations (the topic of Chapter 4). The footnote describes both the issue and terms of each major debt issuance. The interest rates range from 7.37% to 9.4%; the MD&A Market Risk section states that the average interest rate is 8.3%.

Chapter Summary

Corporations raise a significant amount of capital through debt financing. The balance sheet reports the mix of debt and equity financing so that investors and creditors can assess a firm's financial flexibility and credit risk. Regardless of the level of cash interest that is paid each period, net income is reduced by interest expense calculated under the effective interest method. This process matches the cost of financing with the revenues generated by the invested capital.

The concept of present value was used repeatedly in this chapter. Long-term debt represents a series of future cash flows subject to a risk of payment. Although one method of determining the present value of long-term debt is to discount these cash flows using an appropriate interest rate, it is important to remember that an arm's-length exchange between two parties often provides the accountant with a clear measure of present value. In the case of bonds payable, the security market determines the present value of the bond recorded at the date of issue. Chapter 4 deals with leasing, an alternative form of debt financing in which the direct discounting of cash flows is an important activity.

Appendix: Straight-line Method of Amortization and an Example of Bonds Issued at a Premium

This appendix covers two topics: (1) the alternative straight-line method of premium/discount amortization and (2) accounting for a bond premium using the effective interest method.

Straight-Line Method of Premium/Discount Amortization

APB No. 21 specifies that the effective interest method is to be used to compute the amortization of bond premium/discount. The text examples use the effective interest method. The straight-line amortization method may be used if the results are not materially different from those using the effective interest method. Under the ***straight-line method*, the dollar amount of interest income is the same each period, but the percentage of interest income compared to the book value changes each period.** This contrasts with the effective interest method, where the dollar amount of interest income changes each period, but the percentage of interest income compared to the book value is the same each period. The use of the straight-line method illustrates a cost–benefit trade-off. If the benefits are not material, then the costs in complexity of using the effective interest method may not outweigh the benefits of using the less complex, straight-line method.

To illustrate the straight-line method of computing interest expense, we use Example 2 (Worthy Co.) from the text and the straight-line method rather then the effective interest method. When you complete this example, compare the financial statement effects using the straight-line method with those shown in the text using the effective interest method.

Example A1. On January 1, 2001, Worthy Co. issued $1,000,000 in bonds payable. The bonds are dated January 1, 2001, mature in five years (January 1, 2006), and pay 9% interest every year on December 31. The issue sold for $891,857 (rounded to the nearest dollar). The underwriter deducted $10,000 in fees and remitted the proceeds to Worthy. Worthy has a December 31 year-end.

Solution. Under the straight-line method, (1) the discount amortization is the same amount each period, and (2) the interest expense each period equals the amount of interest paid/payable plus discount amortization calculated using the straight-line method. In the example problem, Worthy's discount was $108,143, and the straight-line amortization equals $21,629 per year ($108,143 ÷ 5). Worthy's bond amortization table is as follows:

EXHIBIT 19 Worthy Co. Straight-Line Amortization Table

Date	9% Cash Interest	Interest Expense	Discount Amortization*	Book Value of Debt
01/01/01				$ 891,857
12/31/01	$ 90,000	**$111,629	$ 21,629	913,486
12/31/02	90,000	111,629	21,629	935,115
12/31/03	90,000	111,629	21,629	956,744
12/31/04	90,000	111,628	21,628	978,372
12/31/05	90,000	111,628	21,628	1,000,000
Total	$450,000	$558,143	$108,143	

*Straight-line amortization: $108,143 ÷ 5 = $21,628.60
**Interest paid/payable ($90,000) plus discount amortization ($21,629) = $111,629

To better understand the differences between the effective interest and straight-line methods, compare this amortization table to Exhibit 1.

EXAMPLE A1 2001 Journal Entries

To issue bond on 1/1/01:		
Cash	891,857	
Discount on Bonds Payable	108,143	
Bonds Payable		1,000,000
Unamortized Bond Issue Costs	10,000	
Cash		10,000
12/31/01 journal entries (Entries for following years are similar):		
Interest Expense	111,629	
Discount on Bonds Payable		21,629
Cash		90,000
Bond Issue Expense	2,000	
Unamortized Bond Issue Costs		2,000

Bond Premium Example

The text examples used a bond discount situation. To illustrate a bond premium, see Example A2 below. (This is also Example 2 from the text, except we assume that the bond sold for $1,082,004 rather than $891,857. This sales price implies a 7% effective interest rate: $n = 5$; ordinary annuity payment = $90,000; present value = $1,082,004; future value = $1,000,000; $i = ? = 7.0\%$.)

Example A2. On January 1, 2001, Worthy Co. issued $1,000,000 in bonds payable. The bonds are dated January 1, 2001, mature in five years (January 1, 2006), and pay 9% interest every year on December 31. The issue sold for $1,082,004 (rounded to the nearest dollar). The underwriter deducted $10,000 in fees and remitted the proceeds to Worthy. Worthy has a December 31 fiscal year-end.

Solution. Worthy's effective interest amortization table is as follows:

EXHIBIT 20 Worthy Co. Effective Interest Amortization Table—Bond Premium

Date	9% Cash Interest	7% Effective Interest Expense*	Premium Amortization	Book Value of Debt
01/01/01				$1,082,004
12/31/01	$ 90,000	$ 75,740	$14,260	1,067,744
12/31/02	90,000	74,742	15,258	1,052,486
12/31/03	90,000	73,674	16,326	1,036,160
12/31/04	90,000	72,531	17,469	1,018,691
12/31/05	90,000	71,309	18,691	1,000,000
Total	$450,000	$367,996	$82,004	

*Book value of debt at beginning of interest accumulation period × 7% effective interest rate

EXAMPLE A2 2001 Journal Entries

To issue bond on 1/1/01:		
Cash	1,082,004	
Bonds Payable		1,000,000
Premium on Bonds Payable		82,004
Unamortized Bond Issue Costs	10,000	
Cash		10,000
12/31/01 journal entries (Entries for following years are similar):		
Interest Expense	75,740	
Premium on Bonds Payable	14,260	
Cash		90,000
Bond Issue Expense	2,000	
Unamortized Bond Issue Costs		2,000

Key Terms

bond indenture 103
business risk 103
callable bond 101
collateral trust bond 101
coupon rate 102
debenture bond 100
detachable warrant 101
discounted 104
dividend in arrears 122
effective interest method 105
equipment note 101
financial risk 103
mortgage bond 101
note agreement 103
rate of return 102
serial bond 101
stated rate 102
straight-line method 126
term bond 101
underwriter 103
yield 102
yield-to-maturity 102

Questions

Q1. **Bond Terminology.** Indicate the security backing of the following types of bonds:
a. mortgage bonds
b. collateral trust bonds
c. junk bonds
d. debenture bonds

Q2. **Bonds Terminology.** What distinguishes a term bond from a serial bond?

Q3. **Callable Bond.** What is a callable bond? Why is it important to disclose the call feature in the financial statements?

Q4. **Convertible Bond.** What is a convertible bond? Give two reasons why it is important to disclose this conversion feature.

Q5. **Interest Expense/Paid.** What is the difference between cash interest and effective interest? How is each computed?

Q6. **Market Interest Rate.** Identify several economy-wide factors and firm-specific factors that determine the market's required return (i.e., effective interest rate) for a specific bond.

Q7. **Bond Terms.** Identify five items that are usually covered in a bond indenture.

Q8. **Bond Covenants.** What are the "covenants and restrictions"? What kinds of restrictions are usually present?

Q9. **Bond Issuance.** What is the difference between a private placement and an open-market issue of debt?

Q10. **Bond Payable Financial Statement Presentation.** What is the balance sheet attribute used to measure and report bonds payable?

Q11. **Bond Issue Cost Financial Statement Presentation.** What is the balance sheet attribute used to measure and report bond issue costs?

Q12. **Bond Payable Financial Statement Presentation.** What determines whether a bond payable is reported as current or noncurrent? Considering a bond payable due in the next year, under what two circumstances would it be classified as noncurrent?

Q13. **Bond Premium/Discount.** Indicate in the following situations whether the bond would be issued at face value, a premium, or a discount.
a. The stated cash interest rate and the market effective interest rate are equal.
b. The stated cash interest rate is *higher* than the market effective interest rate.
c. The stated cash interest rate is *lower* than the market effective interest rate.

Q14. **Characteristics of Debt Securities.** What four characteristics of debt securities are discussed in the text?

Q15. **Characteristics of Debt Securities.** What characteristic(s) of debt securities distinguishes between bonds and notes? Between convertible debt and nonconvertible debt?

Q16. **Hybrid Securities.** Why is a security described as a hybrid security? What four hybrid securities are discussed in Chapters 2 and 3, and what makes them hybrid?

Q17. **Bonds Payable versus Preferred Stock.** Compare and contrast the basic financial statement effects of financing a large asset purchase with 10-year bonds (with annual interest payments) or preferred stock (with an annual dividend preference).

Q18. **Effects of Leverage on Cash Flow and Income Variability.** Positive leverage occurs when a company borrows to finance assets and the assets generate a rate of return that is greater than the cost of the financing. In general, what is the effect of three financing alternatives—notes payable, common stock, and preferred stock—on cash flow and income variability? Assume that the preferred stock pays an annual dividend and the common stock pays no dividend.

Short Problems

1. **Compute Bond Sales Price.** Using a financial calculator, compute the price at which the following bonds will issue:
a. Manuel Corp. issued a 20-year, 9%, $100,000 bond, interest payable annually. The market's desired rate of return on this bond is 10%.
b. Parker Bros. issued a 25-year, 8%, $100,000 bond, interest payable annually. The market's desired rate of return on this bond is 8%.
c. Subzero Ice Cream issued a 5-year, non-interest-bearing, $100,000 bond. The market desires a 12% return on this bond.

d. Lancelot Builders issued a 5-year, $200,000 bond. The bond pays 7% interest every six months. The market's desired rate of return on this bond is 6% every six months.

2. **Bond Present Value Computations.** Use a financial calculator to solve the following problems:
   a. Martin Co. issued a $50,000, non-interest-bearing note due in 3 years. The lender gave Martin $43,000. What is the present value of this note? What is the effective interest rate?
   b. Lewis Co. issued a $75,000, 4-year note, bearing interest at 2% annually in exchange for equipment with a known cash price of $48,000. What is the present value of this note? What is the equipment vendor's rate of return?

3. **Financial Statement Effects of Notes Payable with Contradictory Evidence About Value.** On July 1, 2001, Mason performed consulting services for Miller Co., accepting a 3-year, 12%, $50,000 note, interest payable semiannually on January 1 and July 1. A reasonable rate of interest for this note is 15% per year (7.5% per semiannual period). The value of the services are not easily estimated.

Required What is the present value of the note on July 1, 2001? How much interest expense does Miller record in 2001 and in 2002? What is the value of the note payable on Miller's December 31, 2001, balance sheet? What is the amount of interest payable on Miller's December 31, 2001, balance sheet.

Journal Entry Option: Record Miller's 2001 journal entries related to this note.

4. **Financial Statement Effects of Notes Payable Issued at Discount.** On January 1, 2001, Mason lent $40,000 to BillyBob Corp., accepting a $48,400, 2-year, non-interest-bearing note in exchange, with the principal due January 1, 2003.

Required What is the present value of the note on January 1, 2001? How much interest expense does BillyBob record in 2001 and in 2002? What is the value of the note payable on BillyBob's December 31, 2001, balance sheet? What is the amount of interest payable on BillyBob's December 31, 2001, balance sheet?

Journal Entry Option: Record BillyBob's 2001 journal entries related to this note.

5. **Financial Statement Effects of Notes Payable Issued at Premium.** On July 1, 2001, Mason performed consulting services with a well-known market value of $11,500 for Cold Pizza Restaurants, Inc. Cold Pizza issued a 2-year note to Mason that pays 16% annually on June 30 on the maturity value of $10,000. Cold Pizza has issued several notes of varying terms to other companies in recent months. The yields on the notes vary between 5% and 8%.

Required At what value should Cold Pizza record the note on July 1, 2001? How much interest expense does Cold Pizza record in 2001 and in 2002? What is the value of the note payable on Cold Pizza's December 31, 2001, balance sheet? What is the amount of interest payable on Cold Pizza's December 31, 2001, balance sheet?

Journal Entry Option: Record Cold Pizza's 2001 journal entries related to this note. Also, include the July 1, 2002, journal entry to record 2002 interest expense and the interest payment.

6. **Financial Statement Effects of Convertible Bonds.** Starks Co. issued 100, $1,000 bonds on January 1, 2001. The bonds mature on December 31, 2005, and pay 10% interest annually every December 31. Each $1,000 bond is convertible into 90 shares of Stark's $1 par common stock. The bonds were issued at $103,890 (implying an 8.8% effective rate). On December 31, 2002 (after interest was paid), the investors converted all 100 of the bonds into common stock.

Required Use a financial calculator to confirm the 8.8% effective interest rate computation. Compute interest expense for 2001 and 2002. Calculate the book value of the bonds at December 31, 2001 and 2002 (preparing a bond amortization table for 2001 and 2002 will provide these amounts).

Journal Entry Option: Prepare all 2001 and 2002 journal entries related to the issuance of the bonds, interest expense, interest payable, and the conversion of the bonds.

7. **Financial Statement Effects of Bonds Payable with Detachable Warrants.** On January 1, 2001, the Montross Co. issued 100, $1,000 bonds. The bonds mature in five years, pay interest at 10% every December 31, and each bond contains 25 detachable warrants. Each warrant may be redeemed along with $14 to acquire one share of Montross's $1 face value common stock. The entire issue (bonds and warrants) sold at face value of the bonds. On January 1, 2001, immediately after issuance, the warrants began trading on a national stock exchange at $4 per warrant.

Required At issuance, what amounts are allocated to the bonds and the warrants, respectively? What is the effective interest rate on the bonds? Compute interest expense for 2001 and 2002. Calculate the book value of the bonds at December 31, 2001 and 2002 (preparing a bond amortization table for 2001 and 2002 will provide these amounts).

Journal Entry Option: Prepare all 2001 and 2002 journal entries related to the issuance of the bonds, interest expense, interest payable, and the conversion of the warrants.

Analytical and Comprehensive Problems

8. **Note Payable Financial Statement Presentation under Alternative Valuation Possibilities.** On November 1, 2001, in return for consulting services the Chen Co. issued a 4%, 90-day, $5,000 note, interest payable at maturity. The value of the services performed is not well-known, but based upon recent Chen Co. note payable transactions and prevailing market interest rates, an annual interest rate of 10% seems more reasonable than the stated rate of 4%.

Required Compute any amounts related to the note payable that would be reflected in the December 31, 2001, balance sheet and 2001 income statement under the following valuation approaches. Compare the two disclosures on the basis of materiality and cost–benefit trade-off.
a. Value the note at present value.
b. Value the note at face value.

Journal Entry Option: Prepare 2001 journal entries under both alternatives to record the note payable and 2001 interest expense.

9. **Compute Bond Payable Sales Price on a Bond Issued Between Interest Dates.** Bobo Circus intended to issue bonds on July 1, 2001, with the following terms: 4%, 10-year bonds due July 1, 2011, with a face value of $1,000,000 and interest paid annually on July 1. On July 1, 2001, the market rate of interest for these bonds was 15%. The issue was not sold, however, until August 1, 2001, causing the bond to have only a 9-year, 11-month life. On August 1, 2001, the 4% bonds were issued with the market's desired return still at 15%. What was the bonds' sale price on August 1, 2001?

Journal Entry Option: Prepare the August 1, 2001, journal entry to record the issuance of the bond.

10. **Effects of Alternative Financing Arrangements.** Astro Enterprises needs to raise $30 million to finance plant expansion. Sherri Hendricks, CEO, does not want to dilute voting control of Astro; she is considering whether Astro should issue noncumulative preferred stock, cumulative preferred stock, or bonds. This is the first of a series of expansions, and as a result, the CEO is particularly interested in the financial statement effects of these financing arrangements.

Required Prepare a brief memo to Ms. Hendricks that summarizes the effects of the three alternative financing arrangements on the income statement and balance sheet. At this point, summarize the effects on net income only and ignore any EPS effects (we cover the intricacies of EPS computation in Chapter 10).

11. **Bond Financial Statement Presentation.** Monumental Engravers floated a large, 30-year bond issue in 1997. Reference to the bond exchange quotes in *The Wall Street Journal*

indicates a substantial difference between the initial issue price of the bond and its current market value. The bond is carried on Monumental's balance sheet at its carrying value, calculated by applying the effective interest method. Why do the bond's market value and carrying value differ?

12. **Financial Statement Effects.** Using the indicated letters, identify the effects of the following transactions or conditions on the various financial statement components:

I = increases D = decreases NE = no effect

Transaction	Assets	Liabilities	Owners' Equity: Contributed Capital	Owners' Equity: Retained Earn. Direct Effect	Owners' Equity: Retained Earn. through N.I.
a. Note issue					
• for cash					
• for property					
• for expenses					
b. Bond issue costs					
• issuance					
• amortization					
c. Bond issue					
• at par					
• at a discount					
d. Convertible bond issue					
e. Issue of bond with detachable warrants					
f. Passage of time when bond is outstanding					
g. Payment of interest (interest payable not previously accrued)					
h. Payment of interest previously accrued as interest payable					
i. Change in interest rates					
j. Retirement of bond issue					
k. Conversion of bonds to common stock					
l. Exercise of stock warrants					

13. **Compute Net Income.** Presented below are partial comparative balance sheets for Dusey Co. that reflect the effects of a bond payable. The five-year bond, due January 1, 2006, with interest payable annually on December 31, was issued on January 1, 2001.

DUSEY CO.
Balance Sheet
December 31

	2001	2002	2003	2004	2005	2006
Assets						
Current assets						
Cash	791,857	701,857	611,857	521,857	431,857	(568,143)
Other assets						
Bond issue costs	8,000	6,000	4,000	2,000	0	0
Liabilities						
Current liabilities						
Bonds payable					1,000,000	0
Long-term liabilities						
Bonds payable	1,000,000	1,000,000	1,000,000	1,000,000		
Less discount	(91,121)	(72,056)	(50,703)	(26,788)		
	908,879	927,944	949,297	973,212		

Required Compute the effect of the bond transaction on net income for 2002 and 2003 using only the information provided. Ignore income tax effects. What were the bond issue costs at issuance? What was the bond's effective interest rate on the date of issuance? What was the market (sales) price of the bonds on January 1, 2001?

14. **Note Payable Financial Statement Classification.** On December 31, 2001, Flyward Airlines had $2,000,000 of notes payable due September 5, 2002. Although Flyward had not provided a sinking fund to retire these notes, it intended to issue a new long-term note with sufficient proceeds to retire the first note on December 31, 2001. As of December 31, 2001, Flyward had not been able to obtain a refinancing agreement. On February 11, 2002, however, Flyward entered into an agreement with Merchant Bank to refinance the note on September 5. Merchant agreed to provide a loan to Flyward of no more than 80% of Flyward's inventory and receivables balance at September 5, 2002. Past history shows that the sum of Flyward's inventories and receivables will likely range from $1,500,000 to $2,200,000 in September 2002. How should Flyward classify the $2,000,000 note payable in its December 31, 2001, balance sheet assuming that the financial statements are not to be issued until March 1, 2002?

15. **Note Payable Issued at a Discount.** Fantastic Nurseries borrowed $10,000 from the bank on January 1, 2001. Fantastic must pay the bank $13,310 on January 1, 2004, to satisfy the note. No other cash flows are specified in the note agreement (i.e., the note is non-interest-bearing). Violet Bush, owner of the nursery, remembered from her accounting principles class that this is a discount situation and that discounts need to be amortized. She prepared the following disclosures for 2001, 2002, and 2003:

Account	12/31/01	12/31/02	12/31/03
Note payable	$13,310	$13,310	$13,310
Discount	(2,207)	(1,103)	(0)
Net payable	$11,103	$12,207	$13,310
Interest expense	$ 1,103	$ 1,103	$ 1,104

a. Did Violet use the effective interest method or the straight-line method to amortize the discount and recognize interest expense?
b. If Violet used the "theoretically" correct method to amortize the discount and recognize interest expense, what amount would be recorded as interest expense each year and what would be the year-end amounts for the note payable?
c. Compute the ratio of interest expense to the book value of the note at the beginning of each year for both the straight-line and effective interest methods. From this data, describe why the effective interest method is deemed to be a theoretically better method.

http://

16. **Financial Statement Analysis: Texas Instruments.** Refer to the Texas Instruments 1998 annual report at our Web site (http://baginski.swcollege.com). Pay particular attention to the balance sheet's liabilities section, the financing activities section of the statement of cash flows, and the long-term debt and lines of credit footnote. The following questions pertain to the financial statements and footnotes.
a. Compute the following:
   1. What was the amount of change (and percentage change) in total debt from 1997 to 1998? Use loans payable and long-term debt as the definition of total debt.
   2. Reconcile the change in total debt for 1998 using the balance sheet, long-term debt footnote, and statement of cash flows.
b. The income statement shows interest expense of $55 million, $94 million, and $73 million for the years 1998, 1997, and 1996, respectively. The long-term debt footnote indicates (1) the amount of accrued interest incurred in those years, (2) the amount of accrued interest capitalized, and (3) the amount of interest paid, net of amounts capitalized. Prepare a schedule reconciling accrued interest incurred to interest expense (Interest incurred − Amounts capitalized = Interest expense).
c. **Part (c) is to be completed only by students who completed Module A.** The ratio "times interest earned" is defined as income before income taxes and interest divided by interest charges (see Module A). Using the information from the previous requirement, compute "times interest earned" for 1998, 1997, and 1996.

Use the following schedules to report the financial statement effects of items 17–19 for the debtor. Make sure to indicate any subclassifications that should be used. Use a different set of worksheets for each item.

Statement of Cash Flows
(cash outflows in parentheses)

	Year 1	Year 2	Year 3	Year 4	Year 5	etc.
Operating Activities						
Investing Activities						
Financing Activities						
Separate schedule showing "Significant Investing and Financing Activities not Affecting Cash"						

Income Statement

	Year 1	Year 2	Year 3	Year 4	Year 5	etc.
Financial revenues, (expenses), gains, and (losses)						

Balance Sheet
December 31

	Year 1	Year 2	Year 3	Year 4	Year 5	etc.
Assets						
Liabilities						
Owners' Equity						

17. **Financial Statement Effects.** Magic Ltd. issued a $500,000, 5-year bond on January 1, 2001, due January 1, 2006. The bond pays 8% interest annually on January 1. The bond sold for $462,092 (implying an effective rate of 10%). There were no bond issue costs.

18. **Financial Statement Effects.** Porter Properties issued a $200,000, 4-year, 11% bond at par on January 1, 2001, due January 1, 2005. The net proceeds remitted by the underwriter to Porter equaled $196,000, the difference due to issue costs.

19. **Financial Statement Effects.** On January 1, 2001, Mason Inc. performed consulting services for DuBois Inc., accepting a 5-year, $100,000, non-interest-bearing note due December 31, 2005. The services were so unique that their value is not easily estimated. Given DuBois's excellent credit rating, a reasonable rate of interest for the note is 7%.

CFA Exam-Type Problems

Use the following to answer questions 20 and 21.

On June 30, 2001, the Lovatta Co. issued $10,000,000 in 10 year, 9% bonds due June 30, 2011, with interest payable semiannually on December 31 and June 30. The bonds sold for $9,376,889, which reflected an effective interest rate of 10%.

20. On the December 31, 2001, income statement, what amount should be reported as interest expense? (author constructed)
    a. $421,960
    b. $450,000
    c. $468,844
    d. $500,000
21. On the December 31, 2001, balance sheet, what amount should be reported as bonds payable? (author constructed)
    a. $9,376,889
    b. $9,395,733
    c. $9,426,889
    d. $10,000,000

22. When a company issues convertible debt: (author constructed)
    a. The market interest rate attached to the convertible debt is *lower* than it would be if the debt were nonconvertible.
    b. The market interest rate attached to the convertible debt is *higher* than it would be if the debt were nonconvertible.
    c. The current stock price reflects a premium over the bond's market price.
    d. GAAP requires the debt and equity features to be recognized separately.
23. Current GAAP requires material bond issue costs to be: (author constructed)
    a. Expensed immediately as bond issue expense.
    b. Expensed immediately as interest expense.
    c. Netted against bond proceeds, thereby increasing bond discount or decreasing bond premium and increasing the effective interest rate.
    d. Capitalized separately as deferred costs and amortized over the life of the bond, thereby not affecting the effective interest rate.
24. Which of the following statements is true? (author constructed)
    a. Convertible debt and bonds issued with detachable warrants are accounted for in the same manner.
    b. GAAP requires zero-coupon bonds to show zero interest expense each period based upon current period market rates of interest.
    c. Preferred stock dividends reduce net income.
    d. Preferred stock has debt-like characteristics.

Objectives

1 Describe the determinants of a lease versus purchase decision.
2 Understand lease terminology and the characteristics that distinguish different kinds of leasing arrangements.
3 Account for operating leases.
4 Account for capital leases.
5 Identify important footnote disclosures for leases.
6 Analyze the effects of leasing on cash flow and income variability.

Chapter 4

Financing Decisions—Leasing

In Chapter 3, we discussed decisions related to the issuance of debt. In this chapter, we discuss leasing, which is a particular form of debt financing. A common decision faced by many firms is whether to purchase an asset by issuing debt to finance the purchase or to simply lease the asset.

The Lease versus Purchase Decision

1 Describe the determinants of a lease versus purchase decision.

Most corporations purchase property, plant, and equipment (i.e., engage in investment activities) with cash raised through equity or debt issue. However, an alternative to purchasing is leasing. The basics of the leasing arrangement are illustrated by the following diagram:

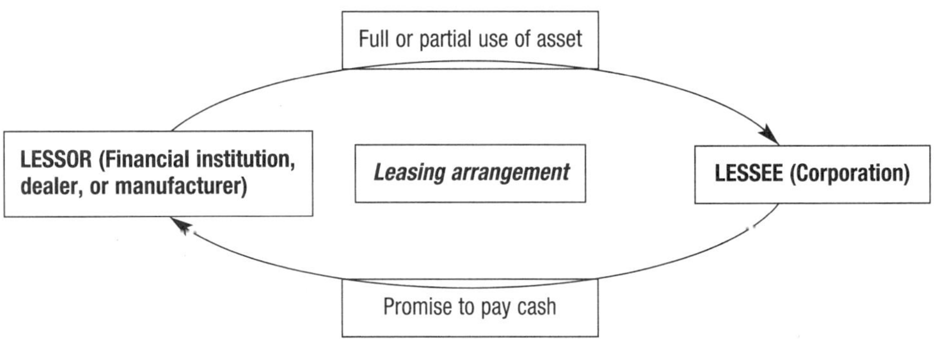

The diagram shows a lessor trading the full or partial use of an asset in exchange for expected future cash flows, which are subject to a risk of realization. As in the case of bonds or notes, the lessor's problem of setting the level of k future cash flows (i.e., the periodic lease payments) to return principal (i.e., the asset FMV) and earn interest at rate i can be expressed by the following present value formulation:

$$\text{Asset value} = \sum_{n=1}^{k} \frac{\text{Periodic lease payments}}{(1 + i)^n}$$

As an example, suppose that you wish to obtain a car. You can either buy the car, financing it with a note payable to a bank, or lease the car from a leasing company. In both cases, you *finance* the purchase. Therefore, ***leasing* is essentially equal to borrowing money, purchasing an asset, and then paying the money back.**

The equivalence of leasing and borrowing to purchase raises the question of "why lease instead of borrow?" The answer to this question, to a great degree, lies in three areas: *potential tax advantages, off-balance-sheet financing, and management of obsolescence risk* (the risk associated with holding assets that become technologically obsolete). The major *tax advantage* of leases created to follow Internal Revenue Service guidelines is the immediate recognition of the full amount of a periodic lease payment as a tax deduction. Off-balance-sheet financing and management of obsolescence risk require more detailed discussion.

Off-Balance-Sheet Financing

Managers frequently attempt to use off-balance-sheet financing when acquiring assets. The use of off-balance-sheet financing can improve financial ratios and increase the likelihood that debt covenants linked to financial statement measures will not be violated. Leasing is a primary example of a technique used to achieve off-balance-sheet financing.

To illustrate the advantages of off-balance-sheet financing, assume the following simplified balance sheet information for the Jefferson Co.:

Current assets	$10,000,000
Long-term assets	70,000,000
Total assets	$80,000,000
Current liabilities	$ 5,000,000
Long-term liabilities	35,000,000
Owners' equity	40,000,000
Total liabilities and equity	$80,000,000

Jefferson has a current ratio (Current assets ÷ Current liabilities) of 2:1 and a total liability to equity ratio (total liabilities ÷ total equity) of 1:1. Assume that Jefferson wants to acquire an additional $20,000,000 in long-term assets. One financing option is that Jefferson can purchase the assets by making a $2,000,000 down payment signing a ten-year note to borrow the remaining 90% from a local bank, with interest and $1,000,000 principal due next year. Alternatively, Jefferson can use a lease structured to qualify for off-balance-sheet financing. The lease terms are that Jefferson can sign a ten-year lease, the present value of which is $20,000,000, with no down payment required. The balance sheets after acquiring the additional long-term assets under the alternative choices would be:

	Purchase	Lease
Current assets	$ 8,000,000	$10,000,000
Long-term assets	90,000,000	70,000,000
Total assets	$98,000,000	$80,000,000
Current liabilities	$ 6,000,000	$ 5,000,000
Long-term liabilities	52,000,000	35,000,000
Owners' equity	40,000,000	40,000,000
Total liabilities and equity	$98,000,000	$80,000,000

If Jefferson borrows from the bank, the current ratio is lowered from 2:1 to 1.33:1 ($8,000,000 ÷ $6,000,000), and the debt to equity ratio is increased from 1:1 to 1.45:1 ($58,000,000 ÷ $40,000,000). However, if Jefferson leases the assets, the ratios remain unchanged. This example illustrates why off-balance-sheet financing, particularly through the use of leasing, is so attractive to managers. The lease obligation is not capitalized, and, consequently, debt ratios are not adversely affected.[1]

Management of Obsolescence Risk

The management of obsolescence risk is one characteristic of leasing that explains the existence of two different kinds of leases—those that do not transfer the risks and rewards of ownership to the lessee, and those that do.

Ownership Risks and Rewards Remain with Lessor—Operating Leases Asset ownership entitles the owner to the benefits of asset use. However, asset ownership also involves risks. In many industries, one of the greatest risks is that of obsolescence. This risk is manageable because some lessors are willing to share obsolescence risk with the lessee corporation by entering into relatively short-term leases. An example of a lease that minimizes the lessee's obsolescence risk is leasing computer equipment for one year. In this short-term lease, a lessor provides only a very small portion of the asset's benefit to the lessee in exchange for lease payments. The short-term nature of this agreement keeps most of the risk of obsolescence with the lessor rather than shifting the risk to the lessee. **Accountants classify leases that do not transfer a substantial portion of the risks and rewards of ownership to the lessee as *operating leases*.**

Ownership Risks and Rewards Transferred to Lessee—Capital Leases On the other hand, leases that transfer substantial portions of the risks and rewards of ownership to the lessee are, in substance, installment purchases. The lessee obtains *substantially all* of the asset's risks and benefits in exchange for future lease payments that return to the lessor *substantially all* of the asset's fair market value. For the most part, the lessee bears the risk of obsolescence. However, some of these leases may still qualify for favorable tax treatment or, depending on the lessor's required rate of return, be more advantageous than borrowing and purchasing the asset outright.[2]

An example of a long-term lease that is in substance an installment purchase is a grocery store chain leasing a store for 30 years. **Accountants classify leases that transfer the risks and rewards of ownership to the lessee as *capital leases*.**

Summary

Leasing is actually a debt financing arrangement. (The decision to incur debt rather than issue equity is discussed in Chapter 2.) Tax advantages, fear of obsolescence, and lessor return preferences may make leasing a more favorable alternative than borrowing and purchasing. An operating lease offers tax advantages, the opportunity to manage obsolescence risk, and the ability to use off-balance-sheet financing. A capital lease is essentially a borrowing and purchase. The following sections show how accountants determine whether a lease is classified as operating or capital and how the two types of leases are reported in the lessee's financial statements.

1. Of 600 companies surveyed, the *1999 Accounting Trends and Techniques* shows that 207 reported both capitalized and noncapitalized leases; 324 reported noncapitalized leases only; 10 reported capitalized leases only; and 59 disclosed no leases. Therefore, 531 of the 600 companies (88.5%) used off-balance-sheet financing through noncapitalized leases.

2. For example, lessors might accept a lower return as a marketing strategy.

Lease Classification: Operating versus Capital

2 Understand lease terminology and the characteristics that distinguish different kinds of leasing arrangements.

The classification of leases as operating or capital is very important to the objective of fair representation of a corporation's financial position. You will discover that there are several financial statement differences between operating and capital leases. The difference that has captured the most attention is the reporting of long-term debt. Upon entering into any lease agreement, the corporation (lessee) promises to pay the lessor in several future periods. This is clearly a long-term debt arrangement. For a capital lease, the long-term debt is reported in the balance sheet. The asset acquired is reported as well because capital leases are, in substance, installment purchases of an asset. With an operating lease, only a minor portion of the asset's risks and benefits are transferred to the corporation. Thus, in operating leases, neither the asset nor the long-term debt are recorded in the balance sheet. That is, the financing arrangement is "off-balance-sheet."

A great deal of concern exists among accounting standard setters about off-balance-sheet financing. The debt-to-equity ratios of firms are an important gauge of financial flexibility and risk. Therefore, the question of whether a lease is operating or capital is an important one to investors, creditors, management, and standard setters. After discussing how to account for the different kinds of leases, we will return to the analysis of financial risk in the presence of operating and capital leases.

To aid in lease classification, the FASB developed practical lease classification criteria to determine whether the risks and rewards of the asset are transferred to the lessee. A lease is considered to be a *capital lease if any one of the following criteria is met*:

1. The lease transfers title from lessor to lessee at the end of the lease term.
2. The lease contains a bargain purchase option.
3. The lease term is greater than or equal to 75% of the economic useful life of the asset.
4. The present value of the minimum lease payments is greater than or equal to 90% of the fair market value of the asset.[3]

In order to understand the importance of these criteria and to learn more about lease accounting, we will consider each criterion in turn. *Note that, to avoid capital lease classification, the lessee only needs to ensure that none of the four criteria are met.*

Title Transfer

This criterion is probably the easiest to understand. If the lessee receives title at the end of the lease, then the risks and rewards of asset ownership have clearly passed to the lessee. The lease payments represent an installment purchase of the asset.

Bargain Purchase Option

A ***bargain purchase option*** **entitles the lessee to obtain title to the asset by making a final payment that is far below the expected fair market value of the asset at the end of the lease term.** The difference between a title transfer and a bargain purchase option is a matter of degree. In a title transfer, the final payment is usually zero, and the transfer of title at a future date is certain. In a bargain purchase option, the final payment is greater than zero (but small relative to the fair value of the asset), and title transfer depends upon a future event—the payment of the bargain purchase option price. A purchase option that is considered to be a bargain when the lease is signed is evidenced by a purchase price that is so attractive (in re-

3. "Accounting for Leases," *FASB Statement of Accounting Standards No. 13*, as amended and interpreted through May 1980 (Stamford, Conn.: FASB, 1980).

lation to the asset's estimated fair value at the purchase option date) that we would expect the lessee to exercise the option, and as a result, enjoy all the benefits of ownership and be subject to all the risks of ownership. A common bargain purchase price is $1.

Length of Lease Term—75% Test

Under title transfer and bargain purchase option situations, the lessee obtains all the risks and rewards of the asset. Receiving all risks and rewards is one end of a continuum. Conceptually, an operating lease falls nearer to the opposite end of the continuum, where only a small part of the risks and rewards of the asset are acquired by the lessee. One way to measure whether the risks and rewards of asset ownership have been acquired by the lessee is to look at the length of time over which the lessee controls the asset. If the lessee has control for most of the asset's life, then capital lease treatment is appropriate. If the lessee has control for only a small part of the asset's life, then operating lease treatment is appropriate. In order to standardize the classification of leases, the FASB provides a practical cutoff of 75% of economic useful life to represent the point on the continuum where operating leases are distinguished from capital leases. If the lease term is greater than or equal to 75% of the asset's economic useful life, then the lessee is deemed to have acquired a sufficiently large portion of risks and rewards, and the lease is classified as a capital lease.

One of the difficult issues in this area is the definition of the lease term. Several standards, technical bulletins, and interpretations have addressed this issue. The underlying theme is determining the probable length of time that the lessee will control the asset. For example, if the lessee has the option to renew the lease at a bargain option price, then we would expect the lessee to do so, and the lease term would include the covered renewal option periods. Also, if the lessee could cancel the lease at any time, but only by paying an extreme penalty, we would not expect the lessee to cancel the lease, and the lease, therefore, would last its full term. GAAP lists five situations in which it should be assumed that the lease will be extended beyond any minimum, noncancelable lease term because of specific renewal option clauses: (1) renewal option periods where the renewal option price is considered to be a bargain; (2) renewal option periods prior to a bargain purchase option date; (3) renewal periods where the lessor has the option to force renewal; (4) renewal option periods after the date of a termination penalty option that is considered so large that it is unlikely that the lessee will pay the termination penalty; and (5) renewal option periods where the lessee is guaranteeing the lessor's debt used to finance the leased asset.[4]

Present Value of Minimum Lease Payments—90% Test

Probably the best measure of the portion of the asset's risks and benefits transferred under the lease agreement is the present value of the consideration provided by the lessee over the life of the lease relative to the fair value of the asset at the time the asset is leased. If the lessee is acquiring a major portion of risks and rewards, then we would expect the present value of the lease payments to be a major portion of the fair market value of the asset. In search of a practical, standardized measure of "major portion," the FASB settled on 90% of the asset's fair market value as the point at which the lessee is deemed to have acquired the risk and rewards of the asset. If the present value of minimum lease payments is greater than or equal to 90% of the estimated fair market value of the leased asset, then it is capitalized.

Two important technical issues in applying this rule are the definition of minimum lease payments and the interest rate used in discounting. ***Minimum lease***

4. *SFAS No. 98* (Stamford, Conn.: FASB, 1988).

***payments* are those transfers of assets from the lessee to lessor that are probable.** Minimum lease payments include the more obvious asset transfers such as periodic cash rental payments; they also include less obvious asset transfers such as a bargain purchase option price, bargain renewal option amounts, cancellation fees (if we expect the lessee to cancel the lease at some time and pay any stipulated cancellation fees), and any guarantees by the lessee to the lessor of residual value at the end of the lease.

The last in this list, ***guaranteed residual value***, is particularly important in the determination of minimum lease payments. At the end of the lease term, the leased asset generally has a residual (salvage) value. If the asset reverts back to the lessor, the contract can specify that such residual value is either guaranteed or unguaranteed. In some leases, **the lessee guarantees that at the end of the lease the asset will be worth a minimum amount** (the guaranteed residual value). If the leased asset is worth less than the guaranteed residual value, then the lessee must make up the difference, usually through an additional cash payment to the lessor. *Guaranteed residual values are used to transfer obsolescence risk from the lessor to the lessee.*

Sometimes a portion of periodic cash payments to the lessor are **reimbursements for the lessor's cost of maintaining and insuring the asset.** These latter costs are referred to as ***executory costs*** and are *not* considered minimum lease payments because they are not paid to *acquire* the asset.

Two different interest rates are primary candidates for use when discounting minimum lease payments. Because capital leases are debt instruments, the ***lessee's incremental borrowing rate*** is one candidate. The lessee's incremental borrowing rate is "the rate that, at the inception of the lease, the lessee would have incurred to borrow the funds necessary to buy the leased asset on a secured loan with repayment terms similar to the payment schedule called for in the lease."[5] Also, **the rate that implicitly links the fair market value of the asset to the minimum lease payments,** called the ***implicit rate*** or the ***lessor's desired rate of return***, is a candidate. Accounting standards require that the lessee use its incremental borrowing rate to discount the payments unless the lessor's implicit rate is lower *and* the implicit rate is known by the lessee. If these conditions are met, then the lessee uses the lower implicit rate to perform the discounting. These requirements lead to the use of a general rule when working lease problems: **the lessee uses the lower of the lessee's incremental borrowing rate or the lessor's implicit rate (if known) when computing the *present value of minimum lease payments*.**

The present value of minimum lease payments is used in the 90% test. If the lease is capitalized, then the leased asset and leased obligation are recorded at the present value of minimum lease payments. Although it is unlikely to occur, the exception to this rule is that the asset cannot be recorded at an amount greater than its fair value. If the present value of minimum lease payments is greater than the asset's fair value, then the leased asset and lease obligation are recorded at the asset's fair value; an effective interest rate must then be computed to use in calculating interest expense related to the lease obligation. This situation implies that the lessee incurred a lease obligation greater than the value of the asset—it would be cheaper for the lessee simply to buy the asset! Implementation of certain tax planning strategies, using the lessor's implicit rate, or the inability to finance the asset's acquisition elsewhere are reasons this exception could occur.

Examples of Accounting for Operating and Capital Leases

Because this section of the text deals primarily with financing activities, we emphasize accounting for the lease obligation and its effect on the lessee's financial statements. The fixed asset purchase is an investing activity—it is explained in greater detail in Chapter 7, where lessor accounting is explained.

5. *SFAS No. 13,* para 5.

3 Account for operating leases.

Simple Example of an Operating Lease

Example 1. On January 1, 2001, Bird Co. leased a delivery van under a four-year, noncancelable lease agreement, which expires on December 31, 2004. The specifics of the lease are as follows:

Van fair market value	$10,000
Useful life	6 years
Residual (salvage) value (12/31/04), not guaranteed by Bird	$3,000
Lessor's required rate of return (known by Bird)	10%
Bird's incremental borrowing rate	11%
Maintenance and insurance costs (paid separately by Bird, beginning of the year)	$200
No transfer of title clause	
No purchase option clause	

Objectives: Compute Bird's annual rental payments and illustrate lease accounting.

Solution. Because no bargain purchase option or title transfer is present, the van will revert back to the lessor at the end of the lease (12/31/04). The problem indicates that the lessor must earn a 10% rate of return over the four years. The lessor will receive $3,000 in value at the end of the lease when the van is returned. Therefore, the unknown in this problem is the amount of the periodic payments from Bird that will allow the lessor to earn the 10% rate of return. The amount of the periodic payment set by the lessor depends upon whether periodic lease payments are made at the beginning of a period (ordinary annuity) or at the end of a period (annuity due). If *ordinary annuity payments* are used, then the lessor calculates lease payments to return the portion of the $10,000 fair value that is *not* collected in the residual value:

$$\$10{,}000 - \frac{\$3{,}000}{(1 + 0.1)^4} = \sum_{n=1}^{4} \frac{\text{Lease payments}}{(1 + 0.1)^n}$$

Solving for the ordinary annuity lease payment yields lease payments = $2,508.[6]

Alternatively, *annuity due lease payments* are calculated as follows:

$$\$10{,}000 - \frac{\$3{,}000}{(1 + 0.1)^4} = \sum_{n=0}^{3} \frac{\text{Lease payments}}{(1 + 0.1)^n}$$

Solving for the annuity due lease payments yields lease payments = $2,280.[7]

The left-hand side of the equations gives the amount that will have to be recovered by the lessor in the form of annual cash lease payments. The lessor will receive an asset with an expected value of $3,000 at the end of the lease term. So, the present value of $3,000 will *not* have to be covered by the annual lease payments. The lease payments are $2,508 if payments are to begin one year hence, and $2,280 if the first payment is due immediately.[8] *For the remainder of this example, we assume that Bird and the lessor negotiate payments at the beginning of each year, making $2,280 the appropriate lease payment.*

Is this an operating or a capital lease? We already know that the first two criteria for lease capitalization are not met (no title transfer or bargain purchase op-

6. Use a financial calculator to confirm the computation (using $n = 4$; $i = 10$; future value = $3,000; present value = $10,000; the ordinary annuity payment = ? = $2,508).
7. Use a financial calculator to confirm the computation (using $n = 4$; $i = 10$; future value = $3,000; present value = $10,000; the annuity due payment = ? = $2,280).
8. You should note that delaying each payment by one period transforms an annuity due into an ordinary annuity at the effective rate of interest. That is, $2,280 × 1.1 = $2,508.

tion). The lease term is four years out of a six year economic life (67%). Thus, the third criterion requiring the lease term to be greater than or equal to 75% of the economic life is not met. The fourth criterion requires the lessee to compute the present value of the minimum lease payments (MLP):

$$\text{Present value MLP} = \sum_{n=0}^{3} \frac{\$2{,}280}{(1 + 0.1)^n} = \$7{,}950^9$$

Note that the lessee's only MLP are the $2,280 periodic rentals; the residual value is not guaranteed by the lessee. The lessee does not have to return an asset worth $3,000 to the lessor. There is no probable future sacrifice of assets by the lessee to make up any deficiency in residual value. Also, the lessor's implicit rate of 10% is used by the lessee to discount the periodic rentals because the implicit rate is smaller than the lessee's incremental borrowing rate, and this fact is known by the lessee. Because $7,950 is less than 90% of the $10,000 fair value of the asset, the fourth criterion is not met as well. *The failure to meet any of the criteria results in an operating lease classification.*

The presentation of an operating lease in the statement of cash flows is straightforward:

EXHIBIT 1 Example 1. Statement of Cash Flows*

BIRD CO.
Statement of Cash Flows*

	2001	2002	2003	2004
Operating Activities				
Payment of lease rentals	(2,280)	(2,280)	(2,280)	(2,280)
Payment of maintenance and insurance	(200)	(200)	(200)	(200)
Net cash outflow	(2,480)	(2,480)	(2,480)	(2,480)

*Cash outflows in parentheses

The correspondence of the lease with Bird's fiscal year causes rental expense and maintenance and insurance expense for one year to be reflected on the income statement:

EXHIBIT 2 Example 1. Income Statement

BIRD CO.
Income Statement

	2001	2002	2003	2004
Operating expenses				
Rent expense (operating leases)	2,280	2,280	2,280	2,280
Maintenance and insurance expense	200	200	200	200

On the balance sheet, cash decreases by $2,480 each year, and retained earnings accumulates the reductions in income from expenses:

9. Use a financial calculator to confirm the computation [using $n = 4$; $i = 10$; future value = 0 (because the lessee owes nothing at the end of the lease); payment (annuity due) = $2,280; and present value = $7,950].

EXHIBIT 3 Example 1. Balance Sheet

BIRD CO.
Balance Sheet
December 31

(Cumulative effect of operating lease)	2001	2002	2003	2004
Assets				
Current assets				
Cash (cumulative effect; year by year effects are shown in the statement of cash flows)	(2,480)	(4,960)	(7,440)	(9,920)
Owners' Equity				
Retained earnings (cumulative effect of lease transactions only, ignoring income taxes)	(2,480)	(4,960)	(7,440)	(9,920)

As always, the accumulated decrease in assets minus liabilities equals the accumulated decrease in owners' equity.

EXAMPLE 1 Journal Entry

1/1 each year		
Rent Expense	2,280	
Maintenance and Insurance Expense	200	
Cash		2,480

Most leases are not signed on January 1. As a result, cash flows and accrual components are unlikely to be equal. To illustrate, assume the same information as before except that the lease was signed on July 1, 2001. (We designate this new example as Example 1A.) The cash flow statement would not change because cash payments are made at the beginning of each year. But, in the first year, only one-half (six out of twelve months) of the expenses would have been *incurred*. The asset would be used for a full year in 2002, 2003, and 2004, and for the final half-year in the first six months of 2005.

EXHIBIT 4 Example 1A. Income Statement

BIRD CO.
Income Statement

	2001	2002	2003	2004	2005
Operating expenses					
Rental expense (operating leases)	1,140	2,280	2,280	2,280	1,140
Maintenance and insurance expense	100	200	200	200	100

Because cash flows occur before expenses are incurred, deferred (prepaid) expenses are created. Recall from Chapter 1 that costs with future economic benefits (i.e., deferred expenses) are assets. These assets will be reflected on the balance sheet, Prepaid Rent and Prepaid Maintenance and Insurance.

EXHIBIT 5 Example 1A. Balance Sheet

BIRD CO.
Balance Sheet
December 31

	2001	2002	2003	2004	2005
Assets					
Current assets					
Cash (cumulative effect of lease transactions)	(2,480)	(4,960)	(7,440)	(9,920)	(9,920)
Prepaid rent	1,140	1,140	1,140	1,140	0
Prepaid maintenance and insurance	100	100	100	100	0
Owners' Equity					
Retained earnings (cumulative effect of lease transactions, ignoring taxes)	(1,240)	(3,720)	(6,200)	(8,680)	(9,920)

On each July 1, a full year's worth of rent and maintenance and insurance are *paid*. By December 31, however, only one-half has been *incurred*. At each December 31, the other half of the expense recognition is deferred and reported in current assets.

EXAMPLE 1A Journal Entries (Assuming a 7/1/01 signing and first payment)

7/1/01–05		
Rent Expense	2,280	
Maintenance and Insurance Expense	200	
Cash		2,480
To reflect cash payments.		
12/31/01–05 adjusting journal entry		
Prepaid Rent	1,140	
Prepaid Maintenance and Insurance	100	
Rent Expense		1,140
Maintenance and Insurance Expense		100
Only one-half of July 1 payment should be expensed each year.		
6/30/02–06		
Rent Expense	1,140	
Maintenance and Insurance Expense	100	
Prepaid Rent		1,140
Prepaid Maintenance and Insurance		100
To reflect first half year rent and maintenance expense.		

4 Account for capital leases.

Illustration of a Capital Lease

Example 2. Example 1 can be changed from an operating lease to a capital lease by altering the lease terms such that one of the four capitalization criteria is met. An example is to change the estimated useful life of the asset in Example 1 from six to five years (and assume the original terms that the lease was signed on January 1, 2001, and periodic annuity due payments occur each January 1).

Solution. Now, the lease term is greater than 75% of the van's economic useful life (four of five years, or 80%), resulting in a capital lease classification. The remainder of the economics of the lease are unchanged. The payments, due each January 1, continue to have a present value at a 10% effective rate of $7,950.

Because the lease is now a capital lease, its financial statement effects mirror those of a borrowing and asset purchase. Long-term debt (lease obligation) is reported at the *present value of the minimum lease payments* ($7,950); a long-term operational asset (equipment) is recorded at the *fair market value of consideration given*, which is equal to the present value of the minimum lease payments at the inception of the lease ($7,950). In this example, the lessee capitalizes the asset cost, depreciating it to zero over the four-year lease term.

Amortization tables are very useful in understanding any long-term debt situation, leases included. The lessee's amortization schedule for a capital lease is similar to a bond or note amortization schedule.

EXHIBIT 6 Example 2. Capital Lease Amortization Schedule

Date	Cash Payment	Interest Expense @ 10%	Amortization (Principal Reduction)	Book Value
1/1/01 (inception)				$7,950
1/1/01	$2,280	$ 0	$2,280	5,670
1/1/02	2,280	567	1,713	3,957
1/1/03	2,280	396	1,884	2,073
1/1/04	2,280	207	2,073	0
Total	$9,120	$1,170	$7,950	

At the inception of the lease (January 1, 2001), Bird promises to pay an annuity of minimum lease payments of $2,280 due at the beginning of each year. The present value of that annuity is $7,950 ($n$ = 4; i = 10; annuity due payment = $2,280; future value = 0). Upon paying the first $2,280 on January 1, 2001, Bird's obligation is reduced to $5,670. Between January 1, 2001, and December 31, 2001, $567 of interest accrues ($5,670 × 10%). On January 1, 2002, an additional $2,280 of cash is paid, of which $567 is interest and $1,713 is a reduction in principal (book value); this leaves a January 1, 2002, obligation of $3,957.

While the amortization schedule is indicative of the economics of the capital lease agreement, its structure does not coincide with balance sheet dates (i.e., December 31 dates). The schedule can be recast as follows to clarify the discussion of financial reporting:

EXHIBIT 7 Example 2. Capital Lease Amortization Schedule (Recast)

Date	Cash Payment	Interest Expense @ 10%	Amortization (Principal Reduction)	Book Value
1/1/01 (inception)				$7,950
1/1/01	$2,280		$2,280	5,670
12/31/01		$ 567	(567)	6,237
1/1/02	2,280		2,280	3,957
12/31/02		396	(396)	4,353
1/1/03	2,280		2,280	2,073
12/31/03		207	(207)	2,280
1/1/04	2,280		2,280	0
Total	$9,120	$1,170	$7,950	

From this schedule, it is easier to see the two economic events that change the lessee's obligation from January 1, 2001, to December 31, 2001. The payments of $2,280 reduce (amortize) the obligation, while interest accruals increase the obligation. It also highlights the classification of each cash flow as an operating or financing outflow. The first $2,280 paid is purely a financial outflow, reducing the outstanding financing. The subsequent January 1 cash flows are a combination of paying for interest accrued to December 31 (an operating activity) and a reduction of lease obligation (a financing activity).

The presentation of a capital lease in the statement of cash flows divides cash flow between operating (interest) and financing activities (principal reduction), and shows the $200 payment for maintenance and insurance as well.

EXHIBIT 8 Example 2. Statement of Cash Flows*

BIRD CO.
Statement of Cash Flows

	2001	2002	2003	2004
Operating Activities				
Payment of interest	0	(567)	(396)	(207)
Payment of maintenance and insurance	(200)	(200)	(200)	(200)
Financing Activities				
Reduction of capital lease obligation	(2,280)	(1,713)	(1,884)	(2,073)
Net cash flow	(2,480)	(2,480)	(2,480)	(2,480)
Separate Schedule of "Significant Investing and Financing Activities Not Involving Cash"				
Acquisition of equipment through capital leases	7,950			

*Cash outflows in parentheses

Also, a separate schedule accompanies the statement of cash flows to disclose significant investing and financing activities that do not involve cash flows. In this schedule, the issuance of debt (financing activity) to acquire equipment (investing activity) would be disclosed. A similar transaction and disclosure was discussed in Chapter 2 when common stock was issued to acquire a building.

In the income statement, interest expense and maintenance and insurance expense are reflected. Additionally, the cost of the equipment must be matched with the periods in which it generates revenues. Thus, depreciation expense appears in each period ($7,950 acquisition cost ÷ 4 years = $1,987.50).

EXHIBIT 9 Example 2. Income Statement

BIRD CO.
Income Statement

	2001	2002	2003	2004
Operating expenses				
Depreciation expense	1,988	1,987	1,988	1,987[10]
Maintenance and insurance expense	200	200	200	200
Financial revenues, (expenses), gains, and (losses)				
Interest expense	(567)	(396)	(207)	0
Total lease-related operating expenses	2,755	2,583	2,395	2,187

On the balance sheet, cash decreases by $2,480 each year. At each balance sheet date, the lease obligation is reported at the present value of remaining future cash flows at the historical effective rate of interest at the inception of the lease. The lease obligation is broken down between current (the $2,280 due next year) and long-term (the remainder). The current portion is further broken down between that portion which represents interest payable and that portion which amortizes the lease obligation.

10. The actual depreciation expense is $1,987.50. The amount is rounded up in alternate periods. Depreciation of a leased asset occurs over the lease term unless there is title transfer or a bargain purchase option. In the latter two cases, the lessee uses the asset over its economic useful life and, thus, depreciates it over this time period to its estimated salvage value to the lessee.

EXHIBIT 10 Example 2. Balance Sheet

BIRD CO.
Balance Sheet
December 31

	2001	**2002**	**2003**	**2004**
Assets				
Current assets				
Cash (cumulative effect of lease transactions)	(2,480)	(4,960)	(7,440)	(9,920)
Property, Plant, and Equipment				
Equipment	7,950	7,950	7,950	0
Less accumulated depreciation	(1,988)	(3,975)	(5,963)	
	5,962	3,975	1,987	
Liabilities				
Current liabilities				
Interest payable	567	396	207	0
Lease obligation	1,713	1,884	2,073	0
Long-term liabilities				
Lease obligation	6,237	4,353	2,280	
Less current portion	(2,280)	(2,280)	(2,280)	
	3,957	2,073	0	0
Owners' Equity				
Retained earnings (cumulative effect of lease transactions, ignoring income taxes)	(2,755)	(5,338)	(7,733)	(9,920)

For example, reference to the recast lease amortization table (Exhibit 7) shows a $4,353 obligation at December 31, 2002, interest accrual being responsible for the $396 increase in the obligation. The long-term liability section at December 31, 2002, reports the $4,353 total, but shows that $2,280 will be paid in the next period (and thus, is not long term). The current liability section shows that $396 of the $2,280 is actually interest payable, while the remainder ($1,884) reduces the lease obligation.

Equipment is shown in the property, plant, and equipment section. The attribute measured for this kind of long-lived asset is historical cost less accumulated depreciation at each balance sheet date.

As always, there are two ways to obtain the decrease in owners' equity. The accumulated decrease in assets minus liabilities equals the accumulated decrease in owners' equity. Also, the accumulation of income statement effects reduces owners' equity. The $5,338 negative balance shown for retained earnings re-ported through December 31, 2002, can be obtained by summing interest, insurance and maintenance, and depreciation expenses for 2001 ($2,755) and 2002 ($2,583).

EXAMPLE 2 Journal Entries

1/1/01 Lease inception								
Equipment (or Leased Asset)	7,950							
Lease Obligation		7,950						
Lease Obligation	2,280							
Cash		2,280						
Lease payment dates after 1/1/01			*1/1/02*		*1/1/03*		*1/1/04*	
Lease Obligation			1,713		1,884		2,073	
Interest Payable			567		396		207	
Cash				2,280		2,280		2,280
Adjusting entries at each year-end	*12/31/01*		*12/31/02*		*12/31/03*		*12/31/04*	
Depreciation Expense	1,988		1,987		1,988		1,987	
Accum. Depr.—Equipment		1,988		1,987		1,988		1,987
Interest Expense	567		396		207			
Interest Payable		567		396		207		

Illustration of a Capital Lease with a Guaranteed Residual Value

The accounting for leases becomes a bit more complicated if the lessee guarantees all (or a portion) of the asset's estimated residual value.

Example 3. Change Example 2 to assume that Bird Co. guaranteed that the van would be worth $3,000 when it was returned to the lessor.

Solution. With the residual value guaranteed, two of the four criteria would lead to capital lease treatment—the lease term is greater than 75% of the van's economic useful life (four of five years = 80%) and the present value of minimum lease payments is greater than 90% of the asset's fair market value. Because the lessee has guaranteed the asset will be worth at least $3,000, GAAP requires that the lessee include the guaranteed residual value in the computation of minimum lease payments. At a 10% effective rate, the minimum lease payments have a present value of $10,000 ($7,950 as with the unguaranteed residual value case, plus the present value of $3,000 received once at the end of the fourth year),[11] and the 90% of FMV criterion is met.

Bird's lease obligation amortization schedule reflects the $10,000 book value at the beginning of the lease.

EXHIBIT 11 Example 3. Capital Lease Amortization Schedule

Date	Cash Payment or Asset Transfer	Interest Expense @ 10%	Amortization (Principal Reduction)	Book Value
1/1/01 (inception)				$10,000
1/1/01	$ 2,280	$ 0	$ 2,280	7,720
1/1/02	2,280	772	1,508	6,212
1/1/03	2,280	621	1,659	4,553
1/1/04	2,280	455	1,825	2,728
12/31/04	3,000	272	2,728	0
Total	$12,120	$2,120	$10,000	

Note that, at January 1, 2004, an obligation exists to deliver $3,000 of fair market value (in equipment or cash) one year hence ($3,000 ÷ 1.10 = $2,728, rounded). By the time the lease is terminated (December 31, 2004), one more year of interest is accrued ($272) to raise the obligation to $3,000. The $3,000 is satisfied by the transfer of the asset to the lessor or, if the fair market value is less than $3,000, by a combination of asset transfer and cash payment.

Again, the amortization schedule can be recast as follows to clarify the discussion of financial reporting:

EXHIBIT 12 Example 3. Capital Lease Amortization Schedule (Recast)

Date	Cash Payment or Asset Transfer	Interest Expense @ 10%	Amortization (Principal Reduction)	Book Value
1/1/01 (inception)				$10,000
1/1/01	$ 2,280		$ 2,280	7,720
12/31/01		$ 772	(772)	8,492
1/1/02	2,280		2,280	6,212
12/31/02		621	(621)	6,833
1/1/03	2,280		2,280	4,553
12/31/03		455	(455)	5,008
1/1/04	2,280		2,280	2,728
12/31/04	3,000	272	2,728	0
Total	$12,120	$2,120	$10,000	

11. Using a financial calculator ($n = 4$; $i = 10$; annuity due payment = $2,280; future value = $3,000; the present value = $10,000). In this example, the present value of minimum lease payments equals the fair market value of the asset. Usually, the present value of minimum lease payments is less than the fair market value of the asset.

The statement of cash flows for Example 3 shows slightly higher total interest payments ($2,120) than Example 2 ($1,170)—the amount borrowed was greater ($10,000 in Example 3 as compared to $7,950 in Example 2). It also shows that $10,000 in equipment was acquired by capital lease and that the last reduction in financing in 2004 was accomplished by transferring the leased asset with a value of $3,000 back to the lessor.

EXHIBIT 13 Example 3. Statement of Cash Flows*

BIRD CO.
Statement of Cash Flows

	2001	2002	2003	2004
Operating Activities				
Payment of interest	0	(772)	(621)	(455)
Payment of maintenance and insurance	(200)	(200)	(200)	(200)
Financing Activities				
Reduction of capital lease obligation	(2,280)	(1,508)	(1,659)	(1,825)
Net cash flow	(2,480)	(2,480)	(2,480)	(2,480)
Separate Schedule of "Significant Investing and Financing Activities Not Involving Cash"				
Acquisition of equipment through capital leases	10,000			
Satisfaction of capital lease obligation by transfer of equipment				3,000

*Cash outflows in parentheses

The noncash transfer of the van worth $3,000 at December 31, 2004, satisfies the $272 interest obligation and the $2,728 principal obligation (see the amortization schedule in Exhibit 12).

Interest expense and maintenance and insurance expense are reflected on the income statement. Depreciation expense also appears for each year ($10,000 acquisition cost minus $3,000 guaranteed residual value ÷ 4 years = 1,750).

EXHIBIT 14 Example 3. Income Statement

BIRD CO.
Income Statement

	2001	2002	2003	2004
Operating expenses				
Depreciation expense	1,750	1,750	1,750	1,750
Maintenance and insurance expense	200	200	200	200
Financial revenues, (expenses), gains, and (losses)				
Interest expense	(772)	(621)	(455)	(272)

The process of preparing the balance sheet is unaffected. Exhibit 15 illustrates Bird's balance sheet for this guaranteed residual value example.

In summary, capital leases are reported much like an installment purchase. On the balance sheet, a long-term asset (e.g., equipment) and a long-term liability (i.e., lease obligation) are both reported. The income statement shows the changes in the long-term asset (i.e., depreciation expense) and the long-term liability (i.e., interest expense). The statement of cash flows shows the cash repayment of interest and principal.

EXHIBIT 15 Example 3. Balance Sheet

	2001	2002	2003	2004
Assets				
Current assets				
Cash (cumulative effect of lease transactions)	(2,480)	(4,960)	(7,440)	(9,920)
Property, plant, and equipment				
Equipment	10,000	10,000	10,000	0
Less accumulated depreciation	(1,750)	(3,500)	(5,250)	
	8,250	6,500	4,750	
Liabilities				
Current liabilities				
Interest payable	772	621	455	0
Lease obligation	1,508	1,659	1,825	0
Long-term liabilities				
Lease obligation	8,492	6,833	5,008	
Less current portion	(2,280)	(2,280)	(2,280)	
	6,212	4,553	2,728	0
Owners' Equity				
Retained earnings (cumulative effect of lease transactions, ignoring income taxes)	(2,722)	(5,293)	(7,698)	(9,920)

EXAMPLE 3 Journal Entries

1/1/01 Lease inception								
Equipment (or Leased Asset)	10,000							
Lease Obligation		10,000						
Lease Obligation	2,280							
Cash		2,280						
Lease payment dates after 1/1/01			*1/1/02*		*1/1/03*		*1/1/04*	
Lease Obligation			1,713		1,884		2,073	
Interest Payable			567		396		207	
Cash				2,280		2,280		2,280
Adjusting entries at each year-end	*12/31/01*		*12/31/02*		*12/31/03*		*12/31/04*	
Depreciation Expense	1,750		1,750		1,750		1,750	
Accum. Depr.—Equipment		1,750		1,750		1,750		1,750
Interest Expense	772		621		455		272	
Interest Payable		772		621		455		272
12/31/04 transfer of guaranteed residual value to lessor								
Lease Obligation							3,000	
Accum. Depr.—Equipment							7,000	
Equipment								10,000

Footnote Disclosures for Leases

5 Identify important footnote disclosures for leases.

The materiality and prevalence of leasing has led the FASB (and its predecessors) to mandate a number of footnote disclosures about leases (see Exhibit 16). One important disclosure, for example, is a general description of the lease arrangements, including the presence of subleases, contingent rental agreements (i.e., additional lease payments contingent on lessee performance), renewal or purchase options, and restrictions of dividends and financing activities.

Probably the most important footnote disclosure is future cash flows under the lease agreement for the next five years and in the aggregate. This kind of disclosure is critical because only in capital leases are such future cash flows shown on the face of the balance sheet (in present value terms). For operating leases, the cash flows are not shown on the balance sheet.

The existence of cash flow footnote disclosures allows investors and analysts to engage in at least a crude transformation of operating into capital leases (i.e., calculating the balance sheet effect of capitalizing operating leases). The resulting lease liability can be used to adjust debt-to-equity ratios, and thus, aid in the assessment of financial flexibility and risk.

Do investors make these calculations? A great deal of finance and accounting research has documented that footnote disclosures are associated with firm valuation, implying that security markets are efficient with respect to publicly disclosed footnote information. One of the most interesting and comprehensive studies to date is found in Abdel-khalik, et al. (1981).[12] Using a variety of research methods, the authors found that the FASB's mandate to capitalize certain leases had little effect on lessee stock prices and valuations of debt paying ability. Therefore, it appears as if (prior to the FASB's mandate) footnote disclosures of cash flows were sufficient for the market to evaluate profitability and riskiness.[13]

For some industries, operating lease commitments are substantial. For example, in the airline industry, many of the planes are leased under operating leases. To illustrate the magnitude of off-balance-sheet leasing, consider UAL Corporation's 1998 annual report—the company reported $18.6 billion in assets, $15.3 billion in liabilities, and $15.1 billion in future minimum lease payments on operating leases. This means that the company has future obligations (undiscounted) under operating leases almost equal to the total reported liabilities on December 31, 1998. The present value of the $15.1 billion in future operating lease payments is not reported. However, if we used a 50% conversion factor and estimated that the present value of the future minimum lease payments was $7.55 billion (15.1 billion × 50%), it would show that by using off-balance-sheet financing UAL was able to exclude $7.55 billion in liabilities from its balance sheet.

EXHIBIT 16 Summary of Important Lease Disclosures

All leases. A general description of the lessee's leasing arrangements is required. The description must include, but is not limited to: (1) the basis for determining contingent rentals; (2) the existence and terms of renewal or purchase options and escalation clauses; and (3) the existence of dividend or other restrictions imposed by lease.

Operating Leases. Rental expense for each period must be disclosed. An income statement must be presented with separate amounts for (1) minimum rentals, (2) contingent rentals (rentals contingent on some variable such as the prime interest rate), and (3) sublease rental income.

Noncancelable Operating Leases of More Than One Year. As of the latest balance sheet, the following must be presented: (1) the minimum aggregate future lease payments and amounts for each of the five succeeding fiscal years and (2) the total minimum future rentals due from noncancelable subleases.

Capital Leases. For *each balance sheet*, the following must be presented: (1) gross amount of assets recorded under capital leases in aggregated and by major classes according to nature or function and the total accumulated amortization and (2) current and long-term portions of lease obligations. For the *latest balance sheet*, the following must be presented: (1) minimum future lease payments in the aggregate and for each of the succeeding five fiscal years; (2) amount of aggregate future minimum lease payments representing (a) executory costs, including profit, and (b) imputed interest to reduce to present value; and (3) total minimum future rentals due to noncancelable subleases to be received. For *each income statement* the following must be presented: (1) separate disclosure of amortization and (2) total contingent rentals actually incurred.

12. *The Economic Effects on Lessees of FASB Statement No. 13, Accounting for Leases* (Stamford, Conn.: FASB, 1981).

13. Not all material in the study supports this view. Some evidence is presented that analysts and bankers look more favorably on firms classifying leases as operating. Also, survey results point to managers altering financing decisions to avoid capital lease classification.

Sale-Leasebacks

In a sale-leaseback transaction, a seller sells an asset to a buyer, and the buyer leases the asset back to the seller. Therefore, two parties are involved, a seller/lessee and a buyer/lessor. From the seller/lessee's perspective, the lease may be classified as an operating lease or as a capital lease. The seller/lessee capitalizes any profit on the sale of the asset and recognizes it over the lease term. Any loss on the sale would be recognized immediately.

Example of Lease Note Disclosures

To illustrate lease note disclosures, we review the following lease disclosure made by Fruit of the Loom, Inc.

EXHIBIT 17 Fruit of the Loom, Inc. Lease Disclosures in 1997 Financial Statements

Lease commitments (in part): Following is a summary of future minimum payments under capitalized leases and operating leases that have initial or remaining noncancelable lease terms in excess of one year at December 31, 1997.

Year Ended December 31 (in thousands of dollars)	Capitalized Leases	Operating Leases
1998	$ 4,700	$ 33,300
1999	3,600	29,100
2000	3,600	11,400
2001	3,600	5,200
2002	3,600	2,200
Years subsequent to 2002	63,800	1,000
Total minimum lease payments	$ 82,900	$ 82,200
Imputed interest	(32,600)	
Present value of minimum lease payments	$ 50,300	
Current portion	(1,500)	
Long-term capitalized lease obligations	$ 48,800	

Assets recorded under capital leases are included in Property, Plant and Equipment as follows (in thousands of dollars)

	December 31	
	1997	1996
Land	$ 8,300	$ 9,000
Buildings, structures and improvements	58,500	61,700
Machinery and equipment	82,500	82,500
	$149,300	$153,200
Accumulated depreciation	(101,900)	(93,200)
	$ 47,400	$ 60,000

Rental expense for operating leases amounts to $33,700,000, $34,100,000, and $30,200,000 in 1997, 1996, and 1995, respectively.

Fruit of the Loom has about the same minimum lease commitments under capitalized leases ($82,900,000) and operating leases ($82,200,000). However, the capital leases cause obligations of $50.3 million to be recorded on the balance sheet, while the operating lease obligations are not recognized on the balance sheet.

Leases: Cash Flow and Income Variability

6 Analyze the effects of leasing on cash flow and income variability.

An examination of the preceding examples of operating and capital leases confirms that there is little difference between the two in income and cash flow effects. Classifications are different for the two kinds of leases—operating leases show rent expense, while capital leases show interest expense and depreciation expense. However, there is not a great deal of difference in the amounts and variability of the resulting net income. For simplicity, cash flow was identical in the leases we examined.

Regardless of the FASB mandate, operating and capital leases are both long-term debt arrangements in concept. They both involve fixed charges, and thus, increase income and cash flow variability relative to equity financing.

Leasing Transactions for Southwest Airlines

Leasing transactions frequently are material in the airline business. The Southwest Airlines 1998 financial statements provide a good example of the financial statement effects of capital and operating leases. Before continuing this section, review the following sections of the Southwest Airlines 1998 financial statements, which appear in Appendix C:

- Balance Sheet—Assets (property and equipment)
- Balance Sheet—Liabilities (long-term debt, deferred gains from sale and leaseback of aircraft)
- Income Statement—Operating Expenses (aircraft rentals, landing fees and other rentals, depreciation)
- Statement of Cash Flows (Financing activities—Proceeds from aircraft sale and leaseback transactions, payment of long-term debt and capital lease obligations; Operating activities—Amortization of deferred gains on sale and leaseback of aircraft)
- Note 1—Summary of Significant Accounting Policies (property and equipment section)
- Note 2—Commitments (entire note)
- Note 3—Accrued Liabilities (see aircraft rentals)
- Note 4—Long-Term Debt (see capital leases)
- Note 5—Leases (entire note)

Leasing and Southwest Airlines' Liabilities

It is evident that leasing has a significant effect on Southwest Airlines' financial statements. On the liability side, capital leases (including current maturities) constituted 20.9% of Southwest's long-term debt in 1998 ($133,190,000 ÷ $637,671,000, see Note 4), and 20.2% in 1997 ($152,324,000 ÷ $752,324,000). Further, using the balance sheet and information in Note 4, capital leases were 9.1% of total liabilities in 1998 ($133,190,000 ÷ $1,467,425,000) and 11.1% in 1997 ($152,324,000 ÷ $1,368,629,000). Also, accrued aircraft rental liabilities related to operating leases were $121,868,000 and $123,669,000 in 1998 and 1997, respectively (see Note 3).

Note 5 indicates how the off-balance-sheet aspect of operating leases affects the balance sheet. At December 31, 1998, total (undiscounted) minimum lease payment cash flows under capital leases over the lives of the lease agreements were $209,867,000 compared to $3,006,092,000 under operating leases. Therefore, of the total minimum lease payments due under capital and operating leases, 93.5% of the amount ($3,006,092,000 ÷ $3,215,959,000) was in the form of operating leases. If the operating lease obligation of $2,368,164,000 were recorded at just 50% of the amount on the balance sheet (50% × $3,006,092,000 = $1,503,046,000), then total liabilities would increase in 1998 from $1,467,425,000 to $2,970,471,000, a 102.4% increase.[14] If the financial statements were adjusted to include the operating lease adjustment, the 1998 total debt to equity ratio would double, increasing from 0.61 ($1,467,425,000 ÷ $2,397,918,000) to 1.24 ($2,970,471,000 ÷ $2,397,918,000).

Leasing and Southwest Airlines' Assets

On the asset side, capital leases are 2.1% of total assets in 1998 [$97,413,000 (Note 5) ÷ $4,715,996,000 (balance sheet)] and 2.5% in 1997 [$105,457,000 (Note 5) ÷ $4,246,160,000 (balance sheet)]. Notice that Note 5 does not provide information about either the fair value or the depreciated value of operating lease assets nor does GAAP require these disclosures. A financial analyst interested in obtaining an estimate of the fair market value of the property, plant, and equipment might simply communicate with Southwest Airlines and request information about the fair value of the assets under operating leases. However, we have only the financial statements to use in calculating a value. One approach would be to simply use the same 50% adjustment factor that we used in the liability computations. This approach has the benefit of making the pro forma increase in net assets the same as the pro forma increase in total liabilities. Using this approach, property and equipment in 1998 would increase from $4,137,610,000 to $5,640,656,000, a 36.3% increase.

Leasing and Southwest Airlines' Income Statement

In the income statement, the expenses related to capital leases are depreciation expense and interest expense. The financial statements and notes do not allow us to determine exactly how much of the depreciation and interest expense is related to leasing. The expenses related to operating leases are reflected primarily in aircraft rentals and terminal operations space (Note 5), with $306,629,000 and $297,158,000 total rental expense related to operating leases in 1998 and 1997, respectively. As indicated in the previous two sections, if a financial analyst wanted to create pro forma financial statements and capitalize the operating leases, then aircraft rentals would decrease because the expenses would no longer be treated as a period expense; depreciation expense (related to the pro forma net assets) and interest expense (related to the pro forma debt) would increase. We could make some crude calculations of pro forma depreciation amounts (using the information in Note 1—Property and Equipment) and interest amounts (from Note 4).

Leasing and Southwest Airlines' Statement of Cash Flows

There are three leasing amounts that are easily identified in the statement of cash flows. First, the payment of long-term debt and capital lease obligations of $118,859,000 appears in the financing activities section as a 1998 cash outflow. Using the information in Note 4, we could make some allocation of this amount between payment of long-term debt and payment of capital lease obligations. Second, the amortization of deferred gains on the sale and leaseback of aircraft ($15,251,000 adjustment in 1998) is found in the operating activities section. The deferred gains are subtracted because they are included in net income but are noncash amounts. Third, in 1996, the financing activities section indicates that South-

14. Note 7 does not provide the present value of the operating lease payments. This means that the financial analyst who wants to assess the effect of capitalizing operating leases must approximate the present value of the operating lease payments. Rather than proceeding through a present value approximation computation, we simply added 50% of the operating lease cash payments for illustrative purposes. The use of the 50% factor is conservative and probably understates the effect.

west had a sale-leaseback transaction. Any gains on a sale-leaseback transaction are deferred and recognized in future periods. The balance sheet indicates that Southwest had deferred gains of $238,412,000 in 1998 and $256,255,000 in 1997.

Commitments

Note 2—Commitments provides interesting information about Southwest Airlines' commitments to purchase and lease aircraft in future years. Southwest reports commitments to purchase 105 aircraft in future years, with options to purchase an additional 62 aircraft. If a financial analyst were preparing pro forma financial statements for future years, this information would be invaluable.

Summary

Leasing transactions are an integral part of Southwest Airlines' business. Southwest extensively uses operating lease transactions both for aircraft and terminal space. A financial analyst would need to thoroughly comprehend lease accounting before being able to understand the business environment and financial statements of Southwest Airlines.

The External Decision Makers' View of Leases

Leases increase the variability of future cash flows and net income because, whether or not capitalized, leases are associated with fixed cash outflows and fixed expenses. However, if leases are not capitalized (i.e., they are "off-balance-sheet"), then debt-to-equity ratios are smaller, giving the impression that a company is less risky and more financially flexible.

The off-balance-sheet nature of operating leases is no mystery to investors and creditors. GAAP rules require note disclosures of future contractual cash outflows under current lease agreements. Investors and creditors transform these future cash flows into measures of debt that are added to the numerators of debt-to-equity ratios. Thus, accounting rules that keep leases off-balance-sheet are more of a minor nuisance than a real problem to informed external decision makers.

Chapter Summary

Off-balance-sheet financing opportunities, the management of obsolescence risk, and possible tax advantages often result in companies acquiring operational assets by entering into leases rather than by borrowing for purchase. The classification of leases as operating or capital is critical for proper financial statement presentation, especially in regard to balance sheet disclosure. Footnote disclosures of future cash flows are particularly important for leases. Financial analysts need the information to determine future obligations under leasing agreements. We review key lease terminology below.

Four Criteria Used to Determine Capitalization Status

A lease is capitalized if it meets any one of the following criteria:

1. The lease transfers title from lessor to lessee at the end of the lease term.
2. The lease contains a bargain purchase option.
3. The lease term is greater than or equal to 75% of the economic useful life of the asset.
4. The present value of the minimum lease payments is greater than or equal to 90% of the fair market value of the asset.

Lease Term

The lease term includes the fixed, noncancelable period plus certain renewal option periods.

1. Renewal option periods where the renewal option price is considered to be a bargain.
2. Renewal option periods prior to a bargain purchase option date.
3. Renewal periods where the lessor has the option to force renewal.
4. Renewal option periods after the date of a termination penalty option that is considered so large that it is unlikely the lessee will pay the termination penalty.
5. Renewal option periods where the lessee is guaranteeing the lessor's debt used to finance the leased asset.

Minimum Lease Payments

Minimum lease payments, excluding executory costs, include the following amounts:

1. Periodic cash rental payments over the lease term. (To maintain simplicity, we use an even, periodic cash flow payment, either an ordinary annuity or annuity due, throughout each problem.)

Minimum lease payments also include any one time payments.

2. Down payment (made at the beginning of the lease term).
3. Bargain purchase option price.
4. Cancellation fees to be paid to terminate the lease (if we expect the lessee to cancel the lease at some time and pay any stipulated cancellation fees).
5. Guaranteed residual value (the amount of residual value guaranteed by the lessee to the lessor at the end of the lease).

Present Value of Minimum Lease Payments

Using the lower of the lessee's incremental borrowing rate or the lessor's implicit rate (if known to the lessee), the lessee computes the present value of the minimum lease payments. This is the amount used in the 90% test; it is also the amount used to record the leased asset and lease obligation if the lease is capitalized. The exception to this rule is that the asset cannot be recorded at an amount greater than its fair value. If the present value of minimum lease payments is greater than the asset's fair value, then the leased asset and lease obligation are recorded at the asset's fair value; an effective interest rate must then be computed to use in calculating interest expense related to the lease obligation.

Key Terms

bargain purchase option 138
capital leases 137
executory costs 140
fair market value of consideration given 144
guaranteed residual value 140
implicit rate 140
leasing 136
lessee's incremental borrowing rate 140
lessor's desired rate of return 140
minimum lease payments 139
operating leases 137
present value of minimum lease payments 140

Questions

Q1. **Lease Characteristics.** What characteristics of long-term leasing agreements make them equivalent to installment purchases?

Q2. **Operating versus Capital Leases.** How do tax consequences and risk management distinguish operating leases from capital leases?

Q3. **Lease Classification Criteria.** What are the four criteria that determine whether a lessee will classify a lease as operating or capital? How many criteria must be met before the lease is treated as a capital lease?

Q4. **Off-Balance-Sheet Financing and Leasing.** What is meant by the term "off-balance-sheet financing" in the context of leasing?

Q5. **Bargain Purchase Option.** What is a bargain purchase option?

Q6. **Lease Term.** Conceptually, how is the length of the lease term determined?

Q7. **Minimum Lease Payments.** What are minimum lease payments? Give several examples.

Q8. **Lease Discount Rate.** What rule should the lessee apply in choosing the appropriate discount rate for leases?

Q9. **Residual Value.** What is the difference between a guaranteed and unguaranteed residual value? How does a guaranteed residual value affect lessee accounting?

Q10. **Executory Costs.** What are executory costs? Are they a part of minimum lease payments?

Q11. **Operating Lease Cash Flows.** Identify the typical cash flows in an operating lease. How does the statement of cash flows report these flows?

Q12. **Capital Lease Cash Flows.** Identify the typical cash flows in a capital lease. How does the statement of cash flows report these flows?

Q13. **Operating versus Capital Lease.** Identify differences in the balance sheet and income statement accounts that will appear on the lessee's books under capital versus operating leases.

Q14. **Sale-leaseback.** What is a sale-leaseback?

Q15. **Lease Footnote Disclosures.** What are two key footnote disclosures concerning leases that are mandated by FASB rules?

Short Problems

1. **Compute Lease Payments.** Using a financial calculator, compute lease payments under the following scenarios (assume a 10% interest payment and an ordinary annuity):

	1	**2**	**3**	**4**
Title transfer	No	No	Yes	No
Bargain purchase option	No	No	No	$5,000
Number of lease payments	10	8	5	5
Residual value:				
Guaranteed	$3,000	0	$1,000	0
Unguaranteed	0	$3,000	$2,000	0
Fair market value of asset	$40,000	$200,000	$150,000	$100,000

Use the following schedules to report the financial statement effects for items 2 through 5. Make sure to indicate any subclassifications that should be used. IGNORE INCOME TAX EFFECTS. Indicate whether the lease is a capital or operating lease and why. You may also find it helpful to prepare an amortization schedule if the lease is a capital lease.

Statement of Cash Flows
(cash outflows in parentheses)

	Year 1	**Year 2**	**Year 3**	**Year 4**	**Year 5**	**etc.**
Operating Activities						
Investing Activities						
Financing Activities						
Separate Schedule of "Significant Investing and Financing Activities Not Involving Cash"						

Income Statement

	Year 1	**Year 2**	**Year 3**	**Year 4**	**Year 5**	**etc.**
Operating expenses						
Financial revenues, (expenses), gains, and (losses)						

Balance Sheet
December 31

	Year 1	Year 2	Year 3	Year 4	Year 5	etc.
Assets						
Liabilities						
Owners' Equity						

2. **Financial Statements Effects.** Chip Co. produces extra-thick chocolate chip cookies. On January 1, 2001, Chip entered into a 5-year, noncancelable lease of a large mixing machine. The cash price of the machine was $70,000, and the machine's economic useful life was estimated to be five years, with an estimated salvage value of $10,000. Under the terms of the lease, Chip must pay $16,787 annually for five years; the first payment is due at the lease signing date. At the end of the lease term on January 1, 2006, title will transfer to Chip. Chip's incremental borrowing rate is 11%. Chip knows that the rate implicit in the lease is 10%. Chip uses straight-line depreciation for long-lived assets. For convenience, assume that the value of the machine on January 1, 2006, is $10,000.

   Journal Entry Option: Prepare any 2001 journal entries related to the lease. Also, make the January 1, 2006, journal entry at the end of the lease.

3. **Financial Statements Effects.** Micro Inc. uses computer monitoring devices for manufacturing quality control. Because the type and speed of manufacturing varies from year to year, Micro has entered into a three-year, noncancelable lease of monitoring equipment. The equipment has a $100,000 market value and a 10-year useful life. The lease, signed on January 1, 2001, specifies that there is no title transfer or bargain purchase option at the end of the lease on January 1, 2004. The equipment should be worth $50,000 at the end of three years, but Micro does not guarantee any of the residual value. The lessor has set the lease payments at $25,106, with the first payment due December 31, 2001. The rate implicit in the lease is 10% (it is unknown to Micro); Micro's incremental borrowing rate is 12%. Micro uses straight-line depreciation.

   Journal Entry Option: Prepare any 2001 journal entries related to the lease. Also, make the January 1, 2004, journal entry at the end of the lease.

4. **Financial Statements Effects.** Repeat the previous problem, assuming that Micro guarantees the entire $50,000 residual value on January 1, 2004. Also, assume that on January 1, 2004, the asset is worth at least $50,000.

   Journal Entry Option: Prepare any 2001 journal entries related to the lease. Also, make the January 1, 2004, journal entry at the end of the lease.

5. **Financial Statements Effects.** On January 1, 2001, Neverland Builders entered into a noncancelable, three-year lease of an office building that expires on January 1, 2004. The lease payments are $289,948, with the first payment due immediately upon signing the lease. The office building is worth $800,000 with a five-year useful life; it has no estimated residual value at the end of three years due to a perceived decay in the safety of the surrounding neighborhood. Title to the building transfers to Neverland at the end of the lease term. The lessor's implicit rate, known to Neverland, is 9%. Neverland's incremental borrowing rate is 14%.

   Journal Entry Option: Prepare any 2001 journal entries related to the lease. Also, make the January 1, 2004, journal entry at the end of the lease.

Analytical and Comprehensive Problems

6. **Financial Statement Effects.** Using the following key, identify the effects of the following transactions or conditions on the various financial statement components: I = Increase, D = Decrease, NE = No effect.

			Owners' Equity		
Transaction	**Assets**	**Liabilities**	**Contributed Capital**	**Retained Earnings Direct Effect**	**Retained Earnings Through Net Income**
A. Inception of a capital lease					
Ordinary annuity					
Leased asset					
Lease obligation					
Annuity due					
Leased asset					
Lease obligation					
First cash payment					
B. Inception of an operating lease					
Ordinary annuity					
Annuity due					
If expensed					
If capitalized as prepaid					
C. Passage of time when a capital lease obligation is outstanding					
D. Lease payment (capital lease)					
E. Transfer of leased asset back to lessor					
Unguaranteed residual value					
Guaranteed residual value (assuming no gain or loss)					

7. **Capital Leases—Guaranteed Residual Value.** Cranberry Corp. is negotiating a relatively long-term lease agreement; Cranberry wants to keep the lease obligation off of its balance sheet. The leased asset has a fair market value of $200,000 and an economic useful life of ten years. The proposed lease contains no transfer of title clause or purchase option clause. To avoid the 75% of useful life criterion, Cranberry proposed a lease term of seven years. Both Cranberry and the lessor agree that the asset will be worth $50,000 at the end of the seventh year. The lessor has set the annual lease payments (due at the end of each year) to equal $35,810.83. Assuming that Cranberry's incremental borrowing rate is 12% per year, and the lessor's implicit rate is unknown to Cranberry, what is the maximum amount of the $50,000 residual value that Cranberry Corp. can guarantee and still keep the debt off of the balance sheet? If Cranberry agreed to a guaranteed residual value of $30,000, what is the present value of minimum lease payments?

8. **Residual Values.** In the chapter coverage of guaranteed versus unguaranteed residual values, we kept the examples simple. When we moved from the unguaranteed residual value situation in Example 2 to the guaranteed residual value situation in Example 3, we did not change the annual lease payments. In reality, what would likely happen to the annual lease payments if the residual value is guaranteed rather than unguaranteed? Why?

9. **Lease Footnote Disclosures.** Foot Happy Mfg. acquired its office building by entering into a relatively long-term operating lease. Footnote disclosures at December 31, 2001, show the annual net cash outflows on operating leases:

	2002	2003	2004	2005	2006	Beyond 2006
Net rental payments on operating leases (in thousands)	51	54	59	48	48	111

Assuming that Foot Happy's incremental borrowing rate is 12%, compute the following:
a. a crude measure of the lease obligation at December 31, 2001.
b. a crude estimate of interest expense for 2002.
What factors will lead to these estimates being crude measures? What evidence might be gathered to establish the incremental borrowing rate at 12%?

10. **Capital Lease—Minimum Lease Payments.** Egg Beaters Inc. entered into a capital lease to acquire an asset with the following characteristics:

Fair market value	$50,000.00
Lease term	5 years
Guaranteed residual value	$0
Implicit rate	10%
Lease payments (annuity due)	$11,991

a. Compute the present value of minimum lease payments assuming the following information about Egg Beaters' incremental borrowing rate and its knowledge about the implicit rate in the lease agreement:
(i) borrowing rate, 9%; implicit rate known
(ii) borrowing rate, 9%; implicit rate unknown
(iii) borrowing rate, 11%; implicit rate known
(iv) borrowing rate, 11%; implicit rate unknown

b. Recall that the leased asset will also be recorded at the present value of the minimum lease payments because this is the best measure of the fair market value of the consideration paid by Egg Beaters. If Egg Beaters knows that the fair market value of the asset is $50,000, do you see any problems with the asset being recorded in any of your answers in (a)? How would you resolve any inconsistencies?

http://

11. **Financial Statement Analysis—Texas Instruments.** Review the Texas Instruments 1998 financial statements presented at our Web site (http://baginski.swcollege.com). For Texas Instruments, leasing is not a major financing source. In fact, no mention of leases is made in the financial statements themselves. However, the footnote "rental expense and lease commitments" provides information about leasing activities. Using the available information, answer the following questions:

a. What is the total amount of Texas Instruments' minimum lease commitments under noncancelable leases at December 31, 1998?

b. What percentage of Texas Instruments' total operating costs and expenses was lease rental expense in 1998?

12. **Capital Lease Problem.** In this problem, we begin with one basic example. We then alter it to illustrate various combinations of minimum lease payments.

Example 1. The Pile Company agrees to lease an automobile for its chief executive. She picks out a 2001 Lexus with a fair market value (FMV) of about $42,000. The three-year lease, which expires January 1, 2004, calls for no down payment and monthly rental payments (due at the end of each month) of $1,068 for three years. (Pile could alternatively borrow the money to purchase the car at 12% per year.) The lease allows Pile to buy the car at the end of the lease period for $12,000, even though the FMV at that date is expected to be $30,000. The lessee pays executory costs directly and depreciates all assets on a straight-line basis. Also, Pile estimates that the car will have an estimated useful life of four years, with an estimated salvage value of $15,000 at the end of this time. The Pile Co. takes advantage of 10% financing made available from the dealer (0.83% per month) rather than borrow from a bank at 12%. The lease is signed on January 1, 2001, and the automobile is delivered on that day. Pile prepares monthly financial statements.

Required Go through the steps to determine whether the lease is a capital or operating lease (*hint*: it is a capital lease). Determine the amount of the lease liability and leased asset on January 1, 2001. Calculate the amount of interest expense and principal reduction to be recorded on January 31, 2001 (you may find it helpful to prepare a lease obligation amortization schedule), as well as the amount of depreciation expense to be recorded on that date. Also calculate the amount of interest expense and principal reduction to be recorded on February 28, 2001, and the depreciation expense recorded on that date. Assuming that at the end of the three-year lease the Lexus is worth $30,000, describe the final January 1, 2004, lease transaction.

Journal Entry Option: Prepare January 1, 2001, January 31, 2001, and January 1, 2004, journal entries.

Example 2. Assume the same facts as in Example 1, except no purchase option is offered. Instead, the lessee guarantees that the automobile will be worth at least $12,000 at the end of the lease term.

Required Answer the same questions as required in Example 1.

Journal Entry Option: With a bargain purchase option no longer involved, prepare the entry on January 1, 2004, to return the Lexus to the dealer.

Example 3. Assume that Pile Co. was offered the same deal as in Example 2 (no bargain purchase option, guaranteed residual). However, the controller wanted to limit the monthly payment to $900 per month instead of the stated $1,068 per month. Accordingly, Pile made a counteroffer regarding the lease: lease payments of $900 per month at the end of each month for 36 months; a guaranteed residual value of $12,000; a down payment of $5,200; and dealer financing at 10% per year (0.83% per month). The automobile dealer accepted the offer.

Required Answer the same questions as required in Example 2.

CFA Exam-Type Problems

13. Compare the impact of a capital lease versus an operating lease on (a) current ratio, (b) debt/equity ratio. (CFA adapted)
14. If a lease is capitalized, as compared to being treated as an operating lease, the effect on the current ratio and the debt/equity ratio will be: (CFA adapted)

	Current Ratio	Debt/Equity Ratio
a.	increase	increase
b.	increase	decrease
c.	decrease	increase
d.	decrease	decrease

15. Dale Mail plans to lease a computer from Cray Computing Services. It will be a 10-year capital lease with annual payments of $2,400 plus a guarantee of a residual value of $4,000 at the end of the lease. The present value of the lease discounted at the appropriate interest rate of 9% is $17,000. The company uses the straight-line depreciation method. In the first year, the reported lease expense is: (CFA adapted)
    a. $1,700
    b. $2,400
    c. $2,830
    d. $3,320
16. For a lessee capitalizing a lease rather than treating it as an operating lease may lead to: (CFA adapted)
    a. lower lease expense at first, but the difference will eventually reverse.
    b. a higher current ratio.
    c. lower funds from operations.
    d. higher operating income, even though net income is initially less.
17. Which of the following is false? (author constructed)
    a. The lessee uses the lower of the incremental borrowing rate or implicit rate when determining whether to capitalize a lease.
    b. An operating lease is an example of off-balance-sheet financing.
    c. Including a guaranteed residual value makes it more likely that a lessee will capitalize a lease.
    d. A lease is capitalized if the present value of minimum lease payments is greater than or equal to 75% of the estimated fair market value of the leased asset.

Objectives

1 Identify reasons to reduce equity financing.
2 Identify methods of equity reduction.
3 Account for liquidating dividends, stock retirements, and treasury stock transactions.
4 Understand the information presented in the statement of shareholders' equity.
5 Identify reasons to reduce debt financing.
6 Identify methods of debt reduction.
7 Account for debt retirements before maturity.
8 Account for troubled debt settlements and term modifications.

Chapter 5

Financing Decisions—Reducing Outstanding Equity and Debt

In previous chapters, we have discussed issuing equity securities, issuing debt securities, and entering into leasing transactions. We will now discuss the decision to retire debt before scheduled maturity and to reduce the amount of outstanding equity.

The Decision to Reduce Outstanding Equity and Debt

Corporations use the resources obtained from financing activities for various investment and operating purposes. In turn, the funds obtained from investing and operating are used to pay debt as it matures and, along with additional financing, provide the capital for future investing and operating activities. Changes in market conditions, however, may limit the existence of profitable projects in the short term, and possibly the intermediate term. **If cash has been used to fund all profitable projects and an excess of cash remains, this excess is referred to as *free cash flow*.** A common use of free cash flow is to pay dividends to shareholders.

The payment of dividends reduces retained earnings, thus reducing total assets and total financing. However, with the exception of liquidating dividends (discussed later in this chapter), dividends are a return *on* investment. Corporations may choose to provide investors with return *of* investment due to the existence of substantial free cash flow. Corporations return investment by reducing outstanding debt and equity.

The existence of free cash flow is not the sole reason for reducing liabilities and owners' equity. In the following sections, we identify other reasons that are equity or debt-specific.

Equity Reduction

1 Identify reasons to reduce equity financing.

Reasons for Reducing Equity

In addition to having available free cash flow, managers may have many reasons to reduce equity. First, the reduction in equity may be temporary. For example, employee compensation plans often grant options to acquire common stock. To service the possible exercise of options, companies need a supply of their own stock on hand, and temporarily repurchasing shares as treasury stock is one way to provide that supply.

Second, the corporation might repurchase stock simply because it desires to shift the mix of debt and equity financing. The target debt-to-equity ratio (if there is one) will likely vary through time, fluctuating due to economic conditions that change the relative costs of debt and equity as forms of financing (e.g., inflation).

Third, stock buy-backs can be used as a signal of higher future earnings expectations. If prevailing investor beliefs about earnings are too low, stock price will be depressed. The corporation signals that the stock is undervalued (i.e., too "cheap") by buying it back.

Fourth, the corporation may repurchase shares to support stock price. During the mid 1990s, companies generated large amounts of free cash flow during an upturn in the business cycle. It was common news for companies to increase dividend levels and/or implement stock repurchase plans in order to placate shareholders (or deter a potential hostile takeover). For example, in 1995, Chrysler Corporation had amassed a huge cash hoard of over $5 billion to prepare for weathering the next down cycle. (Chrysler's goal was to collect $7 billion.) Although, a hostile takeover was launched by investor Kirk Kerkorian, it eventually collapsed when Kerkorian could not obtain the approximately $2.5 billion in financing needed to effect the takeover. After the unsuccessful takeover attempt, Mr. Kerkorian continued to pressure Chrysler to use the cash hoard to the benefit of shareholders. In response to that pressure, Chrysler increased the quarterly dividend and implemented a $2 billion stock buy-back program. Other stock buy-back programs during 1995 included a $1 billion stock buy-back initiated by Toys "R" Us Inc. and a plan to buy back one million shares of stock in the open market announced by TCBY Enterprises.

Finally, fewer shares outstanding means less dilution of voting power. This may be particularly important if the firm is facing a takeover attempt. If an investor (or block of investors) has acquired a significant portion of the firm's voting shares, then corporate management can target the repurchase of these shares to thwart a takeover attempt. Repurchasing these shares enables the voting rights tied to the remaining outstanding shares to be centralized in the hands of friends of current management (at least current management *hopes* that they are friends). In a process dubbed ***greenmail,*** **an investor may acquire a large block of stock and threaten a hostile takeover unless management buys out the "greenmailer" at a price premium.** During the 1990s, several large investors used greenmail to profit from selected investments.

2 Identify methods of equity reduction.

Methods of Equity Reduction

Corporations can take different approaches to repurchasing their own stock. A common approach to acquiring smaller numbers of shares is the ***open-market purchase.*** **The corporation acquires shares in the same manner that an individual investor would normally acquire shares, through the use of a stock broker.**

Larger share purchases are not effectively handled through a broker. For these repurchases, it is better to deal with all shareholders simultaneously, or with a targeted block of shareholders. There are three oft-used methods for achieving this goal. First, a tender offer could be made. A ***tender offer*** **specifies that the corpora-**

tion will pay a certain fixed price for a fixed period of time to acquire a certain number of shares. When the appropriate number of shares have been tendered to the corporation at the specified price, the offer is withdrawn. A successful tender offer occurred in the 1990s when the Walt Disney Company acquired Capital Cities Corporation (the owner of ABC) pursuant to a tender offer.

A second method of dealing with all shareholders simultaneously is simply an interesting modification of the tender offer. Called a ***Dutch auction*, a corporation gathers information from shareholders on the price that shareholders are willing to accept in exchange for the number of shares that they hold.** The corporation establishes a minimum and maximum price that it is willing to pay for a share, thereby assisting shareholders in setting their offers. The corporation then aggregates the offers and constructs a supply curve that indicates the cumulative number of shares that will be tendered at each price. The corporation then moves up the supply curve until it reaches the desired number of shares to repurchase, and it pays the price at that number of shares to every shareholder at or below that price. The obvious advantage of the Dutch auction is that the corporation pays the minimum price possible for all shares. In a more traditional tender offer, the corporation runs the risk of establishing an unnecessarily high price.

A third method is to **target a specific block of shareholders, identify who they are, and negotiate with them directly.** ***Targeted block repurchases*** are an effective means of heading off takeovers and also dealing with greenmail. The targeted block of shareholders is often interested in acquiring the firm.

3 Account for liquidating dividends, stock retirements, and treasury stock transactions.

Accounting for Equity Reduction

In the following sections, we examine three specific kinds of equity reduction:

- Liquidating dividends
- Stock retirements
- Treasury stock transactions

Our discussion focuses on balance sheet effects and, ultimately, on the statement of shareholders' equity. The effects on the statement of cash flows are simple. Reducing equity with cash is a cash outflow reported as a financing activity. Similarly, the effects on the income statement are simple—there are no effects. The reduction of equity is a distribution to owners, a transaction that does not affect income.

Liquidating Dividends ***Liquidating dividends*** **are payments to shareholders that exceed the balance in retained earnings.** Recall that the two components of owners' equity are contributed capital (common and preferred shares at par value plus additional paid-in capital accounts) and retained earnings. When equity funds are initially raised, contributed capital increases. As income is earned, retained earnings increases. Finally, when dividends are paid, retained earnings decreases. In most states, if the dividend is greater than the retained earnings balance, then the increment must be used to decrease contributed capital.

Example 1. In its first year of operations, the Baily Co. issued 100 shares of $1 par value common stock for $500, earned $50 in income, and paid $75 in cash dividends.

Solution. The following columnar format is useful for summarizing the effects of several transactions on financial statements. It is used here to show the effects of each transaction for the Bailey Co. The shaded columns emphasize that Assets − liabilities (the shaded left column) = Total owners' equity (the shaded right column). The other three columns show how the individual accounts within the owners' equity classification are affected.

EXHIBIT 1 Example 1. Bailey Co.—Regular and Liquidating Dividends

		Owners' Equity			
		Contributed Capital			
	Assets − Liabilities	**Common Stock**	**Additional Paid-In Capital**	**Retained Earnings**	**Total Owners' Equity**
Event					
Stock issue	\$500 ↑	\$100 ↑	\$400 ↑		\$500 ↑
Earnings	50 ↑			\$50 ↑	50 ↑
Dividend paid	**75 ↓**		**25 ↓**	**50 ↓**	**75 ↓**
Balance sheet balances	\$475	\$100	\$375	\$ 0	\$475

As shown in Exhibit 1, the stock issue increased contributed capital by \$500 (\$100 par plus \$400 additional paid-in capital). Earnings increased retained earnings by \$50. The total amount of retained earnings is the *maximum* amount of regular (nonliquidating) dividends that can be paid. This schedule shows the effect of paying out in dividends more than has been earned. The portion of the dividend that is a return *on* capital is \$50. The portion of the dividend that is a return *of* capital (i.e., a reduction of outstanding contributed capital to \$475) is \$25. This amount is recorded and reported as a liquidating dividend. The original investment by shareholders is reduced by the amount of dividends that exceed retained earnings (\$75 − \$50 = \$25).

EXAMPLE 1 Journal Entries

Equity issue		
Cash	500	
Common Stock		100
Additional Paid-In Capital		400
Closing of revenues and expenses into retained earnings		
Revenues	XXX	
Expenses		XXX
Retained Earnings		50
Dividends		
Retained Earnings	50	
Additional Paid-In Capital	25	
Cash		75

Stock Retirements In order to illustrate the effects of stock retirement, consider Example 2.

Example 2. Standard Co. originally issued 1,000 shares of \$10 par value stock at \$30 per share. Over time, Standard has not paid all of its earnings out in dividends. As a result, it has a \$5,000 balance in Retained Earnings. Before any additional equity transactions, the owners' equity section shows the following:

Common stock (1,000 shares at \$10 par)	\$10,000
Additional paid-in capital	20,000
Retained earnings	5,000

Solution. The given data is summarized in the columnar format in Exhibit 2.

EXHIBIT 2 Example 2. Standard Co.—Initial Facts

		Owners' Equity			
		Contributed Capital			
	Assets − Liabilities	Common Stock	Additional Paid-In Capital	Retained Earnings	Total Owners' Equity
Event					
Equity issue	$30,000 ↑	$10,000 ↑	$20,000 ↑		$30,000 ↑
Net effect of earnings and dividends	5,000 ↑			$5,000 ↑	5,000 ↑
Balance sheet balances	$35,000	$10,000	$20,000	$5,000	$35,000

Example 2A. Now suppose that Standard decides to retire 250 shares of stock through an open-market purchase. We will examine the retirement under two scenarios. In the first scenario, the market value of the repurchased shares is $35, higher than the original issue price of $30. In the second scenario, the market value of the shares is $26, lower than the $30 original issue price.

Solution. (Scenario 1) If Standard pays more than the original issue price to retire the shares, then its shareholders collectively receive their investment plus an additional amount. Therefore, the amount paid over the initial issue price ($35 − $30 = $5 × 250 shares = $1,250) is recorded similarly to a dividend by reducing Retained Earnings as shown in Exhibit 3. (Note that the $1,250 is not actually reported as a dividend because it was not declared by the board of directors as a dividend.) Cash is reduced by $8,750 (250 shares × $35). The increases that were recorded in the contributed capital accounts when the shares were originally issued are removed as follows:

Common stock:	250 shares × $10 par = $2,500
Additional paid-in capital:	250 shares × $20 premium at original issuance = $5,000

The remaining reduction of cash is shown as a $1,250 reduction of retained earnings ($8,750 − $7,500 removed from the contributed capital accounts).

EXHIBIT 3 Example 2A. Standard Co.—Stock Retirement (Scenario 1)

		Owners' Equity			
		Contributed Capital			
	Assets − Liabilities	Common Stock	Additional Paid-In Capital	Retained Earnings	Total Owners' Equity
Event					
Equity issue	$30,000 ↑	$10,000 ↑	$20,000 ↑		$30,000 ↑
Net effect of earnings and dividends	5,000 ↑			$5,000 ↑	5,000 ↑
Share retirement	**8,750 ↓**	**2,500 ↓**	**5,000 ↓**	**1,250 ↓**	**8,750 ↓**
Balance sheet balances	$26,250	$ 7,500	$15,000	$3,750	$26,250

EXAMPLE 2A Journal Entry (Scenario 1)

Share retirement		
Common Stock	2,500	
Additional Paid-In Capital	5,000	
Retained Earnings	1,250	
Cash		8,750

Solution. (Scenario 2) If the amount paid to retire the shares is less than the original issue price, we treat the transaction as if the shareholders had to make up a deficiency in their capital accounts. During the firm's life, events have occurred that have caused the market value to fall rather than to rise as expected. The interpretation is that capital has been impaired. Shareholder contribution to eliminate the impairment is recognized by their accepting the shortfall in market price ($30 − $26 = $4 × 250 shares = $1,000) and increasing additional paid-in capital as shown in Exhibit 4.[1]

EXHIBIT 4 Example 2A. Standard Co.—Stock Retirement (Scenario 2)

		Owners' Equity			
		Contributed Capital			
	Assets − Liabilities	Common Stock	Additional Paid-In Capital	Retained Earnings	Total Owners' Equity
Event					
Equity issue	$30,000 ↑	$10,000 ↑	$20,000 ↑		$30,000 ↑
Net effect of earnings and dividends	5,000 ↑			$5,000 ↑	5,000 ↑
Share retirement	**6,500 ↓**	**2,500 ↓**	**5,000 ↓** **1,000 ↑**		**6,500 ↓**
Balance sheet balances	$28,500	$ 7,500	$16,000	$5,000	$28,500

EXAMPLE 2A Journal Entry (Scenario 2)

Share retirement		
Common Stock	2,500	
Additional Paid-In Capital	5,000	
Additional Paid-In Capital—Stock Retirement		1,000
Cash		6,500

In summary, note that retiring equity reduces net assets (Assets minus Liabilities) and reduces Owners' Equity. The allocation of the reduction *within* Owners' Equity is determined by comparing the price paid to retire the shares to their original issue price.[2]

Treasury Stock Transactions At previously noted, **firms may repurchase stock for reissue at a later date.** A common reason for reissue is to compensate employees through stock ownership plans. Although there are two acceptable methods to account for ***treasury stock***—the cost method and the par method—the par method is rarely used. Therefore, we limit our discussion to the cost method.[3] The cost method was designed under the assumption that any treasury stock acquired would be reissued.

Example 3. Assume the original information for Standard Co. in Example 2 (1,000 shares of $10 par common issued for $30 per share; $5,000 cumulative retained

1. Although the distinction is not important from a financial statement analysis perspective, a separate account, Additional Paid-In Capital from Retirements, is used to record the shortfall.
2. If the shares were originally issued at different times, a weighted-average of the original issue prices is often used to accomplish the intra-equity allocation.
3. For 600 companies surveyed, the *1999 Accounting Trends and Techniques* shows 396 instances of treasury stock disclosures (392 common stock and 4 preferred stock) by 392 companies. Of the 396 instances, 357 showed the cost of the treasury stock as a stockholders' equity deduction (as a deduction at the bottom of the section); 24 showed the par or stated value as a deduction in the capital stock section; 12 showed the cost as a deduction in the capital stock section; and 3 had other presentations. Therefore, 93% (369 of 396) of disclosures used the cost method.

earnings; and no share retirements made). Additionally, Standard Co. repurchased 500 shares of the 1,000 outstanding shares to hold as treasury stock. These shares were reacquired at $16,000 (500 shares × $32 per share).

Solution. The financial statement effects are illustrated in Exhibit 5.

EXHIBIT 5 Example 3. Standard Co.—Purchase of Treasury Stock (Cost Method)

		Owners' Equity				
		Contributed Capital				
	Assets – Liabilities	Common Stock	Additional Paid-In Capital	Retained Earnings	Contra Equity Treasury Stock	Total Owners' Equity
Event						
Equity issue	$30,000 ↑	$10,000 ↑	$20,000 ↑			$30,000 ↑
Net effect of earnings and dividends	5,000 ↑			$5,000 ↑		5,000 ↑
Treasury stock purchase	**16,000 ↓**				**$ 16,000 ↑ ***	**16,000 ↓**
Balance sheet balances	$19,000	$10,000	$20,000	$5,000	$(16,000)	$19,000

*An increase in a contra equity account decreases total stockholders' equity.

The $16,000 cash disbursement decreases owners' equity. *Treasury stock is not an asset of the corporation*—a corporation cannot own itself. The payment of cash to owners is a distribution to owners. Under the cost method, this distribution is shown as an increase in the contra equity account called treasury stock. "Contra" accounts reduce the accounts with which they are associated. Thus, a ***contra equity account* reduces equity.** Under the cost method, Treasury Stock is usually shown at the bottom of the stockholders' equity section, as shown in Exhibit 6.

EXHIBIT 6 Example 3. Standard Co.—Stockholders' Equity

Stockholders' Equity		
Common stock, $10 par, 1,000 shares issued, 500 shares outstanding	$10,000	
Additional paid-in capital	20,000	
Total contributed capital		$30,000
Retained earnings		5,000
Treasury stock, at cost		(16,000)
Total stockholders' equity		$19,000

EXAMPLE 3 Journal Entry

Repurchase shares		
Treasury Stock	16,000	
Cash		16,000

We examine the reissue of treasury stock under two scenarios. We then consider a third scenario where the decision to reissue is abandoned and the shares are instead retired.[4]

Example 3A—Shares Reissued at Amount Greater than Repurchase Price. First, assume that the treasury shares are reissued for $34 ($2 greater than the cost of acquiring the treasury shares). Exhibit 7 shows that the increase in cash of $17,000 ($34 × 500 shares) increases owners' equity by (1) decreasing the contra equity

4. For simplicity, we assume that the shares are reissued for cash. Distributing shares for employee compensation purposes is covered in Chapter 12.

account treasury stock by the amount of original acquisition cost, and (2) increasing Additional Paid-In Capital by the $1,000 excess.

EXHIBIT 7 Example 3A. Standard Co.—Reissue Shares @ $34 per Share (Cost Method)

		Owners' Equity				
		Contributed Capital				
	Assets − Liabilities	Common Stock	Additional Paid-In Capital	Retained Earnings	*Contra Equity* Treasury Stock	Total Owners' Equity
Event						
Equity issue	$30,000 ↑	$10,000 ↑	$20,000 ↑			$30,000 ↑
Net effect of earnings and dividends	5,000 ↑			$5,000 ↑		5,000 ↑
Treasury stock purchase at $32 per share	16,000 ↓				$16,000 ↑ *	16,000 ↓
Treasury stock reissue at $34 per share	**17,000 ↑**		**1,000 ↑**		**16,000 ↓ ***	**17,000 ↑**
Balance sheet balances	$36,000	$10,000	$21,000	$5,000	$ 0	$36,000

*An increase (decrease) in a contra equity account decreases (increases) total stockholders' equity.

EXAMPLE 3A Journal Entry

Reissue shares at $34 per share		
Cash	17,000	
Treasury Stock		16,000
Additional Paid-In Capital—Treasury Stock		1,000

It is important to remember that treasury stock transactions are transactions with owners. Thus, even though the net assets increase from the reacquisition and reissue of treasury stock by $1,000, the amount is not reported as income, but rather as contributions by owners.

Example 3B—Shares Reissued at Amount Lower than Repurchase Price. If the treasury shares are reissued at an amount less than the original acquisition cost, say $24, the net effect of treasury stock transactions reduces owners' equity. Paying owners more to reacquire shares than is received at reissuance is equivalent to paying a dividend to shareholders. Thus, the excess of the original acquisition price over the subsequent reissue price multiplied by 500 shares is a $4,000 reduction in Retained Earnings ($32 − $24 = $8 × 500 = $4,000) as shown in Exhibit 8.

EXHIBIT 8 Example 3B. Standard Co.—Reissue Shares @ $24 per Share (Cost Method)

		Owners' Equity				
		Contributed Capital				
	Assets − Liabilities	Common Stock	Additional Paid-In Capital	Retained Earnings	*Contra Equity* Treasury Stock	Total Owners' Equity
Event						
Equity issue	$30,000 ↑	$10,000 ↑	$20,000 ↑			$30,000 ↑
Net effect of earnings and dividends	5,000 ↑			$5,000 ↑		5,000 ↑
Treasury stock purchase at $32 per share	16,000 ↓				$16,000 ↑ *	16,000 ↓
Treasury stock reissue at $24 per share	**12,000 ↑**			**4,000 ↓**	**16,000 ↓ ***	**12,000 ↑**
Balance sheet balances	$31,000	$10,000	$20,000	$1,000	$ 0	$31,000

*An increase (decrease) in a contra equity account decreases (increases) total stockholders' equity.

EXAMPLE 3B Journal Entry

Reissue shares at $24 per share		
Cash	12,000	
Retained Earnings	4,000	
Treasury Stock		16,000

Example 3C—Repurchased Shares Retired. Finally, as illustrated in Exhibit 9, consider the situation where management originally intends to reissue the repurchased shares, but later decides to retire the 500 shares. Retirement involves removing the original issue amounts from the contributed capital accounts:

Common stock:	500 shares × $10 par value = $5,000
Additional Paid-In Capital:	500 shares × $20 original issuance premium = $10,000

EXHIBIT 9 Example 3C. Standard Co.—Retire Treasury Shares (Cost Method)

		Owners' Equity				
		Contributed Capital				
	Assets − Liabilities	Common Stock	Additional Paid-In Capital	Retained Earnings	*Contra Equity* Treasury Stock	Total Owners' Equity
Event						
Equity issue	$30,000 ↑	$10,000 ↑	$20,000 ↑			$30,000 ↑
Net effect of earnings and dividends	5,000 ↑			$5,000 ↑		5,000 ↑
Treasury stock purchase at $32 per share	16,000 ↓				$16,000 ↑ *	16,000 ↓
Treasury stock retired	**(no change)**	**5,000 ↓**	**10,000 ↓**	**1,000 ↓**	**16,000 ↓ ***	**(no change)**
Balance sheet balances	$19,000	$5,000	$10,000	$4,000	$ 0	$19,000

*An increase (decrease) in a contra equity account decreases (increases) total stockholders' equity.

EXAMPLE 3C Journal Entry

Retirement of common stock		
Common Stock	5,000	
Additional Paid-In Capital	10,000	
Retained Earnings	1,000	
Treasury Stock		16,000

The $16,000 is removed from Treasury Stock by retiring the stock. Because the $32 reacquisition price for the treasury shares is greater than the $30 original issue price of the common stock, the difference ($2 × 500 shares = $1,000) is shown as a reduction of retained earnings (i.e., as if it were a dividend).

Treasury Stock Financial Statement Presentation

The following information is from Eastman Kodak Company's 1998 financial statements. This illustrates treasury stock financial reporting using the cost method.

Treasury Stock Disclosures—Eastman Kodak Company and Subsidiary Companies

The following Stockholders' Equity section was reported in Kodak's 1998 annual report.

	In $ Millions December 31	
	1998	**1997**
Stockholders' Equity		
Common stock, par value $2.50 per share, 950,000,000 shares authorized; issued 391,292,760 shares in 1998 and 1997	978	978
Additional paid-in capital	902	914
Retained earnings	6,163	5,343
Accumulated other comprehensive loss	(111)	(202)
	7,932	7,033
Treasury stock, at cost, 68,494,402 shares in 1998; 68,225,820 shares in 1997	3,944	3,878
Total stockholders' equity	3,988	3,155

The Statement of Shareholders' Equity

4 Understand the information presented in the statement of shareholders' equity.

The statement of shareholders' equity (Exhibit 10) documents the increases in shareholders' equity from net income and investments by owners and the decreases in shareholders' equity from distributions to owners. A closer look at a typical statement of shareholders' equity shows that the increases and decreases in equity are traced through individual accounts or account classifications. This examination also presents an excellent opportunity to review equity transactions discussed in this and previous chapters.

EXHIBIT 10 Statement of Shareholders' Equity

	Contributed Capital					
	Common Stock	**Additional Paid-In Capital**	**Retained Earnings**	**Treasury Stock (Cost)**	**Accumulated Other Comprehensive Income***	**Total Shareholders' Equity**
Balance at 1/1/01	X	X	X	X		X
Issued common stock	↑	↑				↑
Retired common stock (reacquired at price greater than original issue price)	↓	↓	↓			↓
Retired common stock (reacquired at price less than original issue price)	↓	↓ ↑				↓
Purchased treasury stock (cost method)				↑		↓
Reissued treasury stock (cost method; reissue price greater than acquisition price)		↑		↓		↑
Reissued treasury stock (cost method; reissue price less than acquisition price)			↓**	↓		↓
Cash dividend			↓			↓
Small stock dividend, recorded at fair value	↑	↑	↓			–
Large stock dividend, recorded at par value	↑		↓			–
Property dividend, recorded at fair value			↓			↓
Stock split						No effect
Unrealized gains and losses on available-for-sale security investments*					↑ (gain) ↓ (loss)	
Unrealized foreign currency translation gains and losses*					↑ (gain) ↓ (loss)	
Minimum pension liability adjustments*					↓	
Net income			↑			↑
Balance at 12/31/01	X	X	X	X		X

*We will cover these topics in future chapters when we discuss the transactions that affect accumulated other comprehensive income. (Note that this item appeared in the Kodak stockholders' equity section.)

**In some states and situations, Additional Paid-In Capital might be reduced instead of Retained Earnings. We ignore those situations here.

The statement of shareholders' equity begins with the balances reported in the balance sheet equity section at the end of the previous year. Total equity is divided into contributed capital (Common Stock and Additional Paid-In Capital), earnings retained in the business (Retained Earnings), reductions in equity caused by holding shares in the treasury (Treasury Stock), and items affecting accumulated other comprehensive income. The final column, Total Shareholders' Equity, indicates whether the event caused total shareholders' equity to increase (↑) or decrease (↓). Every item on the list is classified as an investment by owners or a distribution to owners, except for net income, which is an element of the statement in and of itself, and items affecting accumulated other comprehensive income. (The items affecting accumulated other comprehensive income are covered in subsequent chapters.) Reviewing the list of events yields the following observations:

- Issuing common stock increases Contributed Capital.
- Retiring common stock by reacquiring the stock at a price greater than the original issue price reduces Contributed Capital (by the amount of the original issue proceeds) and reduces Retained Earnings (for the excess of price over the original proceeds).
- Retiring common stock by reacquiring the stock at a price less than the original issue price reduces Contributed Capital (by the amount of the original issue proceeds) and increases Additional Paid-In Capital (by the amount that the current market price is less than the original issue price).
- Purchasing treasury stock reduces Total Shareholders' Equity through a contra equity account. Under the cost method, treasury stock is reported at cost at the bottom of the shareholders' equity section.
- Reissuing treasury stock at a price greater than the acquisition price increases Total Shareholders' Equity. This reissue decreases Treasury Stock and increases Additional Paid-In Capital.
- Reissuing Treasury Stock at a price less than the acquisition price decreases Treasury Stock and decreases Retained Earnings. In substance, this difference in prices is treated as a dividend and, therefore, reduces Total Shareholders' Equity.
- Cash dividends reduce Retained Earnings.
- *Small stock dividends* increase Contributed Capital, the amount summing to the decrease in Retained Earnings (also, equal to the stocks' market value). There is no change in Total Shareholders' Equity. *Large stock dividends* increase Common Stock and reduce Retained Earnings for par value of the shares issued, with no effect on Total Shareholders' Equity. (See Chapter 2 for a more complete discussion of stock dividends, which includes additional options regarding how stock dividends affect shareholders' equity.)
- Property dividends reduce Retained Earnings.
- Stock splits do not affect Total Shareholders' Equity.
- Net income increases Retained Earnings.

Debt Reduction

5 Identify reasons to reduce debt financing.

Reasons for Reducing Debt

One of the major reasons for reducing debt is that too much debt has been issued. A good example is a leveraged buy-out (LBO), where a company purchases another company and finances the acquisition with 100% debt. After the buy-out, a portion of the acquired corporation's assets must be sold in order to service and retire debt; or if the debt bears a high interest rate, cheaper equity will have to be issued to raise cash to refund the debt. Allowing the debt to remain outstanding might make it difficult to raise additional capital in either debt or equity markets. As noted in Chapter 2, debt has its advantages, but a corporation may be perceived too risky if it has excessive debt. During the 1980s, LBOs were very popular, frequently financed by junk bonds. However, during the 1990s, LBOs were announced less frequently, and many of the announced LBOs were unsuccessful. For example, in the 1990s, Conseco, Inc. announced a $2.68 billion LBO bid for Kemper Corporation. The LBO was unsuccessful because Conseco was unable to raise the required funds.

Another reason for early debt retirement is the existence of debt covenants and restrictions. For example, in a financial statements note, Courier Corporation disclosed the following:

Courier Corporation footnote information regarding debt covenants. The long-term debt agreements contain various restrictive covenants including provisions relating to the maintenance of working capital and interest coverage ratios, incurrence of additional indebtedness, and limitations on payment of dividends and certain investments.

A corporation might find that it is close to violating the debt covenants and may have to restructure its financing. Alternatively, the corporation might become aware of profitable projects that it could undertake with current financing, but management may be limited in taking on these projects because of the effects on current ratios or working capital restrictions under the debt covenants.

Finally, economic and firm-specific conditions change over time. A sudden drop in expected inflation could make cheaper debt available. Or, a new product line with low operating risk could reduce the riskiness of the entire firm, and hence, enhance its ability to raise capital that is cheaper than maintaining current debt levels.

6 Identify methods of debt reduction.

Methods of Debt Reduction

Several methods may be used to reduce outstanding debt. One method (covered in Chapter 3) would be to wait until maturity and pay off the maturity value. But if retirement before maturity is desired, other methods are necessary. First, as in the case of equity, an open-market purchase could be initiated. Second, because some debt is callable at a premium, a call could be issued to retire the debt. (A call is similar to an open-market purchase with the price prespecified at the debt's original issue date.) Third, some debt is convertible into common stock, and in some instances, the corporation has a right to force the conversion.

7 Account for debt retirements before maturity.

Accounting for Debt Reduction Before Maturity

In this section, we examine accounting for an open-market purchase or a call of debt (both have identical accounting implications). Below is the long-term bond example and financial statement presentation (Exhibits 11, 12, and 14) from Chapter 3. This example illustrates the effects of debt held to maturity.

Example 4. On January 1, 2001, Worthy Co. issued $1,000,000 in bonds payable. The bonds are dated January 1, 2001, mature in five years, and pay 9% interest every December 31. The issue sold for $891,857. The underwriter deducted $10,000 in fees and remitted the proceeds to Worthy. Worthy has a December 31 fiscal year-end.

EXHIBIT 11 Example 4. Statement of Cash Flows*

WORTHY CO.
Statement of Cash Flows

	2001	2002	2003	2004	2005	2006
Operating Activities						
Interest payments	(90,000)	(90,000)	(90,000)	(90,000)	(90,000)	
Financing Activities						
Bond issue proceeds	891,857					
Transactions costs	(10,000)					
Bond retirement						(1,000,000)

*Cash outflows in parentheses

EXHIBIT 12 Example 4. Income Statement

WORTHY CO.
Income Statement

	2001	2002	2003	2004	2005	2006
Financial revenues, (expenses), gains, and (losses)						
Interest expense	(107,023)	(109,065)	(111,353)	(113,916)	(116,786)	
Bond issue expense	(2,000)	(2,000)	(2,000)	(2,000)	(2,000)	

The amortization table shown in Exhibit 13 documents the interest expense amounts.

EXHIBIT 13 Example 4. Effective Interest Amortization Table

Date	9% Cash Interest	12% Effective Interest Expense	Discount Amortization	Book Value of Debt
01/01/01				$ 891,857
12/31/01	$ 90,000	$107,023	$ 17,023	908,880
12/31/02	90,000	109,065	19,065	927,945
12/31/03	90,000	111,353	21,353	949,298
12/31/04	90,000	113,916	23,916	973,214
12/31/05	90,000	116,786	26,786	1,000,000
	$450,000	**$558,143**	**$108,143**	

EXHIBIT 14 Example 4. Balance Sheet

WORTHY CO.
Balance Sheet
December 31

	2001	2002	2003	2004	2005	2006
Assets						
Current assets						
Cash (net cumulative effect of bond transactions only)	791,857	701,857	611,857	521,857	431,857	(568,143)
Other assets						
Bond issue costs	8,000	6,000	4,000	2,000	0	0

(continued)

EXHIBIT 14 (concluded)

	2001	2002	2003	2004	2005	2006
Liabilities						
Current liabilities						
Bonds payable					1,000,000	0
Long-term liabilities						
Bonds payable	1,000,000	1,000,000	1,000,000	1,000,000		
Less discount	(91,120)	(72,055)	(50,702)	(26,786)		
	908,880	927,945	949,298	973,214		
Owners' Equity						
Retained earnings (through cumulative effect on net income, ignoring income taxes)	(109,023)	(220,088)	(333,441)	(449,357)	(568,143)	(568,143)

Now assume that instead of holding the debt to maturity, Worthy decides to retire the debt on December 31, 2004.

Solution. A look at the December 31, 2004, balance sheet indicates that an asset, Bond Issue Costs, has a $2,000 balance, and the long-term liability, Bonds Payable, has a balance of $973,214. Suppose interest rates have fallen to only 6% for a bond of this type. As a result, the bond should be trading in the market at $1,055,002 on December 31, 2004.[5] Therefore, in an open-market purchase, Worthy would pay $1,055,002 for the bonds.[6] Assume that Worthy paid $1,055,002, plus transactions costs of $20,000 to repurchase the bonds. A loss on the retirement would be computed as follows:

Decrease in assets from cash purchase:	
Decrease in cash	$1,075,002
Write-off of bond issue costs	2,000
Decrease in liabilities:	
Write off of bond payable	(973,214)
Loss on bond retirement (extraordinary)	$ 103,788

Worthy used up more assets than the book value of the debt retired, resulting in a loss. The 2004 cash flow statement (Exhibit 15) would reflect the early cash outflow to retire the debt.

EXHIBIT 15 Example 4. Statement of Cash Flows—Debt Repurchase*

WORTHY CO.
Statement of Cash Flows

	2001	2002	2003	2004	2005	2006
Operating Activities						
Interest payments	(90,000)	(90,000)	(90,000)	(90,000)		
Financing Activities						
Bond issue net proceeds	891,857					
Transaction costs	(10,000)					
Bond retirement				(1,075,002)		

*Cash outflows in parentheses

5. Compute this amount using the remaining cash flows on the bond [$n = 2$; $i = 6\%$; payment (ordinary annuity) = $90,000; future value = $1,000,000].
6. If the bond were callable, the call premium would be known in advance. For example, if the bonds were callable at 102, Worthy would have to pay 102% of par value ($1,020,000) to retire the issue.

The income statement (Exhibit 16) has been expanded to show the disclosure of the loss on the early retirement of bonds. As noted in Chapter 1, accounting standard setters have mandated a "bottom-of-the-income-statement" disclosure for certain items that require special analysis to determine their permanence. An extraordinary item is one classification receiving this treatment. Although extraordinary items are defined as material, unusual, and infrequent (the retirement of bonds clearly does not meet all three criteria), gains and losses from early retirement of debt are disclosed as extraordinary items by FASB rule.[7] *The loss on early bond retirement would be shown net of tax.* For simplicity (and because we have been ignoring income tax effects in our illustrations), we show the effect at its gross amount. If we were to assume a 40% tax rate, the loss would be disclosed at $62,273 [$103,788 × (1 − 0.4)].

EXHIBIT 16 Example 4. Income Statement—Debt Repurchase

WORTHY CO.
Income Statement

	2001	2002	2003	2004	2005	2006
Sales						
Less cost of goods sold						
Gross margin						
Less operating expenses						
Income from operations						
Financial revenues and (expenses), gains and (losses)						
Interest expense	(107,023)	(109,065)	(111,353)	(113,916)		
Bond issue expense	(2,000)	(2,000)	(2,000)	(2,000)		
Income from continuing operations before tax						
Income taxes						
Income from continuing operations						
Discontinued operations						
Extraordinary items						
Gain (loss) on early bond retirement*				(103,788)		
Accounting changes						
Net income						

*In an actual financial statement, this would be shown net of tax, at $62,273.

The balance sheet in Exhibit 17 reflects the removal of all bond-related accounts from the books, the reduction of retained earnings (through the extraordinary loss reported on the income statement), and the reduction of cash required to retire the bonds.

EXHIBIT 17 Example 4. Balance Sheet—Debt Repurchase

WORTHY CO.
Balance Sheet
December 31

	2001	2002	2003	2004	2005	2006
Assets						
Current assets						
Cash (cumulative effect of bond transactions)	791,857	701,857	611,857	(553,145)*	(553,145)	(553,145)
Other assets						
Bond issue costs	8,000	6,000	4,000	0	0	0

(continued)

7. "Reporting Gains and Losses from Extinguishment of Debt," *Statement of Financial Accounting Standards No. 4* (Stamford, Conn.: FASB, 1975).

EXHIBIT 17 (concluded)

	2001	2002	2003	2004	2005	2006
Liabilities						
Current liabilities						
Bonds payable					0	0
Long-term liabilities						
Bonds payable	1,000,000	1,000,000	1,000,000			
Less discount	(91,120)	(72,055)	(50,702)			
	908,880	927,945	949,298			
Owners' Equity						
Retained earnings (through cumulative effect on net income, ignoring income taxes)	(109,023)	(220,088)	(333,441)	(553,145)	(553,145)	(553,145)

*Cumulative cash effect prior to bond redemption (see prior example before repurchase) less amount required to repurchase the bonds ($521,857 − $1,075,002).

EXAMPLE 4 Journal Entry

12/31/04 Bond redemption		
Bond Payable	1,000,000	
Extraordinary Loss on Early Retirement of Bond	103,788	
Discount on Bonds Payable		26,786
Bond Issue Costs		2,000
Cash		1,075,002

Exhibit 18 illustrates an open-market purchase of debt.

EXHIBIT 18 Early Extinguishment of Debt: Atlantic Richfield Company

The following income statement and footnote disclosure reflects ARCO's 1997 early extinguishment of debt.

Income Statement ($ Millions)	
Income before extraordinary item	$1,899
Extraordinary loss	(118)
Net income	$1,781

Note 5: Extraordinary Item
During 1997, ARCO retired debt with a face value of $756 million prior to maturity. The debt repurchase resulted in an extraordinary charge of $118 million against net income, after tax of $74 million.

Accounting for Troubled Debt

8 Account for troubled debt settlements and term modifications.

In this section, we examine a special issue in the reduction of debt financing. Sometimes, firms are unable to pay debt when it is due. Special rules govern the accounting for restructuring troubled debt.[8] Because this is a chapter on financing activities, we examine the issue from the side of the debtor. In an investing activities chapter (Chapter 7), we consider the issue from the creditor's side.

From the debtor's perspective, two situations exist for handling troubled debt: settlement or modification of terms.

Settlement

The following example illustrates how the debtor handles a troubled debt restructuring by settlement.

8. In this chapter, we examine troubled debt from the debtor's perspective. GAAP for the debtor is found in "Accounting by Debtors and Creditors for Troubled Debt Restructurings," *FASB No. 15* (Norwalk, Conn.: FASB, 1977).

Example 5. On January 1, 2001, Sample Candies borrowed $100,000 from Banker, Inc., by issuing a 4-year, $100,000, 10% note payable. The interest is due every January 1. Interest was paid on January 1, 2002. As of December 31, 2002, $10,000 of interest has been accrued, but due to financial difficulties, it is clear that Sample will not be able to pay the debt.

(Scenario 1). Banker, Inc., is willing to settle the debt by accepting a tract of land from Sample Candies. The land has a book value of $40,000 but a fair market value of $85,000.

Solution (Scenario 1). It is clear that the concessions made by Banker result in an economic gain to Sample. Sample owes $110,000 at December 31, 2002—$100,000 note payable plus $10,000 accrued (but unpaid) interest. Sample removes $110,000 of debt by transferring an asset (land) with a fair market value of $85,000 (book value of $40,000). Removing a $110,000 liability and a $40,000 asset from the books must increase Owners' Equity by $70,000. This $70,000 gain is disclosed on the income statement and increases Retained Earnings.

The $70,000 book gain is driven by two events. One is the increase of land from an original historical cost of $40,000 to a current market value of $85,000—a $45,000 ordinary gain from disposing of an investment. The remainder of the gain ($70,000 − $45,000 = $25,000) is from early extinguishment of debt and, hence, is reported as an extraordinary item. This transaction is illustrated in the columnar chart in Exhibit 19.

EXHIBIT 19 Example 5. Sample Candies—Settlement of Troubled Debt (Scenario 1)

		Owners' Equity			
		Contributed Capital			
Event	Assets − Liabilities	Common Stock	Additional Paid-In Capital	Retained Earnings (through effect on net income)	Total Owners' Equity
Debt settlement					
Write up assets to be distributed ($85,000 FMV − $40,000 book value)*	$ 45,000 ↑			$45,000 ↑	$45,000 ↑
Asset distribution**	85,000 ↓ 110,000 ↑			25,000 ↑	25,000 ↑
Net effect	$ 70,000 ↑			$70,000 ↑	$70,000 ↑

*The $45,000 ordinary gain is recognized in the income statement.
**Assets valued at $85,000 are distributed, debt with a carrying value of $110,000 is written off, resulting in an extraordinary gain of $25,000. This gain should be presented net of tax in the income statement.

EXAMPLE 5 Journal Entries (Scenario 1)

Write-up of land to fair value		
Land	45,000	
Gain on Revaluation of Land		45,000
Settlement of debt		
Interest Payable	10,000	
Note Payable	100,000	
Land		85,000
Extraordinary Gain on Debt Settlement		25,000

In summary, the settlement of troubled debt results in an economic gain to the debtor. A book gain (or loss) may also result. If a noncash asset is transferred to settle the debt, the total gain must be separated between an ordinary gain (or loss) and an extraordinary gain. The ordinary gain (or loss) is equal to the difference between the fair market value of the asset given up to settle the debt and its book value. The extraordinary gain is equal to the book value of the debts (principal plus any accrued interest) less the fair market value of the consideration given to retire the debt.

(Scenario 2). In order to settle the debt, Sample Candies issues 10,000 shares of its $1 par value common stock with a fair market value of $8.50 per share, a total value of $85,000. (The valuation at $8.50 per share allows a direct comparison with the previous settlement problem.)

Solution (Scenario 2). A second common way that debt is settled is for a company to issue capital stock. In this case, the stock issue is recorded at its fair market value, and the extraordinary gain to the debtor is the excess of the book value of the debt over the fair market value of the stock issued to settle the debt (Exhibit 20).

EXHIBIT 20 Example 5. Sample Candies—Settlement of Troubled Debt (Scenario 2)

		Owners' Equity			
		Contributed Capital			
Event	**Assets – Liabilities**	**Common Stock**	**Additional Paid-In Capital**	**Retained Earnings (through effect on net income)**	**Total Owners' Equity**
Debt settlement					
Equity issue effect	$ 85,000 ↑	$10,000 ↑	$75,000 ↑		$ 85,000 ↑
Debt retirement effect	85,000 ↓ 110,000 ↑			$25,000 ↑	25,000 ↑
Net effect	$110,000 ↑	$10,000 ↑	$75,000 ↑	$25,000 ↑	$110,000 ↑

This transaction is the equivalent of two transactions—(1) stock valued at $85,000 is issued, increasing Cash and Owners' Equity by $85,000; (2) debt with a carrying value of $110,000 is extinguished using the $85,000 cash (a net asset increase of $25,000), resulting in an extraordinary gain of $25,000 (net of tax) recognized in the income statement.

EXAMPLE 5 Journal Entry (Scenario 2)

Settlement of debt by stock issue		
Interest Payable	10,000	
Note Payable	100,000	
Common Stock		10,000
Additional Paid-In Capital		75,000
Extraordinary Gain on Debt Settlement		25,000

Modification of Terms

Rather than accepting an asset or a right of asset ownership to retire the debt, Banker might modify the terms of the debt, hoping that Sample will be able to perform under less stringent debt service requirements. There are many possible modifications, but one set of rules governs them all. The debtor must first compare the total future cash flows of the restructured debt to the current book value of the debt. The following rules are then applied:

- **If total restructured future cash flows are greater than book value,** then
  1. make no adjustment to book value (i.e., record no gain or loss), and
  2. compute the new interest rate that discounts the total restructured future cash flows to the current book value.
- **If total restructured future cash flows are less than book value,** then
  1. reduce book value to the total of new restructured future cash flows, recording an extraordinary gain in the process, and
  2. recognize no future interest expense; all future cash flows represent the repayment of principal (i.e., the discount rate is zero).

We examine the situation where future cash flows are greater than book value in Example 6. Future cash flows less than book value are covered in Example 6A.

Example 6. Recall the following information about Sample Candies. On January 1, 2001, Sample Candies borrowed $100,000 from Banker, Inc., by issuing a 4-year, $100,000, 10% note payable. The interest is due every January 1. Interest was paid on January 1, 2002. As of December 31, 2002, $10,000 of interest has been accrued, but due to financial difficulties, it is clear that Sample will not be able to pay the debt. Now assume that Banker agrees to modify the terms of the debt on January 1, 2003, by forgiving the $10,000 of accrued interest at December 31, 2002; reducing the principal to $95,000 payable on January 1, 2005; and reducing the interest rate to 9%, with interest payable January 1, 2004, and January 1, 2005.

Solution. The comparison of total cash flows of the restructured debt to the current book value is as follows:

Total cash flows under restructured agreement:	
Principal (due 1/1/05)	$ 95,000
Interest (9% × 95,000 × 2 years)	17,100
	$112,100
Current book value:	
Principal	$100,000
Accrued interest	10,000
	$110,000

Because the total restructured cash flows exceed the current book value, no adjustment of the $110,000 current book value of debt is made. As a result, Sample records no gain, even though concessions were made by Banker. A new interest rate is calculated for future recognition of interest expense:

$$\$110{,}000 = \frac{\$8{,}550}{(1+i)^1} + \frac{(\$8{,}550 + \$95{,}000)}{(1+i)^2}$$

Conceptually, the current book value ($110,000) is the present value of future cash flows at the new effective interest rate. Solving the equation for i yields 0.988%.[9] Thus, interest expense is slightly less than 1% effective interest per year.

EXAMPLE 6 Journal Entries

12/31/02 restructuring		
Note Payable	100,000	
Interest Payable	10,000	
Restructured Note Payable		110,000
12/31/03 interest accrual		
Restructured Note Payable	7,463	
Interest Expense	1,087*	
Interest Payable		8,550
*$110,000 note payable × 0.988% new effective interest rate		
1/1/04 interest payment		
Interest Payable	8,550	
Cash		8,550

9. Using a financial calculator to calculate $i = 0.988\%$, the present value parameters are $n = 2$; future value = $95,000; present value = $110,000; and payment (ordinary annuity) = $8,550.

Example 6A. Assume that Banker made all the concessions given in Example 6, except that the principal was reduced to $80,000.

Solution. The comparison of cash flows to book value is as follows:

Total cash flows under restructured agreement:	
Principal (due 1/1/05)	$ 80,000
Interest (9% × 80,000 × 2 years)	14,400
	$ 94,400
Current book value:	
Principal	$100,000
Accrued interest	10,000
	$110,000

Because total cash flows are less than the current book value, Sample recognizes an extraordinary gain of $15,600, equal to the write-down of debt from $110,000 to $94,400 (i.e., a write-off of $10,000 in accrued interest payable and a reduction in notes payable from $100,000 to $94,400). Solving the following equation for *i* yields a zero effective interest rate:

$$\$94{,}400 = \frac{\$7{,}200}{(1+i)^1} + \frac{(\$7{,}200 + \$80{,}000)}{(1+i)^2}$$

Therefore, no future interest expense is recorded by Sample. The receipt of $94,400 of future cash flows reduces the $94,400 book value to zero.

EXAMPLE 6A Journal Entries

12/31/02 restructuring		
Note Payable	5,600	
Interest Payable	10,000	
Extraordinary Gain on Restructuring		15,600
12/31/03 interest accrual		
No entry		
1/1/04 interest payment		
Note Payable	7,200	
Cash		7,200

This accounting can be described as conservative because future cash flows must markedly decrease before the debtor can recognize a gain. However, the accounting is contrived. Did Sample's effective interest rate fall from 10% to less than 1% (or 0%) when Sample experienced financial difficulties? It is more likely that the effective rate rose dramatically due to Sample's increased riskiness. If we applied higher interest rates to the same or lower future cash flows, then the fair market value of the debt would be substantially below its book value. The result of the conservative accounting is to minimize any gains recognized by debtors who experience difficulty and restructure debt agreements. It is easy to see why the FASB did not want those companies experiencing financial distress to be able to record large gains.

The accounting for troubled debt restructurings is controversial to say the least. We consider the accounting from the investor's side when we study investments in Chapters 6–8. The investors are usually banks, savings and loans, and insurance companies. In the current economic environment, the controversy is even more intense on the investment side.

The External Decision Maker's View of Equity and Debt Reductions

Debt Reductions

The decision to retire debt before its maturity is driven primarily by publicly available information about economywide conditions (e.g., changes in interest rates). It is important to remember that any gains and losses reported for early debt reductions occurred during the periods of time when conditions such as interest rates changed. That is, the market value of debt changed even though book value did not. GAAP requires note disclosure of the fair market value of ***financial instruments***, allowing investors to estimate any gains or losses on early debt reduction on a timely basis. Actual extraordinary gains and losses disclosed on the income statement are unlikely to convey new information.

Debt reductions decrease financial risk; with less debt outstanding, financial flexibility of the firm is generally increased. As new profitable projects are discovered, financing with relatively cheap debt will likely be available.

Equity Reductions

For a given level of debt in the capital structure, equity reductions increase financial risk because the debt to equity ratio is also increased. However, this direct effect of equity reduction seems to be less important than the signaling implications of equity reduction. Why did the firm buy back its common stock? Is it running out of profitable products and thus returning capital to investors so that they can reinvest in other firms?

Stock buy-backs have been argued to be a strong signal that managers expect increased future earnings—that managers believe the stock is underpriced because investors have not incorporated increased earnings expectations into security prices. If you are wondering why managers who expect increased earnings don't just issue a press release to forecast higher future earnings, consider the damage to their reputations and potential legal ramifications if their forecasts turn out to be incorrect. Stock buy-backs represent a signaling mechanism that does not impose these dangers on the manager.

Southwest Airlines' Equity and Debt Reduction

In Southwest Airlines' 1998 financial statements, which are provided in Appendix C, review the statement of cash flows (financial activities section), the statement of stockholders' equity, Note 4 (long-term debt), and Note 7 (common stock). Note 4 shows $121,324,000 in current maturities of long-term debt at December 31, 1997. The 1998 statement of cash flows shows that Southwest paid $118,859,000 on long-term debt. (There is no indication why these two amounts are different—it seems that the amount paid in 1998 should be greater than or equal to the December 31, 1997, current portion.) A large portion of the 1998 debt payment relates to the payment of the 9.25% notes due in 1998 (see Note 4). During 1998, Southwest used $100 million to repurchase 4,885,763 shares of treasury stock at an average cost of $20.47 per share (Note 7 and the statement of stockholders' equity). No stock was retired.

Summary

When cash flow from operations exceeds the cash needed to fund all profitable investments, corporations may reduce outstanding equity and debt financing. Reduction of equity financing involves outflows of cash and corresponding reductions in owners' equity. No gains or losses occur on equity transactions. Reductions in equity can be temporary (if the company repurchases treasury stock) or permanent (if the company repurchases and retires the stock). By definition, the treasury stock classification signals that the company intends to reissue the stock.

The accounting for reduction of debt financing depends upon whether the payments are scheduled or unscheduled (normally early). As we discussed in Chapter 3, if debt payments are made according to scheduled maturities, no gain or loss occurs. However, as discussed in this chapter, if debt is repaid early, an extraordinary gain or loss often results because the amount of consideration given to reduce outstanding debt is rarely equal to the amortized book value of the debt.

Accounting for troubled debt depends upon whether the debt is settled (usually by issuing stock or exchanging assets) or whether the terms of the debt agreement are modified. In a settlement, the debt and any related accounts (e.g., Interest Payable, Unamortized Bond Issue Costs) are written off and an extraordinary gain is recorded (we assume that in a troubled debt situation, the debtor always has an economic gain and the creditor always has an economic loss). Additionally, if the company transfers assets to settle the debt, the assets are written up (down) to fair market value before the debt settlement, and an ordinary gain (loss) is recorded. If the terms of the debt are modified, then either no gain is recorded by the debtor (when the total of future cash flows is greater than the current book value of the debt) or an extraordinary gain is recorded (when the total of future cash flows is less than the current book value of the debt).

Changes in the mix of debt and equity affect the riskiness of the firm. This, in turn, affects the return that investors require on the firm's debt and equity securities. Comparative balance sheets and the statement of cash flows describe the accrual and cash flow effects of the reduction of financing.

Key Terms

contra equity account 168
Dutch auction 164
financial instrument 182
free cash flow 162
greenmail 163
liquidating dividends 164
open-market purchase 163
targeted block repurchases 164
tender offer 163
treasury stock 167

Questions

Q1. **Free Cash Flow.** What is free cash flow? How does it relate to the decision to reduce outstanding financing?

Q2. **Dividends—Return of Capital.** Discuss dividend payments in the context of a return *on* capital versus a return *of* capital.

Q3. **Repurchase Common Stock—Open-Market Purchase.** What is an open-market purchase of common stock?

Q4. **Greenmail.** What is greenmail?

Q5. **Repurchase Common Stock.** For what reasons might a corporation repurchase common stock?

Q6. **Dutch Auction.** How does a Dutch auction differ from a more traditional tender offer?

Q7. **Liquidating Dividend.** What is a liquidating dividend?

Q8. **Treasury Stock Classification.** Is treasury stock an asset of the corporation? Why or why not?

Q9. **Treasury Stock Methods.** What are the two acceptable methods of accounting for treasury stock transactions? Which is the preferred method?

Q10. **Reduce Outstanding Debt.** Why might a corporation need to reduce outstanding debt?

Q11. **Reduce Outstanding Debt.** List several specific methods of debt reduction.

Q12. **Early Retirement of Debt.** How is the gain or loss on early retirement of debt computed? How is it reported? What economic events cause the gain or loss to occur?

Q13. **Stockholders' Equity.** What are the components of stockholders' equity?

Q14. **Troubled Debt.** What are the two ways in which borrowers and lenders handle troubled debt?

Q15. **Troubled Debt.** For troubled debt, what is the important comparison in the modification of terms that determines whether a gain will be reported by the debtor?

Q16. **Troubled Debt.** In a troubled debt modification of terms, if a reduction of book value is necessary, will future interest expense be recognized by the debtor? Why or why not?

Short Problems

Use the following schedule to demonstrate the accounting treatment of items 1–5. As shown in the text, use arrows to indicate increases and decreases in the components of owners' equity.

		Owners' Equity				
		Contributed Capital				
Event	**Assets – Liabilities**	**Common Stock**	**Additional Paid-In Capital**	**Retained Earnings**	***Contra Equity* Treasury Stock**	**Total Owners' Equity**

Journal Entry Option: After completing the chart, make any necessary journal entries to reflect the transaction(s).

1. **Effect on Owners' Equity—Liquidating Dividend.** Marin Properties properly issued a liquidating dividend of $2,000,000. Prior to the transaction, Marin had additional paid-in capital of $10,000,000.

2. **Effect on Owners' Equity—Repurchase and Retire Common Stock.** Pebco Inc. decided to retire 10% of its outstanding common stock through an open-market purchase. Pebco originally issued 40,000 shares of $1 par value common stock for $8 per share. Pebco paid $9.50 per share to reacquire and retire the stock.

3. **Effect on Owners' Equity—Repurchase and Retire Stock.** Strawberry Co. originally issued one million shares of $1 par value common stock for $3. Strawberry reacquired and retired 120,000 shares by paying $2.75 per share.

4. **Effect on Owners' Equity—Treasury Stock Transactions.** Popboys Co. has the following shareholders' equity section at the beginning of the year on January 1:

Common stock ($1 par, 300,000 shares issued and outstanding)	$ 300,000
Additional paid-in capital	900,000
Retained earnings	1,000,000

The following treasury stock transactions occurred during the year.
a. Popboys reacquired 10,000 shares to hold as treasury stock, paying $3 per share.
b. Popboys reissued 5,000 of the shares a few months later for $3.25 per share.
c. Popboys retired the remaining 5,000 shares.
Popboys uses the cost method for treasury stock transactions.

5. **Effect on Owners' Equity—Treasury Stock Transactions.** Terra Inc. has the following shareholders' equity section at the beginning of the year on January 1:

Common stock ($1 par, 100,000 shares issued and outstanding)	$ 100,000
Additional paid-in capital	800,000
Retained earnings	1,650,000

The following treasury stock transactions occurred during the year.
a. Terra reacquired 20,000 shares to hold as treasury stock, paying $11 per share.
b. Terra reissued 5,000 of the shares for $10 per share.
c. Terra retired the remaining 15,000 shares.
Terra Inc. uses the cost method to account for treasury stock transactions.

Problems 6–10 do *not* require the use of the preceding schedules.

6. **Bond Retirement—Bonds Called.** On December 21, 2001, Green Co. retired a $1,000,000 bond issue. The bond's original maturity date was December 31, 2003. On the date of retirement, the bonds had a book value of $951,000. Green Co. called the bonds at 102, the pre-established call premium listed in the indenture agreement.
a. Compute Green's gain or loss on bond retirement.
b. How would the gain or loss be disclosed? Why?

Journal Entry Option: Prepare the journal entry to record the retirement.

7. **Bond Retirement—Bonds Called.** Makepeace Co. had the following bond issue outstanding at July 1, 2001:

Bond payable	$1,000,000
Discount on bond payable	150,000
Unrecognized bond issue costs	30,000

Compute the gain or loss on bond retirement assuming Makepeace called the bonds at 101.

Journal Entry Option: Prepare the journal entry to record the retirement.

8. **Troubled Debt—Debt Settlement.** On January 1, 2001, Garden Co. borrowed $200,000 from Insurance Co. by issuing a 5-year, 16% note payable. The interest, due each January 1, was not paid at January 1, 2002, because of Garden's financial situation. Believing that Garden would soon go bankrupt, Insurance accepted land worth $150,000 in settlement of the debt. The land was recorded in Garden's financial records at its cost of $145,000.
   a. Compute Garden's gain or loss related to the settlement of the debt.
   b. How will the gain or loss be disclosed in the financial statements?

Journal Entry Option: Prepare Garden's journal entry to record the debt settlement.

9. **Troubled Debt—Modified Debt Agreement.** Pine Straw Suppliers is indebted to Big Bank in the amount of $50,000 principal plus $5,000 of accrued interest on January 1, 2001. Big Bank restructures this debt to avoid forcing Pine Straw into bankruptcy. Under the terms of the modified agreement, Pine Straw must pay Big Bank $4,000 in interest at the end of each of the next four years (beginning December 31, 2001) and $40,000 at the end of December 31, 2005.
   a. How much gain will Pine Straw report on January 1, 2001, at the date of restructuring?
   b. How much interest expense will Pine Straw report in 2001?

Journal Entry Option: Prepare Pine Straw's 2001 journal entries related to the debt.

10. **Troubled Debt—Modified Debt Agreement.** Chip Building Supply is indebted to National Bank on January 1, 2001, in the amount of $100,000 principal plus $10,000 of accrued interest. National Bank restructures this debt to avoid forcing Chip into bankruptcy. Under the terms of the modified agreement, Chip must pay National $8,000 in interest at the end of each of the next two years (beginning December 31, 2001) and $85,000 on December 31, 2005.
    a. How much gain will Chip report on January 1, 2001?
    b. How much 2001 interest expense will Chip report?

Journal Entry Option: Prepare Chip Building Supply's 2001 journal entries related to the debt.

11. **Effect on Shareholders' Equity.** Using arrows to indicate an increase or a decrease, fill in the following table that summarizes the effects of equity transactions:

	Statement of Shareholders' Equity				
	Common Stock	**Additional Paid-In Capital**	**Retained Earnings**	**Treasury Stock (Cost Method)**	**Total Shareholders' Equity**
Balance at 1/1/01	X	X	X	X	X
Issued par value common stock at a premium					
Retired common stock (reacquired at price greater than original issue price)					
Retired common stock (reacquired at price less than original issue price)					
Purchased treasury stock (cost method)					
Reissued treasury stock (cost method; reissue price greater than acquisition price)					
Reissued treasury stock (cost method; reissue price less than acquisition price)					
Cash dividend					
Small stock dividend					
Large stock dividend					
Net income					
Balance at 12/31/01	X	X	X	X	X

12. **Debt Refunding.** On January 1, 1991, Peterson Co. issued $1,000,000 of 15%, 20-year bonds at par. These bonds were callable at 104, due January 1, 2011, with annual interest payable each December 31. On January 1, 2001, Peterson considers refunding the bonds by calling the old bonds and issuing new ten-year notes. The new notes would be issued for $990,000. The terms of the new notes are as follows: $1,000,000 in 10-year, 9% notes due January 1, 2011, with interest paid annually on December 31.
    a. Determine whether it is economically advantageous for Peterson to refund the debt on January 1, 2001.
    b. Assume that Peterson does refund the debt. Compute the gain or loss on refunding.

Journal Entry Option: Make the journal entry to reflect the refunding.

Analytical and Comprehensive Problems

http://

13. **Financial Statement Analysis: Texas Instruments.** Complete 1998 financial statements for Texas Instruments are available at our Web site (http://baginski.swcollege.com). Review the liabilities and stockholders' equity section of the balance sheet; the financing activities section of the statement of cash flows; the statement of stockholders' equity, and two notes: Lines of Credit and Stockholders' Equity.
    a. What was the amount paid on long-term debt in 1998? How much of this amount was scheduled and how much was unscheduled?
    b. Was any stock repurchased during 1998, either through treasury stock transactions or repurchased and retired?

14. **Effect of Using Free Cash Flow on Financial Statements.** Consider the following December 31, 2001, financial information about the Benard Co.

BENARD CO.
Financial Statement Information

Cash	$10,000,000
Other assets	60,000,000
Total assets	$70,000,000
Current liabilities	$ 1,000,000
Long-term debt (stated rate is 8%, paid annually)	29,000,000
Common stockholders' equity	40,000,000
Total liabilities and stockholders' equity	$70,000,000
2001 net income	$5,000,000
Number of common shares outstanding	1,000,000
Earnings per share	$5.00
Current stock price per share	$40

Benard has $5,000,000 in free cash flow and management is considering the following options: (1) do nothing, in which case Benard can earn 10% by investing the $5,000,000; (2) pay $5,000,000 face value of long-term debt (assume all $29 million in 8% long-term debt was issued at face value and its current fair market value is $5,000,000); or (3) repurchase 125,000 shares of common stock at its current market price of $50. Use a static analysis (i.e., use the numbers above as if they will continue into the future) to compare and contrast the effects of the choices on Benard's financial statements. Assuming that the elements comprising Benard's net income are constant, what should be the effect of each of the alternatives on Benard's stock price (assuming that the current price to earnings ratio does not change). Assume an income tax rate of 40%. Although we have not yet covered the topic of earnings per share (EPS), assume that EPS is defined as Net income ÷ Number of common shares outstanding. What is the effect of each of the alternatives on EPS?

CFA Exam-Type Problems

15. Because of a court-imposed settlement, a creditor enters into a debt restructuring agreement on an overdue note receivable of $600,000 plus accrued interest of $32,000. The agreement requires the debtor to pay the creditor $400,000 two years from now, plus annual interest of $40,000 (10 percent is the current rate on an investment in this risk classification). At the time of the restructuring, the debtor must recognize a gain of: (CFA adapted, with slight modifications by author)
    a. $0
    b. $152,000
    c. $200,000
    d. $232,000

The following information is used for problems 16 and 17. On January 1, 2001, the McVay Co. had a $2,000,000 note payable outstanding to First National Bank. Associated with the note was accrued interest payable of $20,000.

16. If McVay issued common stock with a par value of $1,000,000 and a fair market value of $1,800,000 to satisfy the note payable, the following should be recorded: (author constructed)
    a. $0 gain
    b. $200,000 gain
    c. $220,000 gain
    d. $1,200,000 gain

17. If McVay issued land to satisfy the debt with a book value of $1,900,000 and a fair market value of $1,700,000, the following should be recorded: (author constructed)
    a. A loss on write-up of assets of $200,000 and an ordinary gain of $320,000.
    b. No gain (loss) on write-up of assets and an extraordinary gain of $320,000.
    c. A loss on write-up of assets of $200,000 and an extraordinary gain of $320,000.
    d. A loss on write-up of assets of $200,000 and an extraordinary gain of $300,000.

18. On July 1, 2002, the Taylor Co. repurchased and retired bonds outstanding. These bonds had a principal of $10,000,000, unamortized bond discount of $1,500,000, and unamortized bond issue costs of $75,000. The repurchase price was $8,750,000. Taylor should report the following in its 2002 financial statements: (author constructed)
    a. $175,000 extraordinary loss
    b. $250,000 extraordinary loss
    c. $325,000 extraordinary loss
    d. $2,675,000 extraordinary loss

Objectives

1 Describe cash flows related to debt and equity securities.

2 Explain the effects of debt and equity transactions on the financial ratios identified in Module A.

3 Describe the balance sheet and income statement adjustments made by many external users in the process of analyzing the effects of debt and equity securities on the profitability and risk of the firm.

Module B

The External Users' Assessment of Management's Debt and Equity Financing Activities

In this module, we review the cash flow effects of debt and equity financing activities and several important profitability and risk ratios affected by these activities. We then illustrate how external users (principally financial analysts) can use financial statement information (primarily contained in accompanying notes) to make pro forma adjustments to the financial statements. The main example illustrates how an external user could restate financial statements to reflect the capitalization of operating leases.

The Effects of Financing Activities on Cash Flows—A Review

1 Describe cash flows related to debt and equity securities.

Debt and equity holders primarily make investment decisions based on the cash flows that *they* will receive (i.e., principal and interest for debt investments, dividends for equity investments). A key determinant of cash flows to debt and equity investors is the *firm's cash flow* from operating, investing, and financing activities. To this point in the text, we have examined financing activities. Accordingly, in the first section of this module we review several sources and uses of cash related to financing activities reported in the statement of cash flows. We also discuss potential adjustments to the statement of cash flows made by financial analysts.

Cash Inflows: Debt and Equity Transactions

Cash proceeds from debt and equity issues are reported as cash inflows from financing activities in the statement of cash flows. Occasionally, debt or equity is issued as a means of acquiring an investment rather than as a direct source of cash. If debt or equity is issued for such noncash consideration, a separate schedule listing the noncash transactions accompanies the statement of cash flows. The analyst can use the information in this schedule to adjust the statement of cash flows to show a cash inflow from financing and a cash outflow from investing.

For example, assume that Company A borrowed $10,000,000 from a bank, using the cash to purchase $10,000,000 in equipment; Company B purchased $10,000,000 in equipment by giving the seller a $10,000,000 note payable. These transactions are reported differently on the statement of cash flows. Company A shows a $10,000,000 cash inflow in the financing activities section and a $10,000,000 cash outflow in the investing activities section. Company B shows no cash flow effects—it provides a separate schedule reporting that a $10,000,000 note payable was exchanged for equipment. Many financial analysts would make an adjustment to Company B's statement of cash flows to reflect the issuance of the note payable as a financing transaction and the acquisition of the equipment as an investing transaction.

To illustrate such an adjustment, consider the 1998 statement of cash flows of Suiza Foods Corporation, which reports comparative data for 1998 and 1997. The following supplemental schedule accompanied the statement of cash flows:

Suiza Foods Corporation—Supplemental schedule of significant noncash investing and financing activities:

Year Ended December 31 (in thousands)	1998	1997
Noncash transactions:		
Issuance of notes payable and common and preferred stock in connection with business and property acquisitions	$136,751	$17,049
Issuance of mandatorily redeemable preferred securities and subsidiary preferred and common securities in connection with two acquisitions	220,000	0

This schedule reports that during 1998, Suiza issued notes payable, common stock, and preferred stock with business and property acquisitions. An analyst could use this information to make pro forma adjustments to Suiza's statement of cash flows to show the issuance of notes and stock as financing activities and acquisition of property and businesses as investing activities. Should the analyst make these adjustments? The purpose of adjusting financial statements on a pro forma basis is to provide more refined and/or more standardized information for decision making. If analysts find that such adjustments lead to better decisions, then the adjustments should be made. In the case of noncash transactions, most analysts make the adjustments to convert "financing investment" transactions to the two-step transaction of "financing for cash inflow" and "cash outflow for investment."

Cash Outflows: Interest on Debt and Distribution of Dividends

Periodic payments of interest are required by most debt investors. Similarly, common and preferred equity holders expect dividends on a regular basis.[1] Because the issuance of debt and equity are classified as financing transactions, it would seem logical that making interest payments on debt and dividend payments on equity would also be classified as financing transactions. However, GAAP does *not* specify that all cash outflows related to debt and equity are to be classified as financing transactions. *Under GAAP, cash dividend distributions are classified as financing cash outflows, while interest payments are defined as operating cash outflows.* The FASB classified interest payments as operating activities to reserve the operating

1. With zero coupon bonds, debt investors forego current interest payments for larger maturity values. Common equity investors may also prefer that the corporation reinvest the dividends.

activities section of the cash flows statement to reflect the cash flow counterpart of net income—interest expense is deducted in arriving at net income, while dividends paid are not.

A consequence of this classification of interest payments as operating outflows is that two (otherwise identical) firms that choose different capital structures, one with 100% debt and the other with 100% equity, would report different cash flows from operations. The firm financing with equity will report higher operating cash inflows and higher financing cash outflows than the firm financing with debt. To obtain comparable operating and financing activities cash flows for these firms, a user must make pro forma adjustments to one company's statement of cash flows. The most common adjustment is to treat the interest payment as a financing activity rather than an operating activity. This requires the user to add interest payments back in the operating activities section, thereby increasing cash inflows from operating activities. The interest payments must then be deducted in the financing activities section.[2]

Cash Outflows: Lease Payments

In Chapter 4, we learned that lease payments are classified as operating cash outflows if the lease is classified as an operating lease. If the lease is classified as a capital lease, then the payments are allocated as an operating outflow (interest expense) and as a financing outflow (principal reduction).

Analysts frequently reclassify lease payments within the statement of cash flows because most analysts consider leasing to be a form of financing. Thus, operating lease rent payments are moved from operating activities to financing activities in the pro forma statement of cash flows. For capital leases, the interest portion of the lease payment is moved from operating activities to financing activities. The principal reduction portion of a lease payment does not need reclassification because it is already classified as a financing activity.

For example, assume that Lee Company had operating lease payments of $2,000,000 and that if the lease had been capitalized, interest expense related to the lease would be $175,000, and principal reduction would be $1,825,000. Assume that a financial analyst wants to make pro forma financial statement adjustments to treat all leasing transactions as financing activities. If the lease were an operating lease, then the analyst would increase cash flows from operating activities by $2,000,000 and decrease cash flows from financing activities by $2,000,000. If the lease were a capital lease, then the analyst would increase cash flows from operating activities by $175,000 and decrease cash flows from financing activities by $175,000 (the $1,825,000 would already be classified as a financing activity).

Cash Outflows: Reductions of Debt Principal and Equity

Any cash payments to reduce the principal portion of long-term debt or to reduce outstanding common or preferred shares (either through treasury stock or stock retirement transactions) are classified as financing cash outflows.

Financing Cash Flows of TCBY

In Appendix D, we provide the November 29, 1998, financial statements of TCBY Enterprises, Inc. In this section, we illustrate how to make pro forma adjustments to the TCBY statement of cash flows. Before continuing in this section, briefly review TCBY's statement of cash flows, paying particular attention to the financing activities section.

2. If the indirect method is used in the operating activities section of the statement of cash flows, interest payments may not be disclosed. These amounts can either be obtained from financial statement footnotes, or estimated using the principal amounts of balance sheet debt, stated interest rates, and issue dates disclosed in the notes. The indirect method is explained in Chapter 9.

Near the bottom of the statement of cash flows, the "(Decrease) Increase in Cash and Cash Equivalents" for 1998, 1997, and 1996 is reported. For the years 1996–1998, the increases (decreases) in cash and cash equivalents are $9,353,354; $4,774,685; and ($2,769,550), respectively. Thus, over the three-year period, TCBY went from increasing to decreasing cash and cash equivalents. The "Financing Activities" section of the statement includes cash inflow and outflow transactions typically found in the debt and equity areas. Net cash outflows were large during each of the three years: $15,601,609; $13,888,226; and $12,678,087 in 1998, 1997, and 1996, respectively. The only cash inflows were associated with proceeds from the exercise of common stock options—$3,572,263 in 1998 and $174,975 in 1997.

Cash outflows occur when dividends and interest are paid and when principal amounts of debt and equity are reduced. TCBY reports "Dividends paid" of $4,660,280; $4,828,306; and $5,044,410 in 1998, 1997, and 1996, respectively. Principal payments on long-term debt are $3,345,374; $3,171,448; and $3,171,448, respectively. TCBY was active in repurchasing its own stock as treasury stock, spending $11,168,218; $6,063,447; and $4,462,229 in 1998, 1997, and 1996, respectively.

In following GAAP, the interest paid is *not* listed as a financing activity. If TCBY had used the direct method of presenting the operating activities section, interest paid would be listed separately. Instead, TCBY uses the more common indirect method, in which interest expense is simply part of (buried in) net income. Fortunately, TCBY's Note 4, "Long-term Debt," discloses interest payments for each of the three years.

TCBY Enterprises, Inc., 1998 Financial Statements

Note 4. Long-term Debt (partial presentation)

No interest was capitalized in 1998, 1997, or 1996. During fiscal 1998, 1997, and 1996, the Company paid interest of approximately $546,000, $760,000, and $961,000, respectively.

As with interest payments, TCBY followed GAAP by reporting cash outflows for operating leases as an operating activity. Recall that most financial analysts, however, view operating lease payments as principal and interest payments relating to off-balance-sheet debt, and make adjustments to reclassify the amounts from operating activities to the financing activities section. TCBY reports annual rent expense related to operating leases in Note 7, "Lease Commitments," as follows:

TCBY Enterprises, Inc., 1998 Financial Statements

Note 7. Lease Commitments (partial presentation)

In 1998, 1997, and 1996, rent expense totaled approximately $1,657,000, $1,775,000, and $2,884,000, respectively.

Although the amounts reported in the lease footnote are expenses (not cash outflows), the amounts should be reasonably close to cash outflows because of their annual nature and the fact that most lease payments remain fairly level over time.

Using TCBY's statement of cash flows, the analyst could make the following pro forma adjustments to reclassify interest paid and operating lease payments from the operating activities section to the financing activities section.

Analyst Adjustments to TCBY's Statement of Cash Flows

	1998	1997	1996
Operating Activities			
Net Cash Provided by Operating Activities*	$ 9,460,072	$ 17,135,670	$ 18,927,483
Add back (reclassify): Cash outflows for interest payments	546,000	760,000	961,000
Cash outflows for operating lease payments**	1,657,000	1,775,000	2,884,000
Adjusted Net Cash Provided (Used) By Operating Activities	$ 11,663,072	$ 19,670,670	$ 22,772,483
Financing Activities			
Net Cash Used In Financing Activities*	$(15,601,609)	$(13,888,226)	$(12,678,087)
Deduct (reclassify): Cash outflows for interest payments	(546,000)	(760,000)	(961,000)
Cash outflows for operating lease payments**	(1,657,000)	(1,775,000)	(2,884,000)
Adjusted Net Cash Used In Financing Activities	$(17,804,609)	$(16,423,226)	$(16,523,087)

*Reported in TCBY's statement of cash flows.
**Lease expense, which is assumed to approximate cash flows.

These pro forma adjustments significantly alter the amounts reported—increasing net cash inflows from operating activities and also increasing net cash outflows from financing activities. The changes could possibly affect the decisions and impressions of external users who are seeking to understand the collective effects of management's decisions.

Effects of Financing Activities on Ratio Computations

2 Explain the effects of debt and equity transactions on the financial ratios identified in Module A.

In Module A, we discussed profitability and risk ratios and calculated the ratios for TCBY. In Chapters 2–5, we discussed various financing activities that affect a firm's capital structure. In this section, we review those ratios directly affected by a firm's capital structure.

Financing Activities and Profitability Ratios

The distinction between return on assets (ROA) and return on common equity (ROCE) is important when discussing the effects of a firm's capital structure on the ratio analysis of profitability. Recall that ROA, which represents the return to all capital providers from their investments, is defined as:

$$\text{ROA} = (\text{Net income} + \text{After-tax interest expense}) \div \text{Average total assets}$$

Adding back after-tax interest expense causes ROA to reflect a return *before* considering how assets are financed. Thus, *capital structure has no direct effect on ROA.*[3]

ROCE measures return to the common shareholder. ROCE represents ROA transformed by the use of leverage:

$$\text{ROCE} = \text{ROA} \times \text{Common earnings leverage ratio} \times \text{Capital structure leverage ratio}^{4}$$

The effects on ROCE of debt and preferred stock in the capital structure can be best understood by looking at the common earnings leverage ratio and the capital structure leverage ratio:

$$\text{Common earnings leverage} = \frac{(\text{Net income} - \text{Preferred stock dividends})}{(\text{Net income} + \text{After-tax interest expense})}$$

$$\text{Capital structure leverage} = \text{Average total assets} \div \text{Average common stockholders' equity}$$

3. ROA is affected if interest expense is misclassified as another operating expense under GAAP. This occurs in the area of leasing, which we discuss later in this module.
4. Alternatively, ROCE = (Net income − Preferred dividends) ÷ Average common stockholders' equity.

The *common earnings leverage ratio represents the negative effect of leverage on ROCE*. First, consider the effect of debt (assuming no preferred shareholders). If there is no interest-bearing debt in the capital structure, then the common earnings leverage ratio is equal to one. However, as interest-bearing debt is added to the capital structure the denominator increases, causing the common earnings leverage ratio to become less than one. In the ROCE formula, this causes ROA to be multiplied by a number less than one, which decreases ROCE. Second, consider the effect of preferred stock. If preferred stock is present in the capital structure but debt is not, then preferred stock dividends are subtracted from the numerator with no effect on the denominator. This again makes the common earnings leverage ratio less than one and lowers ROCE as it is multiplied by a ratio of less than one.

The *positive effect of leverage on ROCE is captured by the capital structure leverage ratio*. The positive effect is realized by the firm earning a return on assets that common shareholders did not have to finance. Note that the numerator of the capital structure leverage ratio is average total assets, which are financed by three sources: debt, preferred equity, and common equity. However, the denominator of the capital structure leverage ratio is average common stockholders' equity, which equals the portion of assets financed by common equity. As the company uses more preferred equity and debt financing to acquire assets, the numerator increases but the denominator stays the same. Therefore, the ratio increases, thus leading to an increase in ROCE.

Financing Activities and Risk Ratios

Several key ratios in risk analysis are affected by capital structure. In Module A, we listed several ratios that are useful in assessing *short-term liquidity risk:*

$$\text{Current} = \text{Current assets} \div \text{Current liabilities}$$

$$\text{Quick} = \text{Quick assets} \div \text{Current liabilities}$$

$$\text{Cash flow from operations to current liabilities} = \text{Cash flow from operations} \div \text{Average current liabilities.}$$

Each of these ratios has current liabilities as the denominator. Thus, the listing on the balance sheet of current maturities of capital lease obligations and long-term debt, and the current liability created by the declaration of dividends decreases these ratios. Because current maturities of capital lease obligations and long-term debt are scheduled by contract, very little can be done to manage the effects of capital structure on these ratios. However, dividends declared could be paid by year-end, leading to an increase in the current and quick ratios, which are generally greater than one. Using cash (i.e., reducing the numerator) to extinguish the dividends payable liability (i.e., reducing the denominator) would cause equal changes in the numerator and denominator, which increases a ratio greater than one.

Long-term solvency risk assessment is also affected by capital structure. Consider the following key ratios:

$$\text{Long-term debt to equity} = \text{Long-term debt} \div \text{Shareholders' equity}$$

$$\text{Long-term debt to total assets} = \text{Long-term debt} \div \text{Total assets}$$

$$\text{Interest coverage} = \frac{(\text{Income before income taxes} + \text{Interest expense})}{\text{Interest expense}}$$

$$\text{Operating cash flow to total liabilities} = \text{Operating cash flow} \div \text{Average total liabilities}$$

Clearly, the presence of long-term debt in the capital structure increases the long-term debt to equity and long-term debt to assets ratios. This, in turn, increases the credit analyst's assessment of long-term solvency risk. Higher risk is also indicated by the interest coverage ratio, which falls as interest expense increases. The operating cash flow to total liabilities ratio decreases as liabilities increase, indicating greater risk.

Probably the greatest concern in the calculation of these ratios is the proper measurement and inclusion of all liabilities. Balance sheet liabilities reported in accordance with GAAP may not correspond to the assessments of total balance sheet liabilities according to creditors and investors. As a result, financial analysts, creditors, and investors frequently make numerous adjustments to reported GAAP data. We consider these adjustments in the next section.

Adjustments Used to Remeasure Capital Structure

3 Describe the balance sheet and income statement adjustments made by many external users in the process of analyzing the effects of debt and equity securities on the profitability and risk of the firm.

In this section, we consider how analysts might adjust financial statement data in the area of capital structure. We address the areas of leases, other off-balance-sheet liabilities, and financial instruments.[5]

Lease Adjustments

Leasing is one of the most significant sources of off-balance-sheet financing. Many analysts view all leases as long-term debt. If a company has significant operating leases, the analysts will convert the operating leases to capital leases using a variety of estimation methods. Pro forma capitalization results in adjustments to both long-term debt and assets on the balance sheet, as well as to interest expense and depreciation expense on the income statement. We use TCBY's 1998 financial statements to illustrate financial statement adjustments.[6]

Information about TCBY's leases can be found in Note 7 (Lease Commitments). (Before continuing with this discussion, turn to Appendix D and read TCBY's Note 7—Lease Commitments.) GAAP requires disclosure of any capital leases, but none are reported in Note 7. However, Note 7 does report future minimum rental commitments under operating leases totaling $10,612,000. Pro forma adjustment to capitalize these operating lease payments involves computing their present value, and thus, requires an interest rate assumption. In Note 4, TCBY reports interest rates of 6.20719% on its long-term notes payable. Therefore, we might use 6.21% to capitalize the future operating lease payments. However, there are three problems with using this rate. First, leases are secured by the leased asset, and secured debt bears a lower interest rate than unsecured debt. Second, information on when the leases were signed is not provided. Because interest rates vary through time as firm-specific and general economic conditions change, we cannot be sure of the rates in effect when the leases were signed. Third, as previously noted in Chapter 4, much of the obsolescence risk remains with the lessor in an operating lease, and thus, it is likely that the lessor charged a higher implicit rate to compensate for the added risk.[7] An alternative to using a firm-specific interest rate is to use the same general discount rate for all firms for which pro forma computations will be made. This method enhances comparability, and it is used by some external rating agencies.

Consistent with the approach used by many rating agencies to use the same discount rate for all pro forma computations, *we arbitrarily choose to use a 10% interest rate to discount the operating lease cash flows, and we assume that cash flows occur at the end of the year.* Using a higher interest rate gives a lower capitalized liability than using a lower interest rate, and thus, may somewhat understate TCBY's

5. In later sections of the text, we return to the topic of pro forma financial statement adjustments as we discuss other topics (e.g., after we discuss pensions, we will illustrate pro forma financial statement adjustments).

6. For a similar method of adjustment, and for an interesting discussion of the ratio effects of lease capitalization, see E. Imhoff Jr., R. Lipe, and D. Wright, "Operating Leases: Impact of Constructive Capitalization," *Accounting Horizons* (March 1991): 51–63.

7. Alternative methods of choosing a firm-specific interest rate are discussed in E. Imhoff Jr., R. Lipe, and D. Wright, "Operating Leases: Income Effects of Constructive Capitalization," *Accounting Horizons* (June 1997): 12–32.

lease obligation. Our present value calculations for the future cash flows reported in Note 7 are as follows:

Year	Cash Outflow	Factor	Present Value
1999	$ 1,986,000	$(1.10)^1$	$1,805,455
2000	1,707,000	$(1.10)^2$	1,410,744
2001	1,585,000	$(1.10)^3$	1,190,834
2002	1,175,000	$(1.10)^4$	802,541
2003	1,039,000	$(1.10)^5$	645,137
Thereafter	3,120,000	*see below*	1,468,759
	$10,612,000		$7,323,470

Cash flows for each year beyond five years are generally not disclosed; rather, the total amount to be paid after five years is presented as one amount. To calculate the present value of the $3,120,000 after 2003, we assume a 10-year lease period with equal cash flows of $624,000 ($3,120,000 ÷ 5 years) in years six through ten. The present value of the five year annuity of $624,000 discounted to the balance sheet date equals $1,468,759.[8] The final result of capitalizing the operating lease payments increases assets and liabilities by $7,323,470 (i.e., we have treated the transactions as a capital lease, an installment purchase of assets financed by a note payable).[9]

Recall that the income statement effects of lease capitalization arise from accounting for the long-term asset and the liability created by the capitalization. The changes in these two elements through the passage of time are depreciation expense and interest expense. These are calculated from estimates of balances at the beginning of the year using an estimated depreciation rate and the 10% interest rate.

To calculate a depreciation rate to use in our computation of pro forma depreciation expense related to operating leases, we use TCBY's 1998 financial statements. TCBY's 1998 depreciation expense equals $4,048,305. Although this amount is not separately disclosed in the income statement or in notes to the financial statements, it is disclosed in the statement of cash flows as an add-back in the operating activities section. In TCBY's 1998 balance sheet, we see that net property, plant, and equipment actually decreased from $40,341,282 in 1997 to $35,992,113 in 1998. The investing activities section of the statement of cash flows provides an explanation for this decrease. In 1998, TCBY purchased property, plant, and equipment for $1,982,769, but sold property, plant, and equipment for $4,901,790.

We use all this information to calculate an estimated depreciation rate. Although there are many ways to calculate TCBY's depreciation rate, we calculate it as follows: 1998 depreciation expense ÷ 1998 average gross depreciable assets (computed as the beginning and ending balances for buildings; furniture, vehicles, and equipment; and leasehold improvements, divided by two).

TCBY 1998 depreciation rate estimate = $4,048,305 ÷ [($73,003,980 + $77,365,715) ÷ 2] = 5.38%

A 5.38% approximates an 18- to 19-year life. We use this rate to subsequently compute depreciation expense on the pro forma capitalized lease amounts.

The easiest approach to estimating the beginning balances of the lease obligation and the leased asset involves repeating the capitalization procedure using the

8. The assumption that average leases last 10 years is also reasonable; we see in subsequent calculations that average asset useful lives are around 15 years. Recall that, in order to be an operating lease, the lease term must be less than 75% of the asset's economic useful life.

9. Note that it is cumbersome to compute the present value of each individual future cash payment. Perhaps the easiest way to compute the present value of a large number of irregular cash flows is to use a computer spreadsheet, such as Microsoft® Excel. Excel 7.0 has an NPV (net present value) function that computes the present value of a series of unequal cash flows. The Excel 7.0 syntax for the NPV problem is: = NPV(10%, cell-beginning:cell-ending), where cell-beginning is the cell that contains the first of the 10 cash flows and cell-ending is the cell containing the last of the 10 cash flows.

1997 annual report. However, these amounts are not presented in the 1998 financial statements. Therefore, an estimate of the present value of operating lease payments at November 29, 1997, must be obtained from the current years' financial statements by using our knowledge of the effects of rent payments and interest accrual on the balances. Recall that our pro forma estimated present value of future operating lease payments for the 1998 year-end is $7,323,470. Note 7 indicates that, in 1998, TCBY made a $1,657,000 lease payment. The computation of the present value of operating lease payments as of November 1997 is as follows:

November 1998 balance	$7,323,470
1998 lease rent payment	1,657,000
	$8,980,470
Interest accrual factor	÷ 1.10
Adjusted November 1997 balance	$8,164,064

A chronological proof of the calculation can be shown by beginning with the 1997 balance of $8,164,064, and accruing interest due to the passage of time so that the obligation is 10% higher ($8,980,470). The 1998 rent payment reduced the obligation to the November 1998 balance.

The pro forma income statement effects of operating lease capitalization can now be computed by comparing expenses under the two types of leases:

1998 operating leases expense (rent expense)		$1,657,000
Expenses under capital leases:		
Leased asset depreciation ($8,164,064 × 5.38% depreciation rate)	$439,227	
Lease obligation interest ($8,164,064 × 10% interest rate)	816,406	(1,255,633)
Expense decrease from capitalization		$ 401,367
Tax effect (assume a 34% tax rate)[10]		(136,465)
Increase in net income		$ 264,902

There is no single correct way to constructively capitalize leases given the incomplete information provided in financial statements. Our pro forma computation increases 1998 reported net income by $264,902 (2.6%). Admittedly, the method we used is not complete and is not exactly equal to what would have been shown had GAAP required the capitalization of all leases. Nevertheless, it is important for the analyst to make some attempt to adjust to the economic reality of leases.

Summary of Pro Forma Effects of Lease Capitalization on TCBY's 1998 Financial Statements

A summary of the effects of capitalizing operating leases on TCBY's 1998 financial statements is presented below.[11]

Balance Sheet Adjustments

- Increased November 29, 1998, lease obligation (long-term debt) $7,323,470

1998 adjusted long-term debt = $2,952,634 + $7,323,470 = $10,276,104

- Increased leased asset (property, plant, and equipment) $8,164,064

10. We use a 34% tax rate in this module.
11. Not every effect on the financial statements is presented. One example of an omission is deferred tax effects. In this example, the error in ratios caused by omission of the deferred tax effects is not great. We discuss the issue of deferred taxes in Chapter 11.

1998 adjusted total property, plant, and equipment = \$35,992,113 + \$8,164,064 − \$439,227 adjustment to 1998 depreciation expense = \$43,716,950

1998 adjusted total assets = \$94,452,884 + \$8,164,064 − \$439,227 = \$102,177,721

Adjusted average total assets = (\$99,264,396 + \$8,164,064 + \$102,177,721) ÷ 2 = \$104,803,091.

Income Statement Adjustments

- Increased interest expense decreases pretax income \$(816,406)

1998 adjusted interest expense = \$545,664 + \$816,406 = \$1,362,070

- Increased depreciation expense (operating expenses) decreases pretax income \$(439,227)

1998 adjusted depreciation expense = \$4,048,305 + \$439,227 = \$4,487,532

- Decreased lease rent expense increases pretax income \$1,657,000
- 1998 increased pretax income (\$1,657,000 − \$816,406 − \$439,227) = \$401,367
- Increased pretax income increases tax expense (\$401,367 × 0.34) \$136,465
- Increase in 1998 net income (\$401,367 − \$136,465) = \$264,902
- 1998 adjusted net income (\$10,195,612 + \$264,902) = \$10,460,514

Effects of Pro Forma Changes to TCBY's Financial Statements on Ratio Computations

Constructive lease capitalization can have major effects on financial statement ratios. However, as we observe in our computations below, the pro forma adjustments have almost no effects on ROA and ROCE.

ROA = (Net income + After-tax interest expense) ÷ Average total assets

ROA (adjusted) = [\$10,460,514 + \$1,362,070 × (1 − 0.34)] ÷ \$104,803,091 = 10.84%

ROA (unadjusted; as computed in Module A without financial analyst adjustments) = [\$10,195,612 + \$545,664 × (1 − 0.34)] ÷ \$96,858,640 = 10.90%

ROCE = (Net income − Preferred dividends) ÷ Average common stockholders' equity

ROCE (adjusted) = (\$10,460,514 − \$0) ÷ [(\$76,196,154 + \$264,902 + \$77,425,522) ÷ 2] = 13.60%

ROCE (unadjusted; as computed in Module A without financial analyst adjustments) = \$10,195,612 ÷ \$76,810,838 = 13.27%

Alternatively, the pro forma adjustments have a dramatic effect on the calculation of the 1998 year-end long-term debt to total assets ratio, increasing the ratio from 3.1% to 10.1%.

Long-term debt to total assets = 1998 year-end long-term debt ÷ Total assets

Long-term debt to total assets (adjusted) = \$10,276,104 ÷ \$102,177,721 = 10.1%

Long-term debt to total assets (unadjusted; as computed in Module A) = \$2,952,634 ÷ \$94,452,884 = 3.1%

Other ratios would also change. For example, if the operating lease obligations were capitalized, some portion of the lease obligation would be due during the next 12 months, which would increase current liabilities. This change affects the computation of the current ratio, quick ratio, and any other ratio that uses current or total liabilities.

Other Off-Balance-Sheet Liabilities

Unfortunately, for anyone who wants to make pro forma adjustments to GAAP financial statements, the parade of off-balance-sheet obligations only begins with leases. Despite having little evidence that investors and lenders are fooled by keeping obligations off of the balance sheet, managers continue to engage in transactions to do so. The following list of off-balance-sheet transactions is provided to make you aware of their existence and their link to the measurement of financing activities:

- Sales of accounts and notes receivable
- Pensions
- Other post-employment benefits

We discuss these items in subsequent chapters. We also present the financial statement adjustments for these items in subsequent modules.

Information about Financial Instruments

A *financial instrument* is a right to receive or a requirement to pay cash in the future. Bonds payable is a perfect example of a financial instrument. The borrower is required to pay the lender both interest and principal in the future as evidenced by a contract. Generally, financial instruments are reported on the balance sheet if payment or receipt is probable. There are many examples of financial obligations for which payment is not likely, but that subject the firm to risk. Financial statement note disclosures of these obligations allow the analyst to gain greater understanding of the risks associated with the instrument.

Financial instruments can have two kinds of risk, credit risk and market risk. An example of ***credit risk*** is **provided by the financial guarantee by a company** (Company A) **of the creditworthiness of another company** (Company B, usually a partially owned subsidiary or an important supplier). While any borrowings of Company B are not a part of Company A's liabilities, Company A must disclose the financial guarantee—Company B's default would create a liability for Company A. The risk of Company B's default is a credit risk for Company A.

Market risk is illustrated by an interest rate swap. If Company A has a fixed interest rate debt and Company B has variable rate debt, the companies may enter into a contract to swap interest rates. Fluctuations in interest rates change the market value of Company A's obligation and thus represent a market risk to Company A. Interest rate swaps are an example of a ***derivative financial instrument*—the value of the swap contract is derived from the conditions present in the interest rate contract.**

The FASB has issued several standards to increase disclosure in the financial instrument area.

- *FASB No. 105 disclosure requirements for financial instruments:*
  - The face, contract, or notional principal amount
  - Terms of the instrument, discussion of credit and market risks
  - Cash flows and accounting policies
  - Maximum accounting loss if any party failed to perform and collateral was worthless (accounting loss refers to loss accruable under GAAP)
  - Policies regarding collateral and descriptions of current collateral
- *FASB No. 109 disclosure requirements for derivative financial instruments:*
  - If derivatives are held for hedging rather than trading purposes:
    - The business purpose for holding the derivative instrument
    - Accounting policies
  - If derivatives are held for trading rather than hedging purposes (primarily banks):

- The average ending market values for such instrument distinguishing between asset and liability positions
- Net trading gains and losses for the period segregated by basic business activity for which trades were initiated, and where the gains and losses appear in the financial statements

TCBY's 1998 financial statements have little information related to financial instruments. However, financial instrument disclosures can be substantial. For example, PepsiCo, Inc., reports financial instrument information in three long (and complicated) notes to the 1998 financial statements. The nature of the disclosures is provided in Note 11:

PepsiCo, Inc. Note Disclosure (partial and adapted by authors), 1998

Note 11—FINANCIAL INSTRUMENTS, Derivative Financial Instruments

Our policy prohibits the use of derivative financial instruments for speculative purposes and we have procedures in place to monitor and control their use. The following discussion excluded future contracts to hedge immaterial amounts of our commodity purchases.

Our use of derivative instruments is primarily limited to interest rate and currency swaps, which are used to reducing borrowing costs by effectively modifying the interest rate and currency of specific debt issuances. These swaps are generally entered into concurrently with the issuance of the debt they are intended to modify. The notional amount, interest payment dates, and maturity dates of the swaps match the principal, interest payment, and maturity dates of the related debt. Accordingly, any market risk or opportunity associated with these swaps is fully offset by the opposite market impact on the related debt. Our credit risk related to interest rate and currency swaps is considered low because such swaps are entered into only with strong creditworthy counterparties, are generally settled on a net basis, and are of relatively short duration. Further, there is no concentration with counterparties. See Note 10 for the notional amounts, related interest rates, and maturities of the interest rate and currency swaps. See Management's Discussion and Analysis—Market Risk.

Summary

In Module B, we show how external users, primarily financial analysts, may make pro forma adjustments to financial statements in order to understand the effects of management decisions. For example, a financial analyst may recast financial statements (1) to promote comparability across firms that may use different accounting methods; (2) to provide standardized inputs to certain quantitative models; and (3) because the analyst does not feel that GAAP financial statements appropriately characterize the firm. We demonstrate how these adjustments affect financial statements and related ratio computations. In later chapters and modules, we build on Module B to discuss pro forma adjustments for other items.

http://

In which industries would you expect to see heavy use of off-balance-sheet leasing arrangements? Link to EDGAR or company homepages through our Web site (http://baginski.swcollege.com). Pick companies from three industries that you think might have different magnitudes of future cash flows under operating leases. Look at the total cash flows reported in the leasing notes relative to the total property, plant, and equipment amount reported in the balance sheet. Which company might have the debt to equity ratio most adversely affected by pro forma operating lease capitalization?

Key Terms

credit risk 198
derivative financial instrument 198
financial instrument 198
market risk 198

Analytical and Comprehensive Problems

1. **Pro Forma Adjustments to Southwest Airlines' Financial Statements.** Use the 1998 Southwest Airlines financial statements in Appendix C to make pro forma adjustments to capitalize operating leases. Note 5 presents Southwest's lease information. For convenience, assume a 10% discount rate, cash flows are paid at the end of the year, and the $1,901,005,000 in operating lease payments for the years after 2003 are paid equally over the 10-year period 2004–2013. If capitalized, assume that the leased property has a depreciable life of 20 years and zero salvage. Incorporating these assumptions, calculate the amount that would be added to Southwest's 1998 balance sheet and discuss what balance sheet items would be affected. Compute the following December 31, 1998, ratios before and after the assumed capitalization of the operating leases: ROA, ROCE, long-term debt to total assets ratio, and interest coverage ratio (times interest earned). For long-term debt, use the amount reported in the balance sheet as "long-term debt less current maturities." Use a 1998 effective tax rate of 38.5% in your computations. To simplify the computations, use 1998 ending balance sheet amounts rather than averages.

2. **Effect of Operating versus Capital Lease Classification.** The McVay Co. is considering entering into a lease with the following terms: six-year term; no down payment; annual lease payments of $300,000 at the end of each year; and a guaranteed residual value of $50,000 (management believes that the asset will be worth $70,000 at the end of the lease). Assume that management can either treat the lease as an operating lease or a capital lease, depending upon how the estimated useful life of the asset is defined. The lease's implicit interest rate (which is lower than McVay's incremental borrowing rate) is 8%. If capitalized, the asset would be depreciated over six years to the guaranteed residual amount using the straight-line method.

   You have been asked to determine the effect of the leases on current financial statements under two different scenarios: (1) the lease is recognized as an operating lease and (2) the lease is recognized as a capital lease. Your assignment is to compute and contrast the effect of the two alternative scenarios on each of the following items during the first year of the lease: net income, total assets, long-term debt, return on assets (ROA), return on common equity (ROCE), and long-term debt to total assets. To simplify the assessment of the alternatives, use the following amounts as the starting point in a static analysis: net income = $10,000,000; effective tax rate = 35%; preferred dividends on nonconvertible preferred stock = $500,000; total assets = $120,000,000; common stockholders' equity = $80,000,000; long-term liabilities = $12,000,000. The investment is expected to generate an additional $500,000 in pretax income over each of the six years of the lease. You should ignore any interest expense on other liabilities. Immediately after recognizing the lease, what is the amount that would be shown as a current liability under each of the two alternative scenarios?

3. **Capital Structure.** The Kulsrud Co. is about to invest $100,000,000 in property, plant, and equipment, which is expected to last 10 years, with no salvage value. The investment is expected to earn a 20% pretax return per year on the $100,000,000. The company can either raise the $100,000,000 by issuing $100,000,000 in 8%, 20-year bonds (with interest paid annually at the end of the year), or issue $100,000,000 in 8% cumulative, no par preferred stock (each year's dividend is 8% of $100,000,000). Kulsrud expects to declare and pay the 8% dividend at the end of each year. (Note that we use the 8% rate for both debt and equity so that you can directly compare the effects of the alternatives, without having to factor in different costs for debt and equity.) Determine the effect of the two alternative ways of financing the investment on the following items: net income, ROA, ROCE, long-term debt to equity ratio, and interest coverage ratio. Use the following beginning amounts (before the $100,000,000 is raised) for the purpose of your ratio computations: effective income tax rate of 40%; total assets = $2,000,000,000; long-term debt = $700,000,000, with an average interest rate of 7%; preferred stock = $0; stockholders' equity = $900,000,000; income before income taxes = $300,000,000; and net income = $180,000,000. To simplify the computations, use 1998 ending balance sheet amounts rather than averages.

http://

4. **Pro Forma Adjustments to Texas Instruments' Financial Statements.** Go to our Web site at http://baginski.swcollege.com. Using the 1998 financial statements for Texas Instruments, make pro forma adjustments to capitalize the operating leases (see the "Rental Expense and Lease Commitments" footnote). For convenience, assume a 10% discount rate, cash flows paid at the end of the year, and the $129 million in operating lease payments for the years after 2003 paid equally over the 5-year period (2004–2008). If capitalized, assume that the leased property has a depreciable life of 20 years and zero salvage. Using these assumptions, calculate the amount that would be added to Texas Instruments' 1998 balance sheet and discuss what balance sheet items would be affected. Then, compute the following December 31, 1998, ratios before and after the assumed capitalization of the operating leases: ROA, ROCE, long-term debt to total assets ratio, and interest coverage ratio (times interest earned). For long-term debt, use the amount reported in the balance sheet as "long-term debt"; for interest expense, use the amount reported on the income statement as "interest on loans." To simplify the computations, use 1998 ending balance sheet amounts rather than averages.

5. **Compare Ways of Financing Expansion.** You have been asked to advise Jim Rebele, who is president and CEO of Rebele Consulting. Rebele's balance sheet information at December 31, 2001, and other selected information are provided below.

Rebele Consulting Financial Statement Information
December 31, 2001

Current assets	$100,000	
Long-term investments	15,000	
Property, plant, and equipment	230,000	
Other assets	5,000	
Total assets		$350,000
Current liabilities	$ 60,000	
Long-term debt	0	
Total liabilities		60,000
Common stock ($20 par)	$150,000	
Additional paid-in capital	90,000	
Retained earnings	50,000	
Total stockholders' equity		290,000
Total liabilities and stockholders' equity		$350,000

Selected Information for Year 2001

Net income	$28,000
Effective income tax rate	40%

Rebele has an opportunity to expand his business at a cost of $250,000. He believes that the expansion would enable him to increase net income by $25,000 per year. Rebele seeks your advice regarding how to finance the expansion. Specifically, he asks you to help him understand the 2002 financial statement effects of the following three alternatives: (1) finance with long-term debt borrowed from First National Bank at an annual interest rate of 8%; (2) finance by selling 5,000 shares of common stock to relatives at $50 per share; and (3) finance by selling 10,000 shares of 9%, $25 par, cumulative preferred stock at $25 per share. Prepare a written explanation for Rebele regarding each of the alternatives on the income statement, the balance sheet, ROA, ROCE (using the three component parts introduced in Module A), and long-term debt to equity ratio. Use a static analysis such that current financial statement amounts are expected to carry forward into the future (e.g., assume in your computations that Rebele continues to earn the 2001 net income of $28,000—treat the 2001 net income as permanent). Also, to be conservative in your analysis of the common stock alternative, *assume common dividends will be not paid on a routine basis.* To simplify the computations, use 2001 ending balance sheet amounts rather than averages.

CFA Exam-Type Problems

The following questions relate to information from Chapters 2–5. The effect of capitalizing operating leases is a common CFA question.

6. If a lease is capitalized, as compared with being treated as an operating lease, the effect on the current ratio and the debt/equity ratio will be: (CFA adapted)

	Current Ratio	*Debt/Equity Ratio*
a.	Increase	Increase
b.	Increase	Decrease
c.	Decrease	Increase
d.	Decrease	Decrease

7. Adjusting the financial statements to capitalize an operating lease would: (CFA adapted)
   a. increase return on total assets
   b. not affect return on total assets
   c. decrease times interest earned
   d. decrease long-term debt to equity

8. Which of the following would *increase* the number of shares of a company's common stock outstanding? (CFA adapted)
   I. Paying (issuing) a stock dividend
   II. Instituting a reverse stock split
   III. Purchasing treasury stock
   IV. Exercising outstanding warrants
   a. I and III only
   b. I and IV only
   c. I, II, and III only
   d. II, III, and IV only

Use the following data in answering Questions 9–11.

Arndt Corporation's 2000 financial statement footnotes include the following information:

- Arndt has recently entered into operating leases with total future payments of $60 million and a discounted present value of $40 million.
- Marketable securities carried at their original cost of $15 million are included in long-term assets. Fair market value of these securities is $25 million.
- Arndt has guaranteed a $6 million bond issue, due in 2003, issued by a 30%-owned affiliate.

You decide to adjust the balance sheet for all three items. *Note: the topic of investments in equity securities is discussed in future chapters.* Assume that to adjust the balance sheet for the marketable securities, the assets would be written up to fair value, and the offset to the write-up is to increase stockholders' equity.

9. The effect of these adjustments on the long-term debt-to-equity ratio will be that: (CFA adapted, with modification by author)
   a. all three adjustments will decrease the ratio
   b. all three adjustments will increase the ratio
   c. only the marketable securities adjustment will decrease the ratio
   d. only lease capitalization will affect the ratio

10. The effect of lease capitalization will be to: (CFA adapted, with modification by author)
    a. increase current assets
    b. increase current liabilities
    c. decrease current assets
    d. decrease current liabilities

Note: assume that book value per share is defined as [(Total assets − Total liabilities) ÷ number of common shares outstanding].

11. The effect of the marketable securities adjustment will be to: (CFA adapted, with modification by author)
    a. increase the current ratio
    b. decrease the current ratio
    c. increase book value per share
    d. decrease book value per share

III

How Investing Decisions Are Reflected in Financial Statements

Objectives

1 Understand the decision to invest in productive assets.

2 Apply the general rule to record the acquisition of productive assets.

3 Record the acquisition of productive assets with regard to the kind of consideration given.

4 Determine whether to capitalize or expense the costs incurred in acquiring, exploring, and developing natural resources.

5 Classify and record investments in intangible assets.

6 Account for research and development expenditures.

7 Identify and account for exceptions to the general rule of recording acquired productive assets.

8 Allocate costs by applying the various methods for depletion, depreciation, and amortization.

9 Determine and report asset impairments.

10 Describe where and how information about productive assets is disclosed and discussed in annual reports.

Chapter 6

Investment Decisions—Investing in Productive Assets

Financing activities (discussed in Chapters 2–5) provide the necessary capital for investment activities. Our discussions in Chapters 6–8 will focus on these investment activities. Companies invest resources in several ways, and the duration of the investments ranges from a few days to many years. A general classification of investing activities is provided below.

Direct Investments in Long-Term Productive Assets (Chapter 6)

1. Investments in property, plant, and equipment.
2. Investments in natural resources.
3. Investments in intangible assets.

Indirect Investments in Productive Assets (Chapters 7–8)

4. Investments in the net assets of other firms through the purchase of bonds and equity securities.

Investment Decisions Classified as Operating Activities (Chapter 9)

5. Investments in short-term working capital items.

In this chapter, we consider the first three types of investments—the direct investments in long-term productive assets. These assets are employed in the production, service, and selling activities of the firm (i.e., operating activities). The fourth and fifth types of investments will be covered in Chapters 7–9.

The Investment Decision for Long-Term Productive Assets

1 Understand the decision to invest in productive assets.

The decision to invest in productive assets results in trading current cash for indirect, probable future economic benefits:

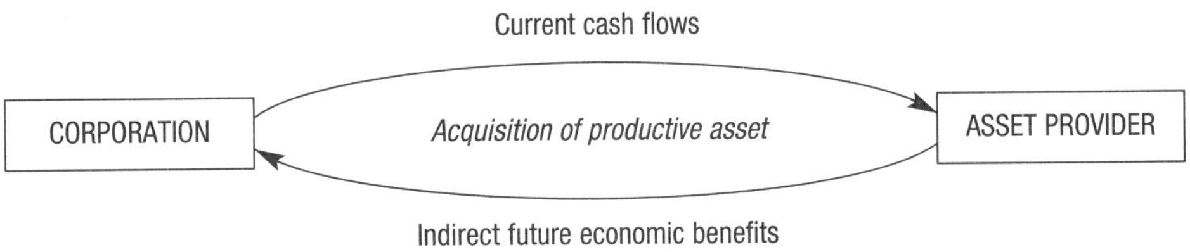

The future benefits acquired by the corporation are *indirect* because certain operating activities must occur to transform the productive asset into other assets before the ultimate transformation into cash. Consider a manufacturer's decision to invest in a machine. The manufacturer trades cash, other assets, or promises to pay cash for a machine. The machine is combined with raw materials and labor in an operating activity to create another asset—inventory. The inventory is most likely transferred to a customer under a credit arrangement in exchange for another asset—accounts receivable. Finally, the accounts receivable is collected, creating a cash asset. This path from cash to cash is quite indirect. As discussed later in this chapter, the indirect cash flow consequences of investments in productive assets are a key determinant of an asset's balance sheet valuation.

Most firms go through **a formal internal decision process to determine whether to accept projects that require investment in productive assets.** This process is referred to as ***capital budgeting.*** The investment decision is driven by the amount and timing of future cash flows and, in most analyses, the cash realization risk. While predicting the level and timing of future cash flows is no easy task, determining the risk of not receiving the cash flows is even more difficult. This risk determines the rate at which a project's future cash flows are discounted. Decision models (such as *net present value* and *internal rate of return*), which incorporate both timing and risk, are used to guide management investment decisions.

One complicating factor in the assessment of project risk is the likely dependence of that project with other projects. Finance theory demonstrates that **the appropriate risk factor in the determination of discount rates** is ***portfolio risk.*** Portfolio risk is determined by the covariance of a project's cash flows with the cash flows of all other projects. From the firm's point of view, the portfolio consists of all other projects of the firm *given* that the firm has chosen to be in a certain risk class. However, from the shareholders' point of view, the relevant portfolio includes all projects in the market. The firm's portfolio of investment projects may not correspond to the market's portfolio if the firm is not well diversified. For example, in the mid-1990s, General Motors' decision whether to make an investment in the long-lived assets needed to produce a faster Chevrolet Camaro began with identifying the cash flows from production and sale of the Camaro. But, the covariance of the Camaro's cash flows with the Chevrolet Corvette's cash flows is likely to be negative, given that both cars are targeted at the same market, and hence, the sale of a Camaro would often replace the sale of a Corvette. Chevrolet needed to both evaluate the Camaro project in light of its effect on Corvette sales and determine the appropriate risk factor in a portfolio setting. Further, General Motors' shareholders evaluated the Camaro project more indirectly, in terms of their holdings of a portfolio of shares in General Motors and other corporations that are not in the same risk class.

Value is created when expected future indirect cash inflows from the investment in a productive asset (appropriately discounted for risk) exceed the initial direct cash outflows to acquire the asset. The reporting of capital outlays and associated cash inflows for each project is not provided to financial statement users. Therefore, users can only assess the success of such decisions at an aggregate level.

Acquisition of Productive Assets

2 Apply the general rule to record the acquisition of productive assets.

Long-term productive assets are initially recorded at the *fair market value of what has been given up* in order to acquire the asset (or the fair market value of the acquired asset if that fair market value is more determinable). This general rule explains how we record the different kinds of productive assets discussed in the following sections.

The fair market value of the asset at acquisition (the initial acquisition price) is often referred to as *historical cost*. Although other attributes of the productive asset could be measured subsequent to acquisition (i.e., the exit value or replacement cost), productive assets are generally reported in financial statements at historical cost during the asset's life. Historical cost is a *reliable* (i.e., verifiable) measure. A different attribute, such as present value, might be more *relevant* to investors because it is based on recent cash flow estimates, but far less reliable. It is difficult to reliably measure the present value of future cash flows because of the indirect nature of productive asset cash flows. The inherent reliability of historical cost is the primary reason that productive assets are reported in GAAP-based financial statements at historical cost rather than the potentially more relevant, but less reliable, current market value.

Once historical cost is determined, the accountant must decide whether the benefits received from using the productive asset will all be recognized in the current period or whether the benefits received will extend beyond the current period. Not all expenditures in the productive asset area yield future benefits. Recall that an expenditure yielding only current benefits is an expense rather than an asset.

The following sections provide specific examples of applying the general rule when productive assets are acquired (i.e., record at the fair market value surrendered) and judging the nature of benefits received (current versus future benefit).

Acquisition of Property, Plant, and Equipment

Land, buildings, and equipment are required in both production and service activities. The general rule of recording acquisitions creates the following balance sheet presentation of property, plant, and equipment *at the date of acquisition:*

Assets	
Property, plant, and equipment	
Property (i.e., land)	Fair value at acquisition (historical cost)
Buildings	Fair value at acquisition (historical cost)
Equipment	Fair value at acquisition (historical cost)

The measurement of historical cost depends upon what type of consideration is given up to acquire a productive asset.

- Long-term assets may be acquired in exchange for other assets, debt, or equity.
  1. Cash (or other assets) surrendered
  2. Debt claims incurred (e.g., notes payable, deferred payment contracts, leases)
  3. Equity claims issued (e.g., common or preferred stock)
- Long-term assets may be acquired by donation, with no consideration given.
- Long-term assets may be acquired by self-construction through the use of company material, labor, and overhead expenditures.

We will now examine how to determine and record acquisition costs when these various forms of consideration are given.

Cash Surrendered

3 Record the acquisition of productive assets with regard to the kind of consideration given.

Cash has a clearly determinable fair market value. The property, plant, or equipment acquired is recorded at the amount of cash surrendered, which includes the purchase price, shipping costs, set-up costs, etc.

Example 1. Applewhite Inc. purchases a machine for $60,000 and pays $400 for shipping.

Solution. The machinery is recorded at an acquisition cost of $60,400.

EXAMPLE 1 Journal Entry

Machinery	60,400	
Cash		60,400

Debt Incurred

Instead of immediately paying cash, corporations can promise to pay in the future by issuing a note payable, signing a lease agreement, or by entering into a long-term deferred payment contract (e.g., installment purchase contract). The general rule stipulates that property, plant, or equipment purchased by the corporation is recorded at the fair market value of the promise to pay. Each *promise to pay* (usually evidenced by a note) specifies future cash payments and also specifies or implies an interest rate. If the note's stated interest rate is reasonable, then the principal amount of the note is recognized as the fair value of the consideration given.[1] In all cases, the present value of cash flows specified in the note, lease agreement, or deferred payment contract defines the fair value of the promise to pay.

However, if the fair market value of what has been given up is difficult to determine, then the accountant can rely on the *fair market value of what has been received* as an approximation. The appropriateness of this estimation procedure relies on the economic assumption that unrelated parties act rationally they trade equal amounts of fair market value.

Examples 2–5 illustrate the initial determination of the amount recorded for a productive asset when a promise to pay is exchanged. (For all note payable examples, assume that interest is due at the end of each year and the entire principal is due at maturity.) Example 2 reflects the more common situation where the note payable's stated interest rate is reasonable; examples 3–5 illustrate the less common situation where the note payable's stated interest rate is not reasonable.

Example 2. Ward Co. purchased land by issuing a $300,000, three-year, 10% note payable. Ward normally pays 10% interest on notes of this kind.

Solution. The interest rate is reasonable because it reflects the rate normally associated with this type of transaction. Therefore, the face value of the note and the fair value of the note are equal. Ward would record the land received at $300,000, the fair value of the promise to pay.

EXAMPLE 2 Journal Entry

Land	300,000	
Note Payable		300,000

Example 3. Bondo Co. purchased land by issuing a $100,000, two-year, non-interest bearing note payable. Bondo normally pays 10% interest on notes of this kind.

Solution. The fair value of the note payable equals its present value at the current market rate of interest. The stated interest rate on this note (0%) is unreasonable because the appropriate market rate of interest is Bondo's borrowing rate, 10%.[2]

1. Usually, when a note payable is issued to purchase an asset, the note's stated rate is reasonable (i.e., it either equals or closely approximates the current market rate of interest appropriate for the transaction). However, situations will arise when a note payable's stated interest rate is unreasonable.
2. Determining whether a stated rate of interest reflects market interest rates (i.e., that it is reasonable) is a process that requires judgment based on experience.

Usually, a note contains two cash flow components—principal and interest. However, in this case only one cash flow is present, the maturity value of $100,000. Because the stated interest rate does not reflect the current market interest rate, we discount the maturity value at 10% [$\$100,000 \div (1 + 0.10)^2$] to calculate the note payable's fair value of $82,645. Thus, Bondo would record the land at $82,645, the fair value of the note payable.

EXAMPLE 3 Journal Entry

Land	82,645	
Discount on Notes Payable	17,355	
Notes Payable		100,000

Example 4. White Co. issued a $100,000, five-year, 4% note payable in exchange for land with a known cash price of $75,000. White has not borrowed recently and would find it impossible to borrow at 4% to purchase the land.

Solution. In this example, it is easier to determine the fair value of what has been received than the fair value of the note payable. Known cash prices provide excellent estimates of fair value—the land would be valued at $75,000.

EXAMPLE 4 Journal Entry

Land	75,000	
Discount on Notes Payable	25,000	
Notes Payable		100,000

Example 5. Foster Co. issued a $100,000, four-year, 3% note payable in exchange for land. Foster normally pays 8% interest on notes of this kind. Foster has three appraisals on the property ($82,000, $84,000, and $86,000) with an average value of $84,000.

Solution. This is the most difficult type of problem to solve because the fair market values of the consideration given and the consideration received are not apparent. The present value of the note ($n = 4$; $i = 8\%$; payment $= \$3,000$; FV $= \$100,000$) is $83,439. Knowing the 8% normal market interest rate implies that the 3% stated interest rate is unreasonably low—therefore, the 8% market rate should be used to compute present value. Although no known cash price exists for the land, the appraisals average $84,000. In this case, the accountant must use judgment in recording this transaction. The presumption is that the fair value of the note payable (the consideration given up) is to be used to value the transaction unless the fair value of the asset received is more determinable. In this case, if the accountant is confident that the 8% is the appropriate market rate of interest, then the asset would most likely be recorded at $83,439. The appraisals are used to confirm the reasonableness of the 8% rate. The accountant would record the appraisal values *only* if an appropriate rate of interest for this type of loan could not be determined.[3]

EXAMPLE 5 Journal Entry

Land	83,439	
Discount on Notes Payable	16,561	
Notes Payable		100,000

3. This example is also useful to illustrate the concept of materiality. The difference between recording the asset at $83,439 or $84,000 is immaterial to the financial statements. The valuation decision would be more difficult if the present value computation for a note was $20,000,000, while three appraisals for the project were $12,000,000, $22,000,000, and $28,000,000.

Equity Claims Issued

Determining the fair value of common or preferred shares issued to acquire a productive asset is a simple matter if the shares are regularly traded on stock exchanges (Example 6). However, if thinly traded shares of closely held corporations are given, the fair market value of the productive asset received is probably the best measure of the fair value of the transaction (Example 7). If the value of neither side of the transaction is known, appraisal may be necessary to estimate the cash price (i.e., fair value) of the transaction (Example 7).

Example 6. Mummy Airlines acquires conveyer belt equipment by issuing 1,000 shares of its $1 par value common stock. The stock trades on a regular basis; its current price is $30 per share.

Solution. The fair value of the stock given up is clearly determinable. The 1,000 shares have a total market value of $30,000. Therefore, the equipment is recorded at $30,000.

EXAMPLE 6 Journal Entry

Equipment	30,000	
Common Stock (1,000 shares @ $1 par)		1,000
Additional Paid-In Capital		29,000

Example 7. HappyValley Products acquires a building by issuing 1,000 shares of its $10 par value common stock. (A similar building in the industrial park recently sold for $500,000 in cash.) HappyValley is closely held; its most recent stock transaction was 18 months ago, at which time a large block of shares was exchanged at $400 per share.

Solution. The fair value of the thinly traded stock is not clearly determinable. The cash price availability of a comparable building allows the accountant to record the transaction at the fair market value of the asset received, $500,000.

EXAMPLE 7 Journal Entry

Building	500,000	
Common Stock (1,000 shares @ $10 par)		10,000
Additional Paid-In Capital		490,000

Long-Term Assets Acquired By Donation

It is common for a governmental unit to offer incentives for a company to move to its locale. Incentives frequently include such items as a donation of property, reduced property taxes, and infrastructure improvements (e.g., road to the property, plus sewer connections and utilities).

Even though no consideration is given to acquire such an asset, it is necessary to assign a value to the asset, which becomes its historical cost. Usually the uniqueness of the donated property makes it difficult (if not impossible) to estimate its fair value except by the use of an appraisal.[4] As we will discuss in subsequent sections of this chapter, the productive asset's original cost must be matched against the future economic benefits generated by the asset's use. This cost allocation process is necessary to properly measure income from the asset's use.

4. *SFAS No. 116*, "Accounting for Contributions Received and Contributions Made" (Norwalk, Conn.: FASB, 1993). The increase in assets that occurs when a contribution is received should be reported as a revenue. Transfers *from* governmental units are exempted from the standard. Therefore, contributed capital is sometimes reported instead of revenue.

Example 8. Clean Industry Inc. receives significant road improvements on its property from the city of Austin as an incentive to remain in its current location. The typical charge for this kind of road improvement is $45,000.

Solution. Clean Industry gave up nothing to receive the road improvements. However, it is important to assign a value to the improvements since they are used up (i.e., turned into expenses) in the process of generating future revenues. The road improvements would be recorded at the $45,000 acquisition price.

EXAMPLE 8 Journal Entry

Road Improvements	45,000	
Revenue from Donations		45,000

Self-Construction

To internally create plant and equipment requires the sacrifice of materials, labor, and overhead. Materials, labor, and some overhead expenditures are variable costs (i.e., they vary directly with production activity). Therefore, a construction project directly causes increases in materials, labor, utilities, and insurance costs. On the other hand, the costs of some assets used in self-construction are fixed overhead costs (i.e., they do not vary with the level of production activity). For example, a self-construction project frequently uses existing equipment and does not create the need for additional expenditures on equipment, plant management supervision, and property taxes. However, these costs are necessary for the construction to occur. Therefore, accountants must allocate part of the fixed overhead costs to self-construction costs.

A company might choose to self-construct an asset for several reasons: to save costs, because the asset is not available externally, or to use employees who would otherwise be idle, to name a few. Initially, accountants compute the cost of a self-constructed asset as the fair value of all costs incurred to construct the asset, which include materials, labor, and allocations of variable overhead and fixed overhead. However, accountants place a ceiling value on a self-constructed asset. If internal expenditures exceed the cost of acquiring the asset externally, then the amount recorded in the self-constructed asset's account is limited to the cost of the external purchase; the excess of costs incurred over the external fair value is recorded as a loss for the period. This process ensures that an asset is not initially recorded at an amount greater than its fair market value.

Example 9. Believing that vendors had overpriced a machine (currently selling for $6,000) used in production, Keady Boilermakers self-constructed the machine. Keady used $4,500 in materials, $1,000 in labor, and applied indirect (i.e., factory overhead) costs at 150% of direct labor cost.

Solution. Keady's total cost to construct the machine is $7,000 ($4,500 materials, $1,000 labor, and $1,000 × 150% = $1,500 indirect costs). But, a self-constructed asset can not be recorded at more than its fair value, in this case, the cash equivalent price of $6,000. Therefore, $6,000 is reported in the machinery account at the date of acquisition.

EXAMPLE 9 Journal Entry

Machinery	6,000	
Loss on Self-Construction of Asset	1,000	
Materials		4,500
Accrued Payroll (labor)		1,000
Factory Overhead Applied (indirect costs)		1,500

Interest Incurred to Self-Construct Assets

In earlier chapters pertaining to bonds, notes, and leases, we indicated that, as a general rule, interest cost is appropriately treated as an expense of the period. The FASB allows an exception to this general rule for interest cost incurred during the self-construction of a productive asset intended for the company's own use.[5] Interest on debt used to finance asset construction is a cost of constructing the asset. By capitalizing interest on self-constructed assets, interest becomes part of the asset's historical cost (depreciation basis) and is then matched with future periods through the depreciation process. To illustrate capitalized interest disclosures, a slightly modified disclosure from the International Paper Company's annual report is shown below.

Capitalized Interest Disclosure: International Paper Company

Interest costs for the construction of certain long-term assets are capitalized and amortized over the related assets' estimated useful lives. For the past three years, the Company capitalized net interest costs of $12 million, $42 million and $36 million. Interest payments for the last three years were $372 million, $363 million and $385 million.

Avoidable interest is the term used to describe **the amount of a company's annual interest cost that should be capitalized.** To compute avoidable interest, **expenditures linked to the self-construction project are weighted by the amount of time that the expenditures were outstanding during the year.** These weighted expenditures, called ***average accumulated expenditures,*** are multiplied by the interest rate on specific borrowings to fund the construction. If the average accumulated expenditures exceed specific construction borrowings, then the excess average accumulated expenditures are multiplied by the weighted-average interest cost of the company's other interest-bearing debt.[6] If the company has no debt, it has no avoidable interest.[7]

Example 10. Vinnie Enterprises began construction of a regional distribution center on January 1, 2001. On that date, Vinnie obtained a $1,000,000 construction loan bearing a 10% interest rate. Interest is paid at the end of each year. Expenditures on the project (i.e., materials, labor, and overhead expenditures) were as follows:

1/1/01	$ 400,000
7/1/01	600,000
10/1/01	280,000
Subtotal through 12/31/01	$1,280,000
5/1/02	900,000
9/1/02	900,000
Total through 12/31/02	$3,080,000

On December 31, 2002, the project was completed. In addition to the construction note, two other interest-bearing debts were outstanding during the construction period:

Bond payable (12%)	$2,000,000	Note payable (15%)	$4,000,000

Compute the amount of avoidable interest to be capitalized in 2001 and 2002.

5. Interest cost may also be capitalized on construction of certain types of inventory (discussed in Chapter 10). *SFAS No. 34,* "Capitalization of Interest Cost" (Stamford, Conn.: FASB, 1979).
6. Alternatives exist for the assignment of interest rates to average accumulated expenditures other than the method we provide in this text. For an analysis of these alternatives, see K. Means and P. Kazenski, "*SFAS No. 34:* Recipe for Diversity," *Accounting Horizons,* September 1998.
7. Public utilities are an exception because they impute interest on equity borrowing when capitalizing interest costs.

Solution.
2001 average accumulated expenditures:[8]

$ 400,000	× 12mo.	÷ 12mo.	=	$400,000
600,000	× 6mo.	÷ 12mo.	=	300,000
280,000	× 3mo.	÷ 12mo.	=	70,000
$1,280,000				$770,000

2001 avoidable interest:
The average accumulated expenditures of $770,000 is less than the $1,000,000 specific construction borrowing. Therefore, the specific borrowing's 10% interest rate is used in the computation of avoidable interest: 2001 avoidable interest = $770,000 × 10% = $77,000. Avoidable interest cannot exceed actual interest:

Construction note	$1,000,000 × 10% =	$100,000
Bond payable	$2,000,000 × 12% =	240,000
Note payable	$4,000,000 × 15% =	600,000
Total actual interest		$940,000

Because avoidable interest is less than actual interest ($940,000), the 2001 interest capitalized is $77,000. The remainder of the interest, $863,000, is reported as interest expense for 2001.

2002 average accumulated expenditures:
The 2002 calculation of accumulated expenditures begins with the balance in the building account brought forward from the prior year ($1,280,000 in expenditures plus $77,000 in capitalized interest = $1,357,000):

$1,357,000	× 12mo.	÷ 12mo.	=	$1,357,000
900,000	× 8mo.	÷ 12mo.	=	600,000
900,000	× 4mo.	÷ 12mo.	=	300,000
$3,157,000				$2,257,000

2002 avoidable interest:
The average accumulated expenditures of $2,257,000 is greater than the $1,000,000 specific construction borrowing. Therefore, to compute avoidable interest, the specific borrowing's 10% interest rate is used for the first $1,000,000 of average accumulated expenditures; a weighted-average interest rate on other borrowings is used for the excess accumulated expenditures:

Avoidable interest:	$1,000,000	× 10% =	$100,000
	1,257,000	× 14%* =	175,980
	$2,257,000		$275,980

*The weighted-interest rate on other interest bearing borrowings is as follows:
[($2,000,000 × 12%) + ($4,000,000 × 15%)] ÷ ($2,000,000 + 4,000,000) = 14%

By the end of construction (2002), the total recorded amount for the regional distribution center is obtained by adding $3,080,000 (the expenditures in 2001 and 2002), $77,000 (the capitalized interest in 2001), and $275,980 (the capitalized interest in 2002). These amounts total to $3,432,980.[9]

8. An alternate way to compute the weighted average is as follows: $200,000 ($400,000 × 6mo./12mo.) + $250,000 ($1,000,000 × 3mo./12mo.) + $320,000 ($1,280,000 × 3mo./12mo.) = $770,000.
9. Temporary investments of funds not used in construction generate interest revenue and are not to be treated as offsets to capitalized interest (*SFAS No. 62*).

EXAMPLE 10 Journal Entries and Selected Ledger Accounts: Capitalized Interest

2001			
1/1/01	Building	400,000	
	Materials, Accrued Payroll, Factory Overhead Applied		400,000
7/1/01	Building	600,000	
	Materials, Accrued Payroll, Factory Overhead Applied		600,000
10/1/01	Building	280,000	
	Materials, Accrued Payroll, Factory Overhead Applied		280,000
12/31/01	Building	77,000	
	Interest Expense	863,000	
	Cash (assuming interest paid at 12/31)		940,000

Building

1/1	400,000	
7/1	600,000	
10/1	280,000	
12/31	77,000	
Bal.	1,357,000	

Interest Expense

12/31	863,000	
Bal.	863,000	

Combined Ledger Account for Cash, Materials, etc.

	1/1	400,000
	7/1	600,000
	10/1	280,000
	12/31	940,000
	Bal.	2,220,000

2002			
5/1/02	Building	900,000	
	Materials, Accrued Payroll, Factory Overhead Applied		900,000
9/1/02	Building	900,000	
	Materials, Accrued Payroll, Factory Overhead Applied		900,000
12/31/02	Building	275,980	
	Interest Expense	664,020	
	Cash (assuming interest paid at 12/31)		940,000

Building

Bal.	1,357,000	
5/1	900,000	
9/1	900,000	
12/31	275,980	
Bal.	3,432,980	

Interest Expense (prior balance closed to retained earnings)

Bal.	0	
12/31	664,020	
Bal.	664,020	

Combined Ledger Account for Cash, Materials, etc.

	Bal.	2,220,000
	5/1	900,000
	9/1	900,000
	12/31	940,000
	Bal.	4,960,000

Acquisition: Natural Resources

4 Determine whether to capitalize or expense the costs incurred in acquiring, exploring, and developing natural resources.

Oil fields, timber tracts, and mineral deposits are examples of natural resources. Because any of the kinds of consideration previously discussed can be used to acquire natural resources, the measurement of the fair value given is similar to the examples we have already discussed. For natural resource accounting, a bigger issue is the classification of costs as expenses or assets. This decision is aided by distinguishing among three types of costs incurred in the natural resource domain:

- Acquisition costs
- Exploration costs
- Development costs

Acquisition Costs

Acquisition costs include the costs of acquiring the natural resources as well as the costs associated with returning the resource site to an acceptable condition. Often, the natural resource is attached to land that is salvageable at the end of production. If that is the case, then the initial cost is separated into two accounts, with the portion of cost attributable to the land reported separately in a land or property account. All other costs of acquisition would be capitalized as part of the natural resources account and reported in the property, plant, and equipment section with other productive, operational assets.

Example 11. Evers Mining acquires a tract of land rich in iron-ore deposits. The purchase price is $6,000,000. Evers expects to sell the land for $1,000,000 after mining is completed.

Solution. The natural resource account is recorded at $5,000,000, the original price less the salvage value of the land. Land is recorded at $1,000,000, its estimated value after mining is completed.

EXAMPLE 11 Journal Entry

Natural Resources—Mineral Deposits	5,000,000	
Land	1,000,000	
Cash		6,000,000

Frequently, a natural resource asset is subject to *reclamation costs* or *restoration costs* at the end of the project's life. For example, for a strip mine used to extract coal, the mine operator incurs substantial costs to fill in the mine and return it to its original contour at the end of the mine's productive life. Reclamation costs must be considered when calculating the amount of costs to be allocated over the life of the asset (depletion is discussed later in the chapter).

Exploration Costs

Exploration costs are incurred to discover the existence and exact location of the natural resource. For example, a petroleum manufacturer purchases an oil field (acquisition cost) and then drills to discover oil. The costs of engaging in the drilling activity (including supplies, labor, and machinery depreciation charges) are exploration costs. The accounting for exploration costs has emerged as one of the most controversial topics in accounting history. At the center of the controversy is the determination of whether the costs of unsuccessful exploration activities are assets or expenses. Two schools of thought on this issue have emerged—successful efforts and full costing.

The ***successful efforts*** argument maintains that if six wells are drilled and only two strike oil, then **the exploration costs of the two successful wells are capitalized in the natural resources account, and the costs of the four unsuccessful wells are expensed.** This argument is rational because only the successful wells yield probable future economic benefits (i.e., the sale of oil) and, hence, should be called assets.

The ***full costing*** approach **capitalizes exploration costs for all six wells as part of the natural resources account.** The argument is that it was necessary to drill all of the wells in order to discover oil. All costs were necessary to generate future economic benefits. Therefore, all costs should be capitalized. This argument is also rational, and it has precedent in other areas of accounting. The cost of producing spoiled goods, for example, is included as part of the cost of producing saleable goods if it is necessary to spoil some goods in the production of those saleable goods.

Since reasonable arguments can be made to support both successful efforts and full costing, both methods are currently used to account for natural resource exploration costs. Managers choose the method they believe is best for their company. Because firms in the same industry often choose different approaches, the resulting financial statements are not comparable across firms.

In the past, many financial statement users complained about the lack of comparability brought about by two such different accounting methods used for the same transaction. At one time, the Securities and Exchange Commission urged the accounting profession to decide on one method, and accounting policy makers chose the successful efforts method. Smaller companies then presented economic consequences arguments in favor of full costing for their firms. They argued that smaller companies would be less likely to raise capital with favorable terms because their income was not sufficiently large to absorb the expensing of unsuccessful wells. As an unfavorable consequence, oil exploration would decrease. In response to the political pressure from firms supporting full costing, the SEC then rejected both the full costing and the successful efforts methods in favor of **a value-based measure, *reserve recognition accounting (RRA)*.** RRA **required the company to estimate the value of the reserves,** which, in substance, required estimates of the magnitude of the reserves, when the reserves would be extracted, how much it would cost to do so, when the goods would be sold, what the selling price would be, and an appropriate interest rate to discount cash flows. Practical implementation problems led the SEC to abandon RRA. Under intense political pressure, the FASB reversed its earlier position and, once again, allowed both the full costing and the successful efforts methods. Currently, the successful efforts method tends to be used by larger producers, while full costing tends to be used by smaller producers.

Development Costs

Once the natural resource has been acquired and exploration has determined the location of deposits, the natural resource must be developed. Development costs are both tangible (e.g., heavy equipment to drill and transport the resource) and intangible (e.g., the costs of drilling and constructing mine shafts, wells, etc.). Tangible development costs are capitalized as part of the equipment (or another property, plant, and equipment) account. Intangible development costs are capitalized as part of the natural resources account because the costs are not separable from the natural resource (e.g., the pipe used to drill an oil well cannot be moved to another well site).[10]

Summary

Acquisition costs, exploration costs (of successful efforts or all efforts, depending on the method used), and intangible development costs are capitalized as part of the natural resources account. The following example from the Quaker State Corporation annual report illustrates partial disclosures related to natural resources.

Natural Resource Footnote Disclosure: Quaker State Corporation

Costs of natural gas and crude oil producing properties are accounted for under the successful efforts method. Lease acquisition costs are capitalized and amortized by the unit of production method based on proved reserves, and equipment and intangible drilling costs are capitalized and amortized by the unit of production method based on proved developed reserves.

Estimated costs of future dismantlement, restoration, reclamation and abandonment of natural gas and crude oil producing properties are accrued through a charge to operations on a unit of production basis.

At this time, we review the asset side of the balance sheet at acquisition for the items already discussed in this chapter.

10. The accounting system captures all costs incurred with respect to natural resources, including additional costs incurred to protect the environment and minimize the environmental risk. For example, in the aftermath of the Exxon Valdez oil spill, double-hull oil tankers, which are more expensive to produce than single-hull tankers, are now used to transport Alaskan crude oil. The direct cost to Exxon to clean up the oil spill and the indirect costs resulting from Exxon's tarnished reputation were substantial.

Assets

Property, Plant, and Equipment	
Property (i.e., land)	Fair value at acquisition (historical cost)
Buildings	Fair value at acquisition (historical cost)
Equipment	Fair value at acquisition (historical cost)
Natural resources	*Fair value at acquisition (historical cost) as incurred in acquisition, exploration, and development*

Acquisition: Intangible Assets

5 Classify and record investments in intangible assets.

Intangible assets usually represent a right, privilege, or competitive advantage.[11] As with any asset, corporations acquire intangible assets at a cost that represents the minimum expected future economic benefits from using the asset in operations. The major issue for intangible assets is whether acquisition costs should be capitalized or expensed. Since the capitalization or expensing decision rests on a reliable determination of the probability of future economic benefits, this decision can be viewed as determining whether probable future economic benefits exist and the timing of their occurrence.

We use the following concepts in our discussion of the accounting for intangible assets:

- Degree of identifiability (specifically identifiable or unidentifiable)
- Manner of acquisition (external purchase or internal creation)
- Period of benefit (indefinite or legally limited)

The following table shows the appropriate accounting treatment for intangible assets (capitalize or expense) based on the interaction of the first two concepts—identifiability and manner of acquisition.

Type of Intangible Asset	**Manner of Acquisition**	
	Purchased	**Internally Created**
Specifically identifiable	Capitalize	Capitalize costs that are not research and development (R&D) expenditures
Unidentifiable	Capitalize	Expense

Specifically Identifiable Intangible Assets

6 Account for research and development expenditures.

Examples of specifically identifiable assets and their legally limited (or GAAP-imposed) periods of economic benefit are:

- Patents—shorter of 20 years or useful life
- Copyrights—shorter of 40 years or useful life
- Trademarks and trade names—shorter of 40 years or useful life
- Franchises—shorter of 40 years or useful life
- Organization costs—40 years or an arbitrarily short period of no less than five years

At the time of the writing of the text, a FASB exposure draft[12] proposed changing the amortization periods for intangible assets as follows.

- *General rule:* Amortize an intangible asset over its estimated economic life, presumed to be 20 years or less.
- The 20-year maximum period presumption can be overcome if the intangible asset generates clearly identifiable cash flows that are expected to continue more

11. APB No. 17, "Intangible Assets" (New York: AICPA, 1970), is the primary standard governing the accounting for intangible assets.
12. "Business Combinations and Intangible Assets," *Proposed Statement of Financial Accounting Standards,* September 7, 1999 (Stamford, Conn.: FASB, 1999).

than 20 years. In this case, amortize the intangible asset over the period (>20 years) expected to be benefitted.

- The exposure draft identified one type of intangible asset that requires no amortization because it has an indefinite useful life (e.g., a broadcast license for a television station). This type of asset should be assessed annually for impairment.

The costs (i.e., the fair value of consideration given) to purchase *or* internally create specifically identifiable, intangible assets are capitalized. For example, costs to purchase a copyright, legally register it, and defend its infringement are capitalized as part of the intangible asset account called Copyrights. Cost of applying for a patent and the legal costs associated with defending a patent are capitalized into the intangible asset account called Patents. Similarly, organization costs such as legal fees and state-imposed registration costs are capitalized as part of the intangible asset account called Organization Costs.

Each of these specifically identifiable intangible assets yields probable future economic benefits. For example, a patent grants exclusive rights to produce a product or operate a process. Because no competitor can do likewise for 20 years, the corporation owning the patent should be able to make superior profits over that period of time. But, it is not likely that the economic useful life of a patent is as long as 20 years. An easily understandable example is a patent on a new kind of computer printing device. Technological advancements by competitors will allow them to produce products to replace the printing device without replicating it.

An important exception to the rule of capitalizing internally developed, specifically identifiable, intangible asset costs is research and development (R&D) costs. The FASB requires that R&D costs be expensed.[13] ***Research*** **is a planned search for new knowledge** that (hopefully) leads to a new product or process or an improvement of an existing product or process. ***Development*** **is the translation of research into a plan or design.** Note that R&D is related to *preproduction* efforts. R&D, if successful, may lead to a patentable product or process.

Historically, the appropriate accounting treatment for R&D has been debated among accountants. Undoubtedly, some portion of R&D expenditures will lead to future economic benefits. However, it is difficult to determine which R&D expenses will lead to successful products and/or processes. For example, a drug company may conduct basic R&D on twenty different projects, in the hope that one or two will lead to commercially viable products. Because of the difficulty in determining which R&D expenses will lead to future economic benefits, the FASB has ruled that research and development costs should be expensed immediately.[14] This accounting rule means that companies uniformly report R&D. *SFAS No. 2* identifies five elements of R&D:

1. Materials, equipment, and facilities, if acquired for a specific R&D project and have no future alternative use (for R&D or otherwise), should be expensed immediately as R&D expense. If materials, equipment, and facilities acquired have alternative future uses, an appropriate portion of the total cost should be allocated to the current R&D project and expensed. If materials, equipment, and facilities are acquired for multiple R&D projects, the cost should be allocated among those projects, with the depreciation expense reported as part of R&D expense.
2. Personnel involved in R&D activities.
3. Purchased intangibles used in R&D.
4. Contract R&D services performed by someone else.
5. Reasonable allocation of related indirect costs.

13. *SFAS No. 2,* "Accounting for Research and Development Costs" (Stamford, Conn.: FASB, 1974).
14. An exception to this rule occurs when R&D services are performed for another company under a contract for reimbursement. Such services yield probable future economic benefits, and thus, the costs are assets (e.g., a contract receivable). See *SFAS No. 68,* "Research and Development Arrangements" (Stamford, Conn.: FASB, 1982).

Research and development costs are common for many companies, particularly for high-technology companies.[15] The following slightly modified disclosure for Intel Corporation illustrates the magnitude of R&D expenses for technology companies.

Research and Development Disclosure—Intel Corporation

In its current year consolidated statements of income, Intel reported research and development expense of $1.808 billion, which was equal to about 8.7% of reported net revenues of $20.847 billion. Over the prior three year period, Intel's research and development expenses as a percent of net revenues ranged from about 8.0% to about 9.6%.

Unidentifiable Intangible Assets—Goodwill

In order to obtain a competitive advantage, corporations spend large amounts to promote customer satisfaction and develop strong supplier relationships (i.e., to develop goodwill with its customers and suppliers) in hopes of obtaining future economic benefits. It is almost impossible, however, to obtain a reliable estimate of the economic value of the goodwill created internally. Thus, accountants expense corporate spending efforts to create goodwill.

Goodwill can be capitalized only if purchased externally in a verifiable transaction that establishes the value of goodwill. Capitalized goodwill is equal to the portion of the total purchase price in an acquisition in excess of the sum of fair market values of identifiable net assets acquired. Under this definition, goodwill serves as a master valuation account. As of the writing of this text, goodwill is amortized over its estimated useful life, not to exceed 40 years.[16] However, a recent FASB exposure draft[17] proposes to change the maximum amortization period to 20 years.

During the late 1990s, many companies purchased technology firms and attributed a large portion of the purchase price to "in-process research and development." After acquisition, a large amount of in-process R&D was expensed because of the uncertainty of future cash flows. The SEC became worried that companies were using this practice to manipulate future income, in particular to reduce expenses in future periods. To the extent that any price premium paid in an acquisition was attributed to in-process R&D rather than to goodwill, companies were willing to recognize current expenses for in-process R&D charges rather than to record future goodwill expense charges. In 1998, the SEC began scrutinizing all in-process R&D write-offs. As an example, in the 1998 acquisition of MCI by WorldCom, MCI WorldCom originally proposed a $7 billion write-off for in-process R&D related to the MCI acquisition. In negotiations with the SEC, the charge was reduced to $3.1 billion. Also in 1998, the SEC required Intellicorp Inc. to reduce a proposed in-process R&D charge from $4.8 million (75% of the purchase price of ICS Deloitte Management LLS's interface technology) to $2.7 million.

Example 12. Assume that Tromp Enterprises acquires Eastern Ice Cream Shop for $1,000,000 in cash. The book value and fair market value of Eastern's net assets are equal at the date of acquisition, except for net property, plant, and equipment (PP&E), which has a fair market value that is $30,000 higher than book value.

15. Financial Statement Disclosures—Research and Development. Of the 600 companies surveyed in the *1999 Accounting Trends and Techniques,* 308 reported research and development type costs.

16. Financial Statement Disclosures—Goodwill. Of the 600 companies surveyed in the *1999 Accounting Trends and Techniques,* 453 reported goodwill recognized in a business combination. Amortization periods were reported as follows: 40 years (166 firms); not exceeding 40 years (94 firms); 25–30 years (37 firms); 20 years (27 firms); 10–15 years (30 firms); legal/estimated life (51 firms); other (117 firms). The number of firms reporting amortization periods sums to more than 453 because firms can make multiple disclosures regarding amortization periods in the financial statements.

17. "Business Combinations and Intangible Assets," *Proposed Statement of Financial Accounting Standards,* September 7, 1999 (Stamford, Conn.: FASB, 1999).

Eastern Ice Cream Shop Balance Sheet—Book Value at Date of Acquisition

Cash	$ 100,000	Current liabilities	$ 50,000
Other current assets	200,000	Long-term liabilities	200,000
PP&E	900,000	Equity	950,000
	$1,200,000		$1,200,000

Solution. Tromp paid $1,000,000 to acquire net assets with individual fair market values that total $980,000 [assets with a fair value of $1,230,000 ($1,200,000 plus $30,000 additional PP&E value) less liabilities of $250,000]. The assumption that individuals trade items with equal fair value implies that Eastern is worth $1,000,000 (the cash acquisition price), and that Eastern has an unrecorded asset of $20,000 ($1,000,000 − $980,000). Tromp records the additional $20,000 of purchase price as goodwill along with the other assets and liabilities purchased at their net fair market value of $980,000.

EXAMPLE 12 Journal Entry

Cash	100,000	
Other Current Assets	200,000	
PP&E	930,000	
Goodwill	20,000	
Current Liabilities		50,000
Long-term Liabilities		200,000
Cash		1,000,000

The following information for Boise Cascade Corp. reflects the presentation of goodwill in the financial statements.

Goodwill Disclosure: Boise Cascade Corp.

Partial Balance Sheet Information (In millions)	1997	1996
Goodwill, net of accumulated amortization of $24,020,000 and $13,139,000	$137.4	$144.8

Note 1 (In Part): Summary of Significant Accounting Policies

Goodwill: Goodwill represents the excess of purchase price and related costs over the value assigned to the net tangible assets of businesses acquired. Goodwill is amortized on a straight-line basis over 40 years. Periodically, the company reviews the recoverability of goodwill. The measurement of possible impairment is based primarily on the ability to recover the balance of the goodwill from expected future operating cash flows on an undiscounted basis. In management's opinion, no material impairment exists at December 31, 1997. Amortization expense was $11,037,000 in 1997, $6,830,000 in 1996, and $2,299,000 in 1995.

Summary

We have extended our review of the asset side of the balance sheet to include intangible assets at acquisition.

Assets

Property, Plant, and Equipment

Property (i.e., land)	Fair value at acquisition (historical cost)
Buildings	Fair value at acquisition (historical cost)
Equipment	Fair value at acquisition (historical cost)
Natural resources	Fair value at acquisition (historical cost) as incurred in acquisition, exploration, and development

(continued)

Intangible Assets[18]	
Patents, Copyrights, Tradenames, etc.	*Fair value at acquisition (historical cost) to purchase externally or create internally*
Goodwill	*Fair value at acquisition (historical cost) to purchase externally*

Acquisition: Exceptions to the Fair Value Rule

7 Identify and account for exceptions to the general rule of recording acquired productive assets.

In the preceding sections, either the fair market value (FMV) of consideration given or the fair value of the asset received was readily determinable. Also, the items traded were dissimilar (e.g., cash for equipment). In this section, we review two exceptions to the rule of recording property, plant, and equipment at fair value. Both occur when nonmonetary assets (e.g., property, plant, and equipment or inventory) are exchanged and (1) neither of the two traded assets' FMVs are determinable, or (2) the exchange results in a *gain* and involves the trade of *similar* assets.[19]

Example 13. A delivery truck (original cost $15,000, accumulated depreciation $9,000) is traded for a computer. Neither asset's fair value is readily determinable.

Solution. Because the fair value of the exchange is not reliably determinable, the asset received would be recorded at the *book value* of what was given up ($15,000 − 9,000 = $6,000).

EXAMPLE 13 Journal Entry

Computer (PP&E)	6,000	
Accumulated Depreciation—Truck	9,000	
Truck (PP&E)		15,000

Example 14. A new asset with a fair value of $42,000 is acquired by giving up an old asset (original cost $50,000, accumulated depreciation $19,000, fair value of $42,000).

Solution. A diagram is useful in solving this problem:

Old asset:
Book value = $31,000 ($50,000 − $19,000)
Fair value = $42,000

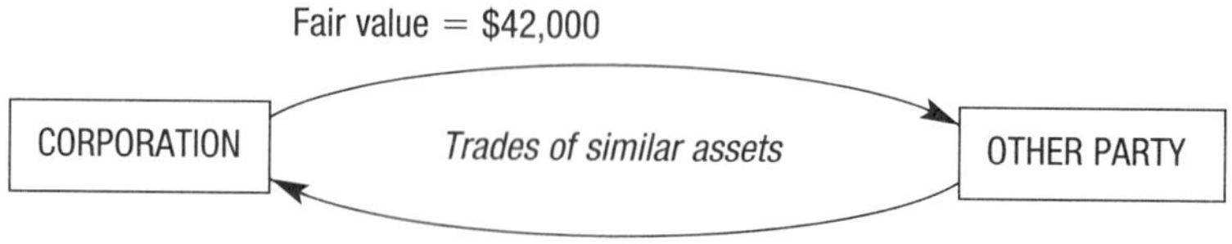

New asset
Fair value = $42,000

If we follow the general rule, the new asset is recorded at the fair value of what was given up, $42,000. The old asset's $31,000 book value would be removed from the books, and an $11,000 gain would be recognized. (Remember

18. Financial Statement Disclosures—Intangible Assets. Of the 600 companies surveyed in the *1999 Accounting Trends and Techniques*, 453 reported goodwill recognized in a business combination; 96 reported trademarks, brand names, and copyrights; 73 reported patents and patent rights; 34 reported licenses, franchises, and memberships; 34 reported technology; 28 reported noncompete covenants; 20 reported customer lists; and 53 reported other types of intangible assets.

19. APB No. 29, "Accounting for Nonmonetary Transactions" (New York: AICPA, 1973). In some exchanges of nonmonetary assets, monetary consideration may also be involved. Monetary consideration includes cash as well as near cash assets such as accounts receivable and notes receivable. If monetary consideration is included in the exchange transaction, the rules for asset valuation and gain recognition are complex and somewhat arbitrary. In this regard, see EITF Issue No. 86–29, "Nonmonetary Transactions: Magnitude of Boot and Exceptions to the Use of Fair Value," *Emerging Issues Task Force Abstracts* (October 1987). To simplify the presentation, we do not illustrate nonmonetary exchanges that also include monetary consideration.

that an increase in net assets from peripheral or incidental transactions is a gain. The corporation increased net assets from $31,000 to $42,000 via the exchange transaction.) Although, in economic terms, the gain had occurred during prior periods, the external verification of the gain through the exchange triggers *accounting* recognition.

If the old asset and the new asset are *dissimilar* (e.g., a truck for a computer), then it is proper to follow the general rule and allow the corporation to record a gain. Property, plant, and equipment is acquired to create product sales revenue or service revenue; revenue is generated by using the property, plant, and equipment. Alternatively, gains can be recognized by selling assets with any unused revenue producing potential to other parties. In our example, the old asset has $42,000 of benefits that would have been recognized in the financial statements as revenues when the asset was used. The $31,000 book value would have been matched (i.e., converted to expenses through depreciation) against these revenues in future periods. Instead, the sale of the old asset accelerates the revenue recognition and cost matching process so that all remaining costs ($31,000) are matched against the benefits received ($42,000) in the current period.

A problem arises, however, in accelerating this recognition process if the assets exchanged are *similar*. If the new asset continues the earnings process of the old asset, then accounting policy makers emphasize that the recognition of gain should wait until the earnings process is complete, when production or services created by the new asset are sold. Delaying gain recognition is equivalent to not writing up the asset from the book value of $31,000 to the fair value of $42,000. To accomplish this gain deferral, the new asset received is recorded at the *book value of what has been given up*, the old asset ($31,000).[20]

EXAMPLE 14 Journal Entries

Assuming the nonmonetary assets exchanged are dissimilar		
Asset (New)	42,000	
Accumulated Depreciation—Asset (Old)	19,000	
Asset (Old)		50,000
Gain on Asset Exchange		11,000
Assuming the nonmonetary assets exchanged are similar		
Asset (New)	31,000	
Accumulated Depreciation—Asset (Old)	19,000	
Asset (Old)		50,000

The importance of the special rule of postponing a resulting gain from a trade of similar assets is evident when the potential for income manipulation in this area is considered, as shown in the following example.

Example 15. Ace Realty owns a parcel of land with a fair market value of $100,000. The land was acquired two years ago at a cost of $65,000. Preferred Realty owns an identical parcel next door. It is a bad year for land sales, and both companies would like to show additional income. Can the two companies trade the land parcels and increase income in the process?

Solution. If the special rule on trades of similar assets did not exist, the two companies could trade the land and increase income. Both would remove $65,000 in cost from their books and record the land received at $100,000 (the FMV surrendered), recognizing a $35,000 gain in the process. Since the special rule (defer gains on the sale of similar assets) exists, a trade would result in both companies recording the new land at $65,000, the *book value* surrendered. No gain would occur because assets simultaneously increased $65,000 and decreased $65,000.

20. Due to conservatism, if the old asset's book value exceeds the fair value of the asset acquired, a loss is recorded (i.e., the rule for nonmonetary exchanges of similar assets is to recognize losses and defer gains).

EXAMPLE 15 Journal Entry

Land (New)	65,000	
Land (Old)		65,000

Expenditures After Acquisition

Each long-term productive asset has an estimated economic useful life. This economic useful life may be expressed in terms of years, or in terms of the total quality and quantity (capacity) of service that the asset will provide over the useful life. For example, Federal Express might expect delivery vans to last 10 years, or to deliver 750,000 packages, or to travel 300,000 miles.

From the time an investment is made in a long-term productive asset to the time the asset is disposed, corporations make additional expenditures on the asset for several reasons. First, certain assets must be repaired and maintained. Since repairs and maintenance do not extend the original estimate of an asset's service potential, expensing such costs is appropriate. **Costs that do not extend the original estimates of an asset's useful life, service quality, or service quantity are** referred to as ***revenue expenditures.*** They are matched against current period revenues (i.e., expensed immediately).

Alternatively, ***capital expenditures*** **increase future service potential by either extending the asset's useful life beyond the original estimated life or increasing service quality or capacity beyond the original estimates.** These expenditures are often referred to as "additions," "replacements," "improvements," or "betterments." These costs become part of the acquisition cost of the asset.

While, conceptually, the distinction between revenue and capital expenditures is apparent, the practical determination of the difference between the two is often difficult, and an opportunity for income manipulation emerges. For example, if large revenue expenditures are capitalized, current period income is freed from an expense charge. Instead, the expenditure is expensed through depreciation charges over the remaining life of the asset. For convenience, some companies use a particular dollar amount threshold in recognizing revenue and capital expenditures. For example, a company may decide that capital expenditures of less than $500 will automatically be expensed. This policy minimizes the record keeping costs associated with capital expenditures (e.g., depreciation and annual physical audits).

The following partial footnote from GenCorp, Inc.'s, financial statements reflects costs after acquisition.

Property, Plant and Equipment Footnote Disclosure: GenCorp, Inc.

Refurbishment costs are capitalized in the property accounts whereas ordinary maintenance and repair costs are expensed as incurred.

Cost Allocation: Depreciation, Depletion, and Amortization

8 Allocate costs by applying the various methods for depletion, depreciation, and amortization.

Once the acquisition cost has been determined, **the cost must be allocated to the periods in which revenues are generated by the asset.** This is accomplished through ***depreciation*** (**of plant and equipment**), ***depletion*** (**of natural resources**), and ***amortization*** (**of intangible assets**). Depreciation can be accomplished through traditional methods—straight-line, sum-of-the-years'-digits, double-declining-balance, and units-of-output). Depletion is normally accomplished by using the units-of-output method, and amortization generally occurs under the straight-line method. But, in substance, each method allocates costs to the periods in which revenues are generated from using the asset.

The cost allocation process involves reducing the property, plant, and equipment (PP&E), natural resource, or intangible asset account and recognizing that the decrease of an asset from its use in normal operations is an expense—depreciation, depletion, or amortization expense, respectively. These decreases in income are matched with increases in income (i.e., revenues from using the asset) in each period of the asset's useful life. On the balance sheet, the asset account is either reduced directly or shown at its **historical cost less the accumulated depreciation, depletion, or amortization to date** (i.e., its ***book value***). The most common example of the *contra account* approach is the use of the accumulated depreciation account for buildings and equipment.[21] For intangible assets and natural resources, most companies do not use a contra account in the cost allocation process.

It is important to realize that the balance sheet reports the *unallocated historical cost* or book value for PP&E, intangible assets, and natural resources. The *fair value is not reported.* Different depreciation methods yield different book values. The use of accelerated methods (e.g., double-declining-balance) quickly reduces book value in the early years of an asset's life, thus yielding a conservative book value relative to straight-line depreciation. The larger depreciation expense charges related to accelerated methods also provide more conservative measures of net income in the earlier years than are obtained using the straight-line method.

Cost Allocation Methods

The most common depreciation method for financial reporting purposes is the straight-line method.[22] The most common amortization method for intangible assets is also the straight-line method, while the most common method of depletion is the units-of-output method. For income tax purposes, most companies use the modified accelerated cost recovery system (MACRS), an accelerated method prescribed by the Internal Revenue Service. We do not discuss MACRS in this text.

In this section, we review four different cost allocation methods: straight-line, double-declining-balance (to illustrate an accelerated method), units-of-output, and present value of remaining cash flows (to illustrate a theoretically preferred method).

Straight-Line In the ***straight-line method,*** **the same percentage of depreciable cost is recognized each year.** *Depreciable cost* equals historical cost less estimated salvage. The percentage used is $1 \div n$, where n equals the estimated useful life of the asset.

Example 16. A depreciable asset is purchased for $30,000. It has an estimated useful life of five years and an estimated salvage value of $5,000.

Solution. Straight-line annual depreciation expense is calculated as follows:

$$\text{Straight-line depreciation expense} = (\text{Original cost} - \text{Estimated salvage value}) \div \text{Estimated life}$$
$$\$5000 = (\$30{,}000 - \$5{,}000) \div 5 \text{ years}$$

Declining Balance Several declining balance accelerated methods [e.g., double-declining-balance (200%), 150% declining balance] may be used. To compute depreciation expense, a ***declining balance*** method **multiplies the asset's beginning of the period book value by some multiple of the straight-line percentage rate.**

21. A contra account is used to accumulate the reductions in another account so that the original cost may be maintained. For example, if a depreciable asset cost $1,000,000, and $400,000 has been depreciated, the depreciation charges are accumulated in the contra account, Accumulated Depreciation. The balance sheet would reflect the assets's historical cost of $1,000,000 less accumulated depreciation of $400,000 for a book value of $600,000. A benefit of the contra account approach is that the asset's original cost is maintained in the accounting records.

22. Financial Statement Disclosures—Depreciation Methods. Of 600 companies surveyed in the *1999 Accounting Trends and Techniques,* depreciation methods were reported as follows: 577 used straight-line, 43 used an unspecified accelerated method, 36 used units-of-production, 25 used declining balance, 9 used sum-of-the-years'-digits, and 9 used other methods. (These numbers sum to more than 600 because some companies used different methods for different types of assets.)

Example 17. A company purchases a $400,000 depreciable asset with an estimated useful life of five years (20% depreciation per year under the straight-line method), and uses the double-declining-balance method to compute depreciation expense.

Solution. The first year's depreciation using the double-declining-balance method is as follows:

$$\text{Double-declining-balance depreciation expense} = \text{Beginning of period book value} \times (200\% \times 20\%)$$
$$\$160{,}000 = \$400{,}000 \times 200\% \times 20\%$$

Please note that of the depreciation methods discussed, declining balance methods are the only ones that do *not* calculate depreciation expense as a portion of depreciable cost.[23]

Units-of-Output A ***units-of-output method*** **allocates costs to a period based upon the usage during the period in some unit of measure** (e.g., machine hours, miles traveled, tons mined) **as a percentage of the total estimated units of production.** When applied to natural resource assets, any estimated reclamation costs at the end of the asset should be treated as a cost to be allocated.

Example 18. A depreciable asset has an original cost of $60,000, an estimated salvage value of $10,000, and an estimated useful life of 100,000 machine hours. In the first year, the asset was used 30,000 machine hours.

Solution.

$$\text{Units-of-output depreciation expense} = (\text{Original cost} - \text{Estimated salvage value}) \times (\text{Current period usage} \div \text{Estimated total usage})$$
$$\$15{,}000 = (\$60{,}000 - \$10{,}000) \times (30{,}000 \div 100{,}000)$$

Present Value Method Although the present value of the remaining cash flows method is not commonly used in financial reports, we review it here because of its theoretical relationship to the asset's purchase price (the present value of future cash flows generated by using the asset). The present value method requires an estimate of the future cash flows from using the machine. At the end of each year, the ***present value of the remaining cash flows*** is computed, with the **current-year depreciation equal to the difference between the beginning and ending book values.** Despite its theoretical superiority, the present value method is rarely applied in practice because of the need to estimate specific future cash flows expected from a particular machine. Therefore, the benefits of using a conceptually superior method do not outweigh its costs.[24] A comparison of traditional depreciation methods to the present value method is illustrated in the next example problem.

Example 19. Martinez Corporation acquires a long-lived asset (equipment, a timber tract, an intangible asset, etc.) for $150,000. The asset's useful life is five years with no expected salvage value at the end of the fifth year. At the time of asset purchase, Martinez expects that the asset will produce a positive net cash flow of $39,570 in each of the five years. Assume that Martinez requires a 10% return on the investment. Compute the depreciation expense and the book value of the long-

23. Another accelerated depreciation method that is frequently discussed in accounting texts is the ***sum-of-the-year's-digits method.*** Under sum-of-the-years'-digits, a **different percentage of depreciable cost is recognized each year.** The percentage used each year is computed as follows:

$$\frac{\text{Remaining useful life at the beginning of the year}}{[n(n+1)] \div 2}$$

For the previous example with a five-year estimated useful life, the denominator is $[n(n + 1)] \div 2 = (5 \times 6) \div 2 = 15$. First year depreciation equals [$25,000 × (5 ÷ 15)] = $8,333. Similarly, second year depreciation equals [$25,000 × (4 ÷ 15)] = $6,667. We do not further illustrate this method because it is used infrequently in practice.

24. This point of view has been dramatically modified in recent accounting practice relating to "asset impairment" (discussed in a later section of this chapter).

lived asset disclosed on the balance sheet under the straight-line, double-declining-balance, and units-of-output cost allocation methods. For the units-of-output method, assume that the machine's expected output is 80,000 units, with production of units over the five years of 15,000; 10,000; 30,000; 15,000; and 10,000 units, respectively. Finally, compute the depreciation each period based upon the present value of the remaining cash flows.

Solution.

Straight-line:	$150,000 ÷ 5 years = $30,000 per year
Double-declining-balance:	$150,000 × 40% = $60,000 (year 1) $90,000 × 40% = $36,000 (year 2) $54,000 × 40% = $21,600 (year 3) $32,400 × 40% = $12,960 (year 4) Remaining balance = $19,440 (year 5)[25]
Units-of-output:	$150,000 × (15,000 ÷ 80,000) = $28,125 (year 1) $150,000 × (10,000 ÷ 80,000) = $18,750 (year 2) $150,000 × (30,000 ÷ 80,000) = $56,250 (year 3) $150,000 × (15,000 ÷ 80,000) = $28,125 (year 4) $150,000 × (10,000 ÷ 80,000) = $18,750 (year 5)

			Present Value Depreciation
Present value of remaining cash flows at the end of each year:[26]	At acquisition date:	$150,000	
	At end of year 1:	$125,430	$24,570
	At end of year 2:	$98,404	$27,026
	At end of year 3:	$68,675	$29,729
	At end of year 4:	$35,972	$32,703
	At end of year 5:	$0	$35,972

The results from these methods are summarized in the following table.

BALANCE SHEET BOOK VALUES UNDER ALTERNATIVE DEPRECIATION METHODS

	Depreciation Method			
	Traditional Methods			
	Straight-Line	Double-Declining-Balance	Units-of-Output	Present Value
Long-lived asset balance sheet disclosure (net of accumulated depreciation, depletion, or amortization)				
12/31/Year 1	$120,000	$90,000	$121,875	$125,430
12/31/Year 2	90,000	54,000	103,125	98,404
12/31/Year 3	60,000	32,400	46,875	68,675
12/31/Year 4	30,000	19,440	18,750	35,972
12/31/Year 5	0	0	0	0

Note that none of the traditional depreciation methods are designed to measure the present value of the future cash flows at each remaining balance sheet date. *Depreciation expense, as shown in the accrual-based financial statements, is simply a systematic and rational allocation of costs to the periods benefitted.*

25. An acceptable variation of the double-declining-balance method is to convert to the straight-line method in the year in which the double-declining-balance amount would be less than the straight-line amount. In this problem, this occurs in year 3 ($21,600 < $30,000). Under the acceptable variation, depreciation in years 3–5 would be [$54,000 (book value at the beginning of year 3) ÷ 3] = $18,000.
26. Use a financial calculator to verify that with $n = 5$, the present value of the cash flows at 10% is $150,000. By reducing n by one each period, we generate the book values for each successive period.

Journal Entries to Record Depreciation, Depletion, and Amortization Expense

Depreciation expense:

Depreciation Expense	XXXX	
Accumulated Depreciation		XXXX

Depletion of a natural resource typically does not involve the use of an accumulated depletion account; a credit is made directly to the natural resource account:

Depletion Expense	XXXX	
Natural Resources		XXXX

Amortization of intangible assets generally involves the direct credit to the intangible asset account:

Amortization Expense	XXXX	
Intangible Asset		XXXX

The expense treatment shown is not proper if the long-lived asset is used in production. Instead, the debit should be to an asset account (e.g., Inventory), or to a cost accumulation account (e.g., Factory Overhead) that is eventually allocated to an asset account.

Impairment of Asset Value

9 Determine and report asset impairments.

What if management knows that the book value and the fair value of the asset do not correspond? As we have learned, PP&E and intangible assets are recorded at historical cost, and those costs are systematically allocated to future periods using an acceptable cost allocation method. The **difference between an asset's book value and its FMV** equals the ***unrealized gain/loss*** on the asset. As a general rule, accountants do not recognize unrealized gains/losses on PP&E in current period's income. However, at each balance sheet date, three situations are possible: FMV exceeds book value, FMV equals book value (an unlikely event), or FMV is less than book value.

Fair Value Exceeds Book Value

If fair value exceeds book value, the unrealized gain can be recognized only if the asset is sold (i.e., the gain is then realized). If the unrealized gain is not recognized through sale, income will be recognized in future periods when the asset generates revenues (the realization of fair value) and is depreciated (the matching of book value against revenues).[27]

Fair Value Less Than Book Value

At a balance sheet date, if management believes that the asset's fair value is less than its book value and that the decline is temporary, then the general rule is to do nothing (i.e., do not recognize the unrealized loss). However, if management believes that the asset may have permanently declined in value at a balance sheet date, then GAAP (*SFAS No. 121*) requires that the asset be assessed for ***impairment.*** The asset impairment is recognized by writing down the asset to its *recoverable value.* Recoverable value equals either (1) the net realizable value if the asset is going to be *sold* or (2) the present value of future indirect cash flows from the asset if the asset is going to be *used.*[28] This write-down violates the general rule of reporting depreciable assets at book value (cost − accumulated depreciation), but it is justified on the basis of conservatism.[29]

27. APB Opinion No. 6 prohibits property, plant, and equipment write-ups to amounts above cost. However, some other countries do allow for the write-up of assets. For example, companies in Great Britain can write up property, plant, and equipment assets.

28. Although the present value of future indirect cash flows from the asset should be computed if the asset is going to be used, in practice, estimating the cash flows may be difficult, if not impossible. Accordingly, an estimate of the asset's fair market value is frequently used as recoverable value.

29. Linda J. Zucca and David R. Campbell, "A Closer Look at Discretionary Write-downs of Impaired

(continued)

Although impaired assets should be written down to the present value of future cash flows (if they will *not* be sold), the determination of whether any write-down should occur is less stringent. The FASB decided that a write-down should not occur unless the *gross* future (undiscounted) cash flows (rather than the present value of future cash flows) are less than the asset's current book value. If the gross future cash flows are less than the asset's current book value, then the asset is deemed to have been impaired, and the asset is written down to its present value. The "loss on asset impairment" is reflected in the income statement. This impairment test based on gross future cash flows is not used if the asset is to be sold. In that case, the asset is simply written down if net realizable value is less than book value at a balance sheet date, and a loss is recognized.[30]

Example 20. Griese Corp. owns a machine with the following characteristics at December 31, 2001:

Original cost	$100,000
Accumulated depreciation	45,000
Present value of future cash flows (estimate of fair value in continued use)	30,000
Net realizable value (estimated cash inflow from immediate sale)	25,000

Under each of the following conditions, at what amount should the machine be reported on the balance sheet?

a. Gross future cash flows from continued use of the machine are estimated to be $60,000 and the asset is in use.
b. Gross future cash flows from continued use of the machine are estimated to be $50,000 and the asset is in use.
c. The asset is being held for sale.

Solution.

a. The asset is in use, and the recoverability test should be applied. Gross future cash flows of $60,000 exceed the machine's book value of $55,000 ($100,000 original cost less $45,000 depreciation). Therefore, the asset is not impaired and should be reported on the balance sheet at the $55,000 book value.
b. The asset is in use, and the recoverability test should be applied. Gross future cash flows of $50,000 are less than the machine's book value of $55,000. Therefore, the asset is impaired and should be reported on the balance sheet at its present value of $30,000 instead of $55,000. Reducing the asset's book value from $55,000 to $30,000 requires the recognition of a $25,000 loss on asset impairment on the income statement.
c. The asset is being held for resale and, therefore, should be shown on the balance sheet at the lower of unamortized cost ($55,000) or net realizable value ($25,000). A $30,000 write-down results in a loss of $30,000 reported on the income statement.

Assets," *Accounting Horizons* (September 1992): 30–41. Seventy-seven write-downs by 67 firms (two-thirds were NYSE firms) were identified during the 1981–1983 period. In each case, the firms' financial statements did not indicate that the assets were going to be sold. An interesting finding of this study was that in 58.4% of the cases, earnings before write-down were lower than expected; in 28.6% of the cases, earnings before write-down were higher than expected; and in 13% of the cases, earnings remained fairly level. These findings suggest that firms took "the big bath," believing that the securities market would not distinguish between bad news and "worse" bad news.

30. If the asset is held for resale and another balance sheet date passes, further write-downs or recoveries of write-downs may need to be recognized.

EXAMPLE 20 Journal Entries

Record a machine purchased for $100,000, accumulated depreciation of $45,000:

Machine	100,000	
Cash (or some kind of payable)		100,000
Depreciation Expense	45,000	
Accumulated Depreciation—Machine		45,000
Record impairment:		
a. No entry. The asset is not impaired and is already at $55,000 book value.		
b. Loss on Asset Impairment	25,000	
Accumulated Depreciation—Machine		25,000
c. Loss on Asset Impairment	30,000	
Accumulated Depreciation—Machine		30,000

As an example of an asset write-down, the following partial footnote disclosure describes an impairment charge for Woolworth Corporation.

Impairment of Long-Lived Assets Disclosure: Woolworth Corporation

Note 2 (partial). The Company adopted Statement of Financial Accounting Standards No. 121 . . . and recorded a non-cash pretax charge of $241 million ($165 million after-tax). Of the total impairment loss, $209 million represents impairment of long-lived assets such as properties, store fixtures and leasehold improvements, $24 million relates to goodwill and $8 million pertains to intangibles . . . Factors leading to the impairment were a combination of historical losses, anticipated future losses and inadequate cash flows.

Disposal and Retirement

If an asset continues to be useful beyond its original useful life estimate, then the asset appears on the financial statements as fully depreciated. That is, accumulated depreciation equals asset cost, and the book value equals zero. When an asset is disposed, accountants update depreciation (if necessary), write-off the asset and its accumulated depreciation, and recognize any gain or loss. A gain (loss) on disposal is reported in the "other income (expense)" section of the income statement.

Example 21. On February 1, 2002, the Falstaff Co. had the following information about certain machinery: cost = $2,500,000; accumulated depreciation calculated to February 1, 2002 = $2,200,000. The asset was sold on February 1, 2002, for $800,000.

Solution. Falstaff records a $500,000 gain because $800,000 cash received exceeds the $300,000 book value at February 1, 2002 ($2,500,000 original cost − $2,200,000 accumulated depreciation).

EXAMPLE 21 2/1/02 Journal Entry

Cash	800,000	
Accumulated Depreciation	2,200,000	
Machinery		2,500,000
Gain on Sale of Machinery		500,000

Capital Budgeting and the Financial Statement Effects of Investing in Productive Assets

In this section, we review the issues addressed in the chapter by illustrating a capital budgeting decision and the resulting financial statement effects. The topic of capital budgeting is discussed thoroughly in management accounting and finance classes. We briefly review that process before working an example problem.

A capital budgeting decision (1) involves deciding whether investing in a particular asset is appropriate, and (2) provides a process for deciding how a company can choose between competing potential investments. Most formal capital budgeting decisions use either a *net present value* (NPV) or *internal rate of return* (IRR) framework. The decision rule normally followed is that all positive NPV projects and those projects with an IRR that is greater than the firm's after-tax cost of capital are acceptable projects. If multiple projects are being considered, the projects can be ranked in desirability based upon the magnitude of the NPV or IRR (i.e., all other things being equal, higher NPV and IRR projects are preferred).

We use the following extended example to illustrate the capital budgeting process and the related financial statement effects.

Example 22. On January 1, 2001, Turner Corporation is deciding whether to acquire a photo color restoration machine and its patent allowing exclusive use of the color restoration process for the next five years. Turner's after-tax cost of capital is 7%. You have gathered the following information about the project.

Initial cost of the machine	$800,000
Initial cost of the patent	$50,000
Machine estimated useful life/salvage value	8 years, no salvage value
Patent life	5 years
Expected machine salvage value at the end of 5 years	$200,000
Tax rate (assume income taxes are paid in the current year)	30%
Estimated annual cash revenues (years 1–5)*	$450,000
Estimated annual cash expenses (supplies, labor, etc.) for years 1–5*	$250,000
Depreciation and amortization method	straight-line

*Cash flows for years 6–8 (after the patent expires) are not estimable.

1. Prepare an analysis of the project's (1) internal rate of return (IRR) and (2) net present value (NPV). To compute an IRR, cash flows need to be estimated from the project. In this example, the machine and the patent have different useful lives. Assume in the cash flow computations that the machinery will be depreciated over an eight-year period, but that it will be sold at the end of year 5, when the patent expires. This allows for the computation of annual cash flows over the five-year period and the use of one future cash flow value at the end of year 5. In this problem, any cash flows from years 6–8 are ignored—the patent expires after five years and estimates of cash flows for years 6–8 are not available. This IRR analysis is conservative (i.e., biased against accepting the project) because it ignores any cash flows from continuing to use the machine beyond year 5.
2. Show how the primary financial statements would reflect the assets if the project were accepted over the 2001–2005 period.

Solution. In order to compute IRR and NPV, the cash inflows and outflows must be identified. In this example, cash flows occur each year (an annuity) and a final cash flow occurs when the machine is sold. Assume that all cash flows occur at the end of each year.

Computation of annual cash flows (for years 2001–2005):

Cash revenues (from services)	$450,000
Cash expenses (for supplies, labor, etc.)	(250,000)
Net annual cash revenues	$200,000
Depreciation expense ($800,000 ÷ 8 years)	(100,000)
Amortization expense ($50,000 ÷ 5 years)	(10,000)
Pretax income	$ 90,000
Income tax expense (30%)	(27,000)
Net income	$ 63,000
Add back noncash expenses:	
Depreciation	100,000
Amortization	10,000
Annual cash inflows	$173,000*

*Alternatively, net annual cash revenues ($200,000) less income taxes paid ($27,000).

It is necessary to subtract the two noncash expenses in order to compute pretax income and the cash flow effects from shielding income taxes. Cash paid out for taxes is $33,000 lower ($110,000 × 30%) because of depreciation and amortization expenses. Note that, after computing net income, depreciation and amortization are added back to compute annual cash flows.

The final cash flow from selling the machine at the end of year 5 is calculated as follows:

Estimated salvage value			$200,000
Tax effect:			
Salvage value		$200,000	
Less book value			
Original cost	$800,000		
Accumulated depreciation, end of year 5	(500,000)	300,000	
Taxable loss		$100,000	
Tax rate		× 30%	
Tax savings			30,000
Net one-time cash flow at end of year 5			$230,000

One component of the year 5 cash flow is the $200,000 from the sale of the machine at its salvage value. Another component is the $30,000 tax savings from the loss on sale. After five years, Turner would have depreciated the asset $500,000. The book value of the asset would be $300,000 ($800,000 original cost less $500,000 accumulated depreciation). A $100,000 tax loss would be generated by receiving only $200,000 cash on the sale of an asset with a $300,000 tax basis. The tax loss times the tax rate equals the cash savings of $30,000.

To compute IRR, enter the following in a financial calculator:

Number of payments = 5
Payment = $173,000 annual cash inflow (ordinary annuity)
Present value = $850,000 ($800,000 machine cost + $50,000 patent cost)
Future value = $230,000 one time cash inflow at the end of year 5

Computing the interest rate yields an internal rate of return of 7.89% (rounded). Finance theory indicates that projects yielding a return greater than the after-tax cost of capital are acceptable. Therefore, the project would be acceptable because the IRR of 7.89% exceeds the 7% after-tax cost of capital. An alternative way to determine the viability of the project is to compute the NPV of the cash flows and compare it to the cost of the project.

To compute NPV, enter the following in a financial calculator:

Number of payments = 5
Interest rate = 7% cost of capital
Payment = $173,000 annual cash inflow (ordinary annuity)
Future value = $230,000 one time cash inflow at the end of year 5

These parameters yield a present value of $873,321. After subtracting the $850,000 initial investment, this yields a NPV of $23,321. Finance theory indicates that projects with a positive NPV are acceptable. Of course, the positive NPV occurs because 7% is used to calculate the present value, and as we determined in the previous calculation, the IRR is > 7%.

Financial Statement Effects

The financial statements reflect both the cash flows and the accrual elements of the decisions. The financial statement with the closest relationship to the decision process is the statement of cash flows.

TURNER CORPORATION
Statements of Cash Flows
(Effects of machinery and patent activities)
(Cash outflows in parentheses)

	2001	2002	2003	2004	2005
Operating Activities					
Collections from customers	450,000	450,000	450,000	450,000	450,000
Payments for labor, supplies, etc.	(250,000)	(250,000)	(250,000)	(250,000)	(250,000)
Payment of income taxes	(27,000)	(27,000)	(27,000)	(27,000)	3,000
Investing Activities					
Purchase of machine	(800,000)				
Purchase of patent	(50,000)				
Sale of machine					200,000
Net cash inflow (outflow)	(677,000)	173,000	173,000	173,000	403,000

In the operating activities section, cash revenues ($450,000) and cash expenses ($250,000) are shown as collections and payments of cash in each of the five years of the project. A $27,000 payment for income taxes is also shown in each year except 2005, when the sale of the machine saved $30,000 in taxes (from the loss on sale). When netted with the $27,000 tax payment, the $30,000 cash savings yields a $3,000 net cash inflow (i.e., refund). In the investing activities section, the cash outflows to purchase the machine and the patent are disclosed in 2001. The anticipated sales price of the machine is a cash inflow in 2005.[31]

The net cash inflow shown for each year agrees with our earlier analysis. Using these numbers and the cost of capital of 7%, you should be able to calculate the NPV and IRR of the project. The purported usefulness of the cash flow statement is now clear—it discloses cash flows used in capital budgeting decisions. The decision rules are developed with the objective of firm value maximization. Thus, the statement is directly linked to firm value (i.e., security prices).[32]

The income statement reflects the accrual elements of the financial statements, revenues and expenses, rather than cash flows. Service Revenue and Supplies and Salary Expense are exactly equal to cash flows only because we so specified in our example. In later chapters on operating activities, we will vary the timing of revenues and expenses so that they do not always occur at the same time as cash inflows and outflows.

31. Remember that a financing activities section would also appear in the statement of cash flows if any of the investment transactions discussed in Chapters 6–8 were financed with debt or equity securities (as discussed in Chapters 2–5).
32. In Module E, we illustrate security pricing methods that do not use cash flows.

TURNER CORPORATION
Income Statements
(Effects of machinery and patent activities)

	2001	2002	2003	2004	2005
Service revenue	$450,000	$450,000	$450,000	$450,000	$450,000
Supplies and salary expense	(250,000)	(250,000)	(250,000)	(250,000)	(250,000)
Depreciation expense	(100,000)	(100,000)	(100,000)	(100,000)	(100,000)
Amortization expense	(10,000)	(10,000)	(10,000)	(10,000)	(10,000)
Operating income	$ 90,000	$ 90,000	$ 90,000	$ 90,000	$ 90,000
Loss on sale of machine					(100,000)
Pretax income	$ 90,000	$ 90,000	$ 90,000	$ 90,000	$ (10,000)
Income tax expense	(27,000)	(27,000)	(27,000)	(27,000)	3,000
Net income (loss)	$ 63,000	$ 63,000	$ 63,000	$ 63,000	$ (7,000)

The income statement reflects the matching of the machine and patent acquisition costs to the revenues generated. The economic benefits of the machine and patent are "used up" over the five-year period. Depreciation and amortization expenses are a recognition of the use of the machine and the patent, respectively.

Operating income is $90,000 in each period. In 2005, the machine sale generates a $100,000 loss. Because this item is not extraordinary, it does not receive net of tax treatment on the income statement. But, because it is not a part of normal operations, it appears as a separate disclosure after operating income.[33] Income tax expense exactly equals income tax payments shown in the statement of cash flows. As discussed in a later chapter, accrued expenses and cash payments for any particular expense item are rarely equal for an accounting period. Thus, income tax expense normally does not equal income taxes paid. Differences in financial and tax reporting methods lead to differences in income tax expense and income taxes paid. For example, although straight-line depreciation is often used for financial reporting, accelerated depreciation methods are used for taxable income determination.

The net cash inflow disclosed in the statement of cash flows totals $245,000 from 2001 to 2005. Similarly, net income disclosed in the income statement totals $245,000. Over a project's life, net cash flow equals net income. Note that income recognition is generally smoother and less variable than cash flow effects over the five-year period.

The following reflects only the effects of the machinery and patent activities:

TURNER CORPORATION
Balance Sheets
December 31
(Effects of machinery and patent activities)

	2001	2002	2003	2004	2005
Assets					
Current assets					
Cash	$(677,000)	$(504,000)	$(331,000)	$(158,000)	$245,000
Property, plant and equipment					
Machinery	$800,000	$800,000	$800,000	$800,000	
Less accumulated depreciation	(100,000)	(200,000)	(300,000)	(400,000)	
	$700,000	$600,000	$500,000	$400,000	
Intangible assets					
Patent (less accumulated amortization)	40,000	30,000	20,000	10,000	0
Total assets	$ 63,000	$126,000	$189,000	$252,000	$245,000
Liabilities and Owners' Equity					
Owners' equity					
Retained earnings	$ 63,000	$126,000	$189,000	$252,000	$245,000

33. If special items (i.e., extraordinary items, discontinued operations, or accounting changes) were present, "net income" would be renamed "income from continuing operations," and the special items would be disclosed after "income from continuing operations."

The balance sheet highlights the conversion of the machine and the patent into the probable future economic benefits that they represent. In the asset section, the cash effect related to the machinery and patent increases as the machine and patent balances decrease. The December 31, 2001, cash balance is equal to the 2001 net cash outflow of $677,000 reported on the statement of cash flows. The machinery balance is the $800,000 original cost reduced each period by the accumulation of depreciation expense reported on the income statement. The patent balance is the $50,000 original cost reduced each period by the accumulation of amortization expense reported on the income statement. As always, retained earnings reflects the accumulation of net income each period, resulting in a balance of $245,000 by the end of the project.

EXAMPLE 22 Journal Entries

January 1, 2001:		
Machines	800,000	
Patent	50,000	
Cash		850,000
In each year, 2001–2004:		
Cash	450,000	
Service Revenue		450,000
Operating Expenses	250,000	
Cash		250,000
Depreciation Expense	100,000	
Accumulated Depreciation—Machines		100,000
Amortization Expense	10,000	
Patents		10,000
Income Tax Expense	27,000	
Cash		27,000
In year 2005:		
Cash	450,000	
Service Revenue		450,000
Operating Expenses	250,000	
Cash		250,000
Depreciation Expense	100,000	
Accumulated Depreciation—Machines		100,000
Amortization Expense	10,000	
Patents		10,000
Loss on Sale of Machine	100,000	
Cash	200,000	
Accumulated Depreciation—Machines	500,000	
Machines		800,000
Cash	3,000	
Income Tax Expense		3,000

The External Decision Makers' View of Investments in Productive Assets

Investments in productive assets are the means by which firms grow. External decision makers attempt to understand a company's operating strategy in order to assess whether the extent and timing of these investments are appropriate. For example, one would expect these investments to take place when a company's strategy is to capture market share in a growing market. Also, if a company is trying to position itself as a low-cost competitor, investments in productive assets can create barriers to entry from economies of scale.

Except for necessary replacements, incremental investments in assets used to produce mature products are generally not expected. The declining profit margins often experienced on mature products do not warrant expansion of production capabilities. External decision makers also monitor operating cash flows to assess whether the operating cash flows are sufficient to increase investments in productive assets when new, profitable projects are discovered.

Investments in Productive Assets—Southwest Airlines

10 Describe where and how information about productive assets is disclosed and discussed in annual reports.

Southwest Airlines' 1998 financial statements are provided in Appendix C. This section should help you become familiar with how and where information related to topics presented in this chapter appears in financial statements. Accordingly, we ask you to read certain portions of the provided financial statements; we then discuss certain aspects of what you read. After completing this chapter, you should be able to read and understand much of the underlying basics of the financial statement discussions related to investments in productive assets.

To review Southwest Airlines' activity related to PP&E, read the following sections in the order given.

1. Management's Discussion and Analysis: Year in Review
   Liquidity and Capital Resources
2. Balance sheet: Property and equipment
3. Income statement: Depreciation expense
4. Statement of cash flows: Investing activities
   Operating activities—depreciation and amortization amounts
5. Accompanying notes: Note 1—Property and Equipment
   Aircraft and Engine Maintenance; Note 2—Commitments; Note 5—Leases

The financial statements reflect that Southwest is a growing company with most of its assets being property and equipment. Significant amounts of cash are being expended each year to purchase property and equipment and to make lease payments. Southwest purchases most of its property and equipment, but it is also using operating leases for a large number of aircraft. Southwest is committed to making significant aircraft purchases in future years. Because Southwest's financial statements are reported in thousands of dollars, *the amounts referenced in the following sections are in thousands of dollars, unless otherwise indicated* (for example, the MD&A section references amounts in millions of dollars).

Aircraft Fleet Size—MD&A and Note 2

To meet expansion needs and to make more frequent flights in existing markets, Southwest is increasing its fleet size: 34 aircraft were added and six retired in 1998 (MD&A), and the Company has plans to add 32 aircraft in 1999 (Note 2). Southwest also has orders for 73 aircraft for 2000–2004, and options for 62 aircraft during the 2003–2006 period (Note 2).

Magnitude of Costs Associated with PP&E—Balance Sheet, Note 1, and Note 5

Total property and equipment increased from $3,435,693 in 1997 to $4,137,610 in 1998, an increase of $701,917 (20.4%). The balance sheets show that property and equipment constitutes most of Southwest's total assets: 87.7% ($4,137,610 ÷ $4,715,996) in 1998, and 80.9% ($3,435,693 ÷ $4,246,160) in 1997. Further, as disclosed in Note 5—Leases, Southwest also acquired the use of property and equipment through capital and operating leases (discussed in text Chapter 4). At year-end, 99 of Southwest's 280 aircraft were accounted for under operating leases, which means that those aircraft are not included in the PP&E balance sheet amount. Operating lease costs were $306,629 and $297,158, respectively, in 1998 and 1997. Note 1 documents that normal repairs are charged to expense. Scheduled airframe overhaul costs are capitalized and amortized over the lesser of ten years or the estimated remaining life. Major repairs that extend an aircraft's life or operating performance are capitalized and amortized over future periods.

Depreciation—Income Statement and Note 1

The income statement indicates that depreciation expense increased to $225,212 in 1998 from $195,568 in 1997. The percentages of depreciation expense to total operating revenues were 5.4% and 5.1% for 1998 and 1997, respectively. Southwest uses the straight-line depreciation method (Note 1, Property and Equipment), with estimated useful lives of 20–25 years for flight equipment and 3–30 years for ground property and equipment. Because Southwest continues to purchase new aircraft, depreciation expense would be expected to rise during future periods.

Statement of Cash Flows

The statement of cash flows shows that Southwest made significant purchases of property and equipment in 1996–1998, with cash outlays of $947,096 and $688,927 in 1998 and 1997, respectively. The MD&A Liquidity and Capital Resources section indicates that the $947.1 million in capital expenditures were used to purchase 22 new 737-700 aircraft, four used aircraft, and to make progress payments for future deliveries. The statement of cash flows also reports the amount of amortization expense associated with capitalized airframe overhaul costs ($22,763 in 1998 and $20,540 in 1997), which is not separately disclosed in the income statement or Note 1. Southwest has entered into contractual purchase commitments to purchase aircraft in the future (Note 2—Commitments). This helps to predict future cash flows for property and equipment, with aggregate commitments at December 31, 1998 of $2,492.5 million. Of these commitments, $715.9 million is committed for 1999.

Chapter Summary

Firms primarily employ cash-based decision models to evaluate whether to invest in long-lived productive assets. After assets are acquired, accountants face the task of determining the initial acquisition value of these assets. The general rule is that investments in long-lived productive assets are initially recorded at the fair value given up to acquire the asset, although exceptions to the rule exist. Once initial valuation is determined, the historical cost of the asset is allocated to the periods benefitted through depreciation, depletion, and amortization. We illustrated four allocation methods: straight-line, double-declining-balance, units-of-output, and present value. Periodically, management must assess long-lived assets to determine if an impairment has occurred. If the asset continues to be used, it is impaired if the undiscounted expected cash flows from the use or sale of the asset are less than the current book value. If an impairment has occurred, the asset is written down to the present value of future cash flows to be generated by use of the asset. A final chapter example illustrated a capital budget decision and the related financial statement effects of acquiring a long-lived asset.

Key Terms

amortization 222
average accumulated expenditures 211
avoidable interest 211
book value 223
capital budgeting 205
capital expenditures 222
declining balance 223
depletion 222
depreciation 222
development 217
full costing 214
historical cost 206
impairment 226
portfolio risk 205
present value of the remaining cash flows method 224
research 217
reserve recognition accounting (RRA) 215
revenue expenditures 222
straight-line method 223
successful efforts 214
sum-of-the-years'-digits method 224
units-of-output method 224
unrealized gain/loss 226

Questions

Q1. **Cash Flows from Productive Assets.** Cash flows from investments in productive assets are indirect. Trace the process by which cash, initially converted into a productive asset, becomes a future cash inflow.

Q2. **Capital Budgeting.** What is capital budgeting? What are the two key inputs into most capital budgeting decisions?

Q3. **Productive Assets: Financial Statement Presentation.** How does the decision to invest in productive assets relate to portfolio risk?

Q4. **Valuing Productive Assets at Acquisition.** What is the general rule for determining the recorded amount of long-term productive assets at the date of acquisition?

Q5. **Productive Assets: Financial Statement Presentation.** In light of the inherent trade-off between relevance and reliability, evaluate the GAAP procedure of reporting a long-lived asset at historical cost rather than current market value.

Q6. **Revenue versus Capital Expenditure Classification.** Why is it important to determine whether an expenditure benefits the current period or a future period? (Use the Chapter 1 definition of an asset to justify your answer.)

Q7. **Acquisition of Productive Assets.** List five text examples of consideration that can be surrendered in order to acquire a productive asset.

Q8. **Valuing Productive Assets at Acquisition.** If the "fair market value of what has been given up" is difficult to determine, at what amount will the accountant record the acquisition of a productive asset? Why?

Q9. **Valuing Productive Assets at Acquisition.** Why might it be difficult to determine the fair market value of common stock given to acquire a productive asset? Of a note payable?

Q10. **Valuing Productive Assets at Acquisition.** What are the two exceptions to the fair market value rule of recording asset acquisition that are discussed in the text?

Q11. **Self-Constructed Assets.** When a corporation self-constructs a building, should part of the plant manager's salary be allocated to the building? Why or why not?

Q12. **Interest Cost Recognition.** What is the general rule for recognizing interest cost in financial statements? What is the exception to the rule for self-constructed assets? Why does this exception exist?

Q13. **Natural Resource Cost Classifications.** What are the three cost classifications of a natural resource?

Q14. **Natural Resource Reclamation Costs.** How should natural resource reclamation costs be treated?

Q15. **Successful Efforts and Full Costing Accounting Methods.** Explain the successful efforts and full costing accounting methods for exploration costs.

Q16. **Reserve Recognition Accounting.** What is reserve recognition accounting (RRA)? Evaluate RRA on its relevance and reliability.

Q17. **Tangible versus Intangible Development Costs.** What are the different treatments accorded tangible and intangible development costs?

Q18. **Intangible Assets.** Give three examples of specifically identifiable intangible assets. Is the accounting for these assets different depending on whether they were purchased or internally created?

Q19. **R&D.** What is R&D? What is its accounting treatment?

Q20. **Goodwill.** What is goodwill? How is it created?

Q21. **Goodwill.** Under what condition is goodwill capitalized? Expensed? Why?

Q22. **Accounting for Asset Trades.** What role does the similarity of traded assets play in the accounting for traded nonmonetary assets such as property, plant, and equipment?

Q23. **Revenue versus Capital Expenditures.** How do revenue expenditures and capital expenditures differ?

Q24. **Depreciation, Depletion, and Amortization.** What is the purpose of depreciation, depletion, and amortization?

Q25. **Book Value versus Fair Value.** Are book value and fair market value equal? Why or why not?

Q26. **Book Value versus Fair Value.** What action should the accountant take if a productive asset will be used in the future and will have a book value that is greater than its fair value? A book value that is less than its fair value?

Q27. **Impairment Accounting.** How does the distinction between gross future cash flows and the present value of future cash flows play a role in asset impairment accounting?

Q28. **Financial Statement Presentation.** Where is a gain or loss on disposition of productive assets reported in the financial statements?

Short Problems

1. **Valuing Productive Assets at Acquisition.** Determine the amount recorded in the land account in each of the following situations:
   a. Kanell Co. purchased land by issuing a $200,000, four-year, 10% note payable. Kanell normally pays 10% interest on notes of this kind.
   b. Shiver Co. purchased land by issuing a $300,000, three-year, non-interest-bearing note payable. Shiver normally pays 9% interest on notes of this kind.
   c. Dunn Co. issues a $200,000, five-year, 3% note payable in exchange for land with a known cash price of $153,000. The market rate of interest on this type of note is unknown.

   Journal Entry Option: Prepare journal entries to record the transactions for a, b, and c.

2. **Valuing Productive Assets at Acquisition.** Microchip acquired an office building by issuing 300,000 shares of its $1 par value stock. The building has an appraised value of $11,000,000. Microchip's stock is regularly traded on the New York Stock Exchange. At

the date of acquisition, the stock traded at $45. At what amount would Microchip record the office building?

Journal Entry Option: Prepare the journal entry to record the transaction.

3. **Valuing Productive Assets at Acquisition.** Lucky Corp. received land valued at $165,000 as a donation from Desperate County. Seven years earlier, Desperate had acquired the land for $40,000 as a right-of-way in a condemnation procedure. (Note: record the gift as revenue from donations.) At what amount should Lucky record the land?

Journal Entry Option: Prepare the journal entry to record the transaction.

4. **Valuing Productive Assets at Acquisition.** On December 31, 2001, Baldwin Mining acquired a timber tract for $2 million in cash. When the timber is harvested, Baldwin will convert the site into a baseball diamond at a cost of $100,000 and donate the land to the city of Joliet. The value of the land will be $400,000 at that time. What is the cost of the natural resource recorded on December 31, 2001?

Journal Entry Option: Prepare the journal entry to record the transaction.

5. **Avoidable Interest.** On January 1, 2001, Maxwell Enterprises began construction of a production plant. Maxwell obtained a $2,000,000 construction loan bearing an 8% interest rate. Expenditures on the project were as follows:

1/1/01	$ 500,000	2/1/02	$1,800,000
4/1/01	1,200,000	6/1/02	1,800,000
12/1/01	240,000		

The project was completed on December 31, 2002, and the production plant was placed into service. In addition to the construction note, two other interest-bearing debt securities were outstanding during the construction period:

Bond payable (10%)	$4,000,000	Note payable (12%)	$6,000,000

a. Compute the amount of avoidable interest to be capitalized in 2001 and 2002.
b. What is the plant's book value in the December 31, 2001, and 2002 balance sheets?

Journal Entry Option: Prepare the 2001 and 2002 annual journal entries to record the capitalized interest. Assume that when the interest was incurred it was recorded as interest expense and later capitalized.

6. **Goodwill Computation.** On December 31, 2001, Gary Enterprises acquired The Great Yogurt Company for $2,000,000 cash. The book values and fair market values of TGYC's net assets are the same at the date of acquisition except for plant and equipment, which has a fair market value that is $30,000 lower than book value. At the date of acquisition, TGYC's balance sheet was as follows:

Cash	$ 300,000	Current liabilities	$ 10,000
Other current assets	100,000	Long-term liabilities	190,000
PP&E	1,000,000	Equity	1,200,000
	$1,400,000		$1,400,000

Compute the goodwill that Gary Enterprises will report in the intangible asset section of the December 31, 2001, balance sheet.

Journal Entry Option: Assuming that assets are recorded at their fair market values, record the acquisition (use account titles from the balance sheet above).

7. **Goodwill and Goodwill Amortization.** On January 1, 2001, the Brown Co. purchased 100% of the assets of the Lyle Co. for $20,000,000 (in a business combination accounted for as a purchase). Lyle's net assets (i.e., Assets − Liabilities) had a book value of $15,000,000, and a fair value of $18,000,000.
a. What is the amount of goodwill to be recorded by Brown?
b. If Brown believed that the goodwill has an estimated useful life of 20 years, what is goodwill amortization for 2001 and 2002, assuming that Brown uses the straight-line method?

(continued)

Journal Entry Option: Prepare Brown's 2001 annual journal entry to record the goodwill amortization expense.

c. Assume that in February 2005 (after the 2004 financial statements had been issued), Brown decided that the goodwill no longer had any future value to the firm. What would the effect of this decision be on the 2005 financial statements?

Journal Entry Option: Prepare Brown's January 2005 journal entry to record the goodwill write-off.

8. **R&D.** The White Co. conducts research and development (R&D) activities in an effort to find viable new commercial products. In 2001, White incurred the following expenses on four R&D projects: (1) $1,000,000 in equipment for which no alternative uses are available after the current research project ends; (2) $3,000,000 in equipment that will be sold for an estimated $750,000 at the end of the research project; and (3) $7,000,000 in salaries for personnel engaged in R&D activities. Management believes that it is reasonable to allocate $10,000,000 in general corporate overhead to the R&D projects. Based upon past experience, management believes that each year's R&D should lead to one viable new product that will be produced over a 10-year period. What amount should be reported for R&D in the 2001 financial statements? How much of the R&D should be expensed and how much should be capitalized?

9. **Exchanges of Similar Assets.** On January 1, 2001, the Schmenner Co. exchanged a fabricating machine, which had a book value of $400,000 ($900,000 historical cost − $500,000 accumulated depreciation), for another fabricating machine. No cash was involved in the exchange.
   a. If the new fabricating machine had a fair value of $350,000, at what value would the new machine be recorded? What is the amount of any associated gain (loss) on exchange?

   Journal Entry Option: Prepare the January 1, 2001, journal entry to record the asset exchange. Use Machinery (Old) and Machinery (New) as account titles.

   b. If the new fabricating machine had a fair value of $525,000, at what value would the new machine be recorded? What is the amount of any associated gain (loss) on exchange?

   Journal Entry Option: Prepare the January 1, 2001, journal entry to record the asset exchange. Use Machinery (Old) and Machinery (New) as account titles.

10. **Cost Allocation Methods.** On January 1, 2001, the Helmkamp Co. acquired a depreciable asset at a cost of $500,000. Accountants believe that the asset's estimated useful life is five years, with an estimated salvage value of $25,000. Engineers estimate that the asset will be able to produce 250,000 units. During 2001 and 2002, the asset was used to produce 60,000 and 75,000 units, respectively. Compute depreciation expense for 2001 and 2002 under the following three depreciation methods: straight-line, 150% declining-balance, and units-of-output.

    Journal Entry Option: Prepare the 2001 annual journal entry to record the straight-line depreciation expense.

11. **Cost Allocation Methods.** On January 1, 2001, the Heerema Co. purchased a milling machine at a cost of $1,000,000. The machine's estimated useful life is 10 years, with an estimated salvage value of 10%. The company that manufactured the machine estimates that it is engineered to produce 10,000,000 units during its life. During 2001 and 2002, the asset was used to produce 800,000 and 1,600,000 units, respectively. Compute depreciation expense for 2001 and 2002 under the following three depreciation methods: straight-line, 200% declining-balance, and units-of-output.

    Journal Entry Option: Prepare the 2001 annual journal entry to record the units-of-output depreciation expense.

12. **Asset Impairment.** On December 31, 2000, the Wheeler Co. had depreciable assets with a book value of $5,000,000 (historical cost of $15,000,000 − accumulated depreciation of $10,000,000) that company management felt might be impaired. Wheeler intends to use the assets for the next five years. Indicate the appropriate accounting treatment for each of the following independent cases. Assume that an annual interest rate of 9% is appropriate for any impairment computations, and that cash flows occur at year-end.
    a. Management believes that the assets will produce $1,500,000 in net cash flows during each of the next five years, 2001–2005.

    Journal Entry Option: Prepare any necessary adjusting journal entry related to the possible impairment.

b. Management believes that the assets will produce $900,000 in net cash flows during each of the next five years, 2001–2005.

Journal Entry Option: Prepare any necessary adjusting journal entry related to the possible impairment.

c. Management cannot reasonably estimate future cash flows from the machine. However, the assets are actively traded, and management estimates that the current fair market value of the assets is $4,600,000. If management were forced to sell the assets in the near-term, management believes that it could receive $4,200,000 net of transactions costs.

Journal Entry Option: Prepare any necessary adjusting journal entry related to the possible impairment.

13. **Capital Budgeting.** The Warren Co. has a formal capital budgeting procedure. Warren uses a 10% discount rate for present value calculations, and it will consider any project that has positive net present value (NPV). Alternatively, Warren will consider any project with an IRR greater than 10%. On January 1, 2001, Warren is considering investing in a project that costs $15,000,000. Cash inflows from the project are estimated at $2,000,000 per year for the next 15 years (for simplicity, assume cash flows occur at the end of the year). Also, at the end of year 10, Warren estimates that equipment used in the project can be sold for $1,000,000. Compute the project's NPV and IRR. Would the project be acceptable for consideration?

Analytical and Comprehensive Problems

14. **Valuing Productive Assets at Acquisition—Assets Traded.** For parts (a)–(d), compute the amount initially recorded in the long-lived asset account for each party.

Journal Entry Option: For parts (a)–(d), record the journal entry for both parties to reflect the transaction. Use the account titles Machinery (Old) and Machinery (New) to differentiate the assets involved in the transaction.

a. Uncle Bill's Rice Co. traded a rice cooking machine to Golden MicroBrewery in exchange for a machine that crates finished product. The rice cooking machine has an original cost of $40,000, accumulated depreciation of $15,000, and a second-hand market cash price of $22,000. The crating machine has an $85,000 original cost and $65,000 of accumulated depreciation.

b. Assume the same facts in (a) except that the rice cooking machine had a market cash price of $30,000.

c. Using the information in (a), assume that Golden MicroBrewery and Uncle Bill exchanged similar rice cooking machines—MicroBrewery's rice cooking machine has an $85,000 original cost and $65,000 of accumulated depreciation. (Uncle Bill's rice cooking machine has a second-hand market value of $22,000.)

d. Using the information in (a), assume that no second-hand market exists for the rice cooking machine or the crating machine.

15. **Asset Impairment.** Realtime Products owns four factories located in four different states. The factory in Danville, Illinois, is unique within the firm. The factory's total output consists of cut and finished metal plates for use in electrical wiring terminals. The book value of the factory located in Danville, Illinois, is $3,000,000, of which $2,500,000 represents the unallocated costs of the *factory building;* $200,000 of unallocated costs of *cutting equipment;* and $300,000 of unallocated costs of *finishing equipment.* Realtime's customers have recently changed their production processes to adapt to new technology. As a result, the demand for cut metal plates has fallen, and the demand for finished metal plates is nearly nonexistent. At December 31, 2001, Realtime provides the following estimates of future cash flows from the building and machines:

- The finishing equipment will be sold early in the year 2004 for $175,000 (assume January 1, 2004, in any cash flow analysis).
- Realtime will continue to cut metal in the Danville plant for the next four years (the remaining useful life of the cutting equipment), realizing $500,000 per year in net cash flows from the sale of cut metal. Treat the $500,000 as associated solely with the cutting equipment (i.e., attribute none to the building or finishing equipment).
- At the end of the fourth year, Realtime will sell the building. The building is highly adaptable, and it is expected that Realtime will receive at least $2,500,000 for the building at that time.

(continued)

Required:

a. Assuming a discount rate of 10%, which of the assets are impaired and why should they be considered impaired?
b. At what amounts should the building, cutting equipment, and finishing equipment be reported on the December 31, 2001, balance sheet?
c. What are the income statement effects (if any) associated with your answer?

Journal Entry Option: Prepare any necessary journal entries for any identified impairments.

16. **Asset Impairment.** The Miller Manufacturing plant has a Ft. Wayne, Indiana, plant that produces fabricated components. On December 31, 2001, the plant, including its contents, has a net book value of $5,000,000. The plant has a remaining expected useful life of six years (i.e., through December 31, 2007), at which time the plant is expected to be torn down. The salvage value of the plant and its equipment is expected to equal the cost of tearing down the building. The plant accountant is performing a review on December 31, 2001, to determine if the plant asset should be treated as impaired. Assume that the plant accountant believes that net cash flows from plant sales will be $800,000 per year over the next six years. Also assume an appropriate interest rate is 8% (Miller's cost of capital) and the net cash flows happen at year-end. Should the plant asset be treated as impaired? If impaired, what would the effect be on the December 31, 2001, financial statements?

Journal Entry Option: If impaired, prepare any necessary journal entries for the impairment.

17. **Financial Statement Recognition.** WendyBird owns and operates an ice cream shop near a local middle school. On January 1, 2001, WendyBird gave $500 worth of coupons to teachers for the purpose of rewarding good students. The coupons allow the purchaser 50 cents off any purchase of $2.00 or more any time during the next two years. WendyBird estimates that 60% of the coupons will be redeemed in 2001, 30% in 2002, and 10% will never be redeemed. On each sale of $2.00, WendyBird realizes a gross profit of $1.00. WendyBird is unsure about whether to record the $500 as goodwill, a capital expenditure, or a revenue expenditure.

Required:

As WendyBird's financial advisor, draft a brief memo discussing each of the three alternative accounting treatments, indicating which treatment you prefer.

18. **Depreciation Methods.** On January 1, 2001, the Double D company purchased a factory machine at a cost of $250,000, with an estimated useful life of four years and an estimated salvage value of 10%. Compute the depreciation expense under the following methods: straight-line, units of-output, 150% declining-balance, and present value. Assume the following information about the units of output: 20,000 units in 2001; 50,000 units in 2002; 30,000 units in 2003; and 30,000 units in 2004. For present value depreciation, assume an 8% discount rate, with net cash flows at the end of each year of $69,932 (excluding salvage value in the last year).

19. **Texas Instruments' Productive Assets.** TI is a highly capital-intensive company. The purpose of this problem is to help you become familiar with how and where information related to topics presented in this chapter appear in financial statements. Complete 1998 financial statements for TI are available at the text Web site, http://baginski.swcollege.com.

Review the assets section of the balance sheet; the investing activities section of the statement of cash flows; the operating activities section of the statement of cash flows (paying particular attention to the amount of depreciation); the 1998 Results of Operations in the MD&A section; and the following five footnotes: Accounting Policies and Practices; Property, Plant and Equipment; Research and Development; Rental Expense and Lease Commitments; and Divestitures.

Required:

a. Compute the percent of net property, plant, and equipment (PP&E) to total assets for 1998 and 1997. Break the percentage down into the separate components (cost, accumulated depreciation, and net).
b. What was the amount of depreciation expense for 1998 and 1997? Calculate the percent of depreciation of net revenues for 1998 and 1997. Which depreciation method(s) did TI use for PP&E?
c. At December 31, 1998, what was the amount authorized to be spent in future years on PP&E?
d. What were capital expenditures (additions to property, plant, and equipment) and R&D expense for 1998 and 1997?

e. During 1998 and 1997, TI sold or terminated certain operations (see Divestiture footnote). Briefly describe these events.

20. **Capital Expenditure Versus Revenue Expenditure.** Assume that the Faulconer Co. recently incurred a capital expenditure of $1,200,000. The accounting staff is unsure how to classify the expenditure. Katherine Plants argues that the future benefits (beyond the current year) of the expenditure are unsure, and conservative accounting supports expensing the expenditure. Kelly Johnson argues that the expenditure will benefit the current year plus two additional years, and the expenditure should be capitalized as a depreciable asset, depreciating it to zero salvage value over the three-year period. Faulconer's effective tax rate is 40%. Using the following exhibits, show the effects of each alternative on the statement of cash flows, income statement, and balance sheet over the three-year period. For the balance sheet presentation, assume that the company began with $2,000,000 cash and $2,000,000 in contributed capital.

FAULCONER CO.
Statement of Cash Flows
(Effects of Capital Expenditures)
(Cash outflows in parentheses)

	Expense			Capitalize		
	Year 1	**Year 2**	**Year 3**	**Year 1**	**Year 2**	**Year 3**
Operating Activities						
Income tax effect						
Investing Activities						
Net cash inflow (outflow)						

FAULCONER CO.
Partial Income Statements
(Effects of Capital Expenditures)

	Expense			Capitalize		
	Year 1	**Year 2**	**Year 3**	**Year 1**	**Year 2**	**Year 3**
Revenues						
No effect						
Expenses						
Effect on net income						

FAULCONER CO.
Partial Balance Sheets*
(Effects of Capital Expenditures)

	Expense			Capitalize		
	Year 1	**Year 2**	**Year 3**	**Year 1**	**Year 2**	**Year 3**
Assets						
Stockholders' Equity						

*Assumes the company began with $2,000,000 in cash and $2,000,000 in contributed capital.

21. **Capital Budgeting.** On January 1, 2001, Big Red Corporation is deciding whether to acquire a machine and a related patent. The machine can restore old newspaper articles by dipping the paper in a chemical solution, and the patent allows exclusive use of the restoration process for the next five years. Big Red's after-tax cost of capital is 6%. The following information about the project is also available:

Initial cost of the machine	$200,000
Initial cost of the patent	$10,000
Machine useful life	10 years
Machine estimated salvage value, end of 5 years	$40,000
Machine estimated salvage value, end of 10 years	$0
Patent life	5 years
Income tax rate	30%
Annual operating cash revenues	$250,000
Annual operating cash expenses	$100,000
Depreciation and amortization methods	straight-line

Required:

a. Prepare an analysis of the project's internal rate of return and net present value.

b. Using the following financial statement templates, show how the primary financial statements would reflect the decision to accept the project.

Statement of Cash Flows
(Cash outflows in parentheses)

	2001	2002	2003	2004	2005
Operating Activities					
Investing Activities					
Financing Activities					
Net cash inflow					

Income Statement

	2001	2002	2003	2004	2005
Operating income					
Pretax income					
Income tax expense					
Net income					

Balance Sheet
December 31

	2001	2002	2003	2004	2005
Assets					
Current assets					
Property, plant, and equipment					
Intangible assets					
Total effect on assets					
Liabilities and Owners' Equity					
Owners' equity					
Retained earnings					

22. **Capital Budgeting.** On January 1, 2001, the Spiller Co. is considering two alternative capital investments and two different financing schemes. Spiller can invest in only one project. Projects A and B both have three-year lives with no estimated salvage value. Project A requires an investment of $21,000,000. This entire amount is depreciable, and estimated year-end cash flows in the years 2001–2003 are $8,000,000 per year ($15,600,000 revenue cash flows less $7,600,000 expense cash flows). Project B requires an investment of $17,000,000. This entire amount is depreciable, and estimated year-end cash flows in the years 2001–2003 are $7,500,000 per year ($11,000,000 revenue cash flows less $3,500,000 expense cash flows). Spiller's after-tax cost of capital is 7%, and its effective tax rate is 40%. For convenience, assume that all revenues and expenses are cash based (except depreciation) and that Spiller uses the straight-line depreciation method.

Spiller has sufficient cash on hand to pay for either project, but Spiller's chief financial officer suggests using 100% debt financing with a note payable that would carry the current market interest rate of 8%, pay interest annually at the end of the year, and be due at the end of the four-year period. An abbreviated and compressed form of Spiller's December 31, 2000, balance sheet is provided.

Required:

a. Determine whether either project should be accepted using both the net present value (NPV) and the internal rate of return (IRR) measures discussed in the text. Spiller considers positive NPV projects and projects with an IRR greater than the after-tax cost of capital to be acceptable. If both projects are acceptable, indicate which is preferable. Calculate the NPV and IRR without regard to the proposed alternative financing methods (i.e., do not include interest paid if financed with debt or opportunity cost if financed with cash).

b. If at least one project is acceptable, show the alternative effects on Spiller's income statement, balance sheet, and statement of cash flows for the three-year period using both methods of proposed financing: cash and 100% debt. Use the following template to prepare your answers. Note that in the years 2001–2003, you are projecting only the effects of the proposed investment—no other effects are to be shown.

c. This analysis is a static analysis, which allows nothing in the future to change. What other considerations might need to be included in the analysis?

SPILLER CO.
Balance Sheets
December 31 (In thousands)
(Under alternative financing arrangements)

		Finance with Cash			Finance with Debt		
	2000	**2001**	**2002**	**2003**	**2001**	**2002**	**2003**
Cash	$ 50,000						
Other assets	400,000						
Property, plant, and equipment (new project)	0						
Total assets	$450,000						
Liabilities	$ 10,000						
Note payable (used to finance new project)	0						
Stockholders' equity	440,000						
Total liabilities and stockholders' equity	$450,000						

(continued)

SPILLER CO.
Income Statements
For Years Ended December 31 (In thousands)
(Under alternative financing arrangements)

	Finance with Cash			Finance with Debt		
	2001	**2002**	**2003**	**2001**	**2002**	**2003**
Revenues						
Expenses						
Net income						

SPILLER CO.
Statements of Cash Flows
For Years Ended December 31 (In thousands)
(Under alternative financing arrangements)
(Cash outflows in parentheses)

	Finance with Cash			Finance with Debt		
	2001	**2002**	**2003**	**2001**	**2002**	**2003**
Operating Activities						
Investing Activities						
Financing Activities						
Net cash inflow (outflow)						

CFA Exam-Type Problems

23. Which of the following statements about straight-line depreciation is *true*? Straight-line depreciation: (CFA adapted)
    a. results in higher total tax payments over the asset's life.
    b. results in a decreasing return on equity over the asset's life.
    c. introduces a built-in increase in return on investment over the asset's life.
    d. recognizes the increasing rate of obsolescence of an asset with the passage of time.

24. Which of the following statements about impaired assets is *true*? (CFA adapted)
    a. When a write-down is based on future cash flows, present value must be used.
    b. Impairment of assets, similar to loss contingencies, must be recognized if material and probable.
    c. Assets to be idled more than three years must be written down on the balance sheet.
    d. The timing and amount of impairment recognition is largely controlled by management.

25. The capitalization of interest cost during construction: (CFA adapted)
    a. increases future net income.
    b. increases future depreciation expense.
    c. decreases net income during the construction phase.
    d. decreases future depreciation expense.

26. To account for the purchase of a machine, a company may use either straight-line depreciation (SLD) or double-declining-balance depreciation (DDB). Return on investment for the machine will: (CFA adapted, with slight modifications by authors)
    a. initially be higher under DDB than under SLD.
    b. remain constant under SLD.
    c. decrease over time under SLD.
    d. initially be higher under SLD than under DDB.

27. A firm using straight-line depreciation reports gross investment in fixed assets of $80 million, accumulated depreciation of $45 million, and annual depreciation expense of $5 million. The approximate average age of the fixed assets is: (CFA adapted)
    a. 7 years
    b. 9 years
    c. 15 years
    d. 16 years

28. For companies in an expansion phase, capitalization of interest may result in a gain in earnings when: (CFA adapted)
    a. the amount of interest amortization will not catch up with the amount of interest capitalized in the current period.
    b. the average projected expenditures for the period exceed specific borrowings.
    c. the cost of financing project debt exceeds the cost of equity financing.
    d. earnings are greater under capitalization than under the expense method over the life of the qualifying asset.

29. A machine is purchased for $3,000 and has an estimated useful life of five years. Its salvage value is estimated to be $500. Using sum-of-the-years'-digits, the depreciation charge for year four is: (CFA adapted) *Note: the sum-of-the-years'-digits method has appeared on several CFA exams. Students planning to take the CFA exam should know this method. (See footnote 23 on page 224.)*
    a. $333.33
    b. $400.00
    c. $500.00
    d. $666.67

30. Research and development (R&D) expenditures: (Author constructed)
    a. should be capitalized and amortized over the future periods benefitted.
    b. on projects performed under contract to outside parties that will lead to future reimbursement should be expensed.
    c. cannot include personnel costs.
    d. should be expensed in the period incurred even if future periods may benefit.

Objectives

1. Account for investments in debt securities.
2. Account for held-to-maturity, trading, and available-for-sale securities, and adjust the financial statements to reflect changes in the market values of these investments when appropriate.
3. Account for loans, loan impairments, and troubled debt restructurings.
4. Account for investments in lease contracts.
5. Explain where information about debt investments is disclosed and discussed in financial reports.

Chapter 7

Investment Decisions—Investing in Other Firms' Debt

In order to maximize firm value, cash should be invested in assets that yield the greatest return per unit of risk.[1] When firms have idle cash, management makes short-term investment decisions that usually entail making investments outside the firm. However, for intermediate and long-term uses of cash, management must decide whether to invest cash internally in operations or to invest cash externally. The best investments may not be found within the firm's own operations. Instead, corporations may find it more beneficial to invest in the operations of other firms by purchasing the claims against the assets used in those operations—debt or equity securities.

Investments in other firms' debt and equity securities result in both direct and indirect payoffs. The direct payoffs from investments in common and preferred stocks are dividends and liquidating market value, and the indirect payoff is the ability to control or influence other firms' activities through voting privileges. The direct payoffs from investments in bonds and notes are interest receipts and maturity value, while the indirect payoff is the control or influence of other firms' activities through the imposition of debt covenants and restrictions. In today's competitive business culture, companies increasingly seek reliable business partners. One way to cement a business partnership is to purchase debt or equity securities of the partner company. For example, we often observe that a customer owns a portion of a supplier's stock to guarantee a steady supply of inventory at potentially favorable prices.

In this chapter, we concentrate on the following three common types of investments in debt-related securities:

1. Moyer, McGuigan, and Kretlow, *Contemporary Financial Management*, 8th Edition (Cincinnati, Ohio, South-Western College Publishing, 2001) provides a background discussion. We concentrate on the link between managers' decisions and finance theory, which traditionally has profit maximization as its goal. Of course, managers' decisions may be based on other altruistic criteria, such as promoting quality and customer service and meeting societal goals, or more self-serving wealth maximization goals.

- long-term investments in bonds
- investments in notes receivable (i.e., loans receivable)
- investments in lease contracts (i.e., lease receivables).

In Chapter 8, we conclude our investment discussion by considering investments in equity securities (i.e., common and preferred stock).

Investments in Debt Securities

1 Account for investments in debt securities.

Debt securities are contracts to trade current cash outflows for future cash inflows from interest and principal.[2] The investor's rate of return (also known as the effective or market rate of interest) is critical in contract valuation. Because the investor's benefit from the contract is a series of future cash receipts, the effective rate of interest discounts the future cash receipts in determining the present value of the investment.

After the original contract is executed, the market rate of interest changes due to supply and demand conditions in the marketplace. Hence, the present value (i.e., market value) of the debt contract changes as well. For example, assume that Montross Corporation purchases a $1,210, two-year, non-interest-bearing note of another company for $1,000. This transaction implies an effective rate of 10%:

$$\$1{,}000 = \$1{,}210 \div (1 + i)^2$$
$$i = 10\%$$

If the market rate of return changes to 9% (i.e., market conditions cause similar notes to trade at prices that imply a 9% effective yield), then the market value of the note increases from $1,000 to $1,018:

$$\text{Market value} = \$1{,}210 \div (1 + 0.09)^2 = \$1{,}018$$

Note that the market rate of interest and the value of the note move in opposite directions (i.e., they are inversely related). As interest rates fall, the financial instrument becomes more valuable because the cash flow stream is discounted at a lower rate—this causes less of the cash flow stream to be allocated to interest and more to principal. Therefore, the market value of debt is affected by market interest rate changes—debt increases in value when interest rates decrease, while debt decreases in value when interest rates increase.

Further, even if the effective rate of interest never changes, the market value of debt will change because of two other events during the life of the contract: (1) the passage of time increases the present value of debt (i.e., we discount the future cash flows over a shorter period of time, which raises the present value), and (2) the payment of interest decreases the total value of debt, which includes contractual interest and principal payments. *Timing the recognition of these changes in value from interest rate changes, passage of time, and interest payments forms the basic accounting framework for the investment in the debt securities of other firms.*

Basic Accounting Treatment of Long-Term Investment in Debt Securities—Bond Investments

We use an example of an investment in bonds to illustrate the basic accounting treatment for long-term investments in debt. In Chapter 3, we reviewed the ac-

2. FASB No. 115 provides the technical definition of a security. "Accounting for Certain Investments in Debt and Equity Securities," *Statement of Financial Accounting Standards No. 115* (Norwalk, Conn: FASB, 1993), paragraph 137. SFAS No. 115 pertains to securities that are registered instruments and are traded in organized exchanges either physically or through memorandum entry in a register. Notes receivable are *not* securities under SFAS No. 115.

counting for debt from the debtor's side of the transaction. Here we are extending the analysis to the investor's (i.e., creditor's) side. We repeat the information for the Worthy Co. from Chapter 3, Example 2, so that you can compare and contrast the accounting for debtors (Chapter 3) and investors.

Long-term bond investors use the *effective interest method* to record interest revenue and any necessary premium or discount amortization.[3] At the end of each accounting period, a long-term bond investment is reported at ***amortized cost*** **(principal plus unamortized premium or minus unamortized discount,** which also equals the present value of the remaining cash flows discounted at the *historical effective interest rate*). As discussed later in the chapter, certain bond investments may be reported on the balance sheet at current market value. For now, we ignore the issue of reporting debt securities at their current value. That is, in terms of the framework presented above for investments in debt, we ignore the interest rate changes and concentrate on the value changes from time passage and interest payment.

Example 1. On January 1, 2001, Worthy Co. issued $1,000,000 in bonds payable. The bonds are dated January 1, 2001, mature in five years on January 1, 2006, and pay 9% interest every December 31. The issue sold for $891,857 (rounded to the nearest dollar). Assume that Laker Co. purchased all the bonds. Laker Co. intends to hold the investment to maturity and has a December 31 fiscal year-end.[4]

Solution. Laker's cash flows from these bonds are as follows:

Cash outflow at issue:	
Purchase price of the bonds	$ 891,857
Annual cash inflows (interest receipts):	
Face amount of issue	$1,000,000
Coupon or stated interest rate	× 9%
Annual interest receipt	$ 90,000
Years received	× 5
	$ 450,000
Cash inflow at retirement date:	$1,000,000

By paying less than $1,000,000 for the bonds, Laker Co. is signaling that it holds an expectation for a return on these bonds that is greater than the 9% stated rate. That is, this investment is sufficiently risky such that a yield or effective rate of interest on this type of investment should be higher than 9%. To solve for Laker's expected rate of return, the following formula is used:

$$\textit{Present value} = \sum_{n=1}^{t} \frac{\text{Cash interest}}{(1+i)^n} + \frac{\text{Maturity value}}{(1+i)^5}$$

$$\$891{,}857 = \sum_{n=1}^{5} \frac{\$90{,}000}{(1+i)^n} + \frac{\$1{,}000{,}000}{(1+i)^5}$$

Using a financial calculator to solve for i shows that $i = 12\%$ ($n = 5$; payment = $90,000; present value = $891,857; future value = $1,000,000). Laker *discounted* the bonds so that it receives a 12% return in two ways—through the receipts of annual interest payments and a $1,000,000 maturity value that exceeds the original $891,857 investment by $108,143.

Laker's total interest revenue on this bond investment is computed by comparing the total cash inflows and outflows over the life of the investment:

3. *APB No. 21* allows the *straight-line method* to be used in lieu of the effective interest method if the results are not materially different. The straight-line method is illustrated in the chapter appendix; the chapter examples use the effective interest method.

4. This example illustrates accounting for a bond discount. The chapter appendix illustrates accounting for a bond premium.

Total cash inflows:		
Maturity receipt	$1,000,000	
Interest receipts	450,000	$1,450,000
Total cash outflows:		
Purchase price		(891,857)
Interest revenue over the life of the investment:		$ 558,143

Recall that increases in assets trigger revenue recognition. Over the life of the issue, Cash increases by $558,143. Thus, $558,143 in revenues are recognized by Laker over the five-year period.

Laker's effective interest amortization table shows the timing of the recognition of this revenue and the book value of the investment at each balance sheet date as shown in Exhibit 1.

EXHIBIT 1 Example 1. Effective Interest Amortization Table

LAKER CO.
Effective Interest Amortization Table

Date	9% Cash Interest	12% Effective Interest Income*	Discount Amortization**	Book Value of Investment (Amortized Cost)***
1/1/01				$ 891,857
12/31/01	$ 90,000	$107,023	$ 17,023	908,880
12/31/02	90,000	109,065	19,065	927,945
12/31/03	90,000	111,353	21,353	949,298
12/31/04	90,000	113,916	23,916	973,214
12/31/05	90,000	116,786	26,786	1,000,000
Total	**$450,000**	**$558,143**	**$108,143**	

*Beginning book value × 12% effective interest rate.
**The difference between cash interest and interest income.
***The prior book value plus discount amortization; also labeled as "Amortized Cost."

The beginning book value represents Laker's investment in Worthy. In the first period, Laker earns a $107,023 return (12%) on the $891,857 initial investment. However, because Laker only receives $90,000 of the $107,023 earned, this difference between the effective interest income and cash interest received (shown in the amortization column as $17,023) increases the book value of the investment.

Financial Reporting of Long-Term Investments in Debt Securities

The goal of the financial statements is to reflect the cash flows each period and the levels and changes in the accrual accounting elements. Laker's statement of cash flows reports the investment, interest receipts, and maturity receipt as shown in Exhibit 2.

EXHIBIT 2 Example 1. Statement of Cash Flows

LAKER CO.
Statement of Cash Flows*
Selected Information

	2001	2002	2003	2004	2005	2006
Operating Activities						
Interest received	90,000	90,000	90,000	90,000	90,000	
Investing Activities						
Investment in Worthy bonds	(891,857)					
Redemption of bond investment						1,000,000

*Cash outflows in parentheses

The statement of cash flows does not reflect the periodic increases in the investment resulting from amortization of the bond discount. It also does not indicate the interest revenue from the investment, which is a function of the effective interest rate. The accrual financial statements reflect these situations through the use of the elements of accrual accounting. The income statement disclosure appears as shown in Exhibit 3.

EXHIBIT 3 Example 1. Income Statement

LAKER CO.
Income Statement Effects

	2001	2002	2003	2004	2005	2006
Financial revenues, (expenses), gains, and (losses)						
Interest revenue (see amortization schedule)	107,023	109,065	111,353	113,916	116,786	0

Interest revenue is the effective interest income as calculated in the effective interest amortization table. It is equal to the increase in the bond investment asset from the passage of time, though it is not necessarily equal to yearly cash interest received. Note that while the statement of cash flows indicates $90,000 cash interest received for each year, the income statement shows more interest revenue every year. Again, the excess of interest income over the amount of interest received reflects the fact that Laker will receive more cash in maturity value than it initially loaned. The matching principle requires that the excess of maturity value over the initial cost be matched against revenue throughout the life of the investment through the amortization process and not recognized in a lump sum in the year of maturity.

On the balance sheet, Laker Co. shows cash and the bond investment as assets. The owners' equity section reflects the income statement effects of interest revenue accumulated in retained earnings (see Exhibit 4).

EXHIBIT 4 Example 1. Balance Sheet

LAKER CO.
Balance Sheet
December 31
(Net cumulative effect of bond investment only)

	2001	2002	2003	2004	2005	2006
Assets						
Current assets						
Cash	(801,857)	(711,857)	(621,857)	(531,857)	(441,857)	558,143
Investments in bonds					1,000,000	
Investments and funds						
Investments in bonds	908,880	927,945	949,298	973,214	0	0
Owners' Equity						
Retained earnings (through cumulative effect on net income, ignoring income taxes)	107,023	216,088	327,441	441,357	558,143	558,143

The negative balance in Cash at December 31, 2001, represents the investment in the bond issue ($891,857) on January 1, 2001, less one $90,000 interest payment received in 2001. The annual receipt of interest increases Cash by $90,000 in each successive year through December 31, 2005. On January 1, 2006, the investment is liquidated when $1,000,000 in cash is received, raising the cash balance to $558,143. The net cash inflow of $558,143 represents Laker's total revenue from investing in Worthy's bonds over the five-year period.

Long-term bond investments are reported in the "Investments and funds" balance sheet section at amortized cost, which equals the present value of future cash flows using the historical effective rate of interest *at the issue date*. The most common practice is for investors to report the bond investment net of premium or discount (i.e., at net present value); the debtor usually shows the face amount of the bonds payable less a discount account (or plus a premium when bonds are issued at a premium). Note that the effective interest amortization table reports the book values of the investment at each year-end; it is not necessary to recompute present value at each balance sheet date. At December 31, 2005, the $1,000,000 maturity value must be reclassified as a current asset because funds will be received within one year of the balance sheet date.

Retained earnings increases each period because it accumulates the increases in net income shown on the income statement. For example, by December 31, 2003, Retained Earnings has increased by $327,441, the total interest revenue for 2001, 2002, and 2003, as reported on the income statement. This illustrates that changes in assets and liabilities from nonowner transactions are reflected in both the balance sheet and the income statement.

EXAMPLE 1 Journal Entries

1/1/01 Purchase of bonds:

Investment in Bonds	891,857	
Cash		891,857

Receipt of cash, recognition of interest revenue, and amortization of discount:

	12/31/01		12/31/02		12/31/03		12/31/04		12/31/05	
Cash	90,000		90,000		90,000		90,000		90,000	
Investment in Bonds*	17,023		19,065		21,353		23,916		26,786	
Interest Revenue		107,023		109,065		111,353		113,916		116,786

*This amount represents discount amortization. As the bond discount decreases, the bond's carrying value increases.

1/1/96 Maturation of bonds:

Cash	1,000,000	
Investment in Bonds		1,000,000

Note: We did not illustrate closing entries in this solution. However, it is a good idea to review the journal entries made to identify which accounts are nominal, and thus, closed to retained earnings in the closing process. The only nominal account shown above is Interest Revenue. Therefore, the changes in Retained Earnings shown in the key ledger accounts below are caused entirely by closing Interest Revenue.

EXHIBIT 5 Example 1. Key Ledger Accounts for Laker Co.

Cash

		1/1/01	891,857
12/31/01	90,000		
		Bal.	801,857
12/31/02	90,000		
		Bal.	711,857
12/31/03	90,000		
		Bal.	621,857
12/31/04	90,000		
		Bal.	531,857
12/31/05	90,000		
		Bal.	441,857
1/1/06	1,000,000		
Bal.	558,143		

Investment in Bonds

1/1/01	891,857		
12/31/01	17,023		
Bal.	908,880		
12/31/02	19,065		
Bal.	927,945		
12/31/03	21,353		
Bal.	949,298		
12/31/04	23,916		
Bal.	973,214		
12/31/05	26,786		
Bal.	1,000,000		
		1/1/06	1,000,000
Bal.	0		

Retained Earnings

		CE	107,023
		Bal.	107,023
		CE	109,065
		Bal.	216,088
		CE	111,353
		Bal.	327,441
		CE	113,916
		Bal.	441,357
		CE	116,786
		Bal.	558,143
		Bal.	558,143

CE indicates that a closing entry generated the ledger entry.

Temporary Investments in Debt Securities

In the preceding discussion, we assumed that Laker purchased the Worthy bonds with the intent to hold them as a long-term investment until maturity. If Laker purchased the bonds intending to temporarily hold the investment (i.e., less than one year), then Laker does not amortize the discount. That is, interest revenue is computed as the face value times the stated rate of interest, *not* the present value times the effective rate of interest. In our example, interest revenue would be $90,000 per year.

Failure to use the effective rate of interest to determine interest revenue is theoretically incorrect. However, the amount of error is relatively small (immaterial) over a very short period (less than one year). Accountants argue that the immaterial error does not make a difference in user decisions. This fact justifies using the simpler method of interest revenue recognition for short-term investments.

Transaction Costs

In Example 1, we ignored transaction costs. Transaction costs related to bond investments are capitalized as part of the bond investment. This causes the effective interest rate to be lower than it would be in the absence of these costs. In the original Laker-Worthy Co. bond example, the effective interest rate on the bonds was 12% (n = 5; payment = $90,000; present value = $891,857; future value = $1,000,000). However, if Laker had incurred $20,000 in acquisition costs, the bond investment would have been recorded at a cost of $911,857, yielding an effective interest rate of 11.41% (n = 5; payment = $90,000; present value = $911,857; future value = $1,000,000). Transaction costs decrease the yield on bond investments.

Contrasting the accounting for bond investment transaction costs with bond payable transaction costs (Chapter 3) reveals that GAAP rules are not always consistent. Recall that bond payable transaction costs are capitalized into a separate account and amortized over the life of the bond without affecting the effective interest rate. The FASB noted in *SFAS No. 3* that transaction costs accounting for bond investments and bond payables is inconsistent, but it has not yet issued a pronouncement to correct this inconsistency.[5] If a pronouncement were issued, it appears that the FASB would change the accounting for bond payable transaction costs to be consistent with the accounting for bond investment transaction costs—the costs would increase the basis of the bonds, which would change the effective interest rate.

Sale of a Bond Investment

Laker's balance sheet reports the bond investment at $949,298 on December 31, 2003. This represents the present value of the remaining cash inflows at the original 9% interest rate. In the following example, we consider how the sale of a bond investment is reported.

Example 2. At December 31, 2003, assume that interest rates on bonds in Worthy's risk class have hit a low of 7%. Also assume that Laker receives the December 31, 2003, $90,000 interest payment as scheduled. What financial statement effects would be reported if Laker sells the investment after the receipt of the interest payment?

Solution. Now that only two interest cash inflows remain, the market value of the investment is computed as follows:

$$\$1{,}036{,}160 = \sum_{n=1}^{2} \frac{\$90{,}000}{(1 + 0.07)^1} + \frac{\$1{,}000{,}000}{(1 + 0.07)^2}$$

5. "Elements of Financial Statements of Business Enterprises," *Statement of Financial Accounting Concepts No. 3* (Norwalk, Conn.: FASB, 1980).

If Laker sells the bond investment at December 31, 2003, it will report a gain on sale of investments equal to the increase in net assets from trading one asset (Investment in Bonds) for another asset (Cash):

Cash received	$1,036,160
Book value of bond investment	949,298
Gain on sale of investment	$ 86,862

EXAMPLE 2 Journal Entry

Cash	1,036,160	
Investment in Bonds		949,298
Gain on Sale of Investment		86,862

Summary of Accounting for Long-Term Investments in Bonds

Long-term investments in bonds are disclosed on the balance sheet at amortized cost, which is equal to the present value of future cash flows using the historical effective rate of interest at the date of the bond issue. The market's effective rate of interest can change during the life of the bond. In a valuation context, an inverse relationship exists between bond prices and the market rate of return (i.e., bond market value and the market rate of interest move in opposite directions): increases (decreases) in the market's required rate of return on the bond decrease (increase) the market value of the bond. The effects of market value changes on bond balance sheet disclosures are considered in the following section.

The income statement effects of bond investments are determined by the effective interest method. The effective interest method recognizes a constant rate of interest earned by the investor on a changing net carrying value. The net investment changes because differences between the stated interest rate and the effective interest rate on a bond result in the investor receiving more (or less) cash interest than is being accrued as interest income. The difference between effective interest income and cash interest received causes a change (i.e., amortization) of the bond's carrying value.

Another Look at the Market Value Issue

2 Account for held-to-maturity, trading, and available-for-sale securities, and adjust the financial statements to reflect changes in the market values of these investments when appropriate.

The financial press provides many examples of corporate financial failure. During the late 1980s and early 1990s, many financial institutions failed. These institutions earned a great deal of revenue from investments in the debt of other entities.

As we previously discussed in this chapter, a change in the effective rate of interest causes a change in the market value of investments in debt. Historically, however, these value changes were not reflected in the financial statements until the 1990s. In 1993, the FASB was bombarded with criticism that the financial reporting of investments played a role in investor surprise over financial failure. In response, the FASB issued a new standard, *SFAS No. 115*, that changed the way in which some debt instruments are reported in financial statements—some bond investments are "marked to market" (written up or down to current market value), while some bond investments are reported at amortized cost (the present value of the remaining cash flows using the historical effective interest rate).

Under *SFAS No. 115*, investments in debt securities are grouped into the following three portfolios at each balance sheet date:

- Held-to-maturity debt securities
- Trading debt securities
- Available-for-sale debt securities

Held-to-maturity debt securities are **those investments for which managers have the *intent* and *ability* to hold to maturity.** While intent is quite subjective, ability is easier to objectively determine. If, for example, a company has a large liability coming due before the debt investment matures, the investment may have to be liquidated in order to extinguish the liability. Thus, the matching of maturities of assets and liabilities that is central to financial management is important in documenting the ability to hold to maturity. Held-to-maturity debt investments are reported at amortized cost at each balance sheet date. *Held-to-maturity debt securities are not marked to market* (i.e., not reported at market value). The preceding Laker Co. example illustrates the reporting of such an investment and the amortization of the related bond discount.

Trading debt securities **have relatively short holding periods.** These securities are bought to avoid the opportunity cost of lost interest; they are sold to meet short-term cash needs. Trading debt securities are "marked to market" at each balance sheet date. The ***unrealized holding gain or loss*** (i.e., **the difference between the book value and the current market value**) is reflected in current income. As previously indicated, premiums and discounts on short-term debt securities are not recorded or amortized.

Available-for-sale debt securities are **those securities that are neither trading debt securities nor held-to-maturity debt securities** (i.e., *the available-for-sale classification is the default category*). While short-run liquidation is not expected, neither has management demonstrated the intent and ability to hold the securities to maturity. Available-for-sale securities may be purchased for either short-term (less than one year) or long-term (greater than one year) purposes. If purchased for the short-term, premiums and discounts are not recorded or amortized. If purchased for the long-term, the bond premium (discount) is amortized over the life of the bond as an adjustment to interest income using the effective interest method. *Available-for-sale debt securities are marked to market at each balance sheet date. Unrealized holding gains and losses are reflected as a component of* ***other comprehensive income;*** *cumulative unrealized holding gains and losses are reported in the owners' equity section of the balance sheet as* ***accumulated other comprehensive income*** *(i.e., the unrealized holding gain or loss is NOT reported on the income statement).*

Example 3. Yogurt Corp. invests cash on January 1, 2000, by purchasing the newly issued \$100,000, 5%, 10-year bonds of Ice Cream Industries for \$79,870 (an 8% yield). Interest is receivable every January 1. The market values of the bonds are \$74,000 at December 31, 2000, and \$75,000 at December 31, 2001. Prepare the relevant portions of the statement of cash flows, balance sheet, income statement, and statement of comprehensive income under the three separate assumptions that the investment is (a) held-to-maturity, (b) available-for-sale, and (c) trading.

Solution. This example is used to compare and contrast the *SFAS No. 115* accounting for each of the three types of securities. Because the investment is held over two years, classification as a trading security in this example is inappropriate—it is held too long to be a trading security. However, greater understanding of *SFAS No. 115* accounting is gained by using the same problem under the three possible classifications.

The amounts reported in the statement of cash flows are identical under each investment assumption (see Exhibit 6). Cash flows associated with available-for-sale and held-to-maturity securities are reported in the investing activities section. However, GAAP requires that cash flows associated with trading securities are classified as operating activities because of the short-term nature of the investment. Every year, Yogurt shows \$5,000 of cash interest receipts as an operating activity. In the year of investment, the bond acquisition is reported as a cash outflow of \$79,870. In the year of disposal (not shown in Exhibit 6), Yogurt reports a cash inflow from operating activities (for the trading classification) or investing activities (for the available-for-sale or held-to-maturity classification) equal to the final disposal price.

EXHIBIT 6 Example 3. Statement of Cash Flows

YOGURT CORP.
Statement of Cash Flows*
Selected Information

	Trading Classification		Available-for-Sale or Held-to-Maturity Classification	
	2000	**2001**	**2000**	**2001**
Operating Activities				
Interest receipts		5,000		5,000
Investment in bonds	(79,870)			
Investing Activities				
Investments in bonds			(79,870)	

*Cash outflows in parentheses

The balance sheet treatment of these security investments (and the related income statement effects) depends on the investment classification. *Held-to-maturity debt securities are reported at amortized cost, while available-for-sale and trading securities are reported at market value.* The following balance sheets in Exhibit 7 show the effects of the investment under each of the three classifications on all accounts except Cash and Retained Earnings:

EXHIBIT 7 Example 3. Balance Sheet

YOGURT CORP.
Balance Sheet
December 31
(Excluding cash balance and retained earnings effect)

	Bond Investment Classification					
	Held-to-Maturity		**Available-for-Sale**		**Trading**	
	2000	**2001**	**2000**	**2001**	**2000**	**2001**
Assets						
Current assets						
Investments in **trading** debt securities (at cost)					79,870	79,870
Less valuation allowance					(5,870)	(4,870)
Investments, at market					74,000	75,000
Interest receivable	5,000	5,000	5,000	5,000	5,000	5,000
Long-term investments and funds						
Investments in **held-to-maturity** debt securities, at amortized cost	81,260	82,761				
Investments in **available-for-sale** debt securities, at amortized cost			81,260	82,761		
Less valuation allowance			(7,260)	(7,761)		
Investments, at market			74,000	75,000		
Owners' Equity						
Accumulated other comprehensive income:						
Cumulative unrealized loss on available-for-sale debt investments	N/A	N/A	(7,260)	(7,761)	N/A	N/A

In the current asset section, a $5,000 interest receivable is reported because the annual interest receipt does not occur until the first day of the following year. The investment itself is reported differently depending on its classification.

Held-to-maturity debt investments are reported at amortized cost at each balance sheet date. Our earlier example of the investment in Worthy Co. bonds is an example of the reporting of held-to-maturity securities. As in that example, the book values at December 31, 2000, and December 31, 2001, for Yogurt are based on effective interest amortization (see Exhibit 8).

EXHIBIT 8 Example 3. Effective Interest Amortization Table (partial)

YOGURT CORP.

Date	5% Cash Interest Received	8% Effective Interest Income	Discount Amortization	Book Value of Investment (Amortized Cost)
1/1/00				79,870
12/31/00	5,000	6,390	1,390	81,260
12/31/01	5,000	6,501	1,501	82,761

Market value accounting is not used for held-to-maturity securities because the annual fluctuations in market value are not indicative of the cash flows that will be realized by Yogurt Co. during the life of the investment. Market value accounting is used, however, for both available-for-sale and trading debt securities. For available-for-sale securities, management has not demonstrated the intent and ability to hold the securities to maturity. In the balance sheet, note that the securities are reported at their market values at each balance sheet date. Market value reporting involves an increase or reduction of amortized cost to market value through the use of a valuation account. At December 31, 2000, the amortized cost is shown in the amortization schedule as $81,260; the current market value is shown in the balance sheet as $74,000. Thus, a valuation allowance of $7,260 has been deducted. Similarly, at December 31, 2001, the amortized cost is $82,761, and a valuation allowance of $7,761 is required to adjust to the $75,000 current market value. In a statement of comprehensive income, each period's unrealized gain (or loss) is recognized as a component of Other Comprehensive Income (Exhibit 10).

Because trading securities are short-term, they do not require amortization of acquisition discounts or premiums. At each balance sheet date, an allowance account adjusts the *original* cost ($79,870), not *amortized* cost, to market.

When market value changes from period to period, when should the change in net assets be reflected in net income? The answer to this question again depends on the classification of the debt investment. The difference between the available-for-sale security's amortized cost ($81,260) and its market value ($74,000) at December 31, 2000, is shown as a reduction in owners' equity ($7,260). The December 31, 2001, difference is treated in a similar manner. The cumulative fluctuation reported in owners' equity shows that net assets have been reduced due to the decline in the investment's market value. However, because the liquidation of the investment is not expected in the near term (i.e., it is not a trading security), the FASB mandated the use of Other Comprehensive Income to report the unrealized gain or loss rather than to report the net asset change in income. Conceptually, this amounts to treating the fluctuation as transitory. Over the period of time the investment is held, the market value will fluctuate in an unknown manner. Since a primary goal of the income statement is to serve as a vehicle for predicting future cash flows, the unrealized gain or loss on available-for-sale securities is not shown on the income statement. Any transitory change in market value would not be a predictor of future cash flows.

The situation is different for a trading security. By definition, a trading security will be liquidated in the short run. Thus, any fluctuation in market value (however short the duration) is reflected on the income statement, as shown in Exhibit 9.

EXHIBIT 9 Example 3. Income Statement Effects

YOGURT CORP. Income Statement Effects						
	Bond Investment Classification					
	Held-to-Maturity		**Available-for-Sale**		**Trading**	
	2000	**2001**	**2000**	**2001**	**2000**	**2001**
Other revenues, (expenses), gains, and (losses)						
Interest revenue	6,390	6,501	6,390	6,501	5,000	5,000
Adjustment to market for trading securities	N/A	N/A	N/A	N/A	(5,870)	1,000

Both the held-to-maturity securities and the available-for-sale securities report interest revenue calculated using the effective interest method (shown in the previous amortization schedule). Trading securities report interest revenue at the cash interest received because, as previously noted, discounts and premiums are not amortized for short-term investments in debt securities. In 2000, the trading securities investment declined from an original acquisition price of $79,870 to a December 31, 2000, market value of $74,000. This $5,870 decline is a reduction of net income. In 2001, market value rose to $75,000. This $1,000 market value increase is reported as an increase in net income.

As illustrated in Exhibit 10, the statement of comprehensive income reports each year's unrealized gains and losses for available-for-sale securities as a component of Other Comprehensive Income. A $7,260 loss is reported in 2000, and a $501 loss is reported in 2001 ($7,761 − $7,260 as shown in Exhibit 7).

EXHIBIT 10 Example 3. Comprehensive Income Effects

YOGURT CORP. Comprehensive Income Effects						
	Bond Investment Classification					
	Held-to-Maturity		**Available-for-Sale**		**Trading**	
	2000	**2001**	**2000**	**2001**	**2000**	**2001**
Net income	(1)	(1)	(1)	(1)	(2)	(2)
Other comprehensive income						
Unrealized gains (losses) on available-for-sale securities	N/A	N/A	(7,260)	(501)	N/A	N/A

(1) Reflects interest revenue (see income statement effects in Exhibit 9).
(2) Reflects interest revenue and unrealized gain (loss) related to market adjustment for trading securities (see income statement effects in Exhibit 9).

It is important to remember that declines in the market values of both available-for-sale and trading securities have similar effects on owners' equity, although the effects are reflected in two different accounts. For available-for-sale securities, the unrealized gain or loss is reflected in owners' equity as Accumulated Other Comprehensive Income. For trading securities, market value changes are recorded as a gain or loss on the income statement. However, remember that all changes in net income become a part of Retained Earnings, an owners' equity account.

EXAMPLE 3 Journal Entries

	Held-to-Maturity Debt Securities			Available-for-Sale Debt Securities			Trading Debt Securities		
1/1/00 Acquisition:	Investment in Bonds	79,870		Investment in Bonds	79,870		Investment in Bonds	79,870	
	Cash		79,870	Cash		79,870	Cash		79,870
12/31/00 Accrue interest revenue:	Investment in Bonds	1,390		Investment in Bonds	1,390		Interest Receivable	5,000	
	Interest Receivable	5,000		Interest Receivable	5,000		Interest Revenue		5,000
	Interest Revenue		6,390	Interest Revenue		6,390			
12/31/00 Market adjustment:	(None)			Unrealized Loss on Market Value Decline	7,260		Unrealized Loss on Market Value Decline	5,870	
				Allowance for Decline In Market Value		7,260	Allowance for Decline In Market Value		5,870
1/1/01 Cash receipt:	Cash	5,000		Cash	5,000		Cash	5,000	
	Interest Receivable		5,000	Interest Receivable		5,000	Interest Receivable		5,000
12/31/01 Accrue interest revenue:	Investment in Bonds	1,501		Investment in Bonds	1,501		Interest Receivable	5,000	
	Interest Receivable	5,000		Interest Receivable	5,000		Interest Revenue		5,000
	Interest Revenue		6,501	Interest Revenue		6,501			
12/31/01 Market adjustment:	(None)			Unrealized Loss on Market Value Decline	501		Allowance for Decline in Market Value	1,000	
				Allowance for Decline in Market Value		501	Unrealized Gain on Market Value Increase		1,000

Exhibit 11 shows a slightly modified portion of Note 2 from Ford Motor Company's 1997 annual report to illustrate the *SFAS No. 115* reporting for securities. Ford separates its financial statements into automotive and financial services components.

EXHIBIT 11 Ford Motor Company's SFAS No. 115 Disclosure

NOTE 2. Marketable and Other Securities

Trading securities are recorded at fair value with unrealized gains and losses included in income. Available-for-sale securities are recorded at fair value with unrealized gains and losses excluded from income and reported, net of tax, in a separate component of stockholders' equity. Held-to-maturity securities are recorded at amortized cost. Equity securities which do not have readily determinable fair values are recorded at cost.

Automotive

Investments in securities at December 31, 1997, were as follows (in millions):

Securities Classification	Amortized Cost	Gross Unrealized Gains	Gross Unrealized Losses	Fair Value	Memo: Book Value
Trading	$14,114	$29	$ 0	$14,143	$14,143
Available-for-sale	395	0	19	376	376
Total investment	$14,509	$29	$19	$14,519	$14,519

Financial Services

Investments in securities at December 31, 1997, were as follows (in millions):

Securities Classification	Amortized Cost	Gross Unrealized Gains	Gross Unrealized Losses	Fair Value	Memo: Book Value
Trading	$ 267	$ 4	$1	$ 270	$ 270
Available-for-sale	1,827	84	5	1,906	1,906
Held-to-maturity	25	0	0	25	25
Total investments in securities with readily determinable fair value	$2,119	$88	$6	$2,201	$2,201
Equity securities not practicable to fair value	6				6
Total investments	$2,125				$2,207

Summary

Bond investments are classified as trading, available-for-sale, and held-to-maturity. The default classification is available-for-sale. Trading securities are short-term investments, and neither bond premiums nor discounts are amortized. Trading securities are recorded at cost and marked-to-market when a balance sheet is prepared. Unrealized gains or losses are included in the income statement.

Held-to-maturity securities are long-term investments, and related bond premiums and discounts are amortized over the life of the bond as adjustments to interest income using the effective interest method. The investments are reported on the balance sheet at amortized cost (principal plus premium or minus discount), which is equal to the present value of future cash flows *discounted at the original effective interest rate*. Held-to-maturity securities are not marked-to-market.

Available-for-sale securities may be purchased for either short-term (less than one year) or long-term (greater than one year) purposes. Available-for-sale securities are recorded at cost. If purchased for long-term purposes, the related bond premium or discount is amortized over the life of the bond as an adjustment to interest income using the effective interest method, and the bonds are marked-to-market when a balance sheet is prepared. Unrealized gains or losses are not included in the income statement; rather, they are shown in the statement of comprehensive income as Other Comprehensive Income and in the stockholders' equity section as a component of Accumulated Other Comprehensive Income.

Investments in Notes (Loans) Receivable

3 Account for loans, loan impairments, and troubled debt restructurings.

The accounting treatment for loans differs slightly from the treatment for investments in debt securities. Technically, loans receivable do not meet the FASB definition of a security, and thus, are not covered by the *SFAS No. 115* mark-to-market standard for investments in securities. A loan receivable should be recorded at the present value of future cash flows using the effective rate of interest at the date of receipt. As in the case of investments in bonds, effective interest recognition of interest revenue is required for notes receivable. To illustrate the accounting for notes receivable, consider the information for Huskie Co. in Example 4. This example sets the effective and stated interest rates as equal. The effective and stated interest rates could, of course, differ, in which case a discount or premium would arise. Any discount or premium would be amortized as an adjustment to interest income in the same manner as previously illustrated in the bond investment example.[6]

Example 4. On December 1, 2001, Huskie Co. loaned $2,000,000 to the city of Seattle, accepting a $2,000,000, 8%, 6-year note as payment. Interest is payable every December 31, and the note matures on December 31, 2006. Assume that the city of Seattle normally borrows at 8% interest.

Solution. The statement of cash flows shows interest receipts of $160,000 ($2,000,000 × 8%) each period as an operating activity. The cash outflow from the 2001 loan and the cash inflow from the 2006 maturation are reported as investing activities for Huskie Co. (See Exhibit 12.)

6. For most note receivables, the stated rate of interest reflects the appropriate market rate of interest on the day the note receivable is executed, and accordingly, no premium or discount is recorded. In this chapter, we assume that the stated rated on the note reflects the appropriate market rate. An exception that would require recording a discount is a note that is non-interest bearing.

EXHIBIT 12 Example 4. Statement of Cash Flows

HUSKIE CO.
Statement of Cash Flows*

	2001	2002	2003	2004	2005	2006
Operating Activities						
Interest receipts:	160,000	160,000	160,000	160,000	160,000	160,000
Investing Activities						
Loan to city of Seattle	(2,000,000)					
Maturity, city of Seattle loan						2,000,000

*Cash outflows in parentheses

Because the effective interest rate and the cash interest rate are identical, cash interest received and interest revenue are the same (see Exhibit 13).

EXHIBIT 13 Example 4. Income Statement

HUSKIE CO.
Income Statement
(Effects of loan only)

	2001	2002	2003	2004	2005	2006
Financial revenues, (expenses), gains, and (losses)						
Interest revenue	160,000	160,000	160,000	160,000	160,000	160,000

On the balance sheet (Exhibit 14), Huskie Co. shows cash and the note receivable as assets. The owners' equity section reflects the cumulative income statement effects of interest revenue in Retained Earnings.

EXHIBIT 14 Example 4. Balance Sheet

HUSKIE CO.
Balance Sheet
December 31
(Net effect of loan only)

	2001	2002	2003	2004	2005	2006
Assets						
Current assets						
Cash	(1,840,000)	(1,680,000)	(1,520,000)	(1,360,000)	(1,200,000)	960,000
Notes receivable					2,000,000	
Investments and funds						
Notes receivable	2,000,000	2,000,000	2,000,000	2,000,000		
Owners' Equity						
Retained earnings (through cumulative effect on net income, ignoring income taxes)	160,000	320,000	480,000	640,000	800,000	960,000

EXAMPLE 4 Journal Entries

1/1/01 Note acquisition:		
Note Receivable	2,000,000	
Cash		2,000,000

(continued)

EXAMPLE 4 (concluded)

12/31/01–06 Interest revenue recognition:		
Cash	160,000	
Interest Revenue		160,000
12/31/06 Note collection:		
Cash	2,000,000	
Note Receivable		2,000,000

Information from the 1999 financial statements for Herman Miller, Inc., is shown in Exhibit 15 and illustrates a note receivable disclosure.

EXHIBIT 15 Illustration of Note Receivable Disclosure

Herman Miller, Inc., Partial Balance Sheet Information (in thousands)

	1999	**1998**
Net Property and equipment	316,719	290,664
Notes receivable, less allowances of $5,469 in 1999 and $8,430 in 1998	17,400	27,522
Other assets	77,285	66,025

Significant Accounting and Reporting Policies (in part)

Notes Receivable. The notes receivable are primarily from certain independent contract office furniture dealers. The notes are collateralized by the assets of the dealers and bear interest based on the prevailing prime rate. Interest income relating to these notes was $3.0, $4.3, and $4.8 million in 1999, 1998 and 1997, respectively.

Defaulted Loan Agreements

Creditors who make loans always face the possibility that debtors will not pay the entire amount of interest and principal contractually owed. Interest rates have a portion attributable to a risk premium that compensates creditors for risk (i.e., the riskier the loan the higher the interest rate). Creditors with large numbers of loans (such as banks and insurance companies) periodically record bad debts expense and an associated allowance for doubtful accounts based upon a general estimate of the amount of loans that will not be collected in the future. The allowance for doubtful accounts amount pertains to the entire portfolio of loans outstanding. Bad debts expense is recognized in the current period income statement. The allowance for doubtful accounts reduces the portfolio of loans to net realizable value, the amount expected to be collected.

GAAP requires creditors to continually assess outstanding loans as to the degree of collectibility. **Whenever a creditor believes that the full amount of interest and principal will not be received as prescribed by the lending agreement, the receivable is considered** to be ***impaired.*** If an impairment is deemed to have occurred, then GAAP requires that the loan receivable be written down to reflect the impairment. Note that at the time of impairment, the creditor has not agreed to take less than the contractual amount of interest and principal. However, the creditor is assessing the likelihood, *ex ante*, that the full amount of principal and interest will not be collected. The accounting for the impairment depends upon whether the creditor has previously recorded bad debts expense and allowance for doubtful accounts for the entire portfolio of loans receivable. If so, the impairment is charged to Allowance for Doubtful Accounts. If not, the impairment is charged to Bad Debts Expense. At the point in time the company deems an impairment has occurred, the loan itself is not written off or reduced because the creditor and debtor have not agreed to change the terms of the agreement.

When a creditor and debtor recognize that a debtor may have trouble paying the full principal and interest amounts on a loan, the two parties may agree to change the terms of the loan in a ***troubled debt restructuring***. In essence, the creditor provides some degree of debt relief to the debtor. The two most common scenarios are ***settlement of debt***, at which point **the creditor receives assets in full payment of the debt,** or ***modification of terms***, at which point **the creditor agrees to reduced payments in the future** (e.g., waive accrued interest, reduce principal, or reduce the stated interest rate).

In the following sections, we discuss accounting for loan impairments, modifications of terms of debt agreements, and debt settlements.

Loan Impairments Most loans are collected according to the terms of the loan. However, it may sometimes be clear to the creditor that the debtor may have trouble paying back the loan. For example (continuing with Example 4), what if Huskie believes that Seattle will have difficulty making future payments? Is the impairment of a loan's value recognized in the financial statements? Under *SFAS No. 114*, any decline in estimated future cash inflows from a loan usually triggers a recognized loss on loan impairment.[7] *The loss amount is the excess of the current carrying value of the loan receivable over the present value of the anticipated remaining cash flows discounted at the loan's historical effective interest rate.*

Example 5. On December 31, 2003, before receiving the $160,000 interest payment currently due, Huskie Co. assessed the likelihood of receiving cash flows in the future from the city of Seattle. Huskie feels that it is probable that it will neither receive the current interest payment due nor the interest payments in any year for the remainder of the note maturity. Further, Huskie expects that Seattle will pay only $800,000 at the maturity date, December 31, 2006.

Solution. Clearly, the loan has been impaired because Huskie believes that it will not receive all future principal and interest to which it is contractually entitled. Although the book value of the receivable is $2,160,000 at December 31, 2003 ($2,000,000 plus $160,000 accrued interest), the present value of the estimated one remaining future cash flow of $800,000 to be received in three years is $635,066. This amount is calculated using the original effective rate of 8% as follows:

$$\$800{,}000 \div (1 + 0.08)^3 = \$635{,}066$$

SFAS No. 114 requires Huskie to recognize a loss of $1,524,934 to reflect the write-down from the book value of the loan ($2,160,000) to its present value ($635,066).

Present value of future cash flows	$ 635,066
Current book value	(2,160,000)
Loss on loan impairment	$(1,524,934)

The statement of cash flows summarizes the cash flow implications of the loan impairment. (See Exhibit 16.)

7. "Accounting by Creditors for the Impairment of a Loan," *Statement of Financial Accounting Standards No. 114* (Stamford, Conn: FASB, 1993).

EXHIBIT 16 Example 5. Statement of Cash Flows

HUSKIE CO.
Statement of Cash Flows*

	2001	2002	2003	2004	2005	2006
Operating Activities						
Interest receipts	160,000	160,000	0	0	0	0
Investing Activities						
Loan to city of Seattle	(2,000,000)					
Maturity, city of Seattle loan						800,000

*Cash outflows in parentheses

For simplicity, we assume that Huskie has not previously recorded bad debts expense based upon a general assessment about the future uncollectibility of all loans receivable. Therefore, the 2003 income statement reflects the impairment loss as bad debts expense. Interest revenue is recognized in future years using the effective interest method because the amount expected to be received on December 31, 2006, ($800,000) is greater than the December 31, 2003, present value ($635,066). (See Exhibit 17.)

EXHIBIT 17 Example 5. Effective Interest Amorization Table

HUSKIE CO.
Effective Interest Amortization Table
Remainder of Loan Life after Impairment Recognized

Date	No Cash Interest	8% Effective Interest Income	Discount Amortization	Book Value of Loan
12/31/03	—			$635,066
12/31/04	0	$50,805	$50,805	685,871
12/31/05	0	54,870	54,870	740,741
12/31/06	0	59,259	59,259	800,000

The revised income statements over the life of the loan reflect the loss (reported as bad debts expense) and the new computation of interest revenue. (See Exhibit 18.)

EXHIBIT 18 Example 5. Income Statement Effects

HUSKIE CO.
Income Statement Effects

	2001	2002	2003	2004	2005	2006
Bad debts expense—loan impairment			(1,524,934)			
Financial revenues, (expenses), gains, and (losses)						
Interest revenue	160,000	160,000	160,000	50,805	54,870	59,259

On the balance sheet, Huskie Co. sets up an allowance for uncollectible notes in order to achieve the note receivable write-down. An allowance account is used rather than a direct write-off of the loan because at this time Huskie has not formally agreed to change the debt agreement. The amortization from effective interest recognition increases the book value of the note receivable in each period by decreasing this allowance account as shown in Exhibit 19.

EXHIBIT 19 Example 5. Balance Sheet

HUSKIE CO.
Balance Sheet
December 31 (Net effect of loan only)

	2001	2002	2003	2004	2005	2006
Assets						
Current assets						
Cash	(1,840,000)	(1,680,000)	(1,680,000)	(1,680,000)	(1,680,000)	(880,000)
Note receivable					2,000,000	
Less allowance for uncollectible notes					(1,259,259)	
					740,741	
Investments and funds						
Note receivable	2,000,000	2,000,000	2,000,000	2,000,000		
Less allowance for uncollectible notes			(1,364,934)	(1,314,129)		
			635,066	685,871		
Owners' Equity						
Retained earnings (through cumulative effect on net income, ignoring income tax effects)	160,000	320,000	(1,044,934)	(994,129)	(939,259)	(880,000)

The $880,000 loss over the life of the loan can be verified by comparing the amount loaned, $2,000,000, to the amount of cash ultimately received under the impaired note, $1,120,000 ($160,000 interest receipt + $160,000 interest receipt + $800,000 final cash flow).

EXAMPLE 5 Journal Entries

1/1/01 Note acquisition:

Note Receivable	2,000,000	
Cash		2,000,000

Interest revenue recognition on 12/31/01 and 12/31/02:

Cash	160,000	
Interest Revenue		160,000

12/31/03 Loan impairment:

Interest Receivable	160,000	
Interest Revenue		160,000
Bad Debts Expense (loss on impairment)	1,524,934	
Interest Receivable		160,000
Allowance for Uncollectible Notes		1,364,934

Interest recognition on:	*12/31/04*		*12/31/05*		*12/31/06*	
Allowance for Uncollectible Notes	50,805		54,870		59,259	
Interest Revenue		50,805		54,870		59,259

12/31/06 Note collection:

Allowance for Uncollectible Notes	1,200,000	
Cash	800,000	
Note Receivable		2,000,000

The following partial note for General Electric illustrates a loan impairment disclosure.

General Electric Company Note 13 (in part, modified by authors)

GE adopted Statement of Financial Accounting Standards (SFAS) No. 114 . . . and the related SFAS No. 118. . . . At year-end, loans that required disclosure as impaired amounted to $867 million, principally commercial real estate loans. For $647 million of such loans, the required allowance for losses was $285 million. The remaining $220 million of loans represents the recorded investment in loans that are fully recoverable, but only because the recorded investment had been reduced through charge-offs or deferral of income recognition. . . .

Troubled Debt Restructuring The previous section illustrated a loan impairment, in which the terms of the loan were not restructured. Alternatively, a creditor and debtor may elect to formally restructure the loan if the debtor is having difficulty meeting the terms of the loan.[8] Two types of restructure are possible: modification and settlement of terms. In a modification of terms, the creditor's loss is the difference between the loan's book value and the present value of cash flows under the new terms of the loan agreement using the historical effective rate of interest at the time the loan was made.[9] In a settlement, the creditor immediately receives cash or other consideration in full settlement of the debt, and the difference between the book value of the loan and the fair value of assets received results in a recorded loss.[10]

Modification of Terms. To illustrate a troubled debt modification of terms, assume that in Example 5 Huskie formally agreed to modify the terms of the debt on December 31, 2003, waiving interest for 2003, 2004, 2005, and 2006, and reducing the debt principal to $800,000. The book value of the debt on December 31, 2003, (before the modification of terms) equals $2,160,000 ($2,000,000 principal plus $160,000 accrued interest). The present value of the future cash flows equals $635,066 [$800,000 $\div$ $(1 + 0.08)^3$]. Therefore, Huskie records a loss of $1,524,934, the excess of the book value at the date of the modification over the present value of the remaining future cash flows *discounted at the historical effective interest rate*. The loss is usually recorded as bad debts expense.

EXAMPLE 5A Journal Entry

12/31/03 Modification of terms:		
Bad Debts Expense—Debt Modification	1,524,934	
Interest Receivable		160,000
Notes Receivable		1,200,000
Discount on Notes Receivable		164,934*

*$800,000 principal − $635,066 new carrying value

Settlement. To illustrate a troubled debt settlement, if on December 31, 2003, Huskie had accepted a parcel of land valued at $900,000 to settle the debt from the city of Seattle, then the carrying value of $2,160,000 would be written off, the land would be recorded at $900,000, and the resulting $1,260,000 loss would be charged to Bad Debts Expense—Debt Settlement.

8. In this analysis, we assume that a debtor only agrees to a restructure if the debtor receives an economic benefit. We assume that the investor always sustains an economic loss in a troubled debt restructuring.
9. This accounting treatment means that the loss is related only to the change in cash flows over time. Any loss associated with changing market rates of interest is not recorded because the original effective rate of interest is used over the entire life of the loan.
10. If the creditor has previously set up an allowance for doubtful accounts for possible loan losses, then the excess of the fair value of the assets received over the book value of the debt is charged to Allowance for Doubtful Accounts. Lending institutions are required to estimate bad debts expense and create appropriate loan loss reserves.

EXAMPLE 5B Journal Entry

12/31/03 Debt settlement:		
Land	900,000	
Bad Debts Expense—Debt Settlement	1,260,000	
Interest Receivable		160,000
Notes Receivable		2,000,000

Summary

Notes receivable are recorded at the present value of the future cash flows. If the present value is different from the maturity value, the resulting premium or discount is amortized over the life of the loan as an adjustment to interest income. *Because most loans have stated interest rates equal to the appropriate market rate of interest, no premium or discount is present.* If notes receivable are impaired, the notes are written down to the present value of the new estimated future cash flows *using the historical effective rate of interest*, and bad debts expense (a loss) is recorded. In a troubled debt situation, the debt can be settled or modified. If settled, the creditor records the assets received at their fair market values, and the difference between the fair values and the book value of the note receivable is recognized as bad debts expense (a loss). In a modification of terms situation, the note receivable is written down to the present value of the new estimated future cash flows *using the historical effective rate of interest*, and bad debts expense (a loss) is recorded.

Investments in Lease Contracts—Lease Receivables

4 Account for investments in lease contracts.

In this chapter, we have discussed investments in long-term notes receivable generated by making loans. In Chapter 9, we will show how firms also invest in receivables when making sales on account (accounts receivable) and in exchange for short-term notes receivable. Here, we discuss an alternative to selling an asset to generate an account or note receivable—leasing the asset in exchange for a lease receivable. In a leasing transaction, an investor (lessor) transfers physical possession of an asset to a lessee but retains legal ownership. While accounting for leases was examined in Chapter 4 from the lessee's point of view as a financing transaction, in this section, we examine the financial reporting of leases for an investor/lessor.[11]

Recall that from the lessee's point of view, a lease is considered to be a *capital lease if any one of the following criteria are met*:

1. The lease transfers title from the lessor to the lessee at the end of the lease term.
2. The lease contains a bargain purchase option.
3. The lease term is greater than or equal to 75% of the economic useful life of the asset.
4. The present value of the minimum lease payments is greater than or equal to 90% of the fair market value of the asset.

These same criteria hold for the lessor. In addition, there are two other criteria that must be met for the lessor to capitalize the lease: no significant uncertainties can exist with respect to the collectability of the lease payments, and the lessor must not have to incur any great amount of cost with respect to the lease. As we will discuss in the chapters covering operating activities (Chapter 9–12), these criteria relate to the question of whether the revenue to be recognized by the lessor is realizable and earned. Because these two criteria are almost always met, we assume that they are met in all chapter examples.

11. Many leasing standards (too many to mention!) have been issued by the FASB over the years. The starting point for further study of this area is *FASB No. 13*, "Accounting for Leases," issued in 1976.

In Chapter 4, we emphasized that lessees frequently want to classify a lease contract as an operating lease rather than a capital lease because the operating lease classification keeps the financing off of the balance sheet. From the lessor's perspective, if the lease is classified as operating, then the asset is retained on the balance sheet. If the lease is capitalized, even though the lessor writes off the asset being leased, it is replaced with another asset, Lease Receivable. Therefore, regardless of the lease classification, the lessor will have an asset related to the lease.

Simple Example of an Operating Lease

To illustrate investor accounting for an operating lease, we repeat the operating lease example used in Chapter 4, Example 1. By using the same example as was used for the lessee you can compare and contrast lessor and lessee accounting for the same situation.

Example 6. On January 1, 2001, Celtic Co. acquired and leased a delivery van to Bird Co. under a four-year, noncancellable lease agreement, which expires December 31, 2004. The specifics of the lease are as follows:

Van fair market value	\$10,000
Van book value	\$10,000**
Useful life	6 years
Residual value (end of year 4), not guaranteed by Bird	\$3,000
Celtic's required rate of return (known by Bird)	10%*
Bird's incremental borrowing rate	11%
Maintenance and insurance costs (paid, beginning of the year by Bird)	\$200
No transfer of title clause	
No purchase option clause	
Annual lease payments (annuity due)	\$2,280

***The rate of return earned by the lessor is also known as the *implicit rate*.**
**For convenience, we assume that the lessor purchases the asset and then leases it to the lessee. Therefore, the fair market value and the book value are the same.

Solution.
Computation of Lease Payments Because the lease contains no bargain purchase option clause or transfer of title transfer clause, the van will revert back to Celtic at the end of the lease. Celtic sets the lease payments to earn a 10% return over the four-year period:

$$\$10{,}000 - \frac{\$3{,}000}{(1 + 0.1)^4} = \sum_{n=0}^{3} \frac{\text{Lease payments}}{(1 + 0.1)^n}$$

Using a financial calculator, $n = 4$; $i = 10\%$; present value = \$10,000; future value = \$3,000; payment (annuity due) = \$2,280. Therefore, lease payments of \$2,280 are made at the beginning of each period (annuity due).

The left-hand side of the equation shows the amount that will have to be recovered by the annual cash lease payments. Celtic will also receive an asset with an expected value of \$3,000 at the end of the lease term. So, the present value of \$3,000 will not have to be covered by the annual lease payments. The lease payments can be set at \$2,280 if the first payment is due immediately.

Is this an operating lease or a capital lease? We have already seen that the first two criteria for lease capitalization have not been met (no title transfer or bargain purchase option). The lease term is four years of a six-year economic life (67%). Thus, the third criterion requiring the lease term to be greater than or equal to 75% of the economic life is not met. The fourth criterion requires the computation of the present value of the minimum lease payments (MLP):

$$\text{Present value MLP} = \sum_{n=0}^{3} \frac{\$2{,}280}{(1 + 0.1)^n}$$
$$= \$7{,}950$$

[$n = 4$; $i = 10\%$; payment = \$2,280 (annuity due); future value = \$0; present value = \$7,950]

Note that the only MLPs are the \$2,280 payments made at the beginning of each period. The residual value is not guaranteed—Bird does not have to return an asset worth \$3,000 to Celtic, and there is no probable future sacrifice of assets by Bird to make up any deficiency in residual value. Celtic uses its rate of 10% to discount the periodic rentals in all cases. Because \$7,950 is less than 90% of the \$10,000 fair value of the asset, the fourth criterion is not met as well. The failure to meet any of the four criteria results in an operating lease classification for Celtic.

Operating Lease Accounting The presentation of an operating lease in the lessor's statement of cash flows is straightforward, as illustrated in Exhibit 20.

EXHIBIT 20 Example 6. Operating Lease Statement of Cash Flows

CELTIC CO.
Statement of Cash Flows
Lessor Operating Lease Accounting
(Cash outflows in parentheses)

	2001	2002	2003	2004
Operating Activities				
Receipt of lease rentals	2,280	2,280	2,280	2,280
Investing Activities				
Acquisition of asset to be leased*	(10,000)			

*Alternatively, if the leasing activity is a *primary activity* of Celtic, the cash outflow to acquire the asset to be leased would be shown as an operating activity. Again, we assume that Celtic purchases the asset and then leases it to Bird.

The correspondence of the lease with Celtic's fiscal year causes one year's worth of rental revenue to be reflected in the income statement. In addition, Celtic would depreciate the asset over its useful life (\$10,000 ÷ 6 years = \$1,667 per year) because it will reacquire the asset at the end of four years and hold it until the end of its estimated life. The classification of lease revenues and depreciation expense depends upon whether leasing is Celtic's primary activity or secondary activity. If it is a primary activity, the leasing revenues are part of operating income and depreciation expense must be matched against these revenues. If it is a secondary activity, the leasing revenues and depreciation expense are part of other expenses, revenues, gains, and losses. In this example, we treat the leasing activity as a secondary activity. (See Exhibit 21.)

EXHIBIT 21 Example 6. Operating Lease Income Statement Effects

CELTIC CO.
Income Statement Effects
Lessor Operating Lease Accounting

	2001	2002	2003	2004
Other revenues, (expenses), gains, and (losses)				
Rent revenue (operating leases)	2,280	2,280	2,280	2,280
Depreciation expense—leased assets	(1,667)	(1,667)	(1,667)	(1,667)

On the balance sheet (Exhibit 22), cash reflects the initial decrease of $10,000 in 2001, plus an increase of $2,280 each year. The leased asset's book value decreases each year from depreciation; Retained Earnings accumulates the reductions in income from depreciation expense and the increase in income from rent revenue.

EXHIBIT 22 Example 6. Operating Lease Balance Sheet

CELTIC CO.
Balance Sheet
December 31
Lessor Operating Lease Accounting
(Net effect of leasing transaction only)

	2001	2002	2003	2004
Assets				
Current assets				
Cash (cumulative effect of lease transactions only)	(7,720)	(5,440)	(3,160)	(880)
Property, plant, and equipment				
Leased asset	10,000	10,000	10,000	10,000
Less accumulated depreciation	(1,667)	(3,334)	(5,001)	(6,668)
	8,333	6,666	4,999	3,332
Owners' Equity				
Retained earnings (ignoring income taxes)	613	1,226	1,839	2,452

EXAMPLE 6 Journal Entries

1/1/01 Purchase of leased asset:		
Equipment	10,000	
Cash		10,000
1/1/01 Lease to Bird:		
Leased Asset	10,000	
Equipment		10,000
1/1/01–04 Receipt of rental payment:		
Cash	2,280	
Rent Revenue		2,280
12/31/01–04 Depreciation:		
Depreciation Expense	1,667	
Accumulated Depreciation—Leased Asset		1,667

Illustration of a Capitalized Lease

When the lessee capitalizes a lease, there is only one accounting treatment available. However, when a lessor capitalizes a lease, two basic accounting treatments are possible: direct financing classification and sales-type classification.[12] In both direct financing and sales-type leases, the leased asset is written off the books, and a new asset, Lease Receivable, is recorded.

Direct Financing Versus Sales-Type Leases The classification of a lease as direct financing or sales-type depends upon the relationship between the book value of the asset to be leased and the asset's fair market value at the time the asset is leased.

12. Although not discussed in the text, a third possible classification is as a *leveraged lease*. A leveraged lease is a special type of direct financing lease.

Direct financing:	Asset fair market value = Asset book value
Sales-type:	Asset fair market value > Asset book value

Direct financing leases are used primarily by banks, finance companies, and insurance companies, where the profit from the lease is based upon the interest income generated by the lease. In a ***direct financing lease*****, the fair market value of the asset is equal to the book value of the leased asset. Sales-type leases are used primarily by dealers and manufacturers that choose to lease rather than to sell inventory.** In a ***sales-type lease*****, the fair market value of the asset is greater than the book value of the asset.** Thus, the lessor earns profit in two ways: the spread between the fair value of the lease and the asset's cost is reported as gross profit (just as if the asset had been sold), and interest income generated by financing the lease is also recorded.

The operating lease in Example 6 can be turned into a capital lease (Example 6A) by changing the estimated useful life of the asset from six to five years. Now, the lease term is greater than 75% of the van's economic useful life (four of five years or 80%), resulting in lease capitalization. The remainder of the economics of the lease are unchanged. The payments, due each January 1, continue to have a present value at a 10% effective rate of $7,950. We use this changed Example 6A to illustrate both a direct financing lease and a sales-type lease.

Direct Financing Lease Celtic has given up the use of an asset (the van) in return for a series of future cash flows. If the lease is capitalized, Celtic removes the van from its books, replacing it with a long-term asset (i.e., Lease Receivable) equal to the fair market value of the leased asset. Over the life of the lease, Celtic will receive lease payments of $2,280 each year. In addition to the minimum lease payments, the leased asset (with an estimated salvage value of $3,000) will be returned to the lessor at the end of four years.[13] Recall from the operating lease example that the present value of minimum lease payments equals $7,950 [$n$ = 4; i = 10%; payment = $2,280 (annuity due); future value = 0]. The present value of the estimated salvage value of the leased asset ($3,000) is $2,050 ($n$ = 4; i = 10%, payment = 0; future value = $3,000). Therefore, the total present value of consideration to be received by Celtic equals $10,000 ($7,950 + $2,050). Because the book value of the asset ($10,000) is equal to the present value of the consideration to be received ($10,000), the lease is a direct financing lease. The difference between the gross receipts of $12,120 [($2,280 × 4) + $3,000] and the fair value of the leased asset, $10,000, is the interest revenue to be recognized over the life of the lease contract.

The amortization table in Exhibit 23 shows how Celtic receives the $10,000 fair market value of the leased asset from the lessee and interest on that fair value.

EXHIBIT 23 Example 6A. Direct Financing Lease Amortization Schedule

CELTIC CO.
Direct Financing Lease Amortization Schedule

Date	Cash Receipt	Interest Income @ 10%	Amortization (Principal Reduction)	Book Value
1/1/01				$10,000
1/1/01	$2,280	$ 0	$2,280	7,720
1/1/02	2,280	772	1,508	6,212
1/1/03	2,280	621	1,659	4,553
1/1/04	2,280	455	1,825	2,728
12/31/04	0	272	(272)	3,000*
Total	**$9,120**	**$2,120**	**$7,000**	

*This is equal to the value of the asset to be received at the end of the lease, December 31, 2004.

13. The lessor must take into account all consideration (both cash and noncash) to be received over the life of the lease and at the end of the lease.

At the inception of the lease (January 1, 2001), Celtic has a lease receivable asset with a carrying value of $10,000. Upon receiving the first $2,280 at the date of inception, Celtic's receivable is reduced to $7,720. Between January 1, 2001, and January 1, 2002, $772 of interest income accrues ($7,720 × 10%), and an additional $2,280 of cash is received on January 1, 2002. The payment amortizes $1,508 in book value ($2,280 − $772), leaving a net receivable of $6,212 on January 1, 2002.

While this amortization schedule is indicative of the economics of the capital lease agreement, its structure does not align with year-end balance sheet dates (i.e., December 31). The schedule is recast in Exhibit 24 to help clarify the discussion of financial reporting.

EXHIBIT 24 Example 6A. Direct Financing Lease Amortization Schedule (Recast)

CELTIC CO.
Direct Financing Lease Amortization Schedule (Recast)

Date	Cash Receipt	Interest Income @ 10%	Amortization (Principal Reduction)	Book Value
1/1/01				$10,000
1/1/01	$2,280	$ 0	$2,280	7,720
12/31/01	0	772	(772)	8,492
1/1/02	2,280	0	2,280	6,212
12/31/02	0	621	(621)	6,833
1/1/03	2,280	0	2,280	4,553
12/31/03	0	455	(455)	5,008
1/1/04	2,280	0	2,280	2,728
12/31/04	0	272	(272)	3,000
Total	$9,120	$2,120	$7,000	

From this recast schedule, it is easier to see the two economic events that change the lessor's receivable from January 1, 2001, to December 31, 2001. A receipt of $2,280 reduces the total lease receivable, while interest accrual of $772 increases the total lease receivable. This schedule also highlights the classification of each cash flow as an operating or investing activity. The first $2,280 received is purely an investing inflow. The subsequent January 1 cash flows are a combination of receiving interest accrued to December 31 (an operating activity) and reducing the lease receivable (an investing activity).

The presentation of a capital lease in the lessor's statement of cash flows depends upon whether the leasing activity is a primary or secondary activity for the lessor. If it is a primary activity, then all cash flows are classified as operating activities. If it is a secondary activity, then cash flow is divided between operating and investing activities. *In the following statement of cash flows, we treat the leasing activity as a secondary activity.* Therefore, the reduction in Lease Receivable is shown as an investing activity, while the interest income is reflected as an operating activity (see Exhibit 25).

EXHIBIT 25 Example 6A. Direct Financing Lease Statement of Cash Flows

CELTIC CO.
Statement of Cash Flows*
Direct Financing Lease Example

	2001	2002	2003	2004
Operating Activities				
Receipt of interest	0	772	621	455
Investing Activities				
Lease receivable reduction	2,280	1,508	1,659	1,825
Purchase of asset to lease	(10,000)			

*Cash outflows in parentheses

Interest revenue is reflected in the income statement. (See Exhibit 26.)

EXHIBIT 26 Example 6A. Direct Financing Lease Income Statement

CELTIC CO.
Income Statement
Direct Financing Lease Example

	2001	2002	2003	2004
Other revenues, (expenses), gains, and (losses)				
Interest revenue	772	621	455	272

Assuming that the leased asset is worth $3,000 on December 31, 2004, when it is returned to the lessor, the asset is recorded at its fair value, as shown in Exhibit 27.

EXHIBIT 27 Example 6A. Direct Financing Lease Balance Sheet

CELTIC CO.
Balance Sheet
December 31
Direct Financing Lease Example
(Cumulative effect of direct financing lease only)

	2001	2002	2003	2004
Assets				
Current assets				
Cash(1)	(7,720)	(5,440)	(3,160)	(880)
Lease receivable—current portion	1,508	1,659	1,825	0
Interest receivable	772	621	455	0
Property, plant, and equipment(2)				3,000
Long-term investments and funds				
Lease receivable	9,840	7,560	5,280	
Less unearned interest	(1,348)	(727)	(272)	
	8,492	6,833	5,008	
Less current portion	(2,280)	(2,280)	(2,280)	
	6,212	4,553	2,728	0
Owners' Equity				
Retained earnings (ignoring income taxes)	772	1,393	1,848	2,120

(1)12/31/01 cash = $2,280 lease payment − $10,000 purchase price.
(2)Alternatively, this could be shown as inventory if the asset is to be sold.

On the balance sheet, Cash initially decreases by $10,000 to acquire the van to be leased, and then increases by $2,280 each year. At each balance sheet date, it is conventional for the lease receivable to be reported as a gross lease receivable less unearned interest, which is equal to the book value shown on the amortization schedule. For example, at December 31, 2001, the lease investment's gross lease receivable is $9,840 [($2,280 × 3) + $3,000] less unearned interest income of $1,348 ($2,120 total interest to be earned less $772 earned in 2001). The lease receivable is broken down between its current portion (the $2,280 receivable on January 1, 2001) and its long-term portion (the remainder). The $2,280 is further broken down between interest receivable ($772) and principal ($1,508).

EXAMPLE 6A Journal Entries

	Debit	Credit
1/1/01 Purchase of leased asset:		
Equipment	10,000	
Cash		10,000
1/1/01 Lease to Bird:		
Lease Receivable*	12,120	
Unearned Interest Revenue		2,120
Equipment		10,000

*[($2,280 × 4) + $3,000]

1/1/01–04 Receipt of rental payments:	1/1/01		1/1/02		1/1/03		1/1/04	
Cash	2,280		2,280		2,280		2,280	
Lease Receivable		2,280		2,280		2,280		2,280

12/31/01–04 Accrual of interest revenue:	12/31/01		12/31/02		12/31/03		12/31/04	
Unearned Interest Revenue	772		621		455		272	
Interest Revenue		772		621		455		272

12/31/04 Receipt of equipment from lessee:	Debit	Credit
Equipment	3,000	
Lease Receivable		3,000

EXAMPLE 6A Key Ledger Accounts

Lease Receivable

1/1/01	12,120		
		1/1/01	2,280
		1/1/02	2,280
		1/1/03	2,280
		1/1/04	2,280
		12/31/04	3,000
		12/31/04	0

Unearned Interest Revenue

		1/1/01	2,120
12/31/01	772		
12/31/02	621		
12/31/03	455		
12/31/04	272		
		12/31/04	0

Sales-Type Lease The previous direct financing lease (Example 6A) can be changed to a sales-type lease (Example 6B) by altering the book value of the asset. Assume the same facts as in Example 6A except that Celtic had acquired the van at a cost of $8,000; therefore, the book value of the van at the time it was leased was $8,000 instead of $10,000. Also, to simplify the lessor accounting, we now assume that the $3,000 residual value is guaranteed. The primary difference between the accounting for a direct financing lease and sales-type lease is that, in a sales type-lease, the lessor records gross profit for the excess of the present value of the consideration to be received over the cost of the asset. Therefore, Celtic records a gross profit of $2,000 ($10,000 − $8,000).[14]

Generally, leasing is a primary activity for lessors involved in sales-type leases. For example, an automobile dealer may lease 30–50% of the cars delivered to its customers. If leasing is a primary activity for dealers, then it should be treated as an operating activity in the statement of cash flows. To compare and contrast the effect of leases as a primary activity versus a secondary activity, we treat this sales-type lease example as a primary activity. You should compare the statement of cash flows in Exhibit 28 for this sales-type lease to the one in the Example 6A to understand the differences in presentation:

14. Technically, gross profit in a sales-type lease is the present value of minimum lease payments less the cost of the asset reduced by the present value of an *unguaranteed* residual value. If we had assumed that the residual value was unguaranteed, the present value of minimum lease payments would remain $7,950 and the cost of the asset reduced by the present value of the residual value ($8,000 − $2,050) would equal $5,950. The difference is still $2,000 gross profit.

EXHIBIT 28 Example 6B. Sales-Type Lease Statement of Cash Flows

CELTIC CO.
Statement of Cash Flows*
Sales-Type Lease Example

	2001	2002	2003	2004
Operating Activities				
Receipt of interest	0	772	621	455
Lease receivable reduction	2,280	1,508	1,659	1,825
Acquire inventory to lease	(8,000)			

*Cash outflows in parentheses

The income statement is where we see the chief difference in accounting for a sales-type lease and a direct financing lease. Compare the income statement in Exhibit 29 with Exhibit 26. The sales-type lease income statement in Exhibit 29 reflects gross profit of $2,000.[15]

EXHIBIT 29 Example 6B. Sales-Type Lease Income Statement

CELTIC CO.
Income Statement
Sales-Type Lease Example

	2001	2002	2003	2004
Sales	10,000			
Cost of goods sold	8,000			
Gross profit	2,000			
Other revenues, (expenses), gains, and (losses)				
Interest revenue	772	621	455	272

The balance sheet for the sales-type lease is shown in Exhibit 30.

EXHIBIT 30 Example 6B. Sales-Type Lease Balance Sheet

CELTIC CO.
Balance Sheet
December 31
Sales-Type Lease Example
(Cumulative effect of sales-type lease only)

	2001	2002	2003	2004
Assets				
Current assets				
Cash(1)	(5,720)	(3,440)	(1,160)	1,120
Lease receivable—current portion	1,508	1,659	1,825	0
Interest receivable	772	621	455	0
Property, plant, and equipment(2)				3,000
Long-term investments and funds				
Lease receivable	9,840	7,560	5,280	
Less unearned interest	(1,348)	(727)	(272)	
	8,492	6,833	5,008	
Less current portion	(2,280)	(2,280)	(2,280)	
	6,212	4,553	2,728	0

(continued)

15. Interest revenue is always accrued on the *fair value* of the leased asset ($10,000 in both the direct financing lease and the sales-type lease examples). Therefore, interest revenue is identical in the two cases.

EXHIBIT 30 (concluded)

	2001	2002	2003	2004
Owners' Equity				
Retained earnings (ignoring income taxes)	2,772	3,393	3,848	4,120

(1) 12/31/01 cash = $2,280 lease payment − $8,000 asset purchase price.
(2) Alternatively, this could be shown as inventory if the asset is to be sold.

EXAMPLE 6B Journal Entries (Journal entry for lease signing only; all other entries are the same as in Example 6A.)

Lease Receivable	12,120	
Cost of Goods sold	8,000	
Unearned Interest Revenue		2,120
Equipment		8,000
Sales Revenue		10,000

Summary: Accounting for Investments in Lease Contracts

Lessor accounting for investments in lease contracts parallels lessee accounting. The lessor *lends* the use of the asset to the lessee and earns an effective rate of return on the transaction. If the lease is capitalized, then the lessor reports interest revenue; if the lease is classified as operating, then rent revenue is reported. In both operating and capitalized leases, the lessor reports a long-term asset in the balance sheet. For an operating lease, the long-term asset being leased is kept on the balance sheet and depreciated (if appropriate). If the lease is capitalized, then the asset being leased is written off of the balance sheet and replaced with a long-term lease receivable, which represents the gross lease receivable less the unearned interest on the transaction.

To be capitalized, the lease must meet one of the four capital lease criteria plus two additional criteria. For direct financing lease classification, the lessor normally is a bank or other type of financial services company, and the present value of the consideration to be received (discounted at the implicit rate) is equal to the cost (carrying value) of the leased asset. For sales-type lease classification, the lessor normally is a dealer or manufacturer, and the present value of the consideration to be received (discounted at the implicit rate) is different from (almost always greater than) the cost of the leased asset. The amount of gross profit recorded in a sales-type lease is equal to the present value of the consideration to be received minus the cost of the leased asset.

Examples of Direct Financing and Sales-Type Leases

Exhibit 31 shows a partial balance sheet and partial footnote information from Pennzoil's 1997 financial statements to provide an example of direct financing and operating lease disclosures.

EXHIBIT 31 Pennzoil Note 9 (in part): Leases

Pennzoil Note 9 (in part): Leases

As lessor, Pennzoil, through Jiffly Lube, owns or leases numerous service center sites, which are leased or subleased to franchisees. Buildings owned or leased that meet the criteria for direct financing leases are carried at the gross investment in the lease less unearned income. Unearned income is recognized in such a manner as to produce a

(continued)

EXHIBIT 31 (concluded)

constant periodic rate of return on the net investment in the direct financing lease. Any buildings leased or subleased that do not meet the criteria for a direct financing lease are accounted for as operating leases. The typical lease period is 20 years, and some leases contain renewal options. . . . The net investment in direct financing leases is classified as other assets in the accompanying consolidated balance sheet.

Future minimum lease payment receivable under noncancellable leasing arrangements as of December 31, 1997, are as follows:

	Amounts Receivable as Lessor (Expressed in thousands)	
Year Ending Dec. 31	**Direct Financing Leases**	**Operating Leases**
1998	$ 4,593	$ 11,996
1999	4,651	11,542
2000	4,723	11,347
2001	4,781	10,532
2002	4,814	10,063
Thereafter	28,648	56,026
Net minimum future lease payments	$52,210	$111,506
Less unearned income	22,626	
Net investment in direct financing leases at December 31, 1997	$29,584	

Note that Pennzoil combines its direct financing lease and operating lease disclosures into the same footnote.

Exhibit 32 shows a partial balance sheet and partial footnote information from Storage Technology Corporation's 1993 financial statements relating to financial reporting for sales-type and operating leases. Although it is old, we include this footnote because it is exceptionally informative.

EXHIBIT 32 Storage Technology Corp. Partial Balance Sheet and Note Information ($000)

	1993	**1992**
Current assets		
Net investment in sales-type leases	171,165	193,078
Long-term assets		
Net investment in sales-type leases	252,678	309,160

Storage Technology Corporation Note 3—
Sales-Type and Operating Leases
The components of net investment in sales-type leases are as follows (*in thousands of dollars*):

	Dec. 31, 1993	**Dec. 31, 1992**
Total minimum lease and maintenance payments	$499,295	$550,201
Less executory costs (maintenance payments)	(50,017)	(41,464)
Net minimum lease payments	449,278	508,737
Estimated unguaranteed residual values	24,879	73,206
Less unearned interest income	(50,314)	(79,705)
	423,843	502,238
Less current portion	(171,165)	(193,078)
Net investment	$252,678	$309,160

(continued)

EXHIBIT 32 (concluded)

Future minimum lease payments due from customers under sales-type leases and noncancellable operating leases as of December 31, 1993, are as follows (*in thousands of dollars*):

	Sales-Type Leases	Operating Leases
1994	$210,110	$17,276
1995	155,363	10,450
1996	86,354	2,775
1997	37,431	170
1998	9,654	23
Thereafter	383	0
	$499,295	$30,694

Sale-Leaseback Transactions

A company may sell an asset, usually at a profit, and then lease the same asset from the buyer. A sale-leaseback transaction involves a seller-lessee and a buyer-lessor. Both the seller-lessee and the buyer-lessor record the lease as an operating or capital lease in the financial records. The accounting issue is what to do with any profits or losses by the seller-lessee. Accountants recognize any losses immediately, but defer recognition of any profits. Deferred profits are amortized over the lease term. An exception to deferring profits is acceptable if the present value of the consideration to be paid by the seller-lessee is less than 10% of the fair value of the asset sold. In this case, accountants record the entire profit.[16]

The following partial footnote (slightly modified by the authors) from Zenith Electronics Corporation's 1997 financial statements illustrates financial reporting for sale-leaseback transactions.

Zenith Electronics Corporation Note Fourteen (in part): Sale Leaseback Transaction

In April 1997 the company entered into an $87 million sale-leaseback transaction whereby the company sold and leased back new and existing manufacturing equipment in its Melrose Park, IL., plant and in its Reynosa and Juarez, Mexico, facilities. The result of the sale was a $10.2 million gain for the company, which was deferred and is being amortized over the 12.5 year lease term. . . . The sale-leaseback agreement contains financial penalties which would be triggered if the company was to terminate the lease early.

Financial Statement Analysis: Southwest Airlines

5 Explain where information about debt investments is disclosed and discussed in financial reports.

Evidently, investments in the debt of other firms is not an important part of Southwest Airlines' activities. Southwest Airlines' 1998 financial statements (presented in text Appendix C) have scant information about investments in other companies' debt securities. In Note 1, Summary of Significant Accounting Policies, the Cash and Cash Equivalents section reports that the caption "cash equivalents" includes investments in certificates of deposit and high-grade commercial paper with maturities of less than three months, with cost approximating market value. The balance sheet reports Cash and Cash Equivalents of $378,511 thousand and $623,343 thousand at December 31, 1998, and 1997, respectively. The financial statements provide no additional information about investments in trading securities, available-for-sale securities, held-to-maturity securities, notes receivable, or lease receivables. In the income statement, the Other Expenses (Income) section reports 1998 interest income of $31,083 thousand, with $36,616 thousand in 1997, and $25,797 thousand in 1996.

16. In slightly more complicated cases, part of the profit is deferred and part is recognized. The goal in this section is to introduce sale leaseback accounting, *not* to cover all cases.

The External Decision Makers' View of Investments in Debt Securities

Investments in debt provide an appropriate employment of a company's excess cash to earn a return. Because investments in debt securities are generally not as risky as investments in equity securities, they generally do not earn as high a return. However, risk is present, and external decision makers rely heavily on accountants and managers to indicate whether these investments have been impaired. Recent standard setting in the investments area has greatly improved disclosures about debt securities (mark-to-market) and other debt investments (consideration of impairment).

Chapter Summary

A company may invest in debt securities (e.g., purchase bond investments, acquire notes receivable and lease receivables). Bond investments are classified as trading, available-for-sale, or held-to-maturity. Notes receivable and lease receivables are not eligible for classification as trading, available-for-sale, or held-to-maturity securities.

Trading securities are marked-to-market for financial statement presentation, with the unrealized gain or loss being recognized in the income statement. Available-for-sale securities are marked-to-market for financial statement presentation, with the unrealized gain or loss being reported as a component of Other Comprehensive Income in a statement of comprehensive income [i.e., the unrealized gains (losses) do not appear in the income statement]. Other comprehensive income items are closed to Accumulated Other Comprehensive Income in owners' equity. Held-to-maturity debt securities are not marked-to-market, and are reported at amortized cost.

Available-for-sale debt securities, notes receivable, and those lease receivables classified as capital leases with maturities of greater than one year at the time of acquisition use the effective interest method to recognize interest income (any premium or discount is amortized over the life of the instrument as an adjustment to interest income). The straight-line method of premium/discount amortization (discussed in the chapter appendix) may be used if the results are not materially different from those obtained using the effective interest method. Available-for-sale debt securities, notes receivable, and those lease receivables classified as capital leases with maturities of less than one year at the time of acquisition do not amortize premium/discount.

From the lessor's perspective, leases are classified as either operating or capital, and capital leases may be recorded as either sales-type or direct financing. A lease is a capital lease if it meets any one of the four primary capital lease criteria (transfer of title, bargain purchase option, 75% test, 90% test) and two additional criteria. In a sales-type lease, the lessor treats the transaction as if a sale were made in exchange for a lease receivable, and the amount of the lease receivable exceeds the book value of the leased asset—sales and cost of goods sold are both recorded. In a direct financing lease, the book value of the leased asset and the amount of the lease receivable are the same—neither sales nor cost of goods sold are recorded. In both sales-type and direct financing leases, the lessor records interest income over the life of the lease using the effective interest method and the lessor's implicit rate.

APPENDIX Straight-Line Method of Premium/Discount Amortization

APB No. 21 specifies that the effective interest method is to be used to compute the amortization of bond premium/discount, and all text examples use the effective interest method. The straight-line amortization method may be used if the results are not materially different from those obtained using the effective interest method. Under the straight-line method, the dollar amount of interest income is the same each period, but the percentage of interest income compared to the book value changes each period. This is the reverse of the effective interest method under which the dollar amount of interest income changes each period, but the percentage of interest income compared to the book value is the same each period. The use of the straight-line method illustrates a cost-benefit trade-off. If the benefits are not material, then the costs in complexity of using the effective interest method may not outweigh the benefits of using the less complex straight-line method.

To illustrate the straight-line method of computing interest expense, we use Example 1 (Laker Co.) from the text.

Example A1. On January 1, 2001, Worthy Co. issued $1,000,000 in bonds payable. The bonds are dated January 1, 2001, mature in five years on January 1, 2006, and pay 9% interest every December 31. The issue sold for $891,857 (rounded to the nearest dollar). Assume that Laker Co. purchased all the bonds. Laker Co. intends to hold the investment to maturity and has a December 31 fiscal year-end.

Solution. Under the straight-line method, interest expense each period equals the amount of interest paid/payable plus (or minus) discount amortization calculated using the straight-line method. Laker's discount was $108,143, and the straight-line amortization equals $21,629 per year ($108,143 ÷ 5). Laker's effective interest amortization table is shown in Exhibit 33.

EXHIBIT 33 Example A1. Straight-Line Amortization Table

LAKER CO.
Straight-Line Amortization Table

Date	9% Cash Interest	Interest Income	Discount Amortization*	Book Value of Investment (Amortized Cost)
1/1/01				$ 891,857
12/31/01	$ 90,000	$111,629**	$ 21,629	913,486
12/31/02	90,000	111,629	21,629	935,115
12/31/03	90,000	111,629	21,629	956,744
12/31/04	90,000	111,628	21,628	978,372
12/31/05	90,000	111,628	21,628	1,000,000
Total	$450,000	$558,143	$108,143	

*$108,143 ÷ 5 = $21,628.60.
**Interest paid/payable ($90,000) plus discount amortization ($21,629) = $111,629.

To better understand the differences between the effective interest and straight-line methods, compare this amortization table to Exhibit 1 (Example 1) in the chapter.

Bond Premium Amortization

The text examples presented a bond discount situation. To illustrate a bond premium situation, we use Example 1 (Laker Co.) from the text, except assume that the bond sold for $1,082,004. This sales price implies a 7% effective interest rate (n = 5; payment = $90,000; present value = $1,082,004; future value = $1,000,000; i = 7%).

Example A2. On January 1, 2001, Worthy Co. issued $1,000,000 in bonds payable. The bonds are dated January 1, 2001, mature in five years on January 1, 2006, and pay 9% interest every December 31. The issue sold for $1,082,004 (rounded to the nearest dollar). Assume that Laker Co. purchased all the bonds. Laker Co. intends to hold the investment to maturity and has a December 31 fiscal year-end.

Solution. Laker's effective interest amortization table is shown in Exhibit 34.

EXHIBIT 34 Example A2. Effective Interest Amortization Table

LAKER CO.
Effective Interest Amortization Table—Bond Premium

Date	9% Cash Interest	7% Effective Interest Income*	Premium Amortization	Book Value of Investment (Amortized Cost)
1/1/01				$1,082,004
12/31/01	$ 90,000	$ 75,740	$14,260	1,067,744
12/31/02	90,000	74,742	15,258	1,052,486
12/31/03	90,000	73,674	16,326	1,036,160
12/31/04	90,000	72,531	17,469	1,018,691
12/31/05	90,000	71,309	18,691	1,000,000
Total	$450,000	$367,996	$82,004	

*Beginning book value × 7% effective interest rate.

To better understand the differences between a bond discount and bond premium situation, compare this amortization table to Exhibit 1 in the chapter.

Key Terms

accumulated other comprehensive income 254
amortized cost 248
available-for-sale 254
direct financing lease 270
held-to-maturity 254
impaired 261
implicit rate 267
modification of terms 262
other comprehensive income 254
sales-type lease 270
settlement of debt 262
trading 254
troubled debt restructuring 262
unrealized holding gain or loss 254

Questions

Q1. **Bond Investment Valuation.** Theoretically, what does the market price of a bond investment represent?

Q2. **Bond Investments.** What are the possible classifications of bond investments under *SFAS No. 115,* "Accounting for Certain Investments in Debt and Equity Securities"? Which one is the default classification, and why?

Q3. **Effective Interest Method.** Without using any numbers, present the steps used in calculating interest income under the effective interest method and any related premium/discount amortization.

Q4. **SFAS No. 115 Classification and Financial Statement Presentation.** On December 31, 2001, the Sheppard Co. had a long-term bond investment due in 10 years. The bond had an amortized cost of $12,750,000 and a fair value of $13,000,000. Where on the balance sheet would the investment be shown if the security were properly classified as held-to-maturity? At what value would it be reported? Where on the balance sheet would the investment be shown if the security were properly classified as available-for-sale? At what value would it be reported? Under either classification, would any amount appear in the accumulated comprehensive income portion of stockholders' equity? If so, how much?

Q5. **Reporting Bonds Investments.** On December 1, 2001, a company purchased a bond investment due on July 1, 2002, at a discount of $150,000. Of the three available classifications (trading, available-for-sale, and held-to-maturity), in the December 31, 2001, balance sheet, which are possible classifications for the investment? Should the bond discount be amortized in 2001? Why or why not?

Q6. **Amortized Cost.** When the effective interest method is applied to a long-term bond, the bond investment is presented on the balance sheet at *amortized* cost. What value does amortized cost reflect on a balance sheet date?

Q7. **Impaired Loan.** If a creditor deems that a loan receivable has been impaired, what must the creditor do? What are the financial statement effects?

Q8. **Troubled Debt—Settlement.** In a troubled debt situation, what does a creditor do if assets are transferred from the debtor to the creditor in settlement of the debt? What are the financial statement effects?

Q9. **Troubled Debt—Modification of Terms.** In a troubled debt situation, what does a creditor do if the terms of the debt are modified such that the future cash flows are reduced? What are the financial statement effects?

Q10. **Capital Lease Classification.** If a lessor capitalizes a lease, what two classifications are available? What determines which classification is used? Briefly describe the accounting for both classifications.

Q11. **Lessor Lease Classification.** What criteria are used by the lessor to determine whether a lease should be capitalized or shown as an operating lease?

Q12. **Straight-Line Method of Computing Interest Income (Appendix).** Compare and contrast the straight-line method of interest income and premium/discount amortization with the effective interest method. When is it appropriate to use the straight-line method rather than the effective interest method?

Short Problems

1. **Accounting for Notes Receivable.** On July 1, 2001, the Neill Co. loaned $2,000,000 to Abdul-Raheem. The loan is a three-year, 9% loan, with principal due on July 1, 2004. Interest is payable annually on July 1. The 9% rate of interest reflects current market conditions.
   a. How much cash will Neill receive in 2001? In 2002?
   b. What is Neill's interest income in 2001? 2002?
   c. What is the total carrying value of the loan (principal and interest) on December 31, 2001?

   Journal Entry Option: Make the journal entry to record the loan on Neill's books on July 1, 2001. Make the December 31, 2001, adjusting journal entry to record interest revenue.

2. **Bond Investments.** On January 1, 2001, the Miller Co. purchased bonds with the following terms: 10-year, 8% bonds due January 1, 2011; maturity value is $5,000,000; interest is paid semiannually on July 1 and January 1; and purchase price was $4,600,000.
   a. What is the annual effective (market) rate of interest that Miller will earn?

   Journal Entry Option: Make the journal entry to record the purchase of the bond on January 1, 2001.

   b. Assume that the January 1, 2002, interest payment has been received by Miller. If the annual market rate of interest on the bonds is 7% on January 1, 2002, what is the total value of the investment?
   c. If the market rate of interest on the bonds is 7% on December 31, 2001, what is the total value of the investment? (Remember that the interest payment will not be received until January 1, 2002.)
   d. If the market value of the bonds on December 31, 2001, is $4,900,000, what are the 2001 income statement effects, the balance sheet presentation of the investment and related accounts, and the statement of comprehensive income effects under each of the following assumptions:
      (1) The investment is classified as trading
      (2) The investment is classified as available-for-sale
      (3) The investment is classified as held-to-maturity?

3. **Impairment.** On December 31, 2001, the Lopez Co. has a note receivable from a supplier, the Cunningham Co. The note receivable is Lopez's only note. The $1,500,000, 10% note, issued on January 1, 2000, is due January 1, 2005, with interest payable annually on January 1. The carrying value of the note on December 31, 2001, is $1,650,000 ($1,500,000 note receivable, $150,000 interest receivable, and $0 note receivable premium/discount), and its historic, effective interest rate is 10%. Cunningham paid its $150,000 January 1, 2001, interest payment as scheduled. The accounting staff believes that Cunningham will not be able to fulfill the terms of the note. The accounting staff's best estimate is that Cunningham will be able to pay $100,000 interest on January 1, 2002, 2003, 2004, and 2005, and will be able to repay only $1,100,000 of the $1,500,000 principal.
   a. Compute the amount of Lopez's loss due to the impairment on December 31, 2001.
   b. How will the impairment loss be reflected in Lopez's 2001 financial statements?

   Journal Entry Option: Prepare the December 31, 2001, adjusting journal entry to record the impairment.

4. **Operating versus Sales-Type Leases.** On July 1, 2001, the Gonzales Co. had an asset on its books at $750,000; the asset had a fair value of $900,000. The asset had an estimated useful life of eight years. Gonzales estimated a salvage value of $0 at the end of eight years, and $250,000 at the end of four years. Gonzales agreed to lease the asset to the Smith Co. under the following terms: four-year lease term; no purchase option; lease pay-

ments of $200,230 made at the beginning of each period; Smith does not guarantee any residual value; and Gonzales requires an 8% rate of return.

a. Should the lease be classified as operating or sales-type? Document your work with reference to the four lease criteria. If it is a sales-type lease, how much gross profit would Gonzales recognize when the lease is signed?

Journal Entry Option: Prepare the July 1, 2001, Gonzales journal entry to reflect the signing of the lease.

b. If the asset's estimated useful life were five years, would the lease be classified as operating or sales-type? Document your work with reference to the four lease criteria. If it is a sales-type lease, how much gross profit would Gonzales recognize when the lease is signed?

Journal Entry Option: Prepare the July 1, 2001, Gonzales journal entry to reflect the signing of the lease.

5. **Direct Financing Lease.** Assume the same information as Problem 4, except change the book value of the leased asset from $750,000 to $900,000, and the estimated useful life from eight years to four years. Should the lease be classified as operating or direct financing? Document your work with reference to the four lease criteria.

Journal Entry Option: Prepare the July 1, 2001, Gonzales journal entry to reflect the signing of the lease.

Analytical and Comprehensive Problems

6. **Bond Investment—Bond Discount.** On January 1, 2001, the Grapevine Co. purchased a five-year bond from Winery Inc. for $6,727,724, including transaction costs of $10,000 as a long-term bond investment. The terms of the bond were as follows: face amount of $7,000,000; maturity date of January 1, 2006; interest paid annually on January 1; stated (coupon) interest rate of 8%.

a. What is the effective interest rate on the bond (round to the nearest one-hundredth of a percent)?

b. Prepare the bond amortization table for this bond investment.

c. On December 31, 2001, how much interest income is reported? What is the amount of the carrying value of the bond investment on the December 31, 2001, balance sheet? Indicate how cash flows associated with the bond investment will appear on the 2001 statement of cash flows.

Journal Entry Option: Prepare the January 1, 2001, journal entry to record the bond purchase and the December 31, 2001, annual summary entry to record interest income.

d. For the purpose of computing Grapevine's December 31, 2001, balance sheet amount, assume that the market rate of interest appropriate for the Winery bond was 7.5% on December 31, 2001. For Grapevine, what would the market value of the bond investment be on December 31, 2001?

e. Describe the 2001 financial statement effects under the following assumptions: (1) the bond investment was classified as available-for-sale; (2) the bond investment was classified as held-to-maturity; and (3) the bond investment was classified as trading (included for completeness; as a long-term investment, this classification would not be appropriate). Use the following schedule to report selected financial statement information.

GRAPEVINE CO.
Balance Sheet

	Available-for-Sale	Held-to-Maturity	Trading
Assets			
Current assets			
Bond investments at cost			
Less valuation allowance			
Bond investments at market value			
Long-term assets			
Bond investments at amortized cost			
Less valuation allowance			
Bond investments at market value			

(continued)

Owners' Equity
Accumulated other comprehensive income
Unrealized gain (loss) on available-for-sale securities

GRAPEVINE CO.
Income Statement

	Available-for-Sale	Held-to-Maturity	Trading
Other revenues, (expenses), gains, and (losses)			
Interest income (expense)			
Unrealized gain (loss) on trading securities			

GRAPEVINE CO.
Statement of Comprehensive Income

	Available-for-Sale	Held-to-Maturity	Trading
Other comprehensive income			

7. **Straight-Line Amortization Method (Appendix).** Using the straight-line amortization method, prepare the bond amortization table for Problem 6(b).

8. **Bond Investment—Bond Premium (Appendix).** On January 1, 2001, the Grapevine Co. purchased a five-year bond from Winery, Inc., for $7,358,196, including transaction costs of $10,000, as a long-term bond investment. The terms of the bonds were as follows: face amount of $7,000,000; maturity date of January 1, 2006; interest paid annually on January 1; stated (coupon) interest rate of 8%. *Note:* Compare the results of this problem to those for Problem 6 to contrast bond discount accounting with bond premium accounting.
   a. What is the effective interest rate on the bond (round to the nearest one-hundredth of a percent)?
   b. Prepare the bond amortization table for this bond investment.
   c. On December 31, 2001, how much interest income is reported? What is the amount of the carrying value of the bond investment on the December 31, 2001, balance sheet? Indicate how cash flows associated with the bond investment will appear on the 2001 statement of cash flows.

   Journal Entry Option: Prepare the January 1, 2001, journal entry to record the bond purchase and the December 31, 2001, annual summary entry to record interest income.

   d. For the purpose of computing Grapevine's December 31, 2001, balance sheet amount, assume that the market rate of interest appropriate for the Winery bond was 7.5% on December 31, 2001.
   e. Describe the 2001 financial statement effects under the following assumptions: (1) the bond investment was classified as available-for-sale; (2) the bond investment was classified as held-to-maturity; and (3) the bond investment was classified as trading (included for completeness; as a long-term investment, this classification would not be appropriate). Use the schedule from Problem 6(d) to report selected financial statement information.

9. **Notes Receivable.** For each of the following situations, indicate (1) the value at which the note should be recorded on January 1, 2001; (2) the amount of interest income reported in 2001; and (3) the carrying value of the note on December 31, 2001.
   a. On January 1, 2001, the Shelton Co. entered into a loan agreement with the Poole Co., an important supplier. Shelton loaned $1,000,000, and received a $1,000,000, five-year note due on January 1, 2006, with interest paid at 10% at the end of each year and principal due on January 1, 2006. The market rate of interest for this type of loan was 10% on January 1, 2001.
   b. On January 1, 2001, the Collie Co. received a $10,000,000, three-year, non-interest-bearing note from the Shepherd Co. in return for 1,000,000 shares of Collie's common stock. The common stock is not publicly traded. The market rate of interest for this type of loan was 8% on January 1, 2001.

(continued)

c. On January 1, 2001, the Collie Co. received a $10,000,000, three-year, non-interest-bearing note due from the Shepherd Co. in return for 1,000,000 shares of Collie's common stock. Collie's stock was publicly traded on January 1, 2001, at $8.50 per share. The market rate of interest for this type of loan was unknown on January 1, 2001.

10. **Bond Investment—Classification as Trading, Available-for-Sale, and Held-to-Maturity.** On January 1, 2001, the Robin Hood Co. purchased Marion Co.'s 10%, $5,000,000, eight-year bond investments for $4,494,705. The bonds are due on January 1, 2009, and pay interest semiannually at a rate of 5%. The market rate of interest for the bond investments on December 31, 2001, is 9%. For each of the three possible balance sheet classifications (available-for-sale, held-to-maturity, and trading), indicate (1) the value at which the bonds would be recorded on January 1, 2001, and where in the balance sheet the bond investments would be reported; (2) any related 2001 income statement effects and where the amounts would be reported; (3) any related 2001 statement of comprehensive income statement effects and where the amounts would be reported; (4) the presentation in the December 31, 2001, balance sheet; and (5) any separate owners' equity effects at December 31, 2001.

ROBIN HOOD CO.
Balance Sheet

	Available-for-Sale	Held-to-Maturity	Trading
Assets			
Current assets			
Bond investments at cost			
Valuation allowance			
Bond investments at market value			
Long-term assets			
Bond investments, principal			
Less bond discount			
Bond investments at amortized cost			
Valuation allowance			
Bond investments at market value			
Owners' Equity			
Accumulated other comprehensive income			
Unrealized gain (loss) on available-for-sale securities			

ROBIN HOOD CO.
Income Statement

	Available-for-Sale	Held-to-Maturity	Trading
Other revenues, (expenses), gains, and (losses)			
Interest income			
Unrealized gain (loss) on trading securities			

ROBIN HOOD CO.
Statement of Comprehensive Income

	Available-for-Sale	Held-to-Maturity	Trading
Other comprehensive income			

11. **Impairment.** On January 1, 2001, the Greer Co. loaned $2,000,000 to the Palmer Co. under the following terms: principal due December 31, 2006, with interest at 10% due on December 31 of each year. (Assume that the 10% reflects market rates of interest for the loan on January 1, 2001.) Palmer made interest payments on December 31, 2001 and 2002. At December 31, 2003, Palmer is in financial trouble and pays $100,000 of the interest owed. After discussions with Palmer, Greer believes that the following future cash flows will result from the loan: interest payments of $100,000 in 2004, 2005, and 2006; principal of $1,750,000 on December 31, 2006. The note is not restructured,

and the terms of the note are not changed. Use the following form to illustrate the 2003 financial statement effects Greer should record on December 31, 2003.

GREER CO.
Effects of Impairment Transaction

	2003
Income Statement	
Balance Sheet	

12. **Troubled Debt.** On December 31, 2001, the Chen Co. informed the First National Bank that it would be unable to fulfill the terms of its loan agreement and wished to discuss alternative courses of action. The original loan was issued for $5,000,000, with principal due on January 1, 2005, and 9% interest payable annually on January 1. The historic, effective interest rate on the bond is 9%. On December 31, 2001, First National's financial records reflected a loan receivable of $5,000,000 and interest receivable of $450,000. As a financial institution, First National routinely makes adjusting journal entries for estimated bad debts attributable to the general portfolio of loans outstanding. The two following situations are independent.
    a. Assume that Chen and First National agree to settle the debt. Chen agrees to issue 100,000 shares of Chen's $10 par common stock and land with a book value of $800,000 to settle the debt in full. On December 31, 2001, the Chen common stock has a fair value of $32 per share, and the land has a fair value of $1,000,000. Describe how First National will record the transaction and how its financial statements will be affected.

    Journal Entry Option: Make the journal entry to record the transaction.

    b. Assume that Chen and First National agree to modify the terms of the loan agreement. First National agrees to waive the January 1, 2002, interest payment; to accept interest payments of $300,000 on January 1, 2003, 2004, and 2005; and to accept $4,000,000 in principal on January 1, 2005. Describe how First National will record the transaction and how its financial statements will be affected.

    Journal Entry Option: Make the journal entry to record the transaction.

13. **Direct Financing Lease.** Although leasing is a secondary activity, the Faulconer Co. occasionally leases automobiles to customers. The customer picks out an automobile, negotiates a price with the dealer, and provides that information to Faulconer. Faulconer purchases the automobile and leases it to the customer. On January 1, 2001, Cheryl Jones, President of Jones Realtors, picked out a 2001 Lexus and negotiated a purchase price of $45,000. Faulconer purchased the Lexus for $45,000 and leased it to Jones Realtors under the following terms: three annual payments of $8,000 due on December 31 (starting December 31, 2001); $5,000 down payment; Faulconer's implicit rate of return is 10% per year; Jones guarantees the auto will be worth at least $26,750 at the end of the lease; and the lease terminates December 31, 2003. If the Lexus is worth less than $26,750 at the end of the lease, Jones can purchase the Lexus for $26,750, or pay the difference between the guaranteed amount and the fair value and return the Lexus to Faulconer. Faulconer believes that the Lexus will be worth about $25,000 at the end of the lease. Faulconer treats the economic useful life of the automobile as three years, after which time the asset will be sold.

Required: Indicate why Faulconer capitalizes this lease. For Faulconer, prepare the following items using the format provided: (1) an amortization table for the lease, and (2) the appropriate sections of the income statement, the statement of cash flows, and the balance sheet. In the financial statements, include only the effects of the lease transactions (i.e., ignore all other account balances and transactions not related to the lease). For the statement of cash flows and the balance sheet, assume that the automobile is worth $25,000 at the end of the lease, and that Jones purchases it for $26,750.

Journal Entry Option: Prepare the January 1, 2001, journal entries to record the lease signing and cash receipt. Also, record any year-end journal entries related to the cash receipt.

FAULCONER CO.
Direct Financing Lease Amortization Schedule

Date	Cash Receipt	Interest Income @ 10%	Amortization (Principal Reduction)	Book Value
1/1/01				
Down payment				
2001				
2002				
2003				
Total				

FAULCONER CO.
Statement of Cash Flows
(Cash outflows in parentheses)

	2001	2002	2003
Operating Activities			
Investing Activities			
Significant noncash financing and investing activities			

FAULCONER CO.
Income Statement

	2001	2002	2003
Other revenues (expenses); gains and (losses)			

FAULCONER CO.
Balance Sheet
December 31
(Cumulative effect of direct financing lease only)

	2001	2002	2003
Assets			
Current assets			
Cash			
Lease receivable—current portion		N/A*	N/A*
Lease receivables	N/A*		
Less unearned interest income			
Net lease receivable			
Long-term investments and funds			
Lease receivables		N/A*	N/A*
Less unearned interest income			
Net lease receivable			
Less current portion			
Total effect on assets			
Owners' Equity			
Retained earnings, ignoring income taxes			

*N/A indicates that this section for the given year would have no disclosures.

14. **Sales-Type Lease.** Assume the same facts as in Problem 13, except assume that Jones leased the Lexus from Luxury Motors Inc., instead of the Faulconer Co. Luxury had the Lexus in stock, and its cost was $38,000. Luxury considers the economic useful life of the automobile to be three years. At the end of the lease term, either the lessee will purchase the asset for $26,750, or the asset will be returned to Luxury Motors for resale.

Required: Indicate why Luxury Motors capitalizes this lease. For Luxury Motors, prepare the following items using the format provided: (1) an amortization table for the lease, and (2) the appropriate sections of the income statement, the statement of cash flows, and the balance sheet. In the financial statements, include only the effects of the lease transactions (i.e., ignore all other account balances and transactions not related to the lease). For the statement of cash flows and the balance sheet, assume that the automobile is worth $25,000 at the end of the lease, and that Jones purchases it for $26,750. (Because Luxury Motors is a dealer, leasing is an operating activity.)

Journal Entry Option: Prepare the January 1, 2001, journal entries to record the lease signing and cash receipt. Also, record any year-end journal entries related to the cash receipt.

LUXURY MOTORS CO.
Sales-Type Lease Amortization Schedule

Date	Cash Receipt	Interest Income @ 10%	Amortization (Principal Reduction)	Book Value
1/1/01				
Down payment				
2001				
2002				
2003				
Total				

LUXURY MOTORS CO.
Statement of Cash Flows
(Cash outflows in parentheses)

	2001	2002	2003
Operating Activities			
Investing Activities			
Significant noncash financing and investing activities			

LUXURY MOTORS CO.
Income Statement Effects

	2001	2002	2003
Sales			
Cost of Goods Sold			
Gross Profit			
Other revenues (expenses); gains and (losses)			

LUXURY MOTORS CO.
Balance Sheet
December 31
(Cumulative effect of sales-type lease only)

	2001	2002	2003
Assets			
Current assets			
Cash			
Lease receivable—current portion		N/A*	N/A*
Lease receivables	N/A*		
Less unearned interest income			
Net lease receivable			
Inventory			
Long-term investments and funds			
Lease receivables		N/A*	N/A*
Less unearned interest income			
Net lease receivable			
Less current portion			
Total effect on assets			
Owners' Equity			
Retained earnings, ignoring income taxes			

*N/A indicates that this section for the given year would have no disclosures.

15. **Leases.** On January 1, 2001, the Foster Co. is in the last stages of negotiating a lease with the Turner Co. The asset is carried in Foster's inventory at a cost of $100,000. The lease does not have a transfer of title clause nor a purchase option clause. The lease terms are as follows: no downpayment; the lessee makes annual lease payments of $27,238 at year-end for four years; the implicit rate is 10%; and the leased asset is to be returned at the end of four years. The accounting staff disagrees about whether the estimated useful life of the leased asset is five or six years, and whether the estimated salvage value of the asset at the end of four years is $20,000 or $0.

Required: Use the following format to illustrate the 2001 financial statement effects of the proposed lease transaction under each of the following sets of assumptions: (1) the asset's estimated useful life is six years, the fair value is $100,000, and the estimated salvage value is $0; (2) the asset's estimated useful life is five years, the fair value is $100,000, and the estimated salvage value is $20,000; and (3) the asset's estimated useful life is five years, the fair value is $100,000, the estimated salvage value is $20,000, and the book value is $80,000 rather than $100,000 (this assumption allows the problem to be changed from a direct financing lease to a sales-type lease). Treat leasing as a primary activity for Foster Co. Also, for each set of assumptions, indicate what type of lease classification is used by Foster.

FOSTER CO.
Statements of Cash Flows
For Year Ended December 31, 2001
(Cash outflows in parentheses)

	Assumption		
	Operating	**Direct Financing**	**Sales-Type**
Operating Activities			

FOSTER CO.
Income Statements
For Year Ended December 31, 2001

	Assumption		
	Operating	**Direct Financing**	**Sales-Type**

FOSTER CO.
Balance Sheet
December 31, 2001
(Cumulative effect of lease transactions only)

	Assumption		
	Operating	**Direct Financing**	**Sales-Type**
Assets			
Current assets			
Cash			
Lease receivable—current portion			
Inventory			
Long-term investments and funds			
Lease receivable			
Less unearned interest			
Net lease receivable			
Less current portion			
Total			
Net cumulative effect on assets			
Owners' Equity			
Retained earnings (ignoring income taxes)			

16. **Texas Instruments' Investments in Debt Securities.** TI's 1998 financial statements are available at the text Web site at http://baginski.swcollege.com. Review the following sections of the 1998 financial statements: (1) balance sheet—short-term investments in the current asset section and investments in the noncurrent asset section; (2) income statement—interest on loans; (3) statement of cash flows—investing activities section; and (4) two footnotes—Cash and Short-Term Investments, and Investments.
    a. What were the December 31, 1998, amounts (if any) of investments in debt securities in (1) cash and short-term investments and (2) noncurrent asset investments? Which debt securities (if any) were listed at December 31, 1998, as trading, available-for-sale, or held-to-maturity securities?
    b. How much interest revenue was recognized in 1998 and 1997?
    c. On the statement of cash flows, investments in debt and other (nondebt) securities are not listed separately. What were the 1998 cash inflows and cash outflows associated with investments?

CFA Exam-Type Problems

17. **Leases.** For a capitalized lease, the implicit interest rate of a lessor is equal to the: (CFA adapted)
    a. weighted-average after-tax cost of capital of the lessor.
    b. weighted-average before-tax cost of capital of the lessor.
    c. interest rate that equates the fair market value of leased equipment to the present value of the lease payments.
    d. interest rate that equates the fair market value of leased equipment to the sum of the present value of the lease payments and the residual value.

18. **Impairment.** If a note receivable is deemed to be impaired by a creditor: (Author constructed)
    a. the creditor records a loss equal to the difference between the current book value and the present value of the new estimated future cash flows on the impaired debt.
    b. the creditor records a gain.
    c. the creditor records a loss equal to the difference between the current book value and the sum of the new estimated future cash flows on the impaired debt.
    d. no gain/loss is recorded until the debtor and creditor agree on new terms.

19. **Impairment.** If a note receivable is deemed to be impaired by a creditor, the interest rate used to compute the loss on the impaired loan is: (Author constructed)
    a. the creditor's after-tax cost of capital.
    b. the creditor's implicit rate.
    c. the current market rate of interest that would apply to the impaired debt.
    d. the creditor's historical, effective interest rate on the loan.

20. **Leases.** Assume that a company is a lessor and has a lease recorded as an operating lease. A financial analyst wants to determine the effect on the financial statements of capitalizing the lease as a direct financing lease. What would be the effect of capitalizing the lease on the company's financial statements if the leased asset is carried on the lessor's books as a depreciable asset? (Author constructed)
    a. The fixed asset turnover ratio increases.
    b. The fixed asset turnover ratio decreases.
    c. The current ratio decreases.
    d. Sales would be recorded.

21. **Debt Investments.** On January 1, a company made a long-term debt investment, properly classified as held-to-maturity. At year-end, the book value of the debt investment is different from its fair market value. Based upon this accounting treatment, which of the following statements is correct? (Author constructed)
    a. The current year's financial statement will report Other Comprehensive Income.
    b. The current year's stockholders' equity will report Accumulated Other Comprehensive Income.
    c. The investment is reported at amortized cost on the balance sheet.
    d. The investment is reported at fair market value on the balance sheet.

Objectives

1 Account for the initial acquisition of equity securities.

2 Describe the effects that the type of investment and the extent of influence have on accounting for equity securities.

3 Account for market value changes in equity investments in the financial statements.

4 Explain how earnings management may be accomplished through gains trading.

5 Describe the difference between the cost and equity methods of accounting for equity investments.

6 Identify the forms of business combination.

7 Account for business combinations at the date of acquisition under the purchase method.

8 Explain how financial statements for parent/subsidiary entities would be prepared in years after the date of acquisition.

9 Identify the effects of minority interests on consolidated financial statements.

Chapter 8

Investment Decisions—Investing in Other Firms' Equity Securities

Like investments in debt securities, investments in equity securities are trades of current cash flow for a stream of future cash flows. Unlike debt investments, the cash inflows of equity investments are not fixed by contract, but are determined by the earnings and cash flows of the firms in which the investments are made (i.e., determined by the investee firm's profitability). Also, investments in common stock equity securities convey voting privileges to the investor, which could lead to some degree of influence or level of control over investee operations.

The major accounting issues related to investments in equity securities are (1) valuation at acquisition; (2) classification of the investment; (3) revenue recognition; and (4) valuation when balance sheets are presented. This chapter concentrates on these four issues.

Investments in Equity Securities

1 Account for the initial acquisition of equity securities.

Investments in equity securities (e.g., common stocks, nonredeemable preferred stocks, and options) are *recorded at the fair value of all consideration given up in order to acquire the investment,* including amounts such as the purchase price, brokerage fees, taxes, and legal fees.

Example 1. Williams Co. purchases 100 shares of common stock at $10 per share. A total of $7 in commissions is also paid on the transaction.

Solution. The asset is recorded in Investment in Equity Securities at $1,007.

EXAMPLE 1 Journal Entry

Investment in Equity Securities	1,007	
Cash		1,007

Investment Classification and Revenue Recognition

2 Describe the effects that the type of investment and the extent of influence have on accounting for equity securities.

The manner in which revenue is recognized on equity security investments depends upon two factors: (1) the investor's extent of influence with the investee (no significant influence, ***significant influence***, or ***control***); and (2) whether the securities are marked-to-market as trading or available-for-sale securities under *SFAS No. 115*. *The appropriate accounting under SFAS No. 115 is discussed in Chapter 7. The presentation in this chapter regarding SFAS No. 115 accounting necessitates that the reader has read and understands that material.* (In Chapter 7, a third *SFAS No. 115* category, held-to-maturity, was discussed. *The held-to-maturity classification is not allowed for investments in equity securities because such securities have no maturity date.*)

The following schedule summarizes the possible combinations of type of investment and extent of influence, and the basis for revenue recognition and balance sheet valuation under each combination:

Combined Effect of Accounting for Common Stock Investments and *SFAS No. 115* Requirements

Type of Investment (*SFAS No. 115*[1] Classification)	Extent of Influence from Common Stock Investments*		
	No Significant Influence (0%–<20% ownership)	Significant Influence (20%–50% ownership)	Control (>50%–100% ownership)
Trading securities	*Cost method:* Mark-to-market with changes in value reported on the income statement	**	**
Available-for-sale securities	*Cost method:* Mark-to-market with changes in value reported cumulatively in owners' equity	**	**
Not applicable for the significant influence and control cases	N/A	*Equity method*	*Consolidate*

*Note that the percentages indicated in each column are default percentages (i.e., we presume that investments of less than 20% do not bring the investor significant influence). Accountants look beyond the default percentages to determine the degree of investor influence.
**Per *SFAS No. 115,* these investments in equity securities may not be classified as trading or available-for-sale.

In the following sections, we examine each possible combination of degree of influence (i.e., ownership percentage) and investment type.

No Significant Influence: Common Stock Investments of Less Than 20 Percent—The Cost Method with Market Valuation

3 Account for market value changes in equity investments in the financial statements.

Investments in equity securities that result in no significant influence (presumed to be of less than 20% ownership) are accounted for under the cost method, with balance sheet valuation adjusted to market at period's end.[2] Under the ***cost method,*** the **investments are recorded at the cost of acquiring shares, including any transaction costs,** and **dividends received are recorded as dividend income (revenue).**

Consistent with the treatment for investment in debt securities, changes in market value from period to period are reported in the owners' equity section for available-for-sale securities and in the income statement for trading securities. If

1. "Accounting for Certain Investments in Debt and Equity Securities," *Statement of Financial Accounting Standards No. 115* (Stamford, Conn.: FASB, 1993).

2. The 1999 *Accounting Trends & Techniques* reports that of 600 companies surveyed, 178 reported marketable securities as *current assets:* 120 reported at market/fair value; 56 at cost; and 2 at lower of cost or market. Although no distinction was made between debt securities (Chapter 7) and equity securities (Chapter 8), of the 56 reported at cost, it is likely that for a large number of companies the complete caption in the balance sheet or footnote read "at cost, which approximates market value." As *long-term assets,* 90 companies reported investments at cost; 77 at fair value; and 3 at lower of cost or market. Again, the investments are not separated into debt and equity security categories. In *stockholders' equity,* 148 companies reported unrealized gains/losses on certain investments.

market value can not be readily determined, then market valuation should not be used. Instead, balance sheet disclosure would be based on cost.

To illustrate these concepts, consider the following investments by Williams Company. Williams had no equity investments prior to the transactions indicated below.

Example 2. During 2001, Williams Company purchased the following common stocks:

Andrew Company	10,000 shares @ $5 per share	$50,000	
Ball Company	5,000 shares @ $4 per share	20,000	
Edwards Company	2,000 shares @ $6 per share	12,000	
Hammer Company	3,000 shares @ $20 per share	60,000	$142,000
Gummi Co.	10,000 shares @ $3 per share	$30,000	
Smurf Co.	10,000 shares @ $2 per share	20,000	50,000
			$192,000

Williams intends to hold the Andrew, Ball, Edwards, and Hammer shares as trading securities and the Gummi and Smurf shares as available-for-sale securities for an indefinite period. Williams does not have significant influence with any of the companies. During 2001 and 2002, Williams received $25,000 and $20,000, respectively, in dividends from the stock investments. Hammer was sold in 2002 for $62,000. At the end of 2001 and 2002, market values were:

	2001	2002
Andrew	$ 30,000	$55,000
Ball	20,000	23,000
Edwards	10,000	10,000
Hammer	63,000	0
Total	$123,000	$88,000
Gummi	$ 25,000	$20,000
Smurf	30,000	22,000
Total	$ 55,000	$42,000

Note that in this example Williams holds three of the trading securities over a two-year period. By definition, a trading security is held for a short period of time (e.g., 90 days). Although a security that is held for two years should not be classified as trading, in this example we hold the trading securities over two periods so that you can compare and contrast the accounting for trading and available-for-sale equity security investments.

Solution. Because Williams has no significant influence with the investee companies, these investments are recorded using the cost method. The statement of cash flows reports the following three cash flow consequences of these transactions, listed in chronological order:

1. The original cash investments (reported as $142,000 and $50,000 cash outflows in 2001).
2. The dividend receipts (reported as cash inflows in 2001 and 2002).
3. The sale of Hammer Company securities (reported as a $62,000 cash inflow in 2002).

In the statement of cash flows, transactions regarding investments in available-for-sale securities (purchases and sales) are listed under Investing Activities, and transactions regarding investments in trading securities (purchases and sales) are listed under Operating Activities. This is reflected in Exhibit 1. Dividends received on investments accounted for under the cost method are reported as revenues on the income statement; GAAP also requires that these cash receipts from dividends be reported in the statement of cash flows under Operating Activities.[3]

3. In contrast, as we discussed in Chapter 2, dividend payments are reported in the financing section of the cash flow statement.

EXHIBIT 1 Williams Co. Statement of Cash Flows

WILLIAMS CO.
Statement of Cash Flows
(cash outflows in parentheses)

	2001	2002
Operating Activities		
Dividends received	25,000	20,000
Investments in trading equity securities	(142,000)	
Sales of trading securities		62,000
Investing Activities		
Investments in available-for-sale equity securities	(50,000)	
Net change in cash	(167,000)	82,000

The balance sheet in Exhibit 2 shows the effects of the investments under both classifications. Because the available-for-sale securities are held for an indefinite period, they are classified as long-term assets. Alternatively, they could be classified as current assets if management's intent was to hold them only for a short period or to sell them whenever needed. The trading securities are classified as current (even though, in this problem, they were held over a two-year period).

EXHIBIT 2 Williams Co. Balance Sheet

WILLIAMS CO.
Balance Sheets
December 31
(Effects of equity investments only)

	2001	2002
Assets		
Current assets:		
Cash	(167,000)	(85,000)
Investments in trading equity securities at cost	142,000	82,000
Valuation allowance	(19,000)	6,000
Investments in trading equity securities at market	123,000	88,000
Long-term investments and funds:		
Investments in available-for-sale equity securities at cost	50,000	50,000
Valuation allowance	5,000	(8,000)
Investments in available-for-sale equity securities at market	55,000	42,000
Net effect on assets	**11,000**	**45,000**
Owners' Equity		
Retained earnings (net effect of equity investment, ignoring income taxes)*	6,000	53,000
Accumulated other comprehensive income:		
Cumulative unrealized gain (loss) on adjustment of equity investments to market	5,000	(8,000)
Net effect on owners' equity	**11,000**	**45,000**

*See the income statement, which is subsequently shown in this example solution.

The cash balance is the cumulative effect of the change in cash reported in the statement of cash flows ($167,000) through 2001 ($192,000 purchase of securities − $25,000 in dividends), and ($85,000) through 2002 [($167,000) from 2001 + 82,000 in 2002, which represents $20,000 in dividends and $62,000 in proceeds from the sale of Hammer]. The investment in equity securities amounts reported in the balance sheet are determined by an analysis of the costs and market values of the two portfolios of investments (trading and available-for-sale) at each balance sheet date:

	Cost and Market Values (in thousands)			
	12/31/01		12/31/02	
	Cost	Market	Cost	Market
Trading securities:				
Andrew	$ 50	$ 30	$50	$55
Ball	20	20	20	23
Edwards	12	10	12	10
Hammer	60	63	–	–
Totals	$142	$123	$82	$88
Valuation allowance needed to increase (reduce) cost to market (reported on balance sheet)	$(19)		$ 6	
Change in valuation allowance from prior year [reported on income statement as unrealized gain (loss)]	$(19)		$25	
Available-for-sale securities:				
Gummi	$ 30	$ 25	$30	$20
Smurf	20	30	20	22
Totals	$ 50	$ 55	$50	$42
Valuation allowance needed to increase (reduce) cost to market (reported on balance sheet in both assets and stockholders' equity sections)	$ 5		$ (8)	
Change in valuation allowance from prior year [reported in other comprehensive income as unrealized gain (loss)]	$ 5		$(13)	

In the current asset section, investments in trading equity securities are reported at the December 31, 2001, and December 31, 2002, market values of $123,000 and $88,000, respectively. In the long-term investments and funds section, the investments in available-for-sale equity securities are also reported at the December 31, 2001, and December 31, 2002, market values of $55,000 and $42,000, respectively. Valuation Allowance represents the cumulative difference between cost and market. This valuation allowance is added to (or subtracted from) the original cost in order to adjust investments to market.

The year-to-year fluctuations in the trading securities market values (i.e., the *change* in the valuation allowance account), a $19,000 unrealized loss in 2001 and a $25,000 unrealized gain in 2002, are reported in the income statement (Exhibit 3). As was the case for debt investments (discussed in Chapter 7), available-for-sale securities have a cumulative adjustment from cost to market reported in Accumulated Other Comprehensive Income in the owners' equity section (instead of in net income), and the current year's change is reported as other comprehensive income.

EXHIBIT 3 Williams Co. Income Statement Effects

WILLIAMS CO.
Income Statement Effects

	2001	2002
Other revenues, (expenses), gains, and (losses)		
Dividend revenue	25,000	20,000
Unrealized gain (loss) on adjustment of trading equity securities to market	(19,000)	25,000
Realized gain on sale of trading equity securities		2,000
Total effect	6,000	47,000

(continued)

EXHIBIT 3 (concluded)

WILLIAMS CO. Statement of Comprehensive Income Effects (Ignoring income tax effects)	2001	2002
Effect on net income (see income statement)	6,000	47,000
Other comprehensive income		
Unrealized gain (loss) on available-for-sale securities	5,000	(13,000)

Dividend revenue is reported in each of the two years, and a realized gain on sale of trading equity securities is reported in 2002. Because the security has been converted to cash, the gain is *realized*. The gain is computed by comparing the original cost to the selling price:

Sales price	$62,000
Original cost of the Hammer securities	(60,000)
Realized gain on sale	$ 2,000

Note that in this example, the realized gain of $2,000 is defined as the excess of the amount received over the original cost.[4] The valuation allowance is not taken into account at the date of sale because the valuation account pertains to the *entire* portfolio of securities rather than to a specific security. Consequently, the valuation account is adjusted at year-end in the cost and market comparison (see the table of cost and market value analysis where the December 31, 2002, valuation adjustment was $25,000 for trading securities). In effect, the result of this accounting process is that any valuation amount and any associated unrealized gain/loss from the prior year mark-to-market adjustment is reversed in the current period (i.e., as part of the $25,000 December 31, 2002, adjustment, the December 31, 2001, $3,000 valuation allowance for the Hammer security is reversed). Therefore, the total 2002 income statement effect associated with the sale of the Hammer security is a net loss of $1,000 (a $2,000 realized gain plus a $3,000 unrealized loss associated with reversing the Hammer portion of the December 31, 2001, trading security valuation). To separate the effect of the Hammer investment on the financial statements, the income statement previously presented is recast in Exhibit 4.

EXHIBIT 4 Williams Co. Income Statement Effects

WILLIAMS CO. Income Statement Effects (Recast to separate the effects of the investment in Hammer)	2001	2002
Other revenues (expenses), gains and (losses)		
Dividend revenue	25,000	20,000
Unrealized gain (loss) on adjustment of trading equity securities to market		
Hammer investment	3,000	(3,000)
Andrew, Ball, and Edwards investments	(22,000)	28,000
Total	(19,000)	25,000
Realized gain on sale of trading equity securities		2,000
Total effect	6,000	47,000

4. In some textbooks, an alternative treatment is to compute the realized gain/loss as the difference between the sales price and the market value at the last balance sheet date (i.e., $62,000 − $63,000 = $1,000 loss). Because we strongly prefer computing the realized gain/loss as the difference between the sales price and the original cost, we do not illustrate this alternative method.

EXAMPLE 2 Journal Entries

2001 purchase of investments:		
Investments in Trading Securities	142,000	
Investments in Available-for-Sale Securities	50,000	
Cash		192,000
2001 dividend receipts:		
Cash	25,000	
Dividend Revenue		25,000
12/31/01 adjustments to market:		
Unrealized Loss on Adjustment of Trading Equity Securities to Market	19,000	
Valuation Allowance—Trading Securities		19,000
Valuation Allowance—Available-for-Sale Securities	5,000	
Cumulative Unrealized Gain/Loss on Adjustments of Available-for-Sale Equity Securities to Market		5,000
2002 dividend receipts:		
Cash	20,000	
Dividend Revenue		20,000
2002 sale of Hammer securities:		
Cash	62,000	
Investment in Trading Securities		60,000
Realized Gain on Sale of Trading Securities		2,000
12/31/02 adjustments to market:		
Valuation Allowance—Trading Securities	25,000	
Unrealized Gain on Adjustment of Trading Equity Securities to Market		25,000
Cumulative Unrealized Gain/Loss on Adjustments of Available-for-Sale Equity Securities to Market	13,000	
Valuation Allowance—Available-for-Sale Securities		13,000

Financial Statement Presentation

The following information (Exhibit 5) about marketable and other securities was provided in the 1998 annual report for General Motors Corporation, Note 3. This footnote ties together material discussed in Chapter 7 (investments in debt securities) and this chapter (investments in equity securities). It has been slightly modified for presentation.

EXHIBIT 5 General Motors Corporation—1998 Annual Report (Note 3)

General Motors 1998 Balance Sheet: Selected Information (Dollars in Millions)

	1998	1997
Cash and cash equivalents	$10,869	$11,262
Other marketable securities	9,155	11,722
Total cash and marketable securities (Notes 1 and 3)	$20,024	$22,984

General Motors Note 3 (partial and modified by authors).
Marketable and Other Securities

Marketable securities held by GM are classified as available-for-sale, except for certain mortgage-related securities of GMAC, which are classified as trading securities. The aggregate

(continued)

EXHIBIT 5 (concluded)

excess of fair value over cost, net of related income taxes, for available-for-sale securities is included as a separate component of stockholders' equity. The excess of fair value over cost for trading securities is included in income on a current basis. GM determines cost on the specific identification basis.

Investments in marketable securities were as follows (in millions):

December 31, 1998—Type of Security	Cost	Fair Value	Unrealized Gains	Unrealized Losses
Bonds, notes and other securities				
United States government and governmental agencies and authorities	$ 736	$ 747	$ 12	$ 1
States, municipalities, and political subdivisions	1,506	1,611	117	12
Mortgage-backed securities	415	383	6	38
Other	1,993	2,031	73	35
Total debt securities available-for-sale	4,650	4,772	208	86
Mortgage-backed securities held for trading purposes	3,173	3,173	0	0
Total debt securities	7,823	7,945	208	86
Equity securities available-for-sale	779	1,210	534	103
Total investment in securities	$8,602	$9,155	$742	$189

Debt securities totaling $453 million mature within one year; $1.6 billion mature after one through five years; $1.5 billion mature after five years through 10 years; and $4.5 billion mature after 10 years.

Proceeds from sales and maturities of marketable securities totaled $8 billion in 1998, $13.6 billion in 1997, and $5.7 billion in 1996. The gross gains and (losses) related to sales of marketable securities were $235 million and ($60) million, $297 million and ($96) million, and $236 million and ($33) million in 1998, 1997, and 1996, respectively.

Other securities classified as cash equivalents, which consisted primarily of commercial paper, repurchase agreements, and certificates of deposit, were $9.4 billion and $10.3 billion at December 31, 1998 and 1997, respectively.

At December 31, 1998, General Motors had about $20 billion in cash and investments in securities, with $9.4 billion in securities (commercial paper, etc.) reported as cash equivalents (highly liquid investments, converted within 90 days), and $9.155 billion reported as other marketable securities.[5] In essence, the $9.4 billion in cash equivalents are trading securities, but they are classified as cash equivalents because they are due within 90 days. Of the $9.155 billion in other marketable securities, $4.772 billion are available-for-sale debt securities, $3.173 billion are trading debt securities, and $1.210 billion are in equity securities classified as available-for-sale. The footnote provides separate amounts for securities with unrealized gains and those with unrealized losses, and also reports separate amounts for realized gains and realized losses.

Earnings Management: Gains Trading

4 Explain how earnings management may be accomplished through gains trading.

The reporting of unrealized gains and losses on available-for-sale securities in owners' equity (rather than income) has the advantage of deferring short-term value fluctuations on longer-term transactions. Keeping these gains and losses out of current income is a reasonable approach because the intent is not to liquidate in the short run. However, earnings management opportunities are created by the special treatment afforded available-for-sale securities—"winners" can be sold, and "losers" can be held in the portfolio. This allows realized gains to be reported as

5. To put this $20 billion in perspective, GM had total assets of about $257 billion. Thus, cash and marketable securities constitute almost 8% of total assets.

income while deferring unrealized losses as a component of owners' equity. For example, suppose that a company made two recent investments in equity securities classified as available-for-sale. The investments were purchased for $10,000 each. Investment A has appreciated to $11,000 during the current period, while Investment B has declined in market value to $9,500. If the company wished to report more income during the current period, Investment A could be sold at a gain of $1,000. Otherwise, the $1,000 would be disclosed as an unrealized gain in the shareholders' equity section. Similar discretion to generate a loss exists with respect to Investment B.[6]

Significant Influence: Common Stock Investments of 20–50 Percent—The Equity Method

5 Describe the difference between the cost and equity methods of accounting for equity investments.

Investments in equity securities that give the investor significant influence over the investee's operations are accounted for under the ***equity method.***[7] In the absence of evidence to the contrary, 20–50% ownership investments are deemed to give the investor significant influence. Note that the default percentage used to indicate significant influence is arbitrary. For example, using the default percentage, a 19.8% ownership does not give the investor significant influence, but a 20.2% ownership does. *The relevant issue is whether an investor has significant influence.* It is unlikely that a movement from a 19.8% to a 20.2% ownership actually resulted in a change from no significant influence to significant influence. In this text, we use the arbitrary 20% cutoff to indicate significant influence (unless we state otherwise).

If an investor has significant influence and the cost method were used to account for equity investments, then the investor could manage earnings by influencing the timing and the extent of dividend declarations and payments. Under the cost method, dividends trigger revenue recognition. Accordingly, the FASB specifies that the equity method be used when the investor has significant influence.

The equity method follows the accrual accounting concept. When an investee earns income, its net assets increase. Under the equity method, the investor accrues its ownership portion of the investee's net income and increased net assets. Income is reported by the investor in the other income, expenses, gains, and losses section of the income statement.[8] The investor's investment account is increased by its portion of the investee's increased net assets.

When an investee declares dividends, it distributes net assets. The investor records the dividends as an increase in cash and a reduction of the investment. Thus, the dividend does not trigger revenue recognition for the investor. The net effect on the investor's balance sheet investment account is that *the investment account changes by the investor's pro rata share of the investee's undistributed earnings.*

Finally, a security accounted for under the equity method is not covered by *SFAS No. 115,* and it is not marked-to-market at year-end (i.e., it cannot be classified as trading or available-for-sale). To summarize, when using the equity method (1) the investor accrues its pro rata share of investee net income (losses) by increasing the investment account and recognizing income (losses); (2) the investor accrues its pro rata share of an investee's declared dividends as an increase in Dividends Receivable and a decrease in Investments; (3) the investor may not classify investments in equity securities accounted for under the equity method as trading or available-for-sale. Accordingly, the investments may not be marked-to-market.

To illustrate these concepts, consider the following example.

Example 3. On January 1, 2001, Lake Co. buys 40% of Pond Co. common stock at a cost of $500,000. Pond Co.'s net assets have a book value of $1,100,000. As-

6. Comprehensive income would not be affected by the choices indicated in this example. All available-for-sale gains and losses, whether realized or unrealized, are a part of comprehensive income.

7. The 1999 *Accounting Trends & Techniques* reports that of 600 companies surveyed, 279 reported using the equity method to account for long-term investments.

8. Investment Income and Equity in Subsidiary Earnings are standard accounts used to report the investee's pro rata share of investee net income.

sume that the individual fair values of identifiable net assets are equal to the book values of Pond's assets. Also assume that any goodwill implied in this transaction is amortized over 10 years. During 2001, Pond has net income of $50,000, and declares dividends of $30,000.

Solution. Lake Co. paid $500,000 to acquire 40% of Pond Co., which implies the $440,000 was paid for identifiable net assets and $60,000 for unidentifiable assets:

Price paid	$500,000
Portion of identifiable net assets acquired ($1,100,000 × 40%)	(440,000)
Unidentifiable assets acquired (implied goodwill)	$ 60,000

The **unidentifiable asset** is generally recognized as ***goodwill***. In this example, we assume that the goodwill has a future economic useful life of 10 years.[9]

If Lake were to use the cost method, Investment in Pond Co. would be marked-to-market at year-end. Further, $12,000 in dividend revenue ($30,000 × 40%) would be reported in the income statement.

Under the equity method, however, the investee's declaration of income, rather than the distribution of dividends, is the event that triggers the investor's revenue recognition. Lake's investment revenue is determined as follows:

Investee earnings ($50,000 × 40%)	$20,000
Amortization of implied goodwill ($60,000 ÷ 10 years)	(6,000)
Investment revenue	$14,000

Pond Co. (the investee) calculated its $50,000 income by matching revenues against the consumption of the book values of its assets (i.e., expenses). Under the equity method, Lake Co. (the investor) records its pro rata share of investee income of $20,000 ($50,000 × 40%). However, from Lake's point of view, the resources committed to generating 40% of Pond's revenues are greater than 40% of Pond's costs because Lake paid an extra $60,000 when purchasing the 40% investment. The cost of that extra investment must also be matched against revenues; hence, the $6,000 goodwill amortization. Rather than reporting it separately, the equity method treats the goodwill amortization as a reduction in investment income.

Investment in Pond Co. is reported in the long-term investments and funds section of the balance sheet at the original cost plus any increases from the investee's income less any decreases from dividend distribution:

Investment in Pond Co. (original cost) at 1/1/01	$500,000
Lake's adjusted share of Pond's earnings	14,000
Lake's share of Pond's dividends ($30,000 × 40%)	(12,000)
Investment in Pond Co. reported at 12/31/01	$502,000

The December 31, 2001, ending balance in the investment account can be reconciled by adding the unamortized excess price paid by Lake to the 40% of Pond's net assets at December 31, 2001:

Pond Co. net assets:	
1/1/01	$1,100,000
Net income	50,000
Dividends	(30,000)
12/31/01	$1,120,000

(continued)

9. As discussed in Chapter 7, goodwill should be amortized over its estimated useful life, not to exceed 40 years. At the time this text went to press, the FASB had proposed, in an exposure draft, that the maximum amortization period be 20 years.

Lake's pro rate share of Pond's net assets at 12/31/01 ($1,120,000 × 40%)	$ 448,000
Unamortized goodwill ($60,000 − $6,000) at 12/31/01	54,000
Investment in Pond reported at 12/31/01	$ 502,000

EXAMPLE 3 Journal Entries

1/1/01 investment purchase:		
Investment in Pond	500,000	
Cash		500,000
2001 dividends:		
Cash	12,000	
Investment in Pond		12,000
12/31/01 recognition of pro rata share of Pond's earnings:		
Investment in Pond	20,000	
Investment Revenue*		20,000

*Alternatively, Equity in Subsidiary Income.

12/31/01 goodwill amortization:		
Investment Revenue	6,000	
Investment in Pond		6,000

Key Ledger Account

Investment in Pond

1/1/01 purchase	500,000		
		Share of dividends	12,000
Share of earnings	20,000		
		Goodwill amortization	6,000
12/31/01 balance	502,000		

In our example, we assumed that the January 1, 2001, fair values of Pond's net assets equaled the book values of the net assets. If the fair values and book values are not equal, the problem becomes more complicated. In the most common situation, the fair values exceed the book values. If this were the situation in our example, the $60,000 premium would be first allocated to specific assets that are undervalued on Pond's books, with any remainder allocated to implied goodwill. To simplify the presentation in this section, we do not illustrate the situation where fair values and book values are not equal. We have, however, provided an extended analysis of the issue in the following section on accounting for controlling interests.

Thus far, we have illustrated the accounting for investments in common stocks. Investors can invest in other equity securities such as preferred stocks or stock options, which normally provide no voting rights to the investor. Without voting rights, the concepts of significant influence underlying the equity method and the control underlying consolidated financial statements become virtually meaningless. Therefore, the cost method is used to record investments in preferred stocks and other equity securities. Because the cost method is used, these investments qualify for classification as trading securities and available-for-securities, and thus, are marked-to-market at each balance sheet date.

Financial Statement Presentation

The financial statement disclosures in the 1998 annual report for Ingersoll-Rand Company illustrate reporting for equity method investments, as shown in Exhibit 6. Note that Ingersoll-Rand's equity in subsidiary earnings is reported after the operating income subtotal. Also, note that the footnote disclosures provide summary income statement and balance sheet information for the partially owned equity affiliates and information about dividends received.

EXHIBIT 6 Ingersoll-Rand Company—Financial Statement Information

Ingersoll-Rand Company Financial Statement Information Related to Use of Equity Method

(in millions)	1998	1997
Balance Sheet Long-Term Investments		
Investments in and advances with partially-owned affiliates	$344.7	$328.0
Income Statement (shown after operating income subtotal)		
Equity in earnings of partially-owned affiliates	46.8	28.8

Note 1, Summary of Significant Accounting Policies, and Note 5, Investments in Partially-Owned Equity Affiliates (in part):

Partially-owned equity affiliates are accounted for under the equity method.

The company has numerous investments, ranging from 20 percent to 50 percent, in companies that operate in similar lines of business.

The company's investments in and amounts due to partially-owned equity affiliates amounted to $380.9 million and $36.2 million, respectively, at December 31, 1998, and $354.2 million and $26.2 million, respectively, at December 31, 1997. The company's equity in the net earnings of its partially-owned equity affiliates was $46.8 million, $28.8 million, and $42.4 million, in 1998, 1997, and 1996, respectively. The company's 1997 earnings were reduced by $13.9 million due to a restructuring charge at one of its partially-owned equity affiliates.

The company received dividends based on its equity interest in these companies of $8.5 million, $8.7 million, and $6.8 million in 1998, 1997, and 1996, respectively.

Summarized financial information for these partially-owned equity affiliates at December 31 and for the year then ended:

(in millions)	1998	1997
Net sales	$1,996.2	$2,048.4
Gross profit	353.6	382.4
Net earnings	90.6	59.4
Balance Sheet		
Current assets	$ 985.1	$ 959.6
Property, plant and equipment, net	490.5	506.7
Other assets	57.7	73.7
Total assets	$1,533.3	$1,540.0
Current liabilities	$ 526.5	$ 610.8
Long-term debt	65.9	75.3
Other liabilities	170.0	227.1
Total shareholders' equity	770.9	626.8
Total liabilities and equity	$1,533.3	$1,540.0

Control: Common Stock Investments of Greater Than 50 Percent—Consolidations

When over 50% ownership occurs, control is obtained by the investor. Although the companies are separate *legal* entities, the investor and investee cease to be treated as separate entities for financial statement purposes, and consolidated financial statements are presented. These consolidated statements combine the individual asset and liability accounts of the two parties, and eliminate any intercompany transfers.[10]

In this section, we address those **investments in other companies that represent controlling interests.** Although there are several forms that these investments can take, we use the term ***business combinations*** to describe the overall phenomenon. Business combinations occur for several reasons. One alleged benefit is diversification. A given corporation can smooth earnings and cash flows by acquiring another company with earnings and cash flow patterns that negatively correlate with its

10. The topics of business combinations and how to prepare consolidated financial statements normally encompass about half of an entire "advanced accounting" course in accounting curricula. Our goal in this chapter is to provide both exposure to basic vocabulary and simple examples to help you understand the concepts. In the 1999 *Accounting Trends & Techniques,* 578 of the 600 companies surveyed provided a description of their accounting policies for consolidated financial statements.

own. For example, a producer of swimming pool accessories could acquire a snow removal company. The earnings stream of the business combination would appear smooth because of the offsetting seasonality of the two combined firms.[11]

Another benefit of combination is the guarantee of steady sales or supplies. For example, if an industry exists with limited production or distribution capacity, vertical integration through the business combination of a producer and a distributor would be beneficial in reducing the sales or supply uncertainty for both firms. This example demonstrates the notion that business combinations can result in the value of the two firms being greater than each firm operating individually. Such synergies can exist in horizontal integration as well. For example, a combination of two retailers could result in a more complete coverage of markets and a reduction in marketing, accounting, and information systems costs through the removal of duplicate employees and systems.

A direct and immediate benefit of some combinations is a tax advantage. Less seasoned firms often become acquisition targets because they are currently profitable *and* because they were terribly unprofitable in the past. As we discuss in Chapter 11 on income taxes, net operating losses can be carried forward to reduce future taxes. If the acquisition was *not* entered into *solely* for tax purposes, then U.S. tax rules permit the acquiring company to offset the potentially large net operating losses against the combined firm profits to generate an immediate tax benefit for itself. Finally, acquisitions can benefit the management of the acquiring firm. Whether intentional or unintentional, executive compensation tends to increase with firm size.

Forms of Business Combination

6 Identify the forms of business combination.

Three types of business combination are possible: ***merger***, ***consolidation***, and acquisition resulting in a ***parent/subsidiary relationship***.[12,13] In the first two types of combination, merger and consolidation, only one corporation remains after the combination. In an acquisition resulting in a parent/subsidiary relationship, two separate corporations remain after the consolidation. For firms A and B, the combinations can be illustrated as follows:

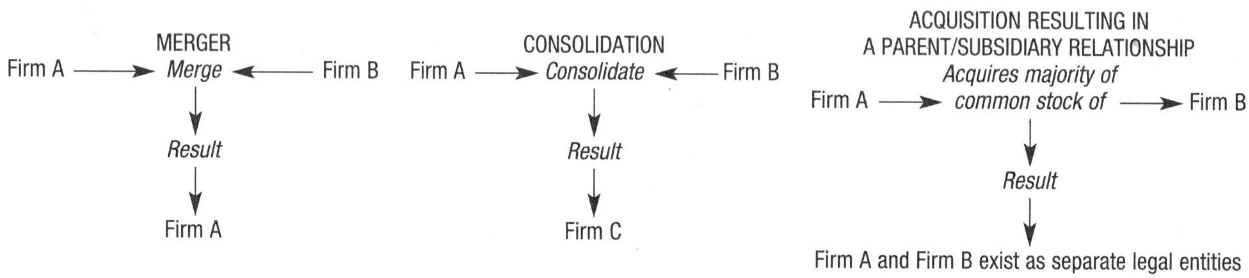

11. Some have questioned the true value of diversification in this context. If the acquiring corporation's shareholders wanted diversification, they could simply buy shares of the acquired corporation, thus avoiding the costs of corporate acquisition. Further, many question whether management skills are generic or firm-specific. Firm value might actually decrease if a single management were to control two unrelated firms in different industries. Each firm might require different managements even at the upper, *strategic* level.

12. A fourth type of combination is possible—a joint venture is a special form of consolidation with a limited life.

13. The vocabulary surrounding business combinations can be confusing. For example, in the general business press the term "merger" is frequently used in place of the more precise term "business combination." In reality, a merger is one type of business combination. The use of the term "consolidation" may also be misleading. In the context of a business combination, a consolidation is one of three ways of effecting the business combination. When applied to a parent/subsidiary relationship (which is one of the three ways of effecting a business combination), consolidation is the process of combining the parent and subsidiary financial statements into consolidated financial statements.

As we continue our discussion of the accounting for these transactions, it is important to note that *only one set of accounting records exists in a business combination accounted for as either a merger or a consolidation. In a business combination accounted for as a parent/subsidiary relationship, two sets of accounting records exist after the combination, one for each legal entity.*

Accounting for Business Combinations at the Date of Acquisition

7 Account for business combinations at the date of acquisition under the purchase method.

As of the writing of this text, business combinations could be accounted for as either a purchase transaction or a pooling of interests. The basic difference between recording an acquisition under purchase and pooling is the valuation basis for net assets acquired. For a ***purchase transaction*****, the net assets acquired are valued at the fair value of the consideration paid by the new owner.** In a ***pooling of interests*****, the net assets acquired are valued at their book value.** In April 1999, the FASB announced in an exposure draft that it would no longer allow pooling of interests as an acceptable method to account for business combinations starting in 2001. We include a discussion of the pooling of interests method because a large number of business combinations have been accounted for as poolings, and these will be reflected in financial statements for many years.

The use of pooling of interests drew a great deal of criticism from the investment public. Periodically during the 1990s, accounting standard setters discussed the idea of eliminating the pooling method. However, use of the pooling method is popular with corporations, and frequently a business combination was completed only if pooling treatment was allowed by the SEC. Also, almost all other countries prohibit the pooling method.

The fundamental problem with pooling (relative to purchase accounting) is that recently acquired assets are shown on the acquirer's financial statements at out-of-date book values. The fact that a new, contemporary valuation has been established through an exchange between the parties is ignored. This basic problem with the pooling of interests method causes two conditions in financial reports: 1) assets are understated, and 2) related expenses are understated in future periods, which results in a series of net income overstatements.

This latter condition, expense understatement, directly results from the first condition, asset understatement. Recall that assets become expenses as they are used up. For example, understating the building account would lead to understating depreciation expense and overstating net income.

This understatement of assets and overstatement of net income causes interpretation problems with ratios such as return on assets (ROA), especially if a comparison is made with the ROAs of firms that use purchase accounting. The ROAs of pooling firms appear to be much higher than those for purchase firms, even though the choice of accounting method is the only difference between the firms.

In order to use the pooling of interests method, 12 criteria had to be met. One of the most important criteria was that at least 90% of the value given up by the buyer had to be common stock. In recent years, some companies have attempted to simulate pooling accounting by using purchase accounting, and subsequently writing off the excess of asset fair values over costs in the period of acquisition (or shortly thereafter). This strategy depresses income in the current period only, while freeing subsequent periods' net income from amortizations of the excess amounts. Book values are also lower due to the asset write-offs. This combination of higher net income and lower asset book values simulates pooling of interests. In the late 1990s, the SEC cracked down on this process and curtailed its use.

Goodwill only arises if purchase accounting is used. Because goodwill is amortized over its estimated useful life, it steadily reduces net income over a long period subsequent to acquisition. The effects on financial statements are even more pronounced when the goodwill asset is thought to no longer have any future value. For example, in 1996, Eli Lilly and Company reported over $1.5 billion in net income. However, in 1997, the company reported a $385 million net loss. This dramatic change came about because Lilly wrote off $2.445 billion in goodwill associated with its 1994 purchase of PCS Health Systems, Inc. If Lilly would have structured the PCS acquisition as a pooling, then the 1997, $2.445 billion charge would have been averted.

The following footnote for Compaq Computer Corporation describes a pooling of interest transaction.

Compaq Computer Corporation—Note 2. Acquisitions (in part, slightly modified by authors)

During the year, Compaq merged with Tandem Computers Incorporated (Tandem) in a stock-for-stock transaction accounted for as a pooling of interests . . . In connection with the merger, Compaq issued 126 million shares of common stock, based upon an exchange ratio of 1.05 shares of Compaq common stock for each share of Tandem common stock. Merger-related costs of $44 million are reflected in the Consolidated Statement of Income as a result of the transaction. The financial data included in these financial statements have been restated to reflect the merger with Tandem. There were no material transactions between Compaq and Tandem during the periods prior to the merger.

The Purchase Method

In a combination accounted for as a purchase, the price paid for the acquired firm is allocated to the fair market values of the assets and liabilities (i.e., net assets) acquired; any excess is then assigned to goodwill.[14] In the unusual event that a negative excess occurs, it is used to revalue long-term assets (other than marketable securities) downward until the negative excess is removed. If any negative excess remains after revaluing the long-term assets to zero, it is called "negative goodwill." We illustrate purchase accounting with the following example.

Example 4. Assume that Co. P acquires Co. S for cash.[15] Prior to the combination, Co. S had the following balance sheet amounts (fair market values are provided in parentheses if different than book value):

Current assets	$120,000	
Building	160,000	(FMV = $200,000)
Land	40,000	(FMV = $50,000)
Liabilities	100,000	
Common stock	150,000	
Retained earnings	70,000	

Case 1. To illustrate the existence of a positive excess leading to the recording of goodwill, assume that the cash price is $300,000.

Case 2. To illustrate the negative excess leading to a reduction of long-term assets, assume that the cash price is $230,000.

Illustrate the balance sheet effects for each case under two assumptions: Co. S is dissolved (i.e., the business combination is effected as a merger), and Co. S con-

14. The 1999 *Accounting Trends & Techniques* reported that of 600 companies surveyed, 453 reported goodwill recognized in a business combination.

15. In business combination problems, it is common to use Company P as the parent and Company S as the subsidiary.

tinues as a separate legal entity (i.e., the business combination is effected as a parent/subsidiary relationship).

Solution. Prior to preparing the balance sheets, we must compute the basis for recording the assets and liabilities received:

Case 1:

Price paid		$300,000
FMV of identifiable net assets:		
Current assets	$120,000	
Building	200,000	
Land	50,000	
Liabilities	(100,000)	270,000
Goodwill		$ 30,000

Co. P paid $30,000 more than the fair values of the net assets it acquired. Thus, another asset was acquired by Co. P—Goodwill. This goodwill is assumed to represent the ability of Co. S to generate profits over and above that which is indicated by the fair values of the individual assets.

Case 2:

Price paid		$230,000
FMV of identifiable net assets:		
Current assets	$120,000	
Building	200,000	
Land	50,000	
Liabilities	(100,000)	270,000
Negative excess		(40,000)
Allocated to long-term assets:		
Building		
$40,000 × (200 ÷ 250)		32,000
Land		
$40,000 × (50 ÷ 250)		8,000
Goodwill		$ 0

In Case 2, the purchase price offered by Co. P is less than the estimates of the individual fair values of the net assets acquired. (Fair value estimates for current assets are usually correct because they are so close to realization; likewise, fair value estimates for liabilities are also usually correct because cash flows are contractual. The greatest difficulty in obtaining fair value estimates is in the long-term asset area, except for marketable securities.) Accordingly, the excess of fair values over the price paid ($40,000) is allocated to the long-term assets in proportion to the fair values as a correction to their fair value estimates.

As a result of this allocation process, Co. P values the entire basket purchase at the total price paid—as one would do in any *purchase* transaction:

	Valuation	
	Case 1	**Case 2**
Current assets	$120,000	$120,000
Building	200,000	168,000
Land	50,000	42,000
Goodwill	30,000	0
Liabilities	(100,000)	(100,000)
Price paid	$300,000	$230,000

For both cases, the balance sheet effects depend on whether Co. S is dissolved or remains as a separate legal entity. Exhibits 7–10 reflect the balance sheet effects under each possibility.

EXHIBIT 7 Case 1: $300,000 cash paid; Co. S dissolved (Merger)

CO. P BALANCE SHEET *Changes* in accounts				CO. S BALANCE SHEET *Balances* in accounts
Assets		**Liabilities**		No longer exists; Co. S has been dissolved.
Current assets*	180,000 ↓	Liabilities	100,000 ↑	
Building	200,000 ↑	**Owners' Equity**		
Land	50,000 ↑	No effect		
Goodwill	30,000 ↑			

*$120,000 of current assets were acquired using $300,000 in cash.

Co. P purchased a basket of assets and liabilities using cash, and Co. S no longer exists. This demonstrates a merger recorded using purchase accounting.

EXHIBIT 8 Case 1: $300,000 cash paid; Co. S remains as a separate legal entity (Parent/subsidiary relationship)

CO. P BALANCE SHEET *Changes* in accounts			CO. S BALANCE SHEET *Balances* in accounts			
Assets		**Liabilities**	**Assets**		**Liabilities**	
Current assets	300,000 ↓	No effect	Current assets	120,000	Liabilities	100,000
Investment in Co. S	300,000 ↑	**Owners' Equity**	Building	160,000	**Owners' Equity**	
		No effect	Land	40,000	Common stock	150,000
					Retained earnings	70,000

To keep Co. S as a separate legal entity, Co. P acquires and holds the rights to Co. S's assets and liabilities (i.e., all common shares) rather than the assets and liabilities directly. Co. P shows only the investment in Co. S at the price paid, $300,000; Co. S continues to report all assets and liabilities at book values, $220,000 (easily determined by totaling owners' equity; remember, A − L = OE).

For Case 2, the balance sheet effects are analogous when only $230,000 is paid for Co. S, except that the long-term assets are recorded at lower amounts and no goodwill exists.

EXHIBIT 9 Case 2: $230,000 cash paid; Co. S dissolved (Merger)

CO. P BALANCE SHEET *Changes* in accounts				CO. S BALANCE SHEET *Balances* in accounts
Assets		**Liabilities**		No longer exists; Co. S has been dissolved.
Current assets*	110,000 ↓	Liabilities	100,000 ↑	
Building	168,000 ↑	**Owners' Equity**		
Land	42,000 ↑	No effect		

*$120,000 of current assets were acquired using $230,000 in cash.

EXHIBIT 10 Case 2: $230,000 cash paid; Co. S remains as a separate legal entity (Parent/subsidiary relationship)

CO. P BALANCE SHEET *Changes* in accounts			CO. S BALANCE SHEET *Balances* in accounts			
Assets		**Liabilities**	**Assets**		**Liabilities**	
Current assets	230,000 ↓	No effect	Current assets	120,000	Liabilities	100,000
Investment in Co. S	230,000 ↑	**Owners' Equity**	Building	160,000	**Owners' Equity**	
		No effect	Land	40,000	Common stock	150,000
					Retained earnings	70,000

In all four Co. P balance sheets, current assets decreased by the amount paid for Co. S less the current assets acquired. Acquisitions accounted for as purchases can also be effected by issuing debt, common stock, preferred stock, or any combination of different types of consideration. The financial statement effects of these various types of financing are similar except for the accounting for the debt or equity claim issued.

EXAMPLE 4 Journal Entries—Co. P Books

Assuming Co. S is dissolved (Merger):		
Case 1—$300,000 paid:		
Current Assets	120,000	
Building	200,000	
Land	50,000	
Goodwill	30,000	
Liabilities		100,000
Cash		300,000
Case 2—$230,000 paid:		
Current Assets	120,000	
Building	168,000	
Land	42,000	
Liabilities		100,000
Cash		230,000
Assuming Co. S remains as a separate legal entity (Parent/subsidiary relationship):		
Case 1—$300,000 paid:		
Investment in Co. S	300,000	
Cash		300,000
Case 2—$230,000 paid:		
Investment in Co. S	230,000	
Cash		230,000

Reporting Goodwill in Financial Statements

Exhibit 11 illustrates how goodwill is reported in financial statements for Safeway, Inc.

EXHIBIT 11 Safeway Inc. Partial Balance Sheet and Note Information

Partial Balance Sheet Information (in millions)	**1998**	**1997**
Total property, net	$5,182.6	$4,115.3
Goodwill, net of accumulated amortization of $211.0 and $157.0	3,348.0	1,824.7

Note A (in part): The Company and significant accounting policies

Goodwill

Goodwill was $3.3 billion at year-end 1998 and $1.8 billion at year-end 1997, and is being amortized on a straight-line basis over its estimated useful life. If it became probable that the projected future undiscounted cash flows of acquired assets were less than the carrying value of the goodwill, Safeway would recognize an impairment loss in accordance with the provision of SFAS No. 121.

Goodwill amortization was $56.3 million in 1998, $41.8 million in 1997 and $10.4 million in 1996. Goodwill and related amortization has increased due to the Vons Merger and Dominick's Acquisition as discussed in Note B.

Goodwill Impairment

Goodwill, like other assets, must be assessed at balance sheet dates for impairment (see Chapter 6 for a discussion of impairment accounting). As an intangible asset, no market exists in which goodwill can be sold. Therefore, in making the impairment decision, a firm must use estimated future cash flows in determining whether goodwill has been impaired. The steps in determining whether an asset impairment has occurred when fair market values of the asset are not obtainable are briefly reviewed below.

1. Compute total future, undiscounted net cash flows associated with the asset.
2. If total undiscounted net cash flows are greater than the asset's book value, no impairment is deemed to have occurred.
3. If total undiscounted net cash flows are less than the asset's book value, an impairment is deemed to have occurred. An impairment charge is recognized equal to the amount of the book value of the asset minus the *present value* of the future, net cash flows associated with the asset.

Exhibit 12 disclosures for Quanex Corporation illustrate goodwill impairment. In 1998, Quanex took a $51.2 million charge for goodwill impairment.

EXHIBIT 12 Quanex Corporation Partial Financial Statement Information Related to Goodwill Impairment

Balance Sheet (in thousands)	1998	1997
Goodwill, net	$52,281	$91,496

Note 1 (in part): Significant Accounting Policies
Long-Lived Assets

Goodwill represents the excess of the purchase price over the fair value of acquired companies and is being amortized on a straight-line basis over forty years for the goodwill resulting from the acquisition of Nichols Homeshield in 1989, and over twenty-five years for the goodwill resulting from the acquisitions of Piper Impact, Inc., in 1996, Piper Impact Europe B.V. in 1997, and Nichols Aluminum-Alabama, Inc., in 1998 (see Note 2). At October 31, 1998 and 1997, accumulated amortization was $9,255,000 and $10,398,000, respectively. During the fourth quarter of 1998, the balance of goodwill associated with Piper Impact was written off in accordance with Statement of Financial Accounting Standard No. 121 (see Note 4).

Note 4 (in part): Piper Impact Impairment Disclosure

During the year ended October 31, 1998, the Company recorded a restructuring charge of $58.5 million related to its subsidiary, Piper Impact. Components of this special charge included $51.2 million for goodwill impairment . . .

Consolidated Statements Subsequent to the Date of Acquisition

8 Explain how financial statements for parent/subsidiary entities would be prepared in years after the date of acquisition.

If an acquisition results in two separate legal entities, then two sets of accounting records will be maintained. At financial statement reporting dates, the two sets of records must be combined to create consolidated financial statements for the single entity. In *form,* two companies exist, but the *economic substance* is that one economic entity exists because the parent *owns* the subsidiary. Although the detailed procedures for such a consolidation are beyond the scope of this text, the basic idea is that the financial statements are combined to simulate a merger in which only the parent company remains. Several issues must be addressed in the consolidation process:

- Any excess price paid over the fair values of a subsidiary's net assets in an acquisition accounted for as a purchase.
- The consolidation of the results of operations for the year.
- The recognition of minority interests arising from less than 100% ownership.

Excess Price The excess price paid by the investor at acquisition to acquire the investee's common stock represents (1) the difference between the subsidiary's book values and fair values of identifiable assets, and (2) the amount of goodwill. Because these differences have not been formally recognized in the accounting records of either company (remember that they were aggregated with other items into Investment in Co. S in the parent/subsidiary example shown previously), the differences must be added in when the balance sheets of the parent and subsidiary are combined (the investment account is eliminated in the process to avoid double counting). This process creates consolidated numbers based on what the parent company paid for net assets.

Consolidating Results of Operations Consolidating the results of operations for the year involves (1) adding the subsidiary's income statement (line by line) to the parent's income statement, (2) removing the effects of any intercompany transactions, and (3) recording amortizations of any excess of purchase price paid over the sum of the identifiable assets computed at the date of acquisition. Because neither company's books record fair value/book value differences, neither do the companies amortize such differences when computing income. As we discussed previously in this chapter, for equity method investments, proper computation of parent company income requires amortizations of any excess paid at acquisition as a reduction of that income.

Income from continuing operations for the consolidated enterprise includes all revenues of both the parent and the subsidiary. Logically, income from continuing operations should also include all of the allocated costs (i.e., expenses) of assets acquired to generate those revenues. If a parent pays a premium to acquire the assets of the subsidiary resulting in the recording of goodwill, then goodwill amortization expense will be reported. Because the goodwill amortization represents an allocated cost of an asset used to generate revenues reported as part of income from continuing operations, then it should be reported as a reduction of income from continuing operations. Under current GAAP, goodwill amortization expense is reported above income from continuing operations, and thus reduces that income statement line item.

As of the writing of this text, acquisition accounting is undergoing a great deal of change. Currently, the FASB is proposing a change for goodwill amortization that would accord goodwill amortization expense special "net of tax" treatment in the income from continuing operations calculation:[16]

Sales revenue	$XXX
Cost of goods sold	(XXX)
Gross margin	$XXX
Operating expenses	(XXX)
Operating income	$XXX
Other financial revenues (expenses), gains and (losses)	XXX
Income before taxes and goodwill amortization	$XXX
Income tax expense	(XXX)
Income before goodwill amortization	$XXX
Goodwill amortization, net of tax	(XXX)
Income from continuing operations	$XXX
Discontinued operations, net of tax	XXX
Extraordinary items, net of tax	XXX
Accounting changes, net of tax	XXX
Net income	$XXX

Although goodwill amortization is still a component of income from continuing operations, the special net of tax treatment is the same treatment given to transitory

16. "Business Combinations and Intangible Assets," *Proposed Statement of Financial Accounting Standards* (Financial Accounting Standards Board, September 7, 1999).

items (e.g., discontinued operations, extraordinary items) and cosmetic items (e.g., accounting changes). Therefore, a potential danger of the proposed disclosure is the misinterpretation of the permanence of the expense. In our opinion, goodwill amortization is not transitory if there was a sound economic basis for the purchaser to pay the premium. That is, in an arms-length transaction, two parties established what would have to be paid to acquire a group of assets to generate a given amount of revenue. There is no reason to expect that they can pay less in the future to generate additional future revenues. Therefore, when those future acquisition costs are allocated to future periods, the current level of expenses will persist.

9 Identify the effects of minority interests on consolidated financial statements.

Minority Interests Finally, consolidation procedures require the recognition of minority interest if the parent owns less than 100% of the subsidiary. If a parent owns only 90% of a subsidiary, minority shareholders represent a 10% claim against assets. Thus, minority shareholders represent a third claim against subsidiary assets, along with debt holders and majority equity holders (i.e., the parent that holds 90% of the equity). These minority shareholders also have a 10% claim against the income of the subsidiary.

Several different theories exist on how consolidated financial statements should be prepared. The parent theory is predominantly used in practice. Under this approach, the income and equity of the consolidated entity reflect the parent's interest. Therefore, minority interest in net income is deducted in arriving at consolidated net income, and minority interest in net assets is reported between liabilities and equities on the balance sheet.[17]

Financial Statement Analysis: Southwest Airlines

The 1998 financial statements for Southwest Airlines (Appendix C) contain no information about investments in trading or available-for-sale equity security investments. In Note 1, Summary of Significant Accounting Policies, Basis of Presentation, Southwest reports that consolidated financial statements for Southwest and wholly-owned subsidiaries are presented. Because Southwest's subsidiaries are wholly-owned, no minority interest appears in the balance sheet. Goodwill is not identified on the balance sheet or in the accompanying notes.[18]

The External Decision Maker's View of Investments in Equity Securities

Many investments in equity securities are strategic in nature. Ownership of large equity stakes creates influence and control over suppliers and customers. Accordingly, external decision makers view equity ownership in conjunction with corporate strategy. For example, equity ownership in a distributor might be important to a company entering new markets and requiring improved distribution channels. Similarly, the desire to leverage management industry expertise in health care might lead to large equity stakes in health maintenance organizations or hospitals.

Chapter Summary

Primarily, investments in the stock of other firms are made to generate excess cash flow equal to the risk-adjusted expected return on the investment. The actual conversion of that return into cash depends on the timing of dividends paid by investee

17. Minority interest is not a liability because it has no maturity date. Also, it is not equity under the view that the parent is the owner of the consolidated entity. Therefore, it is reported between debt and equity (i.e., a "mezzanine" disclosure). The 1999 *Accounting Trends & Techniques* reports that of 600 companies surveyed, 155 separately reported minority interests in the balance sheet after liabilities.
18. Although this information is not available in the 1998 financial statements, in a highly publicized transaction in December 1993, Southwest acquired 100% of the stock of Morris Air Corporation and accounted for the transaction as a pooling of interests.

companies and the liquidation of the investment by the investor company's management. The method used to record investments in common stock depends upon the extent of influence obtained by the investor: cost method (no significant influence); equity method (significant influence); consolidation (control). Investments in noncommon stock securities are not presumed to convey significant influence or control; thus, neither the equity method nor consolidation are appropriate.

The accounting for investments recorded using the *cost method* is largely determined by management intent. Different revenue recognition procedures are used for equity securities depending on whether the securities are classified as short-term trading securities or available-for-sale securities, which is the default category. Changes in market values of securities held for the purpose of short-term trading are reflected in current income. Changes in market values of securities that management intends to hold for longer periods (i.e., available-for-sale securities) are reported as adjustments to owners' equity, and thus, are not reported in current income. Equity securities may *not* be classified as held-to-maturity securities.

An additional reason for larger investments in the stock of other firms is to exercise influence or control. The *equity method* ensures that this influence does not result in investor manipulation of net income by strategic timing of investee dividend distributions. The investor records investment revenue and the corresponding increase in the investment as the investee records net income, not as the investee distributes dividends. Investee dividend distributions reduce the investor's investment account. Investments accounted for using the equity method may not be treated as trading or available-for-sale securities.

Business combinations may be effected in three different ways: *merger* (parent remains and subsidiary dissolved); *consolidation* (parent and subsidiary are both dissolved and a single new entity emerges); and *parent/subsidiary relationship* (both parent and subsidiary remain as separate entities after a business combination). Under proposed new accounting standards, only the *purchase method* can be used to record a business combination. Acquired net assets are revalued to their fair values. Goodwill results from almost all purchase transactions because the book value of net assets is normally less than the fair value of net assets.

If a parent company has control over a subsidiary, consolidated financial statements are prepared by combining the separate statements for the investor (parent) and investee (subsidiary) companies, which are separate *legal* entities.

Key Terms

business combinations 301
cost method 291
consolidation 302
control 291
equity method 298
goodwill 299
merger 302
parent/subsidiary relationship 302
pooling of interests 303
purchase transaction 303
significant influence 291

Questions

Q1. **Common Stock Investments.** What are the three methods used to account for investments in common stock based upon the extent of influence that the investor has on the investee company? What determines which classification is used? How does each method treat investee dividends and investee net income?

Q2. **Investments in Common Stock.** A company's investment in common stocks may be less than 20%, from 20%–50%, or greater than 50%. Explain how these ownership percentages match up with the methods of accounting for investments based upon default percentages specified by the FASB.

Q3. **Investments in Equity Securities.** What are the possible classifications of investments in equity securities under *SFAS No. 115*?

Q4. **Investments in Equity Securities; the Equity Method.** How are investments in common stock accounted for under the equity method classified under *SFAS No. 115*?

Q5. **Investments in Equity Securities; Fair Market Value Not Determinable.** Spike Co. has an investment in the common stock of Circle Co. The investment does not give Spike significant influence or control over Circle, and the stock is not publicly traded so that a fair market value cannot be obtained. How is the investment accounted for? What are the financial statement effects?

Q6. **Available-for-Sale Securities.** How could management manage earnings by using *SFAS No. 115* accounting for available-for-sale securities?

Q7. **Unrealized Gains and Losses.** Describe how unrealized gains and losses are reported in the financial statements on both trading securities and available-for-sale securities.

Q8. **Equity Method Investments.** Briefly describe the accounting process for equity securities accounted for under the equity method.

Q9. **Business Combinations.** At the time of a business combination, the parties must settle on a legal structure that relates to whether the parent and/or subsidiary survive after the combination and whether a new corporation will be created. What are the three ways of effecting a business combination? Briefly describe how each structure affects the investee and investor companies.

Q10. **Purchase versus Pooling of Interests.** Compare and contrast the accounting ramifications of the purchase method versus the pooling of interests method of accounting for a business combination. In general, which method would a business prefer? Why?

Q11. **Impairment.** List the steps that must be periodically used to assess whether goodwill has been impaired.

Q12. **Consolidated Financial Statements.** When a parent owns 100% of a subsidiary's common stock, what process does the parent follow to prepare year-end consolidated financial statements?

Q13. **Minority Interest.** What is a minority interest, and why does it arise?

Short Problems

1. **Investments in Common Stock.** On January 1, 2001, the Sohn Co. purchased 100,000 shares of Benard Co. $5 par common stock at $30 per share. On January 1, 2001, Benard had 800,000 shares of common stock outstanding, and the fair market value of Benard's net assets equaled the book value of the net assets. During 2001, Benard reported net income of $50,000,000, and declared and paid dividends of $4,000,000. At December 31, 2001, Benard's common stock sold for $32 per share.

   a. *Assuming that the purchase did not give Sohn significant influence,* describe the financial statement effects of (1) the purchase, (2) Benard's reporting net income, (3) Benard's declaration and payment of dividends, and (4) the December 31, 2001, increase in market value of stock.

   Journal Entry Option: Prepare the annual 2001 journal entries to reflect these effects.

   b. *Assuming that the purchase gave Sohn significant influence,* describe the financial statement effects of (1) the purchase, (2) Benard's reporting net income, (3) Benard's declaration and payment of dividends, and (4) the December 31, 2001, increase in market value of stock.

   Journal Entry Option: Prepare the annual 2001 journal entries to reflect these effects.

   c. How would your answer to (a) change if the stock did not have a readily determinable fair market value at December 31, 2001?

2. **Investments and Earnings Management.** On December 31, 2001, the Cox Co. owns the following available-for-sale security investments.

	Cost	Market Value
Hill preferred stock	$5,000,000	$6,200,000
Taylor common stock	4,000,000	4,000,000
Dean common stock	5,500,000	3,600,000

   Cox needs to raise at least $3,550,000 by selling one of the investments. The Company intends to keep the other two investments. Write a brief memo to the chief financial officer indicating the pros and cons of selling each security. Ignore any income tax consequences.

3. **Available-for-Sale Securities.** On October 1, 2001, Manning Co. purchased 100,000 shares of Volunteers Co. common stock at $25 per share, incurring transactions costs of $1.00 per share. Manning classifies the security as available-for-sale. On December 31, 2001, and 2002, the fair value of the stock was $22 and $29 per share, respectively. In March 2003, Manning sold the Volunteers stock for $30 per share. During the 2001–2003 period, the Volunteers's stock was Manning's only investment in common stock.

a. At what value would Manning record the investment on October 1, 2001? On December 31, 2001 and 2002?
b. Describe all financial statement effects of the sale of the Volunteers stock in 2003.

Journal Entry Option: Prepare the journal entries to record Manning's investment on October 1, 2001. Also, in relation to this investment, prepare the annual adjusting journal entries on December 31, 2001 and 2002, and the 2003 journal entry related to its sale.

4. **Cost versus Equity Methods.** On January 1, 2001, Kulsrud Co. purchased 100,000 shares of the common stock of Jamison Co. at $20 per share, including transactions costs. The purchase represented 10% of Jamison's outstanding common stock. Kulsrud intends to treat this investment as an intermediate to long-term investment. On January 1, 2001, the book value of Jamison's net assets equaled $20,000,000. (*Note:* To simplify this problem, the purchase price is set equal to Kulsrud's pro rata share of Jamison's net assets.) During 2001, Jamison reported net income of $8,000,000, and declared and paid $1,000,000 in dividends. At December 31, 2001, Jamison's common stock sold for $23 per share. Ignoring income tax effects, show the effects of this transaction on the 2001 balance sheet, income statement, and statement of comprehensive income for each of the assumptions below. Use the provided format to present your answers.
   a. Kulsrud's investment does not provide significant influence over Jamison.
   b. Kulsrud's investment provides significant influence over Jamison.

	Assumption A	Assumption B
Income Statement Effects		
Other income, (expenses), gains, and (losses)		
Dividend income		
Equity in subsidiary net income (losses)		
Comprehensive Income Effects		
Net income		
Other comprehensive income		
Unrealized gain (loss), available-for-sale securities		
Balance Sheet Effects		
Cash		
Long-term investments		
Stockholders' equity		
Retained earnings		
Accumulated other comprehensive income		

Journal Entry Option: Prepare Kulsrud's 2001 summary accounting journal entries to reflect its investment in Jamison's common stock for both (a) and (b).

5. **Cost versus Equity Methods.** On January 1, 2001, Neal Co. purchased 250,000 shares of the common stock of Bonser Co. at $8 per share, including transactions costs. The purchase represented 10% of Bonser's outstanding common stock. Neal intends to treat this investment as an intermediate to long-term investment. On January 1, 2001, the book value of Bonser's net assets equaled $2,000,000. (*Note:* To simplify this problem, the purchase price is set equal to Neal's pro rata share of Bonser's net assets.) During 2001, Bonser reported net income of $600,000, and declared and paid $50,000 in dividends. At December 31, 2001, Bonser's common stock sold for $7 per share. Ignoring income tax effects, show the effects of this transaction on the 2001 balance sheet, income statement, and statement of comprehensive income for each of the assumptions below. Use the provided format to present your answers.
   a. Neal's investment does not provide significant influence over Bonser.
   b. Neal's investment provides significant influence over Bonser.

	Assumption A	Assumption B
Income Statement Effects		
Other income, (expenses), gains, and (losses)		
Dividend income		
Equity in subsidiary net income (losses)		

(continued)

(concluded)	Assumption A	Assumption B
Comprehensive Income Effects		
Net income		
Other comprehensive income		
Unrealized gain (loss), available-for-sale securities		
Balance Sheet Effects		
Cash		
Long-term investments		
Stockholders' equity		
Retained earnings		
Accumulated other comprehensive income		

Journal Entry Option: Prepare Neal's 2001 summary accounting journal entries to reflect its investment in Bonser's common stock for both (a) and (b).

6. **Investments in Common Stock, Equity Method.** On January 1, 2001, Jones Co. purchased 100,000 shares of Chaney Co.'s common stock for $15 per share, paying $30,000 in commissions. The purchase represents 30% of Chaney's outstanding stock and gives Jones significant influence over Chaney. Compute the amount that would appear on Jones' December 31, 2001, balance sheet under the following independent scenarios.
   a. Chaney reports 2001 net income of $3,000,000, and declares and pays dividends of $400,000.
   b. Chaney reports 2001 net income of $2,500,000, and declares (but does not pay) dividends of $300,000.
   c. Chaney reports a 2001 net loss of $1,000,000, and declares and pays dividends of $200,000.

Journal Entry Option: For each scenario, record the summary accounting journal entries to reflect the investment, the dividends, and the pro rata share of investee net income.

7. **Available-for-Sale Securities: Earnings Management.** The Guidroz Co. had the following investments in available-for-sale securities on December 1. On December 10, Jane Lambert, Guidroz's CFO, informs you that the company is $500,000 under budgeted net income for the year ended December 31, and asks your advice on ways to make budget. (Assume that Guidroz's effective tax rate is 40%.) Using the information below, draft a brief memo to Ms. Lambert about how available-for-sale securities might be used to meet budget.

Security		Historical Cost	Fair Market Value December 1
Davis common stock	100,000 shares	$2,000,000	$3,000,000
Cook common stock	50,000 shares	2,500,000	2,300,000
Condermaz preferred stock	10,000 shares	800,000	1,000,000
Payne stock warrants	500,000 warrants	500,000	750,000
		$5,800,000	$7,050,000

8. **Business Combinations.** Using the following chart, indicate for each scenario whether the business combination is a merger, consolidation, or parent/subsidiary relationship.

Scenario	Type of Business Combination
(1) Smith Co. purchased 100% of the common stock of Jones Co. for cash. After the acquisition, Jones Co. was dissolved.	
(2) Snyder Co. purchased 95% of the common stock of Phelps Co. for cash. Immediately after acquisition, Snyder and Phelps were dissolved, and a new entity, Snyder-Phelps, was created. All the assets owned by the former Snyder and Phelps were transferred to Snyder-Phelps.	
(3) Tsay Co. purchased 100% of the common stock of Ho Company solely in exchange for 1,000,000 shares of Tsay's common stock. After the transaction, Tsay and Ho continued to function as separate entities.	

a. For which of the transactions is it possible that the acquiring firm could use the pooling method? Why?
b. For which of the transactions would the company prepare consolidated financial statements at year-end? Why?
c. In which transaction(s) would consolidated financial statements reflect a minority interest? Why?

9. **Purchase Accounting.** On July 1, 2001, Pratt Co. acquired 100% of the outstanding common stock of Maines Co. in exchange for Pratt common stock valued at $15,000,000. On that date, Maines had total assets of $10,000,000; total liabilities of $2,000,000; total paid-in-capital of $1,000,000; and retained earnings of $7,000,000. The fair value of Maines' total liabilities is $2,000,000, and the fair value of Maines' total assets is $12,000,000. Both companies continue to exist after the transaction, and Pratt will prepare year-end consolidated financial statements. Assuming that the *purchase method* is used, at what value will Pratt record its investment in Maines? If Pratt prepares consolidated financial statements immediately after the acquisition, how much goodwill will be shown?

10. **Business Combination Accounted for as a Merger.** On January 1, 2001, Anderson Co. acquired 100% of the net assets of Burgoon Co. in a business combination accounted for as a merger (i.e., Burgoon was dissolved). Anderson issued 1,300,000 shares of $1 par common stock valued at $25 per share. Immediately before the acquisition, Anderson and Burgoon showed the balance sheet amounts provided below. Within Burgoon's property, plant, and equipment, depreciable assets, with a book value of $12,000,000 and a fair market value of $18,000,000, had a remaining depreciable life of five years. All other Burgoon assets had book values equal to market values.

		Burgoon	
	Anderson	**Book Value**	**Fair Value**
Current assets	$200,000,000	$ 4,000,000	$ 4,000,000
Property, plant, and equipment	410,000,000	25,000,000	31,000,000
Total assets	$610,000,000	$29,000,000	
Current liabilities	$ 10,000,000	$ 1,500,000	$ 1,500,000
Long-term liabilities	150,000,000	7,500,000	7,500,000
Stockholders' equity			
Common stock	10,000,000	5,000,000	
Additional paid-in-capital	190,000,000	4,000,000	
Retained earnings	250,000,000	11,000,000	
Total liabilities and stockholders' equity	$610,000,000	$29,000,000	

Under purchase accounting, prepare Anderson's balance sheet immediately after the acquisition.

Journal Entry Option: Prepare the journal entry on Anderson's books to record the merger.

11. **Business Combination Accounted for as a Parent/Subsidiary.** Assume the same information as in Problem 10, except that the business combination was effected to have a parent/subsidiary relationship (i.e., Burgoon was not dissolved). Prepare Anderson's balance sheet immediately after the acquisition.

Journal Entry Option: Prepare the journal entry on Anderson's books to record the transaction.

12. **Goodwill Impairment.** On December 31, the Rabin Co. had goodwill of $4,000,000. As part of the year-end auditing process, the accounting staff conducted a review to determine whether the goodwill had been impaired. For each of the following situations, indicate the appropriate accounting treatment in the year-end financial statements.
    a. The accounting staff estimates that future cash flows associated with goodwill (assumed to occur at year-end) will be $600,000 per year for the next 10 years and the appropriate discount rate is 8%.
    b. The accounting staff estimates that future cash flows associated with goodwill (assumed to occur at year-end) will be $300,000 per year for the next 10 years and the appropriate discount rate is 8%.

Journal Entry Option: Prepare any year-end accounting journal entries to record goodwill impairment.

Analytical and Comprehensive Problems

http://

13. **Financial Statement Analysis: Texas Instruments.** Complete 1998 Texas Instruments financial statements are available at the text Web site at http://baginski.swcollege.com. Review the assets section of the balance sheet (current asset short-term investments and noncurrent asset investments); the investing activities section of the statement of cash flows related to investments; the 1998 Results of Operations subsection of the MD&A; and three footnotes: Accounting Policies and Practices, Cash Equivalents and Short-Term Investments, and Investments.
    a. What were the December 31, 1998, amounts (if any) of investments in equity securities in (1) cash and short-term investments and (2) noncurrent asset investments? Are the equity securities classified as trading or available-for-sale?
    b. Compute the ratio of short-term investments to total assets for both 1998 and 1997.
    c. Reconcile the change in short-term investments from 1997 to 1998. Note the amounts expended to purchase short-term investments and the amounts received for sales and maturities of short-term investments (it is possible that the information provided does not allow for an exact reconciliation).

14. **Equity Method—Fair Value of Net Assets at Acquisition Equals Book Value.** On January 1, 2001, Philipich Co. purchased 30% of the outstanding common stock of McConnell Co. in an open market transaction for $5,000,000. On that date, the book value of McConnell's net assets was $15,000,000. The book values of all identifiable net assets were equal to the fair values. During 2001, McConnell reported net income of $2,000,000, and declared dividends of $400,000. Compute the following in McConnell's December 31, 2001, financial statements: net investment, investment income (i.e., equity in subsidiary net income), dividend income, and goodwill amortization expense. Any unrecorded goodwill should be amortized by McConnell over 20 years.

    Journal Entry Option: Prepare any 2001 summary annual journal entries related to the investment.

15. **Equity Method—Fair Value of Net Assets at Acquisition Exceeds Book Value.** On January 1, 2001, Philipich Co. purchased 30% of the outstanding common stock of McConnell Co. in an open market transaction for $5,000,000. On that date, the book value of McConnell's net assets was $15,000,000. The book value of all net assets was equal to the fair values except that depreciable assets with a book value of $1,000,000 were undervalued by $500,000. The undervalued assets have an estimated useful life of five years. During 2001, McConnell reported net income of $2,000,000, and declared dividends of $400,000. Compute the following in McConnell's December 31, 2001, financial statements: net investment, investment income (i.e., equity in subsidiary net income), dividend income, goodwill amortization expense, and any other adjustments. Any unrecorded goodwill should be amortized by McConnell over 20 years.

    Journal Entry Option: Prepare any 2001 annual journal entries related to the investment.

16. **Investments in Equity and Debt Securities (Encompasses Chapters 7 and 8).** At December 31, 2001, Worley Co. owned 4,000 shares of Phillips common stock, which represented 1% of Phillips' outstanding common stock. Worley classified the investment as available-for-sale. Worley acquired the shares at $25 per share; Phillips' common stock traded at $27 per share on December 31, 2001. Worley Co. had no other investments in debt or equity securities on January 1, 2002. During 2002, Worley had activity related to investments in debt and equity securities as indicated below. Assume that Worley's 2002 net income was $8,000,000, which properly reflected all accounting for investments in debt and equity securities. *Note: This comprehensive problem also includes investments in debt securities, which were discussed in Chapter 7. Combining debt and equity securities into the same problem more clearly reflects business experience. Students who have not completed Chapter 7 should not complete this problem.*

Security	Fair Value December 31, 2002
• On January 1, 2002, acquired Jackson Co. commercial paper at a cost of $14,600 with a maturity value of $15,000 on March 1, 2002. The security was classified as trading.	N/A
• On July 1, 2002, purchased five-year, 8% bonds from Owen Co. The bonds are due on July 1, 2007, have a $5,000,000 maturity value, and were purchased for $4,600,000 (including transactions costs of $100,000). The bonds pay interest semiannually on July 1 and January 1. Worley properly classified this investment as held-to-maturity.	Annual market rate of interest is 11%
• On January 1, 2002, purchased 500,000 shares of Rogers common stock at $10 per share. This purchase represented 30% of Rogers stock and provides Worley significant influence. During 2002, Rogers reported net income of $1,000,000, and declared and paid dividends of $300,000.	$12 per share
• On July 1, 2002, purchased seven-year, 7% bonds from Kulsrud. The bonds are due on July 1, 2009, have a $2,000,000 maturity value, and were purchased for $2,200,000. The bonds pay interest semiannually on June 30 and December 31. Worley properly classified this investment as available-for-sale.	Annual market rate of interest is 5%
• November 1, 2002, acquired 1,000 shares of Stern common stock at $40 per share as a trading security. Stern paid a $3 per share dividend on December 15.	$45 per share
• During 2002, Phillips reported net income of $3,000,000, and declared and paid dividends of $500,000. (Worley owned 4,000 shares at December 31, 2001.)	$24 per share

Use the following partial financial statements to show the December 31, 2002, financial statement effects of these securities and any related 2002 transactions.

WORLEY CO.
Statement of Cash Flows
For the Year Ended December 31, 2002
(Effects of investments only)
(Cash outflows in parentheses)

Operating Activities

Investing Activities

WORLEY CO.
Income Statement
For the Year Ended December 31, 2002
(Effects of investments only)

Other revenues (expenses), gains and (losses)

WORLEY CO.
Statement of Comprehensive Income
For the Year Ended December 31, 2002
(Effects of investments only)

Net income
Other comprehensive income

WORLEY CO.
Balance Sheet
December 31, 2002
(Effects of investments only)

Assets	
Current assets	
Cash	
Trading securities, at cost	
Allowance to adjust to market	
Trading securities, at market	
Interest receivable	
Long-term investments and funds	
Available-for-sale equity securities, at cost	
Allowance to adjust to market	
Available-for-sale equity securities, at market	
Available-for-sale debt securities, at face value	
Bond premium	
Available-for-sale debt securities, at amortized cost	
Allowance to adjust to market	
Available-for-sale debt securities, at market	
Investments accounted for using the equity method	
Held-to-maturity securities, at face value	
Bond discount	
Held-to-maturity securities, at amortized cost	
Total effect on assets	
Owners' Equity	
Retained earnings, ignoring income taxes	
Accumulated other comprehensive income	
Unrealized gains (losses)	
Total effect on owners' equity	

CFA Exam-Type Problems

17. Brown Co. accounts for its investment in Blue, Inc., under the equity method. Brown's investment in Blue: (CFA adapted)
    a. is carried at cost.
    b. is carried at cost plus dividends received.
    c. may generate income without a corresponding cash flow.
    d. is written down to market value if the investment should fall below cost.

18. Marketable equity securities carried as long-term investments and representing less than 50% but more than 20% of the voting stock are: (CFA adapted, with slight modifications by authors)
    a. valued at market, with increases or decreases in portfolio value reflected directly in the equity section.
    b. treated the same as trading securities, but are valued and reported as a separate portfolio.
    c. valued at market, with increases or decreases in portfolio value reflected in net income.
    d. accounted for under the equity method, unless there is evidence of inability to exercise significant influence over the investee.

19. Which of the following categories of marketable securities must a company carry at fair value on the balance sheet? (CFA adapted, with slight modifications by authors)
    I. Trading securities
    II. Held-to-maturity securities
    III. Controlling securities
    IV. Available-for-sale securities

    a. I and II only.

b. I and IV only.
c. II, III, and IV only.
d. I, II, III, and IV.

20. Which of the following *correctly* classifies (as operating or investing cash flow) interest received, dividends received, and interest paid? (CFA adapted) *Note: This problem uses information from Chapters 3, 7, and 8.*

	Interest Received	Dividends Received	Interest Paid
a.	Operating	Operating	Operating
b.	Operating	Operating	Investing
c.	Operating	Investing	Investing
d.	Investing	Investing	Investing

21. In a business combination, how should the assets and liabilities of the acquired corporation be recorded under each of the following? (CFA adapted)

	Pooling-of-Interests	Purchase
a.	Fair market value	Book value
b.	Book value	Book value
c.	Fair market value	Fair market value
d.	Book value	Fair market value

Objectives

1 Review cash flows and other financial statement effects related to investments in debt and equity securities.

2 Review cash flows and other financial statement effects related to investments in long-lived operational assets.

3 Describe the effects of investments on the financial ratios identified in Module A.

4 Identify the balance sheet and income statement adjustments made by many financial analysts in the process of analyzing the effects of investments on the profitability and risk of the firm.

The External Users' Assessment of Investing Activities

In this module, we review the cash flow effects of investing activities and several important profitability and risk ratios affected by these activities. We also discuss the issues faced by financial analysts in interpreting investment activities and the adjustments many analysts make to understand the core operations of the firm. Financial analysts make adjustments to GAAP-based financial statements for several reasons: (1) to facilitate comparisons with companies that use different methods; (2) to incorporate information not present in the body of the financial statements (e.g., using note information to adjust the balance sheet of a lessee to capitalize lease assets and obligations); and (3) to make adjustments related to assessments of items such as *quality of earnings* and *persistence of earnings*. Evaluating the quality of earnings is of particular importance when investing activities are present.

The Effects of Investing Activities on Cash Flows—A Review

1 Review cash flows and other financial statement effects related to investments in debt and equity securities.

A firm's cash inflows and outflows are important both in profitability and risk analysis and in firm valuation. Free cash flows are generated by operating activities and are reduced by investing activities. Because of the importance of investing cash flows in this regard, the first section of this module reviews several sources and uses of cash related to investing activities reported in the statement of cash flows. Because investing in the debt and equity securities of other firms is a peripheral activity, while investing in property, plant, and equipment (PP&E), natural resources, and intangible assets is a core activity, separate analysis of the two kinds of activities is warranted.

Cash Outflows: Investing in the Debt and Equity of Other Firms

Cash used to acquire debt and equity securities and to invest in notes receivable is reported as a cash outflow from investing activities in the statement of cash flows.[1] Classification as an investing activity is appropriate regardless of the degree of influence that the investment represents. Investors closely analyze cash flows related to investing activities. Is this the best use of a company's cash flow? Remember that the company *could* pay dividends to investors who could, in turn, make investments with the risk and return characteristics that they seek. Investments that reflect a long-term strategic alliance yield an expectation of some competitive advantage that might sustain earnings growth.

Cash Inflows: Investing in the Debt and Equity of Other Firms

One major benefit of holding investments in other firms is the expected receipt of periodic interest (on debt investments) and dividends (on investments in common and preferred stock). Because transactions giving rise to these periodic cash increases are investment transactions, one would expect that the interest and dividend receipts would also be classified as investing transactions. However, GAAP requires interest and dividend receipts from investments recorded using the cost method (Chapter 8) to be classified as operating activities because the accrual counterparts, interest revenue and dividend revenue, are part of net income. This operating activity classification occurs because the FASB desires the operating section of the statement of cash flows to be considered the cash flow counterpart of income from continuing operations.

When investments are sold or when debt matures, a cash inflow equal to the proceeds from sale or maturity is realized. This cash flow is reported as an inflow from investing activities because it represents a change in the principal amount of the investment. The one exception to the investing activity classification is that sales of trading securities are classified as operating cash inflows.

For a parent/subsidiary, the parent ownership of more than 50% of subsidiary common shares requires the preparation of a consolidated statement of cash flows. In this case, the individual cash flow statements of the parent and the subsidiary are added together to arrive at consolidated cash flows. Thus, as noted above, the investing activities section reports the acquisition of a more than 50% owned subsidiary, but the operating activities section reports the realization of cash from using the assets acquired.

Cash Outflows: Investing Internally in PP&E, Natural Resources, and Intangible Assets

2 Review cash flows and other financial statement effects related to investments in long-lived operational assets.

When cash payments are made to acquire property, plant, and equipment, natural resources, or intangible assets, a cash outflow is reported in the investing section of the statement of cash flows. As noted in Module B, debt or equity securities are occasionally issued in exchange for an investment instead of paying cash (e.g., issue common stock in direct exchange for land and buildings). The direct exchange of debt or equity securities to acquire another investment is reported in a separate *noncash transactions* schedule that accompanies the statement of cash flows. The analyst can use the information in this schedule to adjust the

1. Recall that an investment made in a debt or equity security classified as trading is not classified as an investing activity. Cash flows related to trading securities are classified as operating activities. Temporary investments lead to the belief that either future dividends or internal investments are planned with the cash to be generated from near-term sale of the temporary investment.

statement of cash flows to show a cash inflow from financing and a cash outflow from investing.

Cash outflows from internal investments are an important area for scrutiny by investors and analysts. These cash flows are not available for dividends, but are incurred with the hope of generating cash inflows for the firm that will be available to the investor in the form of dividends in the future. From these investments, an analyst can understand the average position of the firm in its product life cycle. Using cash flow for internal investment is generally the highest in a company's introduction and growth stages, and it levels off and declines during maturity and decline stages.

Cash Inflows: Investing Internally in PP&E, Natural Resources, and Intangible Assets

Cash inflows from PP&E, natural resources, and intangible assets are realized in two ways: the productive assets are *used* to generate operating cash inflows, and on occasion, the productive assets are *sold* either during or at the end of their useful life. Cash inflows from using productive assets are considered to be operating cash flows because they affect the accountant's computation of operating income (e.g., cash inflow from the sale of inventory created by using long-lived assets has sales revenue as an accrual counterpart). Cash inflows from the sale of productive assets are considered investing transactions because, as in the sale of investments in other firms, sales of productive assets are changes in the principal amounts of such assets.

Statement of Cash Flows: GAAP Rules and Classification

When costs are incurred, accountants must decide whether to capitalize or expense the costs. That is, they must decide whether economic benefits have been created that extend beyond the current period or whether the benefits are related to the current period only. If the costs are capitalized, the amount of long-lived assets changes, and the cash flow portion of the costs is classified as an investing activity. If the costs are expensed, net income is affected, and the cash flow portion of the costs is classified as an operating activity.

The decision to capitalize versus expense is fundamental to all cash outlay situations. In two specific cases, the FASB prescribes accounting that frequently causes financial analysts to make pro forma adjustments when conducting financial statement analysis: (1) *SFAS No. 2* requires that all R&D must be expensed, and (2) *SFAS No. 34* requires that some interest can be capitalized, which provides an exception to the general rule that interest is to be expensed during the period incurred. Many financial analysts believe that the R&D rules are too restrictive, especially for companies with a long history of successful research and development. These analysts view R&D as an investing activity, and if sufficient information is available on R&D cash flows, the analysts will make pro forma adjustments to financial statements by treating the R&D as an investing activity rather than as an operating activity. For example, in 1998, Eli Lilly spent over $1.7 billion on R&D, but, according to generally accepted accounting principles, reported none of it as an investing cash outflow. If an analyst believes that R&D is more properly shown as an investing activity, then the analyst could make a pro forma adjustment and move the $1.7 billion cash outflow from the operating to investing activities section. Regarding interest, some analysts believe that interest should not be capitalized, and move capitalized cash interest (if the information is available) from the investing section to the operating section. Alternatively, if an analyst believes that interest paid should be reflected as an investing activity, a pro forma adjustment could be made to move interest paid from the operating activities section (thereby decreasing cash outflows) to the financing activities section (thereby increasing cash outflows).

Investing Cash Flows of TCBY

Appendix A provides the November 30, 1998, financial statements of TCBY Enterprises, Inc. TCBY has several wholly-owned subsidiaries (e.g., Americana Foods develops and produces its yogurt). Therefore, TCBY and the subsidiaries are treated as a single entity in the preparation of a consolidated statement of cash flows.

The 1998 investing activities section of TCBY's statement of cash flows reports a \$3,371,987 net cash inflow. This net inflow is primarily explained by the sale of property, plant, and equipment totaling \$4,901,790. Generally, net cash inflows from investing activities are regarded as evidence of business contraction. Further evidence of such contraction is provided by a comparison of depreciation with new purchases (writing off versus replacing assets in place). Historical cost depreciation for 1998 is \$4,048,305 (see the operating activities section of the cash flow statement). Purchases of property, plant, and equipment for the same year total \$1,982,769. Depreciation is based on older costs, while recent investments are based on current costs. Therefore, TCBY is spending less in current purchases than it is depreciating, an indication that TCBY's operational capacity in real terms is probably declining.

TCBY's 1998 statement of cash flows reflects two items related to notes receivable (inflows from collecting notes receivables and outflows from originating notes receivable) and two items related to investments in other firms' securities (inflows from maturities of short-term investments and outflows from purchases of short-term investments). While the cash flows related to each of these four items are large, when considered together, their net effects on cash help explain much of the cash flow for 1998. TCBY used \$471,443 to originate notes receivable, but had a higher cash inflow on notes receivable collections (\$1,485,499). TCBY also used \$2,156,893 to purchase short-term investments, but collected \$1,595,803 when some of those investments matured. The net effect of these four items is a cash inflow of only \$452,966. Therefore, the cash inflows from sales of property, plant, and equipment are TCBY's main 1998 investing activity.[2]

Investing Activities: Effects on Ratio Analysis

3 Describe the effects of investments on the financial ratios identified in Module A.

In Module A, we discussed both profitability and risk ratios, and calculated the ratios for TCBY. In Module B, we discussed the effects of financing activities on ratio analysis. In this section, we review those ratios directly affected by a firm's investment decisions. We assume that investments are purchased and sold in cash transactions to keep our analysis independent of the financing decision.

Investing Activities and Profitability Ratios

An important ratio in the assessment of profitability is return on assets (ROA), in which the denominator is average total assets:

$$\text{ROA} = (\text{Net income} + \text{After tax interest expense}) \div \text{Average total assets}$$

Acquisitions of investments with cash are simply exchanges of two different kinds of assets of equal amounts, and thus, have no direct effect on ROA. If those investments yield returns in future years at a rate higher than the pre-investment ROA, then ROA will increase. If not, then ROA will decrease. When using ROA to evaluate investments, it is important to remember that new investments, especially those in other firms, often do not have the same risk as the firm's pre-investment port-

2. In 1998, TCBY sold an aircraft resulting in a \$2.1 million gain (Note 10, Certain Transactions). Therefore, at least half of (and more likely, most of) the net cash inflow from sales of property, plant, and equipment can be explained by this transaction. TCBY replaced this asset by entering into an agreement to occasionally use another aircraft owned by an officer in the company.

folio of projects. As a result, a value-adding investment that yields an ROA commensurate with its risk might reduce overall ROA if the firm's pre-investment projects are risky.

Sales of investments can trigger changes in ROA if the sale involves an investment in productive assets with a book value far different from its market value. Total assets increase or decrease depending on whether the investment is sold at a gain or loss, and the numerator reflects this gain or loss. Material differences at the date of sale will occur far less often for debt and equity investments classified as trading or available-for-sale because the securities are marked-to-market at each balance sheet date. However, marking investments to market creates the denominator effect discussed above due to changing the investments' asset values; in the case of trading securities, it also creates a numerator effect because the investment value change is included in net income. In addition, not all investments in debt and equity securities are marked-to-market, such as an investment accounted for under the equity method.

Equity Method Investments: The Net Profit Margin Ratio

As we learned in Module A, ROA can be broken down into profit margin and asset turnover ratios:

$$\text{ROA} = \text{Net profit margin ratio} \times \text{Asset turnover ratio}$$

The net profit margin ratio is defined as follows:

$$\text{Net profit margin ratio} = [\text{Net income} + (1 - t)\ \text{Interest expense}] \div \text{Sales}$$

Investments accounted for under the equity method (20%–50% ownership) may provide a misleading net profit margin ratio with respect to a company's core operations. The equity method requires that the investor accrue its share of the *net income* of a subsidiary as part of the investor's net income. This accrual causes the numerator of the net profit margin ratio to include a portion of the investee's net income, while the denominator does not include a portion of the investee's sales. Most analysts remedy this interpretive problem by excluding the accrual of investment in subsidiary net income from the numerator when interpreting trends and making comparisons with other companies.

Turnover Ratios and Cost Allocation Methods for Long-Lived Assets

The second element of ROA is the asset turnover ratio:

$$\text{Asset turnover ratio} = \text{Sales} \div \text{Average total assets}$$

Comparisons of both asset turnover ratios and ROAs across companies are greatly affected by the way in which the costs of long-lived assets are allocated across time. Two major issues in this area are the differences in depreciation methods across companies and the immediate expensing of R&D expenditures.

Differences in Depreciation Methods Across Companies Companies that use accelerated depreciation methods for financial reporting purposes will have higher turnover ratios than companies that use straight-line depreciation because the book values of depreciable assets will be substantially lower. If an analyst wishes to compare turnover rates between two companies that have different depreciation methods, it is necessary to adjust one company's depreciable assets. Because the straight-line method is most widely used, financial analysts generally adjust to approximate the straight-line method.[3]

For example, assume that an analyst was interested in whether TCBY should open stores in Japan. As part of the analysis, the analyst might wish to compare TCBY with a Japanese company in the same line of business. Suppose the Japanese company uses accelerated depreciation methods and TCBY uses straight-line depreciation (which it does, see Note 1).[4] To facilitate comparison with the Japanese company, the analyst could convert TCBY's financial statements to reflect accelerated depreciation. The conversion to an accelerated method can be approximated by using the information in TCBY's Note 5 (Income Taxes). (In Chapter 11, we discuss income taxes, and you will become more familiar with the income tax footnote.) Note the line "tax over book depreciation" among deferred tax liabilities in Note 5. The amount reported for 1998, \$3,863,828, represents the tax effects of the cumulative excess of tax depreciation (using an accelerated method) over financial statement depreciation (using straight-line) through time. To find the cumulative excess (instead of the tax effect), we divide \$3,863,828 by the statutory tax rate (35%) to obtain \$11,039,509. This means that, if TCBY had used accelerated depreciation over the years rather than straight-line, then accumulated depreciation, and hence the book values of total assets, would be lower by more than \$11 million.

Also, the difference in "tax over book depreciation" from 1997 to 1998 is \$318,807 (\$4,182,635 − \$3,863,828), representing a decrease from 1997 to 1998. This means that depreciation expense for 1998 would have been \$910,877 lower if TCBY had used an accelerated method on the financial statements (\$318,807 ÷ 0.35). Recall that later in a long-lived asset's useful life, accelerated methods can cause *smaller* depreciation charges than straight-line.

TCBY's statement of cash flows reports \$4,048,305 of depreciation (other than amortization of intangibles) in fiscal 1998, and the balance sheet reports total assets of \$94,452,884 and \$99,264,396 at November 30, 1998, and November 30, 1997, respectively. This information allows an analyst to convert TCBY's financial statements to reflect accelerated depreciation and to recompute asset turnover and net profit margin on the adjusted amounts:

	November 30	
	1998	**1997**
Total assets prior to adjustment	\$94,452,884	\$99,264,396
Excess accumulated depreciation under accelerated method (For 1997, \$4,182,635 ÷ 35%)	11,039,509	11,950,386
Total assets under accelerated depreciation	\$83,413,375	\$87,314,010

	Fiscal 1998
1998 depreciation prior to adjustment (see statement of cash flows)	\$4,048,305
Difference between 11/30/97 and 11/30/98 accumulated difference between tax and book depreciation (equals difference in depreciation expense taken in fiscal 1998 under accelerated depreciation)	(910,877)
1998 depreciation expense under accelerated method	\$3,137,428

3. In the 1999 *Accounting Trends & Techniques*, of 600 companies surveyed, 577 reported using the straight-line method; 77 reported using accelerated methods; 36 reported using units-of-production; and 9 other unidentified (totals sum to more than 600 because a firm may use more than one method for different depreciable items).

4. The Ministry of Finance is the Japanese standard setter in both financial and tax reporting. As a result, Japanese companies use methods in financial statements that are almost identical to what they are allowed to use for tax computations.

The amounts needed to compute TCBY's adjusted financial ratios are recomputed using these adjusted values as follows:

$$\text{Net income adjusted for decreased depreciation} = \$10{,}195{,}612 + [\$910{,}877 \times (1 - 0.35)] = \$10{,}787{,}682$$

$$\text{Average total assets} = (\$83{,}413{,}375 + \$87{,}314{,}010) \div 2 = \$85{,}363{,}693$$

Using these amounts, TCBY's 1998 adjusted ROA, asset turnover ratio, and net profit margin ratio are computed:

Adjusted 1998 ROA:
$\{\$10{,}787{,}682 + [\$545{,}664 \times (1 - 0.35)]\} \div \$85{,}363{,}693 = 13.05\%$

Adjusted 1998 net profit margin ratio:
$\{\$10{,}787{,}682 + [\$545{,}664 \times (1 - 0.35)]\} \div \$93{,}865{,}413 = 11.87\%$

Adjusted 1998 asset turnover ratio:
$\$93{,}865{,}413 \div \$85{,}363{,}693 = 1.10$

For TCBY, the adjusted amounts are very different than the unadjusted amounts (e.g., Module A reports an unadjusted ROA of 10.89%). The adjusted figures are now comparable to those for the Japanese company because both companies reflect a similar basis for depreciation. Of course, if any other accounting methods differ, other adjustments may also be required.

Immediate Expensing of R&D Expenditures Many analysts believe that the FASB rules requiring immediate expensing of all R&D costs cause misleading net profit margin, turnover, and ROA ratios. These analysts capitalize R&D costs by using historical information. We cannot demonstrate this for TCBY because R&D is not dramatic in the frozen yogurt business. Instead, consider selected data from the 1998 annual report of Eli Lilly Company in Exhibit 1.

EXHIBIT 1

ELI LILLY SELECTED DATA
1998 Annual Report
(amounts in millions)

	1998	1997	1996	1995	1994
R&D expenses	$1,738.9	$1,382.0	$1,189.5	$1,042.3	$838.7
Interest expense	$181.3	$234.1	$288.8	$286.3	not used
Net income	$2,097.9	$(385.1)	$1,523.5	$1,306.6	$1,185.1
Total assets	$12,595.5	$12,577.4	$14,307.2	$14,412.5	$14,507.4
R&D ÷ Total assets	13.8%	11.0%	8.3%	7.2%	5.8%

Eli Lilly's statutory tax rate is 35%, and the ROA for years 1996–1998 equals:

$$\begin{aligned} \text{ROA (1998)} &= (\text{Net income} + \text{Interest expense net of tax}) \div \text{Average total assets} \\ &= [\$2{,}097.9 + (\$181.3 \times 0.65)] \div [(\$12{,}595.5 + \$12{,}577.4) \div 2] \\ &= 17.6\% \end{aligned}$$

and using the same formula

$$\text{ROA (1997)} = (1.7\%)$$
$$\text{ROA (1996)} = 11.9\%$$

Assume that an analyst decided that R&D should be capitalized and amortized over five years. The table in Exhibit 2 provides information for the adjustment.

EXHIBIT 2

CAPITALIZATION OF R&D FOR ELI LILLY
(Author constructed; amounts in millions)

	1998	1997	1996	1995	1994
Add back R&D expenses	$1,738.9	$1,382.0	$1,189.5	$1,042.3	$838.7
Amortize R&D 20% per year					
1994 expenditures	(167.7)	(167.7)	(167.7)	(167.7)	(167.7)
1995 expenditures	(208.5)	(208.5)	(208.5)	(208.5)	*
1996 expenditures	(237.9)	(237.9)	(237.9)	*	*
1997 expenditures	(276.4)	(276.4)	*	*	*
1998 expenditures	(347.8)	*	*	*	*
Pretax earnings increase	$ 500.6	$ 491.5	$ 575.4	$ 666.1	$671.0
Total asset increase (accumulation of the previous column from right to left)	$2,904.6	$2,404.0	$1,912.5	$1,337.1	$671.0

*To complete these amounts, we would need the R&D totals from 1993, 1992, etc.

An analyst can recalculate ROA by adjusting the numerator by the pretax earnings increase shown in the schedule multiplied by one minus the tax rate, and adjusting the denominator by the total asset increase as follows:

$$\frac{\text{ROA (1998)}}{\text{Adjusted}} = \frac{[\$2{,}097.9 + (\$181.3 \times 0.65) + (\$500.6 \times 0.65)]}{[(\$12{,}595.5 + \$2{,}904.6) + (\$12{,}577.4 + \$2{,}404)] \div 2} = 16.7\%$$

Note that capitalizing R&D and amortizing it over five years results in a *decrease* of 0.9% in Lilly's 1998 ROA (17.6% − 16.7%). We cannot calculate the adjusted 1997 ROA (nor prior years) from the data available because we would need R&D information for the years 1993 and earlier. The 1998 adjusted ROA results seem counter-intuitive. Why would capitalizing R&D lead to a decreased ROA? As shown below, the adjustment factor, 12.3%, is a smaller percentage than the 1998 ROA of 17.6%, which leads to a reduced adjusted ROA. The adjustment factor equals the dollar increase in net income divided by the dollar increase in total assets. If Lilly's 1998 ROA had been 10%, then the adjustment factor would have increased ROA.

1998 ROA = 17.6%	**Adjustment factor = 12.3%**
$\frac{2{,}097.9 + (181.3 \times 0.65)}{(12{,}595.5 + 12{,}577.4) \div 2}$	$\frac{500.6 \times 0.65}{(2{,}904.6 + 2{,}404.0) \div 2}$

These results also illustrate the effect that assumptions have on pro forma computations. If we chose a ten-year amortization period (rather than five), then the ROA results would not decrease as much (or might even increase) because R&D expenditures in years 1989–1993 were much lower than in more recent years.

Investing Activities and Risk Ratios

Several key ratios in risk analysis are affected by investing activities. In Module A, we listed several ratios that are useful in assessing *short-term liquidity risk*:

Current ratio = Current assets ÷ Current liabilities
Quick ratio = Quick assets ÷ Current liabilities

Whenever cash is used to acquire long-term investments, the current and quick ratios will decrease, indicating more liquidity risk. An analyst should examine the type of long-term investment made, however, to determine whether it is a real increase in risk. If the investments are in long-lived operational assets or represent substantial investments in marketable equity securities (with which management intends to establish long-term strategic relationships), then the investments are not very liquid in a practical sense, and the short-term liquidity risk ratios accurately reflect effects of the investments. If, however, the investment was in a debt or equity security that is classified both as long-term and available-for-sale, then the investment is highly liquid, and liquidity risk has really not increased as indicated by the lower short-term liquidity risk ratios.

Long-term solvency risk assessment is also affected by investing activities. As noted in Module A, long-term creditors and equity investors are both interested in whether a firm has sufficient cash inflows from operations to replace equipment, and possibly, to expand operations through additional capital expenditures. The following ratio is often calculated to provide information about operating cash flow sufficiency:

Operating cash flow to capital expenditures ratio = **Operating cash flow ÷ Capital expenditures**

Clearly, large amounts of new investment in property, plant, and equipment (i.e., capital expenditures) cause this ratio to decrease, an indication of higher long-term solvency risk.

Recently, many companies believe this ratio provides far more information about long-term prospects than ratios based on net income. These companies tend to have recently acquired other companies using purchase accounting, and have recorded large amounts of goodwill in the process. To understand the issue, consider how the operating cash flow to capital expenditure ratio and net income can provide similar information. The operating cash flow to capital expenditure ratio shows how much cash inflow is available to make investments in property, plant, and equipment *before* making those investments. Dividing by capital expenditures gives the analyst an indication of whether the capital expenditures can be "covered." Net income represents net cash inflows (adjusted for accruals) that are left over after "covering" a charge for capital usage (i.e., depreciation and amortization expenses). Companies often argue that the charges for capital usage are excessive (especially amortization of goodwill acquired in an acquisition), and do not represent what will have to be replaced. These companies argue that the capital expenditures in each year are a better measure of what will be replaced.

How soon will long-lived operational assets have to be replaced? Knowing the strategy of the company will help in this regard. However, the following computation provides an understanding of the average ages of assets in place:

Average age of assets in place = **Accumulated depreciation ÷ Depreciation expense**

For TCBY in 1998, the average age of assets in place = approximately 9.8 years [$39,546,174 (from the balance sheet) ÷ $4,048,305 (from the statement of cash flows)]. Although many companies provide the useful lives of broad classes of assets in their footnotes, TCBY does not.

Quality of Earnings Adjustments: Investments

4 Identify the balance sheet and income statement adjustments made by many financial analysts in the process of analyzing the effects of investments on the profitability and risk of the firm.

As discussed throughout this module, a financial analyst may wish to make pro forma adjustments to earnings to evaluate profitability for several different reasons. In this section, we concentrate on two likely adjustments of financial statement data with respect to gains and losses on investment transactions: the persistence of gains and losses on long-lived asset sales and write-downs, and the discretion in unrealized gains and losses on available-for-sale securities.

The Persistence of Gains and Losses on Long-lived Asset Sales and Write-Downs

Long-lived assets used in operations generate revenues and expenses over long periods of time. Occasionally, these assets are sold before their useful lives expire.

Because they are rarely sold at an amount equal to their book value (i.e., original cost less accumulated depreciation), gains and losses on sale are generated. Also, as shown in Chapter 6, companies must now determine whether long-lived assets have been impaired, and if so, write them down at balance sheet dates and show the resulting loss on the income statement.

The peripheral and occasional nature of these sale and impairment write-down transactions imply that the resulting income statement effects are transitory. Analysts wishing to assess the persistence (i.e., sustainability) of current earnings remove these gains and losses from income. A thorough reading of TCBY's annual report reveals that it has some relatively small gains and losses on sales of property, plant, and equipment in each income statement provided. Therefore, any adjustments related to persistence would be negligible. Exhibits 3 and 4 use 1997 financial statement information for Columbia/HCA Healthcare Corporation to illustrate adjustments related to persistence.

EXHIBIT 3 Columbia/HCA Healthcare Corporation

COLUMBIA/HCA HEALTHCARE CORPORATION
Consolidated Statements of Operations
For the Years Ended December 31, 1997, 1996 and 1995
(Dollars in millions, except per share amounts)

	1997	**1996**	**1995**
Revenues	**$18,819**	$18,786	$17,132
Salaries and benefits	**7,631**	7,205	6,779
Supplies	**2,722**	2,655	2,536
Other operating expenses	**4,263**	3,689	3,203
Provision for doubtful accounts	**1,420**	1,196	994
Depreciation and amortization	**1,238**	1,143	976
Interest expense	**493**	488	458
Equity in earnings of affiliates	**(68)**	(173)	(28)
Restructuring of operations and investigation-related costs	**140**	—	—
Impairment of long-lived assets	**442**	—	—
Merger and facility consolidation costs	**—**	—	387
	18,281	16,203	15,305
Income from continuing operations before minority interests and income taxes	**538**	2,583	1,827
Minority interests in earnings of consolidated entities	**150**	141	113
Income from continuing operations before income taxes	**388**	2,442	1,714
Provision for income taxes	**206**	981	689
Income from continuing operations	**182**	1,461	1,025
Discontinued operations:			
Income from operations of discontinued businesses, net of income taxes of $18 in 1997, $29 in 1996 and $26 in 1995	**12**	44	39
Estimated loss on disposal of discontinued businesses, net of income tax benefit of $124	**(443)**	—	—
Extraordinary charges on extinguishments of debt, net of income tax benefit of $67	**—**	—	(103)
Cumulative effect of accounting change, net of income tax benefit of $36	**(56)**	—	—
Net income (loss)	**$ (305)**	$ 1,505	$ 961
Basic earnings (loss) per share:			
Income from continuing operations	**$ .28**	$ 2.17	$ 1.54
Discontinued operations:			
Income from operations of discontinued businesses	**.02**	.07	.06
Estimated loss on disposal of discontinued businesses	**(.67)**	—	—
Extraordinary charges on extinguishments of debt	**—**	—	(.16)
Cumulative effect of accounting change	**(.09)**	—	—
Net income (loss)	**$ (.46)**	$ 2.24	$ 1.44

(continued)

EXHIBIT 3 (concluded)

	1997	1996	1995
Diluted earnings (loss) per share:			
Income from continuing operations	**$ .27**	$ 2.15	$ 1.52
Discontinued operations:			
Income from operations of discontinued businesses	**.02**	.07	.06
Estimated loss on disposal of discontinued businesses	**(.67)**	—	—
Extraordinary charges on extinguishments of debt	**—**	—	(.15)
Cumulative effect of accounting change	**(.08)**	—	—
Net income (loss)	**$ (.46)**	$ 2.22	$ 1.43

The accompanying notes are an integral part of the consolidated financial statements

EXHIBIT 4 Columbia/HCA Healthcare Corporation—Notes to Consolidated Financial Statements

NOTE 6—IMPAIRMENT OF LONG-LIVED ASSETS

The Company adopted Statement of Financial Accounting Standards No. 121, "Accounting for the Impairment of Long-Lived Assets and Long-Lived Assets to be Disposed of" ("SFAS 121"), during the first quarter of 1996. SFAS 121 addresses accounting for the impairment of long-lived assets and long-lived assets to be disposed of, certain identifiable intangibles and goodwill related to those assets, and provides guidance for recognizing and measuring impairment losses. The statement requires that the carrying amount of impaired assets be reduced to fair value. SFAS 121 is not materially different from the Company's prior policy related to regular periodic reviews of long-lived assets for possible impairment.

During the fourth quarter of 1997, in connection with the changes in management and business strategy (see NOTE 3), the Company decided to close or sell twenty hospital facilities and fifteen surgery centers (primarily optical surgery centers) that were identified as not compatible with the Company's operating plans. The carrying value of these facilities was reduced to fair value, based on estimates of selling values, for a total non-cash charge of $402 million. The Company expects to complete the majority of these sales or closures during 1998.

The Company recorded, during the fourth quarter of 1997, an impairment loss of approximately $40 million related to the write-off of intangibles and other long-lived assets of certain physician practices where the recorded asset values were not deemed to be fully recoverable based upon the operating results trend and projected future cash flows. These assets are now recorded at estimated fair value.

The 1997 charges did not have a significant impact on the Company's 1997 cash flows and are not expected to significantly impact cash flows for future periods. As a result of the write-downs, depreciation and amortization expense related to these assets will decrease in future periods. In the aggregate, the net effect of the change in depreciation and amortization expense is not expected to have a material effect on operating results for future periods.

In 1997, Columbia/HCA reported a $442 million charge against earnings under the caption "impairment of long-lived assets." Note 6 (Impairment of Long-Lived Assets) reveals that these charges relate to a combination of impending sales and closings of medical facilities and impairments of assets at continuing physician practices. In the last paragraph of Note 6, management states that operating results in future periods should not be materially affected by these write-offs.[5] This makes sense given the occasional and peripheral nature of such charges. The following adjustment to 1997 net income will likely be made by an analyst interested in the persistence of earnings:

Net income (loss) before adjustment	$(305,000,000)
Remove impairment of long-lived assets	442,000,000
Increase in income tax expense (35% × $442,000,000)	(154,700,000)
Net income (loss) adjusted	$ (17,700,000)

5. Because every cost that is capitalized is eventually expensed, we know that by taking the $442 million write-off in 1997, future income statements will cumulatively report $442 million less expense.

Any adjustment before income from continuing operations requires an adjustment to income tax expense. In this case, the impairment resulted in a loss that reduced income tax expense. Thus, removing the loss increases income taxes by 35% of the $442 million loss. Although the company still has a net loss after the adjustment, the loss is much reduced (by 94%) and more properly reflects the ongoing operations of the firm.

Frequently, a company will highlight for its readers the events that were transitory during the period. For example, Eli Lilly reported a 1997 net loss of $385.1 million. In the Management Discussion and Analysis (MD&A), the company highlighted three unusual events that occurred in 1997: a write-off of $2.4 billion in goodwill; a gain of $631.8 million from the sale of its interest in a joint venture; and a $24 million charge for a litigation settlement. The MD&A narrative then points out that if these three items were eliminated, net income would have been $1.77 billion ($1.57 per share). Clearly, company management wants to focus investor interest on persistent earnings, especially if the earnings news is good.

Discretion in Unrealized Gains and Losses on Available-for-Sale Securities

The investment community has long been concerned that accounting rules allow discretion in calculating earnings of the current period. We identified such a situation in the area of accounting for available-for-sale securities. Gains trading allows management to select appreciated available-for-sale securities to sell in the current period to generate gains. Losses can be deferred and reported as unrealized as a component of owners' equity.

To make financial statements of all companies comparable, some analysts make pro forma adjustments to place all changes in market values of available-for-sale securities in current period income. The comprehensive income disclosure now required by the FASB helps in this regard. Columbia/HCA has chosen the statement of stockholders' equity (shown below) as the vehicle for disclosing comprehensive income. Under "Accumulated Other Comprehensive Income," net unrealized gains and losses on investment securities are reported for each year, beginning in 1995. In 1997, $38 million is reported as the net unrealized gain. This amount can be added, if the analyst desires, to net income on a net of tax basis (i.e., $38 million × 65% = $24.7 million increase in net income). Using this approach, all gains and losses on available-for-sale securities are reported in net income for the period. See Exhibit 5.

EXHIBIT 5 Columbia/HCA Healthcare Corporation

COLUMBIA/HCA HEALTHCARE CORPORATION
Consolidated Statements of Stockholders' Equity
For the Years Ended December 31, 1997, 1996 and 1995
(Dollars in millions)

	Common Stock		Capital in Excess of Par Value	Other	Accumulated Other Comprehensive Income	Retained Earnings	Total
	Shares (000)	Par Value					
Balances, December 31, 1994	662,934	$7	$4,402	$27	$(4)	$1,658	$6,090
Comprehensive income:							
Net income						961	961
Other comprehensive income, net of tax (See NOTE 19):							
Net unrealized gains on investment securities					31		31
Foreign currency translation adjustments					7		7
					38	—	38
Total comprehensive income					38	961	999

(continued)

EXHIBIT 5 (concluded)

	Common Stock		Capital in		Accumulated Other		
	Shares (000)	Par Value	Excess of Par Value	Other	Comprehensive Income	Retained Earnings	Total
Balances Brought Forward	662,934	$7	$4,402	$27	$34	$2,619	$7,089
Cash dividends						(53)	(53)
Stock options exercised, net	5,187		100	(7)			93
Other	607	—	(6)	6			—
Balances, December 31, 1995	668,728	7	4,496	26	34	2,566	7,129
Comprehensive income:							
Net income						1,505	1,505
Other comprehensive income (loss), net of tax (See NOTE 19):							
Net unrealized gains on investment securities					24		24
Foreign currency translation adjustments					(6)		(6)
					18	—	18
Total comprehensive income					18	1,505	1,523
Cash dividends						(54)	(54)
Stock options exercised, net	3,859		81	(5)			76
Other	(1,088)	—	(58)	(7)			(65)
Balances, December 31, 1996	671,499	7	4,519	14	52	4,017	8,609
Comprehensive loss:							
Net loss						(305)	(305)
Other comprehensive income, net of tax (See NOTE 19):							
Net unrealized gains on investment securities					38		38
Foreign currency translation adjustments					2		2
					40	—	40
Total comprehensive loss					40	(305)	(265)
Cash dividends						(53)	(53)
Stock repurchases	(37,895)	(1)	(1,272)				(1,273)
Stock options exercised, net	4,108		100	(4)			96
Other employee benefit plan issuances	3,740		108				108
Other			25	3			28
Balances, December 31, 1997	641,452	$6	$3,480	$13	$92	$3,659	$7,250

The accompanying notes are an integral part of the consolidated financial statements.

Module Summary

In this module, we view investment decisions as would outsiders assessing the risk and profitability of the firm. We show how financial analysts may make pro forma adjustments to financial statements as part of the financial statement analysis process. A financial analyst may recast financial statements (1) to promote comparability across firms that use different accounting methods, (2) to provide standardized inputs to certain quantitative models, and (3) to adjust GAAP financial statements if the analyst does not feel that some elements of GAAP appropriately characterize the firm. We demonstrate how these adjustments affect financial statements and related ratio computations. In later chapters and modules, we build on Module C to discuss pro forma adjustments for other items.

Module C: Financial Statement Ratios

The following financial statement ratios were used in Module C. These ratios help illustrate financial statement analysis concerns related to the investing activities discussed in Chapter 6–8.

Return on assets (ROA) = (Net income + After tax interest expense) ÷ Average total assets
Net profit margin ratio = [Net income + (1 − t) Interest expense] ÷ Sales
Asset turnover ratio = Sales ÷ Average total assets
Current ratio = Current assets ÷ Current liabilities
Quick ratio = Quick assets ÷ Current liabilities
Operating cash flow to capital expenditures ratio = Operating cash flow ÷ Capital expenditures
Average age of assets in place = Accumulated depreciation ÷ Depreciation expense

Questions

Q1. **Statement of Cash Flow Classification.** For the following items, please indicate where the cash flows effects are shown in the statement of cash flows. Use OA, IA, and FA to indicate operating, investing, and financing activities, respectively.

Item	Statement of Cash Flows Placement
Purchases of property, plant, and equipment	
Sales of property, plant, and equipment	
Cash payments for R&D	
Interest received	
Interest paid (general)	
Interest paid, capitalized as part of construction in progress	
Dividends received, available-for-sale securities	
Dividends received, trading securities	
Purchases/sales of debt and equity securities: available-for-sale or held-to-maturity classification	
Purchases/sales of debt and equity securities: trading classification	

Q2. **Financial Analyst Adjustments.** Why might a financial analyst make pro forma adjustments to published GAAP-based financial statements when conducting financial analysis?

Q3. **Unrealized Gains and Losses.** Where are current period changes in unrealized gains and losses shown in the financial statements for (a) trading securities, (b) available-for-sale securities, and (c) held-to-maturity securities? Where are the net cumulative unrealized gains/losses shown in financial statements on (d) trading securities and (e) available-for-sale securities?

Analytical and Comprehensive Problems

1. **Reviewing Investing Activities—The Walt Disney Company.** The following is selected information taken from the 1997 annual report of The Walt Disney Company and Subsidiaries (all amounts are in millions):

Statement of Cash Flows	1997	1996	1995
Operating Activities (partial information)			
Amortization of film and television costs	$ 3,781	$ 2,762	$ 1,383
Depreciation	738	672	470
Amortization of intangible assets	439	301	0
Cash provided by operations	7,064	4,625	3,510
Investing Activities (in its entirety)			
Proceeds from disposal of KCAL	$ 387	$ 0	$ 0
Proceeds from disposal of publishing operations	1,214	0	0
Acquisition of ABC, net of cash acquired	0	(8,432)	0
Film and television costs	(5,054)	(3,678)	(1,886)
Investments in theme parks, resorts, and other property	(1,922)	(1,745)	(896)
Investments in and loan for E! Entertainment	(321)	0	0
Purchases of marketable securities	(56)	(18)	(1,033)
Proceeds from sales of marketable securities	31	409	1,460
Other	(180)	0	67
Total	$(5,901)	$(13,464)	$(2,288)

Required:

a. Write a memorandum describing Walt Disney Company's investment strategy inferred from the cash flow information provided.
b. Which of the investment cash flows do you expect to persist? Why?
c. Is cash flow from operations sufficient to cover capital expenditures? Although we did not provide the financing activities sections, do you believe that there will be a net cash inflow or outflow from financing activities over the three-year period?
d. Does the cash flow statement provide any clue about why amortization started in 1996?

2. **Financial Reporting, Consolidated Statements—General Electric.** One of General Electric Company's investments is its finance subsidiary, General Electric Capital Services, Inc. (GECS). Because GE controls the subsidiary (owns more than 50% of voting shares), it must consolidate the subsidiary under generally accepted accounting principles. It does so in its annual report, but also shows separate results for GE (the parent) and GECS (the subsidiary). Do you believe that financial analysts are helped by such a disclosure practice? (To answer this question, think about the kinds of investing activities that GE might undertake and the kinds of investing activities that a finance subsidiary might undertake.)

3. **Property, Plant, and Equipment—Canon, Inc.** It is important to understand the age of long-lived assets in order to understand when a company is likely to engage in investing activities to replace the assets. Information on property, plant, and equipment taken from the 1997 annual report of Canon, Inc., is shown below (all amounts are in millions of yen).

	1997	1996
Land	¥ 109,386	¥ 107,378
Buildings	550,588	502,133
Machinery and equipment	803,379	704,606
Construction in progress	30,974	31,462
Total	1,494,327	1,345,579
Less accumulated depreciation	797,083	719,452
PP&E (net)	¥ 697,244	¥ 626,127

a. At what stage is Canon's PP&E in terms of estimated useful life?
b. If depreciation expense was ¥139,118 for 1997, approximately how old is PP&E?
c. Is there any evidence that Canon sold assets in 1997?

4. **Investments in Common Stock—Seagram Co. Ltd.** The 1995 consolidated balance sheet of Seagram Co. Ltd includes the following two investments:

Common stock of E. I. du Pont de Nemours and Company, at equity
Common stock of Time Warner, Inc., at market value

a. What conditions could lead Seagram to account for two investments in common stock using two different methods, equity and market value?
b. Describe all the ways in which Seagram's investment in du Pont could change during the period under the equity method. How would Seagram reflect these changes in its income statement?
c. Describe all the ways in which Seagram's investment in Time Warner could change during the period. How would Seagram reflect these changes in its income statement?

5. **Pro Forma Financial Statement Adjustments—LSI Logic.** The 1996 annual report of LSI Logic provides a long-time series of financial data. Such data can be very useful to financial analysts who wish to make pro forma adjustments. Consider the following selected data:

	R&D Expense	Interest Expense	Net Income	Total Assets
1996	184,452	13,610	147,184	1,952,714
1995	123,892	16,349	238,120	1,849,587
1994	98,978	18,455	108,743	1,270,374
1993	78,995			859,010
1992	78,825			
1991	80,802			
1990	60,196			
1989	52,457			
1988	36,964			
1987	28,919			

a. Assuming a 35% tax rate for all years, compute ROA for 1996, 1995, and 1994 using the appropriate data with no adjustment.
b. Many analysts view R&D as an investment that should be capitalized instead of expensed immediately. Prepare a schedule to recompute net income and total assets assuming that R&D is capitalized and amortized over five years, beginning with the year of capitalization.
c. Recompute ROA using the adjusted data for 1996. What additional data would be needed to compute the adjusted ROA for 1995 and 1994?

http://

6. **Texas Instruments.** Access the Texas Instruments 1998 financial statements available at the text Web site at http://baginski.swcollege.com and answer the following questions.
   a. Assume that a financial analyst believes that R&D expense should be capitalized and amortized over a three-year period (including a full one-third amortization in the current period). What effect would following this policy have on TI's 1998 financial statements? (Assume a tax rate of 35%.)
   b. In general, what ratios would be affected by the capitalization policy?
   c. From TI's income statement, what components of net income in 1998 or 1997 would not be expected to persist into future periods?
   d. Using TI's statement of cash flows, what major investments were made in 1998? How were these investments financed?

How Operating Decisions Are Reflected in Financial Statements

IV

Objectives

1 Explain why firms hold inventory.
2 Determine the cost of inventory.
3 Measure newly generated accounts payable.
4 Assign costs using alternative inventory costing methods.
5 Measure inventory for balance sheet valuation.
6 Explain why firms extend credit.
7 Explain how accounts receivable are generated and measured.
8 Report accounts receivable on the balance sheet.
9 Identify methods of raising cash from alternative transfers of accounts receivable.
10 Explain why short-term notes receivable are used as an alternative to accounts receivable and how such notes are measured and reported.
11 Report operating cash flows in the statement of cash flows using the indirect method.

Chapter 9

Preparing for Sales—Building Up Inventory and Establishing Credit Policy

Working Capital Investments

Our discussion of management decision making has taken us from raising capital (financing activities) to using the proceeds to invest in productive assets (investing activities). As we begin our discussion of the final set of management decisions (operating activities), we must first address several kinds of short-term cash investments that are necessary to support operations. These investments in working capital are operating decisions to (1) acquire and hold inventory, (2) negotiate delayed payment to the suppliers of that inventory, and (3) extend credit to buyers for sales of inventory. The corresponding accounts used to record these activities are (1) Inventory, (2) Accounts Payable, and (3) Accounts Receivable.

In this chapter, where we first cover operating activities, we concentrate on accounting measurement and reporting issues generated by these three working capital investment-related operating decisions.

Building Up Inventory to Support Sales

1 Explain why firms hold inventory.

The decision to build up inventory to support sales involves analyzing the trade-off between **the costs of holding inventory** (e.g., insurance and warehousing) and **the costs of not having enough inventory on hand to meet customer demand.** These costs are referred to as ***holding costs*** and ***stockout costs,*** respectively.

Cost accounting texts provide **quantitative models to compute the best quantity to order at a given time** (i.e., the ***economic order quantity,*** or ***EOQ***), as well as when to reorder (i.e., probabilistic models incorporating safety stocks needed to avoid stockouts). These models establish an optimum level of inventory to hold. Recently, **cost management techniques have led to customer/supplier relations that attempt to alter inventory holding costs and the probability of stockouts.** The impact of one of these techniques, ***just-in-time*** inventory systems, has been to decrease the amount of inventory reported in the balance sheet. Smaller quantities of inventory lower holding costs, while arrangements with suppliers for prompt (just-in-time) delivery minimize stockout costs.

In merchandising firms, inventory is normally acquired in three ways: cash payment; issuing short-term, non-interest-bearing promises to pay cash; and issuing short-term, interest-bearing promises to pay cash:

Common Methods Used to Acquire Inventory

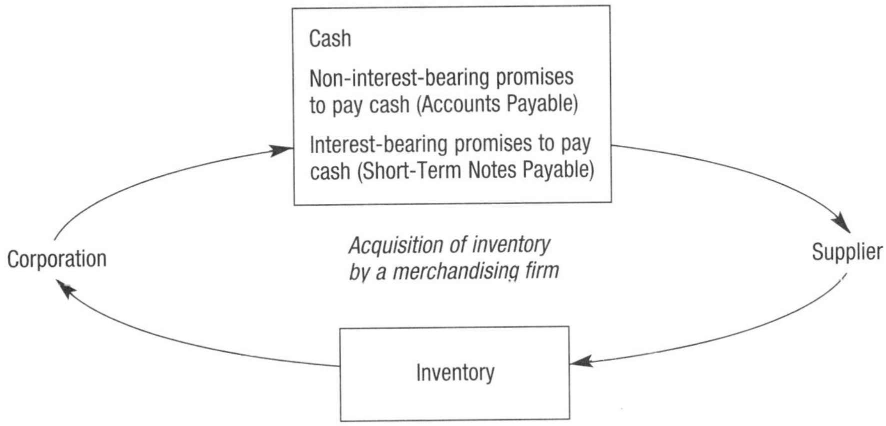

In manufacturing firms, the same kinds of consideration are given to acquire the factors of production (raw materials, labor, and overhead) that are combined to produce inventory.

Initially, accountants are faced with two tasks in the inventory area. First, they must appropriately value the acquisition (i.e., the fair value exchanged becomes the cost basis). Second, as with all costs incurred, accountants must decide how to allocate the costs between assets (costs with future benefit) and expenses (costs with no future benefit). In order to understand how accountants perform these tasks, we address several issues:

- The conceptual cost of inventory
- The purchase of inventory on account (and related accounts payable accounting)
- Inventory costing methods
- Inventory valuation

The Conceptual Cost of Inventory

2 Determine the cost of inventory.

Conceptually, inventory should be *recorded at an amount equal to all costs necessary to acquire and prepare the inventory for sale.* For merchandising firms, the initial purchase price of the inventory should be capitalized, as well as all costs incurred for items such as insurance and freight. For manufacturing firms, costs to acquire raw materials are recorded in Raw Materials Inventory. The costs of raw materials used, direct labor used, and allocated costs of manufacturing overhead are accumulated and reported in Work in Process Inventory for unfinished products and in Finished Goods Inventory for finished products.

A key consideration for determining the cost of inventory is the concept of a *necessary* cost. For example, if goods are being transported in by truck and your company must pay a penalty for not having your dock clear at the scheduled delivery time, then the delivery cost is part of the inventory cost, but the penalty is a loss of the period—it was not necessary to incur the penalty. Examples of necessary and unnecessary costs are also found in bottling operations. Liquid is often spilled in the process of filling a bottle. It is costly to lose product in this manner, but it would be more costly to slow down production to avoid all spills. The cost of spills is referred to as *normal spoilage,* and it is treated as part of the cost of the inventory produced. However, if an employee dropped a case of the product on the floor, the costs associated with the accident would be *abnormal spoilage* because it was unnecessary to drop the product in order to produce good product. These abnormal spoilage costs would be considered a loss of the period rather than part of inventory.

Several kinds of consideration besides cash can be traded to acquire inventory. The most common situation is that the buyer promises to pay the supplier for the inventory within a short period of time (i.e., an account payable). Sometimes, short-term notes payable are issued to acquire inventory. If an interest-bearing promise to pay is traded for inventory, a question arises as to what to do with the interest cost. Should it be expensed, or should it be capitalized as part of the inventory? In the following section, we examine the purchase of inventory on account to answer this question. In addition, the section illustrates the accounting implications of a decision to delay payment to suppliers.

Purchasing Inventory on Account

3 Measure newly generated accounts payable.

In the normal course of business, an interest-free payment period is usually granted by sellers to normal customers (i.e., members of the *trade*). If a firm acquires inventory by making a short-term, interest-free promise to pay, an account payable is generated from the acquirer's point of view. Net income and owners' equity is unaffected by this transaction because current assets (i.e., Inventory) and current liabilities (i.e., Accounts Payable) are increased by an equal amount.

Alternatively, inventory can be acquired by issuing a short-term, interest-bearing promise to pay. Typically, this more formal arrangement is documented by signing a note payable with a duration that is greater than the customary interest-free period associated with an account payable. For example, a seller may be willing to extend 30 days of interest-free credit (an account payable), or alternatively, extend 120 days credit if the buyer is willing to sign a note bearing interest at a reasonable rate. Again, net income and owners' equity are unaffected by the transaction because current assets (i.e., Inventory) and current liabilities (i.e., Notes Payable) are increased by an equal amount.

The measurement of these alternative transactions is illustrated in the following example. (We assume that the credit periods are identical for accounts and notes payable to allow you to compare and contrast the accounting treatment.)

Example 1. Hoosier Corp. acquired $9,800 of inventory, $4,900 in each of two separate transactions under the following arrangements:

A. $4,900 of inventory was acquired by incurring a $5,000 trade accounts payable with terms of 2/30, net 60.
B. $4,900 of inventory was acquired by signing a 12.25%, 60-day note payable, with principal and interest due at maturity.

What is the cost of the inventory and the appropriate amount to record in the payable account under each of the transactions?

Solution.
A. Accounts Payable

The terms of the trade account payable (2/30, net 60) indicate that Hoosier will receive a 2% ***purchase discount*** (i.e., **will pay less than full purchase price**) if paid off within 30 days. Otherwise, the full $5,000 must be paid in 60 days. The net method is the preferred accounting treatment for inventory costs. The ***net method*** **records the inventory** at $4,900, **net of the allowable purchase discount** of $100 ($5,000 × 2%). The 2% purchase discount can be viewed in two ways. One way is to view the fair value of the inventory as $5,000, and argue that the seller is willing to sacrifice $100 ($5,000 × 2%) if Hoosier pays within 30 days. Another way of viewing the discount has more intuitive (and authoritative) support. Although no interest rate is stated in the transaction, an interest cost is clearly present if Hoosier waits to pay until after the 30-day interest free period. Because payment within the interest-free period is $4,900, and it is increased to $5,000 after this period, the value of the inventory is $4,900, and $100 interest is charged for borrowing funds for the last 30 days. Valuing the inventory at $4,900 makes sense because $4,900 is the cash-equivalent price at the date of sale. That is, if no credit had been extended, Hoosier would have paid $4,900 to acquire the inventory.

During the first 30 days, Hoosier reports the trade accounts payable at $4,900. If Hoosier has not paid within the first 30 days, the trade accounts payable valuation is increased to $5,000, and the $100 increase in the liability is recognized as interest expense. The cost of inventory is $4,900, regardless of when Hoosier extinguishes the payable.[1] Normally, companies have a policy of taking all purchase discounts offered because the interest cost associated with not taking a purchase discount is very large. For example, if a 2% discount is not taken to postpone payment for 30 days, the annual effective interest cost is 24% (2% per month × 12 months).

EXAMPLE 1A Journal Entries

Date of acquisition:		
Purchases (or Inventory under a perpetual system)	4,900	
Accounts Payable		4,900

Payment occurs in first 30 days:			*Payment occurs after first 30 days:*		
			When 30-day period expires:		
Accounts Payable	4,900		Interest Expense		
Cash		4,900	(Purchase Discounts Lost)	100	
			Accounts Payable		100
			When payment occurs thereafter:		
			Accounts Payable	5,000	
			Cash		5,000

B. Notes Payable

Inventory is recorded at $4,900, and the final cash outflow on the $4,900 note payable is $5,000. This additional $100 is two months' interest on $4,900 (12.25% × 2/12 × $4,900). The note payable is recorded at $4,900, and Interest Payable is increased by $50 each month with the corresponding monthly interest expense of $50. Thus, the final cash outflow of $5,000 removes a $4,900 note payable and $100 interest payable.

EXAMPLE 1B Journal Entries

Date of acquisition:		
Purchases (or Inventory under a perpetual system)	4,900	
Notes Payable		4,900
Accrual of interest over two-month period:		
Interest Expense	100	
Interest Payable		100
Final payment:		
Notes Payable	4,900	
Interest Payable	100	
Cash		5,000

1. The interest expense computed under the net method of recording inventory purchases on account is often referred to as *purchase discounts lost.* As an alternative (although theoretically incorrect), the *gross method* is often used in practice and justified on materiality grounds. Under the gross method, the purchases are recorded at $5,000 and reduced to $4,900 only if the purchase discount is taken.

Financial Statement Effects To illustrate the financial statement effects, we assume that the purchase discount was not taken. Under this assumption, the combined effects of the two inventory transactions (ignoring income tax effects) are reported in the financial statements as follows:

EXHIBIT 1 Example 1. Financial Statement Effects

Statement of Cash Flows

Operating Activities	
Payments to suppliers	(9,800)
Payments for interest	(200)
Total cash outflows	(10,000)

Balance Sheet

Assets		**Liabilities**	
Current assets:		**Owners' Equity**	
Cash	10,000 ↓	Retained earnings (through effect on net income)*	200 ↓
Inventory	9,800 ↑		

Income Statement

Financial revenues, (expenses), gains, and (losses)	
Interest expense*	(200)

Statement of Owners' Equity

Net income*	200 ↓

*Ignores effect of income taxes

Cash inflows and outflows relating to the firm's normal operating cycle are reported in the operating activities section of the cash flow statement. The balance sheet shows the \$10,000 decrease in cash to purchase inventory (\$4,900 + \$4,900) and pay the \$200 interest on the two transactions.

In summary, interest costs incurred in the acquisition of inventory are charged to interest expense rather than treated as part of the cost of inventory. To understand why, consider how the financial statement elements would be affected by alternative treatments. Most inventory is sold in the period in which it is acquired. The cost of goods sold would reduce income by whatever amount had been originally capitalized as inventory cost. In the Hoosier example, if interest cost is capitalized and goods are sold during the period, cost of goods sold totals \$10,000 (\$9,800 + 200). However, if interest is expensed, cost of goods sold equals \$9,800 and interest expense equals \$200. In either case, \$10,000 is expensed. But, if we do not capitalize interest, we avoid the bookkeeping costs of tracing the interest cost to particular units of inventory. This is a good example of applying a cost/benefit analysis to accounting information production. The bookkeeping costs of interest capitalization may exceed the benefits to the user of having exact classification of the nature of the expense.[2]

Purchase Returns and Allowances

Sometimes a company returns inventory (e.g., wrong item, wrong color, or damaged item), and thus, reduces the cost of inventory still on hand. Companies frequently want to separately track these items. Accordingly, when an item is returned, **a contra account to purchases, *Purchase Returns and Allowances*,** is used. Sometimes, after inventory is delivered, a company may negotiate a purchase allowance

2. The matching principle is also violated on the relatively small amount of inventory held at year-end. Interest cost is incurred in one year, but the goods are sold in another. Again, a cost/benefit analysis leads accountants to expense interest cost when incurred rather than employ capitalization. GAAP treatment for interest expense is consistent across situations; the general rule is that interest expense is expensed as incurred. Only one exception exists. As was discussed in Chapter 6, GAAP allows interest expense on fixed asset self-construction to be capitalized.

(a reduction in the price of the item). For example, assume that a company ordered 25 red basketball backboards at $200 each, and 25 blue backboards were delivered. The company might negotiate to keep the blue backboards if the supplier reduces the price to $150 each. The $50 per backboard represents a purchase allowance, which is recorded in Purchase Returns and Allowances.

Cost of Goods Available For Sale

The cost of goods available for sale, a measure of the total cost of inventory items available for sale during the period, is calculated as Beginning inventory + Net purchases. Net purchases is calculated as Purchases − Purchase Discounts (if the gross method is used) − Purchase Returns and Allowances.

The total cost of goods available for sale during the period is allocated either to ending inventory or to cost of goods sold. This allocation is accomplished by computing ending inventory and subtracting it from cost of goods available for sale to compute cost of goods sold. (The cost of ending inventory is determined by the application of an inventory costing method, which is discussed in the next section.) The following illustrates the computation of cost of goods available for sale and its relationship with cost of goods sold.

Beginning inventory		$14,000,000
Purchases	$12,000,000	
Purchase discounts (not present under net method)	(300,000)	
Purchase returns and allowances	(600,000)	
Net purchases		11,100,000
Cost of goods available for sale		$25,100,000
Ending inventory		(4,600,000)
Cost of goods sold		$20,500,000

This complete reconciliation is useful in understanding all components of inventory cost. In most GAAP financial statements, this reconciliation is not presented; rather, the income statement simply lists cost of goods sold, and the balance sheet lists ending inventory.

Inventory Costing Methods

4 Assign costs using alternative inventory costing methods.

When inventory units exist at year-end, it is necessary to assign a cost to each unit for balance sheet presentation. Also, as noted previously, cost of goods sold is simultaneously determined because all costs incurred by a company for inventory purchases must either be related to goods still on hand or to goods transferred to customers in the sales process.

Inventory costs → allocated to → Goods still on hand (Balance sheet asset—Inventory)
→ Goods sold (Income statement expense—Cost of Goods Sold)

A precise matching of costs with units on hand and units sold can occur **if each product is separately coded so that its acquisition cost can be tracked to the unit. Then, one could simply multiply each unit on hand or sold by its cost to compute total cost of inventory or total cost of goods sold.** This method, known as ***specific identification,*** is useful for large, expensive inventory items. For example, assume that Martin Builders builds three "spec" houses costing $200,000, $220,000, and $250,000. If the $220,000 house is sold, then Martin matches $220,000 cost of goods sold against sales revenue, and reports $450,000 ($200,000 + $250,000) as ending inventory.

A large soft drink manufacturer faces a different kind of inventory situation. Multiple production runs of mass quantities of homogeneous goods are accomplished during the period by using materials and labor acquired at different times and at varying costs. Similarly, a grocery store acquires milk at regular, short time intervals. Does it make sense in a cost/benefit framework to match the revenue from wholesale soft drink sales or retail milk sales against the specifically identified acquisition cost of a particular can of soft drink or carton of milk? Generally, the answer is no. Financial statement users can receive useful information about inventory costs without using the costly specific identification method.[3]

Over time, accountants have developed ***cost flow assumptions*** to aid in the costing of inventory. In this section, we consider the weighted-average, first-in, first-out (FIFO), and last-in, first-out (LIFO)[4] cost flow assumptions. These methods emphasize the cost/benefit trade-off. By sacrificing the preciseness achieved with the specific identification method, record keeping costs are significantly reduced while financial reporting benefits are not significantly affected.

Illustrating Three Cost Flow Assumptions To illustrate and explain these methods, we assume that a company uses a ***periodic inventory system*** in which **costs are accumulated during the period and assigned to inventory and cost of goods sold at the period's end.** Many companies use a perpetual inventory system in which the process we illustrate is done continuously upon each individual inventory purchase and sale. Avoiding an explanation of the more complex perpetual system does not impair understanding how the inventory methods are applied and interpreted. Further, the properties of the resulting numbers do not vary greatly across most practical assumptions about the way input prices move through time. Therefore, we limit our discussions to the periodic inventory system.

Example 2. ProCraft Boat Manufacturers produces small fishing boats. Throughout 2001, increases in the cost of lightweight materials have caused a steady increase in production costs. Information on beginning inventory, the cost of production runs, and sales data (all cost data are in thousands) for 2001 is presented below. Allocate the total costs of goods available for sale to cost of goods sold and ending inventory using (a) weighted-average, (b) first-in, first-out (FIFO), and (c) last-in, first-out (LIFO).

		In Thousands	
	Units	**Cost per Unit**	**Total Cost**
Beginning inventory, 1/1/01	800	$ 4	$ 3,200
Production runs:			
1/15/01	200	5	1,000
4/15/01	250	6	1,500
5/6/01	200	6	1,200
7/15/01	300	7	2,100
9/4/01	100	8	800
11/30/01	150	10	1,500
Total goods available for sale during 2001	2,000		$11,300

	Units	**Sales Price per Unit**	**Total**
Sales:			
2/1/01	400	$ 7	$ 2,800
3/15/01	300	7	2,100
6/30/01	300	8	2,400
8/1/01	200	10	2,000
12/15/01	300	11	3,300
Total sales in 2001	1,500		$12,600

3. Bookkeeping cost is not the only disadvantage of specific identification. In some cases, management could manipulate income by choosing to sell high-cost or low-cost units of a given inventory item.
4. The United States is the only major country allowing the use of LIFO.

Solution (all dollar amounts are in thousands).

(a) Weighted-average. Under the weighted-average method, an average acquisition cost per unit is computed by dividing the cost of goods available for sale by the units available for sale during the period:

$11,300 ÷ 2,000 units = $5.65 per unit

The $11,300 cost of goods available for sale is allocated between ending inventory and cost of goods sold as follows:

Cost of goods sold	1,500 units sold × $5.65 =	$ 8,475
Ending inventory	500 units on hand × $5.65 =	2,825
Total cost allocated		$11,300

Under the weighted-average method, both ending inventory and cost of goods sold reflect the average cost of inventory acquisitions in the current period and prior periods (from beginning inventory).

(b) First-in, first-out (FIFO). The term FIFO relates to the inventory sold during the period. FIFO costing assumes that the first units produced (or purchased) are the first units sold. Consequently, the most recent units produced (or purchased) remain in ending inventory. To compute the cost of the 1,500 units sold in the Pro-Craft problem, we assume beginning inventory was sold first, the units in the January 15, 2001, production run were sold second, and so on:

Cost of goods sold	800 units sold × $4 =	$3,200	
	200 units sold × $5 =	1,000	
	250 units sold × $6 =	1,500	
	200 units sold × $6 =	1,200	
	50 units sold × $7 =	350	$ 7,250
Ending inventory	250 units × $ 7 =	$1,750	
	100 units × $ 8 =	800	
	150 units × $10 =	1,500	4,050
Total cost allocated			$11,300

(c) Last-in, first-out (LIFO). The term LIFO also relates to the inventory sold during the period. LIFO costing assumes that the last units produced (or purchased) are the first units sold, and the first units produced (or purchased) during the period remain in ending inventory. The computation of the cost of the 1,500 units sold assumes that the units in the November 30, 2001, production run were sold first, the units in the September 4, 2001, production run were sold second, and so on:

Cost of goods sold	150 units sold × $10 =	$1,500	
	100 units sold × $ 8 =	800	
	300 units sold × $ 7 =	2,100	
	200 units sold × $ 6 =	1,200	
	250 units sold × $ 6 =	1,500	
	200 units sold × $ 5 =	1,000	
	300 units sold × $ 4 =	1,200	$ 9,300
Ending inventory	500 units × $4 =		2,000
Total cost allocated			$11,300

EXAMPLE 2 Journal Entries

*Assuming a periodic inventory system, with production recorded in Cost of Goods Manufactured:**

Inventory (balance sheet)**	allocated amount	
Cost of Goods Sold (income statement)**	allocated amount	
Inventory (beginning)		3,200
Cost of Goods Manufactured* (total cost of production runs)		8,100

*Cost of Goods Manufactured accumulates the cost of raw materials, direct labor, and factory overhead to document the cost of items manufactured during a period.
**These amounts are determined by applying an inventory costing method (e.g., weighted-average, FIFO, LIFO).

Evaluating the Inventory Costing Methods In the ProCraft example, inventory acquisition costs increased during the period, a common situation with increases in the general price index (i.e., inflation).[5] The following table summarizes the amounts computed in the ProCraft example:

Inventory Method	Cost of Goods Sold	Ending Inventory	Total
Weighted-average	$8,475	$2,825	$11,300
FIFO	7,250	4,050	11,300
LIFO	9,300	2,000	11,300

Note that LIFO cost of goods sold is the highest, and FIFO cost of goods sold is the lowest. Given that sales revenue is the same regardless of the method, LIFO provides the lowest net income of the three methods. A lower LIFO net income is consistent with a lower LIFO ending inventory amount because, with all else equal, a capital maintenance view of income gives a lower value of net income for lower ending asset amounts.

Lower net income and ending inventory under LIFO costing in periods of rising prices is a general result. The reverse is also true, with higher net income and ending inventory for LIFO in periods of falling inventory acquisition prices. The weighted-average amounts fall between the other two costing methods.

If prices are more often rising than not, why do firms use LIFO? Several disadvantages are apparent. First, LIFO firms have smaller earnings and smaller values for ending inventory. Is this a desirable financial picture to paint for investors and creditors? Second, LIFO cost flow is certainly inconsistent with the physical inventory flow for most firms. How many firms sell the most recently produced units and hold old units in inventory?

Still, LIFO remains a popular inventory costing choice because it has several advantages over FIFO and weighted-average. First, LIFO does the best job (of available GAAP methods) in approximating current cost income (sales price minus the cost to replace inventory). For example, assume that a retailer has the following two layers of inventory:

Beginning inventory	300 units @ $4
Purchases	100 units @ $10

Current purchases are higher than beginning inventory because inventory acquisition costs are rising. The retailer increases its selling price to $12 to earn a 20% return on the $10 inventory cost. Further assume that the next piece of inventory will cost the retailer $11 to acquire. The current cost net income on the sale of one unit is computed as follows:

5. Inventory prices on specific goods can decrease, of course, even in the presence of inflation.

Sales	$12
Cost of goods sold (replacement cost)	(11)
Current cost net income	$ 1

The computation of current cost net income involves subtracting the replacement cost of income from sales. An advantage of current cost net income is that physical capital is maintained. The retailer can pay the $1 net income in dividends and still have $11 left to replace the piece of inventory and remain in business. Compare the current cost income computation to LIFO and FIFO:

	Current Cost	LIFO	FIFO
Sales	$12	$12	$12
Cost of goods sold	(11)	(10)	(4)
Net income	$ 1	$ 2	$ 8

Neither generally accepted accounting method yields a current cost net income of $1. But, LIFO is closer because it matches the costs of the more expensive recent purchases with sales.

Another important advantage of LIFO is its tax benefits. If LIFO is used on the tax return, then taxable income and the resulting tax payments are lower in early years. This cash savings can be invested in positive net present value projects to increase firm wealth. If inventory levels are drawn down in later years, additional taxes will be due. But, the increase in firm wealth from the tax break in earlier years should more than offset the additional taxes due in later years.

The Internal Revenue Code's ***LIFO conformity rule*** requires that **firms using LIFO on the tax return must also use LIFO for financial reporting purposes.** However, because some firms receive little or no tax benefit from the use of LIFO, we observe weighted-average and FIFO as the inventory method of choice for many firms. These firms might have smaller inventories, high inventory turnover, or might generate tax deductible losses from other transactions to such an extent that the additional tax deduction presented by LIFO costing is not needed.[6]

Physical Inventories At or near the end of a reporting period, the firm takes a physical inventory. The inventory count provides a basis for allocating the number of units available for sale to ending inventory and cost of goods sold.[7] It is important to realize, however, that inventory possession does not necessarily constitute legal ownership, and lack of possession does not indicate lack of ownership. Consider the following examples:

Example 3. Sandberg Enterprises sold goods to Cubbie Co., shipping them F.O.B. destination on December 26, 2001. The goods arrived at Cubbie Co.'s store on January 1, 2002.

Solution. The contract term F.O.B. (free on board) destination determines when legal title to the inventory transfers. F.O.B. destination means that legal title transfers when the inventory is received at Cubbie Co. Sandberg Enterprises does *not*

6. Of 600 companies surveyed, the 1999 *Accounting Trends & Techniques* indicates that 319 companies used LIFO for at least some inventories, while 281 did not use LIFO for any inventories. The following companies reported using the different methods (the number is greater than 600 because firms may use different methods for certain inventories): FIFO, 409; LIFO, 319; weighted-average, 176; other, 40. Firms reported using LIFO for all inventories, 30; 50% or more of inventories, 152; 50% or less of inventories, 95; not determinable, 42; total, 319.

7. With the advent of bar-code readers at checkouts, many firms also maintain a perpetual updating of units on hand. The physical inventory count remains a good internal control procedure for these firms. Inventory records can be compared to the physical count to ascertain if recording errors have occurred or if inventory has been misplaced, stolen, or simply disappeared due to evaporation, shrinkage, or decay.

have possession of the goods at December 31, 2001, when it takes its physical inventory. However, these goods must be included in Sandberg's physical inventory count because legal title to the goods has not passed to Cubbie Co. by this date. Alternatively, if the terms had been F.O.B. shipping point, then Sandberg would not reflect the inventory at December 31, 2001, but Cubbie Co. should.

Example 4. Vaughn Consignment Shoppe markets used sporting goods. Clients bring their goods to Vaughn, the goods are coded with the client's identification number, and Vaughn remits 75% of the final selling price of the goods to the client when the goods are sold.

Solution. Inventory on consignment belongs to the consignor. Vaughn, the consignee, possesses the inventory at year-end, but does not own it. As a control procedure, Vaughn would probably perform a physical count of the consigned goods to ensure that the goods on hand were appropriately reflected in Vaughn's consignment records.

Example 5. On December 31, 2001, Peterson Products has a short-term need for cash, and Maybelle Co. has a short-term need for inventory. Maybelle Co. does not intend to sell the inventory, but needs to show a purchase on its books to avoid a LIFO layer liquidation. (We discuss the concept of LIFO layer liquidation in the next section.) Peterson sells the inventory to Maybelle with an agreement to buy it back in 30 days.

Solution. Peterson does not have the goods on hand, but must include the inventory in its physical count. GAAP requires that sales with buy-back agreements not be recorded as sales. Maybelle Co. should not include the inventory in its physical count.

Example 6. On December 15, 2001, FastBooks sells 5,000 books on a controversial topic by a new author to Book Retailers Incorporated. Under the terms of the sales agreement, Book Retailers may return unsold units at any time within a 90-day period. Because of the nature of the book and the unknown author, there is no basis for determining how many of the books will be returned by Book Retailers.

Solution. FastBooks counts the 5,000 books in its physical inventory; Book Retailers does not. The general rule for recording book sales is to recognize the sale and estimate sales returns. If returns are expected to be substantial and no basis exists for the estimation of the returns, then a sale should not be recorded until the return privilege expires.

LIFO Layer Liquidation Consider the following LIFO inventory records for Baker Products:

Beginning inventory	100 units @ $1
2001 purchases	100 units @ $15

Assume that Baker sells 120 units during 2001 for $20 each. Sales of $20 are matched with costs of $15 for the first 100 units, yielding a profit of $5 per unit; for the additional 20 units, sales of $20 are matched with costs of $1, yielding a profit of $19 per unit.[8] For tax purposes, eating into previous LIFO layers leads to substantial taxes being paid. Assuming an overall income tax rate of 40% and ignoring all other costs and revenues, the sale of the first 100 units would result in income taxes of $2 per unit ($20 sales price − $15 cost = $5 per unit profit × 40% tax rate). However, the tax on the additional 20 units sold is $7.60 per unit ($20 sales price − $1 cost = $19 per unit profit × 40%). The excess cash outflow

8. Baker receives $20 for the units in beginning inventory because all units are sold at the retail price. Application of LIFO over the years has resulted in old costs being assigned to new units.

from paying additional taxes makes it more difficult to maintain real capital (i.e., buy the next piece of inventory). Because of this detrimental tax effect, most companies try not to eat into inventory layers.

In addition to the detrimental tax effect of LIFO layer liquidation, the layer liquidation also results in excess profits being reported to shareholders that cannot be sustained, and, therefore, costs of managing investor expectations are incurred. For example, managers might have to issue a press release or hold meetings with financial analysts to explain the LIFO layer liquidation problem. Finally, the LIFO layer liquidation problem can lead to suboptimal behavior when a firm buys unneeded inventory at year-end simply to keep from liquidating LIFO inventory layers.

Special Forms of LIFO Special forms of LIFO have been created to avoid the potentially serious problem of LIFO layer liquidation. These forms of LIFO involve an adjustment in the way LIFO is applied to minimize the probability of layer liquidation. Two special forms of LIFO that accomplish this objective are *specific goods pooled LIFO* and *dollar value LIFO*. Both forms are pooled LIFO approaches, with the former pooling in terms of units and the latter pooling in terms of dollars. Pooling diversifies the movements of different goods within the pools. For example, if LIFO is applied to every good individually, layer liquidations will occur for those goods that experience quantity declines. But, if LIFO is applied on a pool of inventory items, some increasing in quantity and others decreasing, a growing firm as a whole minimizes the chance of layer liquidation for the pool. The concept is similar to portfolio diversification of investments.

***Specific goods pooled LIFO* groups substantially identical inventory items.** The number of units and the average cost per unit in the pool at each date are computed. If units increase during a period, a layer is added. If units decrease, then layers are removed in a LIFO fashion (i.e., in the same manner as illustrated earlier for regular LIFO). While it is reasonable for a kitchen supply shop to add units of towels to units of potholders, other firms have more heterogeneous inventory items.

The advantage of ***dollar value LIFO*** is that **pools are formed of items that are similar in use, similar in material, or interchangeable inventory items.** Hence, fewer pools are created, and the probability of LIFO layer liquidation is lowered. Dollar value LIFO avoids replacement problems inherent in the narrow pool definitions used in specific goods pooled LIFO. Wider pools of inventory can be created by adding together an attribute possessed by all goods—dollar cost.

Example 7. Big Retail Co. began operations in 2001. Given the information presented below, compute the annual dollar value LIFO ending inventory of Big Retail Co. for 2001–2004.

December 31	Year-End Cost of Ending Inventory*	Price Index**
2001	$300,000	1.00
2002	451,000	1.10
2003	500,000	1.25
2004	715,000	1.30

*The cost of ending inventory is computed for each item by multiplying the ending inventory times the most recent purchase price.

**The price index may be computed by the company or provided by an outside party such as an industry trade association.

Solution. The first step in dollar value LIFO is to compute the cost of ending inventory using the most recent prices. The most recent purchases are stated in terms of year-end costs. For example, Big Retail counts washing machine units on hand at year-end and multiplies the count by the most recent purchase cost for a washing machine. This computation is performed for every item in the pool (e.g., microwave ovens, refrigerators, etc.), and the extended costs are summed to arrive at the ending inventory in terms of year-end cost.

The second step is to *convert the ending inventory at year-end costs to ending inventory in terms of base year costs.* December 31, 2001, is the year in which Big Retail adopted dollar value LIFO as its inventory costing method. All subsequent ending inventory computations involve a comparison with this "base year."

Because Big Retail began operations in 2001, the *December 31, 2001,* inventory under dollar value LIFO is simply:

$$\$300{,}000 \times 1.00 = \$300{,}000$$

The base year inventory layer of $300,000 serves as a starting point for application of the dollar value LIFO method in subsequent years.

At *December 31, 2002,* ending inventory units are again counted and multiplied by the most recent purchase price. In our example, this total is $451,000. Whenever a LIFO method is applied, the interest is in whether a new layer of inventory has been added from current period unit purchases exceeding current period unit sales, or whether an existing layer of inventory has been eroded from current period unit sales exceeding current period unit purchases. Big Retail began 2002 with one LIFO layer. At first glance, it appears that a new layer of units has been added in 2002. Ending inventory in terms of year-end costs has increased from $300,000 to $451,000. However, this increase could be due to an increase in unit costs (a nominal increase) rather than due to an increase in physical units (a real increase in units). To apply dollar value LIFO, Big Retail must ascertain the extent to which the dollar increase was caused by cost increases. Big Retail will either refer to industry price indices or create its own internal index by comparing current inventory units at beginning-of-the-year costs to the same units at end-of-the-year costs. The information provided in our example indicates an index of 1.10, which means that acquisition costs of inventory in the LIFO pool increased by 10% in 2002, relative to the base year. Inventory at December 31, 2002, is computed as follows:

EXHIBIT 2 Example 7. 2002 Dollar Value LIFO Computations

12/31/02 inventory at year-end prices	$451,000
Divided by the price index*	÷ 1.10
12/31/02 inventory in terms of base year costs*	$410,000
12/31/01 inventory in terms of base year costs (from prior year)	(300,000)
2002 increase (decrease) in terms of base year costs	$110,000

*We can divide by the price index because the base year index = 1.00. To accomplish this computation, we are actually multiplying the 12/31/02 inventory at year-end prices by the ratio of base year index divided by current year index: $451,000 × (1.00 / 1.1) = $410,000.

After removing the 10% increase in acquisition costs from $451,000, the December 31, 2002, inventory is stated in terms of base year costs. When compared to the December 31, 2001, inventory in base year costs, a real increment (net of general price increases) of $110,000 occurred in 2002. Because the increment occurred when prices were 10% higher, the dollar value LIFO inventory record indicates that the base year inventory of $300,000 remains, and an increment of $121,000 (i.e., $110,000 added when prices were 10% higher) during 2002 is also present:

EXHIBIT 3 Example 7. Dollar Value LIFO: December 31, 2002, Ending Inventory Calculation

2001 Layer	$300,000 × 1.00	$300,000
2002 Layer	$110,000 × 1.10	121,000
Total		$421,000

Following the same procedure, *December 31, 2003,* dollar value LIFO ending inventory is computed as follows:

EXHIBIT 4 Example 7. 2003 Dollar Value LIFO Computations

12/31/03 inventory at year-end prices	$500,000
Divided by the price index	÷ 1.25
12/31/03 inventory in terms of base year costs	$400,000
12/31/02 inventory in terms of base year costs	(410,000)
2003 increase (decrease) in terms of base year costs	$ (10,000)

After removing the 25% increase in acquisition costs from $500,000, the December 31, 2003, inventory is stated in terms of base year costs. When compared to the December 31, 2002, inventory in base year costs, a real decrease of $10,000 occurred in 2003. This decrease indicates that, instead of a layer being added to the dollar value LIFO inventory record in 2003, $10,000 of the 2002 layer (in base year dollars) was eroded, thus leaving the following December 31, 2003, inventory information:

EXHIBIT 5 Example 7. Dollar Value LIFO: December 31, 2003, Ending Inventory Calculation

2001 Layer	$300,000 × 1.00	$300,000
2002 Layer	$100,000 × 1.10	110,000
Total		$410,000

The 2002 inventory layer added at 1.10 is reduced from $110,000 @ 1.10 to $100,000 @ 1.10 to reflect the $10,000 base year dollar erosion of the layer. The LIFO record does not contain any goods extended at the 2003 price index of 1.25 because all of those goods were assumed sold in 2003.

December 31, 2004, dollar value LIFO ending inventory is computed as follows:

EXHIBIT 6 Example 7. 2004 Dollar Value LIFO Computations

12/31/04 inventory at year-end prices	$715,000
Divided by the price index	÷ 1.30
12/31/04 inventory in terms of base year costs	$550,000
12/31/03 inventory in terms of base year costs	(400,000)
2004 increase (decrease) in terms of base year costs	$150,000

Because a new layer is added in 2004 when the price index is 1.30, the dollar value LIFO inventory record appears as follows:

EXHIBIT 7 Example 7. Dollar Value LIFO: December 31, 2004, Ending Inventory Calculation

2001 Layer	$300,000 × 1.00	$300,000
2002 Layer	$100,000 × 1.10	110,000
2004 Layer	$150,000 × 1.30	195,000
Total		$605,000

As long as Big Retail increases inventory in nominal dollars each year, the chances are slim that the 2001 base year inventory layer will ever be eroded. The problem of LIFO layer liquidation becomes far less of an issue when the dollar value approach is used. Very few firms that employ LIFO use the basic LIFO approach. Most firms use one of the special forms of LIFO that pool goods to avoid the layer liquidation problem.

Inventory Balance Sheet Valuation

5 Measure inventory for balance sheet valuation.

To this point, we have concentrated on determining the *cost* of inventory. Under GAAP, inventory is reported at each balance sheet date under the ***lower-of-cost-or-market (LCM) method.*** The purpose of LCM is to **recognize a decline in inventory utility** (i.e., impaired future cash flows) **in the period in which the decline occurs rather than when the inventory is sold.** LCM is justified by the matching principle. Further, the recognition of declines (but not increases) in utility is justified by the conservatism principle.

The concept of "market" is replacement cost (i.e., the next inventory acquisition cost). Because sellers normally increase selling prices to offset increases in acquisition costs, changes in replacement cost signal changes in net realizable value (future selling prices less expected disposal costs). If replacement cost is a valid market concept, then **replacement cost should never be higher than net realizable value** (the ***ceiling***), and **should never be lower than net realizable value minus a normal profit margin that the seller is attempting to maintain** (the ***floor***). If replacement cost is greater than the ceiling or less than the floor, then the concept of replacement cost as "market" is not valid, and the ***designated market value*** becomes the **ceiling or floor,** respectively. We use the designated market value in LCM valuation because we should never value inventory at a higher cost than for what it would sell (net realizable value), or write it down so low (below net realizable value less a normal profit margin) such that subsequent sales yield abnormally high profit margins.

Example 8. Consider the following independent cases that illustrate inventory valuation at LCM:

	Market Value Information*					
Case	**NRV**	**RC**	**NRV-PM**	**Designated Market****	**Cost*****	**LCM Balance Sheet Valuation**
A	$80	$60	$30	$60	$ 50	$50
B	80	45	30	45	50	45
C	80	90	30	80	50	50
D	80	90	30	80	100	80
E	80	25	30	30	100	30

*NRV = Net realizable value (the ceiling value); RC = Replacement cost; and NRV-PM = Net realizable value less a normal profit margin (the floor value).

**Note that designated market is the middle of the three market values in all cases, and neither exceeds the ceiling nor is lower than the floor.

***Cost is determined using an appropriate costing method, e.g., specific identification, LIFO, FIFO.

Solution. In *Case A*, inventory has an acquisition cost of $50, and replacement cost (i.e., the cost to purchase the next unit of inventory with the same revenue generating potential) has risen to $60. The inventory's net realizable value (i.e., selling price minus disposal costs) is $80, and the net realizable value minus a normal profit margin for this item is $30. Replacement cost appears to be a valid market concept in this case. Replacement cost valuation of inventory would not be higher than what the inventory would sell for (NRV = $80), or so low as to render future profits that would be greater than the normal profit margin. Thus, replacement cost of $60 is the designated market value to be compared to the $50 original cost. Because the original cost is lower, the inventory under LCM is reported at $50. No adjustment is necessary to reduce inventory to LCM valuation because the inventory is already recorded in the accounting records at $50.

Case B is similar in terms of the appropriateness of a $45 replacement cost as the market concept. Replacement cost is lower than the acquisition cost of $50, however, and inventory must be written down to market from $50 to $45. The remaining $5 is reported as a "loss from decline in inventory market value" in the financial revenues, (expenses), gains, and (losses) section of the income statement.

EXAMPLE 8 Journal Entry

Case B—LCM Write-down:		
Loss from Decline in Inventory Market Value	5	
Inventory (or Allowance to Reduce Inventory to Market Value)		5

Cases C, D, and E illustrate situations in which replacement cost is not a good measure of market value. In *Case C,* the replacement cost of $90 exceeds the net realizable value of $80. Such a situation could occur if input costs are rising, but customer demand for the inventory is elastic, and thus, will not allow selling price increases. Remember, under the notion that replacement cost is a good measure of "market," replacement cost increases are reflected in selling price increases, and, consequently, replacement cost should not be higher than net realizable value. Further, we should not value a saleable asset (such as inventory on the balance sheet) at an amount that is higher than its ultimate sales price. As a result of these conditions, the designated market value in *Case C* is the net realizable value of $80. Under LCM valuation rules, the cost ($50) is lower than the designated market ($80), and no write-down of inventory below its cost is necessary.

Case D is similar to *Case C* in that the designated market is the net realizable value of $80. But, in this case, the acquisition cost is $100, and a $20 write-down of inventory occurs on the balance sheet with a corresponding $20 loss recognition on the income statement.

In *Case E,* replacement cost has fallen so far that it is below the floor for LCM valuation. This case might seem unrealistic. Why would replacement cost fall so far compared to cost ($100) and NRV ($80)? An example is often found in the electronic components industry where prices can fall dramatically. In this case, the floor of $30 becomes designated market, and inventory is written down from the $100 cost to $30. At first glance it would seem that conservatism would suggest that we write down the inventory even further (to $25). But, under the conditions in *Case E,* consider how the firm's profit would look in both the year of the write-down and the following year when the inventory is sold:

Correct Application of LCM

	Year of Write-Down	**Year of Sale**
Loss on write-down	$100 − $30 = $70	
Profit on sale		$80 − $30 = $50

More Conservative Write-Down Below Floor

	Year of Write-Down	**Year of Sale**
Loss on write-down	$100 − $25 = $75	
Profit on sale		$80 − $25 = $55

A correct application of LCM results in the normal $50 profit margin being reported in the year of sale. The more conservative write-down below the floor results in a $5 higher write-down loss in the year LCM is applied, but a $5 higher than normal profit margin in the year of sale. The objective of not recording abnormal profit margins in the year of sale justifies the LCM rule of not writing down inventory below the floor.

Summary of Inventory Accounting

In summary, inventory is initially recorded at historical cost, which is equal to the fair value of consideration sacrificed to prepare the inventory for resale. Cost flow assumptions such as LIFO, FIFO, and weighted-average are used to assign historical costs to the units sold (i.e., Cost of Goods Sold) and to ending inventory. LCM is applied to ending inventory on the balance sheet. Any write-downs from inventory cost to LCM are reported as losses of the period in which the decline in expected future cash flows occurred.

To illustrate inventory information contained in annual reports, the following inventory information comes from Ecolab's 1998 annual report.

Ecolab: Balance Sheet (in thousands of dollars)

	December 31	
	1998	**1997**
Inventory	165,627	154,831

Note Two: Summary of Significant Accounting Policies
Inventory Valuations
Inventories are valued at the lower of cost or market. Domestic chemical inventory costs are determined on a last-in, first-out (lifo) basis. Lifo inventories represented 45 percent and 40 percent of consolidated inventories at year-end 1998 and 1997, respectively. All other inventory costs are determined on a first-in, first-out (fifo) basis.

Note Three: Inventories (in thousands of dollars)

	December 31	
	1998	**1997**
Finished goods	$ 73,983	$ 67,823
Raw materials and parts	93,862	89,716
Excess of fifo cost over lifo cost	(2,218)	(2,708)
Total	$165,627	$154,831

Ecolab has two inventories, Finished Goods and Raw Materials and Parts. Note the amounts listed by the caption "Excess of FIFO cost over LIFO cost." These amounts reported represent *LIFO adjustments*. It is common for firms that use LIFO to actually keep inventory records on a FIFO (or other) basis. Thus, at year-end, an adjustment is needed to restate ending inventory from FIFO to LIFO. A LIFO adjustment is made to effect the change from FIFO cost to LIFO cost.

Establishing Credit Policy

6 Explain why firms extend credit.

To some extent, the ability to make a sale depends on the payment options given to customers. If the only payment option is cash, then some sales will be lost to customers who have short-term cash flow problems, or those who prefer to do business with merchants who will extend credit. Easy credit is a great way to stimulate sales by accommodating the payment preferences of customers.

A great deal of thought goes into the credit extension decision. As policies to determine customer credit worthiness are relaxed, the probability of payment default increases. The goal of the firm is to maximize the trade-off between increased sales revenue and increased bad debts over all possible credit policies. For example, Alabama Co. presently sells $1,000,000 per year on credit, allowing customers 30 days to pay the invoice. Currently, bad debts average 1% of sales. Alabama's credit manager estimates that sales could be increased by 1.6% if a 45-day payment period were implemented. However, bad debts would also increase to 1.3% of sales. A comparison of the two situations reveals a trade-off between increased benefits (more sales revenue) and increased costs (more bad debts):

	Current Situation: 30-days credit, Bad Debts Expense 1% of credit sales	**Proposed Situation: 45-days credit, Bad Debts Expense 1.3% of credit sales**
Sales revenue	$1,000,000	$1,016,000
Bad debts expense	10,000	13,208
Net sales revenue	$ 990,000	$1,002,792

It appears that the credit policy change is warranted because sales net of bad debts expense are expected to rise by $12,792 if credit terms are increased to 45 days. The link between increased sales and increased customer defaults that is created by relaxing the credit policy is central to the accounting for accounts receivable and associated bad debts.

Determining the Amount of Accounts Receivable

7 Explain how accounts receivable are generated and measured.

Accounts receivable are generated in the normal course of business as firms provide services or goods to customers in exchange for short-term promises to pay. These promises do not bear interest if payment is made in a relatively short period of time. Because accounts receivable transactions are common and repetitive and do not bear interest, determining the amount receivable is a simple task. Customers promise to pay the cash equivalent price of the goods or services, and that amount is recorded in Sales (or Services) Revenue and Accounts Receivable.

Previously in the chapter, we illustrated how buyers should record purchase discounts. Sellers follow a similar procedure to record sales discounts using the net method. ***Sales discounts*** offered are treated as a reduction of the sales price, and sales discounts not taken are reported as interest income.

Example 9. Assume that Baumgart Co. made a $100,000 sale to Lively Co. with terms of 2/15, net 30. The goods cost $60,000.

Solution. Baumgart should record the sale and account receivable at $98,000 ($100,000 less 2%), the equivalent cash price. If Lively does not take the discount and remits $100,000 at the end of 30 days, then the additional $2,000 is reported as interest income. Exhibit 8 illustrates Baumgart financial statements if the discount is *not* taken.

EXHIBIT 8 Example 9. Baumgart Co. Financial Statements

Statement of Cash Flows

Operating Activities	
Collections from customers	$ 98,000
Interest receipts	2,000
Total cash inflows	$100,000

Balance Sheet

Assets		**Liabilities**	
Current assets:		**Owners' Equity**	
Cash	$100,000 ↑	Retained earnings (through effect	
Inventory	60,000 ↓	on net income)*	$40,000 ↑

Income Statement*

Sales	$98,000
Cost of goods sold	(60,000)
Gross margin	$38,000
Financial revenues, (expenses), gains, and (losses):	
Interest revenue	2,000
Net income	$40,000

Statement of Owners' Equity

Net income*	$40,000 ↑

*Ignores effect of income taxes

EXAMPLE 9 Journal Entries

Date of sale:

Accounts Receivable	98,000	
Sales Revenue		98,000

Payment received in first 15 days:

Cash	98,000	
Accounts Receivable		98,000

Payment received after first 15 days:

When 15-day period expires:

Accounts Receivable	2,000	
Interest Revenue		2,000

When payment is received:

Cash	100,000	
Accounts Receivable		100,000

Accounts Receivable Valuation

8 Report accounts receivable on the balance sheet.

The final event in the life of an account receivable is conversion to cash. That is, the *realizable* amount becomes *realized*. Therefore, accountants report accounts receivable on the balance sheet at the amount of cash that is expected to be realized (i.e., the "net realizable value"). To accomplish net realizable value reporting, accountants estimate (at each balance sheet date) the amounts that they expect will *not* be collected. These estimates are developed for the two causes of uncollectible receivables: sales returns and bad debts.

Sales Returns If ***sales returns*** are infrequent and small in dollar amount, they are recorded as incurred by simultaneously reducing Sales and Accounts Receivable. Although this approach does not report accounts receivable at net realizable value and mismatches the sales returns of one period with the sales of the next period, these violations are justified by the immateriality of the transactions. If sales returns are material, then they should be accounted for using the ***allowance method.*** Basically, the **expected sales returns are estimated and reported as a subtraction from Sales Revenue in the income statement, and from Accounts Receivable on the balance sheet.**

Example 10. Riley Co. has $1,000 in credit sales. It collects $200 during the period and estimates $50 in sales returns at year-end. How should the income statement and balance sheet report the net effect of these transactions?

Solution. On the income statement, Riley Co. reports $950 in net sales ($1,000 credit sales less $50 expected returns). On the balance sheet assets increase by $950 as well:

Income Statement		
Sales revenue	$1,000	
Less estimated sales returns	(50)	$950
Balance Sheet		
Cash		$200
Accounts receivable	$ 800	
Less allowance for sales returns	(50)	750

EXAMPLE 10 Journal Entries

Sale:		
Accounts Receivable	1,000	
Sales Revenue		1,000
Collections:		
Cash	200	
Accounts Receivable		200
Estimation of sales returns:		
Sales Returns	50	
Allowance for Sales Returns		50

If the return privilege is too great in amount and probability, then the sale is not recorded because realizing the account receivable is questionable.

Bad Debts Bad debts are accounted for using the *allowance method.* Companies traditionally apply either the income statement approach or the balance sheet approach to estimate bad debts under the allowance method. Both approaches accomplish the two goals of the allowance method, (1) the valuation of accounts receivable at net realizable value and (2) the matching of the cost of extending credit (bad debt expense) with the benefits of extending credit (sales revenue).

When using the *income statement approach,* accountants concentrate on estimating the income statement effect of bad debts. Bad Debts Expense is computed by multiplying credit sales by the percentage of expected uncollectible credit sales. The reduction in accounts receivable is reported by leaving Accounts Receivable at its face amount and establishing a contra account, Allowance for Doubtful Accounts. This contra account is then subtracted from accounts receivable on the face of the balance sheet.

The focus changes if the *balance sheet approach* is used. Emphasis is placed on determining the proper balance in the allowance account rather than directly computing bad debts expense. This proper balance is determined either by taking a percentage of total ending accounting receivable or by **applying different percentages to groups of receivables based on age** (an ***aging of receivables***).

An alternative method for accounting for bad debts is the ***direct write-off method.* Accounts receivable are written off to bad debts expense as the account becomes uncollectible.** *The direct write-off method is not allowed by GAAP for financial reporting* because it violates the matching principle by recognizing bad debts in a period other than the period in which credit policy led to increases in sales revenue. Further, because it is probable that some receivables will not be collectible, the direct write-off method's failure to establish a contra account also violates the net realizable value reporting of accounts receivable.

Example 11. Cleaves Company recorded the following in 2001 and 2002, its first two years of operations:

	2001	2002
Credit sales	$1,000,000	$1,200,000
Collections on credit sales	800,000	900,000
Specific accounts identified that will not be collected and should be written off	0	15,000

Compute bad debts expense for 2001 and 2002, and the valuation of accounts receivable at December 31, 2001, and December 31, 2002, under the following two independent scenarios:
(a) Cleaves uses the balance sheet approach, and an aging of accounts receivable indicates that 10% of gross accounts receivable are estimated to be uncollectible at each balance sheet date.
(b) Cleaves uses the income statement approach and estimates bad debts to be 2.1% of credit sales.

Solution.
Scenario (a) By the end of 2001, Cleaves has outstanding accounts receivable of $200,000 ($1,000,000 in credit sales less $800,000 collections). The goal of the *balance sheet approach* is to reflect the expected uncollectible accounts of $20,000 (10% of the $200,000 receivable balance) as a reduction of the gross accounts receivable. Because this is the first year of Cleaves' operations, there is no beginning balance of uncollectible accounts. Therefore, the accountant adjusts the $0 beginning estimated uncollectible balance to a $20,000 ending estimated uncollectible balance. This $20,000 write-down of receivables flows through to the income statement as Bad Debts Expense:

	Beginning Balance	Write-Down	Ending Balance
Accounts receivable	$200,000		$200,000
Allowance for doubtful accounts	0	$20,000	(20,000)
Net realizable value	$200,000		$180,000

The allowance for doubtful accounts disclosure is an expectation that accounts totaling $20,000 will not be collected. In 2002, Cleaves identifies that specific customers will not pay $15,000. This fact is reflected by the accountant as a simultaneous reduction in accounts receivable and the allowance for doubtful accounts in 2002:

	Beginning Balance	Write-Off of Specific Accounts	Ending Balance
Accounts receivable	$200,000	$(15,000)	$185,000
Allowance for doubtful accounts	(20,000)	15,000	(5,000)
Net realizable value	$180,000	$ 0	$180,000

Note that the write-off of specific uncollectible accounts has no effect on net realizable value, and thus, no income statement effect. Instead, the income statement effect was recognized in the prior period (2001) when the bad debts expense was matched with sales.

By the end of 2002, Cleaves has outstanding accounts receivable of $485,000 ($2,200,000 in credit sales in 2001 and 2002 less $1,700,000 in collections and $15,000 of write-offs), and uncollectible accounts are estimated at $48,500 (10% of the receivables balance). Because there is a balance in Allowance for Doubtful Accounts of $5,000 at year-end before adjustment, the accountant simply adjusts the balance to the required $48,500 ending estimated uncollectible balance. This $43,500 write-down of receivables flows through to the income statement as Bad Debts Expense:

	Beginning Balance	Write-Down	Ending Balance
Accounts receivable	$485,000		$485,000
Allowance for doubtful accounts	(5,000)	$43,500	(48,500)
Net realizable value	$480,000		$436,500

Scenario (b) The goal of the *income statement approach* is to properly match the bad debts expense with the sales revenue in each year. Bad Debts Expense for 2001 is $21,000 (2.1% of $1,000,000 in credit sales). This $21,000 flows through to the balance sheet as an adjustment to Allowance for Doubtful Accounts:

	Beginning Balance	Write-Down	Ending Balance
Accounts receivable	$200,000		$200,000
Allowance for doubtful accounts	0	$21,000	(21,000)
Net realizable value	$200,000		$179,000

When, in 2002, Cleaves identifies that specific customers will not pay $15,000, the accountant simultaneously reduces Accounts Receivable and Allowance for Doubtful Accounts:

	Beginning Balance	Write-Off of Specific Accounts	Ending Balance
Accounts receivable	$200,000	$(15,000)	$185,000
Allowance for doubtful accounts	(21,000)	15,000	(6,000)
Net realizable value	$179,000	$ 0	$179,000

As always, a write-off of specific uncollectible accounts has no effect on net realizable value, and thus, no income statement effect.

In 2002, $1,200,000 in credit sales multiplied by 2.1% yields bad debt expense of $25,200, which flows through to the balance sheet as an adjustment to Allowance for Doubtful Accounts:

	Beginning Balance	Write-Down	Ending Balance
Accounts receivable	$485,000		$485,000
Allowance for doubtful accounts	(6,000)	$25,200	(31,200)
Net realizable value	$479,000		$453,800

Both the income statement and the balance sheet method match the bad debts expense with the period in which the sales revenue is generated, and report the net realizable value of accounts receivable. However, the income statement approach concentrates on proper measurement of bad debts expense and can lead to greater error in the net realizable value reporting of receivables. The balance sheet approach leads to better net realizable value reporting but can cause more volatility on the income statement.

EXAMPLE 11 Journal Entries

	2001		2002	
Credit sales:				
Accounts Receivable	1,000,000		1,200,000	
Sales Revenue		1,000,000		1,200,000
Cash collections:				
Cash	800,000		900,000	
Accounts Receivable		800,000		900,000
Write-off of specific uncollectible accounts:				
Allowance for Doubtful Accounts			15,000	
Accounts Receivable				15,000
Bad debt expense accrual:				
Balance sheet approach:				
Bad Debt Expense	20,000		43,500	
Allowance for Doubtful Accounts		20,000		43,500
Income statement approach:				
Bad Debt Expense	21,000		25,200	
Allowance for Doubtful Accounts		21,000		25,200

The following balance sheet information from Ecolab's 1998 annual report illustrates how the allowance for doubtful accounts is reported.

Ecolab: Balance Sheet (in thousands of dollars)

	December 31	
	1998	**1997**
Accounts receivable, net	$246,695	$246,041
Note Three. Accounts Receivable, Net (in thousands of dollars)		
Accounts receivable	$259,588	$256,919
Allowance for doubtful accounts	(12,893)	(10,878)
Total	$246,695	$246,041

Monitoring and Altering the Investment in Receivables

9 Identify methods of raising cash from alternative transfers of accounts receivable.

Financial managers must monitor their investment in receivables in order to ensure that collections of receivables occur as expected. From time to time, changes in the economic environment may alter cash collection patterns. During periods of economic downturn, for example, collections may slow down and strategic cash reserves may become depleted. Fortunately, markets exist in which receivables may be used to obtain cash. Accounts receivable can be used to raise cash in a *general assignment,* a *specific assignment,* or via *factoring.*

General Assignment of Accounts Receivable In a ***general assignment*** of accounts receivable, **the company borrows money and pledges accounts receivable as collateral under the credit arrangement.** Footnote disclosure in the financial statements is normally used to disclose the pledging of assets.

Specific Assignment of Accounts Receivable In a ***specific assignment,*** **the company borrows money and the collection of specific receivables is designated to fund the repayment of the loan.** The company can either collect the receivables for the lender, or it can instruct customers to pay the lender directly. Generally, the dollar amount of the accounts assigned exceeds the dollar amount of the loan in anticipation of uncollectible receivables due to sales returns or bad debts.

If the assigned receivables are material, they should be segregated from other accounts receivable in the current assets section. The financial statement notes disclose the equity in the assigned receivables. (The equity is equal to the amount by which the assigned receivables exceeds the loan.)

The following footnote information for the Nashua Corporation describes the assignment of accounts receivable.

Nashua Corporation: Indebtedness (in part)

The Company negotiated a new secured $18 million line of credit of which $5 million is available exclusively for letters of credit. Borrowings under this facility are collateralized by a security interest in the Company's receivables and inventory.

Factoring of Accounts Receivable In accounts receivable ***factoring,*** **the receivables are transferred to an entity called a "factor" in exchange for cash.** The factor profits by paying less than the face value for the accounts receivable; the risk of receivable collection assumed by the factor determines the amount paid. If the accounts receivable are factored ***without recourse,*** **the factor bears all risk of uncollectibility** because it has no recourse if the receivables are not collected. If the accounts receivable are factored ***with recourse,*** **the factor assumes less risk of uncollectibility** because the company must repay the factor for any receivable that becomes uncollectible. Thus, the factor is willing to pay more for the receivables on a *with recourse* basis.

A fine line exists between assignment and factoring. Differentiation between the two is determined by the extent to which the risks and rewards of the accounts receivable are transferred from the company to the factor. From the company's point of view, accounts receivable have been *sold* if (1) control of the receivables' future economic benefits has been surrendered to the factor, and (2) the factor can only require the company to repurchase the receivables under the recourse provisions (and the expected repurchases can be reasonably estimated). If these criteria are not met, the transaction is more like a specific assignment in which money is borrowed and receivable collections are used to pay the note.[9]

The following footnote information from Cincinnati Milacron, Inc., illustrates the sale of accounts receivable.

9. The use of receivables for financing is widespread. The 1999 *Accounting Trends & Techniques* reported that of 600 companies, 125 (21%) used receivables in financing transactions a total of 128 times: receivables sold (103 times), and receivables used as collateral (25 times).

Cincinnati Milacron: Receivables (in part)

In January, the company entered into a new three year receivables purchase agreement with an independent issuer of receivables-backed commercial paper. This agreement replaced a similar agreement that expired in January. Under the terms of the new agreement, the company agreed to sell on an ongoing basis and without recourse, an undivided percentage ownership interest in designated pools of accounts receivable.

Example 12. Hawkeye Co. has $200,000 of accounts receivable and wishes to raise $150,000 in cash. Assume the following independent scenarios:
(a) Hawkeye borrows the $150,000, pledging the receivables as collateral on the note (general assignment).
(b) Hawkeye borrows the $150,000, specifically assigning the $200,000 of accounts receivable (specific assignment).
(c) Hawkeye factors $160,000 of receivables *without recourse*. The factor charges $10,000 for the transaction, and remits $150,000 to Hawkeye. For simplicity, assume that all the receivables are collectible (factoring without recourse).
(d) Hawkeye factored $155,000 of the receivables *with recourse*. Because the risk of collectibility remains with Hawkeye, the factor charges only $5,000, and remits $150,000 to Hawkeye. Also assume that control of the receivables' future economic benefits has been surrendered to the factor and the factor can only require Hawkeye to repurchase the receivables under the recourse provisions (factoring with recourse).
(e) Repeat requirement (d) assuming that the economic control of the receivables has not been transferred to the factor (e.g., a repurchase agreement exists).

Solution.
Scenario (a) General assignment
The balance sheet effects are as follows:

Assets		**Liabilities**	
Cash	150,000 ↑	Notes payable	150,000 ↑
Accounts receivable	(unchanged)	**Owners' Equity**	
		No cffcct	

Both Cash and Notes Payable increase by $150,000. Accounts Receivable does not change. Hawkeye reports the pledging of receivables as collateral in the notes to the financial statements.

EXAMPLE 12 Journal Entry—(a) General Assignment

Cash	150,000	
Notes Payable		150,000

Scenario (b) Specific assignment
The balance sheet effects are as follows:

Assets		**Liabilities**	
Cash	150,000 ↑	Notes payable	150,000 ↑
Accounts receivable	200,000 ↓	**Owners' Equity**	
Accounts receivable assigned	200,000 ↑	No effect	

Both Cash and Notes Payable increase by $150,000. Accounts Receivable is reclassified as Accounts Receivable Assigned. Hawkeye reports the nature of the arrangement and the equity in the receivables of $50,000 ($200,000 Accounts receivable assigned less $150,000 Notes payable) in the notes to the financial statements. As cash is collected and remitted to the creditor, Accounts Receivable and Notes Payable are both reduced.

EXAMPLE 12 Journal Entry—(b) Specific Assignment

Cash	150,000	
Notes Payable		150,000
Accounts Receivable Assigned	200,000	
Accounts Receivable		200,000

Scenario (c) Factoring without recourse
The balance sheet effects are as follows:

Assets		**Liabilities**	
Cash	150,000 ↑	No effect	
Accounts receivable	160,000 ↓	**Owners' Equity**	
		Retained earnings (via income statement effect)*	10,000 ↓

*The income statement shows $10,000 in losses.

Cash increases by $150,000, and Accounts Receivable decreases by $160,000. The decrease in net assets of $10,000 is reported as Loss on Sale of Accounts Receivable on the income statement with a corresponding reduction in Retained Earnings on the balance sheet.

EXAMPLE 12 Journal Entry—(c) Factoring with recourse

Cash	150,000	
Loss on Sale of Accounts Receivable	10,000	
Accounts Receivable		160,000

Scenario (d) Factoring with recourse (accounted for as a sale)
The balance sheet effects are as follows:

Assets		**Liabilities**	
Cash	150,000 ↑	No effect	
Accounts receivable	155,000 ↓	**Owners' Equity**	
		Retained earnings (via income statement effect)*	5,000 ↓

*The income statement shows $5,000 in losses.

Note that with the exception of the factor only charging $5,000 (causing only $155,000 of receivables to be factored to raise $150,000), the balance sheet effects of a *with recourse* factoring and a *without recourse* factoring are identical.

EXAMPLE 12 Journal Entry—(d) Factoring with recourse, accounted for as a sale

Cash	150,000	
Loss on Sale of Accounts Receivable	5,000	
Accounts Receivable		155,000

Scenario (e) Factoring with recourse (assuming that economic control is not transferred)
The transaction is not treated as a sale if control over the receivables' future economic benefits has not been surrendered to the factor, or if the factor can require the company to repurchase the receivables other than under the recourse provisions.

In this case, the with recourse factoring is, in substance, a loan, and the balance sheet effects are similar to those seen in a general assignment:

Assets		**Liabilities**	
Cash	150,000 ↑	Liability on factored receivables	155,000 ↑
Accounts receivable	(unchanged)		
		Owners' Equity	
		Retained earnings (via income statement effect)*	5,000 ↓

*The income statement shows $5,000 in expenses.

Although the receivables might appear to be transferred to the factor, they are not, in substance, because economic control has not been transferred to the factor. Thus, the balance sheet presentation of accounts receivable does not change. In effect, $155,000 has been borrowed, of which $150,000 has been remitted to Hawkeye yielding a $5,000 reduction in net income. This $5,000 is treated as interest expense, following the idea that it is a charge for borrowed funds. Once the receivables have been collected by the factor, the $155,000 is removed from Accounts Receivable and Liability on Factored Receivables. The simultaneous reduction in an asset and liability in the same amount has no further effect on net income or owners' equity.

EXAMPLE 12 Journal Entry—(e) Factoring with recourse, accounted for as a borrowing

Cash	150,000	
Interest Expense	5,000	
Liability on Factored Accounts Receivable		155,000

The Recourse Liability

Factoring receivables with recourse creates a contingent liability in the amount of the expected uncollectible receivables. GAAP requires the selling party to estimate the liability under the recourse provisions and to record it at the sale date of the receivables. The increase in the ***recourse liability*** increases the loss on the accounts receivable sale as illustrated by the following example.

Example 13. Melrose factors $60,000 of accounts receivable with recourse to Locklear Finance Company. Locklear's finance charge is $2,000. Melrose estimates that $1,500 of the receivables will not be collected.

Solution.

Assets		**Liabilities**	
Cash	58,000 ↑	Recourse liability	1,500 ↑
Accounts receivable	60,000 ↓		
		Owners' Equity	
		Retained earnings (via income statement effect)*	3,500 ↓

*The income statement shows $3,500 in losses.

The factoring causes net assets to decrease $2,000, and liabilities to increase $1,500. The asset decrease and liability increase is a $3,500 loss on sale reflected in the income statement, and through the normal closing process, is then reflected as a decrease in retained earnings.

EXAMPLE 13 Journal Entry

Cash	58,000	
Loss on Sale of Accounts Receivable	3,500	
Accounts Receivable		60,000
Recourse Liability		1,500

Short-Term Notes Receivable

10 Explain why short-term notes receivable are used as an alternative to accounts receivable and how such notes are measured and reported.

If customers request a payment period longer than customary accounts receivable terms, interest is required to compensate the firm for the opportunity cost of the funds tied up in working capital. Short-term notes receivable are simply more formal lending arrangements that bear interest. **Short-term notes received in return for sales of merchandise** are often called ***trade notes receivable.*** Conceptually, the deferred payments inherent in notes receivable should be discounted and the resulting present value used as a valuation basis for the note, with effective interest rates used to calculate interest revenue. Accounting standard setters have decided that the informational gains from the precise measurement of interest revenue are offset by the costs of estimating effective interest rates and present values. *Therefore, notes receivable (and payable) of less than one year's duration are reported at face value less an allowance for estimated uncollectible notes.*

Example 14. Mason accepted a 4%, 90-day, $5,000 note (with interest payable at maturity) in exchange for services.

Solution. Because the note is due in less than one year, it is reported at the $5,000 face amount. Service Revenue is reported at $5,000, and interest revenue is accrued over the 90-day period by multiplying the 4% stated rate by the $5,000 face value times 90 days ÷ 360 days, which equals $50 of interest revenue.

EXHIBIT 9 Example 14. Mason Co. Financial Statement Effects

Balance Sheet
(90 days after note is issued; just before cash collection)

Assets		**Liabilities**	
Notes receivable	5,000 ↑	No effect	
Interest receivable	50 ↑	**Owners' Equity**	
		Retained earnings (via income statement effect)	5,050 ↑

Income Statement		**Statement of Owners' Equity**	
Service revenue	5,000	Net income	5,050 ↑
Financial revenues, (expenses), gains, and (losses)			
Interest revenue	50		

EXAMPLE 14 Journal Entries

Note received for services:		
Note Receivable	5,000	
Service Revenue		5,000
*Accrual of interest over 90 days:**		
Interest Receivable	50	
Interest Revenue		50
*Cash receipt 90 days later:**		
Cash	5,050	
Note Receivable		5,000
Interest Receivable		50

*These two entries could be combined into the following single entry recorded at the note maturity:

Cash	5,050	
Note Receivable		5,000
Interest Revenue		50

Example 15. To illustrate reporting of notes receivable at net realizable value, assume that Mason received twenty, 5%, $1,000, 90-day notes from various customers. The notes pay interest at maturity. Four of the notes are estimated to be uncollectible at year-end.

Solution. Mason reports the following for notes receivable at the balance sheet date:

Notes receivable	$20,000	
Less allowance for uncollectible notes	4,000	$16,000

EXAMPLE 15 Journal Entry

To record uncollectible notes:		
Bad Debt Expense	4,000	
Allowance for Uncollectible Notes		4,000

Preparing the Operating Section of the Statement of Cash Flows—The Indirect Method

11 Report operating cash flows in the statement of cash flows using the indirect method.

Thus far in the text, our illustrations have used a *direct* format in presenting the operating activities section of the statement of cash flows. Although the FASB prefers the direct method, most statements of cash flows are prepared using the indirect method.[10] As shown below, the indirect method starts with net income and adjusts for certain items to reconcile to cash flows from operating activities. These reconciling items are grouped into three categories: noncash expenses and revenues, nonoperational gains and losses, and operational balance sheet amounts for which the accrual basis and cash basis amounts are different.

Cash flow from operating activities:
Net income
Add (Deduct)
- Noncash expenses: e.g., depreciation, depletion, amortization
  (Noncash revenues): e.g., investment income for securities accounted for under the equity method
- Losses (gains) on sale: primarily nonoperational in nature for most companies
- Decreases (increases) in operational current assets and deferred income tax assets
  Increases (decreases) in operational current liabilities and deferred income tax liabilities

Net cash flows from operating activities

Reconciling Items

Noncash Expenses and Revenues Although net income is decreased by noncash expenses such as depreciation, depletion, and amortization expense, cash flow is not affected. Therefore, by adding back the amount of the noncash expenses, the noncash flow effect is removed from the operating activities section. Similarly, by subtracting noncash revenue (such as investment income recorded under the equity method of accounting for common stock investments), the noncash effect is removed from the operating activities section.

Nonoperational Gains and Losses For most companies, the gains and losses on sales of assets and the disposition of some liabilities are nonoperational in nature. By subtracting gains and adding back losses, the effect of the nonoperational gains and losses are removed from the operating activities section.

Changes in Operational Asset and Liability Accounts Increases in working capital items discussed in this chapter (accounts receivable, inventory, and accounts

10. Of 600 companies surveyed in the 1999 *Accounting Trends and Techniques,* 593 used the indirect method to report cash flows from operating activities.

payable) are examples of changes in operational assets and liabilities. To understand how the indirect method reports the cash flows from these activities, consider the following example:

Example 16. Ewing Company began operations on January 1, 2001, with $100,000 in cash and $100,000 in owners' equity. Operating activities for 2001 were as follows:

- Purchased $80,000 in merchandise inventory, paying 90% in cash and owing suppliers the balance.
- Sold inventory costing $70,000 for $120,000, receiving 70% in cash and extending the rest in credit.

Using these facts, the following income statement and comparative balance sheets result:

2001 Income Statement

Sales		$120,000
Cost of goods sold:		
Beginning inventory	$ 0	
Purchases	80,000	
Goods available for sale	$ 80,000	
Ending inventory	10,000	70,000
Net income		$ 50,000

Balance Sheet

	January 1, 2001	December 31, 2001
Cash	$100,000	$112,000
Accounts receivable	0	36,000
Inventory	0	10,000
Total assets	$100,000	$158,000
Accounts payable	$ 0	$ 8,000
Owners' equity	100,000	150,000
Total liabilities and owners' equity	$100,000	$158,000

Prepare the operating activities section of the statement of cash flows under both the direct method and the indirect method.

Solution.

EXHIBIT 10 Example 16. Statement of Cash Flows—Direct Method

Operating Activities	
Collections from customers	$84,000*
Payments to suppliers	(72,000)**
Cash inflows from operating activities	$12,000

*$120,000 sales × 70% collection rate.
**$80,000 purchases × 90% payment rate.

EXHIBIT 11 Example 16. Statement of Cash Flows—Indirect Method

Operating Activities	
Net income	$50,000
Increase in accounts receivable	(36,000)
Increase in inventory	(10,000)
Increase in accounts payable	8,000
Cash inflows from operating activities	$12,000

Both methods explain the $12,000 increase in cash during 2001. The indirect method begins with net income of $50,000 and adjusts for changes in operational assets and liabilities. Net income includes sales revenue of $120,000 of which $36,000 has not been collected in cash (as reflected in the increase in accounts receivable). Therefore, the $36,000 increase is subtracted to reconcile to cash flow. Net income also includes cost of goods sold of $70,000. Cash outflows were $2,000 higher due to the purchase of $10,000 of additional inventory, minus the $8,000 of the purchases that were not paid. Therefore, the increase in inventory is added back and the increase in accounts payable is subtracted.

An alternative way to look at the indirect method reconciliation is provided by the capital maintenance approach to computing net income. From Chapter 1, recall that if transactions with owners are not present, then:

$$\text{Net income} = \text{Increases in assets} - \text{Increases in liabilities}$$

Expanding this equation gives the following:

$$\text{Net income} = \text{Increases in noncash assets} + \text{Increases in cash} - \text{Increases in liabilities}$$

Rearranging the equation yields the indirect method:

$$\text{Increases in cash} = \text{Net income} - \text{Increases in assets} + \text{Increases in liabilities}$$

Therefore, the indirect method adjustments for operational assets and liabilities (1) add decreases in assets and increases in liabilities, and (2) deduct increases in assets and decreases in liabilities.

Financial Statement Presentation

To illustrate the indirect method in an actual annual report, we present the following partial information from the operating activities section of Universal Foods Corporation's 1998 statement of cash flows.

UNIVERSAL FOODS CORPORATION
Statement of Cash Flows, Operating Activities
For the Periods Ended December 1998 and 1997
(Dollars in Thousands)

	1998	1997
Cash flows from operating activities:		
Net earnings	$72,644	$64,688
Adjustment to reconcile net earnings to net cash provided by operating activities:		
Depreciation	38,011	32,399
Amortization	6,221	4,927
(Gain) loss on sale of property, plant and equipment and other productive assets	(3,277)	16
Changes in operating assets and liabilities (net of effects from acquisition of businesses):		
Trade accounts receivable	(1,111)	(13,351)
Inventory	(5,664)	(13,418)
Prepaid expenses, income taxes and other assets	(8,063)	(283)
Accounts payable and accrued expenses	(21,782)	7,844
Salaries, wages and withholdings from employees	1,320	2,882
Income taxes	7,516	2,044
Deferred income taxes	8,058	4,838
Other liabilities	182	1,160
Net cash provided by operating activities	$94,053	$93,746

Southwest Airlines' Financial Statements

Southwest Airlines' 1998 financial statements are provided in Appendix C. Cross reference the following information to the balance sheet (accounts receivable, inventories, and accounts payable) and Note 1: Summary of Significant Accounting Policies—Inventories. Southwest uses both accounts receivable and accounts payable on a routine basis. Southwest had larger amounts of accounts payable ($157,415,000 and $160,891,000) than accounts receivable ($88,799,000 and $76,530,000) in 1998 and 1997, respectively. Southwest's inventory pertains to parts and supplies, and it is reported (at cost) at $50,035,000 and $52,376,000 for 1998 and 1997, respectively. The inventories section of Note 1 reports that inventories of flight equipment expendable parts, materials, and supplies are carried at average cost. Because the inventories are not reported at lower-of-cost-or-market, we assume that market was not materially different from cost.

Southwest uses the indirect method in the operating activities section of the statement of cash flows. While net income for 1998 and 1997 is $433,431,000 and $317,772,000, respectively, cash flow generated from operating activities is $886,135,000 and $610,588,000, respectively, which is about twice as large as net income. The most significant reconciling item in both years is depreciation expense, which is a noncash expense, followed by deferred income taxes, which we discuss in Chapter 11. Because Southwest has a large amount invested in property, plant, and equipment, depreciation expense should be substantial every year.

The External Decision Makers' View of the Building Up of Working Capital

Building up working capital is a necessary part of growing a business. Sales are stimulated by good credit terms to customers, and merchandise inventory often has to be accumulated to support the next period's sales. Therefore, external decision makers expect such buildups for companies with products that are in the introductory or growth stages. However, the buildup of inventory and accounts receivable is a bad sign for firms with most products in the maturity or decline stages. For these latter types of companies, working capital buildups usually lead to downturns in profits; receivable buildups often lead to additional bad debts or losses when the receivables are sold to third parties; and inventory buildups signal future price cuts to move inventory.

Even for firms in the growth stage, external decision makers closely watch for signs of overexpansion. Cash tied up in receivables and inventories (and in the property, plant, and equipment purchases that usually concurrently occur) drain cash flow for dividends and interest payments. This can be a particularly serious problem for firms that already have relatively large amounts of outstanding debt.

Chapter Summary

Preparing for sales involves working capital investments in inventory and accounts receivable. Also, decisions must be made about delaying payment to suppliers by using accounts payable. Each of these decisions creates measurement and reporting issues in published financial statements.

Accountants accumulate all costs to acquire and prepare inventory for sale as part of the cost of inventory. These costs are then allocated to ending inventory (an asset) and cost of goods sold (an expense) using cost flow assumptions such as LIFO, FIFO, and weighted-average. At the end of each period, the cost allocated to ending inventory is compared to the market value of that inventory. If the market value is lower, the inventory is written down to market, and a loss is matched with the current period.

Accounts receivable are reported at the net realizable value at each period-end. Bad debts expense is estimated at the end of each period so that the cost of extending credit is matched against the period in which the related benefits of the credit policy (increased sales revenue) occur.

Estimation is present in the valuation of both inventory and accounts receivable. To the extent that management integrity and established internal control procedures are weak, the estimation process can break down and misstatement can occur. Because of this situation, companies' accounting policies in the inventory and accounts receivable areas receive tremendous scrutiny in the financial press. Often, allegations of fraud are linked to intentional errors in estimating uncollectible accounts or establishing inventory ownership.

The indirect method of reporting cash flows from operating activities in the statement of cash flows is used by almost all public companies. The indirect method starts with the amount of net income and then reconciles to the amount of operating activities cash flows in a series of steps. In the first eight chapters of the text, we used the direct method of reporting cash flows from operating activities in order to show the direct effects of management's decisions. Throughout the remaining chapters, we will use both methods at different times to illustrate how financial statements reflect management decisions.

Key Terms

aging of receivables 357
allowance method 356
ceiling 352
cost flow assumptions 344
designated market value 352
direct write-off method 357
dollar value LIFO 349
economic order quantity (EOQ) 338
factoring 360
floor 352
general assignment 360
holding costs 338
just-in-time 338
LIFO conformity rule 347
lower-of-cost-or-market (LCM) method 352
net method 340
periodic inventory system 344
purchase discount 340
purchase returns and allowances 342
recourse liability 363
sales discount 355
sales returns 356
specific assignment 360
specific goods pooled LIFO 349
specific identification 343
stockout costs 338
trade notes receivable 364
with recourse 360
without recourse 360

Questions

Q1. **Why Firms Choose to Hold Inventory.** Holding inventory is costly, as it must be purchased, stored, and managed. Why do firms choose to hold inventory?

Q2. **Inventory.** In general, what costs should be included in inventory costs?

Q3. **Inventory Financed with Accounts Payable.** What advantages come from purchasing inventory by incurring an accounts payable as opposed to paying cash or issuing trade notes payable? To illustrate, assume that a company purchases $100,000 in inventory and is given the following terms: cash upon purchase or an accounts payable with the terms n/30. Also, assume that the company can purchase temporary investments that earn 6% per year.

Q4. **Accounts Payable Terms.** What do the following terms mean, and what is the approximate annual rate of interest implied by the terms? (a) 2/10, net 30 (b) 3/15, net 45.

Q5. **Accounts Payable versus Notes Payable.** Assume that Jefferson Company makes a $50,000 inventory purchase. The seller offers two different terms: an account payable with terms n/30, or a 90-day note payable with stated rate of 1% per month (i.e., 12% per year). What is the effective interest rate to the buyer who selects the note payable over the accounts payable option?

Q6. **LIFO versus FIFO.** Do the terms LIFO and FIFO describe the assumption about the ending units on hand during the period or the units sold during the period?

Q7. **Inventory Ownership.** For inventory shipped near the end of the year, special attention is necessary to determine whether the inventory should be included in the current year inventory or as a sale. The FOB contract terms provide the information about who owns this inventory at year-end. Assume that on December 28, 2001, McVay Co. ships 500 inventory units to Jordan Company, which receives them on January 4, 2002. For each of the following independent situations, indicate whether McVay should include the 500 units in 2001 year-end inventory or as a 2001 sale.

a. The terms are FOB shipping point.
b. The terms are FOB receiving point.
c. The inventory is shipped from Dallas, Texas, to Ft. Wayne, Indiana, through Indianapolis, Indiana. The terms are FOB Indianapolis, and the goods arrive in Indianapolis on December 30, 2001.
d. The inventory is shipped from Dallas, Texas, to Ft. Wayne, Indiana, through Indianapolis, Indiana. The terms are FOB Indianapolis, and the goods arrive in Indianapolis on January 2, 2002.
e. The goods are shipped on consignment to Jordan. Jordan tracks the inventory and remits proceeds from the sale once a month to McVay.

Q8. **Dollar Value LIFO.** Why do companies use pooled LIFO approaches, such as dollar value LIFO, rather than applying LIFO to each inventory unit individually?

Q9. **Inventory: Lower-of-Cost-or-Market.** Why do accountants report inventory at lower-of-cost-or-market (LCM)? Is LCM consistent with balance sheet valuation for other current assets?

Q10. **Inventory: Lower-of-Cost-or-Market.** In applying lower-of-cost-or-market (LCM), what market value measure is used?

Q11. **Accounts Receivable.** Why do companies sell products and take accounts receivable (a non-interest-bearing promise to pay) in return instead of requiring immediate cash payment or a note receivable?

Q12. **Extending Credit.** Assume that a company allows three choices to customers who want to purchase its goods: (1) cash purchases, which receive a 1% discount; (2) credit card purchases, for which the company pays 2% of the sales price to the credit card company; and (3) accounts receivable, with terms 2/10, net 30 (if not paid within 30 days, the accounts are charged 1.5% per month in interest). Why does the company provide these three choices? Assuming $1,000,000 in sales, discuss the effect the three alternatives have on the company's financial statements. (For convenience, assume that the company and the credit card company settle up immediately.)

Q13. **Accounts Receivable on Balance Sheet.** At what value are accounts receivable reported in a year-end balance sheet? Does the amount recorded as accounts receivable differ between the gross and net methods of recording credit sales if a company offers sales discounts?

Q14. **Assigning and Factoring Accounts Receivable.** Describe the accounts receivable processes of general assignment, specific assignment, and factoring, both with and without recourse.

Q15. **Trade Notes Receivable versus Accounts Receivable.** Why might a company ask a customer to sign a trade note receivable in conjunction with selling inventory rather than offering normal terms on account?

Q16. **Statement of Cash Flows, Indirect Method.** In a statement of cash flows that uses the indirect method in the operating activities section, what are the three groups of reconciling items? Which items are added and which are subtracted?

Short Problems

1. **Cost of Goods Available for Sale.** At the beginning of the current year, Schaefer Co. had $200,000 in inventory. Additionally, Schaefer purchased $750,000 in inventory, took $30,000 in available cash discounts, and returned $40,000 in merchandise during the year. Compute cost of goods available for sale for the year.

2. **LIFO, FIFO, and Average Cost Methods.** The following information is available about Webber Company's 2001 inventory activities. Calculate ending inventory and cost of goods sold under each of the following inventory cost assumptions: LIFO, FIFO, and weighted-average.

WEBBER CO. 2001 INVENTORY DATA

	Units	Cost per Unit	Total Cost
Beginning inventory, 1/1/01	1,800	$10	$ 18,000
Production runs:			
1/30/01	2,000	12	24,000
2/15/01	2,000	11	22,000
5/15/01	1,200	12	14,400
8/15/01	3,000	14	42,000
9/4/01	1,000	17	17,000
12/15/01	2,000	18	36,000
Total goods available for sale during 2001	13,000		$173,400

	Units	Sales Price per Unit	Total
Sales:			
2/1/01	2,000	$15	$ 30,000
3/15/01	2,500	15	37,500
6/30/01	1,000	15	15,000
9/1/01	3,000	22	66,000
12/18/01	2,000	22	44,000
Total sales in 2001	10,500		$192,500

3. **LIFO Layers.** The Taylor Co. began operations on January 1, 2001, with no inventory. Its inventory activity for the years 2001–2004 is as follows.

Year	Purchases Units	Purchases Average $ Per Unit	Sales Units	Sales Average $ Per Unit
2001	10,000	$ 5	8,000	$ 8
2002	13,000	7	12,000	11
2003	18,000	10	15,000	16
2004	22,000	14	20,000	22

a. Compute the December 31, 2004, ending inventory (separate each year's layer).

b. From January 1, 2005, to December 28, 2005, Taylor had purchased 20,000 units of inventory at $12 and sold 24,000 units of inventory at $19. Taylor can purchase up to 8,000 units of inventory at $13 before December 31, 2005. Provide an assessment for management of the financial consequences of the LIFO liquidation. Should Taylor buy additional inventory before year-end?

4. **Inventory: Lower-of-Cost-or-Market.** Assume that lower-of-cost-or-market (LCM) is based on an individual item approach. For each of the items below, indicate the appropriate designated market and LCM amounts.

Inventory Valuation Examples

Inventory Item	Market Value Information* NRV	RC	NRV-PM	Designated Market	Cost**	LCM Balance Sheet Valuation
A	$120	$100	$90		$100	
B	38	40	30		35	
C	20	16	17		15	
D	75	70	65		77	
E	55	60	45		62	
F	45	37	40		42	
G	28	25	22		20	

*NRV = Net realizable value; RC = Replacement cost; and NRV-PM = Net realizable value less a normal profit margin.

**Cost is determined using an appropriate costing method, e.g., specific identification, LIFO, or FIFO.

5. **Sales Discounts and Sales Returns and Allowances.** McBride Co. sold $2,000,000 in merchandise (all subject to terms 3/15, net 45) in its first year of operations, with accounts receivable related to $300,000 of the credit sales outstanding at year-end. McBride uses the net method to record sales subject to sales discounts. Buyers responded by taking $50,000 in sales discounts. Of the $300,000 in accounts receivable at year-end, sales discounts are still available on $250,000 of the receivables (i.e., the 15-day discount period has passed for $50,000 in year-end accounts receivable). During the year, McBride granted $75,000 in sales allowances, and customers returned $120,000 in merchandise, for which McBride granted complete credit for the return (none of these returns and allowances pertain to year-end receivables). At year-end, McBride believes that an allowance of $15,000 should be set up for future sales returns and allowances related to the year-end receivables. How does McBride's income statement and balance sheet reflect these transactions? (Note: Two interpretations are possible for the information about sales returns and allowances—the $75,000, $120,000, and $15,000 amounts could either refer to the gross sales or to the net of cash discount amounts. Assume that these amounts are net of any cash discounts.)

Journal Entry Option: Prepare the summary annual journal entries to reflect the sales on account, sales discounts, and sales allowances.

6. **Bad Debts.** Kennelley Co. began the current period with an allowance for bad debts (doubtful accounts) of $20,000. During the current year, Kennelley had sales of $1,000,000, 80% on credit and 20% for cash, and wrote off $10,000 in accounts receivable that proved to be uncollectible. Kennelley does not offer sales discounts on credit sales. Compute the current year's bad debts expense on the income statement, and the ending balance sheet allowance for bad debts under the following independent assumptions:

a. Kennelley uses the percent of sales method, and management believes that 3% of credit sales should be set aside for bad debts.

b. Kennelley uses the aging method. Based on an aging of accounts receivable, management believes that the ending balance in the allowance for bad debts should be $40,000.

Journal Entry Option: Prepare the summary annual accounting journal entries to reflect the current year information under both alternatives.

Analytical and Comprehensive Problems

7. **LIFO.** The following information appeared in the Shamus Co. annual report.

	2002	2001
Inventories:		
Finished products and parts	$ 55,847,000	$46,061,000
Work in process	27,078,000	25,320,000
Raw materials	2,745,000	2,684,000
Total	$ 85,670,000	$74,065,000
Net income	$102,481,000	$70,345,000
Effective income tax rate	39.62%	38.5%

Additionally, Note 1 contained the following information:

Inventories are stated at cost, which does not exceed market. The last-in, first-out (LIFO) method was used for determining the cost of approximately 89% of total inventories at December 31, 2002, and 89% at December 31, 2001. The cost for the remaining portion of the inventories was determined using the first-in, first-out (FIFO) method. If the FIFO inventory valuation method had been used exclusively, inventories would have totaled $42,268,000 and $40,888,000 higher in the respective years.

What would the 2002 total inventory have been on a FIFO basis? How much would the 2002 income before the cumulative effect of accounting change have been if FIFO had been used?

8. **LIFO and Lower-of-Cost-or-Market.** Consider the following hypothetical footnote in an annual report.

Inventories are principally valued by the last-in, first-out (LIFO) method. In aggregate, such valuations are not in excess of market value at year-end.

Assume that LIFO is applied to individual units. Because LIFO assigns the cost of the latest purchases to the cost of goods sold and the earlier purchases to ending inventory, why would the year-end inventory approximate the market value?

9. **LIFO Reserve.** The following information is from J. C. Nickel's 2002 annual report.

J. C. NICKEL COMPANY, INC.
(In millions)

	2002	2001	2000
Balance Sheet			
Merchandise inventory	$3,935	$3,876	$3,545
Note 4: Merchandise Inventory			
Merchandise inventory, at lower-of-cost (FIFO)-or-market	$4,161	$4,123	$3,791
LIFO reserve	(226)	(247)	(246)
Merchandise inventory, at LIFO cost	$3,935	$3,876	$3,545

No other information about inventories is provided in the annual report. Because GAAP requires inventories to be reported at lower-of-cost-or-market, what interpretation is consistent with J. C. Nickel's presentation?

10. **Inventory.** HTC Corporation owns distilleries. The following information is available from HTC's 2002 annual report.

HTC CORPORATION
(In millions)

	2002	2001	2000
Balance Sheet			
Inventories:			
Barreled whisky	$167	$163	$144
Finished goods	169	123	123
Work in process	59	59	60
Raw materials and supplies	38	37	31
Total inventories	$433	$382	$358

Note 1: Accounting Policies—Inventories

Inventories are stated at the lower-of-cost-or-market. Approximately 84% of the total amount of consolidated inventories at December 31, 2002, 2001, and 2000, are stated on the basis of the last-in, first-out (LIFO) method. All remaining inventories are valued using the first-in, first-out and average cost methods.

If the LIFO method had not been used, inventories would have totaled $85, $70, and $72 million higher than reported at December 31, 2002, 2001, and 2000, respectively.

A substantial portion of barreled whisky will not be sold within one year because of the duration of the aging process. All barreled whisky is classified in current assets in accordance with industry practice. Bulk wine inventories are classified as work in process.

Warehousing, insurance, ad valorem taxes, and other carrying charges applicable to barreled whisky held for aging are included in inventory costs.

a. Why would industry practice allow barreled whisky to be classified as a current asset?
b. Why would bulk wine inventories be classified as work in process?
c. Is it appropriate to capitalize ad valorem taxes and other carrying charges applicable to barreled whisky held for aging as inventory costs? How do you think ad valorem taxes are handled for a company that, for example, turns its inventory every five days?

11. **Inventory Purchases and Sales.** Use the following format to show the complete financial statement effects of the following transactions. On the balance sheet, use arrows (↑) (↓) to indicate the direction of changes. Ignore income taxes.

Statement of Cash Flows

Operating Activities

Balance Sheet

Assets	**Liabilities**
	Owners' Equity
	Retained earnings (through effect on net income)*

Income Statement	**Statement of Owners' Equity**

*Ignores effect of income taxes

a. Parry Co. purchased $40,000 in inventory from Wilson Co. under the terms, 2/10, net 30. Parry took the discount and remitted the amount to Wilson within 10 days. Show the effect on *Parry's* financial statements.

b. Parry Co. purchased $40,000 in inventory from Wilson Co. under the terms, 2/10, net 30. Parry took the discount and remitted the amount to Wilson within 10 days. Show the effect on *Wilson's* financial statements.
c. Parry Co. purchased $40,000 in inventory from Wilson Co. under the terms, 2/10, net 30. Parry did not take the discount, and remitted the amount to Wilson within 30 days. Show the effect on *Parry's* financial statements.
d. Parry Co. purchased $40,000 in inventory from Wilson Co. under the terms, 2/10, net 30. Parry did not take the discount, and remitted the amount to Wilson within 30 days. Show the effect on *Wilson's* financial statements.
e. On January 1, Tiller Co. purchased $100,000 in inventory from Hite Co., agreeing to a four-month note payable at 1% per month, with principal and interest due at maturity. Principal and interest were paid as scheduled. Show the effect on *Tiller's* financial statements.
f. On January 1, Tiller Co. purchased $100,000 in inventory from Hite Co., agreeing to a four-month note payable at 1% per month, with principal and interest due at maturity. Principal and interest were paid as scheduled. Show the effect on *Hite's* financial statements.

Journal Entry Option: Prepare the summary accounting journal entries for each situation. If sales or purchase discounts are offered, assume that the net method is used to record the related credit sale or purchase.

12. **Assigning and Factoring Accounts Receivable.** On December 31, Bailey Co. will need $400,000 in cash. The treasurer is considering four different alternatives to raise the cash: (a) borrowing $400,000 from First National Bank and using $430,000 in general accounts receivable as collateral (no specific assignment); (b) borrowing $400,000 from Gonzales Finance Co. and using $415,000 of Smith's accounts receivables as collateral; (c) factoring with recourse enough receivables (economic control transferred) to raise the $400,000, subject to a 4% discount; or (d) factoring without recourse enough receivables to raise the $400,000, subject to a 7% discount. Use the following format to illustrate the current year financial statement effects of each of the alternatives for Bailey Co. On the balance sheet, use arrows (↑) (↓) to indicate the direction of changes. Ignore income taxes.

BAILEY CO.

Assets	Liabilities
	Owners' Equity

Journal Entry Option: Prepare the journal entries that would be made on December 31 for each alternative.

13. **LIFO versus FIFO.** Herron Company began operations on January 1, 2001. Based on the following information (which was prepared before considering the effect of inventories), prepare an ending 2001 income statement and balance sheet under LIFO, FIFO, and weighted average. Ignore income taxes and fill in stockholders' equity with the amount needed to balance the balance sheet.

Balance Sheet

Cash	$ 100,000
Other current assets, excluding inventory	200,000
Property, plant, and equipment, net	1,000,000
Total assets, excluding inventory	$1,300,000
Current liabilities	$ 150,000
Long-term liabilities	600,000
Stockholders' equity	?
Total liabilities and owners' equity, excluding inventory effect	$1,300,000

Income Statement*

Sales	$1,330,000
Cost of goods sold	?
Other expenses, excluding inventories	200,000

*Ignore income tax effects.

The following inventory flows occurred during 2001.

	Units	Cost per Unit	Total Cost
Beginning inventory, 1/1/01	0	$ 0	$ 0
Purchases:			
1/20/01	20,000	10	200,000
5/15/01	20,000	12	240,000
9/4/01	20,000	14	280,000
12/15/01	20,000	16	320,000
Total goods available for sale during 2001	80,000		$1,040,000

	Units	Sales Price per Unit	Total
Sales:			
2/1/01	10,000	$18	$ 180,000
5/15/01	10,000	19	190,000
6/30/01	10,000	20	200,000
9/15/01	20,000	24	480,000
12/18/01	20,000	24	480,000
Total sales in 2001	70,000		$1,530,000

14. **Dollar Value LIFO.** The following information is available for Young Co., which uses dollar value LIFO for its inventory valuation. Young began operations on January 1, 2000. Prepare a schedule showing the December 31, 2003, ending inventory valuation.

YOUNG CO.—Dollar Value LIFO Information

December 31	Year-End Cost of Ending Inventory*	Price Index**
2000	$1,000,000	1.00
2001	1,500,000	1.20
2002	1,800,000	1.35
2003	2,400,000	1.50

*The cost of ending inventory is computed for each item by multiplying the ending inventory times the most recent purchase price.
**The price index may be computed by the company or provided by an outside party such as an industry trade association. For convenience, the price index has been standardized at 1.00 for the base year in which dollar value LIFO was adopted.

15. **Inventory Costing Methods.** The following information pertains to Hill Company for 2001 (its first year of operations) and 2002.

	Units	Cost per Unit	Total Cost
Beginning inventory, 1/1/01	0	$ 0	$ 0
Purchases:			
5/20/01	10,000	20	200,000
8/15/01	25,000	22	550,000
Subtotal	35,000		$ 750,000
1/4/02	30,000	28	840,000
10/15/02	20,000	32	640,000
Total goods available for sale, 2001–2002	85,000		$2,230,000

	Units	Sales Price per Unit	Total
Sales:			
6/1/01	5,000	$30	$ 150,000
10/15/01	18,000	32	576,000
Subtotal (total sales in 2001)	23,000		$ 726,000
3/30/02	32,000	38	1,216,000
11/15/02	22,000	43	946,000
Total sales in 2001–2002	77,000		$2,888,000

a. Compute the December 31, 2002, ending inventory under the following assumptions: LIFO, FIFO, and weighted-average.

b. Assuming the following information, calculate the designated market value for the inventory on December 31, 2002: replacement cost = $35 per unit; ending inventory could be sold for $43 per unit, less $2 per unit in disposal costs. Assume a normal profit margin on sales of $10 per unit.

c. Compute the December 31, 2002, balance sheet inventory presentation under each of the following methods. Use the designated market value from (b) for the December 31, 2002, market value.

	Cost	Designated Market	Lower-of-Cost-or-Market
LIFO			
FIFO			
Average			

d. Assume the same facts as in (c), except that replacement cost has fallen to $27 per share. Complete the following.

	Cost	Designated Market	Lower-of-Cost-or-Market
LIFO			
FIFO			
Average			

16. **Statement of Cash Flows.** Given the following information for Chan Co., prepare the operating activities section of the statement of cash flows. Amounts are in millions of dollars, and all items appear in the operating activities section.

Net income (loss)	$(90.2)
Depreciation and amortization	176.5
Gain (loss) on sale of investments	40.5
Gain (loss) on sale of assets	(4.3)
Restructuring charge	10.3
Changes in assets and liabilities	
Increase (decrease) in asset accounts:	
Trade receivables	40.1
Inventories	(18.8)
Increase (decrease) in liability accounts:	
Accounts payable	(15.8)
Income taxes payable	9.7
Accrued liabilities	37.3

17. **Statement of Cash Flows.** The following information was taken from Brown Group Inc.'s financial statements. Prepare the operating activities section of Brown's statement of cash flows. Amounts are in thousands of dollars.

Net income (loss)	$23,669
Depreciation and amortization	26,943
Gain (loss) on disposal or impairment of facilities and equipment	(961)
Provision for losses on accounts receivable	2,772
Changes in assets and liabilities	
Increase (decrease) in asset accounts:	
Receivables	(6,768)
Inventories	(17,903)
Prepaid expenses and other current assets	(9,100)
Increase (decrease) in liability accounts:	
Trade accounts payable and accrued expenses	2,904
Income taxes	(5,553)
Other, net (Hint: in the statement of cash flows, this is subtracted as a reconciling item in the operating activities section.)	6,587

BROWN GROUP, INC.
Statement of Cash Flows
Inflows (Outflows), in Thousands

Operating Activities		
Net income (loss)		$23,669
Add (Deduct):		
Depreciation and amortization	$26,943	
Gain (loss) on disposal or impairment of facilities and equipment	961	
Provision for losses on accounts receivable	2,772	
Changes in assets and liabilities		
Increase (decrease) in asset accounts:		
Receivables	6,768	
Inventories	17,903	
Prepaid expenses and other current assets	9,100	
Increase (decrease) in liability accounts:		
Trade accounts payable and accrued expenses	2,904	
Income taxes	(5,553)	
Other, net	(6,587)	55,211
Net cash flow from operating activities		$78,880

http://

18. **Texas Instruments (TI).** Access TI's 1998 annual report at the text Web site (http://baginski.swcollege.com) and review the following information: the balance sheet (accounts receivable, inventories, accounts payable, and accrued expenses), the inventory footnote, and the accounts payable and accrued expenses footnote.
    a. What is the relationship between the year-end accounts receivable and the allowance for doubtful accounts in 1998 and 1997?
    b. What is the relationship between accounts receivable and accounts payable in 1998 and 1997?
    c. If we consider the total of accounts payable to be a short-term, interest-free loan payable, and accounts receivable to be an interest-free loan receivable, what are the effects of both types of interest-free arrangements on the financial statements?
    d. Does TI use the direct or indirect method in the operating activities section of the statement of cash flows? What are the major reconciling items?

CFA Exam-Type Problems

19. During a period of rising prices, the financial statements of a firm using FIFO reporting instead of LIFO reporting would show: (CFA adapted)
    a. higher total assets and higher net income.
    b. higher total assets and lower net income.
    c. lower total assets and higher net income.
    d. lower total assets and lower net income.

20. An analyst gathered the following information about a company for a fiscal year: (CFA adapted)

Quarter	Purchases in Units	Cost per Unit	Purchases in Dollars
1	200	$22	$ 4,400
2	300	24	7,200
3	300	26	7,800
4	200	28	5,600
Total			$25,000

- Inventory at the beginning of the first quarter: 400 units at $20 per unit = $8,000
- Inventory remaining at the end of the fourth quarter: 600 units
- Sales for the fiscal year: 800 units

Reported inventory at the end of the fourth quarter using LIFO and FIFO would be:

	LIFO	FIFO
a.	$12,400	$15,800
b.	$14,200	$12,400
c.	$15,800	$20,600
d.	$20,600	$14,200

21. Given a current ratio greater than 1, if ending inventory is understated by $3,000 and beginning inventory is overstated by $5,000, the effect on net income and the current ratio will be: (CFA adapted)

Net Income	Current Ratio
a. understated by $2,000	lower
b. overstated by $2,000	lower
c. understated by $8,000	lower
d. understated by $8,000	higher

22. If net purchases are overstated by $1,000 and ending inventory is overstated by $4,000, then net income is: (CFA adapted)
a. overstated by $5,000.
b. overstated by $3,000.
c. overstated by $1,000.
d. understated by $4,000.

23. The year-end financial statements for a firm using LIFO accounting show an inventory level of $5,000, cost of goods sold (COGS) of $16,000, and inventory purchases of $14,500. If the LIFO reserve is $4,000 at year-end and was $1,500 at the beginning of the year, what would the COGS have been using FIFO accounting? (CFA adapted)
a. $11,000
b. $12,000
c. $13,500
d. $18,500

24. The following information applies to a company during a recent fiscal year: (CFA adapted)

Cash paid for land	$ 30,000
Cash paid for salaries	60,000
Cash paid to suppliers	40,000
Cash paid for interest to bondholders	20,000
Cash collected from customers	150,000
Cash collected for sale of equipment	75,000
Depreciation expense	10,000

If the company is not subject to income taxes, what is its net cash flow from operations for the fiscal year?
a. $20,000
b. $30,000
c. $50,000
d. $75,000

25. **Statement of Cash Flows.** Soft Corporation (SC) is a rapidly growing company. This rapid growth was largely financed by an initial public offering of 3,000,000 shares at $20 a share on June 27, 2001, and by the exercise of stock options for 1,000,000 shares at $1 per share on January 1, 2002. Tables 2 and 3 present SC's income statements and balance sheets for 2001 and projected for 2002.

TABLE 2

SOFT CORPORATION
Balance Sheets
as of December 31
(In millions)

	Actual 2001	Projected 2002
Cash	$ 24.0	$ 26.0
Accounts receivable	17.0	24.0
Inventory	100.0	150.0
Property, plant, and equipment	100.0	125.0
Accumulated depreciation	(30.0)	(35.0)
Total assets	$211.0	$290.0
Accounts payable	$ 91.0	$101.0
Long-term debt	20.0	40.0
Common stock	80.0	90.0
Retained earnings	20.0	59.0
Total liabilities and stockholders' equity	$211.0	$290.0

TABLE 3

SOFT CORPORATION
Income Statements
as of December 31
(In millions)

	Actual 2001	Projected 2002
Sales	$ 80.0	$198.0
Cost of goods sold	38.0	90.0
Gross profit	$ 42.0	$108.0
Selling, general, and administrative expenses	$ 13.0	$ 30.0
Depreciation expense	3.0	5.0
Operating expenses	$ 16.0	$ 35.0
Interest expense	$ 4.0	$ 5.0
Pretax income	$ 22.0	$ 68.0
Income tax expense	(7.0)	(25.0)
Net income	$ 15.0	$ 43.0
Earnings per share	$ 2.00	$ 4.30
Average share outstanding (millions)	7.5	10.0
Dividends per share	$ 0.10	$ 0.40

Required Prepare a projected statement of cash flows for 2001 based only on the information in Tables 2 and 3. Show cash flow from operations, financing, and investing. *Note to Students:* The CFA problem did not specify which method to use in preparing the operating activities section, indirect or direct, but the CFA Guideline provides answers for both methods. Use the indirect method in your answer. (CFA adapted)

Objectives

1 Identify issues in the timing of revenue recognition for merchandising, manufacturing, and service firms.

2 Explain when revenue is realized and the critical events that determine when revenue is earned.

3 Properly account for sales returns.

4 Explain three practical justifications for matching expenses to revenues.

5 Differentiate between product and period costs.

6 Explain when generally accepted accounting principles permit departure from the general rule of recognizing revenue at the point of sale.

7 Account for the recognition of revenues, expenses, and profits in the construction industry.

8 Account for structural changes in operations, including restructurings and discontinued operations.

9 Identify and account for accounting changes.

10 Learn how to compute Earnings Per Share (EPS) and how EPS is presented on financial statements.

Chapter 10

Operating Activities—Revenue and Expense Recognition

In Chapters 10–12, we continue to examine operating activities. In this chapter, we concentrate on the revenue and expense recognition process for firms that purchase goods (merchandising firms) and those that produce goods (manufacturing firms). In Chapter 11, we introduce property, sales, and income taxes. In Chapter 12, we consider strategies for compensating employees.

Firms that Purchase and Sell Goods—Merchandising Firms

The primary operating activity of merchandising firms is the purchase and resale of goods. After raising cash with financing activities, these firms invest cash in long-term assets such as land, buildings, display racks, and delivery equipment, and in short-term working capital items such as inventory. Upon committing cash to purchase inventory, the firm's operating cycle begins.[1] The firm engages in numerous operating activities to bring about final sale of the inventory.

As a framework for discussion, consider the following partial income statement of Bonilla Co. presented in Exhibit 1. We will refer to this statement throughout the chapter.

In order to generate $1,970,000 net sales revenue, Bonilla had to expend resources related to inventory ($1,000,000), selling activities ($330,000), and general and administrative activities ($175,000). Some of these activities, such as those related to inventory and salespersons' efforts, have *direct relationships* with sales (i.e., for a particular sale, inventory must be acquired and salespersons must be compensated). Other expenses are necessary, but have *indirect relationships* with sales (i.e., advertising, building rent, and management salaries, etc.). The two primary

1. Recall that a firm's operating cycle encompasses purchasing inventory (or materials to manufacture inventory), selling inventory on credit, and receiving cash from collecting the receivable.

EXHIBIT 1

BONILLA CO.
Partial Income Statement
For the year ended December 31, 2001

Net sales		
Sales revenue	$2,000,000	
Less sales returns and allowances	30,000	
Net sales		$1,970,000
Costs and expenses		
Cost of goods sold		1,000,000
Gross profit		$ 970,000
Selling expenses:		
Warranty expense	$ 40,000	
Depreciation expense—delivery trucks	30,000	
Sales salaries and commissions	125,000	
Rent expense—store	110,000	
Advertising expense	25,000	
Total selling expenses		330,000
General and administrative expenses:		
Rent expense—office	$ 50,000	
Office supplies expense	10,000	
Administrative salaries expense	100,000	
Depreciation expense—office equipment	15,000	
Total general and administrative expenses		175,000
Operating profit		$ 465,000

accounting problems that Bonilla faces are (1) timing the recognition of sales revenue, and (2) properly matching expenses with sales.

1 Identify issues in the timing of revenue recognition for merchandising, manufacturing, and service firms.

2 Explain when revenue is realized and the critical events that determine when revenue is earned.

Timing of Revenue Recognition

The General Rule of Revenue Recognition Revenue should be recognized when (1) the revenue is *realized* or *realizable,* and (2) the revenue is *earned.*[2] *As a general rule, firms recognize revenue at the point of delivery (for manufacturing and merchandising firms) and when a service is performed (service firms).*

Realization refers to **the process of converting noncash assets into cash. When cash is received from making a sale or performing a service,** revenue has been ***realized.*** However, strict realization is not necessary for revenue recognition. **Expected realization** (i.e., the revenue is ***realizable***) meets the first condition for revenue recognition. *Realizable* means that an event has occurred that reduces the uncertainty about collecting cash to an acceptable level. To illustrate the opposite ends of the uncertainty spectrum, assume that Bonilla sells inventory to two customers; one is a financially stable customer who promises to pay in 30 days (an accounts receivable), and the other customer can pay only if the goods are resold to a third party. In the case of the customer who must resell the goods in order to have the resources to settle the debt with Bonilla, the accountant must exercise professional judgement as to whether the uncertainty about collecting cash has been reduced to an acceptable level. In this example, revenue recognition will likely occur at the time of sale for the first customer, but not for the second.

The second revenue recognition condition is that the revenue is *earned.* Firms generate revenue by expending resources to sell a product or perform a service. If **the firm has expended all (or nearly all) the resources needed to generate revenue,**

2. "Recognition and Measurement in Financial Statements of Business Enterprises," *Statement of Financial Accounting Concepts No. 5* (Stamford, Conn.: FASB, 1984).

then the revenue is ***earned.*** For example, assume that a magazine publisher contracts with a free-lance writer to produce an article. When the writer delivers the finished article, the revenue is earned by the writer and an expense is incurred by the publisher. However, when a magazine publisher receives cash for a 12-month prepaid subscription, no revenue is recognized because the magazine publisher must expend resources to produce and deliver magazines over the next 12 months. Revenue recognition occurs each month (i.e., one-twelfth of the revenue is earned each month) as the publisher incurs the production and delivery costs, and delivers the magazines.

3 Properly account for sales returns.

Sales Returns Most companies allow sales returns within some prespecified period of time. Although sales returns are an unknown future amount, they must be estimated and recorded in the period of sale in order to measure the actual amount of net sales. If all sales are made on a cash basis, an estimated liability for sales returns must be accrued and recognized to match against sales. For some firms, estimating sales returns is a difficult problem; nevertheless, sales returns must be estimated at the time of sale to match against sales revenue. In the Bonilla Co. income statement, sales revenue totaled $2,000,000, but actual and estimated sales returns totaled $30,000. Thus, *net sales revenue* was $1,970,000.

A Closer Look at the Right of Return In some industries, the estimation of returns is a significant issue. The publishing industry, for example, can experience returns greater than 50% on some products. Does it make sense for revenue recognition to occur at the point of delivery for firms who have high returns (i.e., should a high proportion of returned goods negate the general rule of revenue recognition)? Some accountants feel that no sale should be recorded until the return privilege expires (i.e., make an exception to the general rule of revenue recognition). Others argue that the general rule of revenue recognition should be followed by recording the sales revenue, and estimated sales returns should be recorded as a reduction of sales revenue to match revenues with costs, no matter how large the estimated returns might be. The publishing industry generally records sales when made, and matches against those sales an estimate of the sales returns because management is able to make a reliable estimate.

In order to promote comparability across firms, standard setters have addressed the question of recording revenue when a right of return exists. Under current GAAP, the general revenue recognition rule should be followed *when all the following six conditions are met:*

- There is a fixed or determinable price at the time of sale.
- The price paid or payable and the obligation are not contingent on resale.
- The buyer's obligation is unchanged by theft, damage, etc.
- The buyer has economic substance apart from the seller.
- The seller has no significant obligation to directly bring about resale.
- The amount of future returns can be reasonably estimated.[3]

If one of the conditions is not met, then no sale should be recorded until the return privilege expires.

These conditions illustrate the spirit of revenue recognition. Many of the conditions pertain to whether the uncertainty surrounding the expected future cash flow has been reduced to an acceptable level (i.e., whether the revenue is realizable). These conditions include the "fixed or determinable price," "obligation not contingent on resale," and "obligation unchanged by theft." Other conditions address whether the resource expenditures to produce the sale have been made (i.e., whether

3. "Revenue Recognition When Right of Return Exists," *Statement of Financial Accounting Standards No. 48* (Stamford, Conn.: FASB, 1981).

the revenue is earned). The primary condition addressing the "earning" of revenue is "the seller has no significant obligation to directly bring about resale."

The Critical Event Often the decision regarding whether to recognize revenue boils down to determining whether a *critical event* has occurred. The great diversity in business activities introduces the need for corporations to consistently apply a critical event test. Frequently, critical events are industry specific, and the critical event in one industry (e.g., magazine sales) may be different from the critical event in another industry (e.g., computer sales). Over time, general rules emerge in various industries regarding revenue recognition. *For merchandising firms, the critical event is almost always the delivery of the product.* At the point of delivery, legal title to the goods passes, and the seller has transferred all risks and rewards of ownership to the buyer. The sacrifice of the goods to the buyer represents the *earning* of revenue. Because we cannot discuss all industries, we will use the general revenue recognition rule throughout this chapter, and we point out in any examples where a particular industry's critical event may (seemingly) conflict with the general rule.

Determining When the Critical Event Occurs In the following situations, the timing of revenue recognition depends on identification of the critical event. Each example includes an explanation of when revenue is recognized and why.

Example 1. On December 28, 2000, Dunbar Co. sold merchandise that cost $400 to Tiffany Products for $600. Under the terms of the sales arrangement, Dunbar shipped the merchandise to Tiffany F.O.B. destination, and Tiffany promised to pay for the goods by January 15, 2001. The goods are in route at December 31, 2000 (Dunbar's fiscal year-end), and are delivered January 3, 2001.

Solution. Dunbar should not recognize revenue (and the associated cost of goods sold and other related expenses) until the year 2001. The term F.O.B. destination is short for "free on board" destination, which means that the seller has legal title until the goods arrive at the buyer's place of business. Therefore, legal title to (and, hence, the risks and rewards of) the merchandise inventory does not pass to Tiffany until the goods arrive at Tiffany's location. The critical event is the passage of legal title, which occurred when the goods reached their delivery destination. This is the most common situation for merchandising firms. Hence, the general rule of revenue recognition is to record revenue when the item is delivered.

EXAMPLE 1 Journal Entries

12/28/00 shipping date:		
No entry		
1/3/01 product delivery date:		
Accounts Receivable	600	
Sales Revenue		600
Cost of Goods Sold	400	
Inventory		400
Cash collected in 2001:		
Cash	600	
Accounts Receivable		600

Example 2. Assume the same facts as in Example 1, except the terms of the sale are F.O.B. shipping point.

Solution. The term F.O.B. shipping point means that the buyer acquires legal title as soon as the goods are shipped from the seller. Therefore, legal title to (and, hence, the risks and rewards of) the merchandise inventory passes to Tiffany as soon as Dunbar ships the inventory. Revenue (and all related expenses) are recognized in 2000. The critical event is the passage of legal title.

EXAMPLE 2 Journal Entries

12/28/00 shipping date:		
Accounts Receivable	600	
Sales Revenue		600
Cost of Goods Sold	400	
Inventory		400
Cash collected in 2001:		
Cash	600	
Accounts Receivable		600

We previously indicated that a general rule is to recognize revenue when products are delivered or services are provided. This general rule works well for sales in nearby geographic locations. However, as illustrated in Examples 1 and 2, the *passage of legal title is the actual critical event.* As a practical matter, firms that ship F.O.B. destination (Example 1) record revenues when the items are shipped. At year-end, accountants then pay particular attention to the F.O.B. terms to make sure that sales made around year-end are properly reported in the correct period.

Example 3. Golden Body Gym collected $200 for an eight-month health club membership from Arnold Swartz on December 1, 2000.

Solution. Golden Body records $25 as revenue by providing gym facilities for the month of December ($200 ÷ 8 months). The remaining $175 represents cash received in advance of providing services, which is reflected as Unearned Revenue (a liability) in the balance sheet. Although the collection of cash and the contract signing are important events, they are not the critical event for revenue recognition. Golden Body earns revenue by providing health club services on a monthly basis by expending resources to open and operate the gym each month. The critical event is providing these services through time.

EXAMPLE 3 Journal Entries

12/1/00 cash receipt:		
Cash	200	
Service Revenue Collected in Advance*		200
12/31/00 adjusting journal entry to record one month of revenue earned:		
Service Revenue Collected in Advance	25	
Service Revenue		25

*Reported in the balance sheet with current liabilities. An alternate account title is Unearned Revenue.

Example 4. During November and December 2000, Musicmania sold $245,000 in gift certificates redeemable for CDs, tapes, and music videos any time before December 31, 2001. In 2000, $60,000 of the certificates were redeemed for goods costing $48,000. In 2001, $180,000 of the certificates were redeemed for goods costing $154,000. Certificates totaling $5,000 lapsed.

Solution. Musicmania recognizes revenue only to the extent that the gift certificates are redeemed or lapse. Musicmania has received cash, but has not yet earned revenue—it has simply promised to deliver merchandise in exchange for a gift certificate. Until the time of delivery or certificate lapse, Cash is shown at $245,000, and the obligation to deliver merchandise in the future is reflected on the balance sheet as a liability in the same amount. When either critical event occurs (delivery or certificate lapse), the liability is removed, and the revenues and associated direct expenses (e.g., cost of goods sold) are recognized. Therefore, sales revenues of $60,000 and expenses (cost of goods sold) of $48,000 are recognized in 2000; sales revenues of $180,000 and expenses (cost of goods sold) of $154,000 are recognized in 2001. Revenues of $5,000 from gift certificate lapse are also recognized in 2001.

EXAMPLE 4 Journal Entries

2000 gift certificate sale:		
Cash	245,000	
Liability for Unredeemed Gift Certificates		245,000
2000 redemption:		
Liability for Unredeemed Gift Certificates	60,000	
Sales Revenue		60,000
Cost of Goods Sold	48,000	
Inventory		48,000
2001 redemption:		
Liability for Unredeemed Gift Certificates	180,000	
Sales Revenue		180,000
Cost of Goods Sold	154,000	
Inventory		154,000
12/31/01 gift certificate lapse:		
Liability for Unredeemed Gift Certificates	5,000	
Revenue from Lapsed Gift Certificates		5,000

Example 5. In December 2001, BlackStar Mines extracted 400 carats of diamonds. All mined diamonds can be sold for $300 per carat for the next three months, with no marketing costs and only minor distribution costs. The full cost of mining is $100 per carat.

Solution. BlackStar has performed the critical event by mining the diamonds. The resources needed to bring about sale have been almost entirely expended. The known price makes the revenue realizable. All $120,000 of revenue should be recorded in 2001. Although this solution seems counterintuitive because it is inconsistent with the general rule that revenue is recognized when the goods are delivered, this rule has emerged in some industries (e.g., precious metals and agriculture products) where products have ready markets in which all goods produced (and refined, if necessary) can be sold immediately for known prices. Therefore, the critical event is *not* delivery, but production.

EXAMPLE 5 Journal Entries

Accumulation of production costs:		
Diamond Inventory	40,000	
Cash		40,000
(400 carats × $100 per carat = $40,000)		
2001 completion of mining:		
Diamond Inventory	120,000	
Revenue from Diamond Mining		120,000
(400 carats × $300 per carat = $120,000)		
Cost of Goods Mined and Held for Sale	40,000	
Diamond Inventory		40,000
Sale of diamond inventory:		
Cash	120,000	
Diamond Inventory		120,000

Example 6. Custom Mantles produced a custom fireplace mantle for Clyde Warfington, at a cost of $9,000 and a selling price of $15,000. At December 31, 2001, the mantle was located at the shipping dock awaiting delivery.

Solution. Custom Mantles performed the critical event by producing the special order custom goods. All $15,000 in revenue (and the related actual and estimated expenses) are recorded in 2001. The fact that separates this example from the previous examples is that the item is a special order constructed for a particular customer. Legal title normally passes at the end of production for special order goods. Therefore, the critical event is production of the item, not its delivery.

EXAMPLE 6 Journal Entries

2001 goods are ready to be shipped:		
Accounts Receivable*	15,000	
Sales Revenue		15,000
Cost of Goods Sold	9,000	
Inventory		9,000

*A common occurrence in special order situations is that the producer would require a customer deposit before production. If this is Custom Mantle's policy, then prior to production, the following entry would have been recorded for a $3,000 deposit:

Cash	3,000	
Customer Deposits		3,000

Completion of production would trigger the first entries, with $3,000 Customer Deposits substituted for $3,000 of Accounts Receivable.

The previous examples illustrate how diverse revenue recognition practices are across different industries. The revenue recognition principle has a long history of unintentional misuse and intentional abuse. Controversy continually arises around the revenue recognition practices of companies, primarily those that appear to recognize revenue without reasonably strong evidence that the revenue is realizable. The two events that most often cast doubt on realizability are sales returns and customer defaults. Aggressive companies sometimes underestimate sales returns and overestimate the bill-paying ability of customers.

The Internet revolution has also caused problems in revenue recognition. Internet companies often swap Web site advertising with other Internet companies, booking a revenue and an expense in the same amount. In these bartering transactions, cash flows never actually occur. At first glance, the Internet company revenue recognition practices do not seem to cause a problem in assessing the profitability of the company. Net income equals zero because revenues and expenses are exactly equal. However, many investors believe that revenue growth is the key determinant of Internet companies' values, rather than net income.

In January 2000, the Emerging Issues Task Force reached a consensus opinion that revenues on these Internet bartering transactions should be reported as "net" revenues of zero, rather than revenues and expenses of equal, nonzero amounts. An exception to this rule is allowed if the Internet company has received recent cash flows (in less than a six-month period) on similar transactions, in which case the revenues and expenses should be separately recorded.

Matching Expenses with Revenues

4 Explain three practical justifications for matching expenses to revenues.

Matching expenses with revenues is a fundamental accounting principle. The general rule is to record all expenses necessary to generate a sale in the same period the sale is recognized. In the Bonilla Co. financial statements, a large number of expenses were necessary to bring about sale (e.g, cost of goods sold, sales salaries and commissions, and rent). Conceptually, these expenses should be matched with the period in which the revenues were generated. In practice, three ways used to justify expense recognition are (1) direct cause and effect; (2) lack of future economic benefit; and (3) systematic and rational allocation.[4]

Direct Cause and Effect Some expense items have a direct cause and effect relationship with revenues. For example, the act of selling inventory causes a direct effect, the reduction in Inventory, which is reported as an expense, Cost of Goods Sold. Other items have a direct cause and effect relationship with a sale. Delivery expense is recognized if the seller pays the expenses to deliver inventory to the buyer. Sales commissions must be paid or accrued causing the recognition of sales commissions expense. Warranty expense is directly related to a sale. Although some portion of the warranty costs will be paid in future years, the expense must be matched against sales revenue in the period of sale.

Consider the following example that reflects cost of goods sold, commissions expense, delivery expense, and warranty expense:

Example 7. Mulvaney Co. sells riding mowers with a two-year guarantee on all parts and labor. In 2000, Mulvaney sold 1,000 mowers for $1,300 each; the mowers cost $700 each. Delivery expense is $10 per mower, and Mulvaney pays a sales commission of 5% on each mower sold. Mower repairs over the warranty period are expected to cost Mulvaney $100 per mower. During 2000, Mulvaney spends $35,000 in cash on mower repairs attributable to mowers sold in 2000.

Solution. In 2000, Mulvaney records $1,300,000 in sales revenue. Cost of goods sold in 2000 equals $700,000 (1,000 mowers × $700); delivery expense equals $10,000 (1,000 mowers × $10); and sales commissions expense equals $65,000 ($1,300,000 × 5%). As an enticement for customers to purchase the riding mowers, Mulvaney promised to repair the mowers at no charge during the next two years. The expected cost of the promise is $100,000 (1,000 mowers × $100 estimated repair cost per mower). Because the promise causes a liability to increase, $100,000 of warranty expense is reported in the 2000 income statement, matched against $1,300,000 in sales revenue. Therefore, the event that causes the warranty expense to be recognized is the sale of the mowers. The $35,000 spent to repair mowers in 2000 is not recognized as an expense. Instead it represents the partial satisfaction of the liability. At December 31, 2000, Mulvaney reports Estimated Obligation Under Warranties of $65,000 ($100,000 original promise less $35,000 satisfaction of the promise) in the liabilities section of the balance sheet. Exhibit 2 presents the financial statement effects of this set of transactions.

EXHIBIT 2 Example 7. Mulvaney Co. Financial Statements

MULVANEY CO.
Statement of Cash Flows
December 31, 2000

Operating Activities*	
Receipts from customers	1,300,000
Commissions and delivery charges	(75,000)
Warranty repairs	(35,000)
Cash flows from operations	1,190,000

(continued)

4. Additionally, materiality is sometimes used to justify expense recognition. For example, assume that Lee Co. purchased 4 plastic garbage cans at $15 each, and each garbage can is expected to last 4 years. Conceptually, the garbage cans should be recorded as depreciable assets and depreciated over four years. However, the cost of the garbage cans is most likely to be immaterial (i.e., not very large with respect to the amount of Lee's other expenses and revenues), and recognizing the expenditure as an expense is an acceptable practice.

EXHIBIT 2 (concluded)

Balance Sheet

Assets		**Liabilities**	
Current assets:		Estimated obligation under warranty	65,000 ↑
Cash	1,190,000 ↑	**Owners' Equity**	
Inventory	700,000 ↓	Retained earnings (through effect on net income)**	425,000 ↑

Income Statement		**Statement of Owners' Equity**	
Sales revenue	1,300,000	Net income**	425,000
Cost of goods sold	(700,000)		
Gross margin	600,000		
Delivery expense	(10,000)		
Sales commissions	(65,000)		
Warranty expense	(100,000)		
Net income**	425,000		

*Under the indirect method: Net income of $425,000 + $700,000 decrease in inventory + $65,000 increase in estimated obligation under warranty = $1,190,000.
**Ignores effect of income taxes.

EXAMPLE 7 Journal Entries

2000 sale of mowers:		
Cash	1,300,000	
Sales Revenue		1,300,000
Cost of Goods Sold	700,000	
Inventory		700,000
Delivery Expense	10,000	
Sales Commissions Expense	65,000	
Cash		75,000
Warranty Expense	100,000	
Estimated Warranty Liability		100,000
2000 incurrence of warranty repair cost:		
Estimated Warranty Liability	35,000	
Cash (and/or Parts Inventory, etc.)		35,000

To test your ability to detect expenses recognized because a cause and effect relationship exists, return to Exhibit 1; identify the expenses that are included in the Bonilla Co. income statement because of a cause and effect relationship. When you are finished, check the following footnote for an answer.[5]

Lack of Future Economic Benefit Mulvaney incurred certain other costs to bring about the sale of inventory that are not directly related to the $1,300,000 riding lawnmower sales. These expenses are more related to the period in which the company conducted business than to a particular sale. For example, administrators must be hired and paid; advertising expenditures must be made; office supplies are purchased and used; and rent on the store and the administrative offices is incurred. These costs are all related to and benefit the current period. Thus, they are charged as expenses in the current period. It is possible that some of these expenditures have at least *some* future economic benefit. But, the estimate of the future benefits is un-

5. The items that reflect cause and effect with sales are Cost of Goods Sold ($1,000,000), Warranty Expense ($40,000), and Sales Salaries and Commissions Expense ($125,000).

reliable, and the expense treatment (rather than capitalization as an asset) is accorded these expenditures.[6]

Once again, it is important to understand that expense recognition is an *accrual* concept. It does not matter when the cash flow took place to pay administrators, landlords, and advertisers. In determining which accounting period warrants the expense recognition, two assessments are important: whether the expense was incurred in the current period, and whether the expenditure has a reliably measurable effect on future periods.

Once again, refer to the Bonilla Co. income statement in Exhibit 1. The items that do not have a direct cause and effect relationship with revenues, but are associated with the year 2001 and have (or are assumed to have) a lack of future economic benefit, are Rent Expense—Store ($110,000); Advertising Expense ($25,000); Rent Expense—Office ($50,000); Office Supplies Expense ($10,000); and Administrative Salaries Expense ($100,000). Note that these expenses appear in either the selling expenses category or the general and administrative expense category.

Systematic and Rational Allocation A third reason for expense recognition is related to the need for a systematic and rational allocation of costs to the periods benefitted. Firms raise funds from financing activities and commit them to investing and operating activities. If the investing activities are in the corporation's own productive assets, then the costs of acquiring long-lived assets used in operating activities must be allocated to the periods benefitted. The Bonilla Co. invested in delivery equipment and office equipment that had useful lives of more than one year. Depreciation of those assets represents a systematic and rational allocation of costs to the periods benefitted. Depreciation expense is matched to the periods in which the revenues are generated through the use of the long-lived asset. Bonilla's 2001 income statement reports depreciation expense of $45,000, of which $30,000 is reported as selling expenses and $15,000 as general and administrative expenses.

Summary

Accounting for operating activities primarily involves the timing of revenue recognition and the matching of expenses with revenues. Revenue recognition occurs when revenues are both realized (or realizable) and earned. Expenses are matched against (1) specific revenues, if the act of generating revenues directly caused the expense; (2) the current period, if no cause and effect relationship is apparent and the expenditures benefitted only the current period; and (3) current and future periods to reflect the systematic and rational allocation of the costs of investments in long-lived operating assets.

Firms that Produce and Sell Goods—Manufacturing Firms

Many of the revenue and expense recognition issues present for merchandising firms are also present for manufacturing firms. In the following sections, we concentrate on the following *additional* issues that arise when firms produce rather than buy their inventory:

- Product versus period costs.
- Revenue recognition at the end of production.
- Revenue recognition during production.

6. Advertising is a good example of an expenditure that may have future benefits. A company may invest $1,000,000 in an advertising campaign that is expected to raise the public's awareness of its product. Social scientists may be able to determine that this campaign has an effective life of 18 months in the public's collective consciousness. However, because it is difficult to determine the benefits in future periods, accountants generally expense advertising as incurred (i.e., over the period of service provided by the advertising agency).

Product versus Period Costs

5 Differentiate between product and period costs.

Merchandising firms *purchase* the inventory that they hold for resale. However, manufacturing firms incur costs to *produce* the inventory: the costs to purchase raw materials inventory, costs to pay for direct labor used in the manufacturing process, and other indirect costs of production (e.g., manufacturing overhead). The **costs incurred to produce inventory** are labeled as ***product costs*** because they are directly traceable to the production of a specific product that will later be sold. In contrast, a ***period cost*** is not directly traceable to the production of a specific product but is **traceable to a particular accounting period.**

For illustration, we use labor cost and equipment depreciation to briefly examine the path by which costs become expenses in the manufacturing versus merchandising firms.

Labor and Depreciation in Merchandising Firms The treatment of labor cost and depreciation is simple in a merchandising firm, as the following diagram shows:

Labor cost ⟶ Salaries and Wages Expense (direct cause and effect or lack of future economic benefit)

Depreciation cost ⟶ Depreciation Expense (systematic and rational allocation)

Because labor cost of the period either has a direct cause and effect relationship or no future economic benefit, it is expensed in order to match it with current revenues. Depreciation cost is a portion of the equipment's original cost that is assigned to depreciation expense. Systematic and rational allocation justifies this recognition.

Labor and Depreciation in Manufacturing Firms The treatment of labor cost and depreciation is more complex in a manufacturing firm:

		Balance Sheet		Income Statement
Labor cost *associated with manufacturing*	⟶	Inventory	⟶	Cost of Goods Sold
Labor cost *associated with nonmanufacturing* selling and administrative activities	⟶			Salaries and Wages Expense
Depreciation cost *associated with manufacturing*	⟶	Inventory	⟶	Cost of Goods Sold
Depreciation cost *associated with nonmanufacturing* selling and administrative activities	⟶			Depreciation Expense

Labor costs must be separated into the costs used to produce inventory (a product cost that produces an asset with future economic benefit) and the costs of selling and administration that have no future economic benefit (a period cost that is expensed). Likewise, depreciation cost associated with inventory production is assigned to inventory cost (an asset). Systematic and rational allocation justifies the recognition of depreciation expense associated with selling and administrative activities. Specific systems for achieving these assignments are illustrated in managerial and cost accounting courses.

Revenue Recognition—Situations that Conflict with the General Rule of Revenue Recognition

6 Explain when generally accepted accounting principles permit departure from the general rule of recognizing revenue at the point of sale.

In this section, we provide more detail on three specific situations for which an accounting treatment seemingly conflicts with the general rule of revenue recognition—revenue recognition at the end of production but before sale and delivery, during production, and after sale and delivery.

Revenue Recognition at the End of Production but Before Sale and Delivery As previously noted, the critical event for revenue recognition differs across industries. A good example is the precious metals industry, where revenue is generally recognized when a precious metal is mined and refined. The act of producing and refining the metal has reduced cash flow uncertainty to an acceptable level. The condition of restricted supply in the precious metals market provides a known market price for all quantities. Thus, the realization criterion is met. Also, the bulk of the costs associated with precious metals are the mining and refining costs, with the costs of marketing and distributing the product proving minimal. This is evidence that the revenue is earned at the time of production. Revenue recognition at the end of production is also appropriate for many agricultural products.

7 Account for the recognition of revenues, expenses, and profits in the construction industry.

Revenue Recognition During Production Special revenue and expense recognition rules apply in the construction industry because many construction jobs take more than 12 months to complete.[7] Depending on the ability to estimate revenues and costs, corporations theoretically have two choices for revenue recognition for long-lived construction projects of greater than one year: either applying the general rule of revenue recognition at delivery, or accelerating revenue recognition to a point during production.

The general rule of revenue recognition is illustrated by companies that use the ***completed contract*** method, which **recognizes profit when a long-term contract is complete.** Consistent with the conservatism principle, expected losses on the contract are recognized as soon as estimated. Under this method, revenue for companies with several long-term construction projects can become bunched in the years that projects are finished—it is possible that no revenue would be recognized in some years if the completed contract method is used.

Departing from the general rule of revenue recognition, other companies use the ***percentage of completion*** method, which **recognizes profit as work is performed.** As with the completed contract method, expected losses are recognized as soon as estimated. *GAAP requires using the percentage of completion method for long-term construction projects when dependable revenue and cost estimates exist and the company can reasonably estimate the degree of completion.*[8] By associating revenues and expenses (i.e., income) with the period in which the effort is made, a better matching of expenses and revenues occurs. Also, income fluctuations through time are avoided.[9]

The following example illustrates the two methods of revenue and income recognition in the construction industry.

Example 8. On January 1, 2001, Janus Construction enters into a four-year project to produce a section of an interstate highway. The contract price is $3,000,000. Each year $750,000 is billed to the customer and collected in cash. All costs incurred are paid in cash. Information (in thousands) pertaining to the contract is given at the top of the next page.

7. For example, it may take three years or more to construct an interstate highway section, and it may take a developer five years to acquire raw land, create the required infrastructure, and build houses on 40 acres of land.

8. Two methods are commonly used to determine the percentage of completion. In one method, the percent of completion is estimated with respect to the actual percentage of completion. This can be accomplished through analyzing engineers' reports or by referring to certain standardized guidelines (e.g., once the building is under roof it is 30% complete). The ***cost-to-cost method*** **estimates the percentage complete by dividing the costs incurred to date by the total estimated costs.** *Problems in accounting and financial statement analysis textbooks tend to use the cost-to-cost method for percentage of completion problems.*

9. Of the 600 companies surveyed in 1999 *Accounting Trends and Techniques,* 91 show instances of accounting for long-term contracts with the following: 67 percentage of completion; 21 units-of-delivery (this is a modification of the percentage of completion method); 1 completed contract; and 2 not determinable.

	2001	2002	2003	2004
Contract price	$3,000	$3,000	$3,000	$3,000
Actual costs to date	$ 400	$ 900	$2,200	$3,300
Estimated costs to complete	2,000	1,800	1,000	—
Total expected costs	$2,400	$2,700	$3,200	$3,300
Expected profit	$ 600	$ 300	$ (200)	$ (300)
Percent complete*	16.7%	33.3%	68.8%	100%

*Uses the cost-to-cost method to determine percentage complete (actual cost to date ÷ total expected costs)

Solution. This example is (hopefully) unusual because by the end of the contract Janus sustains a loss. Most long-term contracts result in a profit. A loss situation usually occurs when a contractor enters into a fixed-price contract, with the costs escalating during construction. A contractor can attempt to minimize this possibility by negotiating fixed-cost contracts for all materials and labor with suppliers at the beginning of the construction. We illustrate this loss situation because of the way GAAP requires estimated losses to be reported. The following statements show the financial statement effects of this example.

The statement of cash flows does not differ between the completed contract and the percentage of completion methods. Cash flow is an economic event that is independent of the accrual accounting method chosen. The statement of cash flows reports cash payments for construction costs and cash collections from customers in each year. Note that in 2001 and 2002, net cash flow is positive, but it becomes negative in 2003 and 2004 when construction costs dramatically increase. See Exhibit 3.

EXHIBIT 3 Example 8. Statement of Cash Flows

JANUS CONSTRUCTION
Statement of Cash Flows
Completed Contract and Percentage of Completion Methods
(Cash outflows in parentheses)

(In thousands)	2001	2002	2003	2004
Operating Activities				
Cash payments for construction costs	(400)	(500)	(1,300)	(1,100)
Cash collections from customers	750	750	750	750
Net cash inflow (outflow)	350	250	(550)	(350)

The income statement and balance sheet presentation under the ***completed contract*** *method* are presented in Exhibit 4. Explanations follow the financial statements.

EXHIBIT 4 Example 8. Income Statement and Balance Sheet Effects

JANUS CONSTRUCTION
Income Statement Effects
Completed Contract Method
(In thousands)

	2001	2002	2003	2004
Construction revenues	0	0	0	3,000
Construction expenses	0	0	0	(3,100)
Profit (loss) on long-term construction contracts	0	0	0	(100)
Estimated loss on long-term construction contracts	0	0	(200)	0
Net income	0	0	(200)	(100)

JANUS CONSTRUCTION
Balance Sheet Effects (December 31)
Completed Contract Method
(In thousands)

	2001	2002	2003	2004
Assets				
Current assets:				
Cash	350	600	50	(300)
Liabilities				
Current liabilities:				
Billings on construction in progress	750	1,500	2,250	
Less construction in progress	400	900	2,000	
Billings in excess of construction in progress	350	600	250	
Owners' Equity				
Retained earnings (ignores income tax effects)	0	0	(200)	(300)

2001. Construction revenues, expenses, and profits are not recognized in the 2001 income statement because the contract is not complete. The balance sheet reports Cash of \$350,000 (the net cash flow from the statement of cash flows), and Accounts Receivable of \$0. We assumed that, in each year, Janus bills \$750,000 to the customer and receives \$750,000 in cash. If cash flow lagged behind billings, then an accounts receivable balance would be present at each balance sheet date. The balance sheet also presents the netting of two special accounts, Construction in Progress and Billings on Construction in Progress, that are used throughout the project's life. ***Construction in Progress* is used to accumulate construction costs.** At December 31, 2001, the cumulative construction cost is \$400,000. ***Billings on Construction in Progress* accumulates billings to customers.** At December 31, 2001, billings totaled \$750,000. At the balance sheet date, if construction in progress exceeds billings, then the firm has a current asset, Construction in Progress in Excess of Billings. Janus Construction has the opposite situation. Billings exceed construction in progress by \$350,000 (\$750,000 − \$400,000). Thus, a current liability is shown. Current (rather than long-term) classification is appropriate because the accounts will be liquidated within the operating cycle, which is longer than one year for firms engaged primarily in long-term construction contracts.[10] Owners' equity equals zero because assets minus liabilities equals zero. Also, the only component of owners' equity in this example, Retained Earnings, equals zero because no net income is reported through the end of 2001.[11]

2002. The income statement and balance sheet disclosures in 2002 are determined in a similar manner as in 2001. Construction in Progress and Billings on Construction in Progress are balance sheet accounts (i.e., cumulative). Thus, the \$600,000 balance in Billings in Excess of Construction in Progress in 2002 is computed as follows:

Billings in 2001	\$750,000	
Billings in 2002	750,000	
Total billings		\$1,500,000
Construction costs in 2001	\$400,000	
Construction costs in 2002	500,000	
Total construction in progress		900,000
Billings in excess of construction in progress		\$ 600,000

10. Our example deals with a single project. For firms with multiple projects, those projects with billings in excess of costs are grouped separately from those projects with costs in excess of billings. These firms would show both a current liability and a current asset.

11. Janus will report balance sheet amounts for its investing and financing activities as well. We refrain from this presentation in order to concentrate on the operating accounts.

2003. At December 31, 2003, Janus expects a loss of $200,000 on the entire project ($3,000,000 contract price less $3,200,000 in total expected costs). Accountants justify the immediate recognition of an expected loss by applying the concept of conservatism. The 2003 income statement reports the estimated loss of $200,000. Cumulative construction costs at December 31, 2003, total $2,200,000. Recognizing a $200,000 loss is equivalent to recognizing that Construction in Progress is impaired. As of December 31, 2003, Janus expects that $3,200,000 will be recorded in Construction in Progress by the end of the contract, but that only $3,000,000 will be collected in contract price. Thus, the $200,000 loss represents the write-down (reduction) of the construction in progress asset, and the balance sheet disclosure is determined as follows:

Billings in 2001	$ 750,000	
Billings in 2002	750,000	
Billings in 2003	750,000	
Total billings		$2,250,000
Construction costs in 2001	$ 400,000	
Construction costs in 2002	500,000	
Construction costs in 2003	1,300,000	
Expected total loss on contract	(200,000)	
Total construction in progress		2,000,000
Billings in excess of construction in progress		$ 250,000

2004. When the contract is completed in 2004, total cumulative billings of $3,000,000 are recognized as revenue, and $3,100,000 of cumulative construction costs are recognized as construction expenses, yielding an additional $100,000 loss. The $3,100,000 is the balance in Construction in Progress at the point of contract completion ($3,300,000 in cumulative costs less the $200,000 write-down in 2003). The 2004 balance sheet shows a negative cash effect of $300,000. Retained earnings at December 31, 2004, is obtained by summing the 2003 net loss of $100,000 and the 2004 net loss of $200,000.

EXAMPLE 8 Journal Entries—Completed Contract Method

	2001		2002		2003		2004	
Construction costs:								
Construction in Progress	400		500		1,300		1,100	
Cash		400		500		1,300		1,100
Billings and collections:								
Cash	750		750		750		750	
Billings*		750		750		750		750
Profit and loss accruals:								
Estimated Loss on Contracts					200			
Construction in Progress						200		
Completion of project:								
Construction Expenses							3,100	
Construction in Progress								3,100
Billings*							3,000	
Construction Revenues								3,000

*Complete account title is Billings on Construction in Progress.

Construction in Progress

2001 costs	400		
12/31/01	400		
2002 costs	500		
12/31/02	900		
2003 costs	1,300		
		2003 loss	200
12/31/03	2,000		
2004 costs	1,100		
		Complete	3,100
12/31/04	0		

Billings on Construction in Progress

		2001 bills	750
		12/31/01	750
		2002 bills	750
		12/31/02	1,500
		2003 bills	750
		12/31/03	2,250
		2004 bills	750
Complete	3,000		
		12/31/04	0

Retained Earnings

		2001 profit	0
		12/31/01	0
		2002 profit	0
		12/31/02	0
2003 loss	200		
12/31/03	200		
2004 loss	100		
12/31/04	300		

The income statement and balance sheet presentation under the ***percentage of completion*** *method* (using the cost-to-cost method to estimate percentage of completion) are presented in Exhibit 5. Again, explanations follow the financial statements.

EXHIBIT 5 Example 8. Income Statement and Balance Sheet Effects

JANUS CONSTRUCTION
Income Statement Effects
Percentage of Completion Method

(In thousands)	2001	2002	2003	2004
Construction revenues	500	500	1,063	937
Construction expenses	(400)	(500)	(1,363)	(1,037)
Profit (loss) on long-term construction contracts	100	0	(300)	(100)

JANUS CONSTRUCTION
Balance Sheet Effects (December 31)
Percentage of Completion Method

(In thousands)	2001	2002	2003	2004
Assets				
Current assets:				
Cash	350	600	50	(300)
Liabilities				
Current liabilities:				
Billings on construction in progress	750	1,500	2,250	
Less construction in progress	500	1,000	2,000	
Billings in excess of construction in progress	250	500	250	
Owners' Equity				
Retained earnings (ignores income tax effects)	100	100	(200)	(300)

The percentage of completion method requires the periodic recognition of revenues, expenses, and profits based on the amount of revenue earning "effort" in each year. This recognition is accomplished by accruing annual profits and revenues. These amounts are based on annual updates of estimated total project profits, revenues, and percent of completion (as shown below and discussed thereafter), and accruing expenses to reconcile the profits and revenues.

(In thousands)	2001	2002	2003	2004
Profit recognition:				
Expected profit (loss)	$ 600	$ 300	$ (200)	$ (300)
Percent complete*	× 16.7%	× 33.3%	N/A**	N/A
Profit (loss) to date	$ 100	$ 100	$ (200)	$ (300)
Prior years' recognitions	0	(100)	(100)	200
Current period profit (loss)	$ 100	$ 0	$ (300)	$ (100)

*Using the cost-to-cost method.
**100% should be reflected because the contract has an estimated loss.

(In thousands)	2001	2002	2003	2004
Revenue recognition:				
Expected contract price	$3,000	$3,000	$3,000	$3,000
Percent complete	× 16.7%	× 33.3%	× 68.8%	× 100%
Revenue to date	$ 500	$1,000	$2,063	$3,000
Prior years' recognitions	0	(500)	(1,000)	(2,063)
Current period revenue	$ 500	$ 500	$1,063	$ 937

2001. In 2001, Janus incurs \$400,000 of an expected total \$2,400,000 in construction costs. If costs are an adequate measure of effort, Janus is 16.7% complete (\$400,000 ÷ \$2,400,000)[12] on a job with an expected profit of \$600,000 (\$3,000,000 contract price less \$2,400,000 expected costs). Under the percentage of completion method, 16.7% of the expected revenue (\$3,000,000 × 16.7% = \$500,000) and 16.7% of the expected profit (\$600,000 × 16.7% = \$100,000) are recognized. Construction expenses are recorded at an amount that yields the \$100,000 profit when matched against the \$500,000 recognized revenue (i.e., \$400,000).[13]

The excess of billings over construction in progress for 2001 is calculated as follows:

Billings in 2001		\$750,000
Construction costs in 2001	\$400,000	
Profit recognized in 2001	100,000	
Total construction in progress		500,000
Billings in excess of construction in progress		\$250,000

Note in the Exhibit 5 balance sheet that Construction in Progress equals \$500,000 (\$400,000 costs plus \$100,000 profit). Increasing an asset to recognize profit is consistent with the idea that net income represents increases in net assets from transactions with nonowners.

2002. In 2002, revenue recognized is \$500,000. The project is 33.3% complete, and the \$3,000,000 contract price times 33.3% equals \$1,000,000 in revenue recognition to date. Because \$500,000 in revenue had been recognized in all years prior to 2002, \$500,000 in additional revenue is recognized in 2002. At December 31, 2002, the expected profit on the contract is \$300,000. The percentage of completion method dictates that 33.3% of the profit, or \$100,000, be recorded by December 31, 2002. Because \$100,000 was recognized in 2001, no profit is recognized in 2002 (i.e., \$100,000 profit in 2001 + \$0 profit in 2002 = \$100,000 cumulative profit on December 31, 2002). In order to show \$0 profit in 2002, \$500,000 in expenses is recognized.

The balance sheet is constructed following the same measurement rules as shown for the completed contract method. For example, at December 31, 2002, Billings in Excess of Construction in Progress is \$500,000, determined as follows:

Billings in 2001	\$750,000	
Billings in 2002	750,000	
Total billings		\$1,500,000
Construction costs in 2001	\$400,000	
Profit recognized in 2001	100,000	
Construction costs in 2002	500,000	
Profit recognized in 2002	0	
Total construction in progress		1,000,000
Billings in excess of construction in progress		\$ 500,000

2003. In 2003, the revenue recognized is \$1,063,000. The project is 68.8% complete, and the \$3,000,000 contract price times 68.8% equals \$2,063,000 in revenue recognition to date. Because \$1,000,000 in revenue had been recognized in all prior years, \$1,063,000 in additional revenue is recognized.

In 2003, a \$300,000 loss is recognized. Janus expects a \$200,000 loss overall on the project. Conservatism dictates that on a project-to-date basis, the entire \$200,000 estimated loss must be recognized. Conservatism means that if we antic-

12. Consistent with the idea that resource expenditure is the way firms earn revenue, the cost-to-cost method of determining percentage of completion is the most widely used method.

13. In this example, the estimated expenses recorded of \$400,000 equaled the construction costs incurred in 2001. This does not have to be, but often will be, the case.

ipate a loss on the project, then 100% of the estimated loss on a project-to-date basis is recorded in the period in which the estimated loss situation becomes apparent. Because $100,000 in profit had been recognized in all prior years ($100,000 profit in 2001 + $0 profit in 2002), a $300,000 loss accrual adjusts the $100,000 cumulative profit situation to the needed $200,000 cumulative expected loss situation. The billings in excess of construction in progress amount is computed as in the completed contract example.

2004. The remaining $937,000 in construction revenues is recorded ($3,000,000 less the cumulative revenues of $2,063,000 recognized through December 31, 2003). A loss of $100,000 is recorded to increase the total estimated loss on the project from $200,000 at December 31, 2003, to $300,000 at December 31, 2004. Construction expenses of $1,037,000 are recorded ($3,300,000 total less $2,263,000 cumulative expenses recorded at December 31, 2003).

EXAMPLE 8 Journal Entries—Percentage of Completion Method

	2001		2002		2003		2004	
Construction costs:								
Construction in Progress	400		500		1,300		1,100	
Cash		400		500		1,300		1,100
Billings and collections:								
Cash	750		750		750		750	
Billings*		750		750		750		750
Profit and loss accruals:								
Construction Expenses	400		500					
Construction in Progress	100							
Construction Revenues		500		500				
Construction Expenses					1,363		1,037	
Construction in Progress						300		100
Construction Revenues						1,063		937
Completion of project:								
Billings*							3,000	
Construction in Progress								3,000

*Complete account title is Billings on Construction in Progress.

Construction in Progress

2001 costs	400		
12/31/01	400		
2002 costs	500		
2002 profit	100		
12/31/02	1,000		
2003 costs	1,300		
		2003 loss	300
12/31/03	2,000		
2004 costs	1,100		
		2004 loss	100
		Complete	3,000
12/31/04	0		

Billings on Construction in Progress

		2001 bills	750
		12/31/01	750
		2002 bills	750
		12/31/02	1,500
		2003 bills	750
		12/31/03	2,250
		2004 bills	750
Complete	3,000		
		12/31/04	0

Retained Earnings

		2001 profit	0
		12/31/01	0
		2002 profit	100
		12/31/02	100
2003 loss	300		
12/31/03	200		
2004 loss	100		
12/31/04	300		

The percentage of completion method accelerates revenue and profit recognition to a point before sale and delivery. As emphasized in previous chapters, revenue recognition occurs via increases in assets or decreases in liabilities. In the construction industry, Construction in Progress is increased for profit recognition and decreased for loss recognition.

To illustrate financial statement disclosure of the percentage of completion method, the following partial footnote appeared in the financial statements of Kevlin Corporation:

Kevlin Corporation, Summary of Significant Accounting Policies—Revenue Recognition

For financial statement purposes, revenues and profits are recorded using the percentage-of-completion method for certain contracts based on the product type, contract size and duration of time to completion. The percentage of completion is determined by relating the actual cost of work performed to date to the current estimated total cost of the respective contracts. Revenues and profits on all other contracts are recorded as shipments are made. If estimated total costs on any of these contracts indicate a loss, the entire amount of the estimated loss is recognized immediately.

Costs and estimated earnings in excess of billings on uncompleted contracts, as reflected on the accompanying consolidated balance sheet, comprise amounts of revenue recognized on contracts for which billings have not been rendered. Billings in excess of costs and estimated earnings on uncompleted contracts comprise amounts of billings recognized on contracts for which costs have not been incurred. In accordance with industry practice, the Company includes in current assets and liabilities amounts realizable and payable under long-term contracts.

Revenue Recognition After Sale and Delivery In some situations, revenue is recognized after sale and delivery. The following example from an annual report for Ford Motor Company illustrates a situation where revenue is not recognized at the time of sale and delivery. In this situation, because the buyers had the option to require Ford to repurchase vehicles, Ford recognized revenue over the period the vehicles were rented. The footnote also describes Ford's basic revenue recognition policy, and how sales incentive costs are matched with revenues.

Ford Motor Company—Note 1 (in part):
Accounting Policies (Slightly modified by authors)

Revenue Recognition. Sales are recorded by the company when products are shipped to dealers, except as described below. Estimated costs for approved sales incentive programs are normally recognized as sales reductions at the time of revenue recognition. Estimated costs for sales incentive programs approved subsequent to the time that related sales were recorded are recognized when the programs are approved.

Beginning December 1, sales through dealers to certain daily rental companies where the daily rental company has an option to require the company to repurchase vehicles, subject to certain conditions, are recognized over the period of daily rental service. . . Previously, the company recognized revenue for these vehicles when shipped. The carrying value of these vehicles, included in other current assets, was $1,803 million at December 31.

Two accounting methods are used to recognize revenue after sale and delivery: the installment sales method and the cost recovery method. These methods, closely related to cash basis accounting, are used when cash collection is so uncertain as to make it the critical event. We do not illustrate these two methods in the text.

Structural Changes in Operations

8 Account for structural changes in operations, including restructurings and discontinued operations.

From time to time, company evaluation of operational success leads to the decision to restructure or abandon a portion of operations. These structural changes cause one-time increases or decreases in net income. In recent years, U.S. companies have engaged in downsizing activities to match the lean production capabilities of foreign competitors, thus creating new competitive advantages when entering the global markets of the late twentieth and early twenty-first centuries. Voluntary structural changes include restructurings and discontinuing entire sets of operations. Changes may also be involuntary due to events that are unusual in nature and infrequent in occurrence (i.e., extraordinary items). We consider each of these *real* changes in operations in turn.[14]

Restructurings

In a ***restructuring,*** **companies may lay off workers and rearrange and/or sell a portion of production lines or service-oriented facilities.** These activities will likely result in paying severance benefits to employees, collecting cash on sales of property, plant and equipment, and incurring costs to rearrange plant and other facilities. Restructuring costs are reported as a line item in the income statement above income from continuing operations.[15]

Example 9. In 2001, National Paper Company restructures the fine paper production operations at its Erie Plant. Downsizing the employee work force results in termination benefits of $80,000. The sale of certain assets and rearrangement of the production floor generate $67,000 in losses and $30,000 in costs, respectively.

Solution. National reports $177,000 in *restructuring charges* in its 2001 income statement, whether these amounts have been paid or not.

The stock market seems to love restructurings, even though net income is temporarily reduced. Stock prices often increase at the time of restructurings, indicating investors' beliefs that long-run benefits will accrue to the company from such changes. The FASB is concerned, however, by restructurings. Supposedly, these are one-time (or at least somewhat infrequent) events. However, many companies report restructuring charges in nearly every period. The FASB is concerned that some companies use these charges to manipulate income. Remember that an asset write-down taken today or a noncapitalized rearrangement cost frees future income from such charges.

Discontinued Operations

Discontinued operations result from the **disposal of an entire segment of the business. The date at which the management of the firm decides to dispose of the segment** is called the ***measurement date.*** The following two elements of discontinued operations are measured and reported in financial statements for a hypothetical Division S:

1. **Income (loss) from *operations* of the discontinued Division S** includes the income (loss) from operating the discontinued segment from the beginning of the current fiscal year to the measurement date. Only *actual* amounts are included as a part of this element.

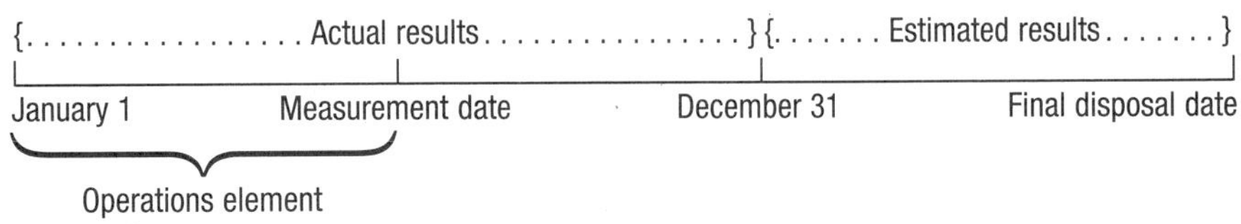

2. **Gain (loss) on *disposal* of discontinued Division S** includes the income (loss) from operating the discontinued segment from the measurement date to the date

14. In the 1999 *Accounting Trends & Techniques,* of the 600 companies surveyed, 197 reported restructuring of operations; 174 reported write-downs of assets; and 28 reported sales of assets. Further, 93 reported current liabilities for estimated costs related to discontinued operations, and 32 reported long-term liabilities related to discontinued operations.

15. Restructuring charges have become a common worldwide event. For example, in November 1999, Japan's Nissan Motor Co. reported ¥368.9 billion in one-time restructuring charges (¥274.2 related to unfunded pension obligations, ¥48.1 billion for vehicle warranties, and ¥46.6 billion for factory-closing charges), and announced plans to take charges of an additional ¥141 billion in the second half of the year

of actual disposal or abandonment *plus* the gain (loss) from the actual disposal of the discontinued segment's net assets. Both *actual* and *estimated* amounts are included as part of this element.

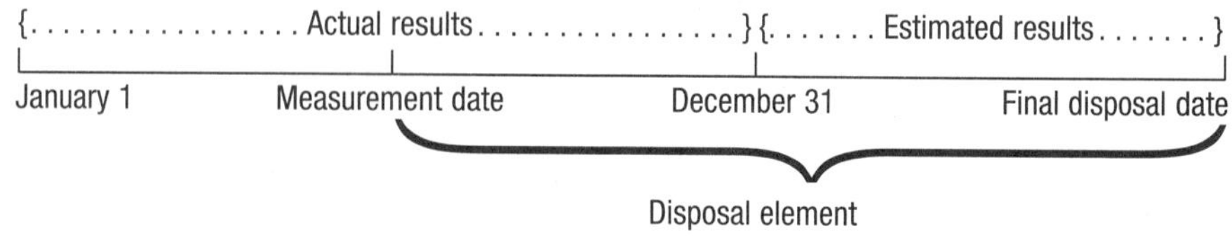

Rules for the current period recognition of the estimated (i.e., post year-end) results, unique to discontinued operations, are illustrated in the following example.

Example 10. In the following cases, three pieces of information are provided that correspond to the time lines presented above: (1) the actual operating income (loss) from the beginning of a company's fiscal year to the measurement date; (2) the actual operating income (loss) and the actual gains (losses) from asset disposals from the measurement date to year-end; and (3) the estimated operating income (loss) and estimated disposal gains (losses) after year-end up to and including the final disposal of the segment. For each case, show what is reported at year-end for the two components of discontinued operations.

		Cases				
Item		**A**	**B**	**C**	**D**	**E**
1	Actual operating income (loss) to measurement date	$ 6,000	$ 9,000	$(4,000)	$(3,000)	$ 1,000
2	Actual operating income (loss) and actual disposal gains (losses) from measurement date to year-end	10,000	10,000	(5,000)	(5,000)	(5,000)
3	Estimated operating income (loss) and disposal gains (losses) after year-end	1,000	(9,000)	6,000	4,000	(1,000)

Solution.

Current year income statement:					
Discontinued operations:					
Income (loss) from operations	$ 6,000	$ 9,000	$(4,000)	$(3,000)	$ 1,000
Gain (loss) on disposal	10,000	1,000	0	(1,000)	(6,000)
Discontinued operations	$16,000	$10,000	$(4,000)	$(4,000)	$ (5,000)

The *first component* of discontinued operations is the income (loss) from operations (of the discontinued segment). For all cases, note that this amount is equal to Item 1 in the example information, which is the actual operating income (loss) from the beginning of the year to the measurement date.

The *second component* of discontinued operations is determined by the sum of all post-measurement date events. Clearly, Item 2 (the actual results of operations from the measurement date to year-end) is recognized in the year-end financial statements. At issue is whether the estimated post-balance sheet date amounts (Item 3) should be recognized in the financial statements at the balance sheet date. *The basic rule under GAAP is to accrue all estimated future losses as of the balance sheet date, and to accrue estimated gains to the extent that they would decrease an actual post-measurement date loss* (Item 2). This rule is actually an application of conservatism. A slight violation of conservatism occurs whenever an estimated gain is accrued as of year-end to offset an actual loss. However, this practice is justified by a desire to avoid fluctuations in net income that artificially arise from applications of conservatism.

In the following section, we apply the rule to the individual cases.

Case A. Estimated post-measurement date results are a $1,000 gain, with actual post-measurement date results equal to a $10,000 gain. Only the $10,000 gain is shown as the second component of discontinued operations. The $1,000 estimated gain should not be recorded as of the balance sheet date. It will be recorded in the next period's financial statements when realized.

Case B. The $9,000 estimated loss should be accrued as of year-end. When it is subtracted from the $10,000 actual gain, a net gain of $1,000 is reported as the second component of discontinued operations.

Case C. The $6,000 estimated gain should be accrued as of year-end to the extent that it reduces the post-measurement date actual loss of $5,000. Therefore, $5,000 of the estimated gain is accrued as of year-end, offsetting the $5,000 actual loss and reducing the second component of discontinued operations to zero. The remainder of the gain not accrued as of year-end, $1,000, is recorded in the next period's financial statements when realized.

Case D. This is similar to *Case C* except that the full $4,000 estimated gain can be offset against the $5,000 actual loss, resulting in ($1,000) being reported as a gain (loss) on disposal.

Case E. This is similar to *Case B* except that the year-end accrual of the estimated ($1,000) loss makes an actual loss bigger, instead of an actual gain smaller.

Charges from discontinued operations are often large enough to swamp the rest of a company's operations. For example, in 1997, Eli Lilly sold PCS, its health-care management operation, and took a $2.401 billion charge under discontinued operations. The charge was bigger than Lilly's $2.016 billion in income from continuing operations, resulting in a net loss for the year of $385 million. This charge was a one-time, transitory charge that would not be expected to repeat.

Involuntary Structural Change— An Extraordinary Item

Extraordinary items are material items that are *both* unusual in nature and infrequent in occurrence. An item may also be classified as extraordinary if so mandated by the FASB. According to Accounting Principles Board Opinion No. 30, items that are not considered to be extraordinary are asset write-offs or write-downs, translation gains and losses on foreign subsidiary financial statements, gains and losses from the disposal of a business, the effects of a strike, and the adjustments of accruals on long-term contracts. Gains and losses from early extinguishment of debt are considered extraordinary because the FASB mandates this treatment. Also, expropriations by government entities and prohibitions under newly enacted laws or regulations are treated as extraordinary items.

Extraordinary items receive disclosure on the bottom portion of the income statement. Unusual *or* infrequent items (but not both) are reported *above* (and thus, as a part of) income from continuing operations. Extraordinary items are rare, except for early debt retirement.[16]

Structural Changes Disclosure

Exhibit 6 shows a summary of the disclosure of structural changes in operations in the income statement.

16. The 1999 *Accounting Trends & Techniques* reveals that 74 companies reported 75 extraordinary items, 73 of which were related to early debt extinguishment.

EXHIBIT 6

XYZ CORPORATION
Multiple-Step Income Statement
For the Year Ended December 31, 20XX

Net sales		$ xxx
Less cost of goods sold		(xxx)
Gross margin (gross profit)		$ xxx
Less operating expenses		(xxx)
Income from operations		$ xxx
Other expenses, revenues, gains, and losses (including **restructuring charges)**		xxx
Income from continuing operations before income taxes		$ xxx
Provision for income taxes (income tax expense)		xxx
Income from continuing operations		$ xxx
Discontinued operations (footnote required):		
Income (loss) from operations of discontinued Division S (less applicable income taxes of $xxx)	**$ xxx**	
Gain (loss) on disposal of discontinued Division S (less applicable income taxes of $xxx)	**xxx**	**xxx**
Income before extraordinary items and cumulative effect of a change in accounting principle		$ xxx
Extraordinary items (less applicable income taxes of $xxx) (footnote required)		**xxx**
Cumulative effect on prior years' income of a change in accounting principle (less applicable income taxes of $xxx) (footnote required)		xxx
Net income		$ xxx

Note that discontinued operations and extraordinary items receive disclosure after income from continuing operations. Presumably, these items are transitory. Other items receiving disclosure on the lower part of the income statement are certain changes in accounting principle. We discuss these changes in *measurement* in the following section.

Changes in Measurement

9 Identify and account for accounting changes.

In addition to real structural changes in operations, accountants occasionally change measurement methods. These changes are cosmetic (i.e., they have no direct cash flow implications), and should be justified by portraying a clearer picture of the success of company operations.

Three Alternative Treatments

We begin by considering possible treatments for a change in accounting measurement. We will first focus on alternatives (both GAAP and non-GAAP) that were considered by accounting standard setters, and then conclude by presenting GAAP in the area.

Consider an asset with a 10-year useful life, purchased for $80,000 on January 1, 2001. The asset had no expected salvage value. Ignoring taxes, the asset would be accounted for as follows:

Balance Sheet	Income Statement	Balance Sheet	Income Statement	Balance Sheet
1/1/01		1/1/02		1/1/03
Asset $80,000		Asset $80,000		Asset $80,000
Acc. depr. 0		Acc. depr. (8,000)		Acc. depr. (16,000)
Book val. $80,000		Book val. $72,000		Book val. $64,000
	Depr. exp. $8,000		Depr. exp. $8,000	

Assume that management changes the total estimated useful life to 8 years on January 1, 2003. The three alternatives for handling this change are prospective treatment, current treatment, and retroactive treatment.

Prospective Treatment Under prospective treatment, an accountant would not restate prior period financial statements for the results of the change. In 2003, depreciation expense would equal the remaining book value divided by the remaining useful life ($64,000 ÷ (8 − 2) = $10,667). The December 31, 2003, balance sheet disclosure would appear as follows:

Asset	$ 80,000
Accumulated depreciation	(26,667)
Book value	$ 53,333

Prospective treatment means that only current and future periods are adjusted for the measurement change.

Current Treatment With current treatment, the cumulative effect of *retroactively* applying the new useful life estimate is calculated:

Prior Years	Depreciation Expense 10-Year Useful Life	Depreciation Expense 8-Year Useful Life	Difference
2001	$ 8,000	$10,000	$2,000
2002	8,000	10,000	2,000
Cumulative	$16,000	$20,000	$4,000

The $4,000 increase that would have occurred in prior periods' depreciation expense if the new method had been in use is reflected as a change in the *current* year's income. However, the prior years' financial statements are *not* restated. Rather, pro forma disclosures are presented about what net income and EPS amounts would have been if the new method had been in use in prior years. These figures represent net income and EPS *as if* a retroactive restatement had occurred. In this example, pro forma net income would be $2,000 less each year.

To illustrate the current approach, assume 2003 net income from continuing operations of $900,000 before the change in accounting principle. The comparative income statements (ignoring income taxes) would be as follows:

Comparative Income Statement

	2003	2002
Income from continuing operations (assumed)	$900,000	$900,000
Cumulative effect of change in accounting principle	4,000	0
Net income	$896,000	$900,000
Pro forma net income (see footnote)	$900,000	$898,000

Retroactive Treatment With retroactive treatment, a cumulative effect of *retroactive* application is computed (as shown before in the current treatment section). However, rather than reporting the total change as a component of net income, the retroactive treatment reports the total change as an adjustment to the beginning balance of *retained earnings*. Each prior period financial statement presented is *restated* (depreciation expense, accumulated depreciation, and retained earnings), and accordingly, no pro forma presentations are necessary. To illustrate, assume that the company had beginning retained earnings of $5,000,000 before the change in depreciation methods. If comparative financial statements are not presented, the following presentation results (ignoring income taxes):

Retained Earnings Statement for 2003
(In thousands)

Retained earnings, 1/1/03 (as previously reported)	$5,000,000	
Cumulative effect of retroactive application of new accounting principle (net of tax)	4,000	
Retained earnings, 1/1/03 (restated)	$4,996,000	
Add net income	xx	
Deduct dividends	(xx)	
Retained earnings, 12/31/03		$ xxx

If comparative financial statements are presented, the first part of the comparative retained earnings statement would appear as shown below.

	2003	**2002**
Retained earnings, 1/1 (as previously reported)	$5,000,000	$ xxx
Cumulative effect of retroactive application	4,000	2,000
Retained earnings, 1/1 (restated)	$4,996,000	$ xxx

Prescribed Treatment Under Generally Accepted Accounting Principles

After considering the alternative approaches for reflecting measurement changes in the financial statements, standard setters have arrived at the following prescribed treatments under GAAP:

Type of Accounting Change	**Treatment**
Change in estimate	Prospective
Change in principle	
General rule	Current
Exceptions *From* LIFO Construction accounting (percentage of completion/completed contract) Extractive industries (full costing/successful efforts) First time issuance of financial statement required by FASB statement If specified by the FASB	Retroactive
Special Exception *To* LIFO (cumulative effect not determinable; beginning inventory becomes first layers for future LIFO calculations; footnote LIFO vs. other method income difference in first year)	Prospective
Change in reporting entity	Retroactive

Accounting uses estimates about the future in applying GAAP. For example, in computing depreciation expense, the estimated useful life and the estimated salvage value are used. When a company changes an estimate that leads to a material effect on the financial statements, it is accounted for as a change in estimate. A ***change in estimate*** includes our example of a **change in estimated useful life, as well as changes in items such as expected uncollectible accounts percentages.** A ***change in principle*** involves a **change in the method instead of a change in the estimate used in the method** (e.g., changing from straight-line to an accelerated method for depreciation of equipment). A ***change in reporting entity*** occurs when **a company significantly changes its structure by acquiring other companies.** An example is when investments in equity cross the 20% and 50% thresholds, as we illustrated in Chapter 8.

It is important to remember that *changes in measurement do not create changes in cash flow.* Thus, the "bottom of the income statement" treatment for changes in accounting principle is appropriate. Such changes are cosmetic and transitory.

Earnings Per Share (EPS)

10 Learn how to compute Earnings Per Share (EPS) and how EPS is presented on the financial statements.

Net income (also labeled earnings or net earnings) is a measure of management performance. The income statement separates transactions that affect net income into various categories (e.g., revenues; selling, general, and administrative expenses; other income and expense; extraordinary items). However, ***earnings per share (EPS)*** rather than net income is the most often quoted statistic about a business enterprise. In fact, a large amount of time and energy is spent by the financial analyst community in understanding current EPS and forecasting future periods' EPS.

EPS is a determinant of firm value. Conceptually, firm value is equal to the present value of all future cash flow streams to owners (dividends and ultimate sales price). Since the ability to pay dividends is related to the ability to produce earnings, financial markets pay strict attention to current earnings and EPS as well as prospective earnings and EPS.

EPS Computation Overview

In 1997, the FASB and the IASB (International Accounting Standards Board) cooperated and issued opinions on how to compute EPS. In issuing *SFAS No. 128*, the FASB changed and simplified its prior EPS presentation to conform to international standards. Reporting EPS is required for companies whose common stock or ***potential common stock*** (e.g., **securities such as options, warrants, and convertible securities that allow the holder to acquire common stock**) trades publicly. Computing EPS depends upon whether a company has a *simple* or *complex capital structure.* A ***simple capital structure*** is one where **the company has no potential common stock securities outstanding,** while a ***complex capital structure*** is one where **the company has issued potential common stock.** Potential common stock securities outstanding can change the number of common shares outstanding, and the ownership percentage of any particular shareholder if the potential common stock securities are exchanged for common stock.

For a simple capital structure, one EPS computation is presented—EPS. For a complex capital structure, two EPS computations are presented—Basic EPS and Diluted EPS.

Simple Capital Structure

A simple capital structure has no potential common stock securities (e.g., stock options or convertible debt); therefore, it may consist of common and preferred stock, as well as various types of debt. For a simple capital structure, only EPS is computed. The computation of EPS is straightforward, and it begins by dividing net income by the ***weighted-average number of common shares outstanding*** during the period. For example, assume that Anderson Company reported 2001 net income of $6,500,000. Also, Anderson had 1,000,000 shares of $10 par common stock outstanding at December 31, 2001. Anderson issued 50,000 common shares at $20 per share on April 1, 2001, and another 50,000 shares on September 1, 2001, at $21 per share. EPS for 2001 is computed as follows:

Reconciliation of 2001 common stock activity:	
1/1/01 shares outstanding (calculated)	900,000
4/1/01 share issue	50,000
9/1/01 share issue	50,000
12/31/01 shares outstanding (given)	1,000,000
Weighted-average number of common shares outstanding:	
900,000 shares × 3/12 (1/1/01–3/31/01)	225,000
950,000 shares × 5/12 (4/1/01–8/31/01)	395,833
1,000,000 shares × 4/12 (9/1/01–12/31/01)	333,333
2001 weighted-average	954,166

$$\text{EPS} = \frac{\$6{,}500{,}000}{954{,}166} = \$6.81223 \approx \$6.81$$

Effect of Nonconvertible Preferred Stock EPS computation becomes slightly more complicated if the simple capital structure contains nonconvertible preferred stock. EPS is a slight misnomer; as computed, EPS is really the "earnings available to a weighted-average common share after meeting preferred dividend requirements." Continuing with the Anderson example, assume that during 2001, Anderson also had 100,000 shares of 10%, $50 par preferred stock outstanding. Therefore, the annual dividend preference per share is $5 ($50 par × 10% preference), and the total dividend preference is $500,000 ($5 per share × 100,000 shares). Preferred dividends are not deducted when computing net income because they are considered to be a return of capital rather than an expense. However, preferred dividends must be paid. In order to compute earnings per share available to an average common share, net income in the EPS numerator is adjusted for the $500,000 preferred stock dividend to compute *net income available to common stockholders.* The revised EPS computation is as follows:

$$\text{EPS} = \frac{\$6{,}500{,}000 - \$500{,}000^{*}}{954{,}166^{**}} = \$6.28821 \approx \$6.29$$

*Nonconvertible preferred dividend preference.
**See the previous computation.

By adding the nonconvertible preferred stock to the capital structure, EPS available to common stockholders is reduced by $0.52 ($6.81 − $6.29, also computed as $500,000 ÷ 954,166).

What if a company has cumulative preferred stock and (1) declares but does not pay the current year dividend, or (2) does not declare the current year dividend? Preferred stock is normally cumulative, which means that **if a company fails to declare a dividend in the current period, the dividend attributable to the period becomes a *dividend in arrears.*** In subsequent periods, dividends in arrears must be declared before declaring a current period dividend. The EPS computation associates dividends on cumulative preferred stock with the period incurred, rather than the period declared. *Therefore, dividends on cumulative preferred stock are subtracted in the EPS numerator in the current year, regardless of whether the dividend was declared or paid.*

Financial Statement Presentation In the 2001 income statement, EPS is presented just below net income.

Net income	$6,500,000
Earnings per share	$6.29

To summarize, *for a simple capital structure, EPS is a computation of net income adjusted for preferred dividends preferences available to an average common share during a particular period.*

Complex Capital Structure— Computation of Basic and Diluted EPS

A complex capital structure is one that has potential common stock securities outstanding. When potential common stock is outstanding, two EPS computations are made. The first, ***basic EPS,*** is the same as computed for a simple capital structure, i.e., **(Net income − Preferred stock dividends) ÷ Weighted-average number of common shares outstanding.** The second computation, ***diluted EPS,*** is computed on a pro forma basis as **what EPS would have been if all potential common stock secu-**

rities had been converted during the period. In a sense, this computation is a worst case scenario for current shareholders—it indicates what EPS could become if all potential common stock securities were converted.

In the diluted EPS computation, potential common stock securities are assumed to have been converted into common stock during the period only if the conversion would **decrease** EPS (i.e., if the conversion would ***dilute*** EPS). **Any assumed conversion that would increase EPS** is deemed to be ***antidilutive.*** Accountants are conservative when computing diluted EPS. Its purpose is simply to show readers how far EPS could fall if potential common stock securities were converted into common stock. Therefore, in computing diluted EPS, we assume the conversion of potential common stock securities when the effect is dilutive, but we do not assume conversion for securities with an antidilutive effect.

To continue our example, assume that Anderson Co. had the additional potential common stock securities.

1. Stock options—Stock options for 50,000 shares of common stock were issued on December 31, 1999. Each option plus $20 is exchangeable for one share of common stock. The options are exercisable between January 1, 2004, and January 1, 2008. The average price of Anderson's common stock during 2001 was $21, and the year-end price was $23.[17]
2. Convertible preferred stock—Anderson issued 25,000 shares of 8%, $100 par convertible preferred stock on January 1, 1999, for $110 per share. Each share of convertible preferred is convertible into three shares of common stock at the option of the holder.
3. Convertible debt—On July 1, 2001, Anderson issued $3,500,000 in 10%, 10-year convertible bonds for $3,360,000. The bonds pay interest annually on July 1, and are due on July 1, 2011. Each $1,000 bond is exchangeable for 33 shares of common stock. Anderson uses the straight-line method of amortizing bond discount.[18]

Assume that Anderson's 2001 effective income tax rate is 40%.

The following solution computes Anderson's 2001 diluted EPS through a series of steps. First, we compute the per share effect on EPS of the assumed conversion of each potential common stock security. Second, we rank the per share effects from the smallest amount to the largest amount. Third, in a series of iterations, we compute an interim diluted EPS amount by using the assumed conversion of each potential common stock security. The purpose of these iterations is to drive down diluted EPS as low as possible.

Steps in Computing Diluted EPS

STEP 1 Compute Basic EPS (i.e., what would EPS be if the capital structure were simple).

Note the addition of convertible preferred stock (a potential common stock security) in this section. For the purposes of computing basic EPS, convertible preferred stock is treated as if it were not convertible.

$$\text{Basic EPS} = \frac{\$6{,}500{,}000 - \$500{,}000^{*} - \$200{,}000^{**}}{954{,}166^{***}} = \$6.07861 \approx \$6.08$$

*Nonconvertible preferred dividend preference.

**Convertible preferred dividend preference: $100 par × 8% preference = $8 per share dividend preference; $8 per share × 25,000 shares = $200,000.

***Computed previously under the simple capital structure example.

17. Although employee stock compensation plans are discussed more completely later in Chapter 12, their effect on EPS is illustrated in this example problem.

18. Recall that the effective interest method should be used for computing bond premium or discount amortization. The straight-line method can be used only if the results do not materially differ. We use the straight line method in this example to simplify the computations involved.

STEP 2 Compute per share effects of assumed conversions of potential common stock securities.

Options. If the options had been converted, Anderson would have received cash and issued common stock. In computing the assumed conversion of options, we take into account the assumed proceeds from the assumed conversion by applying the treasury stock method. The ***treasury stock method*** **assumes that the cash received in exchange for the options is used to repurchase treasury stock at the average market price during the period.** We illustrate the application of the treasury stock method to determined the effect on the EPS denominator (shares) below.

Shares that would be issued if options had been converted	50,000
Exercise price	× $20
Assumed proceeds	$1,000,000
Average market price during period	÷ $21
Shares assumed repurchased	47,619
Net shares assumed issued (50,000 − 47,619)	2,381

This assumed option exercise would have no effect on the EPS numerator (Net income − Preferred stock dividends). The numerator and denominator effects are used to determine how EPS is affected by the assumed conversion. The per share effect of the assumed conversion of the options in the diluted EPS computation is $0 ÷ 2,381 = $0 per share.

The *assumed conversion of options is dilutive only if the options are in the money* (as determined by using the average market price during the period). An option is ***in the money*** if **the option price is less than the current market price.** In this case, the holder of the option can purchase the stock cheaper than going into the open market. If the option is ***out of the money*** during the period (i.e., the **option price is greater than the average market price**), then the assumed conversion would be antidilutive. This determination of whether an option is in or out of the money is made each period, independent of any assessment made in other periods. For example, an option might be out of the money in 2002, but in the money in 2003. Therefore, in the 2002 financial statements, the options would not be assumed to be converted in the diluted EPS computation because the conversion would be antidilutive. In the 2003 financial statements, diluted EPS would reflect the assumed conversion of the options, and the comparative 2002 diluted EPS would not be restated to reflect the options' in the money status in 2003.

Stock options may be subject to minimum vesting periods. An option is vested when the individual has a right to the option regardless of whether the individual continues to work for the company. If the options are in the money, they are assumed converted even if the options have not yet vested. In our example problem, assume that the 50,000 options do not vest until December 31, 2003. As we illustrated, although the options have not yet vested, they are included in diluted EPS because they are in the money.

Convertible Preferred Stock. If the convertible preferred stock were converted, $200,000 in dividends would not have been paid. Additionally, 75,000 shares of common (25,000 shares of convertible preferred × 3 shares of common for each convertible preferred share) would have been issued. Since no cash would be exchanged upon conversion, the ***if converted method*** is used to compute the effect of converting the preferred stock. This method does not require the assumed purchase of treasury stock because no cash would be received by the company. Therefore, the per share EPS effect of the assumed conversion of the convertible preferred stock would be $200,000 ÷ 75,000 shares = $2.67 (rounded).

Convertible Debt. The following computations show the effects of the assumed conversion of the convertible debt.

Diluted EPS denominator effect:	
Number of bonds ($3,500,000 ÷ $1,000)	3,500
Conversion rate (33 shares of stock per bond)	× 33
Number of shares assumed issued	115,500
Diluted EPS numerator effect:	
Face value of bonds	$3,500,000
Stated interest rate	× 10%
Interest paid	$ 350,000
Plus discount amortization of $14,000 using the straight-line method ($3,500,000 − $3,360,000) ÷ 10 = $14,000	14,000
Yearly interest expense	$ 364,000
Effect of income taxes on interest expense (1 − tax rate of 0.4)	× 0.60
Annual interest expense, net of tax	$ 218,400

The numerator and denominator effects must be adjusted for the fact that the bonds were only outstanding for half the year. The denominator effect is that 115,500 shares would be issued. But since the shares were only outstanding for six months (July 1, 2001–December 31, 2001), on a weighted-average basis the 2001 denominator effect is 115,500 ÷ 2 = 57,750 shares. Similarly, 2001 interest expense is $218,400 ÷ 2 = $109,200. Note that interest expense is multiplied by one minus the tax rate to compute the numerator effect (we discuss income taxes in Chapter 11). Since interest expense is tax deductible, the company realizes a tax saving for each dollar of deductible expenses. In this case, by deducting $182,000 in interest expense ($364,000 × $\frac{1}{2}$year), the company achieves a tax savings of $72,800 ($182,000 × 40%). (Note that interest expense of $182,000 minus the tax savings of $72,800 equals $109,200, which we computed above.) Thus, the 2001 per share effect of the assumed conversion of convertible debt is $109,200 ÷ 57,750 shares = $1.89 per share (rounded).

STEP 3 Iterate through computation of diluted EPS and test for antidilution.

First Iteration. Compare the per share effect of the potential common stock security with the smallest per share effect to basic EPS. If the per share effect is smaller than basic EPS, then the assumed conversion will be dilutive (i.e., drive the EPS amount down). From the previous computations, the per share effects of the assumed conversion of potential common stock securities are options, $0; convertible debt, $1.89; and convertible preferred, $2.67. We begin with the security with the smallest per share effect. The per share effect of options is $0 (0 ÷ 2,381 = 0), which is less than $6.08 (basic EPS). Therefore, including options will be dilutive. The resulting new EPS amount should be less than $6.08 and greater than $0.[19] Recalculated EPS to reflect the assumed conversion of the options is as follows.

$$\begin{array}{c}\text{Diluted EPS}\\ \text{1st iteration}\end{array} = \frac{\$6{,}500{,}000 - \$500{,}000^{*} - \$200{,}000^{**} + \$0^{***}}{954{,}166 + 2{,}381^{***}} = \$6.06348 \approx \$6.06$$

*Nonconvertible preferred dividend preference.
**Convertible preferred dividend preference.
***Effect of the assumed conversion of stock options.

The conversion of the stock options would reduce EPS about two cents per share (from $6.08 to $6.06). Note that this EPS reduction aligns with the fact that the resulting diluted EPS computation should be lower than the previous basic EPS computation.

19. Mathematically, we are combining two ratios that have the same base (i.e., per common share). When combining two such ratios, the resulting ratio will fall somewhere between the two original ratios the upper and lower bounds for the combined ratio are the two individual ratios.

Second Iteration. Compare the next smallest per share effect of the assumed conversion of the remaining potential common stock securities with the diluted EPS computed in the first iteration. The per share effect of the assumed conversion of the convertible debt is $109,200 ÷ 57,750 = $1.89, which is less than $6.06. Therefore, including the convertible debt in the diluted EPS computations will dilute EPS. The resulting EPS computation should be less than $6.06, but greater than $1.89. Diluted EPS, including the assumed conversion of the convertible debt, is recalculated as follows.

$$\frac{\text{Diluted EPS}}{\text{2nd iteration}} = \frac{\$6{,}500{,}000 - \$500{,}000 - \$200{,}000 + \$0^{*} + \$109{,}200^{**}}{954{,}166 + 2{,}381^{*} + 57{,}750^{**}} = \$5.82591 \approx \$5.83$$

*Effect of the assumed conversion of stock options.
**Effect of the assumed conversion of convertible debt.

The second iteration reduces diluted EPS by about 23 cents per share (from $6.06 to $5.83).

Third Iteration. Compare the per share effect of the assumed conversion of the remaining potential common stock securities with the diluted EPS computed in the second iteration. The per share effect of the assumed conversion of the convertible preferred stock is $200,000 ÷ 75,000 = $2.67, which is less than $5.83. Therefore, including the convertible preferred will dilute EPS, and the resulting computation should be less than $5.83 and greater than $2.67. Recalculated EPS, including the assumed conversion of the convertible preferred, is as follows.

$$\frac{\text{Diluted EPS}}{\text{3rd iteration}} = \frac{\$6{,}500{,}000 - \$500{,}000 - \$200{,}000 + \$0 + \$109{,}200 + \$200{,}000^{*}}{954{,}166 + 2{,}381 + 57{,}750 + 75{,}000^{*}} = \$5.60839 \approx \$5.61$$

*Effect of the assumed conversion of convertible debt.

Therefore, diluted EPS is $5.61. The conversion of the last security decreases EPS by about $0.22 per share (from $5.83 to $5.61). The combined effect of the assumed conversion of all three securities reduces EPS by about $0.47 per share (from $6.08 to $5.61).

EPS Financial Statement Presentation In the 2001 income statement, both the basic and diluted EPS amounts are presented after net income.

Net income	$6,500,000
Basic earnings per share	$6.08
Diluted earnings per share	$5.61

Additionally, a reconciliation from basic EPS to diluted EPS must be made in a separate footnote disclosure for the numerator, denominator, and per share effects. For Anderson, the following example reflects this disclosure and reconciles the numerators and denominators of basic and diluted EPS.

	Numerator	Denominator (shares)	Per-Share Effects
Basic EPS (Income available to common stockholders)	$5,800,000	954,166	$6.08
Effect of potential common stock securities:			
Stock warrants	0	2,381	(0)
Convertible debt	109,200	57,750	(1.89)
Convertible preferred stock	200,000	75,000	(2.67)
Diluted EPS (Income available to common stockholders adjusted for assumed conversions)	$6,109,200	1,089,297	$5.61

EPS Financial Statement Presentation—Discontinued Operations, Extraordinary Items, and Cumulative Effects of Accounting Changes

The previous examples illustrated EPS presentation for a rather uncomplicated problem. The EPS presentation is expanded if a company has discontinued operations, extraordinary items, or cumulative effects of accounting changes. If any of these items is presented, EPS is calculated for the amounts before and after the item, as well as for the item itself. As an example, assume the following information from the 2001 income statement for Wang Co.

Income before income taxes	$20,000,000
Income tax expense	8,000,000
Income from continuing operations	$12,000,000
Discontinued operations, net of tax	(4,000,000)
Extraordinary item, net of tax	9,000,000
Cumulative effect of accounting change, net of tax	(2,800,000)
Net income	$14,200,000

Assume that Wang has a simple capital structure with a weighted-average of 10,000,000 common shares outstanding and no preferred stock. Wang's 2001 basic EPS would be presented as follows:

Net income	$14,200,000
Basic earning per share	
Income from continuing operations	$1.20
Discontinued operations, net of tax	(0.40)
Extraordinary item, net of tax	0.90
Cumulative effect of accounting change, net of tax	(0.28)
Net income	$1.42

If Wang had a complex capital structure, then the same type of presentation would be made for diluted EPS.

Effect of Stock Dividends and Splits on EPS

If a company changes its capital structure by issuing a stock dividend or stock split (see Chapter 2), an adjustment must be made to the EPS computations to ensure that the EPS amounts are comparable over time. For example, assume that Bulski Co. had (1) net income of $10,000,000 in 2001 and 2002; (2) no preferred stock or potential common stock securities; and (3) 1,000,000 shares of common stock outstanding from January 1, 2001, to December 31, 2002. In this example, basic EPS for 2001 and 2002 is $10.00 ($10,000,000 ÷ 1,000,000 shares).

Now, assume the same facts except that on January 1, 2002, Bulski issued a 2:1 stock split. If EPS is not adjusted, then 2001 basic EPS is $10.00, and 2002 EPS is $5.00 ($10,000,000 ÷ 2,000,000 shares). If we compare the 2002 basic EPS of $5.00 to the 2001 basic EPS of $10.00, it appears that management performed dismally during the year. However, since net income is the same amount each period, the EPS presentation distorts management's performance. When faced with the situation of stock splits and stock dividends, the FASB requires that EPS for all periods presented reflect the stock split. To do this, we restate on a pro forma basis the basic EPS for 2001 from $10.00 to $5.00 (to retroactively adjust for the 2:1 stock split). Therefore, basic EPS for both 2001 and 2002 would be reported as $5.00. Further, the adjustment is made if the stock split or dividend happens any time during the year. For this example, if the 2:1 stock split had occurred on December 31, 2002, then the EPS for 2002 would be computed as if the stock split had occurred on January 1, 2002. This process continually adjusts EPS to make it comparable for changes in capital structure solely related to stock splits and dividends.

Factors Complicating EPS Computation

We discuss items that complicate EPS computation, including contingently issuable shares and other adjustments in the diluted EPS computation numerator.

Contingently Issuable Shares A company may have agreements that require the issuance of shares once certain conditions are met. These contingently issuable shares should be used in the computations of basic EPS and diluted EPS before the shares are actually issued, but once the conditions have been met (after the shares have been issued), they will be included in the weighted-average number of shares outstanding during the period. For example, a company may enter into an agreement with an employee to award stock if certain performance measures are met (e.g., earnings increase by 10% per year over the next three years). These shares shall be assumed to be issued for basic EPS computations if all performance conditions have been met by year-end, and the shares are issuable but have not yet been issued. When computing diluted EPS, if the end of the performance period has not yet arrived, we treat the end of the current period as if it were the end of the performance period. If the performance standards were met by the end of the current year, then the contingently issued shares would be assumed to have been issued in the diluted EPS computation.

Other Adjustments in the Diluted EPS Computation—Numerator In the Diluted EPS computations, the denominator is adjusted for the number of shares that would have been converted if the dilutive security had been converted. If the assumed conversion would also affect net income, then the numerator should also be appropriately adjusted. Consider the following example for Sohn Company.

Example 11. Sohn Co. had 10,000,000 shares of common stock outstanding all year, and also had convertible debt outstanding, which was convertible into 1,000,000 shares of common stock with an annual interest expense of $1,000,000. Sohn had no other potential common stock securities, and an effective tax rate of 40%. Sohn's income before taxes equaled $50,000,000, and net income equaled $30,000,000. Sohn had a bonus agreement in place that awarded employees bonuses equal to 8% of income before taxes.

Solution. In computing Sohn's diluted EPS, the denominator increases by 1,000,000 shares. In the numerator, $600,000 in interest expense, net of tax [$1,000,000 × (1 − 40%)], is added to net income because the interest expense would not have been incurred. However, we must also adjust the numerator for the effect of the reduced interest expense on employee bonuses, which would have increased by $80,000 ($1,000,000 decreased interest expense × 8%). On an after-tax basis, the additional bonus expense decreases net income by $48,000 [$80,000 × (1− 40%)]. Diluted EPS is computed as follows:

$$\text{Diluted EPS} = \frac{\$30{,}000{,}000 + \$600{,}000 - \$48{,}000}{10{,}000{,}000 + 1{,}000{,}000} = \$2.77745 \approx \$2.78$$

Purchased Put or Call Options on the Company's Own Stock If a company has purchased put or call options on its own stock, these options are not considered in the computation of diluted EPS.

A Loss from Continuing Operations If a company reports a loss from continuing operations (even if the presence of discontinued operations, extraordinary items, and/or cumulative effects of accounting changes result in net income being reported), then no potential common stock securities are assumed converted in the dilutive EPS computations.

Southwest Airlines' Financial Statements

The 1998 financial statements for Southwest Airlines appear in Appendix C. As a service provider, the financial statement issues related to this chapter are relatively straightforward. Review the income statement, balance sheet, and statement of cash flows, as well as Note 1 (Summary of Significant Accounting Policies—Revenue Recognition, Frequent Flyer Program, and Advertising sections), and MD&A Results of Operations—Other Expenses.

Note 1, Summary of Significant Accounting Policies—Revenue Recognition, indicates that passenger revenue is recognized when transportation is provided. Revenues for tickets not yet used are reflected on the balance sheet as "Air traffic liability." The balance sheet indicates this amount is \$200,078,000 in 1998, and \$153,341,000 in 1997, which is approximately 20% of current liabilities each year. Note 1 also reports that Southwest accrues an estimated liability for the cost of providing free travel under its frequent flyer program. This liability is not sufficiently large to disclose separately either in the balance sheet or in Note 3, Accrued Liabilities. Note 1, Summary of Significant Accounting Policies—Advertising, indicates that advertising is expensed as incurred. Advertising expenses in 1998, 1997, and 1996 were \$119,739,000, \$112,961,000, and \$109,136,000 respectively, which totaled about 3.0% of total operating revenues during the three-year period (see income statements).

Southwest's income statement reflects interest expense of \$56,275,000 in 1998, and \$63,454,000 in 1997. Also, deductions for capitalized interest of \$25,588,000 and \$19,779,000 are made in 1998 and 1997, respectively. The statement of cash flows shows 1998 and 1997 interest payments, net of amounts capitalized, or \$33,384,000 and \$42,372,000, respectively. Southwest's financial statements do not make it clear as to why some interest is being capitalized. The MD&A—Other Expenses section reports that capitalized interest is related to progress payments, although the nature of the progress payments is not identified.

Chapter Summary

This chapter deals with revenue and expense recognition, and primarily assumes a cash sales and purchase orientation. Revenue and expense recognition present great challenges to accountants. Professional judgement and industry experience guides the determination of the critical event for revenue recognition, as well as the judgement of whether costs have future economic benefits for the purpose of expense recognition or deferral. *Revenue should be recognized when it is (1) realized or realizable and (2) earned.* The general rule of revenue recognition is to recognize revenue when products are delivered or services are performed. However, recognition may be accelerated or delayed depending upon the extent to which a firm has expended resources to earn revenue. Exceptions to the general revenue recognition rule generally are industry specific.

All expenses necessary to generate revenue should be matched against the revenue. When costs are incurred, they are either expensed or capitalized. Capitalized costs are allocated to the current and future periods. Costs are classified as either *product costs,* those directly traceable to the sale of a particular product or service, or *period costs,* those not directly traceable to a particular sale but, rather, to all sales of the period.

Because profit is recognized before completion and delivery, the percentage of completion method of revenue recognition for long-term construction projects is an exception to the general rule of revenue recognition. The percentage of completion method is justified by the long-term (greater than 12 months) nature of the projects. The percentage of completion method records estimated gross profit (and the related revenue and expense amounts) each period as construction occurs.

Key Terms

antidilutive 407
basic EPS 406
billings on construction in progress 393
change in estimate 404
change in principle 404
change in reporting entity 404
completed contract 391
complex capital structure 405
construction in progress 393
cost-to-cost method 391
diluted EPS 406
dilutive 407
discontinued operations 399
dividend in arrears 406
earned 382
earnings per share (EPS) 405
if converted method 408
in the money 408
measurement date 399
out of the money 408
percentage of completion 391
period costs 390
potential common stock 405
product costs 390
realizable 381
realization 381
realized 381
restructurings 399
simple capital structure 405
treasury stock method 408
weight-average number of common shares outstanding 405

Questions

Q1. **Revenue Recognition Criteria.** What two criteria determine the timing of revenue recognition?

Q2. **Revenue Realization.** With respect to revenue recognition, what is meant by the term "realized"? How does "realizable" differ in meaning?

Q3. **Revenue Recognition.** How do firms *earn* revenue?

Q4. **Revenue Recognition.** What is the general rule for the *timing* of revenue recognition?

Q5. **Sales Returns.** Normally, a sale subject to a sales return is recognized. What factors would cause sales subject to sales returns not to be recorded until the right of return expires?

Q6. **Revenue Recognition—When Right of Return Exists.** How does a customer's right to return merchandise affect the timing of revenue recognition?

Q7. **Determining Year of Sale.** For each of the following situations, indicate if the sale should be recorded in 2001 or 2002.

a. Faisala Co. shipped inventory to Fax Co. on December 27, 2001, F.O.B. shipping point. The goods arrived at the Fax Co. loading dock on January 2, 2002.

b. Chaney Co. shipped inventory to Greer Co. on December 28, 2001, F.O.B. destination. The goods arrived at the Greer Co. loading dock on January 3, 2002.

c. Melvin Co. shipped inventory from California to Zap Co. in Florida on December 28, 2001, F.O.B. Dallas, Texas. The goods arrived in Dallas on December 30, 2002, and were delivered to Zap on January 5, 2002.

Q8. **Interest Costs.** What is the general rule for the treatment of interest cost? How is interest treated for long-term construction contracts?

Q9. **Expense Recognition.** In practice, what are three ways to justify expense recognition? Give two examples of each.

Q10. **Product versus Period Costs.** What is the difference between a *product cost* and a *period cost*?

Q11. **Depreciation Expense Recognition—Manufacturing Firm.** For a manufacturing firm, contrast the manner in which the depreciation of office equipment in the corporate headquarters and the depreciation of manufacturing equipment in a manufacturing facility are reflected as expenses in the income statment.

Q12. **Revenue Recognition Prior to Delivery.** Provide an example of when GAAP allows revenue recognition at the end of production but before delivery.

Q13. **Construction Contract Accounting.** How are expected contract losses accounted for under the completed contract method? Under the percentage of completion method?

Q14. **Construction Contract Accounting.** Under what conditions is the percentage of completion method required? Why are those conditions important for the calculation of periodic profit recognition under the percentage of completion method?

Q15. **Construction Contract Accounting.** Explain why the recognition of revenues and profit for construction accounting is a continual change in estimate.

Q16. **Revenue Subsequent to Sale and Delivery.** Why might revenue recognition be delayed past the date of sale and delivery?

Q17. **Restructurings and Discontinued Operations.** Compare and contrast the accounting for restructuring charges and discontinued operations.

Q18. **Extraordinary Items.** What two criteria must be met for an item to be reported as an extraordinary item? What is the most frequent event reported as an extraordinary item? Where and how is an extraordinary item reported on the income statement?

Q19. **Accounting Changes.** What are the three possible treatment options for accounting changes?

Q20. **EPS.** What conditions cause a company's capital structure to be classified as simple? As complex?

Q21. **EPS.** How many EPS amounts are presented if the company has a simple capital structure? A complex capital structure? What are the labels attached to the EPS amounts?

Short Problems

1. **Revenue and Expense Recognition.** For each problem below, indicate the amount of revenue that should be recognized in the company's 2001 income statement. Also, if expenses are mentioned in the problem, indicate the amount of any expenses that should be recognized in 2001.

   Journal Entry Option: Make the December 2001 journal entries to record the revenues and expenses.

   a. Lopez Co. sells computers systems. The selling prices range from $2,500–$4,000. Lopez offers a one-year warranty, and warranty expense is estimated at $150 per unit (regardless of selling price). Cost of goods sold is 75% of the selling price. Also, Lopez allows a free 60-day return privilege for a full refund. Lopez's past experience is that 1% of the systems sold will be returned. In December 2001, Lopez sold 300 systems, at an average price of $3,000.
   b. The Manning Athletic Club sells annual memberships to its health club. Members prepay for an entire year. At December 1, 2001, 100 memberships were sold at an average price of $900.
   c. The law firm of Dewey, Cheetham, and Howe performed legal services for the Tappet brothers in December 2001, and billed them for $20,000 according to an agreement that specified that the law firm would bill for services when completed. The amount was collected in February 2002.
   d. The Splendid Advertising Agency put togther an ad campaign for Sparrow Company. The ad campaign ran in December 2001, and according to the contract, Splendid billed Sparrow for $240,000. Splendid's marketing research group believes that the ad campaign will raise the public's awareness of Sparrow's products and increase sales through June 2002.

2. **Product versus Period Costs.** Indicate whether the following items are period costs or product costs.

	Period Costs	**Product Costs**
a. Inventory purchase price		
b. Transportation-in on purchases		
c. Cost of office supplies for home office		
d. Freight charges on office supplies for home office		
c. Law firm wages paid to lawyers		
e. Labor to machine operator for inventory produced		
f. Bonus paid to company president		
g. Interest expense, not on construction in progress		
h. Advertising expenses		
f. Office equipment lease expense for home office		
g. Commissions paid on sales		
h. Depreciation expense—home office equipment		
i. Depreciation expense—factory equipment		

3. **Interest Costs.** During the period 2000–2002, Greer Construction built a section of an interstate highway for a guaranteed price of $65,000,000. During the project, the company spent $50,000,000 in construction expenses. Additionally, Greer borrowed substantial funds to finance the construction, incurring $3,500,000 in interest cost directly related to the construction over the three-year period. What gross profit should Greer report on the project?

4. **Revenue Recognition.** On January 1, 2000, Lawn Management Co. agrees to provide three years of lawn maintenance service to BigStore in exchange for a $10,000, three-year, non-interest-bearing note due January 1, 2003 (assume that the appropriate market rate of interest is a 10% effective interest rate). This is an unusual entry because Lawn Management is agreeing to provide services over three years and defer any payment for three years. If Lawn Management Co. incurs $2,000 in costs each year, compute the balance in the following accounts for the periods or dates indicated:
   a. Interest Revenue for 2000, 2001, and 2002.
   b. Lawn Services Revenue for 2000, 2001, and 2002.

(continued)

c. Net Income (ignore income taxes) for 2000, 2001, and 2002.
d. Notes Receivable at December 31, 2000, 2001, and 2002.
e. Liabilities (if any) at December 31, 2000, 2001, and 2002.

Journal Entry Option: Prepare the January 1, 2000, journal entry to record the note, the annual journal entries to record Interest Revenue and Lawn Service Revenue, and the January 1, 2003, journal entry to record the receipt of the $10,000.

5. **Structural Changes in Operations.** In the table below, indicate whether each change should be reported as restructuring, discontinued operations, an extraordinary item, or a gain/loss.

Item	Classification*
a. A company takes a $150 million charge related to employee layoffs.	
b. A company sells its entire clothing business.	
c. A company sells its women's dresses factory but retains its women's sportswear business.	
d. A company's plant beside the Mississippi river is destroyed in a flood.	
e. A company's plant in the Nevada dessert is destroyed in a flood, in an area that has never reported a flood.	
f. A company pays off its long-term debt early.	
g. The country of Iran nationalizes an American company's operations.	
h. A company's work force strikes for the first time, resulting in $200 million in losses.	

*Use R = restructuring, DO = discontinued operations, EI = extraordinary item, G/L = gain/loss.

6. **Accounting Changes.** For each of the items below, indicate whether it is accounted for as a change in estimate, principle, or entity. Also, indicate whether the item is accounted for prospectively, currently, or retroactively.

Item	Accounting Treatment
a. A company change from the percent of sales method to the allowance method for computing bad debts expense.	
b. A company switched from FIFO to the weighted-average method of inventory.	
c. A company switches from LIFO to the weighted-average method of inventory.	
d. A company switches from the weighted-average method of inventory to LIFO.	
e. A company buys another company and accounts for the acquisition using the purchase method.	
f. A company has been estimating $1,000 per unit in warranty costs, but because of quality control initiatives, the company now believes that $800 per unit is appropriate.	

7. **Financial Statement Presentation.** Listed below are certain financial statement items and an income statement template. Place the items appropriately in the income statement. Assume that the effective income tax rate is 40%, and that net income from continuing operations (after properly accounting for the items below) is $7,500,000. Fill in the amounts that would be reported as other income, (expenses), gains, and (losses). Finally, complete the partial income statement shown below.

Item	Amount
Restructuring charges	800,000
Gain (loss) on early extinguishment of debt	150,000
Agreed to sell entire manufacturing business, with the deal to close in July of next year:	
Operating income (loss) prior to measurement date	290,000
Operating income (loss) after measurement date, through year-end	75,000
Estimated operating income (loss) next year until disposal date	(330,000)
Estimated gain (loss on disposal)	(250,000)
Gain (loss) on sale of fixed assets	55,000
Current year income (expense) from change in depreciation method from straight-line to declining balance	(300,000)

Partial Income Statement

Other income, (expense), gains, (losses)	
Restructuring charges	
Gain (loss) on sale of fixed assets	
Net income from continuing operations	
Discontinued operations:	
Operating income (expense)	
Estimated gain (loss on disposal)	
Extraordinary item, early extinguishment of debt	
Cumulative effect of accounting change	
Net income	

8. **EPS, Simple Capital Structure.** Show the formula for computing EPS for a simple capital structure.

9. **Diluted EPS.** What is the purpose of computing and reporting diluted EPS?

Analytical and Comprehensive Problems

10. **Revenue and Expense Recognition.** Warehouse Co.'s primary business activity is aging whiskey for a variety of distilleries in a process that takes five aging periods. Under a fixed-price distilleries contract, Warehouse ages the whiskey and receives one-fifth of the contract price each year. Warehouse incurs a great deal of overhead cost each period from the depreciation of buildings and temperature and humidity control units. In addition, small amount of materials and labor are consumed each period. Warehouse estimates that 40%–50% of its costs are incurred in the first aging period; 8%–12% of costs are incurred in each of the next three aging periods; and 20%–30% of costs are incurred in the final aging period.

Required: How should Warehouse Co. recognize revenues and expenses? If Warehouse signs contracts each year that result in several overlapping contracts at one time, would you change your answer? Why?

11. **Revenue Recognition, When Right of Return Exists.** Davis Co. made the following inventory deliveries during 2001. Each item may be returned during a limited period if resale is not achieved. For convenience, assume that payment is due on the day that the right of return expires. Cash collection (or return of the items in saleable condition) is assured for the following deliveries:

Item	Date of Sale	Selling Price	Return Period	Estimated Returns
1	7/1/01	$15,000	90 days	20%
2	8/1/01	$20,000	90 days	no basis for estimation
3	10/1/01	$18,000	120 days	15%
4	12/1/01	$9,000	60 days	no basis for estimation

Required: Compute the net revenues that should be recognized in 2001, and the amount of unearned revenues that should be reported at December 31, 2001.

12. **Revenue Recognition.** For each of the following independent situations, compute net income (ignoring income taxes) for 2001.

Journal Entry Option: For each situation, prepare the summary annual journal entries.

a. On December 28, 2001, Avery Co. sold merchandise costing $6,000 for $9,000, and shipped it F.O.B. destination at a cost of $200 (to be paid upon delivery). Avery pays salespeople a commission of 1% after title legally passes to the buyer. The goods are en route at December 31, 2001.
b. On December 21, 2001, Bass Co. sold merchandise costing $9,000 for $15,000, and shipped it F.O.B. destination at a cost of $400. Bass pays salespeople a commission of 1%. The goods arrived at the customer's place of business on December 30, 2001. Payment is due within 20 days of receipt.

(continued)

c. Golden Body Gym collected $1,200 for a one-year health club membership from Lou Ferry on December 1, 2001. To compute net income, assume that Golden's net income equals 30% of sales.
d. During the months of November and December 2001, Musicmania sold $200,000 in one-year gift certificates redeemable for CDs, cassette tapes, and music videos. Assume that Musicmania has a 10% net income to sales ratio (i.e., net income = 10% of sales). As of December 31, 2001, 75% of the gift certificates had been redeemed.
e. In December of 2001, BlackStar Mines extracted 400 ounces of gold. The mining cost was $100 per ounce. The gold has a known market price (for all quantities) of $360 per ounce for the next three months, with no marketing costs and minor distribution costs.
f. During 2001, Miller Co. delivered printing equipment and collected the contract price of $1,400,000. The printing equipment cost $900,000 to produce, distribute, and market. In addition, Miller has a two-year service warranty on the equipment. Expected costs of servicing the equipment is $175,000 over the two-year period. During 2001, Miller spent $75,000 in materials, labor, and overhead to service the warranties.

Problems 13–15: Using the following formats, prepare the statement of cash flows, income statement, and balance sheet for each of the following independent situations.

Statement of Cash Flows
(Cash outflows in parentheses)

	2000	2001	2002	2003
Operating Activities				
Investing Activities				
Financing Activities				
Net cash inflow (outflow)				

Income Statement Effects

	2000	2001	2002	2003
Net income (ignoring income taxes)				

Balance Sheet Effects
December 31

	2000	2001	2002	2003
Assets				
Liabilities				
Owners' Equity				

13. **Construction Contract Accounting—Profit on Contract.** Tally Builders entered into a four-year, $5,000,000 contract to build an expansion bridge over a portion of Tampa Bay. Tally is allowed to bill $1,250,000 each year. The City of Tampa must pay the entire amount billed in the year of billing. The bridge was completed and accepted by the City in 2003. Cost information on the project is presented below.

	2000	2001	2002	2003
Costs to date*	$1,000,000	$2,400,000	$3,500,000	$4,300,000
Estimated costs to complete	3,000,000	1,600,000	700,000	—

*For convenience, assume that these costs represent cash expenditures.

Required: Prepare the financial statement disclosures under (a) the completed contract method, and (b) the percentage of completion method.

Journal Entry Option: Prepare the annual journal entries over the four-year period to reflect the accounting under each method.

14. **Construction Contract Accounting—Loss on Contract.** (*Note:* This is the same information as in Problem 13, except that the contractor incurs a loss.) Tally Builders entered into a four-year, $5,000,000 contract to build an expansion bridge over a portion of Tampa Bay. Tally is allowed to bill $1,250,000 each year. The City of Tampa must pay the entire amount billed in the year of billing. The bridge was completed and accepted by the City in 2003. Cost information on the project is presented below.

	2000	2001	2002	2003
Costs to date*	$1,000,000	$2,400,000	$4,000,000	$6,000,000
Estimated costs to complete	3,000,000	2,400,000	1,500,000	—

*For convenience, assume that these costs represent cash expenditures.

Required: Prepare the financial statement disclosures under (a) the completed contract method, and (b) the percentage of completion method.

Journal Entry Option: Prepare the annual journal entries over the four-year period to reflect the accounting under each method.

15. **Construction Contract Accounting—Profit on Contract with Interim Estimated Loss.** On January 1, 2000, Kelly Construction entered into a four-year, $1,000,000 contract to build a water irrigation system for Dry County. Kelly bills the annual construction costs to Dry County. Dry County will pay one-half of the amount billed in the year of billing and one-half in the year after billing. Any amounts billed but not collected during the period are reported as Accounts Receivable. The irrigation system was completed and accepted by the Dry County in 2003. Cost information for the project is presented below.

	2000	2001	2002	2003
Costs to date	$300,000	$500,000	$700,000	$950,000
Estimated costs to complete	600,000	600,000	250,000	—

Required: Prepare the financial statement disclosures under (a) the completed contract method, and (b) the percentage of completion method.

Journal Entry Option: Prepare the annual journal entries over the four-year period to reflect the accounting under each method.

16. **Construction Contract Accounting.** On January 1, 2001, Walinski Co. signed a contract with Wang Co. for the construction of an office building. The office building was completed and "delivered" on December 1, 2003. The following information is available for the construction during the period 2001–2003. Use the cost-to-cost method to compute the percentage complete.

	December 31		
	2001	2002	2003
Contract price	$20,000,000	*$21,000,000	*$21,500,000
Actual costs to date	4,000,000	13,000,000	19,750,000
Estimated costs to complete	14,000,000	7,000,000	0
Total estimated costs	18,000,000	20,000,000	19,750,000
Estimated profit	2,000,000	1,000,000	1,750,000
Amounts billed and collected	4,500,000	12,000,000	21,500,000
Percent complete			

*Contract price amended for changes requested by the Walinski Co.

Use the following formats to complete (a) and (b).

a. Assuming that Wang uses the percentage of completion method, show the financial statement effects of the construction project.
b. Assuming that Wang uses the completed contract method, show the financial statement effects of the construction project.

WANG CO.
Statement of Cash Flows
(Cash outflows in parentheses)

	2001	2002	2003
Operating Activities			
Cash payments for construction costs			
Cash collections from customers			
Net cash inflow (outflow)			

WANG CO.
Income Statement Effects

	2001	2002	2003
Construction revenues			
Construction expenses			
Profit (loss) on long-term construction contracts			

WANG CO.
Balance Sheet Effects
December 31

	2001	2002	2003
Assets			
Current assets			
Cash			
Billings on construction in progress			
Less construction in progress			
Construction in progress in excess of billings			
Liabilities			
Current liabilities			
Billings on construction in progress			
Less construction in progress			
Billings in excess of construction in progress			
Owners' Equity			
Retained earnings			

17. **Discontinued Operations.** Manning Co. has traditionally been in two lines of business, manufacturing and consulting services. On June 30, 2001, Manning signed an agreement with James Co. to sell its manufacturing facilities. The sale is to be completed by February 1, 2002. The following information is provided about the manufacturing operations. All amounts are net of income tax effects.

Income (loss) from manufacturing operations, 1/01/01–6/30/01	$2,000,000
Income (loss) from manufacturing operations, 7/01/01–12/31/01	(1,000,000)
Information at 12/31/01	
Estimated income (loss) on manufacturing operations, 1/01/02–2/01/02	(150,000)
Estimated gain (loss) on sale, 2/01/02	(800,000)

a. Compute the amounts that would appear in the 2001 income statement related to discontinued operations.
b. If the estimated gain (loss) on disposal on February 1, 2002, had been an $800,000 gain, compute the amounts that would appear in the 2001 income statement related to discontinued operations.

Journal Entry Option: Prepare any December 31, 2001, adjusting journal entries necessary based on the estimated 2002 results.

18. **Accounting Change—Change in Estimate.** On January 1, 2000, Shefflin Co. purchased property, plant, and equipment at a cost of $4,500,000. The PP&E had an estimated useful life of ten years and a 10% salvage value. Shefflin used the straight-line depreciation method in 2000 and 2001. In late January 2002 (after the 2001 financial statements had been issued), the accounting staff reviewed the equipment and determined that the estimated useful life should be seven years rather than ten, and the estimated salvage value should be zero.
   a. How much depreciation expense should Shefflin report in its 2002 income statement?
   b. If the accounting staff had not made the review until December 2002, how much depreciation expense should Shefflin report in its 2002 income statement?

   Journal Entry Option: Prepare the summary annual adjusting entry to record 2002 depreciation expense.

19. **Accounting Change—Change in Principle.** On January 1, 2000, Cunningham Co. purchased property, plant, and equipment at a cost of $3,000,000. The PP&E had an estimated useful life of eight years, and an estimated salvage value of $200,000. Cunningham used the straight-line method of depreciation in the years 2000–2001. In January 2002 (after the 2001 financial statements were issued), Cunningham decided to change its depreciation method to the 150% declining balance method. (Assume that this change is considered appropriate for GAAP.) Cunningham's effective income tax rate equals 40%.
   a. What amount should Cunningham report in its 2002 income statement for depreciation expense?
   b. What amount (if any) should Cunningham report on its income statement related to the change in depreciation method? Where should the amount be reported?

   Journal Entry Option: Prepare the January 2002 journal entry for the change in depreciation method. (Do not make the separate journal entry related to the income tax effects.)

   c. Would the 2001 financial statements be restated to reflect the change (i.e. restated so that depreciation expense was computed using the 150% declining balance method)?
   d. How would your answers to (a) and (b) change if Cunningham had changed its depreciation method in December 2002?

20. **Statement of Cash Flows.** The cash flows associated with three different companies are shown below. Assume that the current year's cash flow pattern is representative of the cash flow patterns in the three previous years. For each company, use the cash flow patterns to infer general statements and describe the firms' activities.

	Net Cash Flows (In millions)		
Company	**Operating Activities**	**Financing Activities**	**Investing Activities**
A	$1,900	$ 2,300	$(4,000)
B	(50)	(2,250)	1,800
C*	5,000	(500)	(2,000)

*Assume that the company has no debt outstanding.

21. **EPS, Effect of Stock Splits and Dividends.** The following common stock information is available for Lau Co. for 2001 and 2002. Lau had no preferred stock or potential common stock securities outstanding during the two-year period. Net income for 2001 is $28,000,000, and net income for 2002 is $37,000,000.

	Number of Common Shares	
	2001	**2002**
1/01/01, Issued and outstanding	12,000,000	14,000,000
4/01/01: Issuance	2,000,000	
7/01/01: Issuance		5,000,000
12/01/01: Repurchase treasury stock		(1,200,000)
12/31/01	14,000,000	17,800,000

(continued)

a. For the EPS computation, compute the weighted-average number of common shares actually outstanding for 2001 and 2002.
b. Compute EPS for 2001 and 2002.
c. Assume that on December 31, 2002, Lau issued a 5% stock dividend. How would EPS change for 2001 and 2002?

22. **EPS.** Lazy Co. had the following capital structure as of December 31, 2001 (in thousands):

Common stock, $10 par, 6,000,000 shares authorized, 5,000,000 shares issued, and 4,000,000 shares outstanding	$50,000
8% convertible preferred stock (each share convertible into 7 shares of common), $100 par, 100,000 shares authorized, 40,000 shares outstanding	4,000
Stock warrants outstanding (for 50,000 shares)	75
Paid-in capital in excess of par—common	25,000
Retained earnings	36,000
Less treasury stock at cost	(28,000)
Total stockholders' equity	$87,075

Lazy also had $15,000,000 in 10%, 10-year convertible bonds due July 1, 2011. The bonds were issued July 1, 2001, at 96% of face value and pay interest semiannually. Each $1,000 bond is convertible into 25 shares of common stock. Lazy uses the straight-line method of amortizing premium or discount on bonds payable. Each stock warrant plus $32 is exchangeable for one share of common stock. The warrants were issued on October 1, 2000, and expire March 31, 2002. During 2001, Lazy issued 500,000 shares of common stock on June 1. Also, the treasury shares were repurchased on November 30. No shares of convertible preferred were issued. The average market price of Lazy's common stock during 2001 was $33. Lazy's 2001 net income was $14,000,000, with an average income tax rate of 40%.

a. Compute the weighted-average number of shares *actually* outstanding during 2001. (This is necessary for the computations of EPS.) Show your work. (Hint: The answer to part a is 4,708,333. Use this number in parts b and c.)
b. Calculate 2001 basic EPS. Organize and document your work.
c. Calculate 2001 diluted EPS. Organize and document your work.
d. Starting with net income, show (in good form) the 2001 EPS presentation that should be presented in the financial statements. If necessary, document your thought process here.

http://

23. **Texas Instruments.** Access the text Web site (http://baginski.swcollege.com) and retrieve TI's 1998 financial statements. After reading the income statement and the first footnote (Accounting Policies and Practices), answer the following questions.
a. TI had two significant divestitures in 1998 and 1997. How were they accounted for? Was either divestiture accounted for as a discontinued operation? If so, how much was reported on the income statement?
b. What is TI's general revenue recognition policy?
c. Show TI's computation of basic EPS and diluted EPS for 1998 for income from continuing operations. What was TI's weighted average number of common shares outstanding? What dilutive securities were taken into account and not taken into account in computing 1998 diluted EPS? Did TI's basic and diluted EPS increase or decrease in 1998 compared to 1997?

CFA Exam-Type Problems

24. When compared with the "completed contract" method, the percentage of completion method: (CFA adapted)
a. is preferable if reasonable estimates of costs and completion times cannot be made.
b. is more appropriate when a short project is incomplete at the end of the accounting period but will be finished in the next period.
c. is not appropriate if a loss becomes apparent.
d. will lead to less earnings variability over the life of the contract.

25. If a firm uses the completed contract method instead of the percentage of completion method, its financial statements at the mid-point of the contract would show: (CFA adapted)
    a. higher assets and higher net income.
    b. higher assets and lower net income.
    c. lower assets and higher net income.
    d. lower assets and lower net income.

26. **Revenue Recognition.** As a general rule, revenue is normally recognized when it is: (CFA adapted)
    a. measurable.
    b. measurable and received.
    c. realized and earned.
    d. earned.

27. **Diluted EPS.** An analyst gathers the following data:
    - 1,000,000 common shares outstanding (no change during the year)
    - $6,500,000 net income
    - $500,000 preferred dividends paid
    - $600,000 common dividends paid
    - $60 average market price of common stock for the year
    - 100,000 warrants outstanding exercisable at $50

    The company's diluted earnings per share is closest to: (CFA adapted)
    a. $5.45
    b. $5.90
    c. $6.00
    d. $6.39

28. **EPS.** An analyst gathers the following information about a company:
    - The capital structure does not include any potentially dilutive convertible securities, options, warrants, or other contingent securities.
    - Preferred stock dividends of $2 million were paid for the year.
    - Common stock dividends of $3.5 million were paid for the year.
    - Net income for the year was $10.5 million.
    - 20 million shares of common stock were outstanding on January 1, 2001.
    - The fiscal year-end is December 31.
    - The company issued 6 million new shares of common stock on April 1, 2001.

    The company's basic earnings per share for 2001 was closest to: (CFA adapted, with slight modifications by authors)
    a. $0.35
    b. $0.37
    c. $0.43
    d. $0.46

29. **Revenue Recognition.** If a company recognizes revenue faster than justified, which of the following best describes whether accounts receivable, inventory, and retained earnings are overstated or understated? (CFA adapted, with slight modifications by authors)

	Accounts Receivable	Inventory	Retained Earnings
a.	Overstated	Overstated	Overstated
b.	Overstated	Understated	Overstated
c.	Understated	Overstated	Understated
d.	Understated	Understated	Understated

Objectives

1. Explain the accounting for sales taxes paid and sales taxes received.
2. Explain the accounting for property taxes.
3. Describe the differences in the way items are treated for financial accounting and income tax purposes.
4. Compute income tax expense for financial statement reporting purposes.
5. Prepare the balance sheet and income statement disclosures for tax assets and liabilities.
6. Explain how net operating loss carrybacks and carryforwards generate tax assets.
7. Apply special rules for the valuation of deferred tax assets and other unique issues in deferred tax accounting.

Chapter 11

Taxes

Nearly every transaction that increases or decreases the net assets of a company has tax consequences. When selling goods, corporations must serve as a sales tax collection agency for states and municipalities. When buying goods, corporations must pay sales tax. Assets owned are taxed in the form of property taxes. But, the most significant tax is clearly the income tax that corporations must pay on the taxable portion of earnings. We consider each of these taxes in this chapter.

Sales Tax—Collections on Sales and Payments on Purchases

1 Explain the accounting for sales taxes paid and sales taxes received.

When a corporation *collects* sales tax, cash increases and a liability to the state or municipality also increases. Sales tax collections are remitted to the state or municipality at prescribed intervals, which causes both Cash and Sales Tax Liability to decrease. *Sales tax collections have no effect on net income.*

When a corporation *pays* sales tax on purchases of inventory, property, plant, and equipment, and other items, the sales taxes paid are considered to be part of the cost of the asset. These capitalized costs are later expensed when the assets are sold or used. For example, purchasing a unit of inventory with a price of \$100 in a county with a 7% sales tax results in inventory reported at \$107. Cost of goods sold of \$107 is recorded when the inventory is sold. Similarly, a machine purchased for \$10,000 in the same location results in machinery reported at \$10,700. The \$10,700 cost is allocated to depreciation expense over the machine's economic useful life.

Recording sales tax payments on purchased assets as part of the cost of the asset effectively defers expense recognition until the time at which the assets are sold or used to generate revenue. In the computation of periodic net income, this treatment is especially important for the sales tax paid to acquire long-lived assets. For shorter-term assets such as inventory, the deferral treatment is much less important for determining current net income. However, it is important for properly classifying all costs of acquiring inventory as either cost of goods sold (if the goods have been sold) or ending inventory (if the goods are still on hand).

In summary, sales taxes, whether collected on sales to customers or paid on purchases from suppliers, are not separately reported as tax expenses on the income statement. *Sales taxes collected have no effect on earnings. Sales tax payments on asset purchases reduce earnings* through increases in cost of goods sold (if the taxes were paid on inventory purchases), depreciation expense (if the taxes were paid on depreciable asset purchases), and possibly other expenses if expenditures with no future benefit are subject to sales tax. Sales tax payments on purchases of inventory and long-lived assets are reported on the statement of cash flows as operating activities (e.g., purchase of inventory) and investing activities (e.g., purchase of equipment), respectively, but are not segregated from the amounts paid for these assets.

Property Taxes

2 Explain the accounting for property taxes.

Corporate-owned properties are investments that yield revenues. Property taxes, which are levied by state and local governments, are expenses that should be matched against the revenues from property ownership. Property tax rates are based on the *existence* of a valuable asset rather than whether that valuable asset generated revenue in the period covered by the property tax assessment. Therefore, property tax expense is treated as a *period expense,* and it is matched with the period in which properties had potential revenues. Taxing authorities use these tax receipts to provide benefits to the community of which the corporation is a part.

Diversity exists in property tax accounting across various state and local governments. For example, in some cities, property taxes are assessed at the beginning of the city's fiscal year; in other cities, property taxes are assessed at the end of the city's fiscal year. A general rule is to accrue Property Tax Expense and the associated Property Taxes Payable over the period in which the corporation receives benefits from the taxing authority (generally, the taxing authority's fiscal year). Alternative accrual patterns may be used (e.g., the company's fiscal year, the period between lien dates, etc.) if they are consistently applied. Unlike sales taxes, property taxes directly reduce income and appear as Property Tax Expense on the income statement. Property tax cash payments are reported as operating outflows on the statement of cash flows.

If material, the amount of sales taxes and property taxes payable may be reported as a separate line on a company's balance sheet. Otherwise, these taxes payable are usually grouped with other liabilities and reported as other current liabilities.[1]

Income Taxes

Federal, state, and some local authorities levy taxes on corporate income. *In this chapter, we concentrate primarily on federal income taxation.* The concepts that you learn also apply to income taxation by state and local governments. As of the writing of this text, federal corporate tax rates are as follows:

	Tax Rate
First $50,000	15%
Next $25,000	25%
Next layer up to $10,000,000	34%
Above $10,000,000	35%

1. In the 1999 *Accounting Trends & Techniques,* of the 600 companies surveyed, 107 reported taxes other than federal income taxes as a separate balance sheet line item. For example, in its December 1998 balance sheet, Adolph Coors reported $48,332,000 as "taxes other than income taxes."

In the last two layers, surtaxes are also in place that phase out most of the benefits obtained in the lower tax rate layers. Thus, for many corporations, the average tax rate is near 35%.[2] *To simplify our examples in this chapter, we use 35% as the average tax rate for all corporations.*

Two Sets of Income Measurement Rules: GAAP and the Internal Revenue Code

3 Describe the differences in the way items are treated for financial accounting and income tax purposes.

One of the most important concepts to understand in the accounting for income taxes is that there are two sets of rules for determining income. Throughout this text, we illustrate generally accepted accounting principles (GAAP), which rely on the accrual concept in computing ***pretax financial accounting income*** (also known as pretax income, book income, GAAP income, income before income taxes, and income for financial reporting purposes). Financial statements are prepared in accordance with GAAP. In this chapter, we use either the term *pretax income* or *pretax accounting income* to indicate that we are dealing with income taxes in GAAP-based financial statements; we use the term *income tax expense* or ***provision for income taxes*** to indicate **the amount of tax reported in GAAP-based income statements.**

Alternatively, the computation of ***taxable income*** (also known as *income for tax purposes*) is governed by the Internal Revenue Code (IRC) as legislated by the federal government and administered by the Internal Revenue Service (IRS). In this chapter, we use the term *taxable income* to indicate that we are dealing with the income taxes as prescribed by the IRC. *The IRC is not based on GAAP accrual accounting.* More often than not, taxable income is based on cash inflows and outflows.[3]

While the purpose of GAAP is to generate useful information for investment and credit decisions, the purpose of the IRC is to raise revenue for the federal government, and in some cases, to influence corporate behavior to satisfy a political or economic agenda. For example, if the government wishes to stimulate investment, corporations may receive highly accelerated depreciation tax deductions or investment tax credits on newly purchased equipment. Similarly, if investments in municipal securities are a desired objective of federal and state officials, the revenue earned on the investments in municipal securities can be made tax exempt.

The **differences between GAAP and IRC rules** are referred to as ***book/tax differences.*** Several common book/tax differences are listed in Exhibit 1.

EXHIBIT 1 Differences between GAAP and the Internal Revenue Code

Transaction	GAAP (Pretax income)	IRC (Taxable income) (Cash Basis Taxpayer)
Installment sales	Gross profit recognized when sale is made	Gross profit recognized when cash is collected
Long-term construction contracts	Percentage of completion method recognizes profit as work is performed	Completed contract method recognizes profit only when contract is complete
Warranties	Warranty expense estimated and recorded in period of sale	Warranty costs deducted when incurred
Certain accrued losses (litigation losses, asset impairments, etc.)	Generally recognized in period when liability was incurred or asset impaired	Generally recognized when liability paid or lower cash inflow from asset use or sale is realized

(continued)

2. Corporations experiencing smaller net incomes for which average tax rates are less than 35% are required to compute and use average tax rates in the accounting for income taxes as described in this chapter.

3. Corporations may elect to be taxed on the accrual method. However, the IRC rules for accrual method taxation and GAAP rules for accrual accounting are frequently different. To simplify the presentation in this chapter, we assume that corporations are taxed on the cash basis as established in IRC rules and procedures.

EXHIBIT 1 (concluded)

Transaction	GAAP (Pretax income)	IRC (Taxable income) (Cash Basis Taxpayer)
Bad debts	Estimated uncollectible amounts accrued in period of sale using allowance method	Deducted on tax return when debt becomes uncollectible (i.e., the direct write-off method)
Subscriptions, rent, royalties, etc. received in advance of services delivered	Revenue not recognized until services performed	Taxable upon receipt of cash
Prepaid expenses such as insurance premiums, advertising, etc.	Expensed when asset created is consumed	Deductible in periods in which cash was paid
Depreciation	Generally straight-line	Generally accelerated using Modified Accelerated Cost Recovery System (MACRS) in which IRC specifies the depreciation period for each kind of asset (examples: roads, 15 years; trucks, 5 years)
Key person life insurance premium	Expensed as incurred	If the company is the beneficiary, then the premium is not tax deductible
Municipal bond revenue	Recorded as revenue when earned	May be nontaxable if certain conditions are met, otherwise taxable

Temporary versus Permanent Differences

A review of the schedule shows that, for most transactions, both GAAP and the IRC require revenue or expense recognition, but differ on the timing of the recognition. GAAP follows accrual accounting, where the IRC tends to follow cash basis accounting. As discussed in Chapter 1, in the long run, accrual and cash accounting will yield the same lifetime corporate income—only the timing is different. **Transactions that cause timing differences between GAAP and IRC recognition** are referred to as ***temporary differences.***

The last two entries in the schedule (key person life insurance and municipal bond revenue), however, are cases that may lead to either temporary differences or permanent differences. If key person life insurance premiums are tax deductible, or municipal bond revenue is taxable, any book/tax differences are temporary differences. However, if key person life insurance premiums are not tax deductible, or municipal bond revenue is not taxed (i.e., where **GAAP recognizes expenses and revenues but the IRC never allows a deduction on the return** for key person life insurance premiums and never taxes municipal bond revenue), the differences are ***permanent differences.*** When permanent differences are present, in the long run, pretax income never equals taxable income. As we illustrate in following sections, permanent differences have no deferred income tax consequences, but temporary differences are important determinants of income tax expense and have resulting deferred income tax consequences.

Conceptual Determinants of Income Tax Expense

4 Compute income tax expense for financial statement reporting purposes.

Income tax expense is not treated differently from other expenses reported on the income statement. Income tax expense occurs when assets related to income taxes decrease or liabilities related to income taxes increase. The most easily understood liability related to income taxes is the *current income tax liability*. As a firm earns revenues and incurs expenses, a liability for current taxes due to the federal government is computed by filling out the corporation's federal income tax return. **Taxable income is multiplied by the current tax rate(s) to arrive at the *current income tax liability.***

Current income tax liability = Taxable income × Current income tax rate(s)

Payments related to the current income tax liability are reported as payments for income taxes in the operating activities section of the statement of cash flows.

If no differences exist between pretax income and taxable income (i.e., no differences between GAAP and the IRC), then the current tax liability is the only tax-related liability. The increase in this liability justifies the recognition of income tax expense in an equal amount.

Example 1. Georgetown Properties has pretax accounting income and taxable income for the year equal to $2,000,000. No income tax payments were made during the year, and the current tax rate is 35%. What would be disclosed in Georgetown's balance sheet and income statement?

Solution. The current year tax is $700,000, and income tax expense equals $700,000. The portion of current year income taxes payable not remitted to taxing authorities is reported in the current liabilities section of the balance sheet. The bottom portion of the income statement appears as follows:

GEORGETOWN PROPERTIES

(Bottom portion of income statement starting with pretax income)

Income before income taxes	$2,000,000
Income tax expense*	700,000
Net income	$1,300,000

*Alternatively, provision for income taxes.

EXAMPLE 1 Journal Entry

Income Tax Expense	700,000	
Income Taxes Payable (current)		700,000

Deferred Tax-Related Assets and Liabilities

5 Prepare the balance sheet and income statement disclosures for tax assets and liabilities.

Tax-related assets and liabilities other than the current tax liability are created through temporary differences between pretax income and taxable income, or tax loss carrybacks and carryforwards. Changes in the tax-related assets and liabilities created by these items must be considered in conjunction with the current tax liability in order to properly compute income tax expense. **The process of allocating tax expense among accounting periods is called *interperiod tax allocation*.** In the following sections, we examine the effects on income tax expense of temporary differences and tax loss carrybacks and carryforwards.

Deferred Tax Consequences of Temporary Differences

To facilitate the discussion of tax consequences of temporary differences, we need to define several terms. For some transactions, the total amount of revenue or expense over the life of the item is the same for both GAAP and IRC purposes, but the revenue or expense for the item is recognized in different individual periods under GAAP and IRC rules. The differences are related to the timing of revenues and expenses over multiple periods (i.e., timing differences), and are defined as *temporary differences*. Temporary differences may be classified as originating or reversing. An ***originating temporary difference*** **is the first temporary difference in the treatment of a revenue or expense item between GAAP and the IRC for a particu-**

lar transaction (e.g., in year 1, an expense amount reported under GAAP is greater than that allowed under the IRC). A ***reversing temporary difference*** is **the offset in future periods of an originating difference** (e.g., in year 1, an expense amount reported under GAAP greater than that allowed under the IRC is an originating temporary difference; in year 2, an expense amount reported under GAAP that is less than that allowed under the IRC is a reversing temporary difference).

Most temporary differences originate in one period and reverse in the next. Short-term accruals provide good examples of originating differences. For example, assume that a company makes a sale on December 27, 2001, that is subject to a one-year warranty. Accordingly, the company records warranty expense, but no deduction is taken on the income tax return because no warranty costs are actually incurred in 2001. In 2002, any warranty claims result in a tax deduction, but because warranty expense was recorded in 2001, no warranty expense is reported in the 2002 income statement. Another example is bad debts expense. Assume that bad debts expense is estimated at year-end using the allowance method. Bad debts expense is deducted in computing pretax income, but it is not deducted on the tax return in determining taxable income because specific year-end accounts have not yet proved uncollectible (assume that the tax law uses the direct write-off method for bad debts expense). In this situation, an originating difference between pretax income and taxable income occurs—pretax income in the current year is less than taxable income in the current year due to accruing the bad debt expense. In future periods when an account proves to be uncollectible, a tax deduction is taken on the tax return in computing taxable income, but bad debts expense is not deducted in computing pretax income, which causes pretax income to be greater than taxable income in the future periods (a reversing difference).

A look at long-term accruals illustrates that differences may originate over several periods. For example, using MACRS depreciation to compute taxable income provides higher depreciation expense deductions on the tax return for several years relative to, say, using straight-line depreciation to compute pretax income. *(In this chapter, always assume that the straight-line method is used for book purposes and MACRS is used for tax purposes.)* The excess tax depreciation (MACRS) over book straight-line depreciation, which originates in earlier years, is reversed in later years when depreciation expensed on the books (straight-line) exceeds the tax depreciation under tax rules.

Corporations frequently engage in tax planning to shift income tax liability from current periods to future periods.[4] Whenever possible, corporations choose tax methods in the current period to create originating differences that cause taxable income to be less than pretax income, thus saving on current taxes. But, because originating differences become reversing differences in future periods, future ***taxable amounts*** occur, and a higher future tax must be paid. Sometimes rigid GAAP and IRC rules allow no choice, and the opposite situation occurs—originating differences are created in the current period that cause taxable income to be greater than pretax income, resulting in higher current taxes. However, because originating differences become reversing differences in future periods, future ***deductible amounts*** occur, and a lower future tax is paid.

Exhibit 2 summarizes the relations between originating differences, reversing differences, taxable amounts, and deductible amounts for revenue and expense items (*Book* refers to the GAAP rules generating pretax financial income; *Tax* refers to the IRC rules generating taxable income).

4. This statement is not always true. For example, if significant increases in future tax rates are expected, then a corporation might choose to take actions that accelerate income or defer expenses for tax purposes, which results in paying taxes in the current period rather than future periods when tax rates are expected to be higher. The trade-off is between the benefits of minimizing current taxes (current tax savings can be invested to earn additional profits) and the costs of deferring the taxes (higher future tax rates).

EXHIBIT 2 Temporary Differences

Originating Difference	Revenue Item	Expense Item
Book > Tax	*Cell 1* Creates lower current tax liability but creates a *taxable amount* (a higher tax liability in future period when *reversing difference* occurs)	*Cell 2* Creates higher current tax liability but creates a *deductible amount* (a lower tax liability in future period when *reversing difference* occurs)
Tax > Book	*Cell 3* Creates higher current tax liability but creates a *deductible amount* (a lower tax liability in future period when *reversing difference* occurs)	*Cell 4* Creates lower current tax liability but creates a *taxable amount* (a higher tax liability in future period when *reversing difference* occurs)

The second and third columns form the main body of the table. If you want to know the tax consequences when tax expense exceeds book expense, simply find the intersection of "Tax > Book" and "Expense Item" (i.e., Cell 4).

Tax Payment Deferral: Deferred Income Tax Liabilities

First, we consider the table diagonally (Cells 1 and 4). These situations represent the desired tax management strategy for most corporations—shifting tax liability to the future. Cell 1 occurs when book revenue exceeds tax revenue. Cell 4 occurs when tax expense exceeds book expense. In both cells, pretax income exceeds taxable income. This lower taxable income in the years in which the temporary difference originates results in a lower *current* tax liability. But, because these originating differences reverse in future periods, taxable amounts occur in the future, and higher *future* tax payments result. **These future tax payments are probable, and are a result of current transactions.** Therefore, **they are recognized in the current period** as ***deferred income tax liabilities.***

Example 2 (Cell 1). As of December 31, 2001, Matthew Co. had provided gardening services for the City of Orange totaling $60,000. Under the lawn maintenance contract, the City of Orange does not make payment until 2002. Matthew's accountant reports that 2001 pretax income equals $300,000, but the $60,000 amount related to services provided to the City of Orange is not taxable until 2002 when cash is received. (Assume a 35% tax rate for current and future periods.)

Solution.

Computation of *current* income tax liability at 12/31/01:	
Pretax accounting income	$300,000
Temporary difference (service revenue recognized for book purposes, but deferred for tax purposes)	(60,000)
Taxable income	$240,000
Current tax rate	× 35%
Current income tax liability	$ 84,000

In this example, 2001 taxable income is $60,000 lower than pretax income. Therefore, the current tax liability is $84,000. However, the $60,000 temporary difference will reverse in 2002, and $21,000 of tax will then be due. This leads to the computation of deferred income tax liability.

Computation of *deferred* income tax liability as of 12/31/01:	
Service revenue that becomes taxable in the future	$ 60,000
Future tax rate	× 35%
Deferred income tax liability	$ 21,000

Income tax expense represents the change in all tax-related assets and liabilities during the year. Therefore, 2001 income tax expense is computed as follows:

Computation of 2001 income tax expense:		
Increase in *current* income tax liability		$ 84,000
Increase in *deferred* income tax liability		
Ending balance	$21,000	
Beginning balance (assumed)	(0)	21,000
Income tax expense		$105,000

The bottom portion of the income statement appears as follows:

MATTHEW CO.

(Bottom portion of income statement starting with pretax income)		
Income before income taxes		$300,000
Income tax expense		
Current portion	$84,000	
Deferred portion	21,000	105,000
Net income		$195,000

EXAMPLE 2 Journal Entry

Income Tax Expense	105,000	
Income Taxes Payable (current)		84,000
Deferred Income Tax Liability*		21,000

*Alternative account titles include Deferred Income Taxes Payable and Income Taxes Payable—Deferred.

It is no coincidence that income tax expense equals pretax income times the current tax rate ($105,000 = $300,000 × 35%). This relation is true whenever current and future tax rates are equal and no permanent differences exist. In Example 2, the tax rate is 35% for all years, and the service revenue difference is temporary. To illustrate the effect of different future tax rates, assume legislated tax rates of 35% for 2001, and 40% for 2002. Under these circumstances, the 2001 deferred income tax liability equals $24,000 ($60,000 reversing difference × 40%); income tax expense equals $108,000 ($84,000 current + $24,000 deferred); net income equals $192,000; and the income statement's ***effective income tax rate*** equals 36% ($108,000 **tax expense** ÷ $300,000 **pretax income**).

Example 3 (Cell 4). Assume that Valdez Co. prepays $60,000 in equipment rent in 2001 for the use of equipment in 2002. Valdez's accountant reports that 2001 pretax income equals $300,000, and the $60,000 amount is tax deductible in 2001 when cash is paid. (Assume a 35% tax rate for current and future periods.)

Solution. *We constructed this example so that the solution leads to a result identical to the Cell 1 solution* (Example 2). Rent expense is not recognized in 2001 for financial reporting purposes (GAAP) because the asset was not used until 2002. By taking a 2001 tax deduction of $60,000, tax expenses exceed book expenses in the current period, and Valdez loses a tax deduction in 2002 of the same amount. Losing a future tax deduction (Cell 4) is equivalent to having a future taxable amount (Cell 1). In both cases, future taxable income is higher, and the deferred tax liability exists.

Computation of *current* income tax liability at 12/31/01:	
Pretax income	$300,000
Temporary difference (rent paid in advance of use; recognized for tax purposes, deferred for book purposes)	(60,000)
Taxable income	$240,000
Current tax rate	× 35%
Current income tax liability	$ 84,000

Computation of *deferred* income tax liability as of 12/31/01:		
Lost future tax deduction		$60,000
Future tax rate		× 35%
Deferred income tax liability		$21,000

Computation of 2001 income tax expense:		
Increase in *current* income tax liability		$ 84,000
Increase in *deferred* income tax liability		
Ending balance	$21,000	
Beginning balance (assumed)	(0)	21,000
Income tax expense		$105,000

The bottom portion of the income statement appears as follows:

VALDEZ CO.

(Bottom portion of income statement starting with pretax income)		
Income before income taxes		$300,000
Income tax expense		
Current portion	$84,000	
Deferred portion	21,000	105,000*
Net income		$195,000

*Note that the effective income tax rate is $105,000/$300,000 = 35%.

EXAMPLE 3 Journal Entry

Income Tax Expense	105,000	
Income Taxes Payable (current)		84,000
Deferred Income Tax Liability		21,000

Tax Payment Acceleration: Deferred Income Tax Assets

In Exhibit 2, Cells 2 and 3 represent an unfavorable current-year tax situation in that temporary differences cause higher current tax payments to be made. However, because temporary differences reverse, a favorable situation occurs in the future when tax savings result. According to *SFAS No. 106*, **the expectation of lower future costs resulting from an existing transaction** gives rise to ***deferred income tax assets***. This is a departure from an earlier standard (*SFAS No. 96*, "Accounting for Income Taxes") that made deferred tax asset recognition difficult.

Example 4 (Cell 2). Durable Co. sells commercial washing machines that carry a two-year warranty for parts and labor. In 2001, Durable reported $200,000 of pretax accounting income on sales of $3,000,000. A charge to Warranty Expense of 6% of sales ($180,000) is included in the determination of pretax income. Actual warranty expenditures in 2001 totaled $50,000 in parts and labor. The $50,000 is deductible on the 2001 tax return, and the remaining warranty costs will be incurred and tax deductible in 2002. (Assume a 35% tax rate in all years.)

Solution. Taxable income in 2001 is $130,000 higher than pretax income because only $50,000 of the $180,000 warranty expense is currently deductible. As shown below, the 2001 current tax liability is $115,500. Because this temporary difference will reverse in 2002, the remaining $130,000 will become deductible in 2002, resulting in a tax savings of $45,500. The $130,000 deductible amount from the temporary difference leads to the computation of a December 31, 2001, deferred income tax asset. *Combining changes in all tax-related assets and liabilities yields income tax expense of $70,000.*

Computation of *current* income tax liability at 12/31/01:	
Pretax income	$200,000
Temporary difference (Warranty expense: $3,000,000 × 6% = $180,000; only $50,000 deducted on tax return)	130,000
Taxable income	$330,000
Current tax rate	× 35%
Current income tax liability	$115,500

Computation of *deferred* income tax asset as of 12/31/01:	
Warranty costs that become deductible in the future	$130,000
Future tax rate	× 35%
Deferred income tax asset	$ 45,500

Income tax expense for 2001 is as follows:

Computation of 2001 income tax expense:		
Increase in *current* income tax liability		$115,500
Increase in *deferred* income tax asset		
Ending balance	$45,500	
Beginning balance (assumed)	(0)	(45,500)
Income tax expense		$ 70,000

The bottom portion of the income statement appears as follows:

DURABLE CO.

(Bottom portion of income statement starting with pretax income)

Income before income taxes		$200,000
Income tax expense		
Current portion	$115,500	
Deferred portion	(45,500)	70,000*
Net income		$130,000

*Note that the effective income tax rate is $70,000 ÷ $200,000 = 35%.

EXAMPLE 4 Journal Entry

Income Tax Expense	70,000	
Deferred Income Tax Asset	45,500	
Income Taxes Payable (current)		115,500

Example 5 (Cell 3). Q Magazine sells magazine subscriptions lasting one year. As of December 31, 2001 (its first year of operations), Q reported $700,000 in pretax accounting income that properly excluded $200,000 in cash collected on subscriptions to be delivered in 2002. All subscription revenue is taxable when received. (Assume a 35% tax rate in all years.)

Solution. Taxable cash receipts that are not recognized as revenue until subscriptions are delivered causes 2001 taxable income to be $200,000 higher than pretax income. As shown below, the current tax liability is $315,000. When the $200,000 temporary difference reverses in 2002 (i.e., 2001 GAAP income reflects the revenues, but they are not taxed), Q realizes a tax savings of $70,000.

Computation of *current* income tax liability at 12/31/01:	
Pretax income	$700,000
Temporary difference (tax revenues exceed book revenues on unearned subscriptions)	200,000
Taxable income	$900,000
Current tax rate	× 35%
Current income tax liability	$315,000

Computation of *deferred* income tax asset as of 12/31/01:	
Subscriptions revenue not taxable in the future	$200,000
Future tax rate	× 35%
Deferred income tax asset	$ 70,000

Income tax expense for 2001 is as follows:

Computation of 2001 income tax expense:		
Increase in *current* income tax liability		$315,000
Increase in *deferred* income tax asset		
Ending balance	$70,000	
Beginning balance (assumed)	(0)	(70,000)
Income tax expense		$245,000

The bottom portion of the income statement appears as follows:

Q MAGAZINE

(Bottom portion of income statement starting with pretax income)		
Income before income taxes		$700,000
Income tax expense		
Current portion	$315,000	
Deferred portion	(70,000)	245,000*
Net income		$455,000

*Note that the effective income tax rate is $245,000 ÷ $700,000 = 35%.

EXAMPLE 5 Journal Entry

Income Tax Expense	245,000	
Deferred Income Tax Asset	70,000	
Income Taxes Payable (current)		315,000

Multiple Temporary Differences

In Examples 2–5, we illustrated four different temporary differences. What happens in the likely event that a company has multiple temporary differences? *SFAS No. 109* requires that deferred income tax liabilities and deferred income tax assets be separately computed. Therefore, a company can have both deferred income tax assets and deferred income tax liabilities. Increases in deferred income tax liabilities and decreases in deferred income tax assets increase income tax expense during the period. Decreases in deferred income tax liabilities and increases in deferred income tax assets decrease income tax expense during the period.

Tax Consequences: Tax Loss Carrybacks and Carryforwards

6 Explain how net operating loss carrybacks and carryforwards generate tax assets.

So far, we have seen that current taxable income leads to a current tax liability, and temporary differences lead to deferred tax assets and liabilities.

In addition to assessing tax burdens on corporations making a profit, tax laws allow for a corporation to obtain a tax benefit (i.e., asset) from a ***net operating loss (NOL)***. A NOL occurs when **tax deductions exceed taxable revenues (i.e., taxable income on the income tax return is negative)**.

At the writing of this text, corporations have a choice of carrying back NOLs two years and then forward 20 years, or forgoing the carryback option and simply carrying them forward 20 years. The decision to carryback generates a tax asset, Refund Receivable, because the corporation files an amended tax return for past periods, reducing prior period taxable income and income taxes payable. The decision to carryforward results in a tax asset, Deferred Tax Asset.

Example 6. Bad Luck Enterprises began operation in 1998 and generated the following pretax incomes and losses over a six-year period:

Year	Pretax Income (Loss) = Taxable Income (Loss)
1998	$100,000
1999	160,000
2000	(500,000)
2001	300,000
2002	400,000
2003	500,000

Assume a tax rate of 35% for all years and *no temporary or permanent differences* (i.e., taxable income and pretax income are equal in all years). Prepare the income statement disclosures for income tax expense in each year, and describe the changes in the tax assets and liabilities that determine income tax expense. Assume that any NOL is carried back if possible, then carried forward.

Solution. Bad Luck reports the following information for the six-year period:

EXHIBIT 3 Example 6. Bad Luck Enterprises Income Statement Disclosure, 1998–2003

	1998	1999	2000	2001	2002	2003	Total
Pretax/taxable income (loss)	$100,000	$160,000	$(500,000)	$300,000	$400,000	$500,000	$960,000
Current portion of tax expense	(35,000)	(56,000)		(21,000)	(140,000)	(175,000)	(427,000)
Deferred portion of tax expense	0	0		(84,000)			(84,000)
Benefit from loss carryback (reported as Tax Refund in the asset section of the balance sheet)			91,000				91,000
Benefit from loss carryforward (reported as Deferred Tax Asset in the balance sheet)			84,000				84,000
Net income	$ 65,000	$104,000	$(325,000)	$195,000	$260,000	$325,000	$624,000

Before we discuss how each year's tax amounts have been computed, look at the "Total" column. Pretax income for the six-year period is $960,000, and net income is 65% of that amount ($624,000), demonstrating that Bad Luck's income tax expense was 35% over the six-year period. This same relationship holds for every year, and will hold, in general, if no permanent differences exist and if there is no combination of temporary differences and changes in future tax rates.

Also, we purposely set up the example so that Bad Luck had sufficient income to use up the operating loss carryforwards and carrybacks by the end of the six-year period. Because Bad Luck had sufficient income and no temporary differences, the total taxes paid in cash equal the total tax expense over the six-year period. An important point to note is that the *timing* of cash amounts paid or received does not equal the recognition of tax expense or tax benefit in each individual year.

In 1998 and 1999, pretax (and taxable) income equals $100,000 and $160,000, respectively. As a result, current tax liabilities of $35,000 and $56,000, respectively, are recognized and paid. In 2000, Bad Luck has a pretax (and taxable) loss of $500,000. Because tax rates are not expected to increase, it makes sense for Bad Luck to carry the NOL back two years to get an immediate tax refund before carrying any remaining loss forward. Under tax law, Bad Luck carries the NOL back to 1998 (the second year back), and then carries any remaining NOL to 1999, and up to 20 years forward beginning with 2001. Bad Luck offsets the NOL in 2000 against 1998, 1999, and expected future income as follows:

NOL offset against 1998 taxable income	$100,000
NOL offset against 1999 taxable income	160,000
NOL offset against future taxable income	240,000
Total 2000 NOL	$500,000

Because Bad Luck files amended tax returns for 1998 and 1999 and requests a refund, the offsets against 1998 and 1999 income generate immediate tax refunds (Tax Refund Receivable) equal to $91,000. The $91,000 refund is determined by the income tax rates in prior periods on the carryback amounts, ($100,000 + $160,000) × 35%. The expectation that the remaining $240,000 NOL will be offset against future income to reduce future tax payments yields an $84,000 tax benefit (Deferred Income Tax Asset), determined by multiplying the $240,000 by enacted future tax rates (i.e., 35%). The creation of these two assets of $91,000 and $84,000 results in a negative 2000 income tax expense of $175,000, which serves to reduce the pretax loss of $500,000 to a net loss of $325,000. Accrual accounting matches the full $175,000 tax benefit to the period in which it is generated. The $91,000 income tax refund receivable will be collected quickly. Thus, the near-term cash saving is $91,000. The tax savings related to the $84,000 deferred income tax asset will be realized in future years.

In 2001, Bad Luck generates $300,000 pretax (and taxable) income. This amount is sufficient to realize the $240,000 remaining 2000 NOL carryforward, leaving only $60,000 as taxable income ($300,000 − $240,000) and $21,000 as the current tax liability ($60,000 × 35%). Although the $21,000 is the only 2001 cash outflow, total 2001 income tax expense recognition is $105,000 (the increase of current tax liability by $21,000 and the reduction of a deferred income tax asset by $84,000). Deferred Income Tax Asset is reduced by $84,000 because the NOL carryforward tax benefit is used up in the current period. Total 2001 tax expense of $105,000 results in net income of $195,000.

In 2002 and 2003, pretax income equals $400,000 and $500,000 respectively. The current tax liabilities of $140,000 and $175,000, respectively, are recognized and paid.

EXAMPLE 6 Annual Journal Entries

1998:		
Income Tax Expense	35,000	
Income Taxes Payable (current)		35,000
1999:		
Income Tax Expense	56,000	
Income Taxes Payable (current)		56,000
2000:		
Income Tax Refund Receivable	91,000	
Deferred Income Tax Asset	84,000	
Tax Benefit From Loss Carryback*		91,000
Tax Benefit From Loss Carryforward*		84,000
2001:		
Income Tax Expense	105,000	
Income Taxes Payable (current)		21,000
Deferred Income Tax Asset		84,000
2002:		
Income Tax Expense	140,000	
Income Taxes Payable (current)		140,000
2003:		
Income Tax Expense	175,000	
Income Taxes Payable (current)		175,000

*Alternatively, credit Income Tax Expense for $175,000.

Special Issues in Tax Accounting

7 Apply the special rules for the valuation of deferred tax assets and other unique issues in deferred tax accounting.

Several additional issues can complicate the tax accounting that we have illustrated. We examine each of the following items in turn:

- Realizability of deferred income tax assets
- Remeasurement of income tax assets and liabilities for enacted rate changes
- Current versus noncurrent balance sheet classification
- Alternative minimum tax (AMT)
- Income statement presentation for discontinued operations, extraordinary items, and cumulative effects of accounting changes (i.e., intraperiod tax allocation).

Realizability of Deferred Income Tax Assets

One of the greatest controversies in the area of tax accounting is the treatment of deferred income tax assets. In fact, tax asset treatment was one of the biggest reasons why the original overhaul of tax reporting rules (*FASB No. 96*) was not well received and *FASB No. 109*, which currently governs tax accounting, was issued.

The heart of the controversy is the long-held conservatism principle, which makes asset recognition more difficult than liability recognition. Consider the deferred income tax liability. Reporting such a liability implies that the corporation expects to pay future taxes because it was able to defer the tax consequences of current (and, perhaps, past) transactions. For this expectation to be realized, nothing else has to happen. Even if the corporation shuts down its activities, income taxes will be due in the future. Now consider the deferred income tax asset. Reporting such an asset is a statement that the corporation expects to save future taxes. That is, when taxable income is earned in future periods, the future deductible amounts on which deferred income tax assets are based will be taken, and the future taxable income will be shielded from tax liability. Note that future taxable income is necessary for this scenario to work. If future taxable income is not realized, then there is nothing from which to deduct future deductible amounts, and thus, the deductible amounts have no value. What many opponents of current GAAP argue is that we have to *assume future income* to have a reason to currently recognize a deferred tax asset. Assuming future income is not an assumption with which many accountants are comfortable.

To address these concerns, when deductible amount temporary differences exist, the FASB requires that the accountant make a determination about the probability that the company will have future taxable income against which any deferred income tax assets can be offset. To aid the accountant in accomplishing such an investigation, the FASB provides examples of positive and negative evidence of the ability to realize deferred tax assets:

Positive evidence:

- Existing contracts or firm sales backlog yielding sufficient future profits.
- Substantial asset appreciation over tax basis.
- A strong earnings history coupled with evidence that the NOL carryforward or temporary difference yielding the deferred tax asset is transitory rather than permanent.

Negative evidence:

- A history of operating losses.
- A history of unused tax benefits.
- Expected future losses.
- Unsettled circumstances that may unfavorably affect future profitability.
- Substantial quick reversals of large amounts of deferred tax assets that, when considering the length of carryback and carryforward periods, may limit usefulness of the deductions.

After considering all evidence, if it is believed that **it is more likely than not that some or all of the deferred tax asset might not be realized**, then a ***deferred income tax asset valuation allowance*** should be established. This valuation allowance is subtracted from Deferred Income Tax Asset, and because it represents the reduction of an asset, it increases the current period income tax expense. If it becomes necessary to change the valuation allowance in a future period because additional positive or negative evidence is discovered, then the valuation account is changed, with the consequence that income tax expense is also changed.

Example 7. A corporation in its first year of operation computes current income tax liability for the period of $500,000, deferred income tax liabilities of $100,000, and deferred income tax assets of $250,000. Before any assessment about the probability that the deferred income tax asset will be realized in future periods, income tax expense is $350,000, determined as follows:

Increase in income tax-related liabilities:		
Increase in the current income liability	$500,000	
Increase in the deferred income tax liability	100,000	$600,000
Increase in deferred income tax assets		(250,000)
Income tax expense		$350,000

After searching for evidence about the probability of future taxable income, the accountants determine that it is probable that future taxable income will be generated and calculate that it is probable that 80% of the $250,000 deferred income tax asset will be used in future periods. What amount of valuation allowance should be established? How should income tax expense be calculated?

Solution. A valuation allowance of $50,000 ($250,000 × 20%) is established. The computation of income tax expense is as follows:

Increase in income tax-related liabilities:		
Increase in the current income liability	$500,000	
Increase in the deferred income tax liability	100,000	$600,000
Increase in tax-related assets:		
Increase in deferred tax assets	$250,000	
Increase in valuation account	(50,000)	(200,000)
Income tax expense		$400,000

Note that income tax expense needed to be increased $50,000 because the full tax benefit of the deferred income tax asset is not recognized in the current period (i.e., only 80% of the deferred tax asset is recognized).

The balance sheet would report the various tax-related assets and liabilities. Deferred tax assets would be reported at $250,000 less the $50,000 valuation allowance (i.e., at a net realizable value of $200,000).

EXAMPLE 7 Journal Entries

To recognize tax assets, liabilities, and expenses:		
Income Tax Expense	350,000	
Deferred Income Tax Asset	250,000	
Income Taxes Payable (current)		500,000
Deferred Income Tax Liability		100,000
To establish valuation allowance:		
Allowance to Reduce Deferred Income Tax Asset to Realizable Value	50,000	
Income Tax Expense		50,000

When evaluating whether deferred tax assets are realizable, several sources of taxable income should be considered. As noted earlier, a strong earnings history strengthens the expectation of future income. However, other sources of income from which to deduct future deductible amounts (i.e., realized deferred tax assets) also exist. First, future taxable amounts will be created from the reversal of deferred tax liabilities. Second, future deductible amounts can cause NOLs that could be carried back against prior years' profits if tax law permits. Finally, certain tax planning strategies can be implemented to create future income to allow the realization of deductible amounts. Each of these other sources of income should be considered in determining whether a valuation account is necessary.

To illustrate the financial statement presentation of a valuation allowance, in an annual report, IBM reported a gross deferred tax asset of $13,722 million, a valuation allowance of $2,239 million, and a net deferred tax asset of $11,483 million. Similarly, in an annual report, Armco, Inc., reported a gross deferred tax asset of $997.6 million, a valuation allowance of $669.1 million, and a net deferred tax asset of $328.5 million. Clearly, some companies have large valuation allowances associated with deferred tax assets. IBM's valuation allowance was 16.3% of the gross deferred tax asset, while Armco's valuation allowance was 67.1% of the gross deferred tax asset.

Remeasurement of Tax Assets and Liabilities for Enacted Rate Changes

From time to time, corporate tax rates are changed. If this happens, each deferred income tax asset and liability is remeasured at the new tax rate, and income tax expense of the current period is adjusted. For example, a *1% reduction in future tax rates* would decrease income tax expense if the corporation is in a net deferred tax liability situation; it would increase income tax expense if the corporation is in a net deferred tax asset situation.

Current versus Noncurrent Balance Sheet Classification

Several balance sheet accounts arise from tax accounting. The current portion of income taxes payable is a current liability. Similarly, an income tax refund receivable generated from a net operating loss carryback is a current asset. In all examples, we have assumed that the corporation has not paid any taxes until the end of the year when the income tax expense provision is calculated. More likely, the corporation has been prepaying taxes on a quarterly basis much like an individual has taxes withheld from a weekly paycheck. As a result, any balance in Prepaid Taxes would be a current asset.

The classification of deferred tax assets and liabilities in the balance sheet primarily depends on the classification of the asset or liability that gave rise to the difference between the tax and financial accounting records. For example, accounting for bad debts related to accounts receivable initially causes a deferred tax asset because bad debts expense is deducted on the financial records before it is deducted on the tax return. Deferred Income Tax Asset is classified as current because accounts receivable is a current asset. Accounting for depreciation expense on plant and equipment typically creates a deferred tax liability. This deferred tax liability is classified as long-term to match the long-term classification of plant and equipment.

Some deferred tax assets and liabilities do not arise from a given asset or liability. For example, under the equity method of accounting, the investor accrues a portion of an investee's income as part of its own income. IRC rules do not assess taxes on this accrual because no cash (i.e., dividends) have been received from the investee. Thus, a deferred tax liability is created because the amounts will be taxable in the future when cash is received. This deferred tax liability is not related to a single asset or liability, but instead, to the entire operations of the investee. When deferred tax assets and liabilities do not arise from a given asset or liability, balance sheet classification is based on when the difference is expected to reverse. The deferred tax liability would be shown as current if dividend receipt was expected in the next year.

Once deferred tax assets and liabilities are classified as current and noncurrent, *current deferred tax assets and current deferred tax liabilities are netted and reported as one net current amount* (either as an asset or liability), and *noncurrent deferred tax assets and noncurrent deferred tax liabilities are netted and reported as one net noncurrent amount* (either as an asset or liability).[5]

Alternative Minimum Tax (AMT)

For many years (especially in the early 1980s), corporations used tax planning strategies to avoid paying income taxes. As a result, the alternative minimum tax (AMT) was created to ensure that every corporation paid *some* income tax. Each period, the current income tax liability is the greater amount of that calculated under the regular tax rules or the AMT amount. Some corporations have so many tax preference items (generally, excess depreciation deductions allowed under the IRC) that their regular tax liability is substantially smaller than the AMT. When corporations pay the AMT, they are granted a tax credit to be used to reduce future income taxes payable because the tax preferences currently granted will likely reverse. The AMT tax credit results in a deferred tax asset. *Because the computation of the AMT is complex and beyond the scope of our discussion, we do not illustrate it in this text.*

Intraperiod Tax Allocation

GAAP requires the total income tax expense for a period to be allocated to discontinued operations, extraordinary items, and cumulative effects of accounting changes. This process is referred to as ***intraperiod tax allocation.*** These special items are presented at the bottom of the income statement, net of tax effects, after the subtotal income from continuing operations. Therefore, in order to calculate the total income tax expense on the income statement, it might be necessary to look at four different places: provision for income taxes, tax effects of discontinued operations, tax effects of extraordinary items, and tax effects of cumulative effects of accounting changes.

Example 8. In 2001, the Shao Co. had the following information available at year-end. All amounts are gross of tax (i.e., do not reflect tax consequences).

Income before income taxes and discontinued operations, extraordinary items, and cumulative effects of accounting changes	$3,000,000
Discontinued operations	(500,000)
Extraordinary item	750,000
Cumulative effect of accounting change	(300,000)

Shao's income tax rate is 40%. Prepare the bottom section of the income statement starting with Income from continuing operations before income taxes.

5. The 1999 *Accounting Trends & Techniques* reports the following income tax-related information for 600 companies surveyed: 409 reported income taxes payable as current liabilities, and 49 reported tax refunds receivable as current assets; 400 reported deferred income tax assets as current assets, and 47 reported deferred income taxes as current liabilities; and 177 reported deferred income tax assets as noncurrent assets, and 394 reported deferred income tax liabilities as noncurrent liabilities.

Solution.

SHAO CO.
2001 Partial Income Statement

Income from continuing operations before income taxes	$3,000,000
Provision for income taxes	1,200,000
Income from continuing operations	$1,800,000
Discontinued operations, net of tax of $200,000	(300,000)
Extraordinary items, net of tax of $300,000	450,000
Cumulative effect of accounting changes, net of tax of $120,000	(180,000)
Net income	$1,770,000

Comprehensive Example: Multiple Differences

We conclude this chapter with a comprehensive example with multiple differences between GAAP financial accounting and IRC tax treatments of revenues and expenses.

Comprehensive Example. Kenan Co. began operations in 2001. Pretax income determined under GAAP is $600,000 in 2001, $100,000 in 2002, and $300,000 in 2003. The income tax rate is 40% in each year. Additional information is as follows:

Depreciation schedules

Year	Tax Records	Books
2001	$150,000	$50,000
2002	120,000	50,000
2003	100,000	50,000

Warranty cost recognition (assume that Kenan offers one-year warranties)

Year	Tax Records	Books
2001	$ 0	$40,000
2002	20,000	50,000
2003	50,000	60,000

Litigation losses (assume that at the time of financial statement recognition, the company expects to pay the litigation amount in the subsequent year)

Year	Tax Records	Books
2001	$ 0	$ 0
2002	0	400,000
2003	400,000	0

Installment sales used for tax purposes (assume that all installment sales contracts vary between one and two years in length, and that any sales revenue recognized for book purposes, but not for tax purposes, in any calendar year is recognized for tax purposes in the following calendar year)

Year	Tax Records	Books
2001	$20,000	$40,000
2002	30,000	50,000
2003	40,000	60,000

Key person life insurance premiums (assume the premiums are not tax deductible)

Year	Tax Records	Books
2001	$0	$10,000
2002	0	10,000
2003	0	10,000

Prepare the income statement and balance sheet disclosures for Kenan Co. for each year. Assume that any NOL is carried back, if possible.

Solution. We begin by calculating the taxable income and the current portion of income tax expense (i.e., income tax payable or income tax refundable) for each year:

EXHIBIT 4 Comprehensive Example. Kenan Co.

	2001	2002	2003
Pretax income	$600,000	$100,000	$300,000
Temporary differences:			
Excess tax depreciation expense	(100,000)	(70,000)	(50,000)
Excess book warranty expense	40,000	30,000	10,000
Excess book recognition of litigation loss	0	400,000	(400,000)
Excess book installment sales revenue	(20,000)	(20,000)	(20,000)
Permanent difference:			
Key person life insurance premiums	10,000	10,000	10,000
Taxable income (NOL)	$530,000	$450,000	$(150,000)
Tax rate	× 40%	× 40%	
Income taxes payable (current portion of income tax expense)	$212,000	$180,000	
Tax rate in carryback year (2001)			× 40%
Income tax refund receivable generated by NOL carryback (current portion of income tax expense)			$ (60,000)

Kenan Co. owes taxes of $212,000 for 2001, and $180,000 for 2002. However, with a net operating loss of $150,000 in 2003, that amount can be carried back against 2001 income, and Kenan accrues a $60,000 tax refund receivable in 2003.

Explanation of Reconciling Items

The schedule reconciles pretax (book) income to taxable income. The first reconciling amount is *depreciation* (a temporary difference). In each year, tax depreciation deductions exceed book depreciation, which causes taxable income (the amount to which we are reconciling) to be lower than pretax income. Thus, the excess depreciation amount is subtracted to move from the larger pretax income to the smaller taxable income. The 2001 depreciation book/tax difference is originating (tax depreciation expense is greater than book depreciation expense). The temporary differences in 2002 and 2003 are also originating because the tax amounts continue to exceed the book amounts. These originating temporary differences in 2001–2003 are classified as *taxable amounts.* In future periods, when the temporary differences reverse, tax depreciation expense will be lower than book depreciation expense. When this occurs, taxable income will be greater than pretax income, and the income taxes deferred in prior periods will be paid.[6]

The second reconciling amount is *warranty expense* (another temporary difference). In each year, book warranty expense exceeds tax deductions for warranty costs, which causes taxable income (the amount to which we are reconciling) to be higher than pretax income. Thus, the excess warranty expense is added to move from the smaller pretax income to the larger taxable income. The 2001 warranty expense book/tax difference is originating (tax warranty expense is less than book warranty expense). The temporary differences in 2002 and 2003 are also originating because the tax amounts continue to be less than the book amounts. The originating temporary differences in 2001–2003 are classified as *deductible amounts.* In future periods, when the temporary differences reverse, tax warranty expense will be larger than book warranty expense. When this occurs, taxable income will be smaller than pretax income, and the income tax savings will be realized.

6. When you observe, for example, tax depreciation greater than book depreciation in a given year, it could be caused by originating differences that are greater than reversing differences from prior years. Therefore, the *net* difference is originating.

The third reconciling item is related to *litigation losses.* A litigation loss was recognized in the 2002 income statement, but was deducted on the tax return in 2003. Pretax income is smaller than taxable income in 2002 and larger than taxable income in 2003. Thus, the reconciling item is added to obtain the larger taxable income in 2002 and subtracted to obtain the smaller taxable income in 2003. The 2002 litigation book/tax $400,000 difference is originating (tax litigation loss is less than book litigation loss), and the temporary difference reverses in 2003 (tax litigation loss is greater than book litigation loss). The originating temporary difference in 2002 is classified as a *deductible amount.* In 2003, when the temporary difference reverses, tax litigation loss is greater than book litigation loss. Therefore, taxable income is less than pretax income, and the income tax savings are realized.

The fourth reconciling item is related to *installment sales revenue.* For book purposes, sales revenue is recognized when items are sold; for income tax purposes, installment sales revenue is recognized when cash is received. In each year, the amount of installment sales revenue reported in the income statement exceeds the book sales revenue amount, causing taxable income (the amount to which we are reconciling) to be lower than pretax income. Thus, the excess sales revenue amount is subtracted to move from the larger pretax income to the smaller taxable income. The 2001 installment sales book/tax temporary difference is originating (tax installment sales revenue is smaller than book sales revenue). The temporary differences in 2002 and 2003 are also originating because the book amounts continue to exceed the tax amounts. The originating temporary differences in 2001–2003 are classified as *taxable amounts.* In future periods, when the temporary differences reverse, tax sales revenue is higher than book sales revenue. When this occurs, taxable income is greater than pretax income, and the income taxes, which were deferred in prior periods, are paid.

The last reconciling amount is *key person life insurance premiums,* which causes a *permanent difference* because these premiums are not deductible for tax purposes. In each year, book key person life insurance premiums exceed tax deductions for key person life insurance premiums, which causes taxable income (the amount to which we are reconciling) to be higher than pretax income. Because this difference is a permanent difference, it has no deferred tax consequences.

With the exception of the key person life insurance premiums, each of the reconciling items has deferred tax consequences. In this comprehensive example, a key person life insurance premium is a permanent difference because it is never tax deductible. In each of the other differences, however, tax return and financial records will eventually recognize the same total amount. To help understand the deferred tax consequences of the temporary differences, we again provide the matrix of possible relations between tax and book amounts. Here, we indicate how the temporary differences for Kenan Co. are classified within the matrix:

EXHIBIT 5 Kenan Co. Temporary Differences

Originating Difference	Revenue Item	Expense Item
Book > Tax	*Cell 1—Installment Sales* Creates lower current tax liability but creates a *taxable amount* (a higher tax liability in future period when *reversing difference* occurs)	*Cell 2—Warranty Expense* *Litigation Loss* Creates higher current tax liability but creates a *deductible amount* (a lower tax liability in future period when *reversing difference* occurs)
Tax > Book	*Cell 3* Creates higher current tax liability but creates a *deductible amount* (a lower tax liability in future period when *reversing difference* occurs)	*Cell 4—Depreciation Expense* Creates lower current tax liability but creates a *taxable amount* (a higher tax liability in future period when *reversing difference* occurs)

2001 Solution Three originating differences occur in 2001: tax depreciation expense exceeds book depreciation expense (Cell 4), book warranty expense exceeds tax warranty expense (Cell 2), and book sales revenue exceeds tax sales revenue (Cell 1). The depreciation and investment revenue differences (Cells 1 and 4) create a lower current tax liability (note that they are subtracted in the reconciliation), but create taxable amounts in future periods when the differences reverse (that is, they will be added in the reconciliation in future periods when they reverse). Thus, *two deferred tax liabilities* are created:

Deferred tax liabilities at the end of 2001 equal $48,000:	
Related to depreciation expense (noncurrent)	$100,000 × 40% = $40,000
Related to sales revenue (current)	$20,000 × 40% = $8,000

The depreciation-related deferred income tax liability is noncurrent because the related property, plant, and equipment is reported as noncurrent. The deferred income tax liability related to installment sales revenue is current because the installment sales revenue will be recognized within 12 months.

The warranty expense situation (Cell 2) causes a *deferred tax asset* due to its future deductibility:

Deferred tax asset at the end of 2001 equals $16,000:	
Related to warranty expense (current)	$40,000 × 40% = $16,000

Because Kenan offers one-year warranties, any warranty liability on the balance sheet would be classified as a current liability, and, therefore, the deferred tax asset is current.

In summary, the 2001 balance sheet reports:

Current assets:	
Deferred tax assets*	$ 8,000
Current liabilities:	
Income taxes payable**	$212,000
Long-term liabilities:	
Deferred tax liabilities	$ 40,000

*$16,000 current deferred tax asset − $8,000 current deferred tax liability.
**This assumes no tax payments made during the year.

The computation of 2001 income tax expense proceeds as follows:

Increase in *current* tax liability		$212,000
Increase in *deferred* tax liability		
Ending balance	$48,000	
Beginning balance	(0)	48,000
Increase in *deferred* tax asset		
Ending balance	$16,000	
Beginning balance	(0)	(16,000)
Income tax expense		$244,000

The bottom portion of the 2001 income statement (starting with pretax income) is:

Income before income taxes		$600,000
Income tax expense		
Current portion	$212,000	
Deferred portion	32,000	244,000
Net income		$356,000

Note that Kenan's effective income tax rate reflected in the income statement equals 40.67% ($244,000 ÷ $600,000). It is not equal to 40% because of the presence of the permanent difference item (key person life insurance premium of $10,000).

COMPREHENSIVE EXAMPLE Journal Entries

2001:		
Deferred Tax Asset	16,000	
Income Tax Expense	244,000	
Deferred Tax Liability		48,000
Income Taxes Payable (current portion)		212,000

2002 Solution Four tax and book differences occur in 2002. As before, tax depreciation expense exceeds book depreciation expense (Cell 4), book warranty expense exceeds tax warranty expense (Cell 2), and book sales revenue exceeds tax installment sales revenue (Cell 1). In addition, there is a book recognition of a litigation loss that will not be recognized on the tax return until the following year, creating a future deductible amount (Cell 2).

Deferred taxes are balance sheet accounts. They accumulate book and tax differences through time. At each balance sheet date, we measure the cumulative amounts:

Deferred tax liabilities at the end of 2002 equal $84,000:	
Related to depreciation expense (noncurrent)	($100,000 + $70,000) × 40% = $68,000
Related to installment sales revenue (current)	($20,000 + $20,000) × 40% = $16,000
Deferred tax assets at the end of 2002 equal $188,000:	
Related to warranty expense (current)	($40,000 + $30,000) × 40% = $28,000
Related to litigation (current)	$400,000 × 40% = $160,000

In 2002, when the litigation is recognized for book purposes, the company sets up a litigation liability. Because the company expects the litigation amount to be paid in 2003, the liability is a current liability in the 2002 balance sheet. Therefore, the deferred tax asset is current. In summary, the 2002 balance sheet reports:

Current assets:	
Deferred tax assets*	$172,000
Current liabilities:	
Income taxes payable**	$180,000
Long-term liabilities:	
Deferred tax liabilities	$ 68,000

*$28,000 + $160,000 − $16,000
**This assumes no tax payment made during the year.

The computation of 2002 income tax expense proceeds as follows:

Increase in *current* tax liability		$180,000
Increase in *deferred* tax liability		
Ending balance	$ 84,000	
Beginning balance	(48,000)	36,000
Increase in *deferred* tax asset		
Ending balance	$188,000	
Beginning balance	(16,000)	(172,000)
Income tax expense		$ 44,000

The bottom portion of the 2002 income statement (starting with pretax income):

Income before income taxes		$100,000
Income tax expense		
Current portion	$180,000	
Deferred portion	(136,000)	44,000
Net income		$ 56,000

Note that the 2002 effective income tax rate equals 44% ($44,000 ÷ 100,000). Again, it is not equal to 40% because of the presence of permanent differences.

COMPREHENSIVE EXAMPLE Journal Entries

2002:		
Deferred Tax Asset	172,000	
Income Tax Expense	44,000	
Deferred Tax Liability		36,000
Income Taxes Payable (current portion)		180,000

Note that if deferred tax assets and liabilities were not measured, then 2002 pretax income would be reported at $100,000, and tax expense (equal only to taxes paid in the absence of deferred tax measurement) would be reported at $180,000.

2003 Solution The 2003 measurements are affected by the reversal of the litigation loss:

Deferred tax liabilities at the end of 2003 equal $112,000:

Related to depreciation expense (noncurrent)	($100,000 + $70,000 + $50,000) × 40% = $88,000
Related to installment sales revenue (current)	($20,000 + $20,000 + $20,000) × 40% = $24,000

Deferred tax asset at the end of 2003 equals $32,000:

Related to warranty expense (current)	($40,000 + $30,000 + $10,000) × 40% = $32,000
Related to litigation (current)	($400,000 − $400,000) × 40% = $0

The 2003 balance sheet reports:

Current assets:	
Deferred tax assets*	$ 8,000
Income tax refund receivable	$60,000
Long-term liabilities:	
Deferred tax liabilities	$88,000

*$32,000 − $24,000

The computation of 2003 income tax expense proceeds as follows:

Increase in *current* tax asset (refund)		$ (60,000)
Increase in *deferred* tax liability		
Ending balance	$112,000	
Beginning balance	(84,000)	28,000
Decrease in *deferred* tax asset		
Ending balance	$ 32,000	
Beginning balance	(188,000)	156,000
Income tax expense		$124,000

The bottom portion of the 2003 income statement (starting with pretax income):

Income before income taxes		$300,000
Income tax expense		
Current portion	$ (60,000)	
Deferred portion	184,000	124,000
Net income		$176,000

The effective income tax rate equals 41.33% ($124,000 ÷ $300,000).

COMPREHENSIVE EXAMPLE Journal Entries

2003:		
Income Tax Refund Receivable (current portion)	60,000	
Income Tax Expense	124,000	
Deferred Tax Liability		28,000
Deferred Tax Asset		156,000

Computing Cumulative Temporary Differences: An Alternative Way

To this point, we have described temporary differences as the difference between GAAP income statement items and a tax based income statement. In order to compute the cumulative temporary difference at any point in time, we had to track the temporary differences across several years. At any point in time we can also determine the cumulative temporary differences (on which deferred income taxes are computed) if we know the book basis and tax basis of assets and liabilities.

Example 9. The Hingis Co. has the following book bases and tax bases at December 31, 2001. Assume a 40% income tax rate for all computations.

		December 31, 2001 Book/Tax Basis					
		Book Basis		Tax Basis		Deferred Income Tax	
		Asset	Liability	Asset	Liability	Asset	Liability
Depreciable asset	NC*	$240,000		$160,000			$80,000 × 40% = $32,000
Warranty liability**	C		$ 40,000		$0	$40,000 × 40% = $16,000	
Litigation liability**	NC		700,000		0	$700,000 × 40% = $280,000	

*C = current, NC = noncurrent balance classification.
**The tax basis equals zero because Hingis is a cash basis tax payer and no tax liability has been accrued.

Solution. Note that the accounting system must track the book basis and tax basis of assets and liabilities for this process to work. The book basis of *depreciable assets* exceeds the tax basis by $80,000, which leads to a deferred tax liability (current) of $32,000. Cumulatively, 80,000 more in depreciation expense has been reflected on tax returns than in GAAP income statements. In the future, taxable income will exceed pretax income because only $160,000 in depreciation tax deductions will be available, while $240,000 will be deducted in income statements. The $80,000 cumulative difference is a taxable amount, and it leads to the computation of a deferred income tax liability.

For warranty and litigation liabilities, the amounts have been accrued for book purposes, but not for tax purposes. Thus, in future years, tax deductions will exceed book expenses by $40,000 (warranty liabilities) and $700,000 (litigation liabilities). The cumulative differences are deductible amounts, which lead to the computation of deferred tax assets of $16,000, and $280,000, respectively. The deferred tax asset related to the warranty liability is classified as current because the warranty liability is classified as current; the deferred tax asset related to the litigation liability is classified as noncurrent because the litigation liability is classified as noncurrent.

Financial Statement Presentation

Companies present income tax expense, current income tax payable or refund receivable, and deferred tax liabilities and assets in the financial statements. In a footnote, companies include the following information: the current and deferred components of income tax expense, separated into Federal, State, and Foreign components; a listing of the major items affecting deferred income taxes and the deferred tax amounts associated with each item; a reconciliation that demonstrates why the effective income tax rate reflected by provision for income taxes (income tax expense) is different from the statutory tax rate; and, if legislated income tax rates changed during the period, the effect of the change in rates on deferred taxes.

To illustrate how tax information is presented in the financial statements, the following information in Exhibit 6 was reported in Gannett's 1998 annual report. Three types of tax information are included in Note 7: (1) a breakdown of the provision for income taxes into current and deferred components, and federal and state components; (2) a reconciliation from the statutory tax rate to the effective tax rate; and (3) details on the major components of the deferred income tax assets and liabilities.

EXHIBIT 6 Gannett Income Tax Related Information (Modified by authors)

INCOME STATEMENT

(Thousands of dollars)	1998	1997
Income before income taxes	$1,669,413	$1,208,979
Provision for income taxes	669,500	496,300
Net income	$ 999,913	$ 712,679

BALANCE SHEET

(Thousands of dollars)	1998	1997
Current liabilities:		
Income taxes	$ 6,395	$ 12,893
Noncurrent liabilities:		
Deferred income taxes	442,359	402,254

Note 7, Income Taxes (thousands of dollars)

Provision for income taxes. The company's reported income before taxes is virtually all from domestic sources. The provision for income taxes consists of the following:

Federal:		
Current	$ 545,878	$ 443,334
Deferred	34,783	(12,060)
	$ 580,661	$ 431,274
State:		
Current	$ 83,517	$ 67,210
Deferred	5,322	(2,184)
	$ 88,839	$ 65,026
Total	$ 669,500	$ 496,300

Effective tax rate. The provision for income taxes exceeds the U.S. federal statutory rate as a result of the following differences:

U.S. statutory rate	35.0%	35.0%
State/other income taxes, net of federal income tax benefit	3.5%	3.5%
Goodwill amortization not deductible for tax purposes	2.3%	2.5%
Other, net	(0.7%)	0.1%
Effective tax rate	40.1%	41.1%

Deferred tax assets/liabilities. Deferred income taxes reflect temporary differences in recognition of revenue and expense for tax reporting and financial statement purposes. Deferred income tax liabilities and assets were composed of the following at the end of 1998 and 1997.

	1998	1997
Liabilities		
Accelerated depreciation	$392,374	$410,264
Accelerated amortization of deductible intangibles	109,807	106,498
Pension	16,211	16,883
Other	120,475	52,073
Total deferred tax liabilities	$638,867	$585,718
Assets		
Accrued compensation costs	$ (55,718)	$ (41,615)
Postretirement medical and life	(120,177)	(121,712)
Other	(20,613)	(20,137)
Total deferred tax assets	$(196,508)	$(183,464)
Net deferred tax liabilities	$ 442,359	$ 402,254

Statement of Cash Flows Presentation

Income taxes are treated as an operating activity in the statement of cash flows. If a company presents operating activities under the direct method, then the amounts paid during the current period are shown as cash outflows. However, if the indirect method is used (see Chapter 9 for a discussion of the indirect method), an adjustment is made for the difference between income tax expense and income taxes paid. The amount of the adjustment is the difference between the beginning and ending balances in Income Taxes Payable. For example, based on the information presented below, a $30,000 adjustment would be made in the operating activities section to *add* the increase in the income taxes payable.

Income taxes payable:	
Beginning balance	$ 65,000
Add income tax expense	350,000
Deduct income taxes paid	320,000
Ending balance	$ 95,000

Changes in deferred income tax accounts have no cash basis effects. Therefore, no cash flow effect is reported in the operating activities section if the direct method is used. However, if the indirect method is used, the differences between the beginning and ending balances in deferred income tax assets and liabilities are shown as reconciling items as well.

Southwest Airlines' Financial Statements

Southwest Airlines' 1998 financial statements are provided in Appendix C. Review the following information provided in those financial statements: Income statement—provision for income taxes; Balance sheet—deferred income taxes (both current assets and noncurrent liabilities); Statement of cash flows—income taxes paid; Note 10—Income Taxes; and MD&A—Income Taxes.

Balance sheet presentation. The 1998 and 1997 balance sheets report current deferred income tax assets of $20,734,000 and $18,843,000, respectively, with no valuation allowance reported in the balance sheets or notes. Also, the 1998 and 1997 balance sheets report noncurrent deferred income tax liabilities of $549,207,000 and $438,981,000, respectively. Note 10 reveals that the items associated with 1998 deferred tax liabilities are accelerated depreciation ($641,673,000), scheduled airframe maintenance ($40,073,000—Note 1 discusses accounting policy for overhauls), and other ($95,485,000). Items associated with 1998 deferred tax assets are deferred gains from aircraft sale and leaseback ($107,157,000), capital and operating leases ($61,275,000), and other ($80,326,000). Combining the 1998 current deferred income tax asset of $20,734,000 with the noncurrent deferred income tax liability of $549,207,000 equals $528,473,000, which is equal to the net deferred tax liability reported in footnote 10.

Statement of cash flows. The statement of cash flows shows that Southwest paid $147,447,000 in income taxes in 1998, and $107,066,000 in 1997.

Income statement presentation. The income statement reports 1998 income tax expense (provision for income taxes) of $271,681,000, which reflects a 38.5% effective tax rate ($271,681,000 ÷ $705,112,000). The comparative effective income tax rates for 1997 and 1996 are 38.5% and 39.3%, respectively. Note 10 reveals that the current Federal and State portions of the 1998 provision for income taxes are $143,989,000 and $19,357,000, respectively. These amounts reflect the current year's tax liability to Federal and State governments.

Reconciliation of Statutory to Effective Income Tax Rates. Note 10 also details the reasons that the 1998 income statement's effective income tax rate is 38.5%, rather than 35%. The effective tax rate increase from 35% to 38.5% is related to nondeductible items (i.e., permanent differences), state income taxes, and other items. The major influence is state income taxes, net of federal benefit, which increased the 1998 effective tax rate by 2.9% ($20,445,000 ÷ 705,112,000).

Chapter Summary

Corporate taxation in the form of sales taxes on purchases, property taxes, and income taxes is a significant profit-reducing expense. Tax expense is conceptually no different from any other expense in that it is generated by decreases in tax-related assets and increases in tax-related liabilities. One of the most important concepts from this chapter is that the accrual model dictates income tax recognition. Cash payments for current taxes payable and cash receipts from refunds currently receivable are not the sole determinants of income tax expense. Future expected tax payments and tax savings generated from current period transactions are equally important in determining the income tax expense of the current period.

Deferred tax accounting has traveled a controversial path, and many ideas exist on how deferred taxes should be measured. The current GAAP treatment of deferred taxes is consistent with the treatments accorded other assets and liabilities, with one major exception. Deferred tax assets and liabilities classified as long-term are not discounted in a present value computation. That is, the amounts shown are gross expected cash inflows and outflows, not their present values. This fact, coupled with the notion that many firms are able to defer their tax payments for a long time, suggest that many deferred tax liabilities should be substantially reduced by a present value factor.

Key Terms

Questions

Q1. **Sales Tax Collections.** Should sales tax collections be treated as revenue? Why or why not?

Q2. **Sales Tax Payments.** Sales tax payments are costs. When should they be recorded as assets? When should they be expensed? Give an example of each kind of treatment.

Q3. **Property Tax Payments.** How should property taxes paid on an idle factory (i.e., one that is *not* generating revenues) be treated?

Q4. **Pretax versus Taxable Income.** Are pretax financial income and taxable income conceptually the same? How is each determined?

Q5. **Book/Tax Differences.** List and describe three transactions that would be treated differently under GAAP and the IRC.

Q6. **Temporary versus Permanent Differences.** Compare and contrast temporary differences and permanent differences.

Q7. **Compute Current Year's Tax Liability.** What is the formula for computing the *current year's tax liability*?

Q8. **Deferred Tax Assets and Liabilities.** Other than the current tax liability, what are two categories of transactions that create tax assets and liabilities?

Q9. **Originating Difference.** What is an originating difference? Give a specific example.

Q10. **Reversing Difference.** What is a reversing difference? Give a specific example.

Q11. **Tax Planning.** What conditions determine whether a corporation would rather pay taxes in the current or future periods?

Q12. **Book/Tax Differences.** Fill in the following table with the effect of each originating difference on (1) the current tax liability (as opposed to what it would be if the book treatment were used for tax purposes), and (2) the creation of future taxable and deductible amounts.

Originating Difference	Revenue Item	Expense Item
Book > Tax	*Cell 1*	*Cell 2*
Tax > Book	*Cell 3*	*Cell 4*

Q13. **Net Operating Losses.** What are tax loss carrybacks and carryforwards? What is their effect on income tax expense?

Q14. **Deferred Tax Asset Valuation Allowance.** What is the deferred tax asset valuation allowance? How is it used?

Q15. **Deferred Tax Asset.** Give two examples each of "positive" and "negative" evidence of a deferred tax asset's realizability.

Q16. **Deferred Taxes Computation.** Are deferred tax asset and liability measurements based on *enacted* or *expected* tax rates? What would be the balance sheet and income statement effects if either of these rates increased by 2%?

Q17. **Deferred Taxes Balance Sheet Valuation.** Describe the process by which current vs. noncurrent balance sheet classification is obtained for deferred tax assets and liabilities.

Q18. **Alternative Minimum Tax (AMT).** What is the AMT? Does it generate a deferred tax asset or liability?

Q19. **Balance Sheet Classification.** How should the following items be classified on a year-end balance sheet?

a. Year-end accrual for income taxes payable for the current year.

b. Year-end accrual for income tax refund receivable pursuant to a net operating loss carryback.

c. Year-end amounts of current deferred income taxes payable = $75,000; current deferred income tax asset = $225,000; noncurrent deferred income taxes payable = $1,400,000; and noncurrent deferred income tax assets = $800,000.

Q20. **Statement of Cash Flows: The Indirect Method.** When the indirect method is used, how are changes in the following items reflected in the statement of cash flows: income taxes payable, deferred income tax assets, and deferred income tax liabilities?

Short Problems

1. **Deferred Tax Consequences—Bad Debts Expense.** In its first year of operations, Backyard Preschool Books had $60,000 of pretax income. Financial and tax accounting principles were identical except for the treatment of $5,000 of bad debt expense, which was deducted in determining pretax income but is not deductible until the following year in determining taxable income.

a. Backyard pays taxes in the month after year-end. Assuming a 40% current and future income tax rate, what was the amount of current income taxes payable?

b. What is the year-end balance of deferred taxes? Is it an asset or liability?

c. Prepare the income statement disclosures for Backyard beginning with pretax income.

Journal Entry Option: Prepare the tax-related journal entries for the first year of operations.

2. **Deferred Tax Consequences—Construction Contracts.** Phelps Bridge, located in Alaska, constructs custom bridges on interstate roadways. The company specializes in smaller bridges over streams and creeks in rural areas where the contracting municipality wants to preserve the natural lay of the land. The company is able to start and complete all bridges within a very short period of time, usually 30 to 60 days. Due to the climate, Phelps does not accept bridge projects between November 1 and April 1. Phelps has received a contract to build a large bridge over a major river in Oregon. The project is expected to generate $9 million in profit over a three-year period. (Estimated profit is $3 million in each year.) Under generally accepted accounting principles, Phelps uses the percentage of completion method to account for profit recognition on the project. However, Phelps must use the completed contract method for tax purposes, in which all $9 million is taxable in the third year. Assume (1) a 40% income tax rate, (2) no other revenues or expenses during the three years, (3) and that Phelps makes no estimated quarterly tax payments, but instead, pays current taxes payable on the first day of the following year (i.e., the tax bill for year 3 is paid on January 1 of year 4). Prepare the income statement disclosure of income tax expense for each of the three years, beginning with pretax financial income. Also show the balance sheet disclosures with respect to this transaction for each of the three years.

Journal Entry Option: Prepare the tax-related journal entries for each of the four years. Don't forget the tax payments.

3. **Deferred Tax Consequences—Accrued Revenues.** QuickDraw performs drafting services for local builders. At the end of its first year of operations, QuickDraw had performed $10,000 in services (revenue under GAAP) for which cash had not been received (and is not yet taxable under IRC rules). Assuming a 35% tax rate, was a deferred tax asset or liability created? What is the effect of its recognition on income tax expense of the period?

4. **Deferred Tax Consequences—Warranties.** Make-It-Right Corporation produces high-quality kitchen appliances on which a one-year warranty is offered. Warranty deductions for book and tax purposes are as follows:

Year	Book Expense	Tax Deduction
1999	$40,000	$ 0
2000	50,000	35,000
2001	50,000	45,000
2002	50,000	60,000

Assuming a 35% tax rate and pretax income of $300,000 in each year, compute the year-end deferred tax balances and income tax expense for each year.

Journal Entry Option: Prepare the tax-related journal entries for each year.

5. **Deferred Tax Consequences—Life Insurance Premiums.** During the year, Valdez Co. paid life insurance premiums of $400,000 on its president, vice presidents, and members of its board of directors. These life insurance premiums are not tax deductible. Assuming a 40% tax rate and pretax income of $1,500,000, compute income tax expense for the period.

Journal Entry Option: Prepare the tax-related journal entry for the year.

6. **Net Operating Losses.** Good Luck Enterprises began operations in 1999, and generated the following pretax incomes and losses over a six-year period:

Year	Pretax Income (Loss)
1999	$200,000
2000	250,000
2001	(500,000)
2002	100,000
2003	300,000
2004	400,000

Assume a tax rate of 35% for all years, and *no temporary or permanent differences* (i.e., taxable income and pretax income are equal in all years). Using the following schedule, prepare the income statement disclosures for income tax expense in each year. Also, describe the changes in the tax assets and liabilities that determine income tax expense.

GOOD LUCK ENTERPRISES
Income Statement Disclosure, 1999–2004

	1999	2000	2001	2002	2003	2004	Total
Pretax income (loss)							
Current portion of tax expense							
Deferred portion of tax expense							
Benefit from loss carryback (reported as Tax Refund in the asset section of the balance sheet)							
Benefit from loss carryforward (reported as Deferred Tax Asset in the balance sheet)							
Net income (loss)							

Journal Entry Option: Prepare the tax-related journal entries for 2000, 2001, and 2002.

7. **Net Operating Losses.** Goobie Enterprises, which began operation in 1998, generated the following pretax incomes and losses over a six-year period:

Year	Pretax Income (Loss)
1998	$(200,000)
1999	50,000
2000	(100,000)
2001	100,000
2002	300,000
2003	300,000

Assume a tax rate of 35% for all years, and no temporary or permanent differences (i.e., taxable income and pretax income are equal in all years). Using the following schedule, prepare the income statement disclosures for income tax expense in each year, and describe the changes in the tax assets and liabilities that determine income tax expense. Assume the NOLs are carried back whenever possible, and that 100% of any deferred income tax asset related to a NOL is recognized.

GOOBIE ENTERPRISES
Income Statement Disclosure, 1998–2003

	1998	1999	2000	2001	2002	2003	Total
Pretax income (loss)							
Current portion of tax expense							
Deferred portion of tax expense							
Benefit from loss carryback (reported as Tax Refund in the asset section of the balance sheet)							
Benefit from loss carryforward (reported as Deferred Tax Asset in the balance sheet)							
Net income (loss)							

Journal Entry Option: Prepare the tax-related journal entries for each year.

8. **Deferred Income Taxes—Changes in Tax Rates.** Special Industries had the following deferred tax assets and liabilities at December 31, 2001:

Cumulative deductible amounts = $100,000; Deferred tax assets = $35,000
Cumulative taxable amounts = $200,000; Deferred tax liabilities = $70,000

In January 2002, Congress voted to increase future corporate tax rates from 35% to 36%, effective January 1, 2002. Compute the effect of the tax rate change on income tax expense for 2002.

Journal Entry Option: Prepare the journal entry to record the tax rate change.

9. **Deferred Income Taxes—Multiple Temporary Differences.** Mooseneck Co. computed the following deferred tax assets and liabilities at December 31, 2001:

	Deferred Income Tax	
	Asset	**Liability**
Bad debts expense (related to accounts receivable)	$ 60,000	
Depreciation expense		$200,000
Subscriptions revenue (12-month subscriptions)		40,000
Warranty expense		
Current warranty obligations	25,000	
Long-term warranty obligations	30,000	
Estimated litigation loss (estimated to reverse in 2002)	100,000	
Total	$215,000	$240,000

Required: Prepare the 2001 balance sheet disclosures of deferred taxes for Mooseneck Co.

10. **Deferred Income Taxes—Multiple Book/Tax Differences.** Dunn Co. began operations in 2000. Pretax income determined under GAAP was $1,200,000 in 2000, $250,000 in 2001, and $520,000 in 2002. The tax rate is 40% in each year. Additional information is as follows:

	Year	Tax Records	Per Books
Depreciation expense	2000	$250,000	$ 80,000
	2001	200,000	80,000
	2002	150,000	80,000
Warranty expense recognition (all warranties are one year in length)	2000	$ 0	$ 60,000
	2001	60,000	60,000
	2002	70,000	60,000
Litigation losses (expected to be paid in 2002)	2000	$ 0	$200,000
	2001	0	0
	2002	*200,000	0
Municipal bond investment revenue (nontaxable)	2000	$ 0	$ 10,000
	2001	0	10,000
	2002	0	10,000

*Amount recognized in 2000 for book purposes

Required: Prepare the income statement and balance sheet disclosures for Dunn Co. for each year.

Analytical and Comprehensive Problems

11. **Effect of Book/Tax Differences on Financial Statements.** Complete the following table, using *I* for increase, *D* for decrease, and *NE* for no effect. Concentrate only on the effect of the item, and not on the transaction that gave rise to the item.

	Assets	Liabilities	Income Tax Expense
Temporary differences:			
Current period book revenue exceeds tax revenue			
Current period book expense exceeds tax expense			
Current period tax revenue exceeds book revenue			
Current period tax expense exceeds book expense			
Permanent differences:			
Current period book revenue exceeds tax revenue			
Current period book expense exceeds tax expense			
Current period tax revenue exceeds book revenue			
Current period tax expense exceeds book expense			
Net operating losses:			
Carryforward			
Carryback			
Realization of net operating loss carryforward from a prior period			
Other:			
Increase in enacted tax rates			
Increase in deferred tax asset valuation allowance			

12. **Net Operating Losses—Tax Planning.** Monarch Corp. was very profitable during its first several years of operations. Stock prices rose rapidly as investors developed expectations about a rosy future for Monarch's earnings picture. Monarch's success was driven by the creation of a synthetic compound that, when sprayed on the interior of tents, substantially reduced the propensity for the tent to mold and mildew. Also, Monarch recently developed a completely different compound that has similar properties when added to the dyes used in lawn furniture manufacture. In fact, management expects that future earnings and future earnings growth will be dominated by the new product.

In 2000, it was discovered that the original compound was the cause of respiratory problems in campers using Monarch's treatment on their tents. In a class action suit, Monarch sustained a loss of such magnitude that the 2000 net loss was $3,000,000. Since Monarch has no book/tax differences, the 2000 tax net operating loss was also $3,000,000. Monarch had sufficient taxable income in the prior two years to absorb the $3,000,000 loss (i.e., taxable income in the 1998–1999 period exceeded $3,000,000). Income tax rates were 30% in 1998 and 1999. Assume any tax consequences in the NOL carryforward scenario occur at the end of the year.

In 2000, Congress passed a law that increased tax rates to 38% in 2001, and 40% in 2002. Monarch expects to earn $2.5 million in each of those two years. Assuming an 8% weighted-average cost of capital, prepare an analysis to determine whether Monarch should (1) carry the NOL back two years before carrying forward any remaining NOL for 20 years, or (2) forgo the two-year carryback option and carry the NOL forward 20 years. Also, compute income tax expense for 2000, 2001, and 2002 under both scenarios.

13. **Deferred Income Tax Asset Valuation Allowance.** GeeWeeSee Corp., a highly profitable company over the last two decades, prides itself on generating a smooth earnings series through time. Should GeeWeeSee ever have a balance in its deferred tax asset valuation account? Use the positive and negative evidence in the chapter to support your answer.

14. **Deferred Income Tax Liabilities.** How are deferred income tax liabilities different from other balance sheet liabilities such as bonds payable and warranties payable? How are they similar?

http://

15. **Texas Instruments.** The Texas Instruments' 1998 financial statements appear at the text Web site (http://baginski.swcollege.com). Review the income statement (income tax provision, discontinued operations, and extraordinary item), balance sheet (deferred income taxes in current asset and noncurrent liability sections), and income taxes note. After reading this information, answer the following questions. (Be sure to use the financial statement amounts, which are in millions of dollars.)
    a. **Deferred Income Tax Assets and Liabilities.** What are the ending deferred income tax balances on the balance sheet? What are the total *gross* amounts of total deferred income tax assets? Of total deferred income tax liabilities? What is the amount, if any, of the deferred income tax valuation account? Several items are listed as creating deferred income tax assets or liabilities. Explain why the following items have deferred income tax consequences: accrued retirement costs; accrued expenses; operating loss and credit carryforwards; and property, plant and equipment.
    b. **Income Tax Expense.** What is total 1998 income tax expense (provision for income taxes)? What are the amounts of the separate components of income tax expense? Did TI pay income taxes for the 1998 year?
    c. **Effective Income Tax Rate.** What is the 1998 effective income tax rate reflected in the income statement? What are the major reasons that this rate is not 35%, the Federal statutory income tax rate?

16. **Comprehensive Deferred Income Tax Problem—Two Temporary Differences.** The Jennings Co. began operations in 2000. The following 2000 information is available.

Pretax income	$200,000
Depreciation expense:	
Book	40,000
Tax	60,000
Warranty expense:	
Book	30,000
Tax	5,000
Tax rate	40%

No other book/tax differences existed. The depreciable asset was purchased on January 1, 2000, at a cost of $200,000, and with an estimated life of 5 years, and estimated salvage value of $0. The book/tax depreciation differences on the $200,000 depreciable asset for 2000 and subsequent years will be as follows:

	Tax Purposes	Financial Reporting Purposes
2000	$ 60,000	$ 40,000
2001	50,000	40,000
2002	40,000	40,000
2003	30,000	40,000
2004	20,000	40,000
Total	$200,000	$200,000

Assume that the 2000 warranty expense difference is expected to reverse by $15,000 in 2002, and $10,000 in 2003. Scheduled tax rates are 40% in all years. Throughout the problem, assume that 100% of any deferred tax asset value will be realized in future years.

a. Compute income tax expense and income taxes payable for 2000. Prepare a partial income statement starting with income before income taxes to illustrate the presentation of income tax expense (show current and deferred components separately). Show the correct deferred income tax balance sheet presentation. Use the following formats to document your work.

INCOME TAXES PAYABLE

		Temporary difference labeled as:	
	2000 Amounts	**Taxable or Deductible**	**Originating or Reversing**
Pretax income			
Permanent differences*			
Temporary differences*			
Taxable income			
× Income tax rate			
Income taxes payable			

*List book/tax differences used to reconcile from pretax income to taxable income.

DEFERRED INCOME TAX COMPUTATIONS

		Current Year		**Temporary Differences***		**Future Consequences of Current and Past Transactions**
	**T,D*	*2000*	*1/1/00*	*2000*	*12/31/00*	*2000 and beyond*
Pretax income						
**						
Taxable income						
Tax rate						
Income taxes payable						

*Temporary differences are labeled as T = taxable amounts, or D = deductible amounts.
**List individual temporary differences.

b. Assume that 2001 pretax income was $400,000. Also in 2001, (1) tax and book depreciation amounts were as projected in 2000, and (2) the $25,000, 2000 warranty expense difference was still expected to reverse as in the 2000 calculations (i.e., $15,000 in 2002, and $10,000 in 2003). In 2001, Jennings had new book warranty expense of $20,000 and tax warranty expense of $12,000. This difference is a *new originating temporary difference,* and it is unrelated to the 2000 warranty expense. This $8,000 difference is expected to reverse in 2003. Compute income tax expense and income taxes payable for 2001. Prepare a partial income statement starting with income before income taxes to illustrate the presentation of income tax expense (show current and deferred components separately). Show the correct deferred income tax balance sheet presentation. Use the previous formats to document your work (income taxes payable and deferred income taxes payable).

c. Assume that after the 2001 financial statements are issued, in January 2002 the U.S. Congress enacts new tax legislation that changes the Federal 2002 tax rate to 42% for 2002 and beyond. Under *SFAS No. 109,* the deferred tax consequences must be reflected in the period in which the tax rate change was enacted. Accordingly, Jennings would make an adjusting entry in January 2002 to reflect the change in the 2002 beginning deferred income tax balances. Show the correct deferred income tax balance sheet presentation after the January 2002 adjusting journal entry.

CFA Exam-Type Problems

17. White Company has net temporary differences between tax and book income of $90 million, resulting in deferred taxes of $30.6 million. Under *SFAS No. 109,* an increase in the tax rate would have the following impact on deferred taxes and net income: (CFA adapted, with slight modifications by authors)

Deferred Taxes	Net Income
a. Increase	No effect
b. Increase	Decrease
c. No effect	No effect
d. No effect	Decrease

18. When a deferred tax liability account "reverses": (CFA adapted, with slight modifications by authors)
    a. there is a cash drain.
    b. the actual tax bill is lower than the expense in the income statement.
    c. the actual tax paid is the same as the expense in the income statement.
    d. cash outflow is lowered by the amount of the reversal.

19. Which of the following statements about deferred taxes is *true*? Deferred taxes: (CFA adapted)
    a. will decrease only when a cash payment is made.
    b. are not found on the liability side of the balance sheet.
    c. result from permanent differences between taxable and reported earnings.
    d. arising from depreciation of a particular asset will ultimately reduce to zero as the item is depreciated.

20. Differences between taxable income and pretax accounting income arising from transactions that, under applicable tax laws and regulations, will not be offset by corresponding differences or "turn around" in future periods are described as: (CFA adapted)
    a. interperiod tax allocations.
    b. intraperiod tax allocations.
    c. permanent differences.
    d. timing differences.

21. During 2001, the Sanchez Co. incurred and recognized $30,000 in warranty expense on its income statement, but only reported $15,000 in warranty expense on the income tax return, an amount equal to the $15,000 in warranty costs. Sanchez's income tax rate is 40%. This difference leads to the following in the 2001 financial statements: (Author constructed)
    a. deferred income tax asset of $15,000.
    b. deferred income tax liability of $15,000.
    c. deferred income tax asset of $6,000.
    d. deferred income tax liability of $6,000.

22. In its 2001 income statement, the Kim Co. reported municipal bond income of $30,000. However, the bond income is not taxable. Kim's income tax rate is 40%. This difference leads to the following in the 2001 financial statements: (Author constructed)
    a. deferred income tax of $0.
    b. deferred income tax liability of $12,000.
    c. deferred income tax asset of $12,000.
    d. deferred income tax liability of $30,000.

Objectives

1 Explain how employee compensation affects corporate wealth.
2 Account for compensated absences.
3 Describe the economics underlying pensions and other post-retirement benefits.
4 Account for pensions and other post-retirement benefits.
5 Explain the financial statement and note disclosures for pensions and other post-retirement benefits.
6 Account for stock-based compensation.

Chapter 12

Special Compensation Arrangements

1 Explain how employee compensation affects corporate wealth.

For many corporations, employee compensation represents one of the largest ongoing expenditures. Compensation can affect corporate wealth in three ways. First, compensation can benefit the current period by motivating employees to generate current period revenue. A good example is a sales commission paid to a salesperson who sells a specified amount of the company's product. Second, compensated direct and indirect labor in a manufacturing setting benefits current and future periods by creating saleable products. Third, compensation can be used solely to create loyal, highly trained employees.

Accounting treatments vary for typical compensation arrangements. In the case of sales commissions, sales commissions expense is matched to current period sales revenue. For direct and indirect labor to create saleable products, the labor cost is capitalized as finished goods inventory (an asset), and then expensed when the inventory is sold. This treatment matches cost of goods sold with sales revenue. In the case of compensation for the purpose of creating loyal, highly trained employees, the general rule involves expensing the payments in the current period unless reliable estimates of future benefits can be obtained.

In this chapter, we investigate the accounting treatments accorded special compensation arrangements. Each of these arrangements involves deferred compensation of some kind. In the following sections, we consider compensated absences, pensions and other post-retirement benefits (e.g., health insurance), and stock compensation plans.

Compensated Absences

2 Account for compensated absences.

The fact that employees earn future benefits from current service is a central theme in this chapter, and this fact can be easily illustrated by considering compensated absences. Employers provide benefits to employees in the form of vacation pay and sick pay. These benefits are linked to current service by the fact that vacation time and sick pay accruals are typically a function of the length of employee service. For example, one year of service may entitle the employee to two weeks of vacation and five sick days. As much as one would like to believe that employers have generosity as the motivation behind such entitlements, sound economic analysis would treat compensated absences as part of the overall compensation package that must be justified by revenue generation.

Because of the often explicit (and sometimes implicit) link of compensated absences to current service, compensation expense and the related liability for compensated absences should be accrued in the current period if the employer expects to pay the compensation (i.e., *payment is probable*) and the *amount of payment is reasonably estimable*. Not all vacation and sick pay plans are related to current service—some are tied to future service periods, some rights vest or accumulate from period to period (whether taken or not), and some rights do not vest or accumulate. In 1980, the FASB issued *SFAS No. 43,* "Accounting for Compensated Absences," which specifies that *accrual of compensation expense and the related liability should take place only if **all** of the following conditions are met:*

- the obligation is related to services already rendered,
- the rights are vested regardless of whether employment continues, or the rights accumulate from period to period if not taken,
- payment is probable, and
- the amount of payment is reasonably estimable.

If the first three conditions are met but the fourth is not, then note disclosure is required. Vesting is a legal concept that entitles the employee to the benefit even if the employee leaves the job. If benefits are not vested, the employee is not entitled to the benefits when leaving a job.

A special provision exists for sick pay that accumulates but does not vest. In this case, accrual of compensation expense related to sick pay is allowable but not required. The reason for this special provision is that nonvested sick pay depends on whether the employee becomes sick—a future event. We believe that accrual is appropriate for nonvested plans for which benefits accumulate if the employer can reasonably estimate the amount expected to be paid.

Example 1. The Fisher Consulting Group has 20 employees each paid $1,000 per week. A year of service allows an employee to take two weeks of paid vacation and five sick days during the next year. If the vacation is not used up in the next year, it can be traded for cash or accumulated with subsequent years' vacation credits. The sick days lapse if not taken in the next year.

Solution. Fisher must accrue $40,000 of compensation expense for vacation benefits (20 employees × $1,000 per week × 2 weeks) and report a $40,000 (most likely, current) liability for compensated absences. Because the sick pay neither vests nor accumulates, Fisher would make no accrual. If, however, sick pay is vested such that any unused sick days may be carried over to subsequent years, then Fisher would also make an accrual for sick pay expense.

EXAMPLE 1 Journal Entry

Compensation Expense	40,000	
Liability for Compensated Absences		40,000

Pensions and Other Post-Retirement Benefits

3 Describe the economics underlying pensions and other post-retirement benefits.

Most employees derive a substantial portion of their compensation from promises made by employers to provide retirement benefits. The next several sections deal with pension benefits. We also provide a brief summary of similar accounting methods applied to other post-retirement benefits.[1]

To provide for retiree pension benefits, employers sponsor either *defined contribution plans* or *defined benefit plans.*[2] In a ***defined contribution plan,* employers promise to place a certain percentage of an employee's earnings into an investment vehicle as specified by the employee.** During the past decade, more employers have begun to offer defined contribution plans, typically 401(k) plans. Most colleges and universities also offer defined contribution plans, typically 401(b) plans. For example, a college professor typically participates in a defined contribution plan. Based on a percentage of the professor's salary, the university makes a cash contribution each year to an investment company, such as TIAA/CREF. The university's obligation under the plan is satisfied once the funds are placed into the investment account. The university does *not* guarantee a given defined benefit payment when the professor retires. Instead, the fund balance at retirement depends on the investing success of the investment company and the professor's allocation of the investment across different types of investments (e.g., stocks or bonds). The accounting for a defined contribution plan is quite easy. Because of the plan contract, the professor's current service generates the university's obligation to make periodic payments, and the university records pension expense for the amount of the defined contribution obligation. The operating section of the statement of cash flows reports the contribution as a cash outflow in the period in which the funds are contributed to the investment company.

In a ***defined benefit plan,* employers incur the obligation to provide a definite pension payment throughout the employee's retirement period.** The final obligation is determined by the terms of a pension plan, which are frequently negotiated by employers and employees. Many factors affect the determination of the final obligation, including employee longevity, status at retirement, and final pay. The complexity of determining the obligation and assigning pension cost to particular periods creates complex and controversial accounting.

Normally, a corporation hires a third party trustee (usually an insurance or other financial services company) to administer the plan. Each year, the employer makes an annual contribution to the trustee, which is invested in plan assets by the trustee. The trustee keeps records of the plan's obligations to individual employees, and makes pension payments to eligible employees. In some cases, employers may contribute to a multi-employer plan that is set up for a certain class of union members. For example, many trucking firms contribute to a multi-employer plan for the benefit of Teamster union members. The Teamster's union then administers the plan on behalf of the Teamster members.[3]

The Economics of Pension Accounting—A Defined Benefit Plan

4 Account for pensions and other post-retirement benefits.

The underlying economic explanation of defined benefit pension plans involves the understanding and comparison of two key amounts—***pension obligation*** and ***pension assets.***

1. *SFAS No. 87* (issued December 1985) addresses pension plan accounting. *SFAS No. 106* (issued December 1990) deals with post-retirement benefits other than pensions. *SFAS No. 132* (issued February 1998) standardizes disclosure requirements for pension plans and other post-retirement benefit plans.
2. The 1999 *Accounting Trends & Techniques* reports that of 600 firms surveyed, 458 disclosed defined benefit pension plans. (The number of firms having defined contribution plans is not reported.)
3. The presence of multi-employer plans can become a major issue during collective bargaining. For example, it was widely reported in the financial press that a key issue in the 1997 United Parcel Service (UPS) strike was that UPS wanted to withdraw from a multi-employer plan and set up its own plan for its employees. In the strike settlement, UPS agreed to continue to use the multi-employer plan.

Pension Obligation—A Liability In a typical defined benefit arrangement, employees are promised a payment or payments when they retire based on some *plan formula*. A typical ***plan formula*** **considers the years of employee service, a credit for each year of annual service (usually expressed as a percentage), and the final salary at retirement date:**

$$\text{Annual retirement benefits} = \begin{array}{c}\text{Years of service}\\ \text{at retirement}\end{array} \times \text{Annual credit (\%)} \times \begin{array}{c}\text{Salary at retirement date}\\ \text{(or average salary over some period}\\ \text{of time such as last three years)}\end{array}$$

The sequence of events in the plan is illustrated by the following time line:

At any point on the time line, one can apply theoretical, long-term liability valuation rules and compute the *pension obligation as the present value of the annual retirement benefit payments expected to be paid in future years because employees have worked for the company through the current date* (i.e., not including expected retirement benefits to be earned in *future* years). Because of the complexity of the present value computation, an actuarial firm is usually employed to compute the present value of retirement benefit payments. The amount of the actual payments to be made in the future are uncertain and are affected to a great extent by employee mortality.

The FASB defines three possible measures of the pension obligation:

1. Projected benefit obligation (PBO)
2. Accumulated benefit obligation (ABO)
3. Vested benefit obligation (VBO).

Calculated according to the benefit formula (using expected future salary levels), ***PBO*** **is the actuarially determined present value of estimated retirement payments to be paid to employees because employees have worked and earned benefits until the current date. The discount (interest) rate used for the present value computation** is called the ***settlement rate,*** which represents the current market rate at which an outside party would effectively settle the obligation. The current year-end settlement rate is disclosed in the notes to the financial statements.

PBO is based on a projection of estimated future salary levels because most benefit plan formulas are based on final pay. ***ABO*** is identical to PBO in all respects except that ABO is **based on the current salary level rather than an estimated future salary level** (i.e., the expected salary at retirement is deemed to be the current salary). Thus, ABO is substantially smaller than PBO. ***VBO*** is also based on current salary levels, but **represents only the vested portion of ABO.** Recent pension laws have caused rapid vesting, which leads to a VBO that is only slightly smaller than the ABO for companies with a relatively young work force. To summarize, the three amounts of pension benefit obligation reconcile as follows:

Vested benefit obligation
+ Provision for nonvested benefits
Accumulated benefit obligation
+ Provision for increased salary levels
Projected benefit obligation

It is the FASB's position that PBO is the best measure for the pension liability if the pension plan is based on final pay. Accordingly, nearly all calculations use PBO as the measure of the pension liability. All three benefit obligation amounts are frequently disclosed in the company's pension plan footnote.

Pension Assets In order to have the funds available to make pension payments when due, employers accumulate pension assets by either (1) setting aside funds for the purpose (self-administration of the plan), or (2) making cash payments to a plan trustee with the expectation that the trustee will invest the cash and increase the fund by earnings on the investments. **If the employer self-administers the plan, it is referred to as an *unfunded plan*. If a plan trustee is used, the plan is considered a *funded plan*.** *Unless otherwise noted, we assume all plans are administered by a third party trustee.*

Pension fund assets are measured at their fair market value (FMV) at the end of each year. In financial reporting, employers use either the year-end fair market value or the ***market-related fair value,*** which is **an average fair market value over a period of time** (often five years). Determining the fair value of the assets in the fund is usually not a problem because prudent investing of fund assets generally yields funds comprised of cash and widely held, often-traded securities.

The employer and third party trustee, in consultation with an actuary, make planning decisions based upon an assumption about the *expected long-term rate of return on plan assets.* This expected rate is disclosed in the notes to the financial statements. The following information provides a summary of (1) the expected long-term rate of return on plan assets, (2) the year-end settlement rate, and (3) the assumed rate of compensation increase reported in actual financial statements.

For the 600 companies surveyed, the 1999 *Accounting Trends & Techniques* reported the following information about defined benefit pension plans:

	Expected Long-Term Rate of Return On Plan Assets	Assumed Discount (Settlement Rate) on Plan Obligations	Assumed Rate of Compensation Increase
Rate	**Companies Reporting**	**Companies Reporting**	**Companies Reporting**
≤4.5%	0	0	256
5.0%	1	1	115
5.5%	0	4	22
6.0%	4	17	17
6.5%	3	194	2
7.0%	8	201	2
7.5%	10	27	1
8.0%	36	6	2
8.5%	48	1	1
9.0%	135	0	0
9.5%	103	0	0
10.0%	67	0	0
≥10.5%	28	1	1
Nondisclosing	15	6	39
Total	458	458	458

The Economic Status of the Plan—The Theoretical Balance Sheet Implications of Pensions

The economic status of the plan is determined by comparing the two economic amounts, the PBO and the FMV of plan assets:

PBO > FMV of plan assets → Plan is underfunded *(net obligation)*
PBO < FMV of plan assets → Plan is overfunded *(net asset)*

Conceptually, the relationship between PBO and FMV of plan assets represents the balance sheet implications of the pension plan. A pension plan has either a net obligation (i.e., is underfunded) or a net asset (i.e., is overfunded) depending on the relationship between PBO and the FMV of the plan assets at any point in time. In the following sections, we discuss why the employer's balance sheet probably does not reflect this economic fact.

Changes in the Economic Status of the Plan During the Year—The Theoretical Income Statement Implications of Pensions

To understand the economic effects of the pension plan on the employer's income statement, we need to concentrate on what *changes* the economic status of the plan. Because the economic status is a net asset or a net liability, changes in the status caused by nonowner transactions represent theoretical income statement effects.

Changes in PBO—The Pension Plan Liability Five events potentially change the projected benefit obligation (PBO) during a given period: service cost, interest on PBO, prior service cost, liability (actuarial) gains and losses, and benefit payments to retirees. We separately discuss each event below.

Service cost—*employees earn benefits in the current year.* By working one additional year, employees earn an increase in future benefits (see the typical plan formula shown earlier in the chapter). The actuarially-determined present value of the increase in future benefits represents **an increase in the employer's pension liability.** This liability increase is called ***service cost.***

Interest on PBO—*time passes.* PBO represents the present value of future benefits payable to retirees. The process of computing present value involves removing interest from gross future cash outflows. As time passes without the liability being extinguished, the liability moves from current to future value. The process of computing future value involves adding interest at the *settlement interest rate.*[4] That is, the long-term liability PBO grows at a rate of interest equal to the settlement interest rate. **The liability increase due to the passage of time** is called ***interest cost.***

Prior service cost—*plan amendments grant retroactive benefits.* From time to time, employers and employees negotiate and may make a decision to change the pension plan benefit formula. Usually, the negotiation leads to increased retirement benefits, applied retroactively.[5] For example, assume that a pension plan is governed by the following formula:

$$\text{Annual benefits} = \text{Annual credit} \times \text{Years of service} \times \text{Salary at retirement date}$$

If the annual credit is 1%, the interpretation of the formula is that, for each year of service, an employee's annual retirement benefit increases by 1% of the salary at retirement date. An employee who worked 30 years under the plan would retire at 30% of final salary. Now, assume that the employer amends the pension plan agreement to make the annual credit 2%. If the amendment is retroactive, the employee is now entitled to an annual benefit equal to 60% of final salary. This sudden increase in retirement payments translates into a sudden increase in PBO, because PBO is the actuarially-determined present value of the estimated future retirement payments. **The increase in PBO from amending a pension plan and retroactively granting benefits** is defined as ***prior service cost.*** Employers often jus-

4. Under certain circumstances, a pension plan can be terminated. If terminated, the pension plan must provide annuities to the employees that will provide for a defined pension benefit during retirement. The annuities are normally purchased from an insurance or finance company. The interest rate associated with the annuity is called the settlement rate. Note that the settlement rate is associated with current market conditions, and it can change over time.

5. In many labor negotiations, pension benefits are a critical issue. For example, it was widely reported in the financial press that a major factor in avoiding a 1996 strike at Ford Motor Company was the company's willingness to increase pension benefits. *The Wall Street Journal* (September 27, 1996): A4.

tify the sudden increase in the liability by arguing that the current employee group benefitting from the retroactive amendment represents a more loyal work force with a higher morale. These conditions translate into a future economic benefit for the employer over the remaining service life of the affected group.

Liability (actuarial) gains and losses—*actuarial assumptions about future retirement payments change.* Each period, the actuary estimates PBO using the most current assumptions about items such as interest rates, mortality, pay increases, and job classifications. If experience during the period indicates that assumptions should be changed, then the actuary recomputes the PBO based on the new assumptions. **The resulting increase or decrease in PBO** is referred to as a ***liability (actuarial) gain or loss.*** For example, if new information shows that employees are estimated to live longer after retirement than previously thought, increased future retirement payments will occur, and consequently, PBO increases. The unexpected increase in PBO is a liability loss. Other changes in plan assumptions could lead to decreased PBO, which would be classified as a liability gain.

Benefit payments—*retirement benefits are paid.* Finally, actually paying retirement benefits to retired employees reduces the PBO.

Changes in the FMV of Pension Plan Assets Three events may change the FMV of pension plan assets during a given period: employer cash payments to the pension plan, actual return on plan assets, and retirement benefit payments. We separately discuss each event below.

Employer contributions—*employer cash payments are made to the plan trustee.* Funding the plan by making a cash contribution to the pension plan increases the FMV of pension plan assets. Within certain boundaries, company management decides how much cash to contribute to the pension plan each year. The U.S. Federal Government mandates minimum funding amounts for defined benefit pension plans, which becomes the minimum company contribution amount. Internal Revenue Service regulations allow only a certain amount to be tax deductible, which becomes the maximum company contribution amount. Therefore, management normally makes a pension plan contribution between the minimum and maximum amounts.

Return on plan assets—*actual return on invested plan assets.* The pension plan trustee invests the cash contributed by the employer in stocks, bonds, and other assets, which earn a return (e.g., dividends and interest) and change in value. **The change in the FMV of plan assets during the period, adjusted for employer contributions and benefit payments,** equals the ***actual return on plan assets.*** If the return is positive, the FMV of the assets increased during the period. But, the return can also be negative. The actual return can be thought of as being comprised of two components—the expected return on plan assets and the unexpected return on plan assets:

- An ***expected return on plan assets,*** which is always positive, **is based on long-run expected rates of return.**
- An unexpected return on plan assets (***asset gains and losses***) is based upon deviations of the actual rates of return from the expected rates.

For example, if a company expects a 10% return and the actual return is 9%, then the two components of the actual return are an expected return of 10% and an asset loss of 1%. This decomposition is similar to what is previously shown for the PBO. The PBO increases due to accruing interest at the settlement rate. In an analogous fashion, the FMV of plan assets increases based on the expected return. The PBO increases or decreases if the settlement rate (or other assumptions) turn out to be something other than expected. Similarly, the FMV of plan assets increases (a gain) or decreases (a loss) if the actual return turns out to be different than expected.

Benefit payments—*retirement benefits are paid.* Finally, actually paying retirement benefits to retired employees reduces the FMV of available plan assets. Note that this amount is equal to the reduction of the obligation to retiring employees, the PBO.

We have completed our specification of the economic balances and changes in balances associated with a defined benefit pension plan. The next step is to understand how GAAP reflects the economic realities of the pension plan on the face of the employer's balance sheet and income statement, and in the notes to the financial statements. Understanding pension plan accounting is complicated by the fact that the pension plan assets and obligations do not appear on the employer's books if a third party trustee manages the plan. Instead, the financial statements for the pension plan report assets (FMV of plan assets) and obligations (PBO). However, GAAP requires that the employer's financial statements and notes reflect the underlying economics of the pension plan. We begin with a description of how the changes in the PBO and FMV of plan assets are reflected in the income statement.

Income Statement Effects of Defined Benefit Pensions

5 Explain the financial statement and note disclosures for pensions and other post-retirement benefits.

SFAS No. 87 specifies how each change in the pension plan's PBO and FMV of plan assets is to be reflected in the employer's income statement. Each noncash change is given either (1) immediate recognition as a part of pension expense of the current period, or (2) delayed recognition as part of pension expense in future periods.

Changes in PBO	**Changes in FMV of Plan Assets**
Service cost	Employer cash payments to fund trustee
Interest cost on PBO	Actual return on plan assets:
Prior service cost	Expected return on plan assets
Liability gains/losses on PBO	Asset gains/losses
Benefit payments to retirees	Benefit payments to retirees

The last item listed in each column, payments to retirees, has no net effect on the net of PBO and FMV (i.e., it does not change net assets), and thus, can be ignored. Also, cash payments to the fund trustee are determined by financial policy, and represent a cash flow rather than an accrual accounting element.

By eliminating the cash benefit payments to retirees and the employer cash contributions to the trustee from the columns, we are left with the following items, along with their prescribed treatment by the FASB:

Type of Change in Pension Plan	**Treatment in Determining Pension Expense**
Changes in PBO:	
Service cost	Immediate recognition
Interest cost on PBO	Immediate recognition
Prior service cost	Delayed recognition
Liability gains/losses on PBO	Delayed recognition
Changes in FMV of plan assets:	
Actual return on plan assets:	
Expected return on plan assets	Immediate recognition
Asset gains/losses	Delayed recognition

Items receiving immediate recognition are service cost, interest cost, and expected return on plan assets. The FASB delayed recognition of prior service cost to be consistent with the idea that the granting of prior service cost generates future employee goodwill, with the benefits of such goodwill realized over the remaining service period of the employees to whom the retroactive benefits were granted. Accordingly, prior service cost is reflected in pension expense over time using an amortization process.

Both the recognition of liability gains/losses and asset gains/losses are delayed because of a *smoothing* argument. Employers argue that most gains and losses are simply transitory fluctuations, and as such, current recognition should not be given. The rules for the specific delayed recognition given to gains and losses are complex, and we discuss them later in the chapter. The basic idea is that the transitory gains/losses are amortized only if they become very large.

Combining the asset gains and losses with the liability gains and losses and rearranging the components provides the computation of annual pension expense.[6]

Computation of annual pension cost per SFAS No. 87:

	Treatment	Increases (Decreases) Pension Expense
Service cost	Immediate recognition	$XX
Interest cost on PBO	Immediate recognition	XX
Expected return on assets	Immediate recognition	(XX)
Amortizations:		
(Gains)/losses	Delayed recognition	(XX)/XX
Prior service cost	Delayed recognition	XX
Net pension cost (expense)		$XX

The immediate recognition of service cost and interest on PBO increases pension expense because both represent an increase in a liability (PBO), and increases in liabilities increase expenses. The expected return on plan assets is always positive. Because it represents an increase in an asset (FMV of plan assets), it decreases pension expense. As we subsequently illustrate, delayed recognition is achieved through amortizing an outstanding balance. Amortizing (i.e., recognizing) a gain (loss) decreases (increases) pension expense. As in the case of service cost, prior service cost amortization increases pension expense because it is an increase in a liability (PBO) from a plan amendment, and increases in liabilities increase expenses.[7]

The sum of the components, pension expense, is reported as a single amount in the income statement. The following simplified example will strengthen your understanding of pension expense computation, and also illustrate the balance sheet and footnote presentations.

Pension Expense Calculation with Balance Sheet and Note Disclosures—A Simplified Example

Example 2. On January 1, 2000, Robinson Co. adopted a defined benefit pension plan, at which time its PBO equaled zero and FMV of plan assets equaled zero. On December 31, 2001, Robinson granted retroactive benefits of $100,000 to employees who have an average remaining service period of 10 years from that date. Robinson decided to fund the plan at the end of each year by forwarding $60,000 to a plan trustee. Service cost is $50,000 each year. Robinson earns 10% on investments, and could settle the obligation by purchasing an annuity with a 7% interest rate. To simplify this first example, assume that (1) current salaries are 80% of expected future salaries; (2) actual and expected returns on plan assets are equal (i.e., no asset gains or losses); and (3) actual and expected PBO are equal (i.e., no liability gains or losses). Prepare financial statement disclosures for 2000–2002.

6. We use the terms *pension expense* and *net pension cost* interchangeably. This is not always correct because a cost can be either an expense or an asset depending on whether the economic benefits are expected to exist beyond the current period. We have abstracted from the idea that pension cost could be part of inventory (e.g., if it is the pension of a direct laborer) to simplify the discussion. However, if ***pension cost* is deemed to be part of inventory, then it is not reported as pension expense, but instead, it is a part of cost of goods sold when the inventory is sold.**

7. If prior service cost increases PBO, then the employees achieved additional benefits for prior service. In a labor negotiation, it is possible that an employer might achieve reduced pension benefits. In that case, PBO would decrease, and prior service cost would be negative (i.e., prior service cost would reflect a deferred gain rather than a deferred loss). *In this chapter, we always assume that a plan amendment increases PBO and, therefore, prior service cost represents a deferred charge.*

Solution. In order to compute many of the pension disclosures, it is necessary to reconcile PBO and FMV of plan assets. For Robinson Co., the reconciliations are as shown in Exhibits 1 and 2.

EXHIBIT 1 Reconciliation of Robinson Co. Changes in PBO

	2000		2001		2002	
PBO, January 1		$ 0		$ 50,000		$203,500
Service cost		50,000		50,000		50,000
Interest cost on PBO:						
Beginning PBO balance	0		50,000		203,500	
Settlement rate	× 0.07		× 0.07		× 0.07	
Interest cost		0		3,500		14,245
Prior service cost		0		100,000		0
PBO, December 31		$50,000		$203,500		$267,745

EXHIBIT 2 Reconciliation of Robinson Co. Changes in FMV of Plan Assets

	2000		2001		2002	
FMV of assets, January 1		$ 0		$ 60,000		$126,000
Expected return on plan assets:						
Beginning balance	0		60,000		126,000	
Long-term expected return on plan assets	× 0.10		× 0.10		× 0.10	
Expected return				6,000		12,600
Contributions		60,000		60,000		60,000
FMV of assets, December 31		$60,000		$126,000		$198,600

In 2000, PBO began at $0 and increased $50,000 due to employees' current service. Because there was no beginning PBO, it did not grow due to the passage of time, and thus, interest cost on PBO is $0. No other changes in PBO occurred in 2000. (Two other possible changes intentionally not considered in this example are liability gains/losses and payments to retiring employees.) The FMV of plan assets began at $0, no return was earned on the $0 investment, and $60,000 was contributed to the plan trustee at the end of the year. (Again, by construction of the example, no payments were made to retirees.)

Comparing PBO and FMV of plan assets at December 31, 2000, we see that Robinson contributed $10,000 more than the pension plan obligation to retiring employees. Thus, the plan is overfunded by $10,000. That is, the pension plan is in a $10,000 net asset position. On the surface, this seems to be a good thing; however, not all shareholders will be pleased with the decision to overfund the pension plan by $10,000, especially if they feel that the $10,000 excess could have been invested in positive net present value projects, or paid out in dividends.

In 2001, the situation changes dramatically. Again, service cost of $50,000 increases PBO. But now, the $50,000 beginning PBO accrues interest at the 7% settlement rate such that PBO goes up by an additional $3,500 (the interest cost on PBO). More significantly, 2001 is the year in which Robinson granted retroactive benefits in a plan amendment, which caused PBO to increase $100,000 for prior service cost. Therefore, at December 31, 2001, PBO is $203,500. Robinson did not choose to immediately fund the prior service cost PBO increase. The FMV of plan assets increased only by the 10% return on the beginning plan assets plus the annual end-of-period payment to the trustee. Therefore, at December 31, 2001, Robinson is in a net liability position of $77,500, which can be found by comparing the $203,500 PBO to the $126,000 FMV of plan assets. Under certain laws, severe underfunding of a plan can trigger a legal requirement to purchase insurance on the plan. Even if underfunding does not trigger legal actions, employee disenchantment is possible.

The events that change PBO and FMV of plan assets in 2002 are similar. An interesting situation is revealed, however, by the 2002 numbers. Interest on PBO ($14,245) now exceeds the actual return on plan assets ($12,600). When this situation occurs, an employer would have to fund at a rate higher than annual service cost to keep the underfunded position (i.e., a net obligation) from growing.

Income Statement Effects Service cost, interest on PBO, and expected return on plan assets receive immediate recognition as part of pension expense on Robinson's books. Prior service cost (PSC) and gains/losses receive delayed recognition by amortizing the beginning balances over the average remaining service period of employees. See Exhibit 3.

EXHIBIT 3 Robinson Co. Computation of Net Pension Cost

	2000	2001	2002
Service cost	$50,000	$50,000	$50,000
Interest on PBO	0	3,500	14,245
Expected return on assets	0	(6,000)	(12,600)
Amortization of PSC*	0	0	10,000
Amortization of gain/loss	0	0	0
Net pension cost	$50,000	$47,500	$61,645

*The December 31, 2001, prior service cost is amortized beginning in 2002. The amount is amortized over the average remaining service life of the work force at December 31, 2001, which is assumed to be 10 years. Therefore, the prior service cost will be amortized over the period 2002–2011.

Note that the amortization of prior service cost is $0 in 2000, $0 in 2001 (because there was no beginning balance to amortize), and $10,000 in 2002 ($100,000 prior service cost ÷ 10 years). The amortization of prior service cost will continue for nine more years.

Net pension cost is reflected in the income statement in each of the three years. For merchandising firms, it appears as an operating expense. For manufacturing firms, a large portion of the cost is capitalized as a part of inventory, and then expensed as a portion of cost of goods sold as inventory is sold.

Balance Sheet Effects The balance sheet disclosures for defined benefit pension plans can substantially deviate from the economic conditions of the plan as evidenced by a comparison of PBO to FMV of plan assets. The primary balance sheet disclosure is **the cumulative difference between what has been expensed through time** (i.e., pension expense) **and what has been funded** (i.e., cash contributions to trustees) called ***prepaid (accrued) pension cost.*** If cumulative cash contributions to the plan exceed cumulative pension expense, then the amount is reported as prepaid pension cost (an asset). If the cumulative pension expense exceeds the cumulative cash contributions, then the amount is reported as accrued pension cost (a liability).

Minimum Pension Liability—Unfunded ABO A second balance sheet effect may result from the computation of the ***minimum pension liability.*** GAAP does not require that an employer report the pension plan's PBO and FMV of plan assets on the face of the balance sheet. However, if a pension plan's ABO exceeds the FMV of plan assets, GAAP defines **the excess of ABO over FMV as the minimum liability** (also called ***unfunded ABO***), and it may require additional balance sheet disclosure. The GAAP requirements are that if a minimum liability exists, the balance sheet must at least report a liability equal to the minimum liability. To determine whether the existence of a minimum liability results in balance sheet effects, the minimum liability is compared to the balance in Prepaid (Accrued) Pension Cost. If more balance sheet liability is required by the minimum liability computation than exists in Prepaid (Accrued) Pension Cost, then an ***additional pension liability*** is created, which is offset by deferred pension cost, an intangible asset. The following four situations are possible at year-end.

1. *Minimum liability exists, and the balance in Accrued Pension Cost is greater than the minimum liability.* Because a liability already exists on the balance sheet that is greater than the minimum liability, no additional pension liability is required.
2. *Minimum liability exists, and the balance in Accrued Pension Cost is less than the minimum liability.* Because a liability that is less than the minimum liability exists on the balance sheet, additional pension liability is required. The amount is computed as Minimum liability − Accrued pension cost balance.
3. *Minimum liability exists, and Prepaid Pension Cost exists.* In this case, additional pension liability is required to take the balance sheet from a net asset position to a net liability position. The required amount of additional pension liability is calculated as Minimum liability + Prepaid pension cost balance.
4. *Minimum liability does not exist* (i.e., ABO is less than the FMV of plan assets). In this case, no additional pension liability is required.

Exhibit 4 shows how the minimum liability process may result in an additional pension liability.

EXHIBIT 4 Minimum Liability Illustration

	December 31		
	2001	2002	2003
ABO	$(5,000,000)	$(5,400,000)	$(6,200,000)
FV plan assets	4,800,000	5,800,000	5,900,000
Minimum liability	$ (200,000)	$ undefined	$ (300,000)
Balance in prepaid (accrued) pension cost	$ 15,000	$ 25,000	$ (5,000)
Amount of additional pension liability needed to reflect minimum on the balance sheet	(215,000)	none	(295,000)
Ending balance sheet asset (liability)	$ (200,000)	$ 25,000	$ (300,000)

Applying these concepts to Example 2, Exhibit 5 reflects the cumulative difference between the amounts expensed and the amounts funded, and the December 31 differences between the ABO and the FMV of plan assets. The balance sheet effects are presented in bold type. ABO = 80% of PBO because current salaries equal 80% of future salaries.

EXHIBIT 5 Example 2. Robinson Co. Balance Sheet Effects

	Through December 31		
	2000	2001	2002
Cumulative cash payments to trustee	$60,000	$120,000	$180,000
Cumulative amounts recorded as pension expense	(50,000)	(97,500)	(159,145)
Prepaid (accrued) pension cost reported as a balance sheet asset (liability)	$10,000	$ 22,500	$ 20,855
PBO	$(50,000)	$(203,500)	$(267,745)
× 80%	× 80%	× 80%	× 80%
ABO	$(40,000)	$(162,800)	$(214,196)
FMV of plan assets	60,000	126,000	198,600
Minimum liability to be reported	$ 0	$ (36,800)	$ (15,596)
Amount of **additional pension liability**	$ 0	$ (59,300)	$ (36,451)

At December 31, 2000, the cumulative cash payments to the trustee exceed the cumulative amounts recorded as pension expense by $10,000, which results in Prepaid Pension Cost on the balance sheet. Minimum liability is undefined (ABO is less than FMV of plan assets); therefore, no additional pension liability is recorded. In summary, Robinson's balance sheet disclosure is:

Asset	
Prepaid pension cost	$10,000

At December 31, 2001, cumulative cash payments to the trustee continue to exceed pension expense, leading to a $22,500 asset, Prepaid Pension Cost. However, due to the plan amendment that granted retroactive benefits, PBO and ABO have increased dramatically. ABO now exceeds the FMV of net assets by $36,800, which results in a minimum liability of $36,800. This means that Robinson, at a minimum, must report a pension liability in the balance sheet equal to $36,800.[8] Because Robinson has Prepaid Pension Cost (an *asset*) of $22,500 created by increasing funding faster than it is expensed, Robinson must accrue an *additional pension liability* of $59,300 to move from the $22,500 asset to a $36,800 liability. The additional pension liability of $59,300 is combined with the prepaid pension cost of $22,500 to report a single pension liability of $36,800 on the balance sheet. This liability is called Accrued Pension Cost (alternative titles would be Total Pension Liability and Minimum Liability).

Recall from the balance sheet equation that one cannot simply increase liabilities by $59,300 without having an offsetting effect. The FASB decided that the additional liability recognition needed to be offset by recording an intangible asset called ***Deferred Pension Cost.*** The logic behind the intangible asset recognition can best be understood by remembering the reason for the sudden increase in PBO and ABO that triggered the need to recognize the minimum liability in the first place. Robinson incurred prior service cost for the purpose of obtaining future economic benefits from employee goodwill. The prior service cost is given delayed recognition in pension expense. This prior service cost represents a large unrecognized liability incurred to create a large unrecognized intangible asset. If the minimum liability provisions require Robinson to recognize a substantial portion of the large unrecognized liability, then it should also be allowed to recognize a substantial portion of the large unrecognized intangible asset (i.e., employee goodwill). Hence, Robinson's balance sheet disclosures are as follows:

Assets	
Intangible assets	
Deferred pension cost	$59,300
Liabilities	
Accrued pension cost	$36,800

Note that the net of these two amounts is a $22,500 net asset. This equals what would have been shown in the balance sheet if we had ignored the minimum liability provisions altogether, because cumulative cash payments to the trustee exceed cumulative pension expense recognition by $22,500.

Recognition of Deferred Pension Cost as an asset is allowed under GAAP only if the amount shown in the balance sheet is less than the unamortized prior service cost. In Robinson's case, the December 31, 2001, unamortized prior service cost is $100,000, an amount that far exceeds the $59,300 reported as the intangible as-

8. Note that using PBO rather than ABO would be more conservative because it uses a higher value for the estimated liability (PBO of $203,500 to the FMV of plan assets of $126,000 to report a $77,500 minimum liability). However, because of the political process endemic to standard setting, the ABO rather than PBO was chosen for the minimum liability provisions.

set. Therefore, it is reasonable to attribute the unrecognized liability to an unrecognized intangible asset. It is possible, however, for Robinson to have to accrue an additional liability under the minimum liability provisions even though no prior service cost was granted. Both asset and liability gains and losses also receive delayed recognition in pension expense. If Robinson had a large enough unrecognized loss, then an additional liability would have to be recorded. In this case, GAAP does not allow the recognition of an intangible asset. Instead, a contra-equity account, Pension Loss Not Currently Recognized, must be reported. This title is descriptive because the unrecognized losses do not flow through pension expense immediately, and thus, do not decrease owners' equity through the net income effect (i.e., they are not currently recognized). *The amount of pension loss not currently recognized is reported in stockholders' equity as a component of Other accumulated comprehensive income.*

By December 31, 2002, prepaid pension cost is $20,855, and a $15,596 minimum liability is to be reported. The additional pension liability and the deferred pension cost intangible asset are reported at $36,451. The December 31, 2002, balance sheet disclosures are:

Assets	
Intangible assets	
Deferred pension cost	$36,451
Liabilities	
Accrued pension cost	$15,596

Note Disclosures Under *SFAS No. 132*, several pension footnote disclosures are required. The major disclosures are provided in Exhibit 6.

EXHIBIT 6 *SFAS No. 132* Note Disclosures

1. A reconciliation of the beginning balance to the ending balance of Projected Benefit Obligation.
2. A reconciliation of the beginning balance to the ending balance of Fair Value of Plan Assets.
3. A reconciliation of the funded status of the plan to the amounts recognized in the statement of financial position.
4. The components of Net Pension Cost (an expense).
5. The amount included in Other Comprehensive Income for the period arising from a change in the additional minimum pension liability.
6. The following assumptions on a weighted-average basis: the assumed discount (settlement) rate, the rate of compensation increase, and the expected long-term rate of return on plan assets.

The four note disclosures are illustrated for Example 2. First, the note disclosure for pension cost (item #4) is shown in Exhibit 7. To illustrate a complete disclosure, zero amounts are included.

EXHIBIT 7 Example 2. Robinson Co. Note Disclosure: Net Pension Cost

	2000	2001	2002
Components of pension cost:			
Service cost	$50,000	$50,000	$50,000
Interest on PBO	0	3,500	14,245
Expected return on plan assets	0	(6,000)	(12,600)
Amortization of prior service cost	0	0	10,000
Amortization of gain/loss	0	0	0
Net pension cost	$50,000	$47,500	$61,645

Second, as shown in Exhibit 8, a reconciliation from the funded status of the plan and what is disclosed on the face of the balance sheet (Exhibit 6, item #3) is presented.

EXHIBIT 8 Example 2. Robinson Co. Note Disclosure: Reconciliation of Economic Status of Plan to Balance Sheet Amount

	2000	2001	2002
PBO	$(50,000)	$(203,500)	$(267,745)
FMV	60,000	126,000	198,600
Amount plan is over(under)funded	$10,000	$ (77,500)	$ (69,145)
Unamortized prior service cost	0	100,000	90,000
Unamortized loss (gain)	0	0	0
Prepaid (accrued) pension cost	$10,000	$ 22,500	$ 20,855
Additional pension liability	0	(59,300)	(36,451)
Total balance sheet pension asset (liability)	$10,000	$ (36,800)	$ (15,596)

In 2000, the FMV of plan assets exceeds PBO by $10,000. Because there are no items at that time that receive delayed treatment in recognizing pension expense, the prepaid pension cost (and resulting balance sheet disclosure after considering the minimum liability provision) mirrors the economic status of the plan. In 2001, the plan is underfunded by $77,500 (an economic liability). But, because prior service cost (a large increase in liability) of $100,000 is not recognized, prepaid pension cost of $22,500 exits. This asset is not reflective of the economic status of the plan even if defined by a comparison of ABO to FMV; thus the additional liability must be recognized, which leads to an accrued pension cost of $36,800 reported on the balance sheet. The explanation for 2002 numbers is the same.

Finally, as shown in Exhibit 9, a disclosure reconciles beginning PBO to ending PBO (Exhibit 6, item #1), and beginning FMV of plan assets to ending FMV of plan assets (Exhibit 6, item #2).

EXHIBIT 9 Example 2. Robinson Co. Note Disclosures: Reconciliations of PBO and FMV of Plan Assets

	2000	2001	2002
January 1, PBO	$ 0	$ 50,000	$203,500
Service cost	50,000	50,000	50,000
Interest cost	0	3,500	14,245
Prior service cost	0	100,000	0
Benefit payments	0	0	0
December 31, PBO	$50,000	$203,500	$267,745
January 1, FMV of plan assets	$ 0	$ 60,000	$126,000
Company contributions	60,000	60,000	60,000
Benefit payments	0	0	0
Actual return on plan assets	0	6,000	12,600
December 31, FMV of plan assets	$60,000	$126,000	$198,600

Statement of Cash Flows Reporting The statement of cash flows shown in Exhibit 10 reports the three cash outflows of $60,000 (one each year) as an operating activity.

EXHIBIT 10 Robinson Co. Statement of Cash Flows Cash Inflows (Outflows)

	2000	2001	2002
Operating Activities			
Payments to pension plan trustee	$(60,000)	$(60,000)	$(60,000)

EXAMPLE 2 Journal Entries

	2000		2001		2002	
Recognition of annual pension cost:						
Pension Expense	50,000		47,500		61,645	
Prepaid (Accrued) Pension Cost		50,000		47,500		61,645
Payment to the plan trustee:						
Prepaid (Accrued) Pension Cost	60,000		60,000		60,000	
Cash		60,000		60,000		60,000
Minimum liability recognition:						
Deferred Pension Cost*			59,300			
Additional Pension Liability**				59,300		
Additional Pension Liability					22,849	
Deferred Pension Cost						22,849

*The balance in this account is limited to amount of unamortized prior service cost. If additional debits are required because of this limitation, use the contra-equity account, Pension Loss Not Currently Recognized.
**The balance in this account is combined with the balance in Prepaid (Accrued) Pension Cost and reported as a single liability.

Additional Issues in the Pension Area

We now turn to two complexities in defined benefit accounting: gain/loss recognition and how to account for the transition amount when companies adopted *SFAS No. 87*.

Gain and Loss Recognition

To this point, we have assumed that all actual and expected amounts are equal. Gains and losses occur when assumptions turn out to be incorrect. That is:

Expected PBO $\neq$ Actual PBO results in liability gains/losses

and

Expected FMV $\neq$ Actual FMV results in asset gains/losses

Pension plan accounting defers both asset and liability gains and losses. The net deferred gain/loss amount is amortized only if it becomes very large. The FASB set an arbitrary amount, called the ***corridor*** amount, as **the threshold for deferred gain/loss amortization.** The corridor is defined as **10% of the greater of actual PBO or actual FMV.** The logic behind this treatment is simple. Gains and losses are deviations from expectations. If expectations are unbiased, then gains and losses will offset over time and the net gain/loss should average around zero. The FASB assumes that the net deferred gain/loss amount will average around zero, and only prescribes amortization if the balance becomes larger than the corridor. The decision to amortize net deferred gains/losses is made each year, and that decision is independent of any decision made in prior years. Also, the decision is made based upon the *beginning of the year balances* (i.e., using prior year-end balances for net deferred gain/loss, PBO, and FMV).

The following example illustrates the treatment of asset and liability gains/losses.

Example 3. Assume that Mentor Corp. had the following actual and expected amounts for PBO and FMV of plan assets (in $ millions), and that the plan began January 1, 1999. Assume a 15-year amortization period if unrecognized gain/loss is amortized.

	PBO				FMV Assets				Cumulative Unrecognized Loss (Gain) From Asset and Liability Losses (Gains)
			Liability (Gain) Loss*				Asset (Gain) Loss**		
12/31	Actual	Expected	Current Year	Cumulative	Actual	Expected	Current Year	Cumulative	
1999	110	100	10	10	100	100	0	0	10
2000	150	120	30	40	130	120	(10)	(10)	30
2001	200	140	60	100	150	150	0	(10)	90
2002	250	250	0	100	260	220	(40)	(50)	50

*If actual PBO is greater than expected, a loss occurs; if less than expected, a gain occurs.
**If actual FMV is greater than expected, a gain occurs; if less than expected, a loss occurs.

From this information, determine whether any net deferred gain/loss should be amortized, and calculate the ending net deferred gain/loss balance.

Solution. Exhibit 11 provides the solution, which is discussed thereafter.

EXHIBIT 11 Example 3. Mentor Corp. Computation of Amortization of Unrecognized Gain/Loss

	December 31 Balance		As of January 1		
($ millions)	PBO	FMV Assets	*Corridor	**Unamortized Loss(Gain)	***Current Year Amortization
1/1/99	0	0	0	0	N/A
1999	110	100	0	0	0
2000	150	130	11	10	0
2001	200	150	15	30	(30 − 15) ÷ 15 = 1
2002	250	260	20	90 − 1 = 89	(89 − 20) ÷ 15 = 5

*Greater of 10% of the beginning of the period PBO or the FMV of plan assets.
**See the beginning of the year amount from right-hand column of previous table.
***The excess of cumulative unamortized loss (gain) over corridor divided by remaining service life of the current employees (assumed to be 15 years in this problem). For convenience, the amounts are rounded to the nearest million.

1999. As of January 1, 1999, the date of plan adoption, no net deferred gain/loss existed. Therefore, none is subject to amortization. In 1999, a liability loss of $10,000,000 was experienced, but no asset gain/loss was experienced. Therefore, the ending net deferred loss amount is $10,000,000, and it becomes a reconciling amount in the December 31, 1999, notes. *The delay of the current period gains and losses is one way in which pension expense is smoothed.*

2000. The beginning of the period corridor equals $11,000,000 (10% of $110,000,000 PBO, which is higher than 10% of $100,000,000 FMV). The beginning of the period net deferred loss of $10,000,000 is less than the corridor of $11,000,000; therefore, no amortization occurs in 2000. *Requiring a gain or loss to exceed the corridor is a second way that pension cost is smoothed in the gain/loss area.* Reading across the 2000 row in the problem information, a $30,000,000 liability loss occurs (actual PBO exceeds expected PBO by $30,000,000), and a $10,000,000 asset gain occurs (actual FMV exceeds expected FMV). The $10,000,000 beginning loss is added to the net $20,000,000 loss incurred in 2000, yielding an unamortized $30,000,000 loss balance at year-end.

2001. The beginning of the period corridor equals $15,000,000 (10% of $150,000,000 PBO, which is higher than 10% of $130,000,000 FMV). The beginning of the period net deferred loss of $30,000,000 is greater than the corridor of $15,000,000; therefore, amortization occurs in 2001. The amount subject to amortization is the excess of the net deferred gain/loss over the corridor. Thus, $15,000,000 ($30,000,000 net deferred loss − $15,000,000 corridor) is subject to amortization. Amortizing the $15,000,000 over a 15-year period results in $1,000,000 amortization in 2001. The $1,000,000 amortization of a loss increases pension expense of the period. *Amortizing only the amount in excess of the corri-*

dor rather than recognizing it all is a third way that pension expense is smoothed in the gain/loss area. The $89,000,000 net unamortized deferred loss balance at December 21, 2001, is calculated as follows: beginning balance of $30,000,000 loss, minus the $1,000,000 loss amortization, plus $60,000,000 asset loss, and a $0 liability gain/loss. The $89,000,000 loss is carried forward as a reconciling item in the note disclosures and becomes the 2002 beginning balance.

2002. The beginning of the period corridor equals $20,000,000 (10% of $200,000,000 PBO, which is higher than 10% of $150,000,000 FMV). The beginning of the period net deferred loss of $89,000,000 is greater than the corridor of $20,000,000; therefore, amortization occurs in 2002. The amount subject to amortization is the excess of the net deferred gain/loss over the corridor. Thus, $69,000,000 ($89,000,000 net deferred loss − $20,000,000 corridor) is subject to amortization. Amortizing the $69,000,000 over a 15-year period results in $5,000,000 amortization (rounded) in 2002. The $5,000,000 amortization of a loss increases pension expense for the period. The $44,000,000 net unamortized deferred loss balance at December 31, 2002, is calculated as follows: beginning balance of $89,000,000 loss, minus the $5,000,000 loss amortization, plus $0 asset gain/loss, plus a $40,000,000 liability gain. The $44,000,000 loss is carried forward as a reconciling item in the note disclosures and becomes the 2003 beginning balance.

For Mentor, the cumulative net deferred loss exceeded the corridor in 2001 and 2002. However, for many companies the cumulative gains and losses fluctuate within the corridor and are never amortized.

EXAMPLE 3 Journal Entries

Gain and loss amortizations do not generate separate journal entries. Such amortizations serve to determine the pension expense debit.

Transition Amount

It is likely that recent financial statements will reveal an additional component of pension expense and an additional footnote reconciling item. When firms originally adopted *SFAS No. 87,* accountants had to handle the transition from the old *APB Opinion No. 8* rules to the new *SFAS No. 87* rules. We have examined how to treat pensions from the point of plan adoption when PBO and FMV of plan assets start at zero. At the beginning of a plan, there is no difference between the true economic status of the plan and what has been reflected in the balance sheet. The transition rules deal with the adoption of current pension accounting rules when the old rules have resulted in a difference between economic reality and what is reflected in the balance sheet.

Example 4. Although Tarkanian Inc. has always had a pension plan, it adopted *SFAS No. 87* on January 1, 1990. At that date, Tarkanian had plan assets with a FMV of $1,000,000 and a PBO of 800,000. Under *APB Opinion No. 8,* Tarkanian also had an accrued pension cost of $50,000. Compute the transition amount, as well as the 1990 amortization of this transition amount included in pension cost and the unamortized amount to be included as a December 31, 1990, reconciling item.

Solution. *Computation of transition amount.* Computing the transition amount involves identifying a reconciling item at the date of *SFAS No. 87* adoption, and deciding whether the item is a net transition asset or obligation.

PBO, 1/1/90	$ (800,000)
FMV of plan assets, 1/1/90	1,000,000
Overfunded pension plan (net asset)	200,000
Transition amount	?
Accrued pension cost	$ (50,000)

This computation raises the question, "Why do we have an economic asset of \$200,000, but show a \$50,000 liability on the balance sheet?" The answer is that we have *not* recognized a \$250,000 asset on the balance sheet. That is, if we recognized a \$250,000 asset, we would move from a liability position of \$50,000 to an asset position of \$200,000. The \$250,000 reconciling asset is referred to as the transition amount. *This transition amount reflects a deferred gain, which will be amortized as a reduction in pension expense.*[9]

Amortization of transition amount. The transition amount is amortized over the average remaining service life of the employees at the transition date, or over 15 years if that is longer than the average remaining service life. This provision results in a smaller amortization, and also lessens the effect of the transition amount relative to the other components of pension expense. For Tarkanian, assume that the average remaining service life was 25 years. Therefore, the amortization of the transition amount equals \$10,000 (\$250,000 ÷ 25 = \$10,000) in each year, beginning in 1990. This amortization decreases pension cost. For some companies, the amortized amount may be so large that it swamps the other elements of pension cost and creates net pension income.

The *unamortized amount included as a reconciling amount* is equal to \$250,000 minus accumulated amortization to date. For Tarkanian, the December 31, 1990, transition amount equals \$240,000 (\$250,000 beginning amount − \$10,000 amortization).

EXAMPLE 4 Journal Entries

Similar to gain and loss amortizations, transition amount amortizations do not generate separate journal entries. Such amortizations are used to determine the pension expense debit.

Comprehensive Pension Example

Example 5. Grigsby Company's pension plan is administered by a third-party trustee. On January 1, 2001, Grigsby's actuary provided the following amounts related to the defined benefit pension plan. From this information, prepare the financial statement and note disclosures in the pension area for 2001 and 2002.

PBO	\$4,000,000
ABO (current salaries are equal to 90% of future salaries)	3,600,000
FMV of plan assets	3,600,000
Unamortized transition obligation (10-year amortization period)	400,000
Unamortized prior service cost	0
Unamortized gains and losses	0
Prepaid/accrued pension cost reported on the balance sheet	0

	2001	2002
Service cost	\$300,000	\$400,000
Prior service cost (effective from plan amendment on 12/31/01), not to be amortized until 2002	\$250,000	0
Actuarial loss (gain) related to the PBO	\$200,000	\$(105,000)
Actual return on plan assets	\$450,000	\$(350,000)
Pension plan contribution (year-end)	\$600,000	\$600,000
Benefit payments to retirees (year-end)	\$80,000	\$80,000
Settlement rate	9%	9%
Long-term expected rate of return on plan assets	10%	10%
Average expected time until workers retire	10 years	10 years

9. If the transition amount represented a deferred loss, then the amortization would increase pension cost.

Solution. The note disclosures include (1) a reconciliation of PBO and FMV of plan assets from the beginning to the end of the year; (2) the components of pension expense for the year; and (3) a reconciliation from the difference in PBO and FMV of plan assets at year-end to the amount reported as Prepaid/Accrued Pension Cost in the balance sheet.

1. The reconciliation of PBO and FMV of plan assets from the beginning to the end of the year is not only a required disclosure, but it is a first step in understanding how all the other pension amounts are determined. From the information provided by the actuary, the reconciliation is shown in Exhibit 12.

EXHIBIT 12 Grigsby Co., Reconciliation of PBO and FMV of Plan Assets (In thousands)

	2001	2002
PBO:		
Beginning balance	$4,000	$5,030
Service cost	300	400
Interest cost	360	453
Prior service cost	250	0
Liability loss (gain)	200	(105)
Benefit payments	(80)	(80)
Ending balance	$5,030	$5,698
FMV of plan assets:		
Beginning balance	$3,600	$4,570
Actual return on plan assets	450	(350)
Company contributions to pension plan	600	600
Benefit payments	(80)	(80)
Ending balance	$4,570	$4,740

2. While the previous note disclosure shows the economic status of the plan and how it has changed during the year, the pension cost components disclosure in Exhibit 13 shows how those changes were treated in the income statement:

EXHIBIT 13 Grigsby Co. Pension Cost Components (In thousands)

	2001	2002
Service cost	$300	$400
Interest cost	360	453
Expected return on plan assets	(360)	(457)
Amortization of transition amount	40	40
Amortization of prior service cost	0	25
Amortization of unrecognized losses (gains)	0	0
Pension cost	$340	$461

Service cost, interest cost, and the expected return on plan assets receive immediate recognition in Pension Expense. The expected return of $360,000 ($3,600,000 × 10% long-run expected return) is reflected in Pension Expense as a reduction. The difference between the actual and the expected returns (asset gain or loss) is deferred, combined with liability gains and losses (as shown below), and reported as an item that reconciles from the economic status of the plan to the balance sheet disclosure. The amortization of the transition amount is $40,000 ($400,000 ÷ 10 years). Recognizing such a liability increases pension expense. The unamortized portions ($360,000 in 2001 and $320,000 in 2002) are recorded as items that reconcile from the economic status of the plan to the balance sheet disclosure (as shown below). Likewise, the beginning balance of Prior Service Cost ($0 at January 1, 2001, and $250,000 at January 1, 2002) is amortized over a ten-year period.

Recall that the prior service cost represents a sudden jump in the liability, PBO. Amortization is a partial recognition of this liability, and therefore, increases pension expense. The unamortized portion in 2002 ($225,000) is a reconciling item (as shown below).

For 2001, pension cost equals $340,000, and the company contribution equals $600,000; therefore, the company has $260,000 in Prepaid Pension Cost (the excess of the amount paid over the amount recognized). For 2002, pension cost equals $461,000 and the company contribution equals $600,000. The difference of $139,000 increases the balance in Prepaid Pension Cost from $260,000 (the beginning balance) to $399,000. Grigsby is subject to minimum liability provisions, however, and must determine whether an additional pension liability needs to be disclosed by comparing ending ABO with ending FMV of net assets.

(In thousands)	2001	2002
Ending ABO (90% of PBO)	$4,527	$5,128
Ending FMV of net assets	(4,570)	(4,740)
Minimum liability	None	$ 388
Balance in prepaid pension cost	N/A	399
Additional pension liability needed		$ 787

Therefore, on the December 31, 2001, balance sheet, Grigsby would report Prepaid Pension Cost (an asset) at $260,000. On the December 31, 2002, balance sheet, Grigsby would report Accrued Pension Cost (a liability) at $388,000, Deferred Pension Cost (an asset) at $225,000 (because such an intangible asset is limited by the amount of unamortized prior service cost), and Pension Loss Not Currently Recognized (a contra-equity account) at $562,000.

3. Exhibit 14 explains the difference between what is reported in the prepaid or accrued pension cost account on the face of the balance sheet and the economic status of the plan.

EXHIBIT 14 Grigsby Co. Reconciliation of Economic Status to Balance Sheet Amounts (In thousands)

	2001	2002
Reconciliation of ending pension amounts:		
Projected benefit obligation	$(5,030)	$(5,698)
Fair value of plan assets	4,570	4,740
Amount plan is over(under)funded	$ (460)	$ (958)
Unamortized transition obligation	360	320
Unamortized prior service cost	250	225
Unamortized losses (gains)	110	812
Prepaid (accrued) pension cost account before consideration of any necessary additional pension liability	$ 260	$ 399
Additional pension liability	0	(787)
Prepaid (accrued) pension cost	$ 260	$ (388)

In both years, PBO exceeds FMV; therefore, the plan is underfunded. However, because the transition obligation, the prior service cost, and the losses/gains all receive delayed recognition, the balance sheet reports a prepaid pension cost asset of $260,000 in 2001, and only reports a portion of the underfunding as Accrued Pension Cost of $388,000 in 2002 (the portion is equal to the difference between ABO and FMV).

The determination of gain and loss amortization included in Pension Expense and unamortized amounts included in the reconciliation is accomplished by using the corridor approach. The actuary reports that there were no unamortized gains or losses at January 1, 2001. The balance in the unamortized gains and losses can be followed through time:

(In thousands)	
Unamortized losses (gains), 1/1/01	$ 0
Amortization in 2001 ($0 because there is nothing to amortize)	0
Liability loss in 2001	200
Asset gain in 2001 (the difference between the actual and the expected gain that is deferred)	(90)
Unamortized losses (gains), 12/31/01	$110
Amortization in 2002 ($0 because $110 is less than the corridor): 1/1/02 PBO is greater than 1/1/02 FMV; 10% of 1/1/02 PBO is $503; $110 is less than $503.	0
Liability gain in 2002	(105)
Asset loss in 2002 (the difference between the actual and the expected gain that is deferred)	807
Unamortized losses (gains), 12/31/02	$812

Neither 2001 nor 2002 pension expense is affected by gain or loss amortization. The unamortized losses of $110,000 and $812,000 are reconciling items.

To this point, we have shown only the note disclosures. The financial statement disclosures for the two years are shown in Exhibits 15 and 16.

EXHIBIT 15 Example 5. Grigsby Co. 2001 Financial Statements

2001 Balance Sheet

Assets		**Owners' Equity**	
Cash* (an operating activity in the statement of cash flows)	$(600)	Retained earnings (net income effect)	$(340)
Prepaid pension cost	260		

*Cumulative amount associated with pension plan contributions.

2001 Income Statement		2001 Statement of Owners' Equity	
Pension expense	$340	Net income effect on retained earnings	$(340)

EXHIBIT 16 Example 5. Grigsby Co. 2002 Financial Statements

2002 Balance Sheet

Assets		**Liabilities**	
Cash* ($600 outflow reported as an operating activity in the statement of cash flows)	$(1,200)	Accrued pension cost	$388
Deferred pension cost	225	**Owners' Equity**	
		Retained earnings (net income effect)	$(801)
		Accumulated other comprehensive income (pension loss not currently recognized)	(562)

*Cumulative amount associated with pension plan contributions.

2002 Income Statement		2002 Statement of Owners' Equity	
Pension expense	$461	Net income effect on retained earnings	$(461)
		Accumulated other comprehensive income (change in pension loss not currently recognized)	(562)

EXAMPLE 5 Journal Entries

Recognition of annual pension cost:	*2001*		*2002*	
Pension Expense	260		461	
Prepaid/Accrued Pension Cost		260		461
Payment to the plan trustee:				
Prepaid/Accrued Pension Cost	600		600	
Cash		600		600
Minimum liability recognition:				
Deferred Pension Cost			225	
Pension Loss Not Currently Recognized			562	
Additional Pension Liability*				787

*The balance in this account is combined with the balance in Prepaid/Accrued Pension Cost and reported as a single liability.

Actual Pension Plan Disclosures

The following partial retirement plan footnote in Exhibit 17 disclosures (slightly modified by authors) appeared in the Gannet 1998 financial statements.

EXHIBIT 17 Gannet 1998 Note 5: Retirement Plans (In thousands)

Pension cost:	
Service cost (benefits earned during the period)	$ 51,249
Interest cost on benefit obligation	94,171
Expected return on plan assets	(135,484)
Amortization of transition asset	(4,226)
Amortization of prior service (credit) cost	(3,773)
Amortization of actuarial loss	443
Pension expense for company-sponsored retirement plans	$ 2,380
Union and other pension cost	5,357
Total pension cost	$ 7,737
Change in benefit obligation:	
Net benefit obligation at beginning of year	$1,243,188
Service cost	51,249
Interest cost	94,171
Plan amendments	(3,791)
Actuarial loss	57,550
Acquisitions/plan mergers	102,927
Gross benefits paid	(70,883)
Net benefit obligation at end of year	$1,474,411
Change in plan assets:	
Fair value of plan assets at beginning of year	$1,269,090
Actual return on plan assets	151,892
Employer contributions	3,813
Acquisitions/plan mergers	116,914
Gross benefits paid	(70,883)
Fair value of plan assets at end of year	$1,470,826
Reconciliation, funded status to balance sheet amounts:	
Fair value of plan assets at end of year	$1,470,826
Net benefit obligation at end of year	(1,474,411)
Funded status at end of year	$ (3,585)
Unrecognized net actuarial loss	92,081
Unrecognized prior service credit	(39,790)
Unrecognized net transition asset	(1,214)
Net, prepaid benefit cost	$ 47,492
Amounts recognized in consolidated balance sheet:	
Prepaid benefit cost	$ 110,531
Accrued benefit cost	(63,039)
Net, prepaid benefit cost	$ 47,492

Note that Gannet's footnote information is very similar to that discussed in the text. A review of some of the information shows that Gannet's plan is just *barely* underfunded by about \$3.6 million on liabilities of over \$1.47 billion. Gannet made employer contributions to the pension plan of about \$3.8 million, while the plan paid out about \$70.9 million in benefits. The actual return on plan assets was \$151,892,000, around a 9% return on beginning-of-period assets adjusted for company contributions. The actual return of \$151,892,000 exceeded the expected return of \$135,484,000. Acquisitions and plan mergers added \$102,927,000 in pension obligations. However, a plan amendment favored Gannet, reducing its obligation by \$3,791,000. Further, we know that previous plan amendments also favored the company because Gannet has \$39,790,000 in unamortized prior service *credits.* (In all the text examples, we assumed that firms would have unamortized prior service costs.)

Cash Balance Plans

Companies that traditionally offered defined benefit plans generally fell into two groups—those that negotiated the pension plans with unionized employees and those that did not. During the late 1990s, many companies that offered defined benefit plans to nonunion employees converted their pension plans to *cash balance plans.*[10] In a traditional pension plan, employees benefit by spending their entire careers with one employer, because most defined benefit pension plans award pension plans based upon years of service and final salary. A cash balance plan reflects the changing nature of U.S. employment, where it is likely that an employee will work for several employers during a working lifetime. Defined benefit plans do not offer much incentive to an employee who plans on working just a few years for a company.

Because the cash plan fund balances are vested and portable, firms that converted defined benefit plans to cash plans claimed to make the pension plan more attractive to younger employees. **A *cash balance plan* mimics a 401(k) plan in that each employee is given a benefit balance.** Each year, the company makes a contribution to the plan for the employee, and the employee is guaranteed a rate of return on the cash balance (e.g., 5%). If the company invests and earns a rate of return higher than the minimum, then the company keeps the excess. However, if the company earns a rate of return lower than the minimum, the employee is still credited with the minimum return and the company must make up the difference. The cash balance amounts vest quickly and are portable if the employee leaves the company. When cash balance plans were introduced, they were met with opposition by employees who had many years of service with an employer because the traditional defined benefit plan builds up much of its value during the later years of service. Employees in their forties and early fifties believed that when compared to the previous defined benefit plan, the initial cash balance credited to the employee would result in greatly reduced pension benefits at retirement. Many companies either initially, or in response to employee criticism, allowed workers with many years of service to choose whether to keep the defined benefit plan under the old terms, or to move to the cash balance plan. At the writing of this text, the movement to cash balance plans is in its infancy.

Summary of Pension Accounting

To understand the economic effect of pensions on the firm, it is necessary to understand the relationship between the off-balance-sheet economic status of the plan (the difference between PBO and the FMV of net assets) and the on-balance-sheet disclosure of prepaid or accrued pension cost. Not all changes in the economic status of the plan receive current recognition in Pension Expense; and because the balance sheet pension asset or liability is defined as the cumulative difference between

10. In the February 2000 issue of *Journal of Accountancy* (p. 22), an article reported that "an estimated 16% of *Fortune* 100 companies have switched to a so-called cash balance formula."

that pension expense and cash payments to the trustee, the economic status of the plan is rarely reflected on the balance sheet. Three possible reconciling amounts between the economic status of the plan and the balance sheet are unamortized prior service cost, unamortized gains and losses, and the transition amount. These are reconciling amounts precisely because they have never been fully recognized in the accounts due to the delayed treatment that they receive in determining pension expense. An attempt to recognize some of the off-balance-sheet amounts manifests in the minimum liability provisions.

Other Post-Retirement Benefits

Employers also provide other post-retirement benefits to employees and to employees' spouses and dependents. These benefits include medical and hospitalization coverage, college tuition assistance, life insurance coverage, and many others. Just as in the case of pensions, current employee service triggers these promises, and the expected obligation for these benefits can be computed as the actuarially determined present value of future payments.

In the accounting for other post-retirement benefits, GAAP (*SFAS No. 106,* issued in 1990) slightly differs from that used to account for pensions. Although a good understanding of post-retirement benefit accounting can be obtained by adopting the same framework for expense recognition, balance sheet presentation, and note reconciliation as just learned for pensions, there are two major accounting differences. Most companies do not fund other post-retirement benefits because government regulations do not specify minimum funding for post-retirement benefits other than pensions. As a result, the FMV of post-retirement plan assets is $0 for the majority of companies. Therefore, actual return on such assets would also be $0. Second, when they adopted *SFAS No. 106,* employers were allowed to either expense the transition amount, or to capitalize and amortize it over some period of time. Most companies chose to expense the transition amount. For example, when General Motors adopted the prescribed accounting for post-retirement benefits other than pensions (principally related to health care costs), it immediately expensed a transition amount of over $20 billion. In the period of adoption, immediate expensing of the transition amount caused many companies to report all-time record losses because of the sheer size of this unrecognized obligation.[11]

Two additional disclosures are necessary for post-retirement benefits other than pensions: the assumed health care cost trend rate(s) used in actuarial computations, and the effect of both a one-percentage-point increase and a one-percentage-point decrease in the assumed health care cost trend rate on (1) the accumulated post-retirement benefit obligation for health care benefits, and (2) the aggregate of the service and interest cost components of net periodic post-retirement health care benefit cost. To illustrate disclosures for post-retirement benefits other than pensions, the following disclosure (slightly modified by the authors) appeared in Gannett's 1998 annual report.

EXHIBIT 18 Gannett 1998 Note 6: Post-Retirement Benefits Other Than Pensions (In thousands)

Post-retirement benefit cost for health care and life insurance for 1998 included the following components.

Post-retirement benefit cost:	
Service cost (benefits earned during the period)	$ 3,118
Interest cost on benefit obligation	14,378
Amortization of prior service (credit) cost	(5,578)
Amortization of actuarial loss	235
Net periodic post-retirement benefit cost	$ 12,153

(continued)

11. Because companies accrued the post-retirement benefit costs before they were paid, companies that expensed all of the post-retirement benefits generated large deferred tax assets.

EXHIBIT 18 (concluded)

Change in benefit obligation:	
Net benefit obligation at beginning of year	$231,565
Service cost	3,118
Interest cost	14,378
Plan participants' contributions	4,402
Plan amendments	(8,341)
Actuarial loss	13,798
Gross benefits paid	(20,574)
Net benefit obligation at end of year	$238,346
Change in plan assets:	
Fair value of plan assets at beginning of year	$ 0
Employer contributions	16,172
Plan participants' contributions	4,402
Gross benefits paid	(20,574)
Fair value of plan assets at end of year	$ 0
Reconciliation, funded status to balance sheet amounts:	
Fair value of plan assets at end of year	$ 0
Net benefit obligation at end of year	(238,346)
Funded status at end of year	$(238,346)
Unrecognized net actuarial loss	6,154
Unrecognized prior service (credit)	(75,953)
Accrued post-retirement benefit cost	$(308,145)

The accumulated post-retirement benefit obligation was determined using a discount rate of 6.75% and a health care cost trend rate of 8% for pre-age 65 benefits, decreasing to 5% in the year 2005 and thereafter. For post-age 65 benefits, the health care cost trend rate used was 6%, decreasing to 5% in the year 2001 and thereafter.

The company's policy is to fund the above-mentioned benefits as claims for premiums are paid.

The effect of a 1% increase in the health care cost trend rate used would result in increases of approximately $15 million in the 1998 post-retirement benefit obligation and $1 million in the aggregate service and interest components of the 1998 expense. The effect of a 1% decrease in the health care cost trend rate used would result in increases of approximately $13 million in the 1998 post-retirement benefit obligation and $1 million in the aggregate service and interest components of the 1998 expense.

Exhibit 18 shows that at year-end, Gannett's obligation for health care and life insurance is about $308 million, which has been accrued on the balance sheet. Because the plan is pay-as-you-go, the plan has no assets. The cost of 1998 benefits was about $20.6 million, with the company paying approximately 80% of the cost and plan participants paying the remaining 20%.

Stock-Based Compensation

6 Account for stock-based compensation.

Previously in this text, we made the assumption that managers choose investment projects with the objective of maximizing shareholder wealth. Because shareholders are unable to perfectly monitor the actions of managers, it is possible for managers to make decisions that are not in the shareholders' best interest, but that maximize their own wealth. For example, many traditional executive compensation plans have been based on accrual accounting-related performance measures such as return on assets (i.e., operating income before interest divided by average total assets). When faced with declining earnings, managers have the option of choosing accounting principles or making discretionary accruals that might increase income in the short run, but that have no link to firm value, and thus, no link to shareholder wealth.

In response to this problem, a number of companies employ stock-based compensation plans (to at least some extent) for key individuals.[12] The intended effect of stock-based compensation plans is to align the financial interests of managers and shareholders. Simply put, an action by a manager that increases share price for the purposes of personal wealth maximization also increases shareholder wealth. Stock options can be classified as ***fixed options,*** for which **vesting is based solely on continued service,** and ***performance options,*** for which **the number of options or other option terms depend on future performance.** When an option ***vests,*** **the employee has earned the options,** and the award is no longer contingent on remaining with the employer or some future performance level. In a ***cliff vesting*** situation, **all options vest at the end of the vesting period,** while in ***graded vesting,*** **a portion of the options vest each year.**[13]

Historically, valuing stock options has been a vexing issue for accountants. While *put* and *call options* are traded on national exchanges, fixed or performance stock options do not trade on exchanges and can only be exercised by the holder. Therefore, it is difficult to obtain market values for fixed and performance stock options. Prior to 1972, stock options were not valued in any standardized manner. In 1972, accounting standard setters issued *APB Opinion No. 25,* which required that companies value stock options at the *opportunity cost* of the option. The opportunity cost is the excess of market value over the option price on the measurement date (usually the grant date). The opportunity cost would be charged to compensation expense over the vesting period. If **the market price exceeds the option price on the grant date,** then the stock options are labeled as ***compensatory,*** because compensation expense will be recognized over the life of the options. However, if **a company sets the option price equal to the market price on the grant date,** then the stock options are ***noncompensatory,*** because no compensation expense would be recorded. After 1972, virtually all companies tailored their plans so that the plans were noncompensatory. The **opportunity cost accounting used in *APB No. 25*** is called the ***intrinsic value method.***

The FASB issued *SFAS No. 123,* "Accounting for Stock Based Compensation," in October 1995 as a revision of the rules for stock options. *SFAS No. 123 encourages* alternative rules to *APB No. 25, but does not require* a change in the way compensation expense is measured and disclosed in the primary financial statements. The alternate rules require a company to compute the fair market value of the options at the grant date using an appropriate option pricing model. **The fair value accounting used in *SFAS No. 123*** is called the ***fair value method.*** If companies continue to follow *APB No. 25,* they are required to provide note disclosure of measurement under the alternative *SFAS No. 123* rules. Although almost all companies will continue to use the intrinsic value method, we first illustrate the new *SFAS No. 123* fair value method rules. We then apply the intrinsic value method to the same example.

Stock Option Plans—The Fair Value Method versus the Intrinsic Value Method

A common type of stock-based compensation is the stock option plan. For the following example problem, we illustrate alternative solutions based upon whether the company uses the fair value method or the intrinsic value method.

12. Companies may also offer all employees the ability to participate in a stock purchase plan. Because stock purchase plans are not intended as compensation, we do not discuss them in this chapter. Typically, in a stock purchase plan all employees must be able to participate, and employees may purchase stock (either directly or through a payroll deduction) at a slight discount from the current fair market value (e.g., 90%). The 1999 *Accounting Trends and Techniques* reported that of 600 companies surveyed, 123 offered stock purchase plans.

13. In the 1999 *Accounting Trends and Techniques,* the 600 companies surveyed reported 590 instances of stock option plans and 291 instances of stock award plans (a more general term that usually includes stock options).

Example 6. Irish Co. has adopted a stock option plan to compensate key employees. The plan permits executives to purchase shares of Irish $1 par common stock at $21 per share. On January 2, 2001, options to purchase 10,000 shares were equally granted to two key vice presidents. Both must remain employed by Irish continuously through December 31, 2002, before the options may be exercised. These options expire on December 31, 2003. At the grant date, the quoted market price of Irish common stock is $30, and the fair value of the options (calculated using an appropriate option pricing formula) is $2 per option.

Solution 1. *The Fair Value Method (SFAS No. 123 preferred method).* Finance theorists have provided option pricing models that accurately calculate option prices in the real world. For example, Fischer Black and Myron Scholes developed an option pricing model in the early 1970s that required inputs on the number of options granted, current stock price, exercise price, expected life of the options, expected forfeitures per year, risk-free interest rate, expected volatility, and expected dividend yield. For their work, Black and Scholes eventually received a Nobel prize. *SFAS No. 123* encourages companies to measure the value of options using an appropriate option pricing model, and to then allocate that value to the periods benefitted as compensation expense. In our example, an option pricing formula resulted in an option value of $2, which means total compensation expense equals $20,000 ($2 per option × 10,000 options). Because the vice presidents must work for two years before the options may be exercised, the $20,000 in compensation expense is allocated over two years, with $10,000 of compensation expense recognized in 2001, and $10,000 recognized in 2002.

Irish's 2001 financial statements would reflect the amounts shown in Exhibit 19 related to the stock option.

EXHIBIT 19 Example 6. Irish Co. 2001 Financial Statements—Fair Value Method

Balance Sheet

Assets		**Owners' Equity**	
No effect		Contributed capital:	
		Contributed capital from stock option plan	$10,000
		Retained earnings:	
		Income statement effect	(10,000)

Income Statement		**Statement of Owners' Equity**	
Compensation expense	$10,000	Investments by owners:	
		Contributed capital from stock option plan	$10,000
		Net income effect on retained earnings	(10,000)

Assets and liabilities are unaffected.[14] Compensation Expense of $10,000 is reported, which is offset by an increase in contributed capital. In 2002, another $10,000 of compensation expense is recorded, with a corresponding increase in contributed capital of $10,000.

In 2003, the options will either be exercised or they will lapse. If the stock price is below $21 during 2003, the options will not be exercised, and the contributed capital from stock options will be reclassified as contributed capital from expired options.

14. Although this treatment seems to contradict the idea that expenses represent decreases in assets or increases in liabilities, conceptually, one can view the two events as occurring simultaneously—an executive working for cash (assets decrease causing compensation expense) and an executive investing in the firm (owners' equity increases from contribution by an owner).

If the stock price is above $21 during 2003, the options will be exercised by the executives, who will then tender the options and $21 per option to Irish. The increase in cash of $210,000 ($21 exercise price × 10,000 options) is accompanied by a $210,000 increase in owners' equity ($10,000 to Common Stock and $200,000 to total Additional Paid-In Capital).[15] Assuming the 10,000 options were exercised in 2003, the effect on the 2003 financial statements is as shown in Exhibit 20.

EXHIBIT 20 Example 6. Irish Co. 2003 Financial Statements assuming 10,000 options are exercised—Fair Value Method

Balance Sheet

Assets		**Owners' Equity**	
Cash	$210,000	Contributed capital	
		Common stock (10,000 × $1)	$ 10,000
		Additional paid-in capital	220,000
		Retained earnings	
		Cumulative income statement effect	(20,000)

Income Statement	**Statement of Owners' Equity**	
No effect	Investments by owners	
	Common stock issue	$210,000

The combined result of the issuance and the exercise of the options is that assets increase $210,000; contributed capital increases $230,000; and retained earnings decreases $20,000.

EXAMPLE 6 Journal Entries—*SFAS No. 123* Fair Value Method

December 31, 2001:		
Compensation Expense	10,000	
Contributed Capital from Stock Option Plan		10,000
December 31, 2002:		
Compensation Expense	10,000	
Contributed Capital from Stock Option Plan		10,000
2003 exercise:		
Cash	210,000	
Contributed Capital from Stock Option Plan	20,000	
Common Stock		10,000
Additional Paid-In Capital		220,000

The preceding example illustrates cliff vesting. Graded vesting would be similarly handled by dividing the plan into the different vesting periods and using the Black-Scholes option pricing model to separately value each group of options. The example also illustrated a fixed option plan (the number of options is fixed). In a performance based plan, the number of options to be awarded and vested would depend on management's best estimate of the level of future performance expected to occur.

Solution 2. *The Intrinsic Value Method (introduced by APB No. 25) Compensatory stock option.* This stock option plan is *compensatory* because, at the grant date, the option price of $21 is below the quoted market price of $30. The total amount of compensation is clearly determinable at the grant date as $90,000 [($30 − $21) × 10,000 shares], which is the opportunity cost to Irish of committing to issue the

15. $20,000 of contributed capital comes from the stock option plan. When combined with the $200,000 additional paid-in capital from the stock issue, total Additional Paid-In Capital is $220,000 as shown in the 2003 balance sheet.

shares at $21 per share rather than issuing the shares at $30 per share. The two-year service period causes compensation expense of $45,000 to be recognized in both 2001 and 2002. This situation can be viewed as simultaneously recognizing two transactions, service for cash and cash for equity. Therefore, Irish reports an increase in owners' equity of $45,000 in each period. A summary of the financial statement effects appears in Exhibits 21 and 22.

EXHIBIT 21 Example 6. Irish Co. (2001 Financial Statements): Intrinsic Value Method—Compensatory

2001 Balance Sheet

Assets		**Owners' Equity**	
No effect		Contributed capital	
		Contributed capital from stock option plan	$90,000
		Deferred compensation	(45,000)
		Retained earnings	
		Income statement effect	(45,000)

Income Statement		**Statement of Owners' Equity**	
Compensation expense	$45,000	Investments by owners	
		Contributed capital from stock option plan	$90,000
		Deferred compensation	(45,000)
		Net income effect on retained earnings	(45,000)

EXHIBIT 22 Example 6. Irish Co. (2002 Financial Statements): Intrinsic Value Method—Compensatory

2002 Balance Sheet

Assets		**Owners' Equity**	
No effect		Contributed capital	
		Contributed capital from stock option plan	$90,000
		Retained earnings	
		Cumulative income statement effect	(90,000)

Income Statement		**Statement of Owners' Equity**	
Compensation expense	$45,000	Investments by owners	
		Deferred compensation	$45,000
		Net income effect on retained earnings	(45,000)

Because no assets or liabilities are affected, yet compensation expense is recorded, the overall effect of the stock options simply transfers amounts from earned capital (retained earnings) to contributed capital. The statements show the $45,000 compensation expense in each year. The 2001 owners' equity section shows the total estimated contributed capital from the plan, $90,000 less the $45,000 deferred compensation (a contra-equity account) that will not be fully recognized until 2002. The decrease in net income caused by the compensation expense flows through to retained earnings, yielding no net effect on total owners' equity. The 2002 owners' equity section shows that the total contributed capital has increased $90,000 to reflect services performed by the executives. The $90,000 cumulative decrease in net income caused by the compensation expense in 2001 and 2002 flows through to retained earnings, yielding no net effect on owners' equity.

If the stock price is below $21 during 2003, the options will not be exercised, and the contributed capital from the stock options will be reclassified as Contributed

Capital from Expired Options. If the stock price is above $21 during 2003, the options will be exercised by the executives, who will then tender the options and $21 per option to Irish. The increase in cash of $210,000 ($21 exercise price × 10,000 options) is offset by a $210,000 increase in owners' equity. Assuming the 10,000 options were exercised in 2003, the effect on the 2003 financial statements is as shown in Exhibit 23.

EXHIBIT 23 Example 6. Irish Co. 2003 Financial Statements, assuming 10,000 options are exercised—Intrinsic Value Method (Compensatory)

Balance Sheet

Assets		**Owners' Equity**	
Cash	$210,000	Contributed capital	
		Common stock (10,000 × $1)	$ 10,000
		Additional paid-in capital	290,000
		Retained earnings	
		Cumulative income statement effect	(90,000)

Income Statement	**Statement of Owners' Equity**	
No effect	Investments by owners	
	Common stock issue	$210,000

The combined effect of issuing and exercising the stock options increases assets $210,000; increases contributed capital $300,000; and decreases retained earnings $90,000.

EXAMPLE 6 Journal Entries *APB No. 25* Intrinsic Value Method—Compensatory

January 1, 2001 grant date:		
Deferred Compensation	90,000	
Contributed Capital from Stock Option Plan		90,000
December 31, 2001:		
Compensation Expense	45,000	
Deferred Compensation		45,000
December 31, 2002:		
Compensation Expense	45,000	
Deferred Compensation		45,000
2003 exercise:		
Cash	210,000	
Contributed Capital from Stock Option Plan	90,000	
Common Stock		10,000
Additional Paid-In Capital		290,000

Example 6A. *The Intrinsic Value Method (introduced by APB No. 25), Noncompensatory stock option.* What if Irish granted the options on a date when the market price and the exercise price were equal? In Example 6, if we change the original information to a market price of $21 on the grant date, under the intrinsic value method, the option becomes *noncompensatory,* and no compensation expense is recorded in 2001 or 2002. *This approach is most often used because almost all companies choose to use the intrinsic value method. When crafting a stock option plan, the option price is made equal to the market price on the grant date, which ensures that the stock options are noncompensatory.*

Under *SFAS No. 123* accounting, if Irish chooses to use the intrinsic value method rather than the fair value method, the company must disclose the amount of compensation that would have been reported if the company had used the fair value method. (Such disclosures are made in the financial statement footnotes.) Therefore, in its 2001 and 2002 footnotes, Irish would report that $10,000 compensation expense per year would have been recorded if the company had used the fair value method.

If the 10,000 options were exercised in 2003, the financial statements in Exhibit 24 result.

EXHIBIT 24 Example 6A. Irish Co. 2003 Financial Statements, assuming 10,000 options are exercised—Intrinsic Value Method (Noncompensatory)

Balance Sheet

Assets		**Owners' Equity**	
Cash	$210,000	Contributed capital	
		Common stock (10,000 × $1)	10,000
		Additional paid-in capital	200,000

Income Statement	**Statement of Owners' Equity**	
No effect	Investments by owners	
	Common stock issue	$210,000

EXAMPLE 6 Journal Entries *APB No. 25* Intrinsic Value Method—Noncompensatory

At January 1, 2001 grant date:
No entry

December 31, 2001:
No entry

December 31, 2002:
No entry

2003 exercise:

Cash	210,000	
Common Stock		10,000
Additional Paid-In Capital		200,000

Stock Appreciation Rights

Not all stock-based compensation plans involve the issuance of options, nor do they require executives to have the cash available to acquire stock. A good example of an alternative plan that bases compensation on stock appreciation (while not requiring the actual purchase of stock) is the stock appreciation rights (SARs) plan.

Example 7. Seminole Inc. grants the president 20,000 SARs at January 2, 2001. On January 1, 2004, the president will receive cash based on the difference between the quoted market price of Seminole's stock at December 31, 2003, and a price of $10 per SAR. Per share market prices at the end of 2001, 2002, and 2003 were $22, $20, and $16, respectively. Compute the compensation expense and the liability under the SAR plan for each date.

Solution. In a SAR plan, the total amount of compensation expense is unknown at the grant date, and the final amount is not known until the exercise date. Therefore, compensation expense is re-estimated each period, and appropriate adjustments are made to both compensation expense of the period and the liability under the SAR plan. The estimation process assumes that the final stock price is the current stock price. Exhibit 25 illustrates the SAR accounting measurement procedure:

EXHIBIT 25 SAR Measurement Computations

	2001	2002	2003
Market price of common at 12/31	$ 22	$ 20	$ 16
SAR price	(10)	(10)	(10)
Estimated compensation expense per SAR	$ 12	$ 10	$ 6
Number of SARs	× 20,000	× 20,000	× 20,000
Estimated total compensation expense	$240,000	$200,000	$120,000
Proportion of service period to date	× 33.3%	× 66.7%	× 100%
Accrual to date **(liability under SAR plan)**	$ 80,000	$133,334	$120,000
Accruals in prior years	(0)	(80,000)	(133,334)
Compensation expense recognized during the year	$ 80,000	$ 53,334	$ (13,334)

The December 31, 2001, market price is $12 above the SAR exercise price. With 20,000 SARs outstanding and one-third of the service period passed, Seminole estimates its liability to be $80,000 and records that amount as compensation expense. The liability is long-term because the expected cash disbursement date is January 1, 2004. By December 31, 2002, the market price has fallen to $20, yielding an estimate that, once the entire service period is through, compensation expense will be $200,000. Given that two-thirds of the service period is passed, the accrued liability to date should be $133,334. The prior year's accruals total $80,000, so an additional accrual of $53,334 is required in the current period. This accrual increases Compensation Expense by $53,334. Market price continues to fall such that, at December 31, 2003 (the end of the service period), only a $120,000 total liability exists. Because $133,334 had been accrued in prior years, the liability must be reduced by $13,334, which causes a negative expense of the same amount. Market price was the best estimate at each date of the expected SAR liability, and changes in the estimate from period to period are reflected in compensation expense of the period. Restatements of the prior years' financial statements are not made because there were no errors in those statements.

EXAMPLE 7 Journal Entries

12/31/01:		
Compensation Expense	80,000	
Liability Under SAR Plan		80,000
12/31/02:		
Compensation Expense	53,334	
Liability Under SAR Plan		53,334
12/31/03:		
Liability Under SAR Plan	13,334	
Compensation Expense		13,334
1/1/04 payment:		
Liability Under SAR Plan	120,000	
Cash		120,000

Summary of Stock Compensation Plans

Current GAAP for stock compensation plans represents a compromise between theory and political pressure. Most companies simply do not want to recognize compensation expense when stock options vest, even though they are clearly conveying something of value to employees in exchange for services. However, the FASB believes that the value of stock options should be expensed. When the FASB issued *SFAS No. 123*, corporate America prevailed—the FASB allowed the continued use of the intrinsic value method. This method results in no compensation expense, and will be used by almost all companies. However, the effect of the fair value method must still be disclosed in the notes to the financial statements. Research in both accounting and finance demonstrates that note disclosures are used by investors and creditors for decision-making purposes.

Southwest Airlines' Financial Statements

Southwest Airlines' 1998 financial statements are provided in Appendix C. Review the following information provided in those financial statements: Note 8, "Stock Plans" and the related disclosures on the statement of stockholders' equity, the stock-based employee compensation portion of Note 1, "Summary of Significant Accounting Policies"; the statement of cash flows—financing activities; and Note 9, "Employee Profitsharing and Savings Plans."

Benefit Plans

Southwest Airlines does not have a defined benefit pension plan. However, it does have a substantial profit sharing plan, as described in Note 9. Under the profit sharing plan, the company expensed $120,670,000, $91,256,000, and $59,927,000 in 1998, 1997, and 1996, respectively. These amounts represented 2.9%, 2.4%, and 1.8% of total operating revenues, respectively, in 1998, 1997, and 1996. Additionally, the company's matching contributions to an employee 401(k) savings plan were $46,415,000, $39,744,000, and $35,125,000 in 1998, 1997, and 1996, respectively. Note 3 shows that at December 31, 1998, Southwest had accrued liabilities of $123,195,000 for employee profit sharing and savings plans.

Post-Retirement Benefits

Evidently, the amount of post-retirement benefit expense (if any) is immaterial to Southwest—there is no separate note disclosure for post-retirement benefits.

Stock Plans

As expected, Southwest Airlines uses the *intrinsic value method* prescribed in *APB No. 25* for stock plans (see Note 1, "Stock-based employee compensation"). Southwest had seven stock-based compensation plans, with six fixed option plans. No compensation expense is recognized for fixed options, and any compensation expense for the other plans is immaterial. Note 8 provides an extensive description of the plans. The statement of stockholders' equity shows that the company issued 2,803,000, 2,517,000, and 1,079,000 shares in 1998, 1997, and 1996, respectively, under the stock option and stock purchase plans (because the common stock par value equals $1, the dollar amounts reported in the statement of stockholders' equity equal the number of shares issued).

SFAS No. 123 disclosures are required on all options granted after January 1, 1995. The pro forma effects compared to the actual results are as follows:

SOUTHWEST AIRLINES
***SFAS No. 123* Disclosures**

(In thousands)	1998	1997	1996
Net income			
As reported	$433,431	$317,772	$207,337
Pro forma, if *SFAS No. 123* had been applied	421,097	306,553	196,478
Net income per share, basic			
As reported	$1.30	$0.97	$0.64
Pro forma, if *SFAS No. 123* had been applied	1.26	0.93	0.60
Net income per share, diluted			
As reported	$1.23	$0.93	$0.61
Pro forma, if *SFAS No. 123* had been applied	1.20	0.90	0.60

If Southwest had used the *SFAS No. 123* fair value method in 1998, net income would have been reduced by about $12 million, and basic and diluted EPS would have been reduced by $0.04 and $0.03, respectively.

Chapter Summary

Compensation is a critical means of attracting and retaining the human capital necessary for companies to successfully compete. The mix of compensation plans is important in aligning manager and shareholder interests. Of the nonsalary compensation schemes addressed in this chapter, the ones yielding the largest expenses and liabilities are primarily off-balance-sheet in nature. This situation is indicative of the struggle faced by the FASB in deciding between recognition and disclosure.

We have not addressed the personal and corporate tax implications of the different forms of compensation because a thorough tax analysis is beyond the scope of this text. The mix of compensation, however, is greatly affected by tax laws. The 1997 federal budget agreement is likely to impact compensation in many ways, with the most significant being the reduction of the capital gains tax on individuals. However, other provisions will also have an effect on defined contribution pension plans.

Key SFAS No. 132 Disclosures

Under *SFAS No. 132,* several footnote disclosures for pensions and other post-retirement benefits are required. The major disclosures are:

1. A reconciliation of the beginning balance to the ending balance of Projected Benefit Obligation (pensions) and/or Accumulated Post-Retirement Benefit Obligation (other post-retirement benefit plans).
2. A reconciliation of the beginning balance to the ending balance of Fair Value of Plan Assets.
3. A reconciliation of the funded status of the plan to the amounts recognized in the statement of financial position.
4. The components of Net Pension Cost (an expense).
5. The amount included in Other Comprehensive Income for the period arising from a change in the additional minimum pension liability.
6. The following assumptions on a weighted-average basis: the assumed discount (settlement) rate, the rate of compensation increase, and the expected long-term rate of return on plan assets.
7. The assumed health care cost trend rate(s).
8. The effect of both an increase and a decrease of one percentage point in the assumed health care cost trend rate on (1) the accumulated post-retirement benefit obligation for health care benefits, and (2) the aggregate of the service and interest cost components of the net periodic post-retirement health care benefit cost.

Key Terms

Questions

Q1. **Compensated Absences.** What two primary conditions must be present to trigger the accrual of compensated absences that are both vested and related to services already rendered?

Q2. **Compensated Absences.** If all conditions for the accrual of compensated absences are present except for an estimable amount of payment, should the accrual take place? If not, what kind of disclosure is necessary?

Q3. **Sick Pay.** When sick days accumulate but do not vest, the accrual of sick pay related compensation expense is allowable but not required. Why?

Q4. **Defined Contribution versus Defined Benefit Pension Plans.** Compare and contrast defined contribution plans and defined benefit pension plans.

Q5. **Defined Benefit Pension Plan Formula.** Give an example of a typical pension plan formula for a defined benefit pension plan.

Q6. **Pension Plan Obligations.** List and explain the three possible measures of the economic pension obligation.

Q7. **Settlement Rate.** What is the settlement interest rate? How is it used in pension accounting?

Q8. **Pension Plan Assets.** What is the basis for measuring pension plan assets?

Q9. **Economic Status of Pension Plan.** If someone states that the economic status of the pension plan is a "net asset," what do they mean? What does a "net obligation" mean?

Q10. **Events Affecting PBO.** List and describe the five events that change the PBO during a given period. Indicate whether the events receive *no recognition, immediate recognition,* or *delayed recognition* in determining GAAP-based pension expense.

Q11. **Events Affecting the FMV of Pension Plan Assets.** List and describe the three events that change the FMV of net assets during a given period. Indicate whether the events receive *no recognition, immediate recognition,* or *delayed recognition* in determining GAAP-based pension expense.

Q12. **Components of Actual Return on Plan Assets.** What are the two components of the actual return on plan assets? How are they accounted for in determining pension expense?

Q13. **Recognition of Prior Service Cost.** Why is prior service cost given delayed treatment in computing pension cost?

Q14. **Pension Cost versus Pension Expense.** Are pension cost and pension expense always equal? Explain.

Q15. **Stock Options.** What are the two methods in accounting for fixed stock options? Which method do companies use? Why?

Q16. **Stock Options.** Why do companies offer stock options?

Q17. **Stock Options versus Stock Appreciation Rights.** What are the similarities and the major differences in stock options and stock appreciation rights (SARs)?

Short Problems

1. **Reconcile PBO and FMV of Plan Assets.** Given the following information, compute the December 31, 2001, projected benefit obligation (PBO) and the fair market value (FMV) of plan assets for Rogers Co.:

Prior service cost granted in 2001	$110,000
Interest on PBO	70,000
Actual return on plan assets	100,000
Service cost	80,000
Contribution sent to plan trustee	60,000
Benefit payments to retirees	20,000
Liability loss (gain)	(30,000)
FMV of plan assets, 1/1/01	750,000
PBO, 1/1/01	800,000

2. **Reconcile PBO and FMV of Plan Assets, Compute Pension Cost.** Given the following information, compute the December 31, 2001, PBO and FMV of net assets for Roy Co. Also, compute 2001 pension cost.

Prior service cost due to 2001 amendment	$60,000
PBO, 1/1/01	$1,000,000
FMV, 1/1/01	$1,200,000
Settlement interest rate	7%
Expected return on plan assets	9%
Actual return on plan assets	8%
Liability loss (gain)	$(40,000)
Year-end contribution to plan trustee	$100,000
Service cost	$115,000
Payments to retiring employees	$30,000

3. **Reconcile PBO and FMV of Plan Assets, Compute Pension Cost.** Given the following information, compute pension cost for 2001 for the Wong-on-Wing Company.

Service cost	$ 25,000
PBO, 1/1/01	400,000
PBO, 12/31/01	484,000
FMV of plan assets, 1/1/01	500,000
Balance sheet prepaid pension cost, 1/1/01	130,000
Unamortized transition amount, 1/1/01	0
Unamortized gain (loss), 1/1/01	20,000
Unamortized prior service cost, 1/1/01	50,000
Current year prior service cost	0
Actual return on plan assets	100,000
Contribution to trustee	25,000
Prior service cost amortization	10,000
Benefit payments to retirees	15,000
Settlement interest rate	6%
Expected return on plan assets	8%

4. **Defined Benefit Pension Plan Footnote Disclosures.** Using the information provided in problem (3), compute the following footnote disclosures for Wong-on-Wing: (1) reconcile from the beginning to the ending balances of PBO and FMV of plan assets, and (2) reconcile from the amount that the pension plan is over(under)funded to the balance sheet prepaid (accrued) pension cost amount. Ignore minimum liability provisions.

5. **Compute Pension Cost.** Given the following information for Hernandez Co., compute pension cost for 2001:

Payments to retiring employees	$500,000
Contribution to plan trustee	400,000
Interest on PBO	50,000
Expected return on plan assets	75,000
Service cost	100,000
Loss amortization	45,000

6. **Prepaid (Accrued) Pension Cost.** Ignoring the minimum liability, compute the December 31, 2003, balance in Prepaid (Accrued) Pension Cost under the following two scenarios. (Assume a January 1, 2001, prepaid (accrued) pension cost amount of zero for each scenario.)

	Scenario One	**Scenario Two**
Pension expense, 2001	$40,000	$ 65,000
Contributions to plan trustee, 2001	30,000	95,000
Pension expense, 2002	40,000	70,000
Contributions to plan trustee, 2002	40,000	0
Pension expense, 2003	40,000	80,000
Contributions to plan trustee, 2003	45,000	150,000

7. **Minimum Liability.** Given the following information, compute Bell Co.'s minimum liability to be reported as of December 31, 2001.

Cumulative recognitions of pension expense for all years through 12/31/01	$ 800,000
Cumulative payments to plan trustee for all years through 12/31/01	850,000
PBO, 12/31/01	2,000,000
ABO, 12/31/01	1,800,000
FMV of plan assets, 12/31/01	1,500,000

8. **Minimum Liability.** Marony Inc. adopted a defined benefit pension plan on January 1, 2000. On that date, Marony granted benefits to employees based on prior service to the company totaling $50,000 (Marony had no prior pension plan assets or liabilities). Because employees benefitting from the initial grant were expected to be with the company for the next ten years, $5,000 prior service cost is to be amortized each year, beginning with 2000. The following additional information relates to Marony's plan:

	2000	2001	2002	2003
PBO, 12/31	$60,000	$90,000	$120,000	$120,000
ABO, 12/31	40,000	60,000	80,000	80,000
FMV of plan assets, 12/31	0	0	50,000	110,000
Pension expense	10,000	15,000	20,000	15,000
Contributions to trustee	0	0	50,000	50,000

Assume no asset or liability gains or losses for the 2000–2003 period. For each year-end (2000–2003), indicate what pension-related amounts will be shown on Marony's balance sheet. Note that to simplify this problem, we assumed no plan assets at year-end 2000 and 2001. This situation would almost certainly violate ERISA provisions that require minimum funding each period. The scenario could also occur if all assets contributed were paid out to employees.

9. **Pension Plan Note Disclosure.** Using the following information, prepare the note reconciliation between the economic status of Bradshaw Co.'s defined benefit pension plan and the balance sheet amount at December 31, 2001:

PBO, 12/31	$191,000
ABO, 12/31	160,000
FMV of net assets, 12/31	125,000
Unamortized losses (gains), 12/31	67,000
Unamortized prior service cost, 12/31	148,000
Unamortized transition amount, 12/31	0
Cumulative contributions to plan trustee	80,000
Cumulative pension expense recognitions	65,000

10. **Amortization of Unrealized Gain/Loss.** Montego Corporation had the following pension-related amounts at the beginning and the end of the first year of the company's pension plan:

	Beginning	End
PBO	$0	$10,000
FMV of plan assets	0	12,000
Unamortized gains	0	3,000

a. Assuming a 10 year amortization period, how much of the first-year gain was amortized in the first year?
b. Assuming a 10-year amortization period, how much of the first-year gain should be amortized in the second year?

11. **Amortization of Unrealized Gain/Loss.** Assume that Terry Corp. had the following expected and actual PBOs and FMVs of plan assets (in millions of $):

	Actual		Expected	
Dec. 31	**PBO**	**FMV**	**PBO**	**FMV**
2000	$100	$ 90	$110	$ 95
2001	160	160	120	110
2002	200	130	140	160
2003	250	260	250	220

a. Compute the gain/loss amortization included as a component of pension expense for each year of the 2000–2003 period. Assume no unamortized loss (gain) on January 1, 2000. Assume that gains/losses are amortized over a 10-year period for any year in which unrecognized gains/losses are amortized.
b. Compute the unrecognized gain/loss for the note reconciliations at December 31 for each year of the 2000–2003 period. Assume that gains/losses are amortized over a 10-year period for any year in which unrecognized gains/losses are amortized.

12. **Transition Amount.** Wege Welders adopted *SFAS No. 87* on January 1, 1990, to account for its pension plan that had been in place since 1980. At that date, Wege's plan had assets with a FMV of $6,000,000 and a PBO of $6,800,000. Under *APB Opinion*

No. 8, Wege had an accrued pension cost of $500,000 on January 1, 1990, which is treated as part of the transition amount.
a. Compute the transition amount.
b. Compute the 1990 amortization of the transition amount included in pension cost (stating whether the amortization increased or decreased pension cost), and the unamortized amount to be included as a December 31, 1990, reconciling item.

13. **Transition Amount.** Jaworski Brothers Pipeline adopted *SFAS No. 87* on January 1, 1990, to account for its pension plan. At that date, Jaworski's plan had assets with a FMV of $100,000 and a PBO of $60,000. Under *APB Opinion No. 8,* Jaworski had a prepaid pension cost of $5,000 on January 1, 1990, which is treated as part of the transition amount.
    a. Compute the transition amount.
    b. Compute the 1990 amortization of the transition amount included in pension cost (stating whether the amortization increased or decreased pension cost), and the unamortized amount to be included as a December 31, 1990, reconciling item.

14. **Post-Retirement versus Defined Benefit Pension Plan Accounting.** What are two main differences between the accounting for other post-retirement plans and the accounting for defined benefit pension plans?

15. **Fixed versus Performance Stock Options.** Explain the difference between fixed options and performance options.

16. **Cliff versus Graded Vesting in Stock Option Plans.** Explain the difference between cliff vesting and graded vesting of stock option plans.

Note: Problems 17 and 18 are related.

17. **Stock Options: Intrinsic Value versus Fair Value Methods.** On January 1, 2001, Cowboy Company entered into an agreement whereby Cowboy's president, John Jones, was granted stock options. The option agreement stated that Mr. Jones could purchase up to 10,000 shares of Cowboy's $5 par common on January 1, 2003, for $30 per share, *if* Mr. Jones still worked for Cowboy on that date. On January 1, 2001, Cowboy's stock sold for $50 per share. An appropriate option model valued the options at $15,000. Assuming Jones exercises the options on January 1, 2003, when the stock is selling at $53 per share, show all financial statement effects of the plan for 2001–2003 (a) under the intrinsic value approach of *APB No. 25,* and (b) under the fair value approach of *SFAS No. 123.*

18. **Stock Options: Intrinsic Value versus Fair Value Methods.** Repeat problem (17) assuming that on the date of grant, January 1, 2001, Cowboy's common stock trades at $30 per share.

19. **Stock Appreciation Rights (SARs).** On January 1, 2000, Ranger Enterprises issues 900,000 stock appreciation rights, which are exercisable on December 31, 2002, and expire on January 1, 2006. Each SAR allows Ranger's key employees to receive the excess of the stock price at exercise over a predetermined price of $50. The company believes that it will benefit from improved employee performance over the period January 1, 2000–December 31, 2002. The year-end stock prices for 2000, 2001, and 2002 are $60, $54, and $51, respectively. Assuming the key employees exercise the SARs at December 31, 2002, show all financial statement effects of the plan for 2000–2002.

Comprehensive and Analytical Problems

20. **Financial Statement Effects of Alternative Stock Options Methods.** Using I = increases; D = decreases; NE = no effect, identify the effects of the following transactions or conditions on the various financial statement amounts:

Situation (situations 1–4 are the same across all three events, and the situations pertain to the relationship between market price and option price on the grant date)	Contributed Capital: Common Stock	Contributed Capital: Additional Paid-in Capital	Contributed Capital: Other Contributed Capital	Retained Earnings: Direct Effect	Retained Earnings: Indirect Effect (Through Net Income)
Granting of stock options:					
1. Market price exceeds exercise price (*APB No. 25* intrinsic value rules)					
2. Market price exceeds exercise price (*SFAS No. 123* fair value rules)					
3. Market price equals exercise price (*APB No. 25* intrinsic value rules)					
4. Market price equals exercise price (*SFAS No. 123* fair value rules)					
Employee performs service, thus earning any compensation implied by stock options:					
1. Market price exceeds exercise price (*APB No. 25* intrinsic value rules)					
2. Market price exceeds exercise price (*SFAS No. 123* fair value rules)					
3. Market price equals exercise price (*APB No. 25* intrinsic value rules)					
4. Market price equals exercise price (*SFAS No. 123* fair value rules)					
Employee exercises stock options:					
1. Market price exceeds exercise price (*APB No. 25* intrinsic value rules)					
2. Market price exceeds exercise price (*SFAS No. 123* fair value rules)					
3. Market price equals exercise price (*APB No. 25* intrinsic value rules)					
4. Market price equals exercise price (*SFAS No. 123* fair value rules)					

21. **Financial Statement Effects of Pension Plan Events.** Using I = increases; D = decreases; NE = no effect, identify the current year effects of the following transactions or conditions on the various financial statement elements. (Note that the questions pertain to the employer's financial statements, not to the pension plan's financial statements.)

	Assets	Liabilities*	Owners' Equity	Net Income
Pension plan effect of employees performing current service				
Plan amendment grants retroactive benefits				
Projected benefit obligation accrues interest at the settlement rate				
Unexpected increases in PBO due to changes in actuarial assumptions				
Retiring employees are paid				
Contributions made to plan trustee				
Plan assets increase by expected return from investing				
Unexpected decrease in FMV of plan assets due to an asset loss				
Amortization of prior service cost				
Amortization of gain				
Amortization of transition amount				

*Primarily Accrued Pension Cost

22. **Prior Service Cost.** HopeForTheBest Corporation decides not to fund a plan amendment granting prior service to a current employee group. Discuss the effects of this decision on pension expense and the balance sheet disclosures over the next several years. Make sure to consider the direct and indirect effects.

23. **Pension Plan Funding.** You have recently been informed that stock market conditions in the current period have dramatically (and unexpectedly) increased the FMV of your company's pension plan assets by more than 50%. Investment advisors indicate that this effect is a one-time effect that is not expected to reverse. Draft a memo explaining how this event will affect pension expense and the balance sheet disclosures over the next several periods. Make sure to consider the direct and indirect effects.

24. **Fair Value versus Intrinsic Value Method of Accounting for Stock Options.** Your employer has decided to offer a fixed stock option plan to certain key executives. It is necessary to decide whether to use the intrinsic value method or the fair value method to account for the stock options. Briefly describe the financial statement effects of both methods.

http://

25. **Texas Instruments.** The financial statements for Texas Instruments are provided at the text Web site at http://baginski.swcollege.com. Review the balance sheet liabilities (both current and noncurrent) related to accrued retirement costs; the statement of changes in stockholder's equity; the stockholder's equity note; the stock option note; and the retirement and incentive plan note.
   a. **Stock options.** Does the company use the fair value or intrinsic value for stock option plans? What would be the pro forma 1998 net income and earnings per share effects if the fair value method had been used? How many shares were issued in 1998 related to the exercise of stock options?
   b. **Benefit plans.** Did TI offer defined contribution, defined benefit plans, or both? Did TI offer any other post-retirement benefit plans? How much are the defined benefit plan and retiree health care plan over(under)funded in 1998? What was the 1998 expense associated with the two plans? Was TI's 1998 actual return on pension plan assets greater or lesser than the expected return? What was the 1998 asset gain/loss? What was the amount of TI's 1998 pension plan contribution? How much was paid in benefits for the defined benefit and retiree health care plans?

26. **Comprehensive Defined Benefit Pension Plan Problem.** The Peters Co. sponsors a defined benefit pension plan for its 500 employees. The company's actuary provided the following information about the plan, for which *SFAS No. 87* was adopted on January 1, 2001. (Note that the example is artificially created with a beginning PBO and FMV of plan assets on January 1, 2001, in order to include a transition amount.) Amortize the transition amount over ten years.

PETERS CO.
Defined Benefit Pension Plan Information (In thousands)

	January 1	December 31	
	2001	2001	2002
PBO	$2,000,000	$3,850,000	$4,600,000
ABO	$1,975,000	$2,630,000	$3,100,000
FMV plan assets	$1,900,000	$2,800,000	$2,300,000
Current settlement rate	11%	11%	8%
Long-term expected return on plan assets	10%	10%	10%
Service cost	N/A	$400,000	$475,000
Liability loss(gain)	$0	$1,230,000	$(148,500)
Pension plan contribution (made on 12/31)	N/A	$500,000	$550,000
Actual return on plan assets: positive (negative)	N/A	$400,000	$(1,050,000)
Benefit payments to Retirees	$0	$0	$0
Average expected time until workers retire	10 years	10 years	10 years

Required: Present the main *SFAS No. 132* pension disclosures for 2001 and 2002: (1) the reconciliation of PBO and FMV of plan assets, (2) the reconciliation of funded status (adjusted for any minimum liability), and (3) the computation of pension expense for 2001 and 2002.

Note: These requirements are not independent—computations from part (1) are used in part (3), and amounts in the part (3) computations are used in part (1).

CFA Exam-Type Problems

27. **Pensions.** The following information applies to the projected benefit obligation (PBO) for a firm's pension fund.

Opening balance for the PBO	$25,000
Service cost for the year	$3,300
Current year prior service cost	$700
Benefits paid for the year	$400
Projected rate of return	10%
Discount rate	8%

What is the closing PBO balance at the end of the year? (CFA adapted)
a. $30,600
b. $31,100
c. $31,400
d. $31,000

28. **Pensions.** When accounting for pension plans, the change in the projected benefit obligation over a given year will *not* reflect the impact of: (CFA adapted)
a. service cost for the year
b. benefits paid during the year
c. earnings of the pension fund for the year
d. a change in the estimate of compensation growth

29. **Pensions.** In accounting for pension benefits, which one of the following statements is true? (CFA adapted)
a. The difference between the accumulated benefit obligation and the projected benefit obligation is negatively related to the assumed rate of compensation increase.
b. The discount rate used to compute the present value of the benefit obligation is expected to change less often than the rate used in computing return on assets.
c. The benefits must be allocated to years of service using the most conservative applicable method.
d. The difference between the accumulated benefit obligation and the projected benefit obligation is positively related to the assumed rate of compensation increase.

30. **Pensions.** For its year-end 1999 statements, Wahoo Ltd. increased the "pension discount rate" from 9% to 10%, and the "assumed rate of compensation increase" from 8% to 8.5%. The effect of these changes is to: (CFA adapted, with slight modifications by authors)
a. increase the difference between the accumulated benefit obligation and the pension benefit obligation
b. increase the return on assets assumption for 2000
c. increase the service cost element of pension cost in 2000
d. decrease the deferred experience gains or increase the deferred experience losses

31. **Stock Options.** Which of the following statements is *not* true regarding stock compensation plans for fixed stock options with cliff vesting in the future? (Author constructed)
a. Companies prefer the use of the fair value method over the intrinsic value method of reporting for stock options.
b. The use of the fair value method requires companies to obtain quotes from listed exchanges about the fair value of the stock options at the grant date.
c. The use of the intrinsic value method almost always results in the recognition of compensation expense in the income statement.
d. The use of the intrinsic value method almost never results in the recognition of compensation expense in the income statement.

Objectives

1 Describe cash flows related to operating decisions.

2 Analyze the effects of operating decisions on the profit margin.

3 Prepare the balance sheet and income statement adjustments made by many financial analysts in the process of analyzing the success of operations.

Module D

The External Users' Assessment of Management's Operating Decisions

In this module, we review the cash flow effects of operating activities and several important profitability and risk ratios affected by these activities. We also discuss how financial analysts interpret operating activities, and we then consider some of the key adjustments to financial statements that many analysts make in the area.

The analysis of operating cash flows is a cornerstone for many decisions. Early in this text, we described the three primary activities of the firm: operating, investing, and financing. Financing and investing activities exist entirely for the support of operations. Operating cash flows provide the funds to pay dividends and interest (i.e., the returns to investors and creditors for providing financing), and replace and expand operations so that a company can continue to exist and prosper.

Operating Cash Flows

1 Describe cash flows related to operating decisions.

The first section of the statement of cash flows describes cash inflows and outflows from operating activities. These cash flows are important in firm valuation, especially for investors who use free cash flow discounting to determine stock prices. Also, cash flows from operations are very important for creditors to assess the ability of borrowers to make scheduled principal and interest payments. Accordingly, we spend the first part of this module reviewing operating cash flows.

The two core chapters on operations in this text are Chapters 9 and 10. Chapter 9 focuses on the building up of working capital items (inventory, accounts receivable, and accounts payable) to support sales; Chapter 10 describes the revenue and expense recognition process. We first consider how these activities affect operating cash flows by examining TCBY's statement of cash flows.

TCBY's Operating Cash Flows

Appendix D provides the November 30, 1998, consolidated statement of cash flows for TCBY Enterprises, Inc. Like most other companies, TCBY uses the indirect method to arrive at *Net cash provided by operating activities*. TCBY implements the indirect method by beginning with net income of $10,195,612, and then adjusting for accruals that are a part of net income, but not cash flows. First, TCBY adds back changes in (primarily) long-term assets and liabilities that, although reflected in net income, do not involve cash flows. Second, TCBY repeats the process for changes in operating assets and liabilities (primarily short-term).

Expense Recognition Practices in Accrual Accounting—The First Set of Indirect Method Adjustments The costs of long-lived assets (reported as investing activity cash outflows on earlier cash flow statements) are allocated to future periods benefitted through depreciation and amortization. The first two adjustments to net income under the indirect method are addbacks for the amount of depreciation ($4,048,305) and amortization ($262,031). Both of these expenses decreased current period net income, but they did not involve the outflow of cash (in the current period). Thus, they are added back to net income to determine net cash inflow.

Expense recognition and cash outflow also do not occur at the same time for bad debts and deferred taxes. TCBY estimated 1998 bad debts expense on accounts and notes receivable to be $72,500. Although this charge reduced current income, it is indicative of future (not current) reductions in cash. As with depreciation and amortization charges, bad debts expense is added back in determining net cash inflows.

Deferred tax liabilities decreased by $644,802 during 1998. A decrease in a liability increases net assets, and thus, net income. However, the deferred tax liability decrease did not increase cash, and accordingly, it is subtracted from net income in determining net cash inflows from operations.

As previously discussed in the text, cash inflows and outflows from transactions in the principal amounts of long-term assets and long-term debt are reported in the investing and financing activities sections of the cash flow statement, respectively. To avoid double counting, any gains and losses on these transactions must be adjusted to net income in the operating activities section. For example, if a company has property with a book value of $10,000 that it sells for $12,000, net income includes a $2,000 gain. If the company reports the $12,000 as a cash inflow in the investing activities section and does not remove the $2,000 gain from net income in the operating activities section, then that $2,000 amount has been double counted, once as a part of net income and once as a part of cash inflow from sales of property. TCBY has such a gain on sales of property, plant, and equipment ($2,143,990), which it deducts from net income in the operating section to avoid the double counting.

Changes in Working Capital Items—The Second Set of Indirect Method Adjustments The building up of working capital (e.g., inventory, accounts receivable, and accounts payable) to support sales is one of the key operating decisions of management. Net working capital investment drains current cash flow with the expectation of increasing future cash inflows from future sales. For this reason, external parties look at the statement of cash flows to see how working capital items have changed during the period.

With all else equal (that is, assuming no change in accounts payable), a buildup of inventory is a drain on cash. TCBY reports the adverse cash flow effect of such a buildup in a final set of adjustments to net income labeled *Changes in operating assets and liabilities*. An inventory increase of $1,875,644 is subtracted from net income to arrive at net cash provided by operating activities. The subtraction is necessary because cash outflow occurred to build up inventory; however, net income is not reduced when inventory is purchased.

A similar adjustment is made for the $1,408,040 buildup of receivables. Receivables and inventory buildups are one indication of expanding operations. Knowledge of TCBY's plans for expansion in 1999 (relative to actual expansion in 1998) provides investors and creditors with a basis for predicting further cash drains to expand operations.

Accounts payable and accrued expenses decreased by \$54,759 in 1998. Liability decreases also use cash, and they are deducted from net income to arrive at net cash flow. In fact, a review of the other adjustments in the working capital area over the three-year period shows that increases in assets and decreases in liabilities are deducted from net income in arriving at cash flow from operating activities. Decreases in assets and increases in liabilities are added back.

Summary

Net cash provided by operating activities is a primary input into free cash flow-based valuation models and is a key element of several ratios used to assess profitability and risk. Further, because cash flows are free from management's estimation process, many investors rely heavily on cash flow from operations as an indicator of success when they believe that management engages in earnings management.

Effects of Operating Activities on Ratio Analysis

2 Analyze the effects of operating decisions on the profit margin.

In Module A, we discussed profitability and risk ratios, and we calculated those ratios for TCBY. In this section, we review a important set of those ratios directly affected by a firm's operating decisions.

Operating Activities and Profitability: The Profit Margin Ratio

Recall that an important ratio in the assessment of profitability is return on assets (ROA), which can be broken down into ratios for net profit margin and asset turnover:

$$\text{ROA} = \text{Net profit margin ratio} \times \text{Asset turnover ratio}$$

The net profit margin ratio is defined as follows:

$$\text{Net profit margin ratio} = [\text{Net income} + (1 - t)\ \text{Interest expense}] \div \text{Sales}$$

Financial analysts frequently prepare common sized financial statements, where they compute each item as a percentage of a base. For example, a common sized income statement presents all income statement items as a percentage of sales. For TCBY, the common sized income statements for 1996–1998 (with all items expressed as a percentage of sales) are presented below.

Common Sized Income Statement (in %)

	1998	1997	1996
Sales revenue	100.0	100.0	100.0
Cost of sales	(68.3)	(66.7)	(64.5)
Gross margin	31.7	33.3	35.5
Franchising revenues	14.0	15.2	15.5
Selling, general, and administrative expenses	(32.4)	(34.2)	(39.3)
Income from operations	13.3	14.3	11.7
Interest expense	(0.6)	(0.8)	(1.2)
Interest income	1.3	1.3	1.4
Other income	2.4	0.2	0.2
Income tax expense	(5.6)	(5.2)	(4.2)
Net income	10.8	9.8	7.9
Interest expense × (1 − tax rate)/Sales	0.4	0.5	0.7
Profit margin ratio	11.2	10.3	8.6

TCBY's profit margin ratio has steadily increased over the three-year period presented (from 8.6% to 11.2%). Many financial analysts, however, view one element of the profit margin ratio, the gross profit margin ratio, as the least "noisy" indicator of profitability—it does not include the effects of selling, general, and administrative expenses, which are subject to management discretion to a greater extent. Note that the gross profit margin ratio has declined steadily over the three-year period (from 35.5% to 31.7%). A decline in the gross profit margin ratio can occur because selling prices have fallen or because costs of producing or purchasing goods have increased. Franchising revenues as a percentage of sales has also declined (from 15.5% to 14.0%).

Substantial reductions of selling, general, and administrative expenses have been achieved over the same period, however, leading to an increase in the income from operations to sales percentage from 11.7% in 1996 to 14.3% in 1997, and 13.3% in 1998.

As noted during a previous analysis of TCBY, 1998 net income includes a large gain on a peripheral activity, the sale of an aircraft. These one-time gains reported in *Other income* (2.4% of sales in 1998) are unlikely to persist. Thus, even if continued reductions in SG&A expenses can be achieved in future periods to offset declining gross profit margins, the profit margin ratio may still not exceed the 10.3% achieved in 1997. If we remove the 1.43% (of sales) net of tax increase in *Other income* in 1998 [(2.4% − 0.2%) × (1 − tax rate of 0.35)] from the profit margin of 11.2%, the 1998 adjusted profit margin ratio is only 9.77%.

The second element of ROA, the asset turnover ratio is defined as follows:

$$\text{Asset turnover ratio} = \text{Sales} \div \text{Average total assets}$$

Successful operations generate more sales, which increases the asset turnover ratio, and hence, ROA. However, the buildups of receivables and inventory (and the acquisition of capacity in the form of long-lived assets such as building and equipment) decrease asset turnover. Therefore, analysts closely follow the effects of asset turnover on ROA.

Knowledge of the economic environment is very important when interpreting asset turnovers. For example, consider a component of asset turnover, inventory turnover:

$$\text{Inventory turnover ratio} = \text{Cost of goods sold} \div \text{Average inventory}$$

If inventory is built up, the inventory turnover ratio decreases. Analyst projections about future sales are important in interpreting such a decrease. The decrease would be good news if higher future sales were expected. However, if expectations of sales are flat or decreasing, the inventory turnover ratio decrease would be bad news, indicative of difficulty in moving inventory and future price markdowns and lower profitability. In a later section in this module, we return to the inventory turnover issue.

Operating Activities and Risk Ratios

Long-term solvency risk assessment is greatly affected by operating activities. As noted in Module A, long-term creditors and equity investors are both interested in whether a firm has sufficient cash inflows from operations to engage in debt servicing and operating capacity replacement and expansion. The following ratios are often calculated to provide information about operating cash flow sufficiency for these purposes:

$$\text{Operating cash flow to capital expenditures} = \text{Operating cash flow} \div \text{Capital expenditures}$$
$$\text{Operating cash flow to total liabilities} = \text{Operating cash flow} \div \text{Average total liabilities}$$

Operating Cash Flow to Capital Expenditures It is worth repeating a discussion appearing in Module C, relating to the sufficiency of operations to support capital expenditures. Recently, many companies have pointed to the operating cash flow to capital expenditures ratio as providing far more information about long-term prospects than those ratios based on net income can provide. These companies tend to have recently acquired other companies using purchase accounting and have recorded large amounts of goodwill in the process. To understand the issue, consider how the operating cash flow to capital expenditure ratio and net income can provide similar information. The operating cash flow to capital expenditure ratio shows how much cash inflow *before* making investments in property, plant, and equipment is available to make those investments. Dividing by capital expenditures gives the analyst an indication of whether the capital expenditures can be covered. Net income represents net cash inflows (adjusted for accruals) that are left over after covering a charge for capital usage (i.e., depreciation and amortization expenses). Companies often argue that the charges for capital usage are excessive (especially amortization of goodwill acquired in an acquisition), and that these charges do not represent what will have to be replaced. These companies argue that the capital expenditures in each year are a better measure of what will be replaced.

Operating Cash Flow to Total Liabilities The operating cash flow to total liabilities ratio is also increased by successful operations. An increase in this ratio represents lower long-term risk because it indicates more cash available to retire debt principal. Successful operations also increase the following important ratio related to the ability to cover interest:

$$\text{Interest coverage ratio} = \frac{(\text{Income before income taxes} + \text{Interest expense})}{\text{Interest expense}}$$

As noted in Module A, this ratio is based on the accrual model, and it is often preferred to a cash-based ratio because of the existence of zero-interest bearing debt.

Analyst Adjustments in the Operations Area

3 Prepare the balance sheet and income statement adjustments made by many financial analysts in the process of analyzing the success of operations.

Financial analysts monitor the revenue recognition practices of companies. If these practices are not too aggressive and if they are applied consistently through time, pro forma adjustments to revenue are rare. However, adjustments for the expense series are often required to better comprehend company operating profitability. Adjustments can be made to any expense series, and due to the uniqueness of industries and company strategies within those industries, the number of different kinds of adjustments can be many. In the sections that follow, we concentrate on potential adjustments that are common to most firms. We begin with adjustments to inventory and receivables to better interpret profitability and risk. We conclude our discussion with adjustments in the long-term liabilities area for the potential liabilities created by deferred taxes, pensions, and post-employment benefits.

Inventory and Cost of Goods Sold Adjustments

The first note to the financial statements, generally titled "Summary of Significant Accounting Policies," provides a description of the method used to value inventory on the balance sheet. When an analyst compares two firms in an industry, differences in the inventory method often make the firms' ratios not comparable. For example, consider the following disclosure taken from Pharmacia Upjohn's 1998 annual report Note 1, Summary of Significant Accounting Policies:

Inventories are valued at the lower of cost or market. Cost is determined by the last-in, first-out (LIFO) method for substantially all U.S. inventories and the first-in, first-out (FIFO) method for substantially all non-U.S. inventories.

If comparison to a firm using FIFO were desired, the financial analyst could adjust Upjohn's inventory (and related cost of goods sold) to FIFO using additional note information. As required by GAAP, Upjohn reports information in Note 8 that would allow such an adjustment:

Upjohn Note 8 (in part; amounts in millions)

	1998	1997
Inventories (FIFO basis)	$1,186	$1,118
Less reduction to LIFO cost	(154)	(160)
	$1,032	$ 958

A reconstruction of the 1998 cost of goods sold (CGS) section for Upjohn reveals (in millions):

	As Reported (LIFO)	Adjustment	Restated (FIFO)
Beginning inventory	$ 958	$160	$1,118
Purchases (plug)	2,105		2,105
Goods available for sale	3,063		3,223
Ending inventory	(1,032)	(154)	(1,186)
Cost of goods sold (income statement)	$2,031	$ 6	$2,037
Inventory turnover ratio [CGS/Average inventory]	2.04		1.77

The inventory turnover ratio is substantially smaller when restated to FIFO. Note, however, that the cost of goods sold does not change much because of the restatement. This lack of effect on cost of goods sold will generally be the case because cost of goods sold is based on the *change* in the adjustment.

The difference between LIFO and FIFO inventory is referred to as the ***LIFO reserve.*** It is important to identify reserves in financial statements and adjust for them when making comparisons across companies. Although the illustrated inventory reserve is one related to a short-term operating accrual, some of the largest reserves are related to long-lived assets (i.e., investing activities). For example, some companies have large amounts of expenses in earlier periods and smaller amounts of expenses in later periods because they use accelerated depreciation methods or they engage in research and development activities. Financial statements prepared under German GAAP, for example, are likely to have large hidden reserves due to quick write-offs of fixed assets.

Adjustments to the Provision for Bad Debts—Bad Debts Expense

Collection of receivables is an important part of any business. The cost of a credit policy is realized when customers do not pay amounts due. The costs of the company credit policy are reflected in the financial statements in two ways: estimated uncollectible accounts are subtracted from accounts receivable on the balance sheet to arrive at the net realizable value of the receivables, and bad debts expense is reported on the income statement.

Methods used to estimate the annual cost of a credit policy involve a great deal of discretion. Accordingly, analysts closely watch the bad debts expense provision process, especially the relationship between bad debts expense and sales.

TCBY does extend credit to its customers. The following information comes from its 1998 annual report:

	1998	1997
Short-term trade and notes receivable	$11,774,162	$10,877,535
Allowance for uncollectible receivables	439,223	833,447
Sales revenue	93,865,413	90,577,654
Bad debts expense*	72,500	48,705

*Shown as provision for doubtful accounts in the statement of cash flows, operating activities section.

From these amounts, we can compute relevant ratios and observe if the ratios are changing over time:

	1998	1997
Ratio of allowance to receivables balance	3.73%	7.66%
Ratio of bad debts expense to sales	0.08%	0.05%

A somewhat inconsistent picture is portrayed by these ratios. On the one-hand, the allowance account as a percentage of receivables has fallen dramatically between 1997 and 1998, an indication of possible under-reserving for credit losses. One would expect this ratio to stay fairly constant unless the underlying customer base had dramatically improved in terms of credit-worthiness. On the other hand, the bad debts expense to sales ratio increased over the two-year period, indicating that the cost of generating sales (by granting favorable credit terms) had increased.

If an analyst believes that management has not sufficiently reduced income for bad debts in a given period, then a pro forma adjustment to increase bad debts expense (and reduce income tax expense by the tax effect) could be made.

Measuring Liabilities: Adjustments for Taxes, Pensions, and Other Post-Employment Benefits

The final two operating chapters in this text (Chapters 11 and 12) discuss two other important operating activities, paying taxes and compensating employees. Interestingly, the major issues in these areas relate to how liabilities should be determined from analysis of the financial statements.

Deferred Taxes Proper tax planning generally leads to net deferred tax liabilities shown at each balance sheet date. TCBY is no exception, showing deferred tax liabilities of $3,319,847 and $3,846,858 at fiscal year-ends 1998 and 1997, respectively. These amounts are between 3% and 4% of total assets, a significant portion of total financing.

Although shown as liabilities under generally accepted accounting principles, the question of whether deferred taxes are truly liabilities remains unresolved. Recall from Chapter 11 that deferred tax liabilities arise from showing larger expenses or smaller revenues on the tax return relative to what is reported on financial statements. These originating tax/book differences reverse in later years, which causes higher taxable income and higher future tax payments. But, what if the company is growing and generates new originating differences that are greater than (or at least offset) the reversals? Good tax planning could delay the tax payments inherent in deferred tax liabilities for a long time. In present value terms, long payment delays dramatically shrink, and possibly eliminate, the liability.

Financial analysis in the deferred tax area requires a prediction as to when, and if, the deferred tax liabilities become due. If the analyst believes that the operations generating the deferred tax amounts are in a maturity stage or a harvest stage, then the new investments that generally cause offsetting, new originating differences will not occur, and the deferred tax liability amounts will shortly become due. Therefore, the analyst would treat deferred taxes as a liability. If the analyst believes that conditions present in introduction or growth stage companies are such that deferred tax liabilities will remain deferred for the foreseeable future, then treatment as equity is reasonable.

Pensions and Other Post-Employment Benefits (OPEB) As we learned in Chapter 12, many companies make long-term promises to employees to provide them with pensions, health care, and other benefits when they retire. We also learned that recognition of amounts associated with these promises often do not show up in the financial statements.

The general format of disclosure of pension and OPEB is as follows:

	Pensions	**OPEB**
Present value of obligations	$(XXX)	$(XXX)
Fair value of assets set aside to fund obligations	XXX	XXX
Funded status of plan: net asset (liability)	(XXX)	(XXX)
Unrecognized prior service cost	XXX	XXX
Unrecognized losses (gains)	XXX	XXX
Unrecognized transition liability (asset)	XXX	XXX
Additional liability under minimum liability provisions	(XXX)	(XXX)
Prepaid (accrued) liability disclosed on *balance sheet*	$XXX	$XXX
Service cost	$XXX	$XXX
Interest cost on obligation	XXX	XXX
Expected return on assets set aside to fund obligation	(XXX)	(XXX)
Amortization of prior service cost	XXX	XXX
Amortization of unrecognized losses (gains)	XXX	XXX
Amortization of transition liability (asset)	XXX	XXX
Net cost reported on *income statement*	$XXX	$XXX

Analyst treatment of pensions widely varies. Most analysts view the *Funded status of the plan: net asset (liability)* as the true economic liability, and they consider adjustment from the reported balance sheet amount to the true economic liability. The following three approaches are generally followed to accomplish the adjustment:

- Adjust from the balance sheet amount to the economic status of the plan regardless of whether the economic status is an asset or liability.
- Adjust from the balance sheet amount to the economic status of the plan if the economic status of the plan is a liability, and it is a larger liability than the balance sheet liability amount (a conservative approach).
- Consolidate the pension plan with the company. Treat plan obligations as liabilities and plan assets as investments on the balance sheet. Treat service cost, interest cost, and expected return on plan assets as line items on the income statement.

The most often used approach is the second, more conservative approach, in which analysts make adjustments only when plans are underfunded (i.e., a net economic liability), but the balance sheet liability is not sufficiently large to cover the entire underfunded amount. Because recent stock market performance has significantly increased the fair value of plan assets, material underfundings are far less frequent, making the likelihood of analyst adjustment rare for pensions. Also, although other post-employment benefits are often not funded, analyst pro forma adjustments are not likely because most companies expensed the entire transition amount which makes the balance sheet liability large already. The other two approaches are followed far less often because they both involve the assumption that a company has control of the net asset from overfunding the plan. Recent pension laws make it very difficult for companies to withdraw funds from the plan.

Module Summary

In this module, we view operating decisions from the point of view of outsiders assessing the risk and profitability of the firm. We review the cash flow implications of operating decisions, and also show how financial analysts may make pro forma adjustments to financial statements as part of the financial statement analysis process.

Significant disagreements exist among analysts regarding appropriate pro forma adjustments to assess the success of operations. This disagreement is a direct result of differing beliefs about whether generally accepted accounting principles yield financial statements that are useful in assessing firm value and making credit decisions.

In recent years, more emphasis in the financial statement analysis area has been placed on whether managers are engaged in income manipulation within GAAP. Manipulation can occur via management's estimation process (e.g., bad debts), choice of accounting method (e.g., LIFO versus FIFO), and timing the dispositions of investments discussed in Module C.

Key Terms

Analytical and Comprehensive Problems

1. **Analysis of Statement of Cash Flows—Federated Department Stores.** Federated Department Stores is a leading operator of premier department stores, with more than 400 department stores in 33 states, two fashion catalogs, and other retail operations. Federated's operating units include Bloomingdale's, The Bon Marche, Burdines, Macy's, Rich's, Lazarus, Goldsmith's, Bloomingdale's by Mail, Macy's by Mail, and Macys.com. A recent consolidated statement of cash flows for Federated is presented below (in millions; wording slightly adapted by authors):

	1/30/99	1/31/98	2/1/97
Cash flows from operating activities:			
Net income	$ 662	$ 536	$ 266
Adjustments to reconcile net income to net cash provided by operating activities:			
Depreciation and amortization of property and equipment	596	563	504
Amortization of intangible assets	27	27	27
Amortization of financing costs	7	20	27
Amortization of unearned restricted stock	1	0	2
Loss on early extinguishment of debt	23	39	0
Changes in assets and liabilities:			
Decrease in accounts receivable	235	194	223
(Increase) decrease in merchandise inventories	(20)	7	(151)
(Increase) decrease in supplies and prepaid expenses	(2)	(5)	67
(Increase) decrease in other assets	31	(7)	(12)
Increase (decrease) in accounts payable and accrued liabilities	6	(36)	177
Increase in current income taxes	25	103	2
Increase in deferred income taxes	103	138	84
Increase (decrease) in other liabilities	(4)	(6)	4
Net cash provided by operating activities	$1,690	$1,573	$1,220

Required:

a. Discuss how Federated has been able to substantially increase its net cash provided by operating activities over the three-year period.
b. Provide a detailed explanation of why depreciation and amortization of property and equipment is added back in determining net cash provided by operations.
c. Much like the TCBY example in the text, Federated adjusts net income to cash flow under the indirect method in two stages. What are the two stages? How are they different?

d. Is it likely that an analyst would treat deferred income taxes as a liability for Federated? Why or why not?

2. **Analysis of Profit Margin—Eli Lilly and Company.** A portion of the Consolidated Statement of Income for Eli Lilly and Company shown in the 1997 annual report is presented below (in millions; wording slightly changed by authors):

	1997	1996	1995
Net sales	$8,517.6	$7,346.6	$6,763.8
Cost of sales	2,362.9	2,118.4	1,885.7
Research and development	1,382.0	1,189.5	1,042.3
Marketing and administrative	2,314.4	1,991.9	1,854.0
Loss on asset impairment	2,443.0	0.0	0.0
Gain on sale of DowElanco	(631.8)	0.0	0.0
Interest expense	234.1	288.8	286.3
Other income—net	(97.2)	(273.3)	(70.1)
	8,007.4	5,315.3	4,998.2
Income from continuing operations before income taxes	510.2	2,031.3	1,765.6
Income taxes	895.3	507.8	459.0
Income (loss) from continuing operations	(385.1)	1,523.5	1,306.6
Discontinued operations: divestiture of Medical Devices	0.0	0.0	984.3
Net income (loss)	$ (385.1)	$1,523.5	$2,290.9

Required: Analyze the change in Eli Lilly's profit margin over the three-year period.

3. **Analysis of Inventory—Eli Lilly and Company.** The first note to the 1997 financial statements of Eli Lilly, "Summary of Significant Accounting Policies," reports the following information:

The company states all of its inventories at the lower-of-cost-or-market. The company uses the last-in, first-out (LIFO) method for substantially all of its inventories located in the continental United States, or approximately 55% of its total inventories. Other inventories are valued by the first-in, first-out (FIFO) method for substantially all non-U.S. inventories. Inventories of December 31 consisted of the following (in millions):

	1997	1996
Finished products	$262.0	$294.5
Work in process	459.4	423.4
Raw materials and supplies	191.0	171.7
	912.4	889.6
Less reduction to LIFO cost	11.7	8.2
	$900.7	$881.4

Required: Given Lilly's 1997 cost of good sold of $2,362.9 million, compute the 1997 inventory turnover ratio under LIFO and FIFO. If FIFO had been used instead of LIFO, would it have made much difference in the current year computations? (*Note*, do not answer this question as if you were being asked to compute the cumulative effect of an accounting change.)

4. **Deferred Income Taxes.** Deferred tax assets and liabilities arise from temporary differences in the treatments of revenues and expenses on the tax return and the financial statements. Provide a rationale for the treatment of the following items:
   a. deferred tax liabilities as liabilities
   b. deferred tax liabilities as equity
   c. deferred tax assets as assets.

5. **Profit Margin—Federated Department Stores, Inc.** Federated Department Stores, Inc., has shown consistent increases in net income over the last three years as indicated by the recent annual report (amounts in millions):

	For the 52 Weeks Ended		
	1/20/99	1/31/98	2/1/97
Net sales	$15,833	$15,668	$15,229
Cost of sales	9,616	9,581	9,354
Selling, general, and administrative expenses	4,762	4,746	4,982
Operating income	1,455	1,341	893
Interest expense	(304)	(418)	(499)
Interest income	12	35	47
Income before income taxes and extraordinary items	1,163	958	441
Federal, state, and local income tax expense	(478)	(383)	(175)
Income before extraordinary items	685	575	266
Extraordinary items	(23)	(39)	0
Net income	$ 662	$ 536	$ 266

Additional information about one component of selling, general, and administrative expense, *bad debts expense,* and accounts receivable is provided in Note 3 (in millions; adapted by authors):

	1/30/99	1/31/98
Due from customers	$2,099	$2,322
Allowance for doubtful accounts	77	100

Changes in the allowance for doubtful accounts are as follows:

	For the 52 Weeks Ended		
	1/20/99	1/31/98	2/1/97
Balance, beginning of year	$100	$ 96	$ 83
Charges to costs and expenses (bad debts expense)	112	167	172
Net uncollectible balances written off	(135)	(163)	(159)
Balance, end of year	$ 77	$100	$ 96

Required: Analyze the change in Federated Department Stores' profit margin over the three-year period. Analyze the information from Note 3 to see if it raises concerns with respect to the accounting for uncollectible accounts. Comment on how your findings impact your assessment of profit margin trends.

6. **Pension Disclosures—Tyco International Ltd.** In Note 17 to its 1998 Annual Report, Tyco International Ltd. reported the following items related to post-retirement promises made to its employees as of September 30, 1998 (in millions; author adapted):

	Assets Exceed Accumulated Benefits	Accumulated Benefits Exceed Assets	Total
Pension plan:			
Projected benefits obligation	$750.8	$256.1	$1,006.9
Plan assets at fair value	801.7	145.3	947.0
Plan assets (in excess of) less than projected benefits obligation	(50.9)	110.8	59.9
Unrecognized transition asset (liability)	11.4	(0.1)	11.3
Unrecognized prior service cost	(1.6)	(16.6)	(18.2)
Additional minimum liability	0.0	35.8	35.8
Unrecognized net loss	(36.2)	(25.3)	(61.5)
Accrued (prepaid) pension costs	$ (77.3)	$104.6	$ 27.3

(continued)

	September 30, 1998
Post-retirement benefit plan:	
Accumulated post-retirement benefit obligation	$109.2
Unrecognized prior service benefit	21.0
Unrecognized net gain	14.2
Accrued post-retirement benefit cost	$144.4

Required:

a. What is the total amount of pension-related asset or liability shown on Tyco's balance sheet?
b. By what amounts are Tyco's pension and post-retirement plans overfunded (or underfunded) at September 30, 1998?
c. So that risk might be better assessed, what alternative pro forma adjustments might an analyst make to Tyco's financial statement related to pensions? Provide a rationale for each alternative approach.

7. **Texas Instruments.** Access the Texas Instruments 1998 financial statements at the text Web site (http://baginski.swcollege.com). Answer the following questions related to operating activities.
    a. Compute TI's gross profit margin, gross profit margin percentage, and net profit margin ratio for the 1996–1998 period. Is there any trend?
    b. Compared to 1997, did TI have a greater or smaller investment in working capital in 1998?
    c. What happened to TI's interest coverage ratio over the 1996–1998 period?
    d. Cash flow from operations was positive and larger than net income (loss) from continuing operations during each year of the 1996–1998 period. What were the major adjustments in reconciling from net income to cash flow from operations? What were their effects?
    e. For 1997 and 1998, compute the operating cash flow to total capital expenditures ratio and the operating cash flow to total liabilities ratio. Describe what the ratios reveal about TI's operations.
    f. What inventory method does TI use? (*Hint:* you will need to read TI's first footnote.)
    g. What is the relation between allowance for losses and accounts receivable at December 31, 1998, and 1997? If you were a financial analyst, what general action would you take after calculating these numbers? (Answer in general rather than listing specifics.)

Objectives

1 Perform a time-series analysis of profitability.

2 Explain how financial statements can be used to value common stock.

3 Perform a time-series analysis of risk.

4 Explain how accrual accounting-based ratios can be used to predict bankruptcy.

Module E

Valuation and Risk Assessment Using Accrual Accounting Information

If financial statements meet the objective of providing useful information for investment and credit decisions, then we should be able to combine financial statement numbers in a way that can support such decisions. In this module, we perform an historical time-series analysis of profitability and risk, and we introduce two models of investor and creditor decisions that use the knowledge gained from the historical analysis as input. First, investors make decisions on whether to purchase, hold, or sell shares of common stock. Accordingly, we illustrate a recently-developed model that estimates a company's stock price using accrual-based accounting numbers.[1] Second, creditors must assess the ability of debtors to repay loans. Accordingly, we provide a model of bankruptcy prediction that uses current financial statement profitability and risk-related ratios.

Expectations for the future begin with an understanding of the past. In Module A, we compared the most recent financial ratios of TCBY Enterprises, Inc., with industry averages. (Financial statements and related information for TCBY are included in Appendix D.) In this module, we perform a time-series analysis of TCBY's profitability and risk ratios, paying close attention to the prediction of profitability and risk necessary in valuation and credit extension decisions.

Time-Series Analysis of TCBY's Profitability

1 Perform a time-series analysis of profitability.

The following EXCEL® spreadsheet in Exhibit 1 presents TCBY's profitability ratios for the fiscal years 1996–1998, computed from TCBY's 1998 annual report and a prior year's annual report. (We present TCBY's risk ratios later in this module.)

1. Our discussion is based on the Edwards/Bell/Ohlson (EBO) model. Our understanding of this model is attributable to several works, including theoretical analysis by James Ohlson and Gerald Feltham, explanations by Victor Bernard, and useful tutorials by Charles M. C. Lee.

EXHIBIT 1

Profitability Analysis	**1996**	**1997**	**1998**
ROA	0.07	0.09	0.11
Common earnings leverage	0.91	0.95	0.97
Capital structure leverage	1.29	1.29	1.26
ROCE	0.08	0.11	0.13
ROA analysis			
Profit margin	0.09	0.10	0.11
Turnover	0.81	0.90	0.97
Profit margin analysis			
Sales	1.00	1.00	1.00
Other revenues and gains	0.15	0.15	0.14
Cost of goods sold	−0.65	−0.67	−0.68
Selling and administrative expenses	−0.39	−0.34	−0.32
Other revenues and gains	0.02	0.01	0.04
Interest expense	−0.01	−0.01	−0.01
Income taxes	−0.04	−0.05	−0.06
Profit margin	0.08	0.10	0.11
Profit margin for ROA	0.09	0.10	0.11
Turnover analysis			
Accounts receivable turnover	8.41	9.10	8.78
Number of days receivables	43.39	40.11	41.56
Inventory turnover	4.73	5.49	5.52
Number of days Inventories	77.17	66.48	66.15
Fixed assets turnover	1.91	2.16	2.46

The year 1996 is a good starting point for the time-series analysis because TCBY underwent a restructuring in 1995. This restructuring coincided with a major strategic change in operations. In the mid-1990s, TCBY implemented an enhanced "service and convenience" strategy. This strategy involved a new emphasis on the co-branding of products and nontraditional store locations. The 1996–1998 period provides a good indication of how the strategy played out, and helps the analyst develop expectations about profitability trends.

The table begins with an ROCE analysis. ROCE is clearly increasing (0.08 to 0.13) from 1996 to 1998, with relatively little of this change due to changes in the use of debt financing. The common earnings and capital structure leverage ratios stay fairly constant, exhibiting only slight movements consistent with slight decreases in TCBY's use of debt financing, which is already low. Most of TCBY's ROCE change is explained by operating and investing activities (i.e., ROA) rather than financing activities. ROA steadily climbed from 0.07 in 1996 to 0.11 in 1998. The effects of decreasing interest-bearing financing did have a positive effect. The common earnings leverage ratio changed over the period from 0.91 to 0.97.

Breaking down ROA into profit margin and turnover shows that TCBY simultaneously increased profit margin during the three years from 0.09 to 0.11, and in creased turnover from 0.81 to 0.97. Because these two ratios are multiplied in determining ROA, the increases interacted to cause the healthy increase in ROA over the three-year period.

In Module D, we took a close look at the three-year change in profit margin. We found that TCBY has decreased selling and administrative expenses more than enough to offset the upwardly trending cost of goods sold so that profit margin has increased over time. We noted, however, that *Other revenue and gains* included a large, one-time gain on an airplane sale. Removing this after-tax gain from the profit margin reduced the reported profit margin of 0.11 to closer to 0.10. However, TCBY had healthy increases in accounts receivable, inventory, and fixed asset turnover ratios over the three-year period. Therefore, the financial statements reveal that TCBY established an increase in profitability over the three-year period examined.

Earnings-Based Valuation

2 Explain how financial statements can be used to value common stock.

One of the primary uses of profitability analysis is to value the common share price of a company. In the following section, we demonstrate an "earnings-based valuation" technique that follows directly from our analysis of ROCE.

A popular approach to the estimation of equity value per share or "price" (P) involves two steps:

1. Forecasting a company's free cash flows per share (CF) based upon analysis of the statement of cash flows and other nonfinancial statement information.
2. Discounting at an appropriate rate (r) over an infinite horizon using the following formula:

$$P_t = \sum_{\tau=1}^{\infty} = \frac{CF_{t+\tau}}{(1+r)^{\tau}}$$

This approach is typically the focus of a course in investments. The demand for cash flow information to implement the discounted free cash flow approach is one reason why accountants provide a statement of cash flows to supplement the three accrual-based financial statements.

We focus this module on an alternative approach to equity valuation (the EBO model) that uses the accrual-accounting financial statements as input. The earnings-based approach to equity valuation also involves generating forecasts and discounting using appropriate rates of interest. However, the following forecasts are derived from accrual-based financial statements:

1. Forecasts of earnings per share (e), and
2. Forecasts of book value of common equity per share (bv) derived from the forecasts of earnings per share and the dividend payout ratio.

These forecasts can be translated into an estimate of price per share of equity (i.e., common stock price) using the following formula:[2]

$$P_t = \underbrace{bv_t}_{\text{book value}} + \underbrace{\sum_{\tau=1}^{\infty} \frac{e_{t+\tau} - (r \times bv_{t+\tau-1})}{(1+r)^{\tau}}}_{\text{discounted abnormal earnings}}$$

Prior analytical research has demonstrated that this formulation is equivalent to the popular free cash flows (available for dividends) discounting if the "clean surplus" relation holds. The clean surplus relation holds if all changes in book value (except net dividends, which equals dividends minus investments by owners) are reflected in earnings. GAAP financial statements exhibit the clean surplus relation except for three items: unrealized holding gains and losses on available for sale securi-

2. Victor Bernard, "The Feltham-Ohlson Framework: Implications for Empiricists," *Contemporary Accounting Research* (Spring 1995), presents this EBO valuation model.

ties (Chapter 8), pension losses not currently recognized in income (Chapter 12), and translation gains and losses arising from the consolidation of foreign subsidiaries (not covered in this text). If these items exist, then the success of the valuation formula may require analysts to use an earnings number that includes these items. Fortunately, GAAP financial statements now provide such a number—comprehensive income.

The earnings-based valuation formula transacts on an important property of clean surplus accounting to overcome an often-cited deficiency in using earnings for equity valuation—earnings are a function of the accounting method employed. Due to the clean surplus relation, valuation does not depend on the accounting methods used. For example, current value accounting, conservatism, and earnings manipulation each cause a different value for bv_t. However, bv_t appears in the equation not only as a positive number, but also as a negative number (i.e., a "hurdle" in the determination of abnormal earnings). The effects of the accounting method on book value offset, so that the accounting method has no resulting effect on price (P_t).

If we factor out book value and rearrange the equation, we obtain an expression of the formula in terms of an important ratio that we have studied in earlier modules, ROCE:

$$\frac{P_t}{bv_t} = 1 + \sum_{\tau=1}^{\infty} \frac{ROCE_{t+\tau} - r}{(1+r)^{\tau}} \times \frac{bv_{t+\tau-1}}{bv_t}$$

Before we discuss the properties of this formula, let's examine what it measures. The left-hand side of the formula is the price-to-book ratio. This ratio measures the price per common share relative to the book value per common share of equity. Investors who purchase a share of common stock have a right to one share's worth of the book value of the company (i.e., Assets − Liabilities). The price-to-book ratio is almost always greater than one because the market value of the company is almost always greater than what accountants have recorded as book value. In Chapter 8, we discussed why investors pay more for a company than its book value; the excess of price over book value occurs because net assets have a fair market value greater than their book value, and the fair value of the company as a whole is greater than the fair value of its individual assets. In other words, book value represents the "normal" earnings capability of net assets, while stock price incorporates both the normal earnings capability and the ability of the company to use these assets in a way that generates additional or "abnormal" earnings.

This discussion helps explain the right-hand side of the equation. First, assume only one right-hand side component of value:

$$\frac{P_t}{bv_t} = 1$$

Price exactly equals book value if the company can only generate normal earnings. This situation could occur if the future cash flows from net assets (i.e., the returns on equity) are not superior relative to other firms (e.g., a perfectly competitive market).

However, due to the ability of companies to benefit from their competitive advantages, earnings greater than normal earnings are generated, and price exceeds book value. Accordingly, the second right-hand side component of price-to-book is necessary to complete the value determination:

$$\sum_{\tau=1}^{\infty} \frac{ROCE_{t+\tau} - r}{(1+r)^{\tau}} \times \frac{bv_{t+\tau-1}}{bv_t}$$

ROCE is the forecasted future return on common equity, and r is the cost of equity capital (i.e., the expected normal return on investment given the equity risk of the firm). If a company can not generate abnormal returns, then ROCE = r, and the second component of value equals zero. However, competitive advantages cause ROCE to be greater than r. The second component is the infinite sum of these abnormal returns discounted by the cost of equity capital, r.

The last part of the second component is the growth in book value, expressed as each successive future book value divided by the previous period's book value. Future book values are computed by adding current book value and future expected earnings, and subtracting expected future dividends (the clean surplus relation). Future dividends can be estimated by multiplying future expected earnings by the current dividend payout rate because companies are reluctant to change payout rates.

Practical application of any valuation model requires an assumption about terminal value because infinite horizon forecasting is impractical. In other words, in practical applications, the forecasting period is shortened to a reasonable length, and all periods beyond the forecasting period are combined into a terminal value term.

The popular discounted cash flow (DCF) approach results in extremely large terminal value estimates, ranging from 56–125% of total value after eight years. This large terminal value occurs because the DCF terminal value is based on *all* expected cash flows beyond the forecast horizon. In contrast, terminal value estimates under the earnings-based approach are based only on *abnormal* earnings beyond the forecast horizon. Accrual accounting has already produced a book value (bv) that provides an accurate estimate of most of terminal value. If accrual accounting is unbiased, then the terminal value equals zero in a relatively short period of time because competitive pressures force ROCE towards r in a relatively short time period (10–15 years). The following equation is a terminal value formulation of the earnings-based approach to equity valuation:

$$\frac{P_t}{bv_t} = \left(1 + \sum_{\tau=1}^{T} \frac{ROE_{t+\tau} - r}{(1+r)^{\tau}} \times \frac{bv_{t+\tau-1}}{bv_t}\right) + \left(\frac{ROE_{t+T+1} - r}{r(1+r)^{T}} \times \frac{bv_{t+T}}{bv_t}\right)$$

An estimate of value using this equation is presented in the following example.

Practical Application of the Earnings-Based Model to TCBY

In order to determine the November 29, 1998, implied price of TCBY's shares of common stock, we need four "fundamentals" to apply the model: current book value per common share, expected dividend payout rate, expected future earnings, and the discount rate. We also need an assumption about terminal value.

Current Book Value Per Common Share (bv_t)

Book value per common share can be computed from TCBY's November 29, 1998, financial statements. Shareholders' equity reported on the balance sheet at November 29, 1998, is \$76,196,154. The equity section also reports that 27,759,021 common shares have been issued, of which 4,839,952 shares are not outstanding because they are held as treasury stock. Therefore:

$$bv_t = \$76{,}196{,}154 \div (27{,}759{,}021 - 4{,}839{,}952) = \$3.32$$

Expected Dividend Payout Rate

Historically, TCBY has paid \$0.20 per share, regardless of earnings. As earnings per share grows, it is likely that this amount will also increase. Over the last ten years, TCBY has reported nine positive earnings per share amounts. The dividend payout rate has averaged close to 40% over those nine years. We use 40% as our expected future payout rate. To verify this rate, a January 1999 *Value Line Investment Survey* reports analyst expectations of TCBY dividend payout over the next two years of 48% and 38%.

Expected Future Earnings ($e_{t+\tau}$)

Our ratio profitability analysis indicated that TCBY had ROCE during 1996, 1997, and 1998 of 0.08, 0.11, and 0.13, respectively. We also noted that a one-time gain explained a substantial portion of the ROCE increase in 1998. We take a conservative view of TCBY's ability to generate increases in ROCE at the rate that has occurred over the prior three years. We forecast ROCE to be 0.12 in fiscal 1999, to increase by 0.015 each year over the next five years, and then to remain constant at 0.209 (0.014 higher than the prior year) in perpetuity. To check the reasonableness of our expectations, we provide Exhibit 2 that shows our ROCE expectation and the forecasted EPS that it presents by each fiscal year. The last column of the table shows median analyst earnings forecasts of TCBY earnings per share from the *Institutional Brokerage Estimate System* (IBES) shortly after the release of TCBY's 1998 annual report:

EXHIBIT 2

Fiscal Year	ROCE Forecast	EPS Implied by ROCE Forecast	IBES Forecast of EPS
1999	0.120	$0.40	$0.45
2000	0.135	$0.48	$0.57
2001	0.150	$0.58	$0.68
2002	0.165	$0.69	$0.82
2003	0.180	$0.83	$0.98
2004	0.195	$0.99	$1.18
2005	0.209	$1.19	$1.42
2006	0.209	$1.34	Not available
2007	0.209	$1.51	Not available
2008	0.209	$1.76	Not available

Both the EPS implied by our ROCE forecast and the IBES forecast of EPS grow 20% per year after 2000. The primary differences between our forecasts and the IBES forecasts are the first two years' expectations for EPS.

The Discount Rate (r)

Currently, the application of the EBO valuation method requires an estimate of the discount rate from historical security price performance via the capital asset pricing model specification of required return (r):

$$r = \text{risk free rate of interest} + \text{beta (Expected market return} - \text{Risk free rate of interest)}$$

Risk free rates of interest have remained around 7% in recent years, and the market return has averaged 13% over the last few decades. Beta can be historically estimated by the analyst using past realized rates of return for a given firm and the market as a whole. Alternatively, *Value Line* provides beta estimates. Using these values for TCBY:

$$\begin{aligned}\text{Required return} &= 0.07 \text{ risk free rate} \\ &\quad + [0.80 \text{ beta from } \textit{Value Line} \times (0.13 \text{ historical market return} - 0.07)] \\ &= 0.118\end{aligned}$$

Terminal Value Assumption

Because infinite forecasting is not practical, an assumption must be made about how ROCE will persist after some future date. Our assumption is that 2005 abnormal ROCE persists from 2006 on as a perpetuity. This is a liberal assumption if we believe that the value attributable to TCBY's brand equity will someday dissipate. Abnormal ROCE should approach zero as competitors replicate TCBY's value chain (i.e., its unique operations and image).

Worksheet Solution

Exhibit 3 provides an EXCEL® worksheet to solve the model; the cells are explained below. Consistent with most discussions of the EBO model, we have set up the model using our implied EPS forecasts as the starting point. EXCEL® worksheet inputs are in bold.

Forecasted EPS:	**1999–2000 are as we forecast ($0.40 and $0.48, respectively)** based on our ROCE estimates; 2001+ = EPS prior period × (1 + EPS growth rate)
EPS growth forecast:	Our forecasted ROCE increase leads to **EPS growing at 20% per year from 2001–2005;** 2006+ set based on 2005 ROCE to ensure persistence of 2005 ROCE
Dividend payout rate:	**40%**
bv (beginning of year):	**1999 taken from TCBY financial statements ($3.320);** 2000+ = bv prior period + EPS prior period (1 − Dividend payout rate)
ROCE:	1999–2000 = Forecasted EPS ÷ bv; 2006+ set to 2005 value
Required ROCE:	**Estimated from capital asset pricing model (0.118)**
Abnormal ROCE:	ROCE − Required ROCE
Period:	$t = 1, 2, \ldots, 10$
Discount factor:	$(1 + \text{Required ROCE})^t$
Price before terminal value:	bv_{1999} + Summation over t of (Abnormal $ROCE_t \times bv_t$) ÷ Discount $factor_t$
Terminal value:	[Abnormal $ROCE_T$ ÷ (Required ROCE × Discount $factor_T$)] × bv_T
Implied price:	Price before terminal value + Terminal value

EXHIBIT 3 TCBY Equity Valuation

Computation of implied price											
Year		FY1999	FY2000	FY2001	FY2002	FY2003	FY2004	FY2005	FY2006	FY2007	FY2008
EPS growth forecast				**0.200**	**0.200**	**0.200**	**0.200**	**0.200**	0.125	0.125	0.125
Forecasted EPS		**0.400**	**0.480**	0.576	0.691	0.829	0.995	1.194	1.344	1.512	1.701
Dividend payout rate	**0.400**	0.400	0.400	0.400	0.400	0.400	0.400	0.400	0.400	0.400	0.400
bv (beginning of year)		**3.320**	3.560	3.848	4.194	4.608	5.106	5.703	6.420	7.226	8.133
ROCE		0.120	0.135	0.150	0.165	0.180	0.195	0.209	0.209	0.209	0.209
Required ROCE	**0.118**	0.118	0.118	0.118	0.118	0.118	0.118	0.118	0.118	0.118	0.118
Abnormal ROCE		0.002	0.017	0.032	0.047	0.062	0.077	0.091	0.091	0.091	0.091
Period		1.000	2.000	3.000	4.000	5.000	6.000	7.000	8.000	9.000	10.000
Discount factor		1.118	1.250	1.397	1.562	1.747	1.953	2.183	2.441	2.729	3.051
Price before terminal value		4.915									
Terminal value		2.056									
Implied price		6.971									

The 1999 implied price from the worksheet for TCBY is $6.97 per share. Between the balance sheet date (November 29, 1998) and the end of January 1999, TCBY's common stock fluctuated in price between $7.00 and $7.19 per share, indicating that investors shared expectations about continuing TCBY profitability that were fairly close to our expectations. Interestingly, if IBES analyst forecasts of

EPS are used in the model instead of our expectations, implied price is approximately \$8.50 per share, indicating that these analysts had far higher expectations about TCBY's future profitability.[3]

Summary

The earnings-based valuation model that we estimated is simple; yet, accounting researchers have demonstrated that it explains a great deal of variation in security prices across firms. The jury is still out on whether it dominates other models such as free cash flow discounting. However, early evidence seems to indicate that it performs *at least as well* as the more popular cash flow based models in terms of correctly estimating prices.

Time-Series Analysis of TCBY's Risk

3 Perform a time-series analysis of risk.

Creditors are also interested in the profitability of potential borrowers. As we demonstrated in Module A, risk ratios can also be calculated, and most lenders view the risk ratio analysis as an important input into the lending decision. The analysis is viewed in conjunction with more qualitative factors such as the character of management and why the loan is needed, and other predictions of future economic conditions and risks that are not yet reflected in financial statements.

In Exhibit 4, we present a time-series of TCBY's risk ratios:

EXHIBIT 4 TCBY Risk Analysis

	1996	1997	1998
Short-term liquidity risk			
Current ratio	4.15	3.95	3.91
Quick ratio	2.69	2.75	2.61
Operating cash to current liabilities	1.76	1.53	0.80
Accounts payable turnover	28.09	31.32	32.66
Number of days payables	12.99	11.65	11.18
Number of days receivables	43.39	40.11	41.56
Number of days inventories	77.17	66.48	66.15
Interest coverage ratio	11.42	18.86	29.34
Long-term solvency risk			
Long-term debt ratio	0.11	0.08	0.04
Debt-to-equity ratio	0.12	0.08	0.04
Long-term debt to total assets ratio	0.09	0.06	0.03
Operating cash flow to total liabilities	0.81	0.76	0.47
Operating cash flow to capital exp.	7.88	9.17	4.77

3. Because of the lead times necessary to publish a textbook, we worked with 1998 financial statements, and in this chapter we projected future amounts for Module E analysis. At the time the chapter material was being sent to press, 1999 results became available for TCBY. It is interesting to compare the 1999 actual results with the 1999 projected results. For the year ended November 29, 1999, TCBY reported net income of \$7,244,000, basic EPS of \$0.32, and diluted EPS of \$0.31. Note that the EPS amounts are below those projected. In Exhibit 3, we projected a 1999 share price of \$6.97. During fiscal 1999, TCBY's share price actually ranged from about \$7.00 per share to about \$3.50 per share. In February 2000, TCBY announced that it a signed an agreement with Capricorn Investors III, LP., to be acquired for \$6.00 per share. As projected, TCBY paid dividends per share of \$0.20. The 1999 results demonstrate how difficult it is to project earnings amounts, even in the short term. Consequently, financial analysts continually go through computations such as the one demonstrated in Module E in order to make, buy, sell, and hold recommendations/decisions.

Short-term liquidity is not an issue for TCBY. The current and quick ratios remain at very high levels, which indicates low risk. Although the operating cash flow to current liability ratio fell a great deal during the three years (from 1.76 to 0.80), it is still very high. Accounts payable turnover has increased, indicating quicker payment to suppliers. Accounts receivable and inventory turnover are also high indicating no problems in converting these short-term assets into cash. The interest coverage ratio has also dramatically increased from 1996 to 1998, when interest expense is covered by net income by more than 29 times.

TCBY also has very low long-term solvency risk. Not only are the long-term debt, debt-to-equity, and long-term debt to total assets ratios extremely low, they are decreasing through time. Operating cash flow also appears more than adequate to retire debt and to engage in capital expenditures. Operating cash to total liabilities and to capital expenditure ratios are decreasing through time, but remain very high.

The risk ratios are indicative of a low-risk firm. However, our analysis is somewhat *ad hoc*. Have more sophisticated methods been developed that will estimate the likelihood that TCBY will suffer financial distress and be unable to pay back a loan? The answer is yes, and we present such an analysis in the next section.

Bankruptcy Prediction

4 Explain how accrual accounting-based ratios can be used to predict bankruptcy.

Financial distress can manifest through debt covenant violation, missed dividends, and many other ways. However, the most serious form of financial distress is bankruptcy. Sophisticated statistical analyses have been developed to combine financial statement ratios into a single probability of bankruptcy. Ohlson identified a set of ratios that best discriminate bankrupt from nonbankrupt firms, and produced a model from these ratios that can be used to obtain a probability of bankruptcy.[4] His multivariate logistic regression model is as follows:

y = −1.32 − 0.407 [natural log of (Total assets ÷ GNP implicit price deflator index one year previous)]
+ 6.03 (Total liabilities ÷ Total assets)
− 1.43 [(Current assets − Current liabilities) ÷ Total assets]
+ 0.0757 (Current liabilities ÷ Current assets)
− 2.37 (Net income ÷ Total assets)
− 1.83 (Working capital from operations ÷ Total liabilities)
+ 0.285 [1 (0) if last two years net income was negative (otherwise)]
− 1.72 [1 (0) if total liabilities are greater than total assets (otherwise)]
− 0.52 [(Net income in current year − Net income in previous year) ÷ (Sum of the absolute values of net income in current year and net income in previous year)]

After a given firm's financial ratios are substituted into the equation, the value of *y* obtained is substituted into the following equation to obtain the probability of bankruptcy:

$$\text{Probability of bankruptcy} = 1 \div (1 + e^{-y})$$

4. James A. Ohlson, "Financial Ratios and the Probabilistic Prediction of Bankruptcy," *Journal of Accounting Research* (Spring 1980): 109–131. A number of different statistical models exist that forecast financial distress. However, they are similar in spirit to the one shown here.

Applying the model to TCBY:

$$
\begin{aligned}
y = &-1.32 \\
&- 0.407\ [\ln (\$94{,}452{,}884 \div 214.87^{[5]})] \\
&+ 6.03\ [(\$11{,}984{,}249 + 2{,}952{,}634 + 3{,}319{,}847) \div \$94{,}452{,}884] \\
&- 1.43\ [(\$46{,}833{,}211 - 11{,}984{,}249) \div \$94{,}452{,}884] \\
&+ 0.0757\ [\$11{,}984{,}249 \div \$46{,}833{,}211] \\
&- 2.37\ [\$10{,}195{,}612 \div \$94{,}452{,}884] \\
&- 1.83\ [\$12{,}620{,}911^{[6]} \div \$11{,}984{,}249] \\
&+ 0.285\ [0] \\
&- 1.72\ [0] \\
&- 0.52\ [(\$10{,}195{,}612 - \$8{,}879{,}215) \div (\$10{,}195{,}612 + 8{,}879{,}215)] \\
= &-8.17003
\end{aligned}
$$

$$
\begin{aligned}
\text{probability of bankruptcy} &= 1 \div (1 + e^{-(-8.17003)}) \\
&= 0.028\%
\end{aligned}
$$

This is an extremely low probability of bankruptcy. In fact, Ohlson defines 3.8% as the cutoff for minimizing bankruptcy assessment errors (i.e., predicting bankruptcy for a healthy firm and predicting no bankruptcy for a failing firm).

Module Summary

The purpose of this module was to introduce how the process of analyzing a company's financial statements can be used to support decisions. Specifically, we performed a time-series analysis of profitability and risk ratios, and we presented two models of specific investor and creditor decisions: earnings-based security price valuation and bankruptcy prediction.

As you continue your study of financial accounting, it is important to remember the objectives of financial reporting. Although we have only provided an introduction in the area, it is clear that financial ratios are valuable to investors and creditors. The field of financial statement analysis is an exciting, rewarding, and ever-evolving area. We hope that a knowledge of financial accounting and its link to management decisions provides you with a comparative advantage as you continue your study of the measurement, reporting, and use of financial accounting information.

5. The coefficient on this variable (−0.407) was derived by Ohlson using 1978 as the base year. The *Survey of Current Business* (available in most business libraries) reports a fourth quarter 1997 GNP implicit price deflator of 112.57, defining 1992 as the base year of 100. To convert to the proper deflator for Ohlson's model, we divide 112.57 by the fourth quarter 1978 deflator reported in the survey, 52.39, and then multiply by 100. That is, (112.57 ÷ 52.39) times 100 equals 214.87.

6. Working capital from operations is obtained from the cash flow statement by adjusting net income for the first set of adjustments shown in the operating activities section.

Analytical and Comprehensive Problems

http://

1. A ratio analysis worksheet for Texas Instruments is provided below. (Our text Web site at http://baginski.swcollege.com provides an EXCEL® file and annual financial information.) Using the worksheet, the Texas Instruments Annual Report, and any other available library resources, complete the following:
   a. Prepare a time-series profitability analysis for Texas Instruments. Also, comment on the levels of the 1998 ratios relative to the electronics industry.
   b. Prepare a time-series risk analysis of Texas Instruments. Also, comment on the levels of the 1998 ratios relative to the electronics industry.
   c. Estimate the price per share of Texas Instruments' common stock. Use a beta of 1.45. Develop expectations for earnings per share based on your analysis in part (a). Or you may use analyst expectations for earnings per share. In March of 1999, IBES estimates

1999 and 2000 EPS at $3.00 and $3.92, respectively, and an annual EPS growth rate of 20% beyond 2000.

d. Estimate the probability that Texas Instruments will go bankrupt. Use 215 as the appropriate GNP deflator.

Ratio Analysis Worksheet				
(Amounts in millions)				
Texas Instruments	**Fiscal Year Ending**			
	1995	**1996**	**1997**	**1998**
Balance Sheet				
Cash	1,364	964	1,015	540
Marketable securities	189	14	2,005	1,709
Accounts and notes receivable	2,079	1,799	1,705	1,343
Inventories	978	703	742	596
Other current assets	835	974	636	658
Current Assets	5,445	4,454	6,103	4,846
Investments			69	2,564
Property, plant and equipment	4,880	6,712	7,414	6,379
Less accumulated depreciation	1,986	2,550	3,234	3,006
Other assets	409	744	497	467
Total assets	8,748	9,360	10,849	11,250
Accounts payable—trade	2,313	1,940	2,082	1,582
Notes payable—nontrade				
Current portion of long-term debt	27	314	71	267
Other current liabilities	539	232	343	347
Current liabilities	2,879	2,486	2,496	2,196
Long-term debt	804	1,697	1,286	1,027
Deferred taxes			288	381
Other noncurrent liabilities	970	1,080	865	1,119
Minority interest in subsidiaries				
Total liabilities	4,653	5,263	4,935	4,723
Preferred stock				
Common stock	190	190	390	392
Additional paid-in capital	1,081	1,116	1,183	1,178
Retained earnings	2,881	2,814	4,488	4,795
Cumulative translation adjustment				
Other cumulative adjustments	−45	−11	−53	296
Treasury stock	−12	−12	−94	−134
Shareholders' equity	4,095	4,097	5,914	6,527
Total liabilities and shareholders' equity	8,748	9,360	10,849	11,250
Income Statement				
Sales	11,409	9,940	9,750	8,460
Other revenues and gains				
Cost of goods sold	7,401	7,146	6,067	5,394
Selling and administrative expenses	2,569	2,820	3,068	2,667
Other income	79	76	192	293
EBIT	1,518	50	807	692
Interest expense	48	73	94	75

Income tax expense	474	23	411	210
Minority interest in earnings				
Income—continuing operations	996	−46	302	407
Income—discontinued operations	92	109	1,525	
Extraordinary gains (losses)			−22	
Changes in accounting principles				
Net Income	1,088	63	1,805	407
Preferred stock dividend				
Net income available to common	1,088	63	1,805	407
Statement of Cash Flows				
Net income—continuing operations	996	−46	302	407
Depreciation and amortization	681	904	1,109	1,144
Other addbacks	119	278	483	67
Other subtractions	−54	−152	−3	−286
Working cap. from operations				
Inc. (dec.) in receivables	−795	250	−39	289
Inc. (dec.) in inventories	−221	245	−34	74
Inc. (dec.) in other current assets	9	9	−19	−17
Inc. (dec.) in accounts payable	691	−404	−36	−427
Inc. (dec.) in other current liab.	267	−286	102	0
Cash from cont. operations	1,693	798	1,865	1,251
Cash from discontinued operations				
Cash from extraordinary items			−22	
Net Cash Flow from Operations	1,693	798	1,843	1,251
Fixed assets sold				
Investments sold	1,076	352	2,794	2,637
Fixed assets acquired	−1,351	−2,063	−1,238	−1,031
Investments acquired	−733	−340	−2,761	−2,396
Other investing transactions				−680
Net Cash Flow from Investing	−1,008	−2,051	−1,205	−1,470
Increase in short-term borrowing	12	288	0	0
Increase in long-term borrowing	24	871	28	0
Issue of capital stock	111	35	140	196
Decrease in short-term borrowing	0	−2	−314	−4
Decrease in long-term borrowing	−12	−199	−256	−68
Acquisition of capital stock			−86	−253
Dividends	−111	−129	−131	−133
Other financing transactions	−1	−1	−2	0
Net Cash Flow from Financing	23	863	−621	−262
Cash effect of exchange rates	10	−16	−23	6
Net Change in Cash	718	−406	−6	−475
Other information:				
Tax rate	0.35	0.35	0.35	0.35

2. Appendix D provides the 1998 annual report of Southwest Airlines. Using the annual report and available library resources, prepare an EXCEL® worksheet to accomplish the following (a worksheet example is provided in Problem 1, and an EXCEL® template is provided at our Web site, http://baginski.swcollege.com):
   a. Prepare a time-series profitability analysis for Southwest Airlines. Also, comment on the levels of the 1998 ratios relative to the airline industry.
   b. Prepare a time-series risk analysis for Southwest Airlines. Also, comment on the levels of the 1998 ratios relative to the airline industry.
   c. Estimate the price per share of Southwest Airlines' common stock. Use a beta of 1.30. Develop expectations for earnings per share based on your analysis in part (a). Alternatively, use analyst expectations for earnings per share. In March 1999, IBES estimates 1999 and 2000 EPS at \$1.37 and \$1.56, respectively, and an annual growth rate of 13% beyond 2000.
   d. Estimate the probability that Southwest Airlines will go bankrupt. Use 215 as the appropriate GNP deflator.
   e. Given the nature of the airline industry, what would be the most likely adjustment made by a financial analyst to assess the risk of Southwest Airlines?

Appendix A Comprehensive Review Problem: Reviewing Transactions and Preparing Financial Statements

A

This text builds on material covered in a principles of accounting course. In your accounting principles class, you may have learned a *user approach* (journal entries using debits and credits are not used to reflect how the accounting system processes data) or you may have learned a *traditional accounting approach* (journal entries using debits and credits are used to reflect how the accounting system processes data). This appendix contains a short comprehensive example problem that illustrates how financial statements reflect the various management decisions and transactions in the life of a company. We document the computations underlying the problem in two separate ways: the user approach and the traditional accounting approach. As a student, you should review the section of the problem that is consistent with the approach considered appropriate by your instructor.

- Under the *user approach,* we present information associated with the financial statement production cycle and document the computations underlying the financial statements.
- Under the *traditional accounting approach,* we illustrate each step in the accounting cycle including the preparation of journal entries, an unadjusted trial balance, end-of-period adjusting journal entries, an adjusted trial balance, and closing journal entries.

Comprehensive Review Problem

Joe Russ is a landscape architect who has always dreamed of owning his own landscaping business. On January 1, 2001, Russ incorporated his new business, Russ Landscaping. On January 1, 2001, Russ paid an attorney $1,500 to prepare and file all the appropriate incorporation documents and pay all initial incorporation fees. Russ appropriately treated the legal bills associated with incorporation as a business expense. Russ bought 100 shares of Russ Landscaping $1 par common stock at $20 per share. Then, he signed a one-year lease at $500 per month for an abandoned filling station, and proudly hung out a beautiful wooden sign: Russ Landscaping.

Russ maintains two primary business activities. First, he provides landscape architect consulting services, for which he charges $50 per hour. Second, he installs trees and shrubs to his design specifications. He does most of the installation work himself, but he needs help from his brother who will work for $20 per hour.

In order to raise additional working capital, Russ went to First National Bank on January 1, 2001, to apply for a $20,000 loan. To support the loan, Russ submitted a conservative budget for the first year, which covers all estimated revenues and expenses excluding any loan (see Exhibit A.1). Because Russ has been working in the area, he already has several clients. First National Bank provided instant loan approval, and Russ received $20,000 under the following terms: principal is due January 1, 2005, and annual interest at 10% is payable on every January 1. On his way home from the bank, Russ stopped by a local equipment dealer and purchased a used tractor for $15,000. The tractor has an estimated useful life of five years and no salvage value. Assume that Russ uses the straight-line depreciation method for both financial reporting and income tax purposes.

EXHIBIT A.1 Russ Landscaping 2001 Budget

RUSS LANDSCAPING 2001 Budget*	
Landscape consultation fees	
(10 hours per week, 50 weeks at $50 per hour)	$ 25,000
Sales of plants and landscaping materials	200,000

(continued)

EXHIBIT A.1 (concluded)

Total estimated revenues		$225,000
Cost of plants and landscaping materials (50% of sales price)	$100,000	
Rent ($500 per month)	6,000	
Wages (Russ, $1,000 per month)	12,000	
Wages (brother)	8,000	
Truck lease, gas, oil, and maintenance ($600 per month)	7,200	
Telephone, office supplies ($350 per month)	4,200	
Other expense ($1,000 per month)	12,000	
Total estimated expenses		149,400
Income before income taxes		75,600
Estimated income taxes (at 20%)		15,120
Estimated net income		$ 60,480

*Excludes the effects of any loan.

2001 Activities

1. Russ provided 600 hours of landscape consultation in 2001, and billed his clients at $50 per hour. All consulting jobs are billed under the terms net 30 days (i.e., Russ bills the client, records an account receivable, and the client has 30 days to pay the bill). By December 31, 2001, clients had paid for 550 hours.
2. During 2001, Russ purchased plants and landscaping materials at a cost of $95,000. Russ normally pays cash for all plants and landscaping materials. However, on December 27, 2001, Russ purchased $5,000 in materials and agreed to pay the supplier on January 5, 2002 (this amount is included in the 2001, $95,000 total).
3. As indicated in the budget, Russ billed all plants and materials used on jobs at a markup of 100% on cost. Of the $95,000 in plants and materials purchased, $80,000 worth were used on completed jobs during 2001, and clients were billed for $160,000 for landscaping services. All landscaping jobs are billed to clients under the terms net 30 days (i.e., Russ bills the client, records an account receivable, and the client has 30 days to pay the bill). At December 31, 2001, clients owed $7,000 for landscaping services.
4. The 2001 rent expense was as budgeted, and the truck-related expenses were $8,000. Russ paid his brother $9,000 in wages during the year, owing him an additional $1,000 at December 31, 2001, for work completed on December 29, 2001. Russ paid himself $1,100 per month in wages instead of the budgeted $1,000. Telephone and office supplies for the year totaled $5,000. Supplies on hand at year-end were negligible. Miscellaneous expenses during the year were $15,000, including $500 owed to various companies at December 31, 2001. (For convenience, ignore any payroll taxes and sales taxes in this problem.)
5. Russ paid himself $5,000 in dividends during 2001. He also made estimated income tax payments during 2001 totaling $6,000.

User Approach

Note: Students using the traditional accounting approach should proceed to the "Traditional Accounting Approach" section.

Under the user approach, students must systematically accumulate information about Russ's activities in order to prepare the financial statements. Although several different processes may be used, our documentation proceeds in three steps:

1. Compute balances before year-end adjustments.
2. Review the information necessary for year-end adjustments, and compute year-end adjusted balances.
3. Prepare the financial statements: income statement, balance sheet, statement of stockholders' equity, and statement of cash flows.

Compute Balances Before Adjustments

All accounts related to Russ Landscaping are listed below. If more than one transaction affected an account, the underlying detail is presented. The account balances are *before* year-end adjustments.

RUSS LANDSCAPING
Account Balances Before Year-End Adjustments

Cash	
Issued stock	$ 2,000
Paid legal fees	(1,500)
Proceeds from bank loan	20,000
Purchased tractor	(15,000)
Consulting revenues	27,500
Purchased inventory	(90,000)
Landscaping revenues	153,000
Operating expenses—rent, transportation, wages, telephone and office supplies, and other (excludes income tax expense and cost of goods sold)	(55,700)
Paid dividends	(5,000)
Income tax payments	(6,000)
Balance, December 31, 2001	$ 29,300
Accounts Receivable	
Consulting services ($30,000 – $27,500)	$ 2,500
Landscaping services ($160,000 – $153,000)	7,000
Balance, December 31, 2001	$ 9,500
Inventory	
Purchases	$ 95,000
Used on jobs	(80,000)
Balance, December 31, 2001	$ 15,000
Equipment (purchase)	$ 15,000
Operating Expenses	
Cost of goods sold	$ 80,000
Legal fees	1,500
Rent expense	6,000
Transportation expense	8,000
Wages expense ($10,000 brother, $13,200 Russ)	23,200
Telephone and office supplies	5,000
Other expenses	15,000
Balance, December 31, 2001	$138,700
Income Tax Expense	$ 6,000
Consulting Revenues	30,000
Landscaping Revenues	160,000
Notes Payable	20,000
Accounts Payable	5,000
Accrued Expenses Payable ($1,000 in wages, $500 other expenses)	1,500
Retained Earnings	(5,000)
Common Stock	100
Additional Contributed Capital	1,900

Information for Year-End Adjustments

1. As previously noted, Russ provided 600 hours of landscaping consultation in 2001, and billed his clients at $50 per hour. Of the 600 hours, Russ had collected for 550 hours at year-end. Russ believed that a bill for 8 hours would prove to be uncollectible, and decided to write off the account as bad debts expense.
2. Recall that Russ purchased $95,000 in plants and landscaping materials during the year. Of this $95,000, plants and materials with a cost of $80,000 were used on completed jobs. Additionally, a year-end inventory count showed that $2,000 of plants had died or the materials were not usable. The remaining plants and materials (with a cost of $13,000) were on hand in usable condition at Decem-

ber 31, 2001. Russ charges the cost of damaged/lost plants and unusable materials to cost of goods sold.

3. Russ determined that he should accrue interest expense and record depreciation expense for the year.
4. Recall that Russ made estimated income tax payments during 2001 of $6,000. At December 31, 2001, Russ's accountant computed that Russ would owe an additional $380 when the 2001 tax return was filed.

Compute Year-End Adjusted Balances

After making the year-end adjustments, we can compute Russ's adjusted account balances. These adjusted balances are then used to prepare the year-end financial statements.

RUSS LANDSCAPING
Account Balances After Year-End Adjustments

Cash	
Issued stock	$ 2,000
Paid legal fees	(1,500)
Proceeds from bank loan	20,000
Purchased tractor	(15,000)
Consulting revenues	27,500
Purchased inventory	(90,000)
Landscaping revenues	153,000
Operating expenses—rent, transportation, wages, telephone and office supplies, and other (excluding income tax expense and cost of goods sold)	(55,700)
Paid dividends	(5,000)
Income tax payments	(6,000)
Balance, December 31, 2001	$ 29,300
Accounts Receivable	
Consulting services ($30,000 − $27,500)	$ 2,500
Landscaping services ($160,000 − $153,000)	7,000
Write-off	(400)
Balance, December 31, 2001	$ 9,100
Inventory	
Purchases	$ 95,000
Used on jobs	(80,000)
Written off at year-end	(2,000)
Balance, December 31, 2001	$ 13,000
Equipment (purchase)	$ 15,000
Accumulated Depreciation	$ 3,000
Operating Expenses	
Cost of goods sold ($80,000 + $2,000)	$ 82,000
Legal fees	1,500
Rent expense	6,000
Transportation expense	8,000
Wages expense ($10,000 brother, $13,200 Russ)	23,200
Telephone and office supplies	5,000
Other expenses	15,000
Bad debts expense	400
Depreciation expense	3,000
Interest expense	2,000
Balance, December 31, 2001	$146,100
Income Tax Expense ($6,000 + $380)	$ 6,380
Consulting Revenues	30,000
Landscaping Revenues	160,000
Notes Payable	20,000
Accounts Payable	5,000
Accrued Expenses Payable ($1,000 in wages, $500 other expenses)	1,500
Retained Earnings	(5,000)
Common Stock	100
Additional Contributed Capital	1,900

Financial Statements

From the adjusted balances, we can prepare an income statement, balance sheet, statement of stockholders' equity, and statement of cash flows.

RUSS LANDSCAPING
Income Statement
For the Year Ended December 31, 2001

Landscaping revenues		$160,000
Cost of landscaping materials		82,000
Gross margin		78,000
Consulting revenues		30,000
Total gross margin and consulting revenues		108,000
Operating expenses:		
Wages expense	$23,200	
Rent expense	6,000	
Transportation expense	8,000	
Telephone and office supplies	5,000	
Other expenses	15,000	
Depreciation expense	3,000	
Legal fees	1,500	
Bad debts expense	400	62,100
Operating income		45,900
Other expenses—interest expense		2,000
Income before income taxes		43,900
Income tax expense		6,380
Net income		$ 37,520
Earnings per share		$375.20

RUSS LANDSCAPING
Balance Sheet
December 31, 2001

Assets		
Current assets:		
Cash	$29,300	
Accounts receivable	9,100	
Inventory	13,000	
Total current assets		$51,400
Equipment (net of accumulated depreciation of $3,000)		12,000
Total assets		$63,400
Liabilities		
Current liabilities:		
Accounts payable	$ 5,000	
Accrued expenses payable	1,500	
Interest payable	2,000	
Income taxes payable	380	
Total current liabilities		$ 8,880
Notes payable		20,000
Total liabilities		28,880
Stockholders' Equity		
Common stock	$ 100	
Additional contributed capital	1,900	
Retained earnings	32,520	
Total stockholders' equity		34,520
Total liabilities and stockholders' equity		$63,400

RUSS LANDSCAPING
Statement of Stockholders' Equity
For the Year Ended December 31, 2001

	Common Stock	Additional Contributed Capital	Retained Earnings
Beginning balance, January 1, 2001	$ 0	$ 0	$ 0
Net income			37,520
Dividends			(5,000)
Stock issue	100	1,900	
Ending balance, December 31, 2001	$100	$1,900	$32,520

RUSS LANDSCAPING
Statement of Cash Flows
For the Year Ended December 31, 2001
Cash Inflows (Outflows)

Cash flows from operating activities		
Consulting revenues	$ 27,500	
Landscaping revenues	153,000	
Purchase inventory	(90,000)	
Operating expenses*	(57,200)	
Income taxes	(6,000)	
Net cash flows from operating activities		$ 27,300
Cash flows from investing activities		
Purchase equipment		(15,000)
Cash flows from financing activities		
Issue common stock	$ 2,000	
Borrow from bank (note payable)	20,000	
Pay dividends	(5,000)	
Net cash flows from financing activities		17,000
Net increase in cash		$ 29,300
January 1, 2001 cash balance		0
December 31, 2001 cash balance		$ 29,300

*$62,100 (on income statement) − $400 (bad debts expense) − $3,000 (depreciation expense) − $1,500 (accrued expenses at year-end for which payment has not been made).

Traditional Accounting Approach: Journal Entry Option

Under the traditional accounting approach, in which the accounting system uses debits and credits to capture and categorize the effects of the transactions, we present the following items: journal entries; an unadjusted trial balance; adjusting journal entries; an adjusted trial balance; closing journal entries; and T accounts.

Russ Landscaping 2001 Journal Entries

	Debit	Credit
January 1, 2001:		
Cash	2,000	
Common Stock		100
Additional Contributed Capital		1,900
To record issuance of common stock.		
Legal Fees	1,500	
Cash		1,500
Cost of incorporation.		

(continued)

(concluded)

Cash	20,000	
Notes Payable		20,000
Borrowed from First National Bank, four-year note at 10%.		
Equipment	15,000	
Cash		15,000
Purchased tractor.		

Journal Entries for 2001 Transactions After January 1, 2001

Accounts Receivable	2,500	
Cash	27,500	
Consulting Revenues		30,000
To record revenue: 600 hours × $50 = $30,000.		
550 hours × $50 = $27,500.		
Inventory—Plants and Landscaping Materials	95,000	
Cash		90,000
Accounts Payable		5,000
To record purchase of inventory.		
Cost of Goods Sold	80,000	
Inventory		80,000
To record plants and landscaping materials used.		
Accounts Receivable	7,000	
Cash	153,000	
Landscaping Revenues		160,000
To record sales and cash collections:		
$160,000 billed less $7,000.		
Rent Expense	6,000	
Transportation Expense	8,000	
Wage Expense—Brother	10,000	
Wage Expense—Russ	13,200	
Telephone and Office Supplies	5,000	
Other Expenses	15,000	
Accrued Expenses Payable ($1,000 brother, $500 other)		1,500
Cash		55,700
To record operating expenses, including year-end accruals.		
Retained Earnings	5,000	
Cash		5,000
To record payment of dividends.		
Income Tax Expense	6,000	
Cash		6,000
To record estimated tax payments.		

Unadjusted Trial Balance

A trial balance is simply a list of the accounts and their balances. Summarizing the beginning balances and Russ's 2001 activities before year-end adjustments leads to the following trial balance.

RUSS LANDSCAPING
Unadjusted Trial Balance
December 31, 2001

	Debit	Credit
Cash	$ 29,300	
Accounts Receivable	9,500	
Inventory	15,000	
Equipment	15,000	
Accounts Payable		$ 5,000
Accrued Expenses Payable		1,500
Notes Payable		20,000
Common Stock		100
Additional Contributed Capital		1,900
Retained Earnings	5,000	
Consulting Revenues		30,000
Landscaping Revenues		160,000
Cost of Goods Sold	80,000	
Legal Fees	1,500	
Rent Expense	6,000	
Transportation Expense	8,000	
Wages Expense	23,200	
Telephone and Office Supplies	5,000	
Other Expenses	15,000	
Income Tax Expense	6,000	
Total	$218,500	$218,500

Year-End Adjusting Journal Entries

December 31, 2001:		
Bad Debts Expense	400	
Accounts Receivable		400
To write off an uncollectible account (8 hours × $50).		
Cost of Goods Sold	2,000	
Inventory		2,000
Cost of unusable plants and materials.		
Interest Expense	2,000	
Interest Payable		2,000
Interest expense on note payable ($20,000 × 10%).		
Depreciation Expense	3,000	
Accumulated Depreciation		3,000
To record depreciation expense [($15,000 – 0) ÷ 5].		
Income Tax Expense	380	
Income Taxes Payable		380
To accrue income tax expense.		

Year-End Adjusted Trial Balance

RUSS LANDSCAPING
Adjusted Trial Balance
December 31, 2001

Cash	$ 29,300	
Accounts Receivable	9,100	
Inventory	13,000	
Equipment	15,000	
Accumulated Depreciation		$ 3,000
Accounts Payable		5,000
Accrued Expenses Payable		1,500
Interest Payable		2,000
Income Taxes Payable		380
Notes Payable		20,000
Common Stock		100
Additional Contributed Capital		1,900
Retained Earnings	5,000	
Consulting Revenues		30,000
Landscaping Revenues		160,000
Cost of Goods Sold	82,000	
Legal Fees	1,500	
Rent Expense	6,000	
Transportation Expense	8,000	
Wages Expense	23,200	
Telephone and Office Supplies	5,000	
Other Expenses	15,000	
Bad Debts Expense	400	
Interest Expense	2,000	
Depreciation Expense	3,000	
Income Tax Expense	6,380	
Total	$223,880	$223,880

Year-End Closing Journal Entries

The following journal entries close out the revenue and expense accounts to retained earnings.

Russ Landscaping 2001 Closing Journal Entries

December 31, 2001:		
Consulting Revenues	30,000	
Landscaping Revenues	160,000	
Cost of Goods Sold		82,000
Legal Fees		1,500
Rent Expense		6,000
Transportation Expense		8,000
Wages Expense		23,200
Telephone and Office Supplies		5,000
Other Expenses		15,000
Bad Debts Expense		400
Interest Expense		2,000
Depreciation Expense		3,000
Income Tax Expense		6,380
Retained Earnings		37,520
To close revenue and expense accounts to retained earnings.		

Note: This closing journal entry closes the revenue and expense accounts directly to Retained Earnings. An alternative process is to close revenues and expenses to a temporary account, Income Summary, and then to close Income Summary to Retained Earnings.

T Accounts

The following T account information reflects the journal entries to record the year's activities, year-end adjusting journal entries, and year-end closing journal entries. All of these journal entries are posted to these accounts.

Cash

Beginning balance	0		
Issue common stock	2,000	Pay legal fees	1,500
Bank loan	20,000	Purchase equipment	15,000
Consulting revenues	27,500	Purchase inventory	90,000
Landscape revenues	153,000	Rent expense	6,000
		Transportation expense	8,000
		Wages expense ($23,200 − $1,000)	22,200
		Telephone and office supplies	5,000
		Other expenses ($15,000 − $500)	14,500
		Dividends paid	5,000
		Income taxes paid	6,000
Ending balance	29,300		

Accounts Receivable

Beginning balance	0		
Consulting revenues	2,500		
Landscaping revenues	7,000		
Unadjusted ending balance	9,500		
		Year-end adjusting entry, write-off	400
Adjusted ending balance	9,100		

Inventory

Beginning balance	0		
Purchases	95,000		
		Cost of goods sold	80,000
Unadjusted ending balance	15,000		
		Year-end adjusting entry write-off	2,000
Adjusted ending balance	13,000		

Equipment

Beginning balance	0		
Purchase	15,000		
Ending balance	15,000		

Accumulated Depreciation—Equipment

		Beginning balance	0
		Year-end adjusting journal entry	3,000
		Adjusted ending balance	3,000

Notes Payable

		Beginning balance	0
		Bank loan	20,000
		Ending balance	20,000

Accounts Payable

		Beginning balance	0
		Purchase inventory	5,000
		Ending balance	5,000

Accrued Expenses Payable

		Beginning balance	0
		Wages expense	1,000
		Other expenses	500
		Ending balance	1,500

Interest Payable

		Beginning balance	0
		Year-end adjusting entry	2,000
		Adjusted ending balance	2,000

Income Taxes Payable

		Beginning balance	0
		Year-end adjusting entry	380
		Adjusted ending balance	380

Common Stock

		Beginning balance	0
		Issue stock	100
		Ending balance	100

Additional Contributed Capital

		Beginning balance	0
		Issue stock	1,900
		Ending balance	1,900

Retained Earnings

		Beginning balance	0
Pay dividend	5,000		
Unadjusted ending balance	5,000		
		Year-end closing entry	37,520
		Adjusted ending balance	32,520

Revenues*

		Beginning balance	0
		Consulting revenues	30,000
		Landscaping revenues	160,000
		Unadjusted ending balance	190,000
Year-end closing entry	190,000		
		Adjusted ending balance	0

*For convenience, one account is used with the amounts listed separately. In practice, each of the accounts would have its own T account.

Expenses*			
Beginning balance	0		
Legal fees	1,500		
Cost of goods sold	80,000		
Rent	6,000		
Transportation	8,000		
Wages	23,200		
Telephone and office supplies	5,000		
Other	15,000		
Income taxes	6,000		
Unadjusted ending balance	144,700		
Year-end adjusting entries:			
Bad debts expense	400		
Cost of goods sold	2,000		
Interest expense	2,000		
Depreciation expense	3,000		
Income tax expense	380		
Adjusted ending balance	152,480		
		Closing journal entry	152,480
Ending balance	0		

*For convenience, one account is used with the amounts listed separately. In practice, each of the accounts would have its own T account.

Financial Statements

The financial statements are presented at the end of the User Approach section. The financial statements are the same whether a user approach or the traditional accounting approach is used.

Comprehensive Example Problem

Juanita Lopez recently graduated from Purdue University with a degree in computer science. Instead of working for a large company, she decided to open her own consulting business, specializing in Web-page designs, computer systems recommendations to small clients, and computer systems installation. Lopez incorporated her business on January 1, 2001, under the name Lopez Consulting. She used most of her savings to purchase 1,000 shares of $1 par common stock for $10 per share. The following information is provided about her 2001 business activities and year-end adjustments.

1. On January 1, 2001, Lopez borrowed $25,000 from the Citizens National Bank, under the following terms: principal due January 1, 2004; interest rate is 10% per year, with interest paid semiannually on July 1 and January 1 (i.e., 5% every six months). Lopez made the July 1, 2001, interest payment as scheduled.
2. On January 1, Lopez purchased computer and other office equipment costing $10,000. Because of the rapid obsolescence of computer-related equipment, she estimates that the equipment has a three-year life with an estimated $1,000 salvage value. Assume that Lopez uses straight-line depreciation for both financial reporting and income tax purposes. Also, on January 1, Lopez signed a one-year lease on office space at $700 per month, with rent due on the first day of each month. Lopez made the rent payments during 2001 as scheduled.
3. Because Lopez's business is a service business, she has no inventory. Clients buy any needed equipment directly from other vendors. During 2001, Lopez did purchase $2,500 in supplies, accounting for the purchase as Supplies Expense.
4. Lopez billed clients for $140,000 in services performed during 2001, and she collected $120,000. Lopez's services were not subject to sales tax.
5. Lopez incurred $20,000 in advertising expenses during 2001. She owed $1,000 of that amount to the advertising agency at December 31, 2001. She intends to pay in January 2002.

6. Lopez incurred $15,000 in miscellaneous (other) expenses during the year. Of these, she owed $2,000 at year-end.
7. Lopez paid income taxes during the year of $10,000.
8. Lopez paid herself a $1,200 salary per month. (For convenience, ignore payroll taxes and other payroll-related expenses.)

Information for year-end adjustments:

1. Of the $2,500 in supplies, supplies costing $200 were still on hand at December 31, 2001.
2. At December 31, 2001, of the $20,000 in accounts receivable outstanding, Lopez decided that one receivable for $4,000 would not be collected, and that the remaining accounts receivable of $16,000 would be collected in 2002. The $4,000 amount was written off as Bad Debts Expense.
3. At December 31, 2001, Lopez's accountant calculated that Lopez would owe an additional $680 when she filed her 2001 tax return.
4. At year-end, Lopez recorded annual depreciation expense and six months' interest expense for the interest due January 1, 2002.

User Approach

Required: Use some system to track how accounts are affected by the activities described in the problem. Compute all account balances after adjustments. Prepare a complete set of financial statements for Lopez Consulting as of December 31, 2001 (income statement, balance sheet, statement of owners' equity, and statement of cash flows).

Traditional Accounting Approach

Journal Entry Option: Complete each step of the accounting cycle: prepare 2001 journal entries; an unadjusted trial balance; year-end adjusting journal entries; an adjusted trial balance; closing journal entries; and T accounts (post each amount to the appropriate account). Finally, prepare an income statement, balance sheet, statement of stockholders' equity, and statement of cash flows.

Appendix B The Time Value of Money—A Review

B

This appendix provides a brief *review* of the time value of money concepts. We assume that students have learned time value of money concepts in a previous class, and that students will work time value of money problems with either a financial calculator or a computer spreadsheet program such as Excel®.

Time value of money concepts are important in transactions involving contracts that specify cash flows to be paid or received over a period of several years. Long-term assets and liabilities are often recognized as a result of these contracts. For example, a company holding a long-term note receivable might receive an annual cash inflow (if the note bears a stated interest rate) and a final cash inflow at the note's maturity date.

There are three basic cash flow patterns associated with long-term assets and liabilities:

1. A single cash payment or receipt in the future.
2. An *ordinary annuity* series of cash payments or receipts in the future, with the first cash flow at the end of the period.
3. An *annuity due* series of cash payments or receipts in the future, with the first cash flow occurring immediately.

With CF = Cash flow; PV = Present value; and the number of periods (n) = 3, we can illustrate a general time line applying to all time value of money situations as follows:

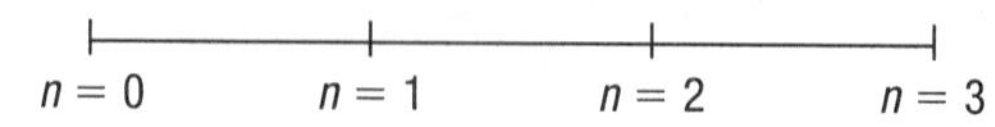

where $n = 0$ is the present time, and $n = 1$, 2, and 3 are one, two, and three periods in the future.

The three basic cash flow patterns are:

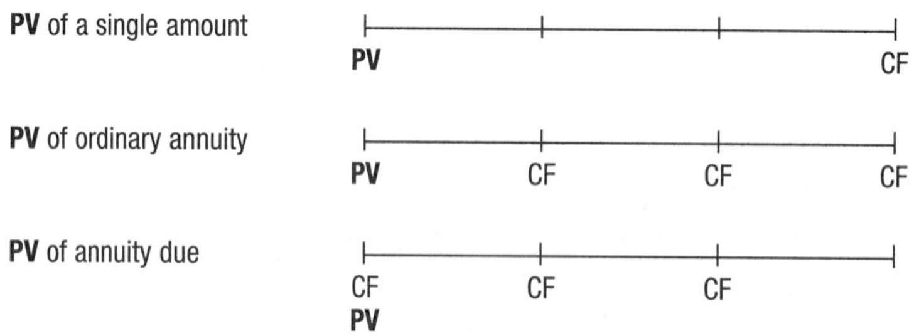

Present Value Computations

In a present value problem, the future cash flow stream represents a combination of both interest and principal. The computation of present value (PV) at $n = 0$ involves removing the interest component from the future cash flows by dividing the cash flow by one plus the risk-adjusted interest rate.

PV of a Single Amount

To estimate the value of a receivable that promised to deliver $100 at the end of three years and has a 10% discount rate, we would move the cash flow to the current period as follows:

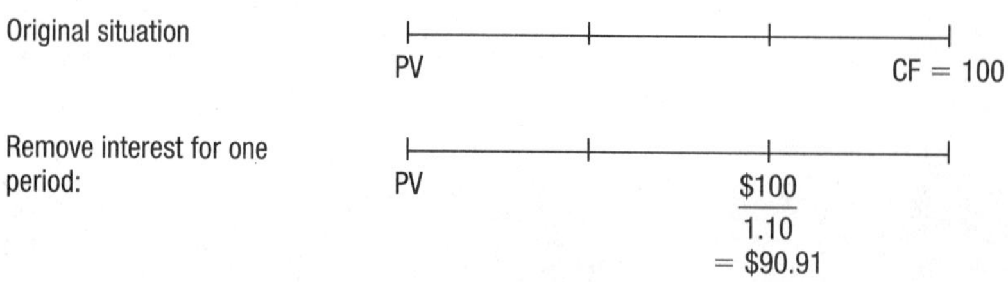

Remove interest for second period:

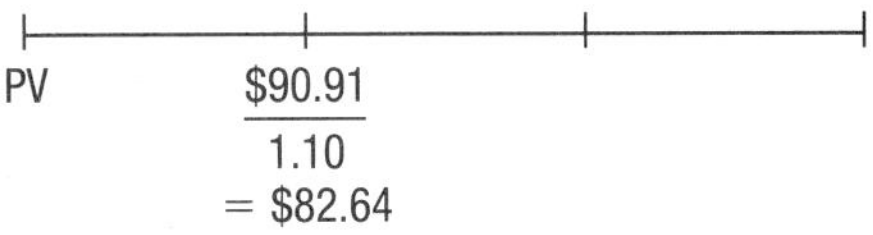

Remove interest for third period:

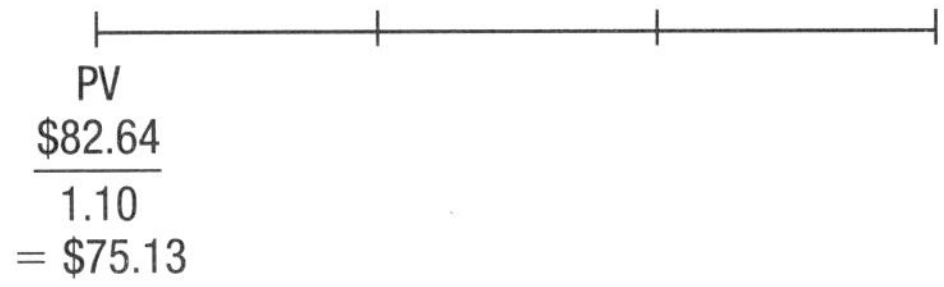

Interest is removed for each period by dividing by one plus the interest rate until the value is expressed in *present* period dollars ($75.13). The general formula for computing present value of a single amount is:

$$\text{PV} = \text{CF} \div (1 + i)^n$$

In our example, this equation is as follows:

$$\text{PV} = \$100 \div (1 + 0.10)^3 = \$75.13$$

Given that we desire a 10% return for allowing this receivable to remain uncollected for three years, we would establish the present value of this receivable at $75.13.

Future Value of a Single Amount

Thus far, we have only discussed the process of computing present values. The reverse process is to compute future values. By looking at the previous transaction from the debtor's point of view, we transform the problem into one of *future value.* The debtor receives in cash today only the present value of the amount promised to be paid in the future. The debtor has a choice of repaying the $75.13 immediately or waiting to pay and allowing interest to accrue at the 10% effective interest rate. As illustrated below, the $75.13 grows each period as interest is added until the amount due at the end of the three years is $100.

Original situation

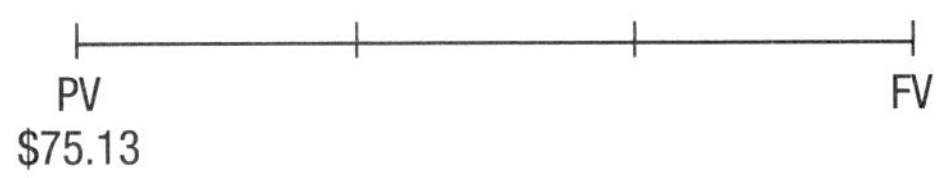

Add first period's interest

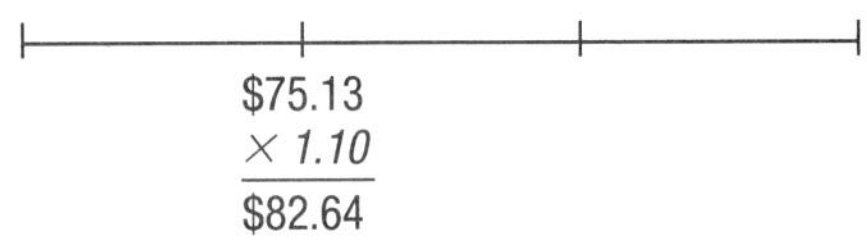

Add second period's interest

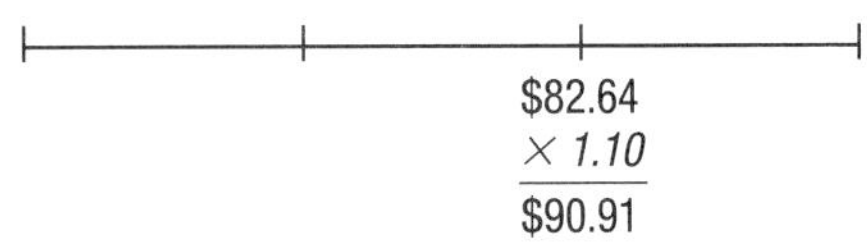

Add third period's interest

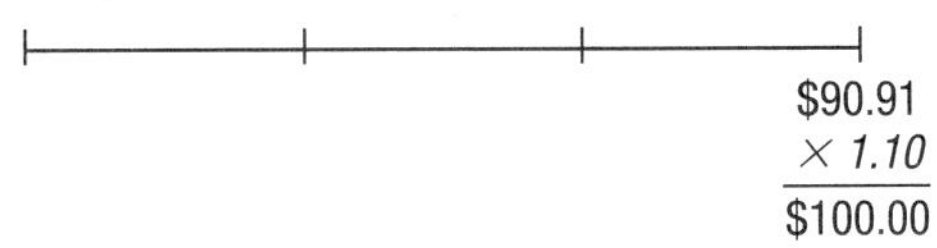

Interest is added each period by multiplying by one plus the interest rate until the value is expressed in *future* period dollars ($100.00). The general formula for computing future value of a single (present value) amount is:

$$\text{FV} = \text{PV} \times (1 + i)^n$$

In our example, this equation is as follows:

$$\text{FV} = \$75.13 \times (1 + 0.10)^3 = \$100.00$$

Although almost all accounting problems are present value rather than future value, we have included this future example to remind you that time value of money concepts can be applied both forward and backward in time.

Present Value of Annuities

Present value computations for annuities can be handled in the same fashion as present value computations for single amounts. **If the annuity payments occur at the end of a period, the annuity is an *ordinary annuity*. If the annuity payments occur at the beginning of a period, the annuity is an *annuity due*.**

Ordinary Annuity Assume that we are determining the value of a receivable that promises to pay \$100 at the end of each year for the next three years plus 10% interest:

PV of ordinary annuity

PV | CF = \$100 | CF = \$100 | CF = \$100

We can determine the present value of this receivable by computing the present value of the three different future cash payments and adding these amounts together:

$$PV = \frac{\$100}{(1 + 0.10)^1} + \frac{\$100}{(1 + 0.10)^2} + \frac{\$100}{(1 + 0.10)^3} = \$248.68$$

Alternatively, the following general formula for the PV of an ordinary annuity (OA) can be used:

$$PV\ (OA) = \text{Annuity amount} \times (\{1 - [1 \div (1 + r)^n]\} \div r)$$

where r equals the appropriate discount (interest) rate and n equals the number of periods. By plugging in the amounts from the previous problem, the present value is computed as follows:

$$\$100 \times \{[1 - (1 \div (1 + 0.10)^3)] \div 0.10\} = \$100 \times 2.48685 = \$248.69$$

Annuity Due The following computation shows the present value of the previous example assuming that the annuity payment occurs at the beginning of the period rather than at the end of the period.

PV of annuity due

CF = \$100 (PV) | CF = \$100 | CF = \$100

The present value equals the sum of the present values of the three cash flows, computed as follows:

$$PV = \frac{\$100}{(1 + 0.10)^0} + \frac{\$100}{(1 + 0.10)^1} + \frac{\$100}{(1 + 0.10)^2} = \$273.55$$

Again, the following general formula for the PV of an annuity due (AD) can be used:

$$PV\ (AD) = \text{Annuity amount} \times (1 + \{1 - [1 \div (1 + r)^{n-1}]\} \div r)$$

where r equals the appropriate discount (interest) rate and n equals the number of periods. By filling in the amounts from the previous problem, the present value is computed as follows:

$$\$100 \times (1 + \{1 - [1 \div (1 + 0.10)^2]\} \div 0.10) = \$100 \times 2.7355 = \$273.55$$

Present Value Computation Using a Financial Calculator

Throughout the text we use present value computations, and we illustrate the solutions using present value formulas. However, it is more expedient to use a financial calculator or a common spreadsheet software such as Excel® to make these present value computations. Accordingly, we also document the present value computations with the appropriate present value parameters entered into a financial calculator. Although financial calculators differ with respect to nomenclature and the manner of data entry, they all follow the same general pattern. We use the following present value parameters throughout the text to document our solutions:

n = Number of payment (annuity) periods

i = Market (effective) rate of interest per n

Payment = Annuity payment per n (normally computed by multiplying the face or maturity value times the stated rate of interest per n). When using a calculator or computer spreadsheet program, you must indicate whether the payment is an annuity due or an ordinary annuity.

Future value = One-time lump sum payment made in the future

Present value = Present value of future cash flows discounted at the market (effective) rate of interest

To illustrate the documentation using a financial calculator, consider the three previous examples.

Present Value of a Single Amount To solve for the present value of a receivable that promised to deliver $100 at the end of three years and has a 10% discount rate, we calculate using a financial calculator as follows: n = 3; i = 10%; payment = 0 (no annuity payments are involved); future value = $100; and present value = ? = $75.13. Note that $75.13 is also the amount we previously computed using the formulas.

Present Value of Ordinary Annuity To document the present value for the annuity that promises to pay $100 at the end of each year for the next three years plus 10% interest, the following information is used to solve the problem using a financial calculator: n = 3; i = 10%; payment = $100 ordinary annuity; future value = $0 (no future, single, lump-sum payment is made); present value = ? = $248.69 (rounded).

Present Value of Annuity Due To document the present value for the annuity that promises to pay $100 at the beginning of each year for the next three years plus 10% interest, the following information is used to solve the problem using a financial calculator: n = 3; i = 10%; payment = $100 annuity due; future value = $0 (no future, single, lump-sum payment is made); present value = ? = $273.55 (rounded).

Present Value of Combined Lump Sum Payment and Annuity Payments

We can combine the previous present value examples into one that has both a lump sum at the end of the time line *and* annuity payments. For example, assume the following cash flow pattern over a three-year period: $100 ordinary annuity payments over the three-year period, a lump sum of $200 at the end of three years, and a market interest rate of 10%.

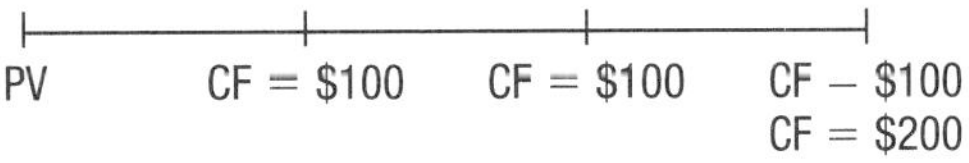

Using a financial calculator to solve the problem: n = 3; i = 10%; payment = $100 ordinary annuity; future value = $200; present value = ? = $398.95.

Key Terms

annuity due B-4

ordinary annuity B-4

Problems

To solve the time value of money problems, students may use a financial calculator, a computer spreadsheet program, or the appropriate formula.

1. **Present Value of an Ordinary Annuity Payment.** Compute the present value of a contract that promises to pay $500 at the end of each year for the next three years. Assume an interest rate of 9%.
2. **Present Value of an Annuity Due Payment.** Compute the present value of a contract that promises to pay $500 at the beginning of each year for the next three years. Assume an interest rate of 9%.
3. **Present Value of Lump Sum Payment.** Compute the present value of $1,000,000 to be received 10 years from today. Use an annual effective interest rate of 8%.
4. **Present Value of Multiple, Uneven Payments.** Compute the present value of a contract that promises to pay $700 at the end of year one, $1,100 at the end of year two, and $3,000 at the end of year three. Assume an interest rate of 7%.
5. **Solving for Effective Interest Rate (*i*).** A note receivable specifies that a company will receive a single cash flow of $48,400 at the end of two years. If the present value of this note is $40,000, what interest rate is used to determine present value?
6. **Solving for Effective Interest Rate (*i*).** Using the following parameters, solve for i: $n = 8$ years; present value = $3,600,000; annual payments = $240,000 ordinary annuity; and future value = $3,000,000.
7. **Future Value.** If we invest $600 today at 5% interest, how much will we have in four years?
8. **Balance Sheet—Note Payable.** On December 31, 2001, the president of Margolis Inc. was reviewing the preliminary balance sheet for the year ended December 31, 2001. The long-term liability section included a note payable. Because Margolis planned to issue additional debt in March 2002, the president was concerned about how the note will be presented in the final December 31, 2001, balance sheet. The documentation you obtain from the financial manager's records indicates the following information about the note:

> We issued a four-year, non-interest-bearing note payable on January 1, 2001, to acquire land. Even though the land had a cash-equivalent price of only $100,000, the note's face amount (the amount we have to pay on January 1, 2005) is $146,410. Because the note was constructed as a non-interest-bearing note (we normally pay 10% interest on notes of this type), we agreed to the face amount of $146,410.

Hint: GAAP requires that a non-interest-bearing note be recorded at its present value using the current market rate of interest for loans of the same riskiness (i.e., 10%). At any point in time, a note payable is reported on the balance sheet at the present value of the remaining cash flows using the historical effective rate of interest (in this problem, 10%).

a. At what amount should the note payable be shown on January 1, 2001?
b. At what amount should the note payable be shown on the December 31, 2001, balance sheet?
c. At what amount will the note be shown on the December 31, 20049i, balance sheet (the day before the note payable is due)?

Appendix C
Southwest Airlines Co.
1998 Annual Report

C

MANAGEMENT'S DISCUSSION AND ANALYSIS OF FINANCIAL CONDITION AND RESULTS OF OPERATIONS

YEAR IN REVIEW

In 1998, Southwest posted a record annual profit for the seventh consecutive year and a profit for the 26th consecutive year. The Company also posted record operating revenues; record operating income; the highest net profit margin since 1981 of 10.4 percent; and the highest operating profit margin since 1981 of 16.4 percent. The Company experienced strong revenue growth, low unit costs, and continued strong demand for our product.

At the end of 1998, Southwest served 52 cities in 26 states. We added service to Manchester, New Hampshire, in June 1998 and have been very pleased with the results. We have plans to add new service to Islip, New York, on Long Island in March 1999 and will begin serving at least one other new city in 1999. With the net addition of at least 28 aircraft in 1999 (32 new Boeing 737-700s, two used -300s, and the retirement of six older -200s), we will also continue to add additional flights to cities we already serve. We are actively pursuing the acquisition of additional used 737-300s that would add to our 1999 expansion efforts.

During 1998, Boeing experienced production delays related to the 737 production line. These production delays, for the most part, have been remedied by Boeing and we currently do not anticipate any significant delays in 1999.

Also during 1998, the Company's Customer Service and Reservations Sales Agents, represented by the International Association of Machinists and Aerospace Workers, AFL-CIO, and Flight Dispatchers, represented by the Southwest Airlines Employees Association, ratified collective bargaining agreements which will run through the years 2002 and 2009, respectively. In addition, in September 1998, the Company's pilots voted to continue their ten-year agreement with the Company which next becomes amendable in 2004.

RESULTS OF OPERATIONS

1998 COMPARED WITH 1997 The Company's consolidated net income for 1998 was $433.4 million ($1.23 per share, diluted), as compared to the corresponding 1997 amount of $317.8 million ($.93 per share, diluted), an increase of 36.4 percent. The prior years' earnings per share amounts have been restated for the 1998 three-for-two stock split (see Note 7 to the Consolidated Financial Statements).

OPERATING REVENUES Consolidated operating revenues increased by 9.1 percent in 1998 to $4,164.0 million, compared to $3,816.8 million for 1997. This increase in 1998 operating revenues was derived primarily from an 8.9 percent increase in passenger revenues as a result of a 10.8 percent increase in revenue passenger miles (RPMs) offset by a 1.7 percent decrease in passenger revenue yield per RPM. While Southwest's passenger revenues increased 8.9 percent in 1998, the RPM yield decline resulted from the higher load factors, a 6.0 percent increase in passenger trip lengths, and higher federal excise taxes on domestic tickets. Assuming load factors and passenger trip lengths continue to be above year-ago levels, RPM yields will continue this trend. (The immediately preceding sentence is a forward-looking statement which involves uncertainties that could result in actual results differing materially from expected results. Such uncertainties include, but may not be limited to, competitive responses from other air carriers and general economic conditions.)

The 10.8 percent increase in RPMs in 1998 exceeded the 6.9 percent increase in available seat miles (ASMs), resulting in an increase in load factor from 63.7 percent in 1997 to 66.1 percent in 1998. The 1998 ASM growth resulted from the net addition of 19 aircraft during the year. The load factor was 59.2 percent in January 1999, up 5.2 points from January 1998.

Freight revenues in 1998 were $98.5 million, compared to $94.8 million in 1997. The 3.9 percent increase in freight revenues fell short of the 6.9 percent increase in ASMs for the same period. United States mail revenue declined 2.5 percent in 1998 and 9.4 percent for fourth quarter 1998 as the postal service continues to shift away from commercial carriers. This trend is expected to continue in 1999. Other air freight revenues increased 8.5 percent in 1998 due to increased capacity.

Other revenues increased by 22.7 percent in 1998 to $101.7 million, compared to $82.9 million in 1997. This increase is primarily due to increased revenues from the sale of frequent flyer segment credits to participating partners in the Company's Rapid Rewards frequent flyer program.

OPERATING EXPENSES Consolidated operating expenses for 1998 were $3,480.4 million, compared to $3,292.6 million in 1997, an increase of 5.7 percent, compared to the 6.9 percent increase in capacity. Operating expenses per ASM decreased 1.1 percent in 1998, compared to 1997, primarily due to a 26.9 percent decrease in average jet fuel price. The decrease in average jet fuel prices was offset by a $36.1 million increase in Profitsharing and Employee savings plan contributions and an increase in maintenance costs primarily due to unusually low aircraft engine overhaul costs in the first half of 1997.

Unit costs are expected to continue to benefit in first quarter 1999, versus first quarter 1998, from lower jet fuel prices. Excluding jet fuel costs, operating expenses per ASM are expected to increase in first quarter 1999 compared to first quarter 1998 primarily due to higher Profitsharing and Employee savings plan contributions and increased advertising primarily related to the opening of Islip, New York, on Long Island on March 14, 1999. (The immediately preceding two sentences are forward-looking statements which involve uncertainties that could result in actual results differing materially from expected results. Such uncertainties include, but may not be limited to, the largely unpredictable levels of jet fuel prices.)

Operating expenses per ASM for 1998 and 1997 were as follows:

OPERATING EXPENSES PER ASM

	1998	1997	INCREASE (DECREASE)	PERCENT CHANGE
Salaries, wages, and benefits	2.35¢	2.26¢	.09¢	4.0%
Employee profitsharing and savings plans	.35	.30	.05	16.7
Fuel and oil	.82	1.11	(.29)	(26.1)
Maintenance materials and repairs	.64	.58	.06	10.3
Agency commissions	.33	.35	(.02)	(5.7)
Aircraft rentals	.43	.45	(.02)	(4.4)
Landing fees and other rentals	.45	.46	(.01)	(2.2)
Depreciation	.47	.44	.03	6.8
Other	1.48	1.45	.03	2.1
Total	7.32¢	7.40¢	(.08)¢	(1.1)%

Salaries, wages, and benefits per ASM increased 4.0 percent in 1998. This increase resulted primarily from a 6.9 percent increase in 1998 average salary and benefits cost per Employee. The increase in average salary and benefits cost per Employee primarily is due to higher effective wage rates, lower productivity in 1998 caused by Boeing aircraft delivery delays, and increased health care and workers' compensation costs.

Profitsharing and Employee savings plans expense per ASM increased 16.7 percent in 1998, primarily due to higher earnings available for profitsharing.

Fuel and oil expenses per ASM decreased 26.1 percent in 1998, primarily due to a 26.9 percent decrease from 1997 in the average jet fuel cost per gallon. The average price paid for jet fuel in 1998 was $.4567 compared to $.6246 in 1997. During fourth quarter 1998, the average cost per gallon decreased 28.0 percent to $.4346 compared to $.6040 in fourth quarter 1997. In January 1999, fuel prices averaged approximately $.38 per gallon. Year-over-year decreases in jet fuel prices are expected to continue in first quarter 1999 due to the continued oversupply of crude oil and related products, along with the effects of the Company's current fuel hedging positions. (The immediately preceding sentence is a forward-looking statement which involves uncertainties that could result in actual results differing materially from expected results. Such uncertainties include, but may not be limited to, the largely unpredictable levels of jet fuel prices.)

Maintenance materials and repairs per ASM increased 10.3 percent in 1998, compared to 1997, primarily as a result of an unusually low number of aircraft engine overhauls in the first six months of 1997. Fourth quarter 1998 maintenance materials and repairs per ASM increased 3.2 percent over fourth quarter 1997. We expect modest year-over-year unit-cost growth for maintenance materials and repairs in 1999. (The immediately preceding sentence is a forward-looking statement which involves uncertainties that could result in actual results differing materially from expected results. Such uncertainties include, but may not be limited to, any unanticipated required aircraft airframe or engine repairs.)

Agency commissions per ASM decreased 5.7 percent in 1998, when compared to 1997, primarily due to a decrease in the percentage of commissionable sales.

Aircraft rentals per ASM decreased 4.4 percent in 1998, compared to 1997, primarily due to a lower percentage of the aircraft fleet being leased.

Depreciation expense per ASM increased 6.8 percent in 1998, compared to 1997, primarily due to a higher percentage of the aircraft fleet being owned. Effective January 1, 1999, the Company will revise its estimated useful lives of its Boeing 737-300/500 aircraft from 20 years to 23 years. This change in accounting estimate will decrease aircraft depreciation by approximately $25 million in 1999.

Other operating expenses per ASM increased 2.1 percent in 1998, compared to 1997, primarily due to increased costs resulting from the Year 2000 remediation program and increased revenue related costs such as credit card processing and communications, offset by lower insurance costs. Advertising costs are expected to increase in first quarter 1999 as a result of opening a new city in March 1999. (The immediately preceding sentence is a forward-looking statement which involves uncertainties that could result in actual results differing materially from expected results. Such uncertainties include, but may not be limited to, competitive responses from other air carriers and general economic conditions.)

OTHER "Other expenses (income)" included interest expense, capitalized interest, interest income, and nonoperating gains and losses. Interest expense decreased $7.2 million in 1998 primarily due to the February 1998 redemption of $100 million of senior unsecured 9 1/4% Notes originally issued in February 1991. Capitalized interest increased $5.8 million in 1998 as a result of higher 1998 progress payment balances. Interest income for 1998 decreased primarily due to lower invested cash balances. Nonoperating gains in 1998 primarily included contractual penalties due from Boeing as a result of aircraft delivery delays.

INCOME TAXES The provision for income taxes, as a percentage of income before taxes, was unchanged from 1997 to 1998.

1997 COMPARED WITH 1996 The Company's consolidated net income for 1997 was $317.8 million ($.93 per share, diluted), as compared to the corresponding 1996 amount of $207.3 million ($.61 per share, diluted), an increase of 53.3 percent.

OPERATING REVENUES Consolidated operating revenues increased by 12.1 percent in 1997 to $3,816.8 million, compared to $3,406.2 million for 1996. This increase in 1997 operating revenues was derived primarily from an 11.3 percent increase in passenger revenues as a result of a 4.7 percent increase in RPMs and a 6.4 percent increase in passenger revenue yield per RPM. Southwest's passenger revenues benefited from a strong U.S. economy, strong demand for air travel, increased fares, and a favorable mix of higher yielding fares.

The 4.7 percent increase in RPMs in 1997, coupled with a 9.2 percent increase in ASMs, resulted in a decrease in load factor from 66.5 percent in 1996 to 63.7 percent in 1997. The decrease in load factor was primarily the result of less promotional fare activity in 1997. The 1997 ASM growth resulted from the addition of 18 aircraft during the year.

Freight revenues in 1997 were $94.8 million, compared to $80.0 million in 1996. The 18.4 percent increase in freight revenues exceeded the 9.2 percent increase in ASMs for the same period primarily due to an increase in United States mail services and increased air freight volumes resulting, in part, from the United Parcel Service labor strike during third quarter 1997.

Other revenues increased by 45.6 percent in 1997 to $82.9 million, compared to $56.9 million in 1996. This increase is primarily due to the sale of frequent flyer segment credits to participating partners in the Company's Rapid Rewards frequent flyer program.

OPERATING EXPENSES Consolidated operating expenses for 1997 were $3,292.6 million, compared to $3,055.3 million in 1996, an increase of 7.8 percent, compared to the 9.2 percent increase in capacity. Operating expenses per ASM decreased 1.3 percent in 1997, compared to 1996, primarily due to lower jet fuel prices; lower aircraft engine repair costs; and favorable results from numerous Companywide cost reduction efforts.

Salaries, wages, and benefits per ASM increased 1.8 percent in 1997. This increase resulted primarily from a 2.4 percent increase in 1997 average salary and benefits cost per Employee, partially offset by slower growth in the number of Employees. The increase in average salary and benefits cost per Employee primarily is due to increased health care costs.

The Company's Flight Attendants are subject to an agreement with the Transport Workers Union of America, AFL-CIO (TWU), which became amendable May 31, 1996. The Company reached an agreement with the TWU, which was ratified by its membership in December 1997. The new contract becomes amendable in May 2002.

Profitsharing and Employee savings plans expense per ASM increased 30.4 percent in 1997, primarily due to higher earnings available for profitsharing.

Fuel and oil expenses per ASM decreased 6.7 percent in 1997, primarily due to a 4.6 percent decrease from 1996 in the average jet fuel cost per gallon, coupled with a slight decrease in the average fuel burn rate from 1996. The average price paid for jet fuel in 1997 was $.6246 compared to $.6547 in 1996. During fourth quarter 1997, the average cost per gallon decreased 17.5 percent to $.6040 compared to $.7323 in fourth quarter 1996.

Maintenance materials and repairs per ASM decreased 6.5 percent in 1997, compared to 1996, primarily as a result of lower engine overhaul costs in the first three quarters of 1997, when compared to the same periods in 1996.

On August 1, 1997, the Company signed a ten-year engine maintenance contract with General Electric Engine Services, Inc. (General Electric). Under the terms of the contract, Southwest will pay General Electric a rate per flight hour in exchange for General Electric performing substantially all engine maintenance for the CFM56-3 engines on the 737-300 and 737-500 aircraft. The Company has a similar agreement with General Electric with respect to the engines on the 737-700 aircraft. Maintenance on the Pratt & Whitney JT8-D engines on the 737-200 aircraft will continue to be performed by General Electric on a time and materials basis. By consolidating its engine repair work and committing to ten years, Southwest believes it will spend substantially less over the course of the contract versus what it would have spent absent this new agreement. (The immediately preceding sentence is a forward-looking statement which involves uncertainties that could result in actual results differing materially from expected results; such uncertainties include the number of unscheduled engine removals, labor rates, and competition in the engine overhaul market.)

Agency commissions per ASM remained unchanged in 1997, when compared to 1996, as the mix of commissionable sales was relatively unchanged.

Aircraft rentals per ASM decreased 4.3 percent in 1997, compared to 1996, primarily due to a lower percentage of the aircraft fleet being leased.

Depreciation expense per ASM decreased 2.2 percent in 1997, compared to 1996, due to an increase in the average life of depreciable assets.

Other operating expenses per ASM decreased 4.0 percent in 1997, compared to 1996, primarily due to lower credit card processing costs, insurance rates, passenger costs, communications costs, and favorable results from numerous other Companywide cost reduction efforts.

OTHER "Other expenses (income)" included interest expense, capitalized interest, interest income, and nonoperating gains and losses. Interest expense increased $4.2 million in 1997 primarily due to the February 1997 issuance of $100 million of senior unsecured 7 3/8% Debentures due March 1, 2027. Capitalized interest decreased $2.5 million in 1997 as a result of the timing of payments related to aircraft purchase contracts. Interest income for 1997 increased $10.8 million primarily due to higher invested cash balances.

INCOME TAXES The provision for income taxes, as a percentage of income before taxes, decreased in 1997 to 38.5 percent from 39.3 percent in 1996. The decrease resulted from lower effective state tax rates, including a reduced California income tax rate.

LIQUIDITY AND CAPITAL RESOURCES

Cash provided from operations was $886.1 million in 1998, compared to $610.6 million in 1997.

During 1998, capital expenditures of $947.1 million primarily were for the purchase of 22 new 737-700 aircraft and four used 737-300 aircraft along with progress payments for future aircraft deliveries. In February 1998, the Company redeemed $100 million of senior unsecured 9 1/4% Notes originally issued in February 1991. At December 31, 1998, capital commitments of the Company primarily consisted of scheduled aircraft acquisitions and related flight equipment.

As of July 22, 1998, the Board of Directors increased the Company's authorization to repurchase shares of its outstanding common stock to $100 million. The Company completed this repurchase program during third quarter 1998, resulting in the repurchase of approximately 4.9 million post-split shares.

As of December 31, 1998, Southwest had 105 new 737-700s on firm order, including 32 to be delivered in 1999, with options to purchase another 62. Aggregate funding required for firm commitments approximated $2,492.5 million through the year 2004, of which $715.9 million related to 1999. See Note 2 to the Consolidated Financial Statements for further information.

The Company has various options available to meet its capital and operating commitments, including cash on hand at December 31, 1998, of $378.5 million, internally generated funds, and a revolving credit line with a group of banks of up to $475 million (none of which had been drawn at December 31, 1998). In addition, the Company will also consider various borrowing or leasing options to maximize earnings and supplement cash requirements.

The Company currently has outstanding shelf registrations for the issuance of $318.8 million of public debt securities, which it currently intends to utilize for aircraft financings in 1999 and 2000.

MARKET RISK

In 1997, the Securities and Exchange Commission issued new rules (Item 305 of Regulation S-K) which require disclosure of material risks, as defined in Item 305, related to market risk sensitive financial instruments. As defined, Southwest currently has market risk sensitive instruments related to jet fuel prices and interest rates.

Airline operators are inherently dependent upon energy to operate and, therefore, are impacted by changes in jet fuel prices. Jet fuel consumed in 1998 and 1997 represented approximately 11.2 and 15.0 percent of Southwest's operating expenses, respectively. Southwest endeavors to acquire jet fuel at the lowest prevailing prices possible.

The Company has historically hedged its exposure to jet fuel price market risk only on a conservative, limited basis. In December 1998, in order to take advantage of historically low jet fuel prices, Southwest increased its fuel hedging activity by entering into fixed price swap agreements hedging approximately 77 percent and 56 percent of its jet fuel needs in first and second quarter 1999, respectively. In January 1999, the Company increased its hedging position for second quarter 1999 to 74 percent. During 1999, the Company may continue its fuel hedging activities at these higher levels to take advantage of the historically low jet fuel prices.

The fair values of outstanding fixed price swap agreements and purchased crude oil call options related to the Company's jet fuel price market risk at December 31, 1998 and 1997, and during the years then ended, were not material. A hypothetical ten percent increase or decrease in the underlying fuel related commodity prices from the December 31, 1998, prices would correspondingly change the fair value of these derivative commodity instruments and their related cash flows by approximately $10 million.

Airline operators are also inherently capital intensive, as the vast majority of the Company's assets are aircraft, which are long lived. The Company's strategy is to capitalize itself conservatively and grow capacity steadily and profitably. While Southwest does use financial leverage, it has maintained a strong balance sheet and "A-" or equivalent credit ratings on its senior unsecured debt with three rating agencies (Standard & Poor's, Moody's, and Duff & Phelps).

As disclosed in Note 4 to the Consolidated Financial Statements, the Company had outstanding unsecured debt of $500 million and $600 million at December 31, 1998 and 1997, respectively, of which only $500 million was long-term at December 31, 1997. This long-term debt represents only 12.1 percent and 14.5 percent of total noncurrent assets at December 31, 1998 and 1997, respectively. The Company currently has an average maturity of ten years for the long-term debt at fixed rates averaging 8.3 percent, which is comparable to average rates prevailing over the last ten years.

At December 31, 1998, the Company operated 112 aircraft under operating and capital leases at rates that are substantially fixed. As defined in Item 305, leases are not market risk sensitive financial instruments and, therefore, are not included in the interest rate sensitivity analysis below. Commitments related to leases are disclosed in Note 5 to the Consolidated Financial Statements.

The Company does not have significant exposure to changing interest rates on its long-term debt because the interest rates are fixed and the financial leverage is modest. Additionally, the Company does not have significant exposure to changing interest rates on invested cash, which was $379 million and $623 million at December 31, 1998 and 1997, respectively. The Company invests available cash in certificates of deposit and investment grade commercial paper that have maturities of three months or less. As a result, the interest rate market risk implicit in these investments at December 31, 1998, is low, as the investments mature within three months. The Company has not undertaken any additional actions to cover interest rate market risk and is not a party to any other interest rate market risk management activities.

A hypothetical ten percent change in market interest rates over the next year would not impact the Company's earnings or cash flow as the interest rates on the Company's long-term debt are fixed and its cash investments are short-term. A ten percent change in market interest rates would not have a material effect on the fair value of the Company's publicly traded long-term debt or its short-term cash investments.

The Company does not purchase or hold any derivative financial instruments for trading purposes.

IMPACT OF THE YEAR 2000

The Company is in the process of converting its computer systems to be Year 2000 ready. This project encompasses information technology systems as well as embedded technology assets. The project also includes an assessment of material third-party relationships and associated risks. The project as it relates to internal systems and equipment consists of four phases: identification, assessment, remediation, and testing. This project is expected to be substantially completed by June 30, 1999.

FLIGHT SAFETY SYSTEMS The Company has completed all phases of its Year 2000 project as it relates to its aircraft fleet and onboard support systems. The Company has determined there are no safety issues with these systems.

The Company also utilizes ground computer systems and equipment essential for the maintenance of aircraft and the management of flight operations. The identification, assessment, and remediation phases of the project with respect to these systems and equipment are completed. The Company expects to complete testing by mid-1999.

INTERNAL SYSTEMS The Company's critical internal systems include computer hardware, software, and related equipment for customer reservations, ticketing, flight and crew scheduling, revenue management, accounting functions, and payroll, as well as airport activities including aircraft ground handling, bag handling, and security. The computing hardware and telecommunications equipment in the Company's central data center are essentially Year 2000 ready at this time. The majority of the Company's vital and critical software systems are either in testing or have already been made Year 2000 ready. While some systems are currently in the testing phase, with a small number in the remediation phase, the Company expects the majority of vital and critical systems to be Year 2000 ready by mid-1999.

THIRD PARTIES The Company has categorized its third party vendors with respect to their potential impact on Company operations in the event any such third party vendor has Year 2000 issues which are not dealt with on a timely basis. The Company is also identifying and assessing the impact of Year 2000 issues as they may affect the vendors' businesses (which, in turn, could affect the Company). The Company has made initial contacts with all of its material third party vendors and is in the process of evaluating their statements of Year 2000 compliance. In addition, the Company continues to work with other members of the Air Transport Association, the airline industry trade group, to share information and resources regarding vendors which are common to the entire industry.

In management's experience, it is not always possible to obtain written certification of Year 2000 compliance from third party vendors. Accordingly, in such cases, the Company is basing its assessment on its own testing, other materials made available by such vendors, and other publicly available information. Upon the conclusion of such assessment, the Company will evaluate the need for contingency plans which may be needed in the event any such vendor cannot demonstrate to the Company, on a timely basis, its Year 2000 compliance.

The Company expects this evaluation and assessment will be an ongoing process through the balance of 1999.

YEAR 2000 COSTS The Company has expensed $11.0 million ($7.1 million in 1998) of costs incurred to date related to the Year 2000 issue. The total remaining cost of the Year 2000 project is presently estimated at approximately $7 million, which will be expensed as incurred.

RISK OF YEAR 2000 ISSUES The Company believes its project to convert its computer systems to be Year 2000 ready will be completed in a timely manner and Year 2000 issues will not have a material adverse effect on operations. However, it is possible the Company's or third parties' systems and equipment could fail and result in the reduction or suspension of the Company's operations. The Company is currently in the process of developing contingency plans related to internal business critical systems and for those critical relationships with third parties. There can be no guarantee, however, that the Company's systems and equipment or third parties' systems and equipment on which Southwest relies will be Year 2000 ready in a timely manner or that contingency plans will mitigate the impact of any failure to complete plans in a timely manner.

The costs of the project, the dates on which the Company believes it will complete the Year 2000 modifications and assessments, and the Company's analysis of its risk in this area are based on management's best estimates, which were derived utilizing numerous assumptions of future events, including the continued availability of certain resources. There can be no guarantee that these estimates will be achieved and actual results could differ materially from those anticipated. Specific factors that might cause such material differences include, but are not limited to, the availability and cost of personnel trained in this area and the ability to locate and correct all relevant computer code, as well as the cooperation needed from third party vendors and others upon whom the Company must rely.

CONSOLIDATED BALANCE SHEET

(In thousands except share and per share amounts)	DECEMBER 31, 1998	1997
ASSETS		
Current assets:		
Cash and cash equivalents	$ 378,511	$ 623,343
Accounts receivable	88,799	76,530
Inventories of parts and supplies, at cost	50,035	52,376
Deferred income taxes (Note 10)	20,734	18,843
Prepaid expenses and other current assets	36,076	35,324
Total current assets	574,155	806,416
Property and equipment, at cost (Notes 2 and 5):		
Flight equipment	4,709,059	3,987,493
Ground property and equipment	720,604	601,957
Deposits on flight equipment purchase contracts	309,356	221,874
	5,739,019	4,811,324
Less allowance for depreciation	1,601,409	1,375,631
	4,137,610	3,435,693
Other assets	4,231	4,051
	$ 4,715,996	$ 4,246,160
LIABILITIES AND STOCKHOLDERS' EQUITY		
Current liabilities:		
Accounts payable	$ 157,415	$ 160,891
Accrued liabilities (Note 3)	477,448	426,950
Air traffic liability	200,078	153,341
Current maturities of long-term debt (Note 4)	11,996	121,324
Other current liabilities	3,716	6,007
Total current liabilities	850,653	868,513
Long-term debt less current maturities (Note 4)	623,309	628,106
Deferred income taxes (Note 10)	549,207	438,981
Deferred gains from sale and leaseback of aircraft	238,412	256,255
Other deferred liabilities	56,497	45,287
Commitments and contingencies (Notes 2, 5, and 10)		
Stockholders' equity (Notes 7 and 8):		
Common stock, $1.00 par value: 850,000,000 shares authorized; 335,904,306 and 221,207,083 shares issued in 1998 and 1997, respectively	335,904	221,207
Capital in excess of par value	89,820	155,696
Retained earnings	2,044,975	1,632,115
Treasury stock, at cost: 3,601,121 shares in 1998	(72,781)	-
Total stockholders' equity	2,397,918	2,009,018
	$ 4,715,996	$ 4,246,160

CONSOLIDATED STATEMENT OF INCOME

(In thousands except per share amounts)	YEARS ENDED DECEMBER 31, 1998	1997	1996
OPERATING REVENUES:			
Passenger	$ 3,963,781	$ 3,639,193	$ 3,269,238
Freight	98,500	94,758	80,005
Other	101,699	82,870	56,927
Total operating revenues	4,163,980	3,816,821	3,406,170
OPERATING EXPENSES:			
Salaries, wages, and benefits (Note 9)	1,285,942	1,136,542	999,719
Fuel and oil	388,348	494,952	484,673
Maintenance materials and repairs	302,431	256,501	253,521
Agency commissions	157,766	157,211	140,940
Aircraft rentals	202,160	201,954	190,663
Landing fees and other rentals	214,907	203,845	187,600
Depreciation	225,212	195,568	183,470
Other operating expenses	703,603	646,012	614,749
Total operating expenses	3,480,369	3,292,585	3,055,335
OPERATING INCOME	683,611	524,236	350,835
OTHER EXPENSES (INCOME):			
Interest expense	56,276	63,454	59,269
Capitalized interest	(25,588)	(19,779)	(22,267)
Interest income	(31,083)	(36,616)	(25,797)
Nonoperating (gains) losses, net	(21,106)	221	(1,732)
Total other expenses (income)	(21,501)	7,280	9,473
INCOME BEFORE INCOME TAXES	705,112	516,956	341,362
PROVISION FOR INCOME TAXES (NOTE 10)	271,681	199,184	134,025
NET INCOME	$ 433,431	$ 317,772	$ 207,337
NET INCOME PER SHARE, BASIC (NOTES 7, 8, AND 11)	$1.30	$.97	$.64
NET INCOME PER SHARE, DILUTED (NOTES 7, 8, AND 11)	$1.23	$.93	$.61

CONSOLIDATED STATEMENT OF STOCKHOLDERS' EQUITY

	YEARS ENDED DECEMBER 31, 1998, 1997, and 1996				
(In thousands except per share amounts)	COMMON STOCK	CAPITAL IN EXCESS OF PAR VALUE	RETAINED EARNINGS	TREASURY STOCK	TOTAL
Balance at December 31, 1995	$ 144,033	$ 162,704	$ 1,120,581	$ -	$ 1,427,318
Issuance of common stock upon exercise of executive stock options and pursuant to Employee stock option and purchase plans (Note 8)	1,079	14,513	-	-	15,592
Tax benefit of options exercised	-	4,433	-	-	4,433
Cash dividends, $.0195 per share	-	-	(6,368)	-	(6,368)
Net income – 1996	-	-	207,337	-	207,337
Balance at December 31, 1996	145,112	181,650	1,321,550	-	1,648,312
Three-for-two stock split (Note 7)	73,578	(73,578)	-	-	-
Issuance of common stock upon exercise of executive stock options and pursuant to Employee stock option and purchase plans (Note 8)	2,517	37,818	-	-	40,335
Tax benefit of options exercised	-	9,806	-	-	9,806
Cash dividends, $.0221 per share	-	-	(7,207)	-	(7,207)
Net income – 1997	-	-	317,772	-	317,772
Balance at December 31, 1997	221,207	155,696	1,632,115	-	2,009,018
Three-for-two stock split (Note 7)	111,894	(111,894)	-	-	-
Purchase of shares of treasury stock (Note 7)	-	-	-	(100,000)	(100,000)
Issuance of common and treasury stock upon exercise of executive stock options and pursuant to Employee stock option and purchase plans (Note 8)	2,803	24,434	(10,184)	27,219	44,272
Tax benefit of options exercised	-	21,584	-	-	21,584
Cash dividends, $.0283 per share	-	-	(10,387)	-	(10,387)
Net income – 1998	-	-	433,431	-	433,431
Balance at December 31, 1998	$ 335,904	$ 89,820	$ 2,044,975	$ (72,781)	$ 2,397,918

CONSOLIDATED STATEMENT OF CASH FLOWS

(In thousands)	YEARS ENDED DECEMBER 31, 1998	1997	1996
CASH FLOWS FROM OPERATING ACTIVITIES:			
Net income	$ 433,431	$ 317,772	$ 207,337
Adjustments to reconcile net income to net cash provided by operating activities:			
Depreciation	225,212	195,568	183,470
Deferred income taxes	108,335	81,711	67,253
Amortization of deferred gains on sale and leaseback of aircraft	(15,251)	(15,414)	(18,263)
Amortization of scheduled airframe overhauls	22,763	20,540	20,539
Changes in certain assets and liabilities:			
Accounts receivable	(12,269)	(3,090)	6,341
Other current assets	1,589	6,243	(19,534)
Accounts payable and accrued liabilities	53,194	8,751	132,096
Air traffic liability	46,737	(4,757)	26,942
Other current liabilities	19,293	(4,204)	5,334
Other	3,101	7,468	3,713
Net cash provided by operating activities	886,135	610,588	615,228
CASH FLOWS FROM INVESTING ACTIVITIES:			
Purchases of property and equipment	(947,096)	(688,927)	(677,431)
Net cash used in investing activities	(947,096)	(688,927)	(677,431)
CASH FLOWS FROM FINANCING ACTIVITIES:			
Issuance of long-term debt	-	98,764	-
Proceeds from aircraft sale and leaseback transactions	-	-	330,000
Payment of long-term debt and capital lease obligations	(118,859)	(12,665)	(12,695)
Payment of cash dividends	(9,284)	(6,593)	(6,216)
Proceeds from Employee stock plans	44,272	40,335	15,592
Repurchase of common stock	(100,000)	-	-
Net cash provided by (used in) financing activities	(183,871)	119,841	326,681
NET INCREASE (DECREASE) IN CASH AND CASH EQUIVALENTS	(244,832)	41,502	264,478
CASH AND CASH EQUIVALENTS AT BEGINNING OF PERIOD	623,343	581,841	317,363
CASH AND CASH EQUIVALENTS AT END OF PERIOD	$ 378,511	$ 623,343	$ 581,841
CASH PAYMENTS FOR:			
Interest, net of amount capitalized	$ 33,384	$ 42,372	$ 36,640
Income taxes	147,447	107,066	66,447

NOTES TO CONSOLIDATED FINANCIAL STATEMENTS

DECEMBER 31, 1998

1. SUMMARY OF SIGNIFICANT ACCOUNTING POLICIES

BASIS OF PRESENTATION Southwest Airlines Co. (Southwest) is a major domestic airline that provides shorthaul, high-frequency, point-to-point, low-fare service. The consolidated financial statements include the accounts of Southwest and its wholly owned subsidiaries (the Company). All significant intercompany balances and transactions have been eliminated. The preparation of financial statements in conformity with generally accepted accounting principles requires management to make estimates and assumptions that affect the amounts reported in the financial statements and accompanying notes. Actual results could differ from these estimates. Certain prior year amounts have been reclassified for comparison purposes.

CASH AND CASH EQUIVALENTS Cash equivalents consist of certificates of deposit and investment grade commercial paper issued by major corporations and financial institutions that are highly liquid and have original maturities of three months or less. Cash and cash equivalents are carried at cost, which approximates market value.

INVENTORIES Inventories of flight equipment expendable parts, materials, and supplies are carried at average cost. These items are charged to expense when issued for use.

PROPERTY AND EQUIPMENT Depreciation is provided by the straight-line method to estimated residual values over periods ranging from 20 to 25 years for flight equipment and 3 to 30 years for ground property and equipment. Property under capital leases and related obligations are recorded at an amount equal to the present value of future minimum lease payments computed on the basis of the Company's incremental borrowing rate or, when known, the interest rate implicit in the lease. Amortization of property under capital leases is on a straight-line basis over the lease term and is included in depreciation expense. The Company records impairment losses on long-lived assets used in operations when events and circumstances indicate that the assets might be impaired and the undiscounted cash flows to be generated by those assets are less than the carrying amounts of those assets.

AIRCRAFT AND ENGINE MAINTENANCE The cost of engine overhauls and routine maintenance costs for aircraft and engines are charged to maintenance expense as incurred. Scheduled airframe overhaul costs are capitalized and amortized over the estimated period benefited, presently the lesser of ten years or the remaining life of the aircraft. Modifications that significantly enhance the operating performance or extend the useful lives of aircraft or engines are capitalized and amortized over the remaining life of the asset.

REVENUE RECOGNITION Passenger revenue is recognized when transportation is provided. Tickets sold but not yet used are included in "Air traffic liability," which includes estimates that are evaluated and adjusted periodically. Any adjustments resulting therefrom are included in results of operations for the periods in which the evaluations are completed.

FREQUENT FLYER PROGRAM The Company accrues the estimated incremental cost of providing free travel awards earned under its Rapid Rewards frequent flyer program. The Company also sells flight segment credits to companies participating in its Rapid Rewards frequent flyer program. The revenue from the sale of flight segment credits is recognized when the credits are sold.

ADVERTISING The Company expenses the costs of advertising as incurred. Advertising expense for the years ended December 31, 1998, 1997, and 1996 was $119,739,000, $112,961,000, and $109,136,000, respectively.

STOCK-BASED EMPLOYEE COMPENSATION Pursuant to Statement of Financial Accounting Standards No. 123 (SFAS 123), *Accounting for Stock-Based Compensation*, the Company accounts for stock-based compensation plans utilizing the provisions of Accounting Principles Board Opinion No. 25 (APB 25), *Accounting for Stock Issued to Employees* and related Interpretations.

DERIVATIVE FINANCIAL INSTRUMENTS The Company utilizes purchased crude oil call options and fixed price swap agreements to hedge a portion of its exposure to fuel price fluctuations. The cost of purchased crude oil call options and gains and losses on fixed price swap agreements are deferred and charged or credited to fuel expense in the same month that the underlying fuel being hedged is used. Gains and losses resulting from hedging positions terminated or settled early are recorded to fuel expense in the month of termination or settlement. Gains and losses on hedging transactions have not been material.

In 1998, the Financial Accounting Standards Board issued Statement of Financial Accounting Standards No. 133 (SFAS 133), *Accounting for Derivative Instruments and Hedging Activities*, which is required to be adopted in years beginning after June 15, 1999. SFAS 133 permits early adoption as of the beginning of any fiscal quarter after its issuance. The Company expects to adopt the new Statement effective January 1, 2000. SFAS 133 will require the Company to recognize all derivatives on the balance sheet at fair value. Derivatives that are not hedges must be adjusted to fair value through income. If the derivative is a hedge, depending on the nature of the hedge, changes in the fair value of derivatives will either be offset against the change in fair value of the hedged assets, liabilities, or firm commitments through earnings or recognized in other comprehensive income until the hedged item is recognized in earnings. The ineffective portion of a derivative's change in fair value will be immediately recognized in earnings. The Company has not yet determined what the effect of SFAS 133 will be on the earnings and financial position of the Company.

2. COMMITMENTS

The Company's contractual purchase commitments consist primarily of scheduled aircraft acquisitions. Thirty-two 737-700 aircraft are scheduled for delivery in 1999, 21 in 2000, 21 in 2001, 21 in 2002, five in 2003, and five in 2004. In addition, the Company has options to purchase up to 62 -700s during 2003–2006. The Company has the option, which must be exercised two years prior to the contractual delivery date, to substitute 737-600s or 737-800s for the 700s scheduled subsequent to 2000. Aggregate funding needed for firm commitments is approximately $2,492.5 million, subject to adjustments for inflation, due as follows: $715.9 million in 1999, $520.2 million in 2000, $498.7 million in 2001, $515.8 million in 2002, $152.8 million in 2003, and $89.1 million in 2004.

3. ACCRUED LIABILITIES

(In thousands)	1998	1997
Employee profitsharing and savings plans (Note 9)	$ 123,195	$ 92,857
Aircraft rentals	121,868	123,669
Vacation pay	54,781	50,812
Other	177,604	159,612
	$ 477,448	$ 426,950

4. LONG-TERM DEBT

(In thousands)	1998	1997
9 1/4% Notes due 1998	$ -	$ 100,000
9.4% Notes due 2001	100,000	100,000
8 3/4% Notes due 2003	100,000	100,000
8% Notes due 2005	100,000	100,000
7 7/8% Notes due 2007	100,000	100,000
7 3/8% Debentures due 2027	100,000	100,000
Capital leases (Note 5)	133,190	152,324
Other	4,481	-
	637,671	752,324
Less current maturities	11,996	121,324
Less debt discount	2,366	2,894
	$ 623,309	$ 628,106

On February 28, 1997, the Company issued $100 million of senior unsecured 7 3/8% Debentures due March 1, 2027. Interest is payable semi-annually on March 1 and September 1. The Debentures may be redeemed, at the option of the Company, in whole at any time or in part from time to time, at a redemption price equal to the greater of the principal amount of the Debentures plus accrued interest at the date of redemption or the sum of the present values of the remaining scheduled payments of principal and interest thereon, discounted to the date of redemption at the comparable treasury rate plus 20 basis points, plus accrued interest at the date of redemption.

On March 7, 1995, the Company issued $100 million of senior unsecured 8% Notes due March 1, 2005. Interest is payable semi-annually on March 1 and September 1. The Notes are not redeemable prior to maturity.

On September 9, 1992, the Company issued $100 million of senior unsecured 7 7/8% Notes due September 1, 2007. Interest is payable semi-annually on March 1 and September 1. The Notes are not redeemable prior to maturity.

During 1991, the Company issued $100 million of senior unsecured 9 1/4% Notes, $100 million of senior unsecured 9.4% Notes, and $100 million of senior unsecured 8 3/4% Notes due February 15, 1998, July 1, 2001, and October 15, 2003, respectively. Interest on the Notes is payable semi-annually. The 9 1/4% Notes due February 15, 1998, were paid in full upon maturity. The remaining Notes are not redeemable prior to maturity.

In addition to the credit facilities described above, Southwest has an unsecured Bank Credit Agreement with a group of banks that permits Southwest to borrow through May 6, 2002, on a revolving credit basis, up to $475 million. Interest rates on borrowings under the Credit Agreement can be, at the option of Southwest, the greater of the agent bank's prime rate or the federal funds rate plus .5 percent, .17 percent over LIBOR, or a fixed rate offered by the banks at the time of borrowing. The commitment fee is .08 percent per annum. There were no outstanding borrowings under this agreement, or prior similar agreements, at December 31, 1998 or 1997.

5. LEASES

Total rental expense for operating leases charged to operations in 1998, 1997, and 1996 was $306,629,000, $297,158,000, and $280,389,000, respectively. The majority of the Company's terminal operations space, as well as 99 aircraft, were under operating leases at December 31, 1998. The amounts applicable to capital leases included in property and equipment were:

(In thousands)	1998	1997
Flight equipment	$ 230,486	$ 227,803
Less accumulated amortization	133,073	122,346
	$ 97,413	$ 105,457

Future minimum lease payments under capital leases and noncancelable operating leases with initial or remaining terms in excess of one year at December 31, 1998, were:

(In thousands)	CAPITAL LEASES	OPERATING LEASES
1999	$ 20,245	$ 247,208
2000	16,871	235,955
2001	17,391	222,688
2002	17,561	208,311
2003	17,750	190,925
After 2003	120,049	1,901,005
Total minimum lease payments	209,867	$ 3,006,092
Less amount representing interest	76,677	
Present value of minimum lease payments	133,190	
Less current portion	9,400	
Long-term portion	$ 123,790	

The aircraft leases generally can be renewed, at rates based on fair market value at the end of the lease term, for one to five years. Most aircraft leases have purchase options at or near the end of the lease term at fair market value, but generally not to exceed a stated percentage of the lessor's defined cost of the aircraft.

6. FINANCIAL INSTRUMENTS

The Company utilizes purchased crude oil call options and fixed price swap agreements to hedge a portion of its exposure to fuel price fluctuations. Prior to December 1998, outstanding call options and swap agreements were not material. At December 31, 1998, the Company had hedged its exposure to fuel price fluctuations on approximately 77 percent of its first quarter 1999 and 56 percent of its second quarter 1999 anticipated fuel requirements, or 290 million gallons of fuel products. The fair value of these agreements at December 31, 1998, representing the amount the Company would receive if the agreements were settled early, was not material.

Any outstanding call options or fixed swap agreements expose the Company to credit loss in the event of nonperformance by the counterparties to the agreements, but the Company does not expect any of the counterparties to fail to meet its obligations. The credit exposure related to these financial instruments is represented by the fair value of contracts with a positive fair value at the reporting date. To manage credit risks, the Company selects counterparties based on credit ratings, limits its exposure to a single counterparty, and monitors the market position of the program and its relative market position with each counterparty. At December 31, 1998, the Company had no collateral or other security interests supporting these agreements but was in the process of negotiating such agreements with a majority of the counterparties.

The Company does not hold or issue any financial instruments for trading purposes.

The fair values of the Company's long-term debt were based on quoted market prices. The carrying amounts and estimated fair values of the Company's long-term debt at December 31, 1998, were as follows:

(In thousands)	CARRYING VALUE	FAIR VALUE
9.4% Notes due 2001	$ 100,000	$ 108,929
8 3/4% Notes due 2003	100,000	112,702
8% Notes due 2005	100,000	109,648
7 7/8% Notes due 2007	100,000	111,390
7 3/8% Debentures due 2027	100,000	106,657

The carrying values of all other financial instruments approximate their fair value.

7. COMMON STOCK

The Company has one class of common stock. Holders of shares of common stock are entitled to receive dividends when and if declared by the Board of Directors and are entitled to one vote per share on all matters submitted to a vote of the shareholders.

At December 31, 1998, the Company had common stock reserved for issuance pursuant to Employee stock benefit plans (69,453,206 shares) and upon exercise of rights (405,357,512 shares) pursuant to the Common Stock Rights Agreement, as amended (Agreement).

Pursuant to the Agreement, each outstanding share of the Company's common stock is accompanied by one common share purchase right (Right). Each Right entitles its holder to purchase one share of common stock at an exercise price of $7.41 and is exercisable only in the event of a proposed takeover, as defined by the Agreement. The Company may redeem the Rights at $.0049 per Right prior to the time that 15 percent of the common stock has been acquired by a person or group. If the Company is acquired, as defined in the Agreement, each Right will entitle its holder to purchase for $7.41 that number of the acquiring company's or the Company's common shares, as provided in the Agreement, having a market value of two times the exercise price of the Right. The Rights will expire no later than July 30, 2006.

On September 25, 1997, the Company's Board of Directors declared a three-for-two stock split, distributing 73,577,983 shares on November 26, 1997. On July 22, 1998, the Company's Board of Directors declared a three-for-two stock split, distributing 111,894,315 shares on August 20, 1998. Unless otherwise stated, all per share data presented in the accompanying consolidated financial statements and notes thereto have been restated to give effect to the stock splits.

As of July 22, 1998, the Company's Board of Directors increased the Company's authorization to repurchase shares of its outstanding common stock to $100 million. The Company completed this repurchase program during third quarter 1998, resulting in the repurchase of 4,885,763 shares at an average cost of $20.47 per share. All of the acquired shares are held as common stock in treasury, less shares reissued under the Employee stock option and purchase plans. When treasury shares are reissued, the Company uses a first-in, first-out method and the excess of repurchase cost over reissuance price, if any, is treated as a reduction of retained earnings.

8. STOCK PLANS

At December 31, 1998, the Company had seven stock-based compensation plans and other stock options outstanding, which are described below. The Company applies APB 25 and related Interpretations in accounting for its stock-based compensation. Accordingly, no compensation expense is recognized for its fixed option plans because the exercise prices of the Company's Employee stock options equal or exceed the market prices of the underlying stock on the dates of the grants. Compensation expense for other stock options is not material.

The Company has six fixed option plans. Under the 1991 Incentive Stock Option Plan, the Company may grant options to key Employees for up to 20,250,000 shares of common stock. Under the 1991 Non-Qualified Stock Option Plan, the Company may grant options to key Employees and non-employee directors for up to 1,687,500 shares of common stock. All options granted under these plans have ten-year terms and vest and become fully exercisable at the end of three, five, or ten years of continued employment, depending upon the grant type.

Under the 1995 Southwest Airlines Pilots' Association Non-Qualified Stock Option Plan (SWAPA Plan), the Company may grant options to Pilots for up to 40,500,000 shares of common stock. An initial grant of approximately 32,788,000 shares was made on January 12, 1995, at an option price of $8.89 per share, which exceeded the market price of the Company's stock on that date. Options granted under the initial grant vest in ten annual increments of ten percent. On September 1 of each year of the agreement beginning in 1996, additional options will be granted to Pilots that become eligible during that year. Additional options granted on September 1, 1998, 1997, and 1996, vest in six annual increments of 16.7 percent, seven annual increments of 14.3 percent, and eight annual increments of 12.5 percent, respectively. Options under all grants must be exercised prior to January 31, 2007, or within a specified time upon retirement or termination.

Under the 1996 Incentive Stock Option Plan, the Company may grant options to key Employees for up to 13,500,000 shares of common stock. Under the 1996 Non-Qualified Stock Option Plan, the Company may grant options to key Employees and non-employee directors for up to 1,293,750 shares of common stock. All options granted under these plans have ten-year terms and vest and become fully exercisable at the end of three, five, or ten years of continued employment, depending upon the grant type.

Under the 1998 Southwest Airlines Employee Association Non-Qualified Stock Option Plan (SAEA Plan), the Company may grant options to Dispatchers for up to 1,050,000 shares of common stock. An initial grant of 738,000 shares was made on September 10, 1998, at an option price of $19.62 per share, which exceeded the market price of the Company's stock on that date. Options granted under the initial grant vest in annual increments of varying percentages, depending on seniority level, through 2006. On December 1 of each year of the agreement beginning in 1998 and through December 1, 2008, additional options will be granted to Dispatchers that become eligible during that year. No options were granted on December 1, 1998. Options under all grants must be exercised prior to June 30, 2012, or within a specified time upon retirement or termination.

Under all fixed option plans, except the SWAPA and SAEA Plans, the exercise price of each option equals the market price of the Company's stock on the date of grant. Under the SWAPA and SAEA Plans, for additional options granted each September 1 and December 1, respectively, the exercise price will be equal to 105 percent of the fair value of such stock on the date of the grant.

Information regarding the Company's six fixed stock option plans, as adjusted for stock splits, is summarized below:

	INCENTIVE PLANS		NON-QUALIFIED PLANS	
	OPTIONS	AVERAGE EXERCISE PRICE	OPTIONS	AVERAGE EXERCISE PRICE
Outstanding December 31, 1995	11,726,729	$ 5.99	33,421,656	$ 8.83
Granted – Incentive Plans	3,758,274	11.19	-	-
Granted – SWAPA Plan	-	-	1,048,950	10.59
Granted – Other Non-Qualified Plans	-	-	155,525	11.19
Exercised	(890,658)	4.57	(653,367)	7.95
Surrendered	(563,504)	8.96	(213,716)	8.89
Outstanding December 31, 1996	14,030,841	7.35	33,759,048	8.91
Granted – Incentive Plans	3,682,737	9.67	-	-
Granted – SWAPA Plan	-	-	1,323,000	13.19
Granted – Other Non-Qualified Plans	-	-	218,109	9.67
Exercised	(1,727,889)	6.03	(2,657,746)	8.85
Surrendered	(1,005,019)	9.72	(148,818)	9.06
Outstanding December 31, 1997	14,980,670	7.91	32,493,593	9.09
Granted – Incentive Plans	2,738,597	17.72	-	-
Granted – SWAPA Plan	-	-	902,475	19.36
Granted – SAEA Plan	-	-	738,013	19.62
Granted – Other Non-Qualified Plans	-	-	256,191	17.69
Exercised	(2,360,733)	6.27	(2,521,455)	9.07
Surrendered	(834,289)	10.52	(247,252)	9.95
Outstanding December 31, 1998	14,524,245	$ 9.89	31,621,565	$ 9.69
Exercisable December 31, 1998	3,132,557		12,271,309	
Available for granting in future periods	11,995,971		6,768,712	

The following table summarizes information about stock options outstanding under the six fixed option plans at December 31, 1998:

RANGE OF EXERCISE PRICES	OPTIONS OUTSTANDING			OPTIONS EXERCISABLE	
	NUMBER OUTSTANDING AT 12/31/98	WEIGHTED-AVERAGE REMAINING CONTRACTUAL LIFE	WEIGHTED-AVERAGE EXERCISE PRICE	NUMBER EXERCISABLE AT 12/31/98	WEIGHTED-AVERAGE EXERCISE PRICE
$2.68 to $3.47	3,307,850	2.03 yrs	$ 2.74	1,195,748	$ 2.86
$5.04 to $7.50	485,476	3.07	5.35	141,557	5.36
$8.36 to $10.83	32,844,404	7.85	8.97	12,009,216	8.94
$11.19 to $16.64	5,061,066	6.85	12.23	1,472,115	12.99
$17.71 to $19.62	4,447,014	9.59	18.37	585,230	18.57
$2.68 to $19.62	46,145,810	7.44 yrs	$ 9.75	15,403,866	$ 9.19

The Company has granted options to purchase the Company's common stock related to employment contracts with the Company's president and chief executive officer. Depending upon the grant, these options have terms of ten years from the date of grant or ten years from the date exercisable and vest and become fully exercisable over three or four years. No options were granted in 1998 or 1997. In 1996, the Company granted 325,000 options with an exercise price of $1.00 per share and 1,125,000 options with an exercise price of $10.44 per share related to the 1996 employment agreement. At December 31, 1998, 1997, and 1996, total options of 3,688,000, 3,916,000, and 4,270,000 were outstanding, respectively. At December 31, 1998, total options of 3,108,000 were exercisable at exercise prices ranging from $1.00 to $10.44 per share. Options for 228,000, 354,000, and 379,500 shares were exercised in 1998, 1997, and 1996, respectively.

Under the 1991 Employee Stock Purchase Plan (ESPP), at December 31, 1998, the Company is authorized to issue up to a balance of 855,000 shares of common stock to Employees of the Company at a price equal to 90 percent of the market value at the end of each purchase period. Common stock purchases are paid for through periodic payroll deductions. Participants under the plan received 451,000 shares in 1998, 660,000 shares in 1997, and 696,000 shares in 1996 at average prices of $17.45, $10.67, and $10.25, respectively.

Pro forma information regarding net income and net income per share is required by SFAS 123 and has been determined as if the Company had accounted for its Employee stock-based compensation plans and other stock options under the fair value method of SFAS 123. The fair value of each option grant is estimated on the date of grant using the Black-Scholes option pricing model with the following weighted-average assumptions used for grants under the fixed option plans in 1998, 1997, and 1996, respectively: dividend yield of .16 percent, .22 percent, and .16 percent; expected volatility of 38.20 percent, 38.23 percent, and 35.37 percent; risk-free interest rate of 4.66 percent, 5.80 percent, and 5.89 percent; and expected lives of 5.0 years for all periods. Assumptions for the stock options granted in 1996 to the Company's president and chief executive officer were the same as for the fixed option plans except for the weighted-average expected lives of 8.0 years.

The weighted-average fair value of options granted under the fixed option plans, except the SAEA Plan, during 1998, 1997, and 1996 was $7.17, $4.08, and $4.52, respectively, for the incentive plans; $7.14, $5.11, and $4.11, respectively, for the SWAPA Plan; and $7.15, $4.08, and $4.52, respectively, for other non-qualified plans. The weighted-average fair value of options granted in 1998 under the SAEA Plan was $7.25. The weighted-average fair value of options granted in 1996 to the Company's president and chief executive officer relative to an employment contract was $6.21. No such options were granted in 1998 or 1997. The weighted-average fair value of each purchase right under the ESPP granted in 1998, 1997, and 1996, which is equal to the ten percent discount from the market value of the common stock at the end of each purchase period, was $1.94, $1.19, and $1.14, respectively.

The Black-Scholes option valuation model was developed for use in estimating the fair value of traded options which have no vesting restrictions and are fully transferable. In addition, option valuation models require the input of highly subjective assumptions including expected stock price volatility. Because the Company's Employee stock options have characteristics significantly different from those of traded options and because changes in the subjective input assumptions can materially affect the fair value estimate, in management's opinion, the existing models do not necessarily provide a reliable single measure of the fair value of its Employee stock options.

For purposes of pro forma disclosures, the estimated fair value of stock-based compensation plans and other options is amortized to expense primarily over the vesting period. The Company's pro forma net income and net income per share is as follows:

(In thousands except per share amounts)	1998	1997	1996
NET INCOME:			
As reported	$ 433,431	$ 317,772	$ 207,337
Pro forma	$ 421,097	$ 306,553	$ 196,478
NET INCOME PER SHARE, BASIC:			
As reported	$ 1.30	$.97	$.64
Pro forma	$ 1.26	$.93	$.60
NET INCOME PER SHARE, DILUTED:			
As reported	$ 1.23	$.93	$.61
Pro forma	$ 1.20	$.90	$.60

As required, the pro forma disclosures above include only options granted since January 1, 1995. Consequently, the effects of applying SFAS 123 for providing pro forma disclosures may not be representative of the effects on reported net income for future years until all options outstanding are included in the pro forma disclosures.

9. EMPLOYEE PROFITSHARING AND SAVINGS PLANS

Substantially all of Southwest's Employees are members of the Southwest Airlines Co. Profitsharing Plan. Total profitsharing expense charged to operations in 1998, 1997, and 1996 was $120,697,000, $91,256,000, and $59,927,000, respectively.

The Company sponsors Employee savings plans under Section 401(k) of the Internal Revenue Code. The plans cover substantially all full-time Employees. The amount of matching contributions varies by Employee group. Company contributions generally vest over five years with credit for prior years' service granted. Company matching contributions expensed in 1998, 1997, and 1996 were $46,415,000, $39,744,000, and $35,125,000, respectively.

10. INCOME TAXES

Deferred income taxes reflect the net tax effects of temporary differences between the carrying amounts of assets and liabilities for financial reporting purposes and the amounts used for income tax purposes. The components of deferred tax assets and liabilities at December 31, 1998 and 1997 are as follows:

(In thousands)	1998	1997
DEFERRED TAX LIABILITIES:		
Accelerated depreciation	$ 641,673	$ 543,547
Scheduled airframe maintenance	40,073	33,202
Other	95,485	83,607
Total deferred tax liabilities	777,231	660,356
DEFERRED TAX ASSETS:		
Deferred gains from sale and leaseback of aircraft	107,157	112,659
Capital and operating leases	61,275	61,747
Other	80,326	65,812
Total deferred tax assets	248,758	240,218
Net deferred tax liability	$ 528,473	$ 420,138

The provision for income taxes is composed of the following:

(In thousands)	1998	1997	1996
CURRENT:			
Federal	$ 143,989	$ 102,938	$ 59,101
State	19,357	14,535	7,671
Total current	163,346	117,473	66,772
DEFERRED:			
Federal	96,237	75,990	60,967
State	12,098	5,721	6,286
Total deferred	108,335	81,711	67,253
	$ 271,681	$ 199,184	$ 134,025

The Company received a statutory notice of deficiency from the Internal Revenue Service (IRS) in July 1995 in which the IRS proposed to disallow deductions claimed by the Company on its federal income tax returns for the taxable years 1989 through 1991 for the costs of certain aircraft inspection and maintenance procedures. The IRS has proposed similar adjustments to the tax returns of numerous other members of the airline industry. In response to the statutory notice of deficiency, the Company filed a petition in the United States Tax Court on October 30, 1997, seeking a determination that the IRS erred in disallowing the deductions claimed by the Company and that there is no deficiency in the Company's tax liability for the taxable years in issue. It is expected that the Tax Court's decision will not be entered for several years. Management believes the final resolution of this controversy will not have a material adverse effect upon the results of operations of the Company.

The effective tax rate on income before income taxes differed from the federal income tax statutory rate for the following reasons:

(In thousands)	1998	1997	1996
Tax at statutory U.S. tax rates	$ 246,789	$ 180,935	$ 119,477
Nondeductible items	5,099	5,893	5,168
State income taxes, net of federal benefit	20,445	13,166	9,072
Other, net	(652)	(810)	308
Total income tax provision	$ 271,681	$ 199,184	$ 134,025

11. NET INCOME PER SHARE

The following table sets forth the computation of basic and diluted earnings per share:

(In thousands except per share amounts)	1998	1997	1996
NUMERATOR:			
Net income, available to common stockholders – numerator for basic and diluted earnings per share	$ 433,431	$ 317,772	$ 207,337
DENOMINATOR:			
Weighted-average shares outstanding, basic	333,342	328,631	325,676
Dilutive effect of Employee stock options	19,824	12,557	11,810
Adjusted weighted-average shares outstanding, diluted	353,166	341,188	337,486
NET INCOME PER SHARE:			
Basic	$ 1.30	$ .97	$ .64
Diluted	$ 1.23	$ .93	$ .61

REPORT OF ERNST & YOUNG LLP
INDEPENDENT AUDITORS

**THE BOARD OF DIRECTORS AND SHAREHOLDERS
SOUTHWEST AIRLINES CO.**

We have audited the accompanying consolidated balance sheets of Southwest Airlines Co. as of December 31, 1998 and 1997, and the related consolidated statements of income, stockholders' equity, and cash flows for each of the three years in the period ended December 31, 1998. These financial statements are the responsibility of the Company's management. Our responsibility is to express an opinion on these financial statements based on our audits.

We conducted our audits in accordance with generally accepted auditing standards. Those standards require that we plan and perform the audit to obtain reasonable assurance about whether the financial statements are free of material misstatement. An audit includes examining, on a test basis, evidence supporting the amounts and disclosures in the financial statements. An audit also includes assessing the accounting principles used and significant estimates made by management, as well as evaluating the overall financial statement presentation. We believe that our audits provide a reasonable basis for our opinion.

In our opinion, the financial statements referred to above present fairly, in all material respects, the consolidated financial position of Southwest Airlines Co. at December 31, 1998 and 1997, and the consolidated results of its operations and its cash flows for each of the three years in the period ended December 31, 1998, in conformity with generally accepted accounting principles.

Ernst & Young LLP

Dallas, Texas
January 20, 1999

QUARTERLY FINANCIAL DATA (UNAUDITED)

	THREE MONTHS ENDED			
(In thousands except per share amounts)	MARCH 31	JUNE 30	SEPT. 30	DEC. 31
1998				
Operating revenues	$ 942,653	$ 1,078,841	$ 1,094,830	$ 1,047,656
Operating income	111,693	208,548	203,919	159,451
Income before income taxes	114,057	216,547	211,055	163,453
Net income	70,008	133,393	129,645	100,385
Net income per share, basic	.21	.40	.39	.30
Net income per share, diluted	.20	.38	.37	.29
1997				
Operating revenues	$ 887,095	$ 956,892	$ 997,241	$ 975,593
Operating income	87,203	156,407	151,770	128,856
Income before income taxes	83,401	153,823	150,387	129,345
Net income	50,874	93,832	92,511	80,555
Net income per share, basic	.16	.29	.28	.24
Net income per share, diluted	.15	.28	.27	.23

COMMON STOCK PRICE RANGES AND DIVIDENDS

Southwest's common stock is listed on the New York Stock Exchange and is traded under the symbol LUV. The high and low sales prices of the common stock on the Composite Tape and the quarterly dividends per share, as adjusted for the November 1997 and July 1998 three-for-two stock splits, were:

PERIOD	DIVIDENDS	HIGH	LOW
1998			
1st Quarter	$ .00667	$ 21.42	$ 15.33
2nd Quarter	.00667	20.71	16.83
3rd Quarter	.00750	23.38	17.19
4th Quarter	.00750	23.75	15.31
1997			
1st Quarter	$ .00513	$ 11.11	$ 9.45
2nd Quarter	.00513	12.45	9.55
3rd Quarter	.00513	14.75	11.55
4th Quarter	.00667	17.50	12.55

TEN-YEAR SUMMARY

SELECTED CONSOLIDATED FINANCIAL DATA [1]

(In thousands except per share amounts)	1998	1997	1996	1995
Operating revenues:				
Passenger	$ 3,963,781	$ 3,639,193	$ 3,269,238	$ 2,760,756
Freight	98,500	94,758	80,005	65,825
Other	101,699	82,870	56,927	46,170
Total operating revenues	4,163,980	3,816,821	3,406,170	2,872,751
Operating expenses	3,480,369	3,292,585	3,055,335	2,559,220
Operating income	683,611	524,236	350,835	313,531
Other expenses (income), net	(21,501)	7,280	9,473	8,391
Income before income taxes	705,112	516,956	341,362	305,140
Provision for income taxes [3]	271,681	199,184	134,025	122,514
Net income [3]	$ 433,431	$ 317,772	$ 207,337	$ 182,626
Net income per share, basic [3]	$1.30	$ .97	$.64	$.56
Net income per share, diluted [3]	$1.23	$ .93	$.61	$.55
Cash dividends per common share	$.02834	$ .02206	$.01955	$.01778
Total assets	$ 4,715,996	$ 4,246,160	$ 3,723,479	$ 3,256,122
Long-term debt	$ 623,309	$ 628,106	$ 650,226	$ 661,010
Stockholders' equity	$ 2,397,918	$ 2,009,018	$ 1,648,312	$ 1,427,318

CONSOLIDATED FINANCIAL RATIOS [1]

	1998	1997	1996	1995
Return on average total assets	9.7%	8.0%	5.9%	6.0%
Return on average stockholders' equity	19.7%	17.4%	13.5%	13.7%

CONSOLIDATED OPERATING STATISTICS [2]

	1998	1997	1996	1995
Revenue passengers carried	52,586,400	50,399,960	49,621,504	44,785,573
RPMs (000s)	31,419,110	28,355,169	27,083,483	23,327,804
ASMs (000s)	47,543,515	44,487,496	40,727,495	36,180,001
Passenger load factor	66.1%	63.7%	66.5%	64.5%
Average length of passenger haul	597	563	546	521
Trips flown	806,822	786,288	748,634	685,524
Average passenger fare	$75.38	$72.21	$65.88	$61.64
Passenger revenue yield per RPM	12.62¢	12.84¢	12.07¢	11.83¢
Operating revenue yield per ASM	8.76¢	8.58¢	8.36¢	7.94¢
Operating expenses per ASM	7.32¢	7.40¢	7.50¢	7.07¢
Fuel cost per gallon (average)	45.67¢	62.46¢	65.47¢	55.22¢
Number of Employees at yearend	25,844	23,974	22,944	19,933
Size of fleet at yearend [10]	280	261	243	224

(1) The Selected Consolidated Financial Data and Consolidated Financial Ratios for 1992 through 1989 have been restated to include the financial results of Morris Air Corporation (Morris)

(2) Prior to 1993, Morris operated as a charter carrier; therefore, no Morris statistics are included for these years

(3) Pro forma for 1992 through 1989 assuming Morris, an S-Corporation prior to 1993, was taxed at statutory rates

(4) Excludes cumulative effect of accounting changes of $15.3 million ($.05 per share)

(5) Excludes cumulative effect of accounting change of $12.5 million ($.04 per share)

1994	1993	1992	1991	1990	1989
$ 2,497,765	$ 2,216,342	$ 1,623,828	$ 1,267,897	$ 1,144,421	$ 973,568
54,419	42,897	33,088	26,428	22,196	18,771
39,749	37,434	146,063	84,961	70,659	65,390
2,591,933	2,296,673	1,802,979	1,379,286	1,237,276	1,057,729
2,275,224	2,004,700	1,609,175	1,306,675	1,150,015	955,689
316,709	291,973	193,804	72,611	87,261	102,040
17,186	32,336	36,361	18,725	6,827 [6]	(13,696) [7]
299,523	259,637	157,443	53,886	80,434	115,736
120,192	105,353	60,058	20,738	29,829	41,231
$ 179,331	$ 154,284 [4]	$ 97,385 [5]	$ 33,148	$ 50,605	$ 74,505
$.56	$.48 [4]	$.31 [5]	$.11	$.17	$.24
$.54	$.47 [4]	$.30 [5]	$.11	$.17	$.24
$.01778	$.01719	$.01570	$.01481	$.01433	$.01382
$ 2,823,071	$ 2,576,037	$ 2,368,856	$ 1,854,331	$ 1,480,813	$ 1,423,298
$ 583,071	$ 639,136	$ 735,754	$ 617,434	$ 327,553	$ 354,150
$ 1,238,706	$ 1,054,019	$ 879,536	$ 635,793	$ 607,294	$ 591,794
6.6%	6.2% [4]	4.6% [5]	2.0%	3.5%	5.5%
15.6%	16.0% [4]	12.9% [5]	5.3%	8.4%	12.9%
42,742,602 [8]	36,955,221 [8]	27,839,284	22,669,942	19,830,941	17,958,263
21,611,266	18,827,288	13,787,005	11,296,183	9,958,940	9,281,992
32,123,974	27,511,000	21,366,642	18,491,003	16,411,115	14,796,732
67.3%	68.4%	64.5%	61.1%	60.7%	62.7%
506	509	495	498	502	517
624,476	546,297	438,184	382,752	338,108	304,673
$ 58.44	$ 59.97	$ 58.33	$ 55.93	$ 57.71	$ 54.21
11.56¢	11.77¢	11.78¢	11.22¢	11.49¢	10.49¢
8.07¢	8.35¢	7.89¢	7.10¢	7.23¢	6.86¢
7.08¢	7.25¢ [9]	7.03¢	6.76¢	6.73¢	6.20¢
53.92¢	59.15¢	60.82¢	65.69¢	77.89¢	59.46¢
16,818	15,175	11,397	9,778	8,620	7,760
199	178	141	124	106	94

(6) *Includes $2.6 million gains on sales of aircraft and $3.1 million from the sale of certain financial assets*

(7) *Includes $10.8 million gains on sales of aircraft, $5.9 million from the sale of certain financial assets, and $2.3 million from the settlement of a contingency*

(8) *Includes certain estimates for Morris*

(9) *Excludes merger expenses of $10.8 million*

(10) *Includes leased aircraft*

CORPORATE DATA

TRANSFER AGENT AND REGISTRAR

Registered shareholder inquiries regarding stock transfers, address changes, lost stock certificates, dividend payments, or account consolidation should be directed to:

Continental Stock Transfer & Trust Company
2 Broadway
New York, New York 10004
(212) 509-4000

STOCK EXCHANGE LISTING

New York Stock Exchange
Ticker Symbol: LUV

INDEPENDENT AUDITORS

Ernst & Young LLP
Dallas, Texas

GENERAL OFFICES

P.O. Box 36611
Dallas, Texas 75235-1611

ANNUAL MEETING

The Annual Meeting of Shareholders of Southwest Airlines Co. will be held at 10:00 a.m. on May 20, 1999, at the Southwest Airlines Corporate Headquarters, 2702 Love Field Drive, Dallas, Texas.

FINANCIAL INFORMATION

A copy of the Company's Annual Report on Form 10-K as filed with the U.S. Securities and Exchange Commission (SEC) may be obtained without charge, as well as other financial information, by writing or calling:

Southwest Airlines Co.
Investor Relations
P.O. Box 36611
Dallas, Texas 75235-1611
Telephone (214) 792-4908

Company documents filed electronically with the SEC can also be found on the SEC's web site (http://www.sec.gov). A copy of this Annual Report and other financial information can be found on Southwest's web site (http://www.southwest.com).

Appendix D
TCBY 1998 Annual Report

D

MANAGEMENT'S DISCUSSION AND ANALYSIS OF FINANCIAL CONDITION AND RESULTS OF OPERATIONS

Results of Operations 1998 Compared to 1997

The Company's total sales for 1998 increased four percent over 1997. The 1997 sales include several items that impact the comparison to current revenues, including: sales of approximately $2.5 million to a private label customer on a one-time basis and sales of approximately $1.2 million from Carlin Manufacturing, Inc. ("Carlin"), a TCBY subsidiary which was sold in July, 1997. The following table sets forth sales by category within the Company's segments (food products and equipment) of operation:

(dollars in thousands)

	1998 Sales	%	1997 Sales	%	1996 Sales	%
Food Products:						
TCBY® frozen products sales for distribution to TCBY® locations	$46,934	50%	$47,851	53%	$49,705	60%
Sales of specialty products	29,284	31	25,103	28	14,973	18
Retail sales by Company-owned stores	424	1	680	1	2,599	3
	76,642	82	73,634	82	67,277	81
Equipment:						
Sales by the Company's equipment distributor	16,062	17	14,624	16	11,779	14
Sales of manufactured specialty vehicles	-	-	1,228	1	2,874	4
	16,062	17	15,852	17	14,653	18
Other	1,161	1	1,092	1	1,034	1
Total Sales	$93,865	100%	$90,578	100%	$82,964	100%

Sales from the Company's food products segment include (i) wholesale sales of frozen yogurt and ice cream products to ProSource Distribution Services (now a division of AmeriServe Food Distribution, Inc.) and other foodservice distributors, which distribute yogurt, ice cream, and other products to TCBY® stores and non-traditional locations, and sales to international master franchisees of frozen products and proprietary ingredients for the manufacture of frozen products in the countries that produce locally, and (ii) sales of TCBY® frozen packaged products and other specialty dairy food products to customers including supermarkets, convenience stores, dairies, foodservice distributors, club stores, and private label suppliers, and (iii) retail sales of yogurt, juices, and related food items by Company-owned stores.

Wholesale sales of frozen yogurt and ice cream products decreased two percent during 1998 compared to 1997. The decrease is attributed primarily to a reduction in the number of domestic traditional TCBY® stores in operation and, to a lesser extent, decreased sales to international franchisees due to economic challenges primarily in Asia. These decreases were partially offset by increased purchases by TCBY® non-traditional locations.

The following table sets forth TCBY® and Juice Works® location activity for 1998 and 1997:

	Franchised Stores	Company Owned Stores	International Locations	Non-Traditional Locations	Total Locations
Locations Open at December 1, 1996	1,198	2	201	1,297	2,698
Opened	47	1	52	350	450
Closed	(132)	-	(24)	(184)	(340)
Net Stores Purchased (Sold) Between Franchisees & Company	(3)	(1)	-	4	-
Locations Open at November 30, 1997	1,110	2	229	1,467	2,808
Opened	30	-	22	347	399
Closed	(109)	-	(35)	(103)	(247)
Locations Open at November 29, 1998	1,031	2	216	1,711	2,960

During 1998, significantly more TCBY® non-traditional locations than traditional locations opened. While the Company has placed and continues to place equal emphasis upon both traditional and non-traditional locations, the Company has experienced more non-traditional development in the last few years. The Company believes this trend will continue in 1999. The rate of development of non-traditional locations is partially determined by co-branding partners, who must approve each location in a process not controlled by the Company, and in some cases, delays have been experienced while the Company and the prospective TCBY franchisee awaited such approval; new development may also be slowed when existing franchisees express their concerns regarding new TCBY® locations; and the desire of the Company to maintain good relationships with all franchisees in the markets under consideration results in occasional delays in development while those concerns are addressed. The non-traditional locations include sites at airports, travel plazas, colleges, hospitals, theme parks, stadiums, and locations in conjunction with petroleum stores and other food concepts (co-branded locations). The majority of the 347 non-traditional openings in 1998 were co-branded. Of the 1,711 non-traditional locations open at year-end, approximately 800 are co-branded locations. As of November 29, 1998, there are over 300 locations under agreement, many of which will be co-branded with petroleum or other food operations. Co-branding has made the Company's products available to more customers as we have opened locations with many national or regional brands including Subway®, Exxon®, Texaco®, Wall Street Deli®, Blimpie®, Shell®, and others. TCBY is a strong partner for these brands because its products complement their operations. During 1998, 103 non-traditional locations closed. These locations generally purchased low volumes of yogurt from the Company. These closings are not expected to have a material impact on yogurt sales. The Company expects that there may be additional closings of low volume non-

Management's Discussion and Analysis of Financial Condition and Results of Operations

traditional locations as they are not efficient for the Company to service or the customer to operate.

During 1998, a total of 109 franchised stores were closed by franchisees. Each store closed is the result of the franchisee's evaluation of its financial condition, cash flow, lease expiration, profitability, and store operations, among other things. Of the locations closed, 77 operated for a portion of 1998, with the remainder having originally closed for relocation in prior years. Included in the franchised store information are 87 and 111 TCBY® stores closed for relocation or for the season at November 29, 1998 and November 30, 1997, respectively. During 1999, the Company will continue to intensify its focus on the traditional locations and pursue measures to improve the performance of these stores. The Company has been working with several research and design firms to address the positioning of traditional stores for both the short and long-term. These efforts will require investments in 1999 that are being undertaken for the long-term benefit of the Company and its franchise system. We will work with franchisees to relocate marginal stores or pursue co-branding to provide additional day-part sales. The benefits experienced by other brands adding TCBY® products to their operations can be realized in TCBY® stores by adding these brands to TCBY® locations. In addition, marketing efforts will be strategically targeted to maximize the benefits in the trade area of each of our stores. The Company will be working with a nationally known firm to evaluate and pursue neighborhood store marketing approaches which will assist the franchisees in their marketing planning for 1999. We will also increase the number of store visits to evaluate the operational standards of the stores. All of these efforts are occurring to improve our customers' experience in the stores. The above measures will be evaluated on a continual basis and may change if the Company deems appropriate. In addition, barriers may be encountered in implementing the above strategies, including lack of availability of co-branded partners due to existing locations, size of TCBY® store, lease restrictions, financial capability and willingness of existing franchisees, and limitations of corporate resources. Even with the successful implementation of these programs, store sales may decline and store closings may continue. However, we believe that the programs can lay the foundation for future success and development of traditional TCBY® franchised locations.

Average store sales (the average of sales by domestic traditional stores open the entire year) for Company-owned and franchised TCBY® stores increased to $208,000 in 1998 from $207,000 in 1997. This increase is due to the closing of lower volume stores as stores open at year-end experienced a slight decline in unit volume during 1998.

Sales of specialty products increased 17 percent during 1998 as compared to 1997. The increase is attributed primarily to increased sales of private label products even after consideration of $2.5 million of sales in 1997 to a private label customer on a one-time basis. The Company continues to pursue private label opportunities at its manufacturing facility in Dallas.

Retail sales by Company-owned stores declined in 1998 due to the sale of a Company-owned Juice Works® store during 1997.

Sales in the Company's equipment segment include (i) sales from the distribution of equipment to the foodservice industry and (ii) 1997 sales of manufactured mobile kitchens and other specialty vehicles primarily to businesses and governments. The increased sales at the Company's equipment distributor for 1998 are due to the opening of non-traditional TCBY® locations, some of which purchased a portion of their original equipment packages from the Company. This increase was partially offset by the sale of the Company's equipment manufacturer, Carlin, in July, 1997. The Company had sales from Carlin of $1.2 million during 1997. In the Carlin transaction, the real estate and certain finished goods inventory were retained by the Company. The real estate was leased to the purchaser (formerly the president of Carlin under the Company's ownership) with the ultimate intent to sell the property. The purchaser is assisting the Company in marketing the remaining inventory and receives a commission on the sale of this inventory. Future sales in the equipment segment are primarily dependent upon the Company's ability to develop new TCBY® locations.

As a percent of sales, cost of sales for 1998 and 1997 for the Company and its two primary segments are presented below:

	1998	1997
Food Products Segment	**67%**	65%
Equipment Segment	**77%**	78%
Company Total	**68%**	67%

The increased cost of sales percentages in 1998 are primarily due to lower gross margins for the food products segment, which were partially offset by improved gross margins for the equipment segment as a result of the sale of Carlin in July 1997 which had low gross profit margins.

The increase in the food products segment cost of sales percentage is due to a number of factors including sales of specialty products, which generally have a higher cost of sales percentage than the other food segment categories, being a larger component of the food products segment sales in 1998 compared to the prior year. (See earlier discussion related to sales increases.) In addition, dairy costs, which are a significant portion of the segment's cost of sales, increased during 1998 compared to 1997. Dairy costs include the value assigned to milk solids and milk fats which are two of the components of milk utilized in most products manufactured and sold by the segment. The cost of these two components are currently tied to the federal milk orders system. This market fluctuates based on supply and demand with prices being variable from month to month. The price paid for milk is based on the Basic Formula Price (BFP) plus any applicable surcharge (based on the use of the milk). Of the price paid for milk, the Butter Fat Differential (BFD) is the market value assigned to milk fats (used in butter, cheese, ice cream, etc.), with the remainder of the milk price being assigned to milk solids. The prices for BFP and BFD exceeded historical levels during 1998. The BFP has continued to increase in fiscal 1999 with the December price reaching an all-time record high of $17.34 per hundredweight. The BFD began to decline in early November and has returned to more traditional levels.

Although dairy prices have increased during 1998 over the same period in the prior year, the food products segment did not bear the full impact of the increases due to the product mix manufactured and sold within the segment in 1998. Because the BFD prices increased more than the prices for BFP, the cost for milk solids remained comparable to the prior year until the fourth quarter when the BFD declined rapidly. The segment's core yogurt products do not utilize high levels of milk fat, which tempered the impact of higher BFP and BFD prices until the decrease of BFD in the fourth quarter. The Company did not change its pricing on TCBY® products and has absorbed the higher cost of products for the TCBY® locations. This resulted in additional cost of sales of approximately $750,000 compared to 1997. The Company was not significantly impacted by dairy prices for products produced for private label customers as these higher costs were passed on to the customer. The prices for BFP are expected to remain above historical levels during the first half of 1999, while BFD should remain closer to historical levels. This results in higher cost for TCBY® products. The Company is evaluating all available options for 1999 to reduce the financial impact of the increases. These actions will likely include price increases for TCBY® products. While the price increases are expected to offset the increases in BFP, further increases in cost or material changes in product mix may change this outcome.

Franchising revenues consist of initial franchise and license fees and royalty income. For 1998, initial franchise and license fees decreased 32 percent while royalty income increased four percent from 1997. The decrease in franchise and license fees result from fewer initial international franchise fees. This is due in part to the economic challenges in certain international markets, but also due to a record level of fees experienced in 1997. There are still new markets to enter, but international growth will come primarily through expansion within existing markets. The Company remains committed to long-term growth in international markets and, during 1999, will begin local production in Europe. This production will result in lower costs to our franchisees in Europe and the Middle East and should enhance our opportunity for development in future years. The increase in royalty income is primarily attributable to more non-traditional locations. The increase was partially offset by fewer traditional TCBY® stores and decreased purchases by international franchisees.

Total international revenues represented approximately three percent of the Company's sales and franchising revenues in 1998 compared to five percent in 1997.

Operating expenses decreased two percent in 1998 compared to 1997. The decrease is due to the sale of Carlin in July, 1997, and reductions in other corporate operating costs. For 1998 and 1997, operating expenses as a percentage of combined sales and franchising revenues were 28 percent and 30 percent, respectively. Included in operating expenses for 1998 is the settlement of a claim by a customer for whom Americana Foods produces private label products, who alleged damages due to production defects. Immediate and voluntary recalls of limited quantities of products were undertaken in 1997. The Company, after negotiations with the customer and the Company's liability insurance carrier, has, with the participation of the liability insurance carrier, settled all claims. The relevant settlement agreement contains a confidentiality clause; however, the amount paid by the Company to obtain settlement exceeded prior accruals by approximately one million dollars. While the Company believed it had meritorious defenses to and disagreed with the customer's claim, settlement was agreed to by the Company in order to avoid the uncertainty of outcome, cost of litigation, and disruption to the Company.

During the third quarter of 1998, the Company's aircraft was sold to a third party resulting in a gain of approximately $2.1 million which is included in Other Income on the Consolidated Statement of Income. The after-tax gain on the sale of the Company assets was approximately $1.4 million or $.06 per share (basic and diluted). The Company contemporaneously entered into an agreement whereunder an aircraft owned by the Chairman and Chief Executive Officer could be made available to the Company from time-to-time at an hourly rate consistent with the cost of operating the aircraft it divested; this hourly rate is substantially below the fair market rate which normally would be charged to the Company for use of a similar aircraft. Under the new arrangement, any use of the aircraft which is charged to the Company is reviewed by the Board of Directors of the Company on a regular basis.

Interest expense decreased approximately $214,000 in 1998 compared to 1997. This decrease is due to reductions in outstanding debt.

Income tax expense as a percentage of pre-tax income was 34 percent and 34.5 percent in 1998 and 1997, respectively. Assuming no significant change in federal and state tax laws, the Company expects its future tax rate to approximate 35 percent. Deferred tax assets of $3.5 million are expected to be realized through the offset of existing taxable temporary differences.

1997 Compared to 1996

The Company's total sales for 1997 increased nine percent from sales in 1996. As described below, the Company experienced improved sales in the specialty products and equipment distribution categories. These increases were partially offset by decreased sales by Company-owned stores due to the franchising of these stores during 1996; the divestiture of Carlin Manufacturing in July, 1997; and decreased sales to traditional TCBY® stores. The Company's total sales excluding TCBY® Company-owned units and Carlin Manufacturing increased 15 percent in 1997 compared to 1996.

Wholesale sales of frozen yogurt and ice cream products decreased four percent in 1997 compared to 1996. The decrease was attributed primarily to a reduction in the number of domestic traditional TCBY® stores in operation and a decline in yogurt purchased by operating stores during 1997 compared to 1996. This decrease was partially offset by increased purchases by TCBY® non-traditional locations.

Management's Discussion and Analysis of Financial Condition and Results of Operations

1997 Compared to 1996 (continued)

During 1997, significantly more TCBY® non-traditional locations than traditional locations opened. While the Company has placed and continues to place emphasis upon both traditional and non-traditional locations, the Company experienced more non-traditional development in the last two years. While different in size and character, each TCBY® location is treated the same in the site evaluation process, and the Company intends to avoid approving the placement of a new TCBY® location, be it traditional or non-traditional, so close to any existing TCBY® location that sales of the two locations would be materially impacted. The non-traditional locations include sites at airports, travel plazas, colleges, hospitals, theme parks, stadiums, and locations in conjunction with petroleum stores and other food concepts (co-branded locations). The majority of the 350 non-traditional openings in 1997 were TCBY® co-branded locations. The Company's experience was that the volume of yogurt and ice cream at co-branded locations exceeded that of other types of non-traditional locations with the exception of airports. During 1997, 184 non-traditional locations were closed. These locations generally purchased low volumes of product from the Company. During 1997, a total of 132 TCBY® franchised stores were closed by franchisees. Each TCBY® store closed was the result of the franchisee's evaluation of its financial condition, cash flow, lease expiration, profitability, and store operations, among other things. Of the 132 locations closed, 64 operated for a portion of 1997, with the remainder having originally closed for relocation in prior years. Included in the franchised and Company-owned store information are 111 and 147 TCBY® stores closed for relocation or for the season at November 30, 1997 and 1996, respectively.

Average store sales for Company-owned and franchised TCBY® stores were $207,000 in 1997 and 1996.

Sales of specialty products increased 68 percent in 1997 as compared to 1996. A majority of this increase was attributed to increased sales of private label products. The Company has pursued private label opportunities to utilize available capacity at its manufacturing facility in Dallas. Sales improvements also occurred due to the introduction of new TCBY® novelty products primarily through club stores.

Retail sales by Company-owned stores declined in 1997 due to the Company's implementation during 1996 of its decision to franchise or close most of its TCBY® Company-owned stores. The Company took this action as it believed the stores could operate more effectively with local ownership.

Sales in the equipment segment increased eight percent in 1997 as compared to the prior year. This improvement in sales was primarily due to the opening of non-traditional TCBY® locations, some of which purchased a portion of their original equipment packages from the Company's equipment distributor. The increase was partially offset by decreased sales by the Company's equipment manufacturer. In July, 1997, the Company sold a portion of the equipment manufacturer's assets to a company controlled by the subsidiary's president. The assets sold included certain inventory, plant equipment, furniture and fixtures, and intangibles. The transaction was partially financed by the Company. The Company retained certain inventory items. In addition, the real property was retained by the Company and leased to the purchaser with the ultimate intent to sell the property. The purchaser is assisting the Company in marketing the remaining inventory and receives a commission on the sale of this inventory.

As a percent of sales, cost of sales for 1997 and 1996 for the Company and its two primary segments are presented below:

	1997	1996
Food Products Segment	65%	63%
Equipment Segment	78%	76%
Company Total	67%	65%

The increase in the food products segment cost of sales percentage was due to a number of factors including the Company's decision to franchise or close most of its TCBY® Company- owned stores. These stores had a lower cost of sales percentage than the other categories of the food products segment noted above. Therefore, as such stores were sold or closed, cost of sales as a percent of sales increased in the food products segment.

In addition, sales of specialty products, which generally have a higher cost of sales percentage than the other food segment categories, were a larger component of the food products segment sales during 1997 compared to the prior year. (See earlier discussion related to these sales increases.) Cost of sales during 1997 were favorably impacted by a decrease in dairy prices which were a major component of the Company's cost of sales.

The change in the equipment segment's cost of sales percentage results from increased sales of new location equipment packages which included large items with lower margins than other sales components of the equipment segment.

Franchising revenues consist of initial franchise and license fees and royalty income. In 1997, initial franchise and license fees increased 37 percent while royalty income was flat compared to the prior year. The improvement in franchise and license fees resulted primarily from increased initial international franchise fees, increased development of TCBY® non-traditional locations, and Juice Works® locations. The flat royalty income was primarily attributable to a decrease in domestic royalties resulting from the decrease in the number of traditional TCBY® stores and the decline in frozen products purchased by the operating stores. This decrease was offset by the increase in the number of non-traditional locations and expanded distribution in international markets.

Five percent of combined sales and franchising revenues were generated from international activity in 1997 and 1996.

MANAGEMENT'S DISCUSSION AND ANALYSIS OF FINANCIAL CONDITION AND RESULTS OF OPERATIONS

Operating expenses decreased five percent in 1997 compared to 1996. The decrease related to reduced operating expenses of corporate stores due to the franchising or closing of these units as discussed above. As a percentage of combined sales and franchising revenues, operating expenses were 30 percent and 34 percent for 1997 and 1996, respectively.

Interest expense decreased approximately $201,000 in 1997 compared to 1996. This decrease was due to reductions in outstanding debt.

Income tax expense as a percentage of pre-tax income was 34.5 percent and 34.6 percent in 1997 and 1996, respectively.

Liquidity and Capital Resources

The Company has historically generated cash from operations sufficient to meet its normal operating requirements. Cash provided by operating activities amounted to $9.5 million in 1998 compared to $17.1 million in 1997 and $18.9 million in 1996. The decrease in 1998 is due to higher levels of inventory and accounts receivables related to the growth in the private label business and also due to changes in deferred income taxes. The decrease in 1997 from 1996 results primarily from a tax refund of approximately $4.1 million and the proceeds of sales of assets held for sale of approximately $2.4 million in 1996 which did not reoccur in 1997.

The following summarizes statistics related to the Company's financial position:

	1998	1997
Current Ratio	**3.9 to 1.0**	4.0 to 1.0
Working Capital (in millions)	**$34.8**	$34.5
Long-Term Debt to Equity Ratio	**.04 to 1.0**	.08 to 1.0
Tangible Net Worth (in millions)	**$71.9**	$73.1

The Company's cash and cash equivalents and short-term investments decreased approximately $2.2 million in 1998. This decrease resulted primarily from purchases of treasury stock (see discussion below).

Long-term debt was reduced by $3.3 million in 1998, and $3.2 million in 1997 and 1996, respectively.

Cash generated from operations has been used to finance all capital expenditures. Purchases of property, plant, and equipment amounted to $2.0 million, $1.9 million, and $2.4 million in 1998, 1997, and 1996, respectively. The Company had no material commitments for capital expenditures at November 29, 1998. The Company estimates $2.5 to $3.5 million for capital expenditures in 1999. It is expected that operating cash flows will be used to finance these capital expenditures, although other financing options may be considered. In addition, from time to time the Company may evaluate strategic alternatives. Any acquisition may require the use of operating cash flows, short or long-term financing, issuance of equity, or other financing sources in order to consummate such acquisition or to fund operating and capital expenditures of any acquired business.

Cash provided by operating activities has also been used by the Company in the past to provide financing to franchisees for the purpose of acquiring equipment and other fixed assets for the development or purchase of stores. The principal collected on notes receivable primarily from franchisees exceeded origination of notes receivable by approximately $1.0 million, $1.4 million, and $1.6 million in 1998, 1997, and 1996, respectively.

The Company's foreseeable cash needs for operations and capital expenditures are expected to be met through cash flows from operations; however, the Company has available a $5 million unsecured credit line to meet seasonal cash needs.

In December, 1995, the Company was authorized to repurchase up to three million shares of its outstanding common stock. The final repurchases under this authorization were completed during the second quarter of 1998. In December, 1997, the Company was authorized to repurchase an additional two million shares of its outstanding stock. As of November 29, 1998, 452,883 shares have been purchased under this authorization. During 1998, the Company has purchased 1,324,683 shares of common stock at a cost of $11,168,218. All repurchases have been funded with cash flows from operations. Future repurchases may be funded with cash flows from operations or long-term financing.

Cash dividends of 20 cents per share were paid to stockholders during 1998, 1997, and 1996. The Company will consider adjustments to the dividend rate after giving consideration to return to stockholders, profitability expectations, financing and cash needs of the Company, and other factors.

Any forward-looking statements contained herein are based on certain assumptions regarding U.S. and foreign economic conditions, competition, costs of raw materials, unit openings and closings, sales volumes per unit, other manufacturing opportunities, no changes in governmental regulation of the food industry or dairy industry, and no material event which would impact the reputation of the Company's manufacturing facility or the Company's ability to utilize that facility. Should the Company's performance differ materially from the assumptions regarding these areas, actual results could vary significantly from the performance noted in the forward-looking statements. Thus, the Company cautions readers not to place undue reliance on any forward-looking statements, which speak only as of the date made.

Year 2000

The worldwide "Year 2000 problem" has arisen due to the fact that many computer hardware and software systems along with components of certain automated equipment utilize only the last two digits of a date to refer to the year, failing to distinguish dates within the twentieth century from those of the twenty-first or other centuries. If not corrected, these systems could fail or produce erroneous results with the advent of the twenty-first century.

Year 2000 (continued)

The Company is substantially complete in its assessment of the Year 2000 impact on systems being utilized within the Company. The Company's primary hardware platform is Year 2000 compliant. The Company has completed a review of its inventory of personal computers (PC's) and will either remediate or replace those PC's found not to be compliant. Additionally, a review of automated equipment other than computer systems has been performed to ascertain if remediation of any of this equipment is necessary. While the Company is continuing its detailed assessment of its automated equipment, the Company has not identified any problems thus far that would have a material impact upon its operations.

The Company's primary manufacturing and accounting software is sourced from an external vendor and has been independently certified as being Year 2000 compliant. The Company has performed testing that supports this certification. Software developed internally along with other purchased software has been reviewed for compliance and is in the process of being remediated where necessary. This remediation effort is expected to be complete in the second quarter of 1999. The Company currently estimates the cost to remediate both its Year 2000 hardware and software issues to be approximately $250,000. Approximately $100,000 of this cost represents redeployment of existing SG&A toward this effort.

The Year 2000 issues may have an impact on certain of the Company's material business partners, potentially causing disruptions in the supply of raw materials, services and/or the ability of customers to take delivery of products which could in turn have a material effect upon the Company's results of operation. The degree of this effect is uncertain. The Company has developed a structured methodology for evaluating the Year 2000 readiness of these business partners and expects this process to be completed during the second quarter of 1999. Contingency plans, where possible, will be developed for those business partners deemed to be at an unacceptable level of risk. A contingency plan for the failure of the Company's overall Year 2000 remediation plan has not been completed at this time.

The forward-looking statements contained herein with regard to the timing and overall cost estimates of the Company's efforts to address the Year 2000 problem are based upon the Company's experience thus far in this effort. Should the Company encounter unforeseen difficulties either in the continuing review of its computerized systems, their ultimate remediation, or the responses of its business partners, the actual results could vary significantly from the estimates contained in these forward-looking statements.

Quantitative and Qualitative Disclosures About Market Risk

The Company is exposed to market risk from changes in interest rates and changes in commodity prices.

The Company's earnings are affected by changes in short-term interest rates due to cash, cash equivalents, and short-term investments held in interest earning accounts, as well as, interest bearing notes receivable primarily from franchisees. Cash, cash equivalents, and short-term investments are held in accounts that have interest rates that are fixed for less than one year. Most of the interest bearing notes receivable reprice annually and bear interest at market rates. If interest rates averaged one percent less in 1999 than they did during 1998, the Company's interest income would decrease by approximately $192,000.

In addition, earnings are affected due to notes payable to a bank. The notes bear interest at the bank's base rate less 0.75% or at a match-funding rate of the adjusted Eurodollar rate plus 1.0%. The notes payable balance at November 29, 1998 was $6,124,082. If interest rates averaged one percent more in 1999 than they did during 1998, the Company's interest expense would increase by approximately $23,000 after consideration that the interest rate on the debt was set for approximately 180 days as of November 29, 1998. The Company manages short-term interest rate risk on debt by tracking projections on interest rate trends when choosing the periodic time-frame (30 days to 180 days) for locking in a certain interest rate on the debt.

The primary commodities purchased by the Company are dairy products. See discussion on pages 18 and 19 for information regarding the market for dairy products. The Company has not used financial instruments to hedge commodity prices in the past; however, the Company may consider such instruments in the future.

This market risk discussion contains forward-looking statements. Actual results may differ materially from this discussion based upon general market conditions and changes in domestic and global financial markets.

Report of Ernst & Young LLP, Independent Auditors

The Board of Directors and Stockholders
TCBY Enterprises, Inc.

We have audited the accompanying consolidated balance sheets of TCBY Enterprises, Inc. and subsidiaries as of November 29, 1998 and November 30, 1997, and the related consolidated statements of income, stockholders' equity, and cash flows for each of the three years in the period ended November 29, 1998. These financial statements are the responsibility of the Company's management. Our responsibility is to express an opinion on these financial statements based on our audits.

We conducted our audits in accordance with generally accepted auditing standards. Those standards require that we plan and perform the audit to obtain reasonable assurance about whether the financial statements are free of material misstatement. An audit includes examining, on a test basis, evidence supporting the amounts and disclosures in the financial statements. An audit also includes assessing the accounting principles used and significant estimates made by management, as well as evaluating the overall financial statement presentation. We believe that our audits provide a reasonable basis for our opinion.

In our opinion, the financial statements referred to above present fairly, in all material respects, the consolidated financial position of TCBY Enterprises, Inc. and subsidiaries at November 29, 1998 and November 30, 1997, and the consolidated results of their operations and their cash flows for each of the three years in the period ended November 29, 1998, in conformity with generally accepted accounting principles.

Ernst + Young LLP

January 14, 1999
Little Rock, Arkansas

Consolidated Balance Sheets

TCBY Enterprises, Inc.

Assets	November 29 1998	November 30 1997
Current Assets:		
Cash and cash equivalents	$ 16,924,143	$ 19,693,693
Short-term investments	2,967,135	2,406,045
Receivables:		
Trade accounts	10,078,733	8,750,207
Notes	1,695,429	2,127,328
Allowance for doubtful accounts and impaired notes	(439,223)	(833,447)
	11,334,939	10,044,088
Refundable income taxes	156,951	12,472
Deferred income taxes	1,204,197	1,086,406
Inventories	12,554,875	10,679,231
Prepaid expenses and other assets	1,540,971	1,549,643
Assets held for sale	150,000	754,652
Total Current Assets	46,833,211	46,226,230
Property, Plant, And Equipment:		
Land	2,534,307	2,866,820
Buildings	22,763,194	23,753,155
Furniture, vehicles, and equipment	46,637,567	49,987,506
Leasehold improvements	3,603,219	3,625,054
Allowance for depreciation	(39,546,174)	(39,891,253)
Net Property, Plant, And Equipment	35,992,113	40,341,282
Other Assets:		
Notes receivable, less current portion (less allowance for doubtful and impaired notes of $8,029,658 in 1998 and $7,741,180 in 1997)	4,525,970	5,495,337
Intangibles (less amortization of $2,226,511 in 1998 and $1,964,433 in 1997)	4,250,684	4,326,193
Other	2,850,906	2,875,354
Total Other Assets	11,627,560	12,696,884
Total Assets	$ 94,452,884	$99,264,396

See accompanying notes.

CONSOLIDATED BALANCE SHEETS

TCBY ENTERPRISES, INC.

Liabilities And Stockholders' Equity	November 29 1998	November 30 1997
Current Liabilities:		
Accounts payable	$ 2,130,430	$ 1,910,414
Accrued expenses	6,682,371	6,612,146
Current portion of long-term debt	3,171,448	3,171,448
Total Current Liabilities	11,984,249	11,694,008
Long-Term Debt, less current portion	2,952,634	6,298,008
Deferred Income Taxes	3,319,847	3,846,858
Commitments And Contingencies		
Stockholders' Equity:		
Preferred Stock, par value $.10 per share, authorized 2,000,000 shares	-	-
Common Stock, par value $.10 per share, authorized 50,000,000 shares; issued 27,759,021 shares in 1998 and 27,095,620 shares in 1997	2,775,902	2,709,562
Additional paid-in capital	30,098,602	25,761,424
Retained earnings	74,751,431	69,216,099
	107,625,935	97,687,085
Less treasury stock, at cost (4,839,952 shares in 1998 and 3,515,269 shares in 1997)	(31,429,781)	(20,261,563)
Total Stockholders' Equity	76,196,154	77,425,522
Total Liabilities And Stockholders' Equity	$ 94,452,884	$99,264,396

See accompanying notes.

CONSOLIDATED STATEMENTS OF INCOME

TCBY ENTERPRISES, INC.

	Three Years Ended November 29		
	1998	1997	1996
Sales	**$ 93,865,413**	$90,577,654	$ 82,964,258
Cost of sales	**64,098,811**	60,398,466	53,548,245
Gross Profit	**29,766,602**	30,179,188	29,416,013
Franchising revenues:			
Initial franchise and license fees	**2,285,646**	3,347,773	2,439,125
Royalty income	**10,828,217**	10,406,033	10,400,873
	13,113,863	13,753,806	12,839,998
	42,880,465	43,932,994	42,256,011
Selling, general, and administrative expenses	**30,393,591**	30,974,594	32,601,401
Income From Operations	**12,486,874**	12,958,400	9,654,610
Other income (expense):			
Interest expense	**(545,664)**	(759,766)	(961,154)
Interest income	**1,213,662**	1,209,393	1,147,484
Other income	**2,293,024**	148,029	168,669
	2,961,022	597,656	354,999
Income Before Income Taxes	**15,447,896**	13,556,056	10,009,609
Income tax expense (benefit):			
Current	**5,897,086**	3,466,300	1,585,861
Deferred	**(644,802)**	1,210,541	1,875,383
	5,252,284	4,676,841	3,461,244
Net Income	**$ 10,195,612**	$ 8,879,215	$ 6,548,365
Earnings Per Share:			
Basic	**$.44**	$.37	$.26
Diluted	**$.43**	$.36	$.26
Average Shares Outstanding:			
Basic	**23,230,863**	24,061,999	25,156,994
Diluted	**23,917,772**	24,339,828	25,162,825

See accompanying notes.

Consolidated Statements of Stockholders' Equity

TCBY Enterprises, Inc.

	Common Stock Shares	Common Stock Par Value	Additional Paid-in Capital	Retained Earnings	Treasury Stock	Total
Balance at December 1, 1995	27,062,345	$2,706,235	$25,547,184	$ 63,661,235	$ (9,735,887)	$82,178,767
Cash dividends–$.20 per share	-	-	-	(5,044,410)	-	(5,044,410)
Purchase of treasury stock-1,037,700 shares	-	-	-	-	(4,462,229)	(4,462,229)
Net income	-	-	-	6,548,365	-	6,548,365
Balance at November 30, 1996	27,062,345	2,706,235	25,547,184	65,165,190	(14,198,116)	79,220,493
Exercise of stock options, including tax benefit of $42,592	33,275	3,327	214,240	-	-	217,567
Cash dividends–$.20 per share	-	-	-	(4,828,306)	-	(4,828,306)
Purchase of treasury stock–1,090,500 shares	-	-	-	-	(6,063,447)	(6,063,447)
Net income	-	-	-	8,879,215	-	8,879,215
Balance at November 30, 1997	27,095,620	2,709,562	25,761,424	69,216,099	(20,261,563)	77,425,522
Exercise of stock options, including tax benefit of $831,255	**663,401**	**66,340**	**4,337,178**	-	-	**4,403,518**
Cash dividends–$.20 per share	-	-	-	**(4,660,280)**	-	**(4,660,280)**
Purchase of treasury stock–1,324,683 shares	-	-	-	-	**(11,168,218)**	**(11,168,218)**
Net income	-	-	-	**10,195,612**	-	**10,195,612**
Balance at November 29, 1998	**27,759,021**	**$2,775,902**	**$30,098,602**	**$ 74,751,431**	**$(31,429,781)**	**$76,196,154**

See accompanying notes.

Consolidated Statements of Cash Flows

TCBY Enterprises, Inc.

	Three Years Ended November 29		
	1998	1997	1996
Operating Activities			
Net income	**$10,195,612**	$ 8,879,215	$ 6,548,365
Adjustments to reconcile net income to net cash provided by operating activities:			
Depreciation	**4,048,305**	4,915,965	5,156,622
Amortization of intangibles	**262,031**	264,022	217,131
Provision for doubtful accounts and impaired notes	**72,500**	48,705	88,205
Deferred income taxes	**(644,802)**	1,210,541	1,875,383
Tax benefit from stock options	**831,255**	42,592	-
Gain on sales of property and equipment	**(2,143,990)**	(51,144)	(43,531)
Changes in operating assets and liabilities:			
Receivables	**(1,408,040)**	(877,273)	937,579
Inventories	**(1,875,644)**	692,926	1,608,413
Prepaid expenses	**(23,128)**	193,158	357,870
Assets held for disposal	-	-	2,413,438
Intangibles and other assets	**345,211**	579,951	(391,497)
Accounts payable and accrued expenses	**(54,759)**	916,611	(3,926,558)
Income taxes	**(144,479)**	320,401	4,086,063
Net Cash Provided By Operating Activities	**9,460,072**	17,135,670	18,927,483
Investing Activities			
Purchases of property, plant, and equipment	**(1,982,769)**	(1,869,282)	(2,403,694)
Purchase of business, net of cash acquired	-	-	(952,800)
Proceeds from sales of property and equipment	**4,901,790**	139,866	325,122
Origination of notes receivable	**(471,443)**	(1,098,771)	(334,551)
Principal collected on notes receivable	**1,485,499**	2,508,921	1,898,270
Purchases of short-term investments	**(2,156,893)**	(1,838,338)	(1,457,224)
Proceeds from maturity of short-term investments	**1,595,803**	3,684,845	6,028,835
Net Cash Provided By Investing Activities	**3,371,987**	1,527,241	3,103,958
Financing Activities			
Proceeds from exercise of Common Stock options	**3,572,263**	174,975	-
Dividends paid	**(4,660,280)**	(4,828,306)	(5,044,410)
Treasury stock transactions	**(11,168,218)**	(6,063,447)	(4,462,229)
Principal payments on long-term debt	**(3,345,374)**	(3,171,448)	(3,171,448)
Net Cash Used In Financing Activities	**(15,601,609)**	(13,888,226)	(12,678,087)
(Decrease) Increase In Cash And Cash Equivalents	**(2,769,550)**	4,774,685	9,353,354
Cash and cash equivalents at beginning of year	**19,693,693**	14,919,008	5,565,654
Cash And Cash Equivalents At End Of Year	**$16,924,143**	$ 19,693,693	$ 14,919,008

See accompanying notes.

NOTES TO CONSOLIDATED FINANCIAL STATEMENTS

TCBY ENTERPRISES, INC.
NOVEMBER 29, 1998

1. Accounting Policies

Principles of Consolidation: The consolidated financial statements include the accounts of the Company and its wholly owned subsidiaries. All significant intercompany accounts and transactions have been eliminated in consolidation.

Description of Business: The Company manufactures and sells soft serve frozen yogurt, hardpack frozen yogurt and ice cream, and novelty frozen food products through Company-owned and franchised retail stores ("TCBY® stores"), non-traditional locations (e.g., airports, schools, hospitals, convenience stores, and travel plazas), and the retail grocery trade (e.g., grocery stores and wholesale clubs). In addition, the Company sells equipment related to the foodservice industry and develops locations under the Juice Works® brand in conjunction with the TCBY® brand.

The following summarizes the number of TCBY® and Juice Works® locations:

	1998	1997	1996
Franchised or licensed	1,247	1,339	1,399
Company-owned	2	2	2
Non-traditional	1,711	1,467	1,297
	2,960	2,808	2,698

Cash and Cash Equivalents: The Company considers all highly liquid investments with an original maturity of 90 days or less to be cash equivalents.

Short-term Investments: Short-term investments consist of certificates of deposit and other income producing non-equity securities with an original maturity of greater than 90 days and less than one year. These investments are recorded at cost which approximates market value and are intended to be held to maturity.

Inventories: Inventories consist primarily of yogurt and ice cream products and related manufacturing materials, and foodservice equipment. Inventories are carried at the lower of cost or market.

Receivables: A majority of the Company's trade accounts receivable are due from customers throughout the United States and internationally in the food products segment. In addition, the Company from time to time extends credit in the form of notes receivable to franchisees. Notes receivable from franchisees are primarily collateralized by equipment located in TCBY® stores. Many of these notes receivable are intended to be paid over five years and bear interest at market rates. Notes receivable are placed on a non-accrual status when the collectibility of principal or interest becomes uncertain.

Also included in notes receivable are amounts due related to the sale of the rights for the exclusive manufacturing and distribution of the TCBY® refrigerated yogurt product line throughout the United States. Mid-America Dairymen, Inc., now Dairy Farmers of America ("DFA"), purchased these rights in April, 1995 and the Company's consideration included a receivable of $10.6 million. Subsequent to the transaction, sales of the TCBY® refrigerated yogurt line declined significantly due to competitive factors. After further negotiations with DFA, the Company agreed to waive certain required payments and accordingly provided an impairment allowance in the fourth quarter of 1995 based on the revised estimate of future discounted cash flows. The loan balance at November 29, 1998 was $8,041,000 with an associated allowance of $6,610,000. These balances are included in the investment in notes considered to be impaired in the following paragraph. During 1998, Suiza Foods Corporation acquired the rights to the TCBY® refrigerated product line from DFA and the associated liabilities.

At November 29, 1998 and November 30, 1997, the recorded investment in notes considered to be impaired under Statement of Financial Accounting Standards ("SFAS") No. 114 was $11,205,000 and $10,507,000, respectively. The entire 1998 and 1997 balances were impaired notes which had allowances for credit losses of $8,403,000 and $8,492,000, respectively. The impairment losses are recorded in the food products segment. The average recorded investment in impaired notes was $10,958,000 during 1998, $11,671,000 during 1997, and $12,901,000 during 1996. The Company recognized interest income on impaired notes of $14,000 in 1998, $19,000 in 1997, and $1,000 in 1996 using the cash basis method of income recognition.

The following presents changes in the allowance for doubtful accounts and impaired notes:

	1998	1997	1996
Balance at beginning of year	$8,574,627	$9,682,024	$11,178,017
Provision for doubtful accounts and impaired notes	72,500	48,705	88,205
Charge-offs	(218,354)	(1,173,093)	(1,586,704)
Recoveries	40,108	16,991	2,506
Balance at end of year	$8,468,881	$8,574,627	$9,682,024

NOTES TO CONSOLIDATED FINANCIAL STATEMENTS

1. Accounting Policies (continued)

Long-lived Assets: Property, plant, and equipment is recorded at cost and is depreciated by the straight-line method for financial reporting purposes over the estimated useful lives of the individual assets. For tax reporting purposes, accelerated cost recovery depreciation methods are used.

Intangibles include the cost in excess of net assets of businesses acquired, trademarks, and non-compete agreements. These intangibles are being amortized over the estimated future periods benefited, ranging from 3 to 40 years.

The Company reviews long-lived assets used in operations and impairment losses are recorded when indicators of impairment are present and the undiscounted cash flows estimated to be generated by those assets are less than the assets' carrying amount. Impairment losses are recorded on long-lived assets to be disposed of when the carrying value of the asset exceeds the fair value (usually based on discounted cash flows) less the estimated selling costs.

Revenue Recognition: Franchising revenues consist of initial franchise and license fees and royalty income. Initial franchise and license fees are recognized as revenue when the Company has substantially completed its obligations under the franchise or license agreement. Royalty income is earned on sales by franchisees and is recognized as revenue when the related sales are made.

The Company recognizes revenue from product sales upon shipment or, for sales by Company-owned stores, when purchased by customers.

Income Taxes: The liability method is used in accounting for income taxes. Under this method, deferred tax assets and liabilities are determined based on differences between financial reporting and tax bases of assets and liabilities and are measured using the enacted tax rates and laws that will be in effect when the differences are expected to reverse.

Net Income Per Share: In February 1997, the Financial Accounting Standards Board ("FASB") issued SFAS No. 128, "Earnings per Share". SFAS No. 128 replaced the calculation of primary and fully diluted earnings per share with basic and diluted earnings per share. Unlike primary earnings per share, basic earnings per share excludes any dilutive effects of stock options. Diluted earnings per share is very similar to the previously reported fully diluted earnings per share calculation. All earnings per share amounts for all periods have been presented and, where necessary, restated to conform to SFAS No. 128 requirements.

Fair Value of Financial Instruments: The carrying amount of financial instruments including cash and cash equivalents, accounts and notes receivable, and accounts payable approximates fair value at November 29, 1998, because of the relatively short maturity of these instruments or valuation allowances which have been recorded to report the balances at fair value. The carrying amount of long-term debt also approximates fair value due to its variable interest rate which is adjusted every 30 to 180 days depending upon certain elections made by the Company.

Fiscal Year: Effective December 1, 1996, the Company changed its fiscal year end from November 30 to a 52 or 53 week year ending on the Sunday nearest November 30. All general references to years relate to fiscal years unless otherwise noted.

Use of Estimates: The preparation of consolidated financial statements in conformity with generally accepted accounting principles requires management to make estimates and assumptions that affect the amounts reported in the financial statements and accompanying notes. Actual results could differ from those estimates.

New Pronouncements: In June 1997, the FASB issued SFAS No. 130, "Reporting Comprehensive Income." SFAS No. 130 is effective for fiscal years beginning after December 15, 1997 and establishes standards for the reporting and display of comprehensive income and its components in a full set of financial statements. The adoption of this statement in 1999 is not expected to have a material affect on the Company's financial statements.

In June 1997, the FASB issued SFAS No. 131, "Disclosures about Segments of an Enterprise and Related Information." Effective for fiscal years beginning after December 31, 1997, SFAS No. 131 requires companies to disclose certain information about their operating segments, their products and services, their major customers and the geographic areas in which they operate. The determination of reportable segments under SFAS No. 131 is based on material segments of a company whose operating results are regularly reviewed by the Company's chief operating decision maker in determining allocation of resources between the segments and assessing their performance. The Company is presently evaluating its reporting requirements under this standard, but believes it will continue reporting information for two segments - food products and equipment.

In June 1998, the FASB issued SFAS No. 133, "Accounting for Derivative Instruments and Hedging Activities," which is effective for years beginning after June 15, 1999 and requires that all derivatives be recognized on the balance sheet at fair value. SFAS No. 133 establishes "special accounting" for fair value hedges, cash flow hedges, and hedges of foreign currency exposures of net investments in foreign operations. Derivatives that are not hedges must be adjusted to fair value through income. If the derivative is a hedge, depending on the nature of the hedge, changes in the fair value of derivatives will

NOTES TO CONSOLIDATED FINANCIAL STATEMENTS

either be offset against the change in fair value of the assets, liabilities, or firm commitments through earnings or recognized in other comprehensive income until the hedged item is recognized in earnings. The ineffective portions of a derivative's change in fair value will be immediately recognized in earnings. As the Company had no derivatives or hedges at November 29, 1998, the adoption of SFAS No. 133 would not have had a material impact on the Company's financial condition or results of operations.

Reclassification: Certain amounts in the 1997 and 1996 consolidated financial statements have been reclassified to conform to the 1998 presentation.

2. Earnings Per Share

The following table sets forth the computation of basic and diluted earnings per share:

	1998	1997	1996
Numerator:			
Net income	$10,195,612	$ 8,879,215	$ 6,548,365
Denominator:			
Denominator for basic earnings per shares–weighted average shares	23,230,863	24,061,999	25,156,994
Potential dilutive effect of employee stock options	686,909	277,829	5,831
Denominator for diluted earnings per share–weighted average shares and assumed conversions	23,917,772	24,339,828	25,162,825
Basic earnings per share	$.44	$.37	$.26
Diluted earnings per share	$.43	$.36	$.26
Anti-dilutive employee stock options excluded	118,404	1,006,760	2,126,017

3. Inventories

Inventories consisted of the following:

	1998	1997
Manufacturing materials and supplies	$ 5,088,456	$ 4,307,719
Finished yogurt and other food products	4,526,777	2,929,034
Equipment and other products	2,939,642	3,442,478
	$12,554,875	$10,679,231

4. Long-term Debt

Long-term debt consisted of the following:

	1998	1997
Unsecured notes payable	$6,124,082	$9,469,456
Less current portion	3,171,448	3,171,448
	$2,952,634	$6,298,008

Two unsecured notes bear interest at the bank's base rate less 0.75% or at a match-funding rate of the adjusted Eurodollar rate plus 1.0%. The interest rate at November 29, 1998 was 6.20719% for both notes. The notes are due in monthly installments of approximately $264,000 plus interest and mature on June 1, 2000 and December 31, 2001. The loan agreement requires, among other things, a fixed charge coverage ratio of greater than 1.25 to 1.0 be maintained. This ratio is defined as the sum of net income and non-cash charges adjusted for extraordinary and non-recurring items divided by the sum of the current portion of long-term debt, cash dividends paid, and capital expenditures incurred to maintain or replace existing property, plant, and equipment. The Company was in compliance with these covenants at November 29, 1998.

Annual maturities of long-term debt are $3,171,448 in 1999, $1,953,967 in 2000, and $998,667 in 2001.

The Company has available a $5 million unsecured credit line.

No interest was capitalized in 1998, 1997, or 1996. During 1998, 1997, and 1996, the Company paid interest of approximately $546,000, $760,000, and $961,000, respectively.

5. Income Taxes

Deferred income taxes reflect the net tax effects of temporary differences between the carrying amounts of assets and liabilities for financial reporting purposes and the amounts used for income tax purposes. Significant components of the Company's deferred tax assets and liabilities are as follows:

	1998	1997
Deferred tax assets:		
Impairment allowance on fixed assets	$ 675,128	$ 811,158
Claims settlement accrual (see Note 8)	517,500	-
Accrued expenses	959,728	973,490
Other	1,333,596	1,063,130
Total deferred tax assets	3,485,952	2,847,778
Deferred tax liabilities:		
Tax over book depreciation	3,863,828	4,182,635
Other	1,737,774	1,425,595
Total deferred tax liabilities	5,601,602	5,608,230
Net deferred tax liabilities	$2,115,650	$2,760,452

NOTES TO CONSOLIDATED FINANCIAL STATEMENTS

5. Income Taxes (continued)

Significant components of the provision for income taxes are as follows:

	1998	1997	1996
Current:			
Federal	$5,862,225	$3,443,225	$1,420,321
State	34,861	23,075	165,540
Total current	$5,897,086	$3,466,300	1,585,861
Deferred	(644,802)	1,210,541	1,875,383
	$5,252,284	$4,676,841	$3,461,244

The reconciliation of income tax computed at the United States federal statutory tax rates to income tax is:

	1998	1997	1996
Income tax at the statutory federal rate	$5,306,764	$4,644,620	$3,403,267
State income taxes, net of federal benefit	22,660	14,999	(28,430)
Other, net	(77,140)	17,222	86,407
Total income tax	$5,252,284	$4,676,841	$3,461,244

The Company made income tax payments of approximately $5,210,000, $3,088,000, and $1,105,000, in 1998, 1997, and 1996, respectively.

6. Accrued Expenses

Accrued expenses consisted of the following:

	1998	1997
Rent	$ 602,272	$ 662,224
Compensation	2,234,893	2,534,394
Other	3,845,206	3,415,528
	$6,682,371	$6,612,146

Accrued expenses at November 29, 1998 and November 30, 1997 includes $.8 million and $1.0 million, respectively, of costs primarily related to the Company's sale of TCBY® Company-owned stores and the related restructuring of its organization in 1995. The original balance of these reserves was $3.4 million. The remaining liabilities will be primarily utilized over the life of the leases for stores sold or closed where sublease payments are less than the Company's required lease payment.

7. Lease Commitments

In 1998, 1997, and 1996, rent expense totaled approximately $1,657,000, $1,775,000, and $2,884,000, respectively. The future minimal rental commitments for all non-cancelable operating leases with initial or remaining terms in excess of one year are as follows: 1999–$1,986,000; 2000–$1,707,000; 2001–$1,585,000; 2002–$1,175,000; 2003–$1,039,000; and thereafter–$3,120,000.

Certain of the leases relating to corporate stores are renewable for substantially the same rentals for up to five additional years. The rental commitments (net of subleases) for closed Company-owned locations totaled approximately $88,000 at November 29, 1998 and are excluded from the future minimum commitments as this amount was accrued in a prior year. The future minimum rental commitments for stores, which total approximately $2,181,000, relate primarily to the remaining Company-owned stores and stores sold where the lease commitment has been assumed by the buyer but the Company remains on the lease as a responsible party. These future commitments are expected to be offset by future minimum rentals to be received under non-cancelable subleases of approximately $1,716,000 at November 29, 1998.

The lease commitments also include a lease for the corporate headquarters which was renegotiated effective January 1, 1997 with a new 10-year term. The base rent escalates 3% annually and the lease contains a 10-year renewal option at the rental rate effective at the end of the initial term. The rate would continue to increase 3% annually during the renewal period.

8. Contingencies

A customer for whom Americana Foods produces private label products asserted a claim alleging damages due to production defects. Immediate and voluntary recalls of limited quantities of products were undertaken in 1997. The Company, after negotiations with the customer and the Company's liability insurance carrier, has, with the participation of the liability insurance carrier, settled all claims. The relevant settlement agreement contains a confidentiality clause; however, the amount paid by the Company to obtain settlement exceeded prior accruals by approximately one million dollars. While the Company believed it had meritorious defenses to and disagreed with the customer's claim, settlement was agreed to by the Company in order to avoid the uncertainty of outcome, cost of litigation, and disruption to the Company.

NOTES TO CONSOLIDATED FINANCIAL STATEMENTS

8. Contingencies (continued)

Other than as set forth above, there is no material litigation pending against the Company. Various legal and administrative proceedings are pending against the Company which are incidental to the business of the Company. The ultimate legal and financial liability of the Company in connection with such proceedings and that discussed above cannot be estimated with certainty, but the Company believes, based upon its examination of these matters, its experience to date, and its discussions with legal counsel, that resolution of these proceedings will have no material adverse effect upon the Company's financial condition, either individually or in the aggregate; of course, any substantial loss pursuant to any litigation might have a material adverse impact upon results of operations in the quarter or year in which it were to be incurred, but the Company cannot estimate the range of any reasonably possible loss.

9. Employee Benefit Plans

The Company's Stock Option Plans made available options for the purchase of the Company's Common Stock to certain officers, employees, and non-employee directors. The options are exercisable in one, two, or four equal annual installments, beginning six months or one year after the date of grant with a 10 year life.

The Company has elected to follow Accounting Principals Board Opinion No. 25, "Accounting for Stock Issued to Employees" ("APB No. 25") and related Interpretations in accounting for its employee stock options versus the alternative fair value accounting provided for under SFAS No. 123, "Accounting for Stock-Based Compensation". Under APB No. 25, because the exercise price of the Company's employee stock options equals the market price of the underlying stock on the date of grant, no compensation expense is recognized.

Pro forma information regarding net income and earnings per share is required by SFAS No. 123 and has been determined as if the Company had accounted for its stock options under the fair value method of that Statement. The fair value of these options was estimated at date of grant using a Black-Scholes option pricing model with the following weighted-average assumptions for 1998, 1997, and 1996, respectively: risk free interest rates of 5.71%, 6.34%, and 6.22%; dividend yields of 3.0%, 3.0% and 4.0%; volatility factors of the expected market price of the Company's common stock of .26, .26 and .30; and the weighted-average expected life of four years.

For purposes of pro forma disclosures, the estimated fair value of the stock options is amortized to expense over their respective vesting periods. Pro forma net income and earnings per share, assuming the Company had elected to account for its stock option grants in accordance with SFAS No. 123 for the three years ended November 29, 1998, is as follows:

	1998	1997	1996
Pro forma net income	**$9,768,000**	$8,603,000	$ 6,447,000
Pro forma earnings per share:			
Basic	**$.42**	$.36	$.26
Diluted	**$.41**	$.36	$.26

Pro forma results are not necessarily indicative of the effect on future years.

A summary of the Company's stock option activity, and related information for the three years ended November 29, 1998 follows:

	Shares Under Option	**Weighted Average Option Price Per Share**
Outstanding at December 1, 1995	2,055,263	$6.33
Granted	810,000	4.61
Terminated	(467,575)	6.71
Outstanding at November 30, 1996	2,397,688	5.68
Granted	958,500	4.70
Exercised	(33,275)	5.26
Terminated	(13,472)	9.20
Outstanding at November 30, 1997	3,309,441	5.30
Granted	**630,000**	**6.15**
Exercised	**(663,401)**	**5.39**
Terminated	**(129,790)**	**6.23**
Outstanding at November 29, 1998	**3,146,250**	**$5.41**

The number of shares exercisable was as follows: November 29, 1998–1,416,058; November 30, 1997–1,469,835; and November 30, 1996–773,271. The weighted-average option price for exercisable shares as of November 29, 1998 and November 30, 1997 and 1996 was $5.73; $5.84; and $6.59, respectively. The weighted-average fair value of options granted was $1.35 in 1998, $1.07 in 1997 and $1.04 in 1996.

NOTES TO CONSOLIDATED FINANCIAL STATEMENTS

9. Employee Benefit Plans (continued)

The following table summarizes information concerning outstanding and exercisable stock options as of November 29, 1998:

	Options Outstanding			Options Exercisable	
Range of Exercise Prices	Shares Outstanding	Weighted Average Remaining Contractual Life (Years)	Weighted Average Exercise Price	Shares Exercisable	Weighted Average Exercise Price
$4.00-7.44	3,068,899	7.07	$ 5.29	1,338,707	$ 5.46
8.38-18.13	77,351	3.12	10.36	77,351	10.36
	3,146,250			1,416,058	

The Company maintains a pre-tax savings plan in accordance with the provisions of Section 401(k) of the Internal Revenue Code (the "Plan"). Employees who have reached age 21 and fulfill the statutory minimum hours of service (1,000) during the plan year are eligible to participate in the Plan. Under the Plan, employees are eligible to contribute up to the lesser of 15% of compensation or the statutory limit, with the Company matching 50% of the first 5% of compensation contributed by the employee. The Company's matching portion of employee contributions resulted in expense of approximately $220,000, $251,000, and $213,000 in 1998, 1997, and 1996, respectively.

10. Certain Transactions

In 1996, the Company paid approximately $75,000 to a marketing consulting firm whose chief executive officer is a shareholder and director of the Company. There were no payments in 1998 and 1997.

In 1998, 1997, and 1996, the Company had sales totaling approximately $183,000, $307,000, and $437,000, respectively, to a foodservice distributor whose chief executive officer is a director of the Company.

On October 2, 1995, nine Company-owned stores were sold to franchisee groups which included a shareholder and director of the Company. In addition, the franchisee groups manage six additional stores and receive $130,000 annually for these services; the Company retains ownership of these stores for research and development and training purposes. These stores are all classified as licensed units in Note 1. In August 1998, the stockholder and director of the Company divested his interest in the franchisee groups.

In 1998, the Company aircraft was sold. The Company contemporaneously entered into an agreement whereunder an aircraft owned by the Chairman and Chief Executive Officer could be made available to the Company from time-to-time at an hourly rate consistent with the cost of operating the aircraft it divested; this hourly rate is substantially below the fair market rate which normally would be charged to the Company for use of a similar aircraft. In an associated transaction, the Chairman and Chief Executive Officer leased the Company's flight operations which included personnel, equipment, and facilities. Payments made by the Company for use of the plane totaled $99,000 in 1998. Payments received on rental of the flight operations totaled $196,000 in 1998.

11. Operations by Industry Segment

Financial information for each of the Company's segments is set forth below:

1998	Food Products	Equipment	Other	Total
Net sales and franchising revenues	$89,755,318	$16,062,038	$ 1,161,920	$106,979,276
Income (loss) from operations	17,875,608	1,229,818	(6,618,552)	12,486,874
Identifiable assets	61,506,093	7,442,212	25,504,579	94,452,884
Capital expenditures	1,601,821	106,359	274,589	1,982,769
Depreciation	3,452,224	203,219	594,522	4,249,965

1997				
Net sales and franchising revenues	$ 87,388,000	$15,851,821	$ 1,091,639	$104,331,460
Income (loss) from operations	20,960,498	799,267	(8,801,365)	12,958,400
Identifiable assets	57,675,539	13,718,822	27,870,035	99,264,396
Capital expenditures	1,333,458	78,059	457,765	1,869,282
Depreciation	3,891,182	287,381	737,402	4,915,965

1996				
Net sales and franchising revenues	$ 80,117,290	$ 14,651,976	$ 1,034,990	$ 95,804,256
Income (loss) from operations	18,973,050	841,617	(10,160,057)	9,654,610
Identifiable assets	63,557,411	15,678,242	23,232,794	102,468,447
Capital expenditures	2,153,862	61,155	188,677	2,403,694
Depreciation	4,157,198	224,227	775,197	5,156,622

(a) Inter-segment sales and transfers are insignificant.

(b) The Company's business segments are described and discussed in Management's Discussion and Analysis of Financial Condition and Results of Operations.

(c) The "Other" segment is composed of unallocated corporate expenditures and other sundry operations.

Substantially all frozen yogurt products sold to domestic TCBY® traditional stores are distributed exclusively by ProSource. Sales by the Company's manufacturing subsidiary to ProSource totaled approximately $43.0 million, $42.9 million, and $43.2 million in 1998, 1997, and 1996, respectively. Approximately $2.8 million and $2.5 million were receivable from ProSource as of November 29, 1998 and November 30, 1997, respectively.

Notes to Consolidated Financial Statements

12. Acquisition/Disposition

In July, 1997, the Company sold a portion of Carlin Manufacturing's assets to a company controlled by the subsidiary's president. The assets sold included certain inventory, plant equipment, furniture and fixtures, and intangibles. The transaction was partially financed by the Company. In the Carlin transaction, the real estate and certain finished goods inventory were retained by the Company. The real estate was leased to the purchaser with the ultimate intent to sell the property. The purchaser is assisting the Company in marketing the remaining inventory and receives a commission on the sale of this inventory.

On September 11, 1996, the Company acquired certain assets of Whatever Works Inc. and Juice Works International Franchise Corporation (collectively "Juice Works"), a Phoenix-based juice bar concept, for a purchase price of $1 million. The acquisition was accounted for as a purchase and the results of operations of Juice Works from the date of acquisition are reflected in the consolidated statement of income of the Company. The results of operations of Juice Works prior to its acquisition by the Company were not significant. Goodwill of approximately $867,000 associated with the purchase is being amortized on a straight-line basis over 20 years.

13. Quarterly Results of Operations (Unaudited)

Financial results by quarter for 1998 and 1997 are summarized below:

	Quarters			
1998	**First**	**Second**	**Third**	**Fourth**
Sales	$16,728,701	$27,083,951	$28,791,737	$21,261,024
Gross profit	5,436,186	8,944,943	10,026,062	5,359,411
Franchising revenues	2,479,824	3,813,639	4,076,691	2,743,709
Net income	741,588	3,526,968	5,676,067	250,989
Net income per share:				
Basic	$.03	$.15	$.25	$.01
Diluted	.03	.15	.24	.01
Average shares outstanding:				
Basic	23,468,430	23,270,022	23,130,874	23,054,740
Diluted	24,164,665	24,158,257	23,872,098	23,476,682
1997				
Sales	$ 15,884,887	$26,802,645	$30,018,752	$17,871,370
Gross profit	5,201,922	8,773,122	10,236,144	5,968,000
Franchising revenues	2,586,812	4,381380	4,119,155	2,666,459
Net income	251,651	3,124,990	4,325,146	1,177,428
Net income per share:				
Basic	$.01	$.13	$.18	$.05
Diluted	.01	.13	.18	.05
Average shares outstanding:				
Basic	24,471,597	24,148,523	23,880,545	23,742,831
Diluted	24,491,551	24,349,540	24,318,308	24,195,412

Corporate Information

TCBY Enterprises, Inc.

Corporate Offices
TCBY Enterprises, Inc.
1200 TCBY Tower, 425 West Capitol Avenue
Little Rock, Arkansas 72201
(501) 688-8229

Independent Auditors
Ernst & Young LLP
Little Rock, Arkansas

Transfer Agent and Registrar
Continental Stock Transfer and Trust Co.
2 Broadway
New York, NY 10004
(212) 509-4000

Investor Relations
Stacy L. Duckett
Vice President

Form 10-K
The Company's Annual Report on Form 10-K, filed with the Securities and Exchange Commission for the year ended November 29, 1998, will be sent without charge to each stockholder upon request to the Investor Relations Department at the Corporate offices.

Business
TCBY Enterprises, Inc., through subsidiary companies, manufactures and sells soft serve frozen yogurt and sorbet, hardpack frozen yogurt, sorbet, and ice cream, and frozen novelty products, and markets foodservice equipment. The Company, through subsidiaries, develops locations and products under the TCBY® and Juice Works® brands.

Annual Meeting
The Annual Meeting of Stockholders of TCBY Enterprises, Inc., will be held at 10:00 a.m., April 13, 1999, at the Excelsior Hotel in Little Rock, Arkansas.

Common Stock
The Company's Common Stock is traded on the New York Stock Exchange under the symbol TBY. The following table sets forth, for the periods indicated, the high and low composite sales prices.

Fiscal 1998	**High**	**Low**
First Quarter	**$ 9 7/16**	**$6**
Second Quarter	**10 1/8**	**8 1/2**
Third Quarter	**9 7/8**	**5 7/8**
Fourth Quarter	**7 3/4**	**5 5/16**

Fiscal 1997	**High**	**Low**
First Quarter	$ 4 1/2	$ 4
Second Quarter	6	4 5/8
Third Quarter	6 15/16	6
Fourth Quarter	7	6 1/16

As of November 29, 1998, there were 4,467 shareholders of record of the Company's Common Stock and 27,759,021 shares issued.

Dividend Policy
The Company will consider adjustments to the dividend rate after giving consideration to return to stockholders, profitability expectations, financing and cash needs of the Company, and other factors. See Note 4 to Consolidated Financial Statements.

Dividends Per Share	**1998**	**1997**
First Quarter	**$.05**	$.05
Second Quarter	**.05**	.05
Third Quarter	**.05**	.05
Fourth Quarter	**.05**	.05
Total	**$.20**	$.20

Ten Year Summary of Selected Financial Data

TCBY Enterprises, Inc.

($000, Except Per Share Amounts)

	1998	1997	1996	1995	1994	1993	1992	1991	1990	1989
Sales	**$93,865**	$ 90,578	$ 82,964	$ 109,808	$ 140,445	$109,525	$107,633	$116,679	$134,832	$131,730
Franchising revenues	**13,114**	13,754	12,840	11,762	12,026	10,952	11,063	12,231	16,475	19,593
Net income (loss)	**10,196**	8,879	6,548	(21,373)	7,552	6,409	5,073	8,017	19,950	29,493
Total assets	**94,453**	99,264	102,468	111,625	142,280	128,691	131,925	134,806	141,537	133,559
Long-term debt	**2,953**	6,298	9,469	12,641	15,910	11,487	14,799	17,330	19,696	21,258
Per share:										
Earnings, Basic	**$ .44**	$ .37	$ .26	$ (.83)	$ .30	$ .25	$ .20	$ .31	$ .75	$ 1.11
Earnings, Diluted	**.43**	.36	.26	(.83)	.29	.25	.20	.31	.75	1.10
Cash dividends	**.20**	.20	.20	.20	.20	.20	.20	.35	.18	.07
Total stockholders' equity	**3.32**	3.28	3.22	3.20	4.23	4.13	4.09	4.10	4.15	3.69

NOTE: The 1995 results included pre-tax charges of $27.6 million, or $.72 per share net of taxes, due to the adoption of new accounting standards, and an additional $1.4 million dollars, or $.04 per share net of taxes, resulting from a restructuring of the Company during the fourth quarter of 1995.

Glossary

ABO *See* **accumulated benefit obligation.**/12

Accounts payable turnover ratio Purchases ÷ Average accounts payable./MA

Accounts receivable turnover ratio Sales ÷ Average accounts receivable./MA

Accrual-basis accounting The accrual basis of accounting seeks to measure and link effort and accomplishment rather than simply match cash inflows and outflows. Accrual accounting records revenues as they are earned, rather than when cash is received, and records expenses as they are incurred, rather than when cash is paid./1

Accrued expenses Recognition of an expense *before* the cash outflow occurs./1

Accrued pension cost *See* **prepaid (accrued) pension cost.**/12

Accrued revenues Recognition of income *before* the cash inflow occurs./1

Accumulated benefit obligation (ABO) In a defined benefit pension plan, ABO is the actuarially determined present value of estimated retirement payments calculated according to the pension plan benefit formula (using current salary levels) to be paid to employees because employees have worked and earned benefits until the current date./12

Accumulated other comprehensive income A component of stockholders' equity. The items reported as other comprehensive income on the statement of comprehensive income are transferred to accumulated other comprehensive income at the end of each annual accounting period./7

Actual return on plan assets In a defined benefit pension plan, the change in the fair value of pension plan assets during the period, after adjusting for additional employer contributions to the plan and for pension payments made to employees. The actual return can be positive (fair value increased) or negative (fair value decreased) in any particular period. The actual return on plan assets is comprised of two parts: the expected return on plan assets and the unexpected return on plan assets (i.e., an asset gain/loss). The expected return on plan assets receives immediate recognition as a part of pension expense, while the unexpected return does not receive immediate recognition as part of pension cost in the period generated. Instead, recognition of the unexpected return as an element of pension cost is delayed and occurs only if the total unamortized gain/loss is greater than the corridor amount./12

Actuarial gain/loss *See* **liability gain/loss.**/12

Additional pension liability In a defined benefit pension plan, additional pension liability is the amount of liability that is recognized because either the minimum liability amount is greater than accrued pension cost balance or a prepaid pension cost balance exists./12

Agency costs Costs arising from activities undertaken by owners to ensure that managers make decisions that maximize owner wealth (e.g., monitoring costs by independent auditors, use of costly managerial evaluation and compensation schemes, etc.)./2

Aging of receivables A process in which receivables are classified as current (not yet past due) or past due. If past due, the receivables are classified further according to timing: e.g., 1–30 days past due, 31–60 days past due, etc. Based upon historical data and other available information, a general estimate of the appropriate amount of the allowance for doubtful accounts is made based upon the aging: e.g., not past due, 2%; 1–30 days past due, 7%; 31–60 days past due, 22%; etc./9

Allowance method A method used to account for bad debts that provides an allowance at year-end to reduce accounts receivable to net realizable value and recognize bad debts expense. Two approaches are used in practice: (1) balance sheet approach and (2) income statement approach. In the *balance sheet approach*, emphasis is placed on determining the proper balance in the "allowance for doubtful accounts" account (rather than direct computation of bad debts expense), which is generally determined by "aging" accounts receivable. Any change in the allowance account is also recognized as bad debts expense. In the *income statement approach*, bad debts expense is computed by multiplying credit sales by the percentage of expected uncollectible credit sales, and the offset is to "allowance for doubtful accounts." The allowance method acceptable is for GAAP (*see also* the **direct write-off method,** which is not acceptable for GAAP)./9

Amortization Refers to a cost allocation process: amortization of intangible asset cost, amortization of bond premium/discount./3, 6, 7

Amortize *See* **amortization.**/6

Amortized cost The carrying value of a bond investment (principal plus unamortized premium or minus unamortized discount, which also equals the present value of the remaining cash flows discounted at the *historical effective interest rate)*./7

Annuity due A series of equal cash payments or receipts in the future at the same interval (e.g., monthly, annually), with the first cash flow occurring immediately./Appendix B

Antidilutive With respect to a diluted EPS computation, the assumed conversion of a dilutive security is antidilutive if the resulting diluted EPS amount would increase. Antidilutive computations are not allowed./10

Asset gain/loss (unexpected return on pension plan assets) In a defined benefit pension plan, an asset gain/loss is the difference between the *actual* return on plan assets and the *expected* return on plan assets. A gain results if the actual return exceeds the expected return, and a loss results if the actual return is less than the actual return. The unexpected return on plan assets does not receive immediate recognition as part of pension cost in the period generated. Instead, recognition as pension cost is delayed and occurs only if the total unamortized gain/loss is greater than the corridor amount./12

Asset turnover ratio Sales ÷ Average total assets./MA

Assets Probable future economic benefits obtained or controlled by a particular entity as a result of past transactions or events./1

Available-for-sale securities Those debt or equity security investments that are not classified as either trading securities nor held-to-maturity securities under *SFAS No. 115* (i.e., *available-for-sale classification is the default classification*). Available-for-sale securities are "marked to market" at each balance sheet date. The unrealized holding gain or loss (i.e., the difference between the book value and their current market value) is not reflected in current income, but it is reflected as a component of other comprehensive income./7, 8

Average accumulated expenditures A term used in the process of calculating the amount of *avoidable interest*, the interest amount capitalized on self-constructed assets. It is computed as the weighted average of expenditures linked to a self-construction project. The average accumulated expenditure is multiplied by the interest rate on specific borrowings used to fund construction and/or the interest rate(s) on general borrowings used to fund construction to compute avoidable interest./6

Average number of days receivables outstanding ratio The number 365 ÷ Accounts receivable turnover ratio./MA

Avoidable interest The term used to describe the amount of a company's annual interest cost that should be capitalized on self-constructed assets. *See also* **average accumulated expenditures.**/6

Balance sheet equation Assets equals liabilities plus owners' equity: A = L + OE./1

Bargain purchase option price In a lease, the lessee may be given the opportunity to purchase the leased asset at a future date. If at the time the lease is signed that purchase option price is considered so low that it virtually ensures that the lessee will purchase the asset (e.g., $1), then the purchase option price is designated as a bargain purchase option price, and the amount of the option price is included when computing minimum lease payments./4

Basic EPS If a company has a complex capital structure, two amounts are computed: basic EPS and diluted EPS. Basic EPS is computed as: (Net income − Preferred dividends) ÷ Weighted average number of common shares outstanding during the period./10

Billings on construction in progress The account that accumulates the total amounts billed to customers for a long-term construction project. Billings on construction in progress are subtracted from the costs incurred for construction in progress to compute the net amount./10

Bond discount Equal to the excess of the face value of a bond over the carrying value of a bond. If a bond is sold at a price below face value, it is sold at a discount./3, 7

Bond indenture The debt contract that specifies the terms related to a bond issuance./3

Bond premium Equal to the excess of the carrying value of a bond over the face value of a bond. If a bond is sold at a price above face value, it is sold at a premium./3, 7

Book value A general term that refers to the amount at which an item is recorded in a company's financial records. With respect to long-term assets, book value equals the historical cost less any portion expensed as part of the depreciation, depletion, and amortization process./6

Book value per share Common shareholders' equity (i.e., contributed capital associated with common stock plus retained earnings) ÷ Number of common shares outstanding./2

Book/tax differences Differences between the way that GAAP and the Internal Revenue Code account for an item./11

Business combinations A general term that applies when one company (parent) acquires a controlling interest in another company (subsidiary). Business combinations can be effected as a merger, consolidation, or a parent/subsidiary relationship./8

Business risk With reference to a debt agreement, business risk is primarily determined by the risk of generating sales and/or service revenues sufficient to service the debt./3

Callable bond A bond for which the issuing corporation (debtor) has the discretion to require the holder of the bond (creditor) to redeem it under prespecified terms./3

Capital budgeting A formal internal investment decision process used to determine whether to accept projects that require investment in productive assets./6

Capital lease Accountants classify leases that transfer the risks and rewards of ownership from the lessor to the lessee as capital leases. Determination of whether a lease is a capital lease or an operating lease is made independently by the lessee and lessor. To be classified as a capital lease, a lease should meet one of four stipulated criteria. If classified as a capital lease to the lessee, the leased asset and lease obligation are recognized by the lessee in its financial statements. A lease classified as a capital lease by a lessor is further classified as either a sales-type lease or a direct financing lease. (lessees)/4, (lessors)/7

Capital maintenance approach The capital maintenance approach measures income (loss) during an accounting period as the amount of increase (decrease) in net assets, after adjusting for any investments by owners and distributions to owners. Under the capital maintenance approach, individual transactions during a period need not be identified./1

Capital structure The mix of debt and equity used to finance a company's assets./2

Capital structure leverage ratio Average total assets ÷ Average common stockholders' equity./MA

Capitalization The act of increasing an asset account to recognize probable future economic benefits of a past or expected cash outflow./1

Cash balance plans A type of defined benefit plan that mimics a 401(k) plan. During the late 1990s, employers began switching to cash balance plans as a way of making their pension plans more attractive to younger, more mobile employees./12

Cash dividends Dividends paid in cash./2

Cash flow from operations to current liabilities ratio Cash flow from operations ÷ Average current liabilities. This ratio is frequently labeled as the cash flow from operations ratio./MA

Ceiling Used when determining the designated market value to apply in the lower of cost or market balance sheet valuation of inventory. The ceiling is the *maximum* amount allowable as designated market value, and it equals the inventory's net realizable value (estimated sales price less costs to complete and dispose)./9

Change in estimate Accountants use estimates about the future throughout the accounting process (e.g., estimated useful life, estimated salvage value, estimated warranty costs, etc.). Almost all estimates eventually prove not to be exact. When conditions change and accountants believe that new estimates are warranted, accountants change the estimated amounts used in the accounting process./10

Change in principle This term is better described as a change in accounting method. In a change in principle, a company changes from one generally accepted method of accounting for an item to another generally accepted method of accounting (e.g., from the straight-line method to a declining balance method of depreciation). A change in principle is reported, net of income tax effect, on the income statement after income from continuing operations./10

Change in reporting entity A situation in which the reporting entity fundamentally changes: e.g., a company acquires another company./10

Classified balance sheet A form of balance sheet in which assets and liabilities are grouped into current and noncurrent portions. These classifications help users assess a company's creditworthiness./1

Cliff vesting In a stock option plan, a situation where all options vest at the end of the vesting period./12

Collateral Assets pledged by a borrower to a lender to secure a loan./3

Collateral trust bonds Bonds secured by investments in lower risk securities that are held in trust./3

Common earnings leverage ratio (Net income − Preferred stock dividends) ÷ [Net income + $(1 - t)$ Interest expense]./MA

Compensatory A stock option plan is compensatory if accounting for the stock options requires compensation expense to be recorded. Most firms craft their stock option plans so that when the intrinsic value method is used, the options are noncompensatory and no compensation expense is recorded./12

Completed contract method One of two possible methods used to account for long-term construction contracts. The completed contract method recognizes revenues and expenses when the contract is completed. The alternate method, percentage of completion, is the preferred method under GAAP./10

Complex capital structure A term that pertains to how a company's assets have been financed. A complex capital structure is one in which the company has at least one dilutive security outstanding./10

Comprehensive income Change in equity (net assets) of an entity during a period from transactions and other events and circumstances from nonowner sources. It includes all changes in equity during a period except those resulting from investments by owners and distributions to owners./1

Consolidated financial statements Financial statements that reflect the combination of a parent company and subsidiary company's financial statements; they reflect an economic entity rather than a legal entity./8

Consolidation Refers to the process of combining the financial statements of a parent company with those of a subsidiary company to create consolidated financial statements. When referring to a specific type of business combination, a consolidation is one in which one firm (Company A) purchases another company (Company B), resulting in a new company, Company C, after the transaction is completed./8

Construction in progress The account that accumulates all the costs incurred to construct the project in long-term construction contact accounting. If the percentage of completion method is used, the amount of profit/loss recognized to date is also accumulated in the construction in progress account./10

Contra account A contra account is used by accountants to reduce a related account indirectly. By using a contra account, the account of interest can be kept at its previous book value. Examples of contra accounts are treasury stock (a contra equity account) and accumulated depreciation (a contra asset account)./5, 6

Contributed capital A portion of owners' equity. Contributed capital is equal to the resources (assets) contributed to the firm by its owners. It includes the proceeds from issuance of common stock, preferred stock, options, and warrants./1

Convertible debt Outstanding bonds that at the creditor's option may be converted into common shares at a prespecified exchange rate./2

Convertible preferred stock Similar to preferred stock, except that the holder has the option to exchange the convertible preferred stock for common stock under some preagreed exchange ratio./2

Core competencies Key economic assets and processes that allow delivery of goods and services in the value chain./MA

Corridor In a defined benefit pension plan, the corridor is defined as 10% of the greater of the beginning-of-the-period projected benefit obligation or the fair market value of plan assets. The cumulative balance in the unamortized gains/losses account is amortized only if the beginning-of-the-period amount exceeds the corridor./12

Cost method A method used to account for investments in common stocks in which the investor does not have significant influence or control over the investee company's operations. Under the cost method, dividends are recognized as income. Securities accounted for under the cost method can be classified as trading or available-for-sale if they have readily determinable market values./8

Cost method—treasury stock Under the cost method, treasury stock is recorded at its cost. Upon reissuance of the treasury stock, any economic gain/loss is computed as the difference between its cost and reissue price./5

Cost-to-cost method Used when the percentage of completion method is used in long-term construction project accounting. In the cost-to-cost method, the project's percentage of completion is computed as the total costs incurred divided by the total estimated project costs./10

Credit risk For a financial instrument, credit risk relates to the fact that the creditworthiness of the issuer of the financial instrument can change./MB

Cumulative effect of changes in accounting principles An amount presented, net of tax, on the income statement after income from continuing operations. The amount represents the effects on prior period's revenues and expenses of changes in the way assets and liabilities are measured because a company changes the accounting principle it uses./1

Cumulative preferred stock The cumulative feature is a normal attribute of preferred stock. Any missed dividend payments in prior periods must be paid before common shareholders receive current dividends. Dividends not paid in prior periods on cumulative preferred stock are dividends in arrears./2

Current asset An asset is classified as current because it will be realized (i.e., converted to cash) within one year or within one operating cycle, whichever is longer./1

Current income tax liability Calculated on a yearly basis, the current income tax liability is the amount owed during the current year to the Internal Revenue Service (and state and local governments). Because corporations normally pay estimated taxes during the year, the current liability for the income taxes payable represents the amount owed less amount paid./11

Current liabilities A liability is classified as current because it is expected to be liquidated within the current year or operating cycle (normally by using current assets)./1

Current ratio Current assets ÷ Current liabilities./1, MA

Cyclicality The tendency of sales and expenses to ebb and flow over the business cycle./MA

Date of declaration In the dividend process, the date that a company's board of directors obligates the firm to distribute a dividend./2

Date of payment (distribution) In the dividend process, the date that a company distributes a dividend./2

Date of record In the dividend process, the cutoff date that establishes who will receive a dividend./2

Debenture bond A bond that is secured not by a particular asset but by a general claim against all of a firm's assets./3

Debt covenants and restrictions The portion of debt agreements that allow creditors to maintain some control over future management activities through prespecified restrictions on management behavior (e.g., restrictions on (1) the amount of dividends that can be paid, (2) the ability of the firm to issue new debt and equity, and (3) maintenance of minimum ratios such as a debt to equity ratio)./2

Declining balance Used to describe a family of accelerated cost allocation methods (e.g., double-declining-balance, also known as 200% declining balance; 150% declining balance) that are most commonly used to compute depreciation expense. A declining balance method multiplies the asset's beginning-of-the-period book value by some multiple of the straight-line percentage rate. For example, if the straight-line percentage rate is defined as $1 \div n$ (where n is the asset's estimated useful life), double declining balance depreciation expense for any period is computed as follows: beginning-of-the-period book value $\times (1 \div n) \times 200\%$./6

Deductible amounts Temporary book/tax differences that will cause taxable income to be less than pretax income in periods when they reverse. Deductible amounts lead to the computation of deferred income tax assets./11

Deferred expenses Recognition of an expense *after* the cash outflow occurs. Deferred expenses are reported on the balance sheet as assets./1

Deferred income tax asset valuation allowance account Used when 100% of a NOL carryforward is not expected to be used. The valuation allowance account reduces the deferred income tax asset associated with the NOL./11

Deferred income tax assets Result from book/tax temporary differences that are classified as deductible amounts and lead to the acceleration of tax payments before income tax expense is recognized in the income statement. Deferred tax assets are computed by multiplying end-of-year cumulative deductible amounts by the future income tax rates scheduled for the years in which the deductible amounts are estimated to reverse./11

Deferred income tax liabilities Result from book/tax temporary differences that are classified as taxable amounts and lead to the deferral of tax payments after income tax expense is recognized in the income statement. Deferred tax liabilities are computed by multiplying end-of-year cumulative taxable amounts by the future income tax rates scheduled for the years in which the taxable amounts are estimated to reverse./11

Deferred pension cost In a defined benefit pension plan, if additional pension liability is increased (decreased), the corresponding account affected is deferred pension cost. To the extent that deferred pension cost is less than any unamortized prior service cost balance, it is reported as an asset. To the extent that deferred pension cost is greater than any unamortized prior service cost balance, it is reported in stockholders' equity as a component of accumulated other comprehensive income./12

Deferred revenues Recognition of income *after* the cash inflow occurs. Deferred revenues are reported on the balance sheet as liabilities./1

Defined benefit plan In a defined benefit plan, employers incur the obligation to provide a definite pension payment to employees throughout the employee's retirement period, as determined by the pension plan's benefit formula./12

Defined contribution plan In a defined contribution plan [e.g., a 401 (k) or 403 (b) plan], employers incur the obligation to provide an annual cash payment on behalf of the employees to the employees' plan. Unlike a defined benefit plan, the company has no obligation to make certain payments to the employees after they retire. An employee's retirement fund depends upon the employee's investment choices and the investment success of the fund chosen by the employee./12

Deplete *See* **depletion**./6

Depletion Refers to a cost allocation process for long-lived natural resource assets./6

Depreciation Refers to a cost allocation process for long-lived tangible assets (e.g., property, plant, and equipment)./6

Derivative financial instrument A financial instrument that derives its value from another item (e.g., put and call options derive their value from the value of the stock on which the options are made)./MB

Designated market value Used when determining the lower or cost or market balance sheet valuation of inventory. Designated market is the replacement cost of the inventory, but it can not be greater than a ceiling value or lower than a floor value./9

Detachable warrants Attached to bonds that are sold, detachable stock warrants give buyers the right to become owners by exercising the option to purchase stock conveyed by the warrants./3

Development costs A term used to refer both to natural resources and tangible assets. When related to natural resource assets, development costs are both tangible (e.g., heavy equipment to drill and transport the resource) and intangible (e.g., the costs of drilling and constructing mine shafts, wells, etc.). Tangible development costs are capitalized as part of the equipment account. Intangible development costs are capitalized as part of the natural resources account because the costs are inseparable from the natural resource (e.g., the pipe used to drill an oil well cannot be moved to another well site). When related to tangible assets, particularly in the context of research and development costs, development is the translation of research into a plan or design./6

Diluted EPS If a company has a complex capital structure, two amounts are computed: basic EPS and diluted EPS. In computing diluted EPS, the computation of basic EPS is adjusted for the assumed conversion of dilutive securities (potential common stock securities), which results in diluted EPS being less than basic EPS. The intent is to show the worst case to current and potential investors, how low EPS could go if dilutive securities outstanding had been converted during the period./10

Dilutive securities Securities that allow the holders to convert them and obtain common stock (e.g., convertible debt, convertible preferred stock, stock rights, warrants, and options). The diluted EPS computation assumes the conversion of outstanding dilutive securities./10

Dilutive With respect to a diluted EPS computation, the assumed conversion of a dilutive security is dilutive if the resulting diluted EPS amount would decrease./10

Direct financing lease A lessor lease classification when the lease is treated as a capital lease. Direct financing leases are used primarily by banks, finance companies, and insurance companies, where the profit from the lease is based upon the interest income generated by the lease. In a direct financing type lease, the fair market value of the asset is equal to the book value of the leased asset./7

Direct write-off method A method of accounting for bad debts that is not acceptable for GAAP, in which bad debts expense is recognized in the period in which the accountant writes off the receivable as uncollectible./9

Discontinued operations The result from the disposal of an entire segment of a company's business. Discontinued operations amounts are reported, net of income tax effect, in the income statement after income from continuing operations. Two amounts are reported: (1) the operating loss for the discontinued segment prior to the measurement date and (2) the actual/estimated operating loss for the discontinued segment between the measurement date and disposal date, plus (minus) the actual/ estimated gain (loss) on disposal./1, 10

Discount *See* **bond discount.**

Discounted (Discounting) This term can be used in several ways. (1) In a present value problem, discounting is the process of computing the present value of future cash flows. Therefore, present value represents the discounted value of future cash flows. (2) In a retail situation, discounting is the process of reducing the price of goods to be sold. (3) With regard to accounts receivable, discounting is the process of selling the accounts receivable for cash at below face value./3

Distributions to owners Decreases in net assets of a particular enterprise resulting from transferring assets, rendering services, or incurring liabilities by the enterprise to owners. Distributions to owners decrease ownership interest (or equity) in an enterprise./1

Dividends Distributions of assets to owners. Types of dividends include cash, property, scrip, liquidating, and stock. Cash, property, and scrip are deemed returns on investment, and a liquidating dividend is deemed to be a return of investment. A stock dividend is a misnomer in that no assets are distributed; rather, the company issues new shares on a pro rata basis to its existing shareholders./2

Dividends in arrears Dividend amounts on cumulative preferred stock that were not paid in prior periods./2

Dollar value LIFO A special case of LIFO inventory valuation where LIFO is applied to pools of goods rather than specific goods. The records of the LIFO pools are kept in terms of dollars rather than units./9

Dutch auction A type of tender offer to repurchase outstanding shares. In a Dutch auction, after establishing a minimum and maximum price, a corporation gathers information from shareholders on the price that shareholders are willing to accept in exchange for the number of shares that they hold. The corporation aggregates the bids and constructs a supply curve that indicates the cumulative number of shares that will be tendered at each price. The corporation then moves up the supply curve until it reaches the desired number of shares to repurchase, and it pays the price at that number of shares to every shareholder at or below that price./5

Earned Related to income recognition, revenue is earned if the firm has expended all or nearly all of the resources needed to generate revenue./10

Earnings per share (EPS) A summary statistic that standardizes a company's performance in generating net income based on the number of common shares outstanding. Chapter 10 discusses how to make EPS computations. If a company has a simple capital structure, one EPS amount, labeled EPS, is presented. If a company has a complex capital structure, two EPS amounts are presented: basic EPS and diluted EPS./10

Economic consequences This term refers to a given party's misfortune to bear some harm as a result of a given accounting rule or to a comparative advantage by one party over another created by an accounting rule. The FASB considers the economic consequences of proposed accounting standards./1

Economic order quantity (EOQ) A computation of the optimum amount of inventory to order at any particular time. Ways to compute EOQ are discussed in managerial and cost accounting courses and are not covered in the text./9

Effective income tax rate For financial accounting purposes, this is computed as follows: Income tax expense ÷ Income before income taxes./11

Effective interest method The GAAP method used to compute interest expense/income and discount/premium amortization on bonds and notes. Under the effective interest method, interest expense/income each period is computed as the beginning-of-period book value times the effective interest rate per period. Any difference between interest expense/income and interest payable/receivable is recognized as bond discount/premium amortization./3

Effective interest rate Computed at the date a bond or note is executed, the effective interest rate is the interest rate in a present value computation that discounts the future cash flows back to the issue (market) price of a bond or note./3

Emerging Issues Task Force (EITF) A committee that assists the FASB. The charge of the EITF is to reach consensus (15 of 17 members) on quickly emerging, high-profile accounting issues that are likely to have material effects on financial statements./1

EOQ *See* **economic order quantity.**/9

EPS *See* **earnings per share.**/10

Equipment note A note payable secured by equipment. Usually, the money is borrowed to buy the specific equipment used as collateral./3

Equity method A method used to account for investments in common stocks in which the investor has significant influence over the investee company's operations but does not have control. Under the equity method, the investor company (1) accrues its pro rata share of the investee company's net income and reports it as income and (2) reports its pro rata share of dividends as a reduction of its investment. Securities accounted for under the equity method cannot be classified as trading or available-for-sale./8

Equity Residual interest in the assets of an entity that remains after deducting its liabilities. In a business enterprise, the equity is the ownership interest./1

Equity security A security that gives the holder ownership of the firm (i.e., common and preferred stock) or the right to acquire ownership (e.g., stock options, rights, warrants)./2

Executory contract An agreement that is mutually unperformed by both parties, under which both parties agree to take future action (e.g., lease contracts, purchase commitments)./2

Executory costs In a lease arrangement, executory costs are the normal costs of maintaining and insuring the asset. Executory costs are excluded when computing minimum lease payments because they are not paid in order to acquire the asset./4

Exit barriers Impediments to a company leaving an industry (e.g., firms that have substantial special purpose assets may find it difficult to sell the assets and exit the industry)./MA

Expected long-term rate of return on plan assets In a defined benefit pension plan, this amount is estimated by the employer, the pension plan, and actuaries representing both the employer and pension plan. This expected rate of return is the basis for planning future employer contributions to the pension plan and pension plan investment strategies. The expected return on plan assets is computed as the beginning-of-the-period long-term expected rate of return on plan assets multiplied by the beginning-of-the-period fair value of plan assets./12

Expenses Outflows or other using up of assets or incurrences of liabilities during a period from delivering or producing goods, rendering services, or other activities that constitute the entity's ongoing major or central operations./1

Extraordinary items An amount presented, net of tax, on the income statement after income from operations. Extraordinary items are events that are both *unusual in nature* and *infrequent in occurrence*./1

Factoring In accounts receivable factoring, receivables are transferred to an entity called a "factor" in exchange for cash. The factor profits by paying less than face value for the accounts receivable. How much less than face value is determined by the risk of receivable collection that the factor assumes (i.e., the factoring is with or without recourse)./9

Fair market value of plan assets In a defined benefit pension plan, the fair market value of the assets held by the pension plan are determined at the end of each period (with reference to quoted market prices for stocks and bonds and appraisals for property)./12

Fair value method In a stock option plan, the fair value method measures the amount of compensation expense related to the stock option as its fair value, computed using a appropriate option pricing model, on the measurement date (assumed to be the grant date). Most companies do not use the fair value method; rather, they use the intrinsic value method./12

FASB *See* **Financial Accounting Standards Board.**

FIFO (first-in, first-out) An inventory cost flow assumption that assumes the inventory units sold during a period were the first ones acquired, leaving the last ones acquired in ending inventory./9

Financial Accounting Standards Board (FASB) The private sector organization that promulgates accounting standards./1

Financial capital maintenance The capital maintenance approach computes net income (loss) as the change in net assets during a period, adjusted for any contributions by owners and distributions to owners. The financial capital maintenance approach measures net assets in terms of dollars. GAAP-based financial statements reflect a financial capital maintenance approach./1

Financial instrument A security that gives the holder a right to receive or a requirement to pay cash in the future./MB

Financial risk A fixed-charge phenomenon related to the presence of debt financing. Financial risk is the risk that fixed interest payments cannot be made./3

Financing activities A company's activities related to raising capital to fund investment and operating activities. Firms issue common stock, preferred stock, stock options, long-term notes, bonds, and other hybrid securities (e.g., convertible debt) in order to obtain cash.

First-in, first-out *See* **FIFO**./9

Fixed asset turnover ratio Sales ÷ Average property, plant, and equipment./MA

Fixed options In a stock option plan, a situation where vesting is based solely on continued service./12

Floor used when determining the designated market value to apply in the lower or cost or market balance sheet valuation of inventory. The floor is the *minimum* amount allowable as designated market value, and it equals the inventory's net realizable value minus normal profit margin (estimated sales price less costs to complete and dispose less normal profit margin)/9.

Free cash flow [*Students should be careful because this term does not have a universal definition.*] We define free cash flow as the excess of cash flow after meeting operating requirements and investing in all profitable projects. Free cash flow can be used to pay dividends, repurchase and retire stock, and repurchase and retire debt./5

Full costing One of two alternative methods used to account for natural resource exploration costs. All exploration costs are capitalized, even if the results were unsuccessful, under the rationale that all costs necessary to find usable natural resources are capitalizable. *See also* the alternative method, **successful efforts**./6

Funded In a defined benefit pension plan, the plan is funded if a third party trustee administers the plan and employers make annual contributions to the plan./12

GAAP *See* **generally accepted accounting principles.**

Gains Increases in net assets from peripheral or incidental transactions of an entity and from all other transactions and other events and circumstances affecting the entity during a period except those that result from revenues or investments by owners./1

Generally accepted accounting principles (GAAP) GAAP is comprised of rules, procedures, and historical precedents that are used to prepare U.S. financial statements./1

Goodwill An intangible asset recorded when the fair market value paid exceeds the sum of the fair market values of the net assets acquired in a business combination accounted for using the purchase method. Goodwill is amortized over its estimated useful life not to exceed a maximum period (40 years at the time the text was written, but proposed to be 20 years beginning in 2001 in an FASB exposure draft outstanding at the time the text was written). /8

Graded vesting In a stock option plan, a situation where a portion of the options vests each year./12

Greenmail A process in which an investor may acquire a large block of stock and threaten a hostile takeover unless management buys out the greenmailer at a price premium./5

Gross margin Also call *gross profit*, gross margin equals sales minus cost of goods sold./1

Gross margin percentage Also call *gross profit percentage*, gross margin equals gross margin divided by sales./1

Gross profit margin ratio (or **gross profit ratio**) Gross profit margin ÷ Sales./MA

Gross profit percentage *See* **gross margin percentage.**/1

Gross profit *See* **gross margin.**/1

Guaranteed residual value In a lease arrangement, the leased asset has a residual value (also known as a market value or salvage value) at the end of the lease. If the lessee guarantees that the asset will be worth at least a minimum amount at the end of the lease, that amount is designated as a guaranteed residual value, and the amount is included in the computation of minimum lease payments./1

Held-to-maturity securities Investments in debt securities for which managers have the intent and ability to hold to maturity. Investments in equity securities cannot be classified as held-to-maturity./7

Historical cost The fair market value of the asset at acquisition (the initial acquisition price) is often referred to as historical cost. Therefore, an asset's historical cost is it acquisition price./1, 6

Impairment A term applied to different types of assets (e.g., property, plant, and equipment; intangible assets; long-term bond investments), reflecting the situation that an asset's fair market value has permanently declined below the asset's carrying value. The rules determining whether an asset has been impaired are different for long-term productive assets and for financial assets./6

Implicit rate In a lease, the implicit rate is computed from the lessor's point of view. The implicit rate is the lessor's rate of return on the leasing transaction./4, 7

Individual expense ratios Individual expense amount ÷ Sales./MA

Interest cost In a defined benefit pension plan, interest cost is computed as the beginning of the period PBO multiplied by the beginning-of-the-period settlement interest rate./12

Interest coverage ratio (Income before income taxes + interest expense) ÷ Interest expense. This ratio is frequently labeled as *times interest earned*./MA

Interperiod tax allocation The process of allocating income tax expense among accounting periods because of temporary book/tax differences. Interperiod tax allocation results in deferred tax assets and deferred tax liabilities being recognized in financial statements./11

In-the-money Regarding stock options, an option is "in the money" if the option price is less than the stock's current market price./10

Intraperiod tax allocation The process of allocating total income tax expense on the income statement to: income from continuing operations, discontinued operations, extraordinary items, and cumulative effects of accounting changes./11

Intrinsic value method In a stock option plan, the intrinsic value method measures the amount of compensation expense related to the stock option as follows: (Stock fair market value at grant date minus option price) × (Number of shares under option) Most companies use the intrinsic value method, and craft the stock option plan so that it is noncompensatory by setting the option price equal to the market price on the grant date./12

Inventory turnover ratio Cost of goods sold ÷ Average inventory./MA

Investing activities A company's activities related to the purchase or creation of tangible items such as land, operating plants, rental properties, equipment, and delivery vehicles, and the purchase or creation of intangible items such as copyrights, patents, and franchise rights./1

Investments by owners Increases in net assets of a particular enterprise resulting from transfers to it from other entities of something of value to obtain or increase ownership interest (or equity) in it. Investments by owners are most commonly received as assets but may also include services or satisfaction or conversion of liabilities of the enterprise./1

Last-in, first-out *See* LIFO./9

Leasing The process of using an executory contract such that the lessee obtains the right to use an asset in the future in return for certain stipulated cash flows, and the lessor relinquishes the right to use the asset in return for stipulated cash flows./4

Lessee's incremental borrowing rate In a lease transaction, the lessee's incremental borrowing rate is the interest rate at which lessee could borrow to finance the purchase of an asset under similar terms to that contained in the lease./4

Liabilities Probable future sacrifices of economic benefits arising from present obligations of a particular entity to transfer assets or provide services to other entities in the future as a result of past transactions or events./1

Liability (actuarial) gain/loss In a defined benefit pension plan, the increase in PBO (liability loss) or decrease in PBO (liability gain) that results from the actuary using new assumptions. Each period, the actuary estimates PBO using the most current assumptions about items such as interest rates, mortality, pay increases, and job classifications. The liability gain/loss does not receive immediate recognition as part of pension cost in the period generated. Instead, recognition as pension cost is delayed and occurs only if the total unamortized gain/loss is greater than the corridor amount./12

LIFO (last-in, first-out) An inventory cost flow assumption that assumes the inventory units sold during a period were the last ones acquired, leaving the first ones acquired in ending inventory./9

LIFO conformity rule The Internal Revenue Code's LIFO conformity rule requires that firms using LIFO on the tax return also use LIFO for financial reporting purposes./9

LIFO reserve The amount necessary to adjust the financial statements to a LIFO basis when the inventory cost method used is different, usually FIFO. The use of a LIFO reserve allows a company to keep its internal records on one basis but to use LIFO for financial reporting purposes./MD

Liquidating dividend A dividend deemed to be a return of capital, which occurs when dividends are declared and the corporation has no retained earnings./2

Liquidity Refers to how long it will take until the asset is converted into cash (i.e., how close an asset is to realizing its economic benefits)./1

Long-term debt to equity ratio Long-term debt ÷ Shareholders' equity. Shareholders equity can be defined either as the *book value of shareholders' equity* or the *market value of shareholders' equity*./MA

Long-term debt to total assets ratio Long-term debt ÷ Total assets./MA

Losses Decreases in net assets from peripheral or incidental transactions of an entity and from all other transactions and other events and circumstances affecting the entity during a period except those that result from expenses or distributions to owners./1

Lower-of-cost-or-market (LCM) The amount at which inventory is reported on the balance sheet. Market is "designated market," and cost is determined either by applying specific identification or a cost flow assumption (e.g., FIFO, LIFO, weighted average)./9

Market risk For a financial instrument, market risk relates to the fact that the underlying interest rates in financial markets change./MB

Market value A general term that indicates the monetary value of an exchange in an arm's-length transaction between two independent parties./1

Market-related fair value In a defined benefit pension plan, the average of several years of the end-of-year fair value of plan assets of a pension plan./12

Market-to-book ratio Market price per share ÷ Book value per share./2

Material *See* **materiality.**

Materiality A concept underlying financial reporting. An item is material to the financial statements if it is large enough to make a difference in the decisions of investors and creditors./1

Measurement date In a discontinued operation situation, the date that the company formally agrees to dispose of a business segment./10

Merger A term sometimes used in the popular press as a synonym for business combination. When referring to a specific type of business combination, a merger is one in which one firm (Company A) purchases another company (Company B), after which only Company A remains./8

Minimum lease payments In a lease transaction, the minimum lease payments are computed as the sum of the following: (1) minimum rental payments over the lease term (excluding executory costs), (2) any down payment, (3) and any one-lump-sum payment at the end of the lease (e.g., bargain purchase option price, guaranteed residual value)./4

Minimum pension liability In a defined benefit pension plan, at year-end, the excess of ABO over fair value of plan assets. If ABO is less than fair value of plan assets, minimum liability is undefined. Therefore, the minimum pension liability represents the unfunded portion of ABO./12

Modification of terms Applies in a troubled debt situation in which the creditor agrees to modify the terms of an existing debt agreement in order to provide relief for a debtor./7

Modified accelerated cost recovery system (MACRS) A depreciation method used on tax returns. [This method is not illustrated in the text.]/6

Mortgage bonds Bonds secured by real estate./3

Net assets Assets minus liabilities./1

Net method As a general term in accounting, the net method can be used to describe a process that takes two or more accounts and combines them into one amount (i.e., the amounts are netted). With respect to inventory, the preferred method is to record credit sales net of any allowable sales discounts for early payment, and record purchases net of any allowable purchase discounts for early payment./9

Net operating loss (NOL) A tax term, a NOL is generated when expenses deducted on a tax return exceed revenues included on a tax return. A NOL can be carried back for two years or forward for 20 years. If carried back, a tax refund receivable occurs. If carried forward, a deferred tax asset is recognized. A deferred income tax asset valuation allowance account may be used to reduce the amount of the deferred income tax asset./11

Net profit margin ratio (sometimes called *net profit margin*), computed as [Net income + (1 − t) Interest expense] ÷ Sales./MA

Net realizable value As a general term, it is an indication of an item's current market value when selling an asset. It equals the amount that would be received upon selling the item in the normal course of business./1. The term net realizable value is also used in two specific contexts. With respect to *inventory*, net realizable value is the estimated sales price less the estimated cost to complete and dispose. With respect to *accounts receivable*, net realizable value is the face value of the receivables less the amount estimated not to be collected (face less allowance for doubtful accounts./1, 9

NOL *See* **net operating loss.**/11

Noncompensatory A stock option plan is noncompensatory if accounting for the stock options requires no compensation expense to be recorded./12

Noncurrent asset An asset is classified as noncurrent because it will be realized (i.e., converted to cash) after one year or one operating cycle, whichever is longer./1

Noncurrent liabilities A liability is classified as noncurrent because it is expected to be liquidated beyond the current year or operating cycle./1

Off-balance-sheet financing Off-balance-sheet financing occurs when a company obtains the right to use an asset in return for an agreement to make future cash payments but the arrangement is not required by GAAP to be recognized on the company's books as an asset and liability. Leasing is frequently used to achieve off-balance-sheet financing./4

Operating activities A company's activities related selling its products or performing services. These activities include the purchase inventory and how to pay for purchases, whether to make or buy inventory, how to implement credit policy, how to establish distribution channels, and other decisions such as employee compensation (including setting levels of executive compensation, deciding whether to establish a pension plan, and selecting appropriate health-care plans)./1

Operating cash flow to capital expenditures ratio Operating cash flow ÷ Capital expenditures./MA

Operating cash flow to total liabilities ratio Operating cash flow ÷ Average total liabilities./MA

Operating cycle The operating cycle is defined as the length of time that it takes a firm to begin with cash and end with cash. The cycle usually involves cash payment for acquiring inventory or producing inventory (materials, labor, and overhead), sale, and finally, cash collection./1

Operating lease Accountants classify leases that do not transfer the risks and rewards of ownership to the lessee as operating leases. Determination of whether a lease is a capital lease or an operating lease is made independently by the lessee and lessor. To be classified as an operating lease, a lease should fail each of the four stipulated criteria. If classified as an operating lease by a lessee, the asset and lease obligation are *not* recognized by the lessee in its financial statements. If classified as an operating by a lessor, the leased asset remains on the lessor's financial statements. (lessees)/4, (lessors)/7

Ordinary annuity A series of equal cash payments or receipts in the future at the same interval (e.g., monthly, annually), with the first cash flow occurring one period in the future (at the *end* of each period)./Appendix B

Originating temporary difference The first temporary book/tax difference in the treatment of a particular revenue or expense item (e.g., in year 1, an expense amount reported under GAAP is greater than allowed under the Internal Revenue Code)./11

Other comprehensive income Reported on the statement of comprehensive income, other comprehensive income reflects changes in net assets that are not deemed to be transactions with owners and which do not affect net income (e.g., unrealized gains/losses on available-for-sale securities)./7

Out-of-the-money Regarding stock options, an option is "out of the money" if the option price is greater than the stock's current market price./10

Owners' equity *See* **equity.** In an accounting system, owners' equity equals assets minus liabilities. For a corporation, owners' equity is called stockholders' equity or shareholders' equity./1

Parent/subsidiary relationship When referring to a specific type of business combination, a parent/subsidiary relationship exists when one firm (Company A) purchases another company (Company B), and both Company A and Company B remain as separate legal entities after the transaction is completed./8

Participating preferred stock A feature of preferred stock that allows a preferred shareholder to share in additional dividends beyond normal dividend preference. Typically, preferred stock is nonparticipating./2

PBO *See* **projected benefit obligation.**/12

Pension cost In a defined benefit pension plan, the amount is computed annually. Its components are service cost, interest cost, expected return on pension plan assets, amortization of prior service cost, amortization of gains/losses, and amortization of any transition amount. This amount is normally expensed, but amounts related to activities that have future benefits (e.g., pension cost for employees who manufacturer inventory) may be capitalized./12

Pension expense *See* **pension cost.**/12

Pension obligation In a defined benefit pension plan, the pension obligation is a measure of the amounts owed because of employees' past service. Three pension obligation amounts are computed, projected benefit obligation (PBO), accumulated benefit obligation (ABO), and vested benefit obligation (VBO), with PBO being the primary measure used to compute pension cost./12

Percentage of completion method One of two possible methods used to account for long-term construction contracts. The percentage of completion method is the preferred method, and it recognizes revenues, expenses, and profits during construction based upon the percent of the project's completion. *See also* the **completed contract method.**/10

Performance options In a stock option plan, a situation where the number of options or other option terms depend on future performance./12

Period costs A cost that is not directly traceable to the production of a specific product, but rather is traceable to a particular accounting period./10

Periodic inventory system A system in which costs are accumulated during the period and assigned to inventory and cost of goods sold at period's end. Although most companies use a perpetual inventory system in which costs are assigned continuously upon each individual inventory purchase and sale, we have used only the periodic inventory system, in order to simplify the text presentation. Perpetual inventory systems are covered thoroughly in managerial/cost accounting courses./9

Permanent difference Related to an item that is treated differently over its life for book and tax purposes. Deferred income taxes are not computed on permanent differences./11

Physical capital maintenance The capital maintenance approach computes net income (loss) as the change in net assets during a period adjusted for any contributions by owners and distributions to owners. The physical capital maintenance approach measures net assets in terms of the productive capacity of the company's assets. GAAP-based financial statements do not reflect a physical capital maintenance approach./1

Plan formula In a defined benefit pension plan, the plan formula specifies how pension benefits at retirement are to be computed. Usually, the plan formula is a function of three items: years of service at retirement, final pay (or average of the last few years of pay), and a percent amount for each year of service./12

Pooling of interests method A method used to record a company's controlling investment in the common stock of a subsidiary company. The pooling of interests method records the investment at the book value of the assets acquired. As of the date the text was written, the FASB had issued an exposure draft that would prohibit the pooling of interests method beginning in 2001./8

Portfolio risk A complex topic covered in finance classes, portfolio risk is determined by the covariance of a project's cash flows with the cash flows of all other projects./6

Potential common stock *See* **dilutive securities.**/10

Preferred stock is an equity security that has debt-like features. Typically, preferred stock is cumulative, nonvoting, not convertible, and nonparticipating./2

Premium *See* **bond premium.**

Prepaid (accrued) pension cost In a defined benefit pension plan, an employer records its (1) annual pension cost and (2) annual contribution to the pension plan, with the difference being recorded as prepaid (accrued) pension cost. At the end of a period, if the cumulative amount recorded for pension cost exceeds the cumulative cash pension payments, then the difference is reported as *accrued pension cost, a liability*. If the cumulative amount recorded for pension cost is less than the cumulative cash pension payments, then the difference is reported as *prepaid pension cost, an asset.*/12

Prepaid expenses *See* **deferred expenses.**

Present value Present value is a concept used in time value of money problems. In a present value computation, the interest component of a future series of cash flows is removed, leaving only the noninterest portion, which is its present value. Present value is a measure of current value applied to financial instruments: the market price of financial instruments such as bonds and notes is the present value of future cash flows discounted at the current market interest rate.

Present value depreciation method Not commonly used in financial reports. Depreciation expense for the current year equals the present value of the remaining cash flows to be generated by the depreciable asset at the beginning of the year minus the present value of the remaining cash flows to be generated by the depreciable asset at the end of the year./6

Present value of minimum lease payments In a lease, the computation of the present value of the minimum lease payments. In the present value computation, the lessor uses the implicit rate, and the lessee uses the lower of the lessee's incremental borrowing rate or the lessor's implicit rate (if known)./4

Price/Earnings Ratio (PE Ratio) Stock price per share ÷ EPS./MA

Prior service cost In a defined benefit pension plan, the increase in PBO from amending a pension plan and retroactively granting benefits is defined as prior service cost. Although the amount could represent a decrease in PBO (i.e., a prior service credit), we assume in the text that plan amendments increase PBO./12

Product costs Costs incurred to produce inventory that are directly traceable to the production of a specific product that will later be sold./10

Projected benefit obligation (PBO) In a defined benefit pension plan, PBO is the actuarially determined present value of estimated retirement payments calculated according to the pension plan benefit formula (using expected future salary levels) to be paid to employees because employees have worked and earned benefits until the current date./12

Property dividend A dividend in which the assets distributed are noncash assets (e.g., stock investments in other companies)./2

Purchase discount From the buyer's point of view, a purchase discount is a potential reduction in the purchase price of an item purchased on account (i.e., on credit) if the buyer pays off the account within a stipulated period of time. For example, in the terms 2/10, net 30, the seller offers a 2% discount if the account is paid within ten days; otherwise, the account is due in 30 days. The preferred method is to record purchases net of any available purchase discounts./9

Purchase method A method used to record a company's controlling investment in the common stock of a subsidiary company. The purchase method records the investment at its fair market value, and if the fair market value exceeds the sum of the fair market values of the net assets acquired, goodwill is recorded./8

Purchase returns and allowances An account that accumulates the reduction of amounts owed to suppliers because a purchaser either returned goods for credit or negotiated additional cost reductions after the sale was made. Purchase returns and allowances are reductions of the purchase price of inventory./9

Quick ratio (Cash + Marketable securities + Accounts receivable) ÷ Current liabilities./MA

Rate of return *See* **effective interest rate.**

Realizable Revenue is realizable when an event has occurred that reduces the uncertainty about collecting cash to an acceptable level./10

Realization Refers to the process of converting noncash assets into cash./10

Realized When cash is received from making a sale or performing a service, revenue has been realized./10

Replacement cost An indication of an item's current market value when buying an asset. It represents the amount that it would currently take to acquire an asset with the same productive characteristics./1

Research costs Costs related to a planned search for new knowledge. Under GAAP, research and development (R&D) costs are expensed as incurred./6

Restructurings In a restructuring, companies may lay off workers and rearrange and/or sell a portion of production lines or service-oriented facilities. Restructuring costs are reported as a line item in the income statement above income from continuing operations./10

Retained earnings A portion of owners' equity. Retained earnings is equal to the amount of assets that have been accumulated over time through operational activities (as measured by net income) but have not been distributed to owners./1

Return on Assets (ROA) (Net income + Interest expense, net of income taxes) ÷ Average total assets. Alternatively, ROA equals the net profit margin ratio multiplied by asset turnover ratio./MA

Return on Common Equity (ROCE) = ROA × Common earnings leverage ratio × Capital structure leverage ratio. In reduced form, ROCE = (Net income − Preferred stock dividends) ÷ Average common stockholders' equity./MA

Revenue expenditures One of two methods for deciding how to account for a cost that has been incurred. If a cost benefits the current period only, it is expensed and referred to as a revenue expenditure. If a cost benefits future periods, it is referred to a capital expenditure and is capitalized as an asset and allocated to future periods using some cost allocation method. GAAP has some exceptions to capital expenditure treatment (e.g., research and development expenses)./6

Revenues Inflows or other enhancements of assets of an entity or settlement of its liabilities (or a combination of both) during a period from delivering or producing goods, rendering services, or other activities that constitute the entity's ongoing major or central operations./1

Revenue recognition accounting Refers to a depletion method used by the SEC for a short period of time. The method is no longer used./6

Reversing temporary difference The offset in future periods of an originating temporary book/tax difference (e.g., in Year 1, an expense amount reported under GAAP that is greater than allowed under the Internal Revenue Code is an originating temporary difference; and in Year 2, an expense amount reported for the expense item under GAAP that is less than allowed under the Internal Revenue Code is a reversing temporary difference)./11

Sales discount From the seller's point of view, a sales discount is a potential reduction in the sales price of an item sold on account (i.e., on credit) if the buyer pays off the account within a stipulated period of time. For example, in the terms 2/10, net 30, the seller offers a 2% discount if the account is paid within ten days; otherwise, the account is due in 30 days. The preferred method is to record sales net of any available sales discounts./9

Sales returns and allowances An account that accumulates the amounts credited to purchasers because a purchaser either returned goods for credit or negotiated additional cost reductions after the sale was made. Sales returns and allowances are reductions of the amount of sales./9

Sales-type lease A lessor lease classification where the lease is treated as a capital lease. Sales-type leases are used primarily by dealers and manufacturers, where the profit from the lease is based upon both (1) the spread between the fair value of the leased asset and its book value and (2) interest income generated by the lease. In a sales-type lease, the fair market value of the asset is almost always greater than the book value of the leased asset./7

Scrip dividend A dividend that is declared with the cash payment delayed for a period of time beyond the normal time to pay dividends (e.g., payable in three months)./2

SEC *See* **Securities and Exchange Commission.**/1

Securities and Exchange Commission (SEC) The public sector organization that has statutory authority to set accounting standards. The SEC has delegated accounting standard setting to the FASB./1

Serial bond A bond that has several maturity dates (i.e., installments)./3

Service cost In a defined benefit pension plan, the actuarially determined present value of the increase in future benefits because an employee worked during the current year (service cost represents an increase in the employer's PBO)./12

Settlement Applies in a troubled debt situation in which the creditor agrees to settle the debt by canceling the debt agreement in return for consideration (cash, property, or the debtor's common stock). In a settlement, it is virtually certain that the fair value of the consideration received by the creditor is less than the carrying value of the debt, which leads to the creditor recognizing an extraordinary loss on the debt settlement./7

Significant influence A term used to describe the degree of influence that an investor company has on an investee company because the investor purchased the investee's common stock. *APB No. 18* discusses factors that reflect significant influence, the most important of which is that representatives put forth by the investor are elected to the investee's board of directors. In absence of evidence to the contrary, significant influence is deemed to occur when the investor owns 20% or more of the investee's common stock (ownership of greater than 50% would reflect control by the investor)./8

Simple capital structure A term that pertains to how a company's assets have been financed. A simple capital structure is one in which the company has no dilutive securities outstanding. In a simple capital structure, one amount is presented, labeled EPS, and it is computed as follows: (Net income − Preferred dividends) ÷ Weighted average number of common shares outstanding during the period./10

Specific assignment With respect to accounts receivable, a company borrows money, and the collection of specific receivables is designated as collateral for the repayment of the loan./9

Specific goods pooled LIFO A special case of LIFO inventory valuation where LIFO is applied to pools of goods rather than specific goods. The records of LIFO pools are kept in terms of units./9

Specific identification An inventory method that uses a precise matching of costs with units on hand and units sold by coding each inventory item separately. Instead of specific identification, most companies use cost flow assumptions such as FIFO, LIFO, and weighted average./9

Stated rate The stated interest rate is designated in a debt agreement, and it determines the amount of cash interest that will be paid. Cash interest equals the stated interest rate times the face value of the debt./3

Stock dividend A pro rata distribution of a company's own stock to its current owners. No assets are distributed, and the par value of the shares is not changed./2

Stock purchase right *See* **stock right.**

Stock right A security that allows the holder to acquire com-mon stock at a prespecified price. As a takeover defense, a company may issue stock purchase rights, which allows current shareholders to purchase an additional number of shares in the event that an outside party either acquires or attempts to acquire a substantial equity stake in the company./2

Stock split A pro rata distribution of a company's own stock to its current owners with the intent of reducing the company's stock price. No assets are distributed, and the par value of the stock is adjusted such that the total par value of the shares outstanding is the same before and after the split./2

Stock subscription agreement In order to market shares in initial (and, less often, seasoned) public offerings, firms sometimes enter into stock subscription agreements whereby the company agrees to issue shares in the future and a potential buyer agrees to pay for the shares in the future at a prespecified price./2

Stockholders' equity See **Owners' equity.**

Stockout costs The costs of not having enough inventory on hand to meet customer demand (e.g., lost sales, special ordering costs, overnight delivery charges)./9

Straight-line Used to describe a cost allocation method for various balance sheet amounts (e.g., long-term tangible and intangible assets; bond premium/amortization). Under a straight-line method, an equal amount of a capitalized cost is allocated to each period benefit. The straight-line percentage rate is defined as $1 \div n$ (where n is the item's estimated benefit period)./6

Straight-line method When applied to bonds and notes, the straight-line method determines the amount of bond premium/discount amortization. When applied to depreciable assets, the straight-line method determines the amount of depreciation expense. Under the straight-line method, the amount to be expensed (or recognized as revenue) is allocated equally over the number of periods affected./3

Successful efforts One of two alternative methods used to account for natural resource exploration costs. Exploration costs are capitalized only if the results were successful, under the rationale that only costs that lead to future revenue streams should be capitalized. *See also* the alternative method, **full costing.**/6

Sum-of-the-years' digits Used to describe a cost allocation method applied to depreciable assets. The depreciable amount is computed as the asset's cost minus estimated salvage value times a percentage that varies each year, which is computed as follows: (Remaining useful life at the beginning of the year) $\div$ {[n (n + 1)] $\div$ 2}, where n is the original estimated useful life of the asset./6

Taxable amounts Temporary book/tax differences that will cause taxable income to be greater than pretax income in periods when they reverse. Taxable amounts lead to the computation of deferred income tax liabilities./11

Taxable income On an income tax return, this is the excess of revenues over expenses; it is the amount on which income taxes payable is computed./11

Temporary difference Related to an item that is treated the same over its life for book and tax purposes, but for which different amounts for book and tax purposes are recognized during a particular year. Deferred income taxes are computed on temporary differences./11

Tender offer A process by which a company seeks to buy back and retire its shares. The company specifies that it will pay a certain fixed price for a fixed period of time to acquire a certain number of shares./5

Term bond A bond with a single maturity date./3

Times interest earned (see **Interest coverage ratio)** = (Income before income taxes + Interest expense) $\div$ Interest expense./MA

Trade notes payable Short-term notes issued in return for purchases of merchandise./9

Trade notes receivable Short-term notes received in return for sales of merchandise./9

Trading securities Those debt and equity security investments that have relatively short holding periods. These securities are bought as a means of avoiding the opportunity cost of lost interest and are sold to meet short-term cash needs. Trading debt securities are "marked to market" at each balance sheet date. The unrealized holding gain or loss (i.e., the difference between the book value and their current market value) is reflected in current income./7, 8

Transactions approach The accounting system classifies each change in net assets during the period for each transaction. Individual transactions and events are recorded as individual changes in financial statement elements. An income statement summarizes and lists revenues, expenses, gains, and losses; net income is the sum of these items./1

Treasury stock A company's own stock that it has repurchased temporarily with the intent to reissue the stock at a future date./5

Treasury stock method Used in computing diluted EPS. If the assumed conversion of a dilutive security would generate cash (as would normally be the case for the exercise of stock rights, warrants, and options), the treasury stock method assumes that the cash received upon issuance would be used to repurchase treasury stock at the average market price during the period./10

Troubled debt Troubled debt is the name given to the situation where a debtor is having trouble or may have trouble meeting its obligations under outstanding debt agreements. If the debtor cannot service the debt as required by the debt agreement, the debtor frequently negotiates with the creditor to either settle the debt or modify the terms of the debt./5

Troubled debt restructuring A general term that can apply to both debt settlements and modification of terms. In a troubled debt restructuring, a creditor provides debt relief to a creditor, and the creditor almost always recognizes an extraordinary loss on the restructuring./7

Underwriter The party, usually an investment banker, that guarantees an issue price (*firm underwriting*) or promises to obtain the best price possible for the issue (*best efforts underwriting*) when debt or equity securities are sold to the public./3

Unexpected return on pension plan assets *See* **asset gain/loss.**/12

Unfunded ABO *See* **minimum liability.**/12

Unfunded plan In a defined benefit pension plan, the plan is referred to as an unfunded plan if an employer self-administers the plan rather than hires a third party trustee to administer the plan./12

Unguaranteed residual value In a lease arrangement, the leased asset has a residual value (also known as a market value or salvage value) at the end of the lease. The unguaranteed residual value is defined from the lessor's perspective, and it equals the excess of any estimated residual value at the end of the lease term over the amount that is guaranteed by the lessee./7

Units-of-output Used to describe a cost allocation method applied to both tangible and intangible assets. The depreciation/depletion amount assigned to each period is based upon the usage during the period in some unit of measure (e.g., machine hours, miles traveled, tons mined) as a percentage of the total estimated units of production. When applied to natural resource assets, any estimated reclamation costs at the end of the asset should be treated as a cost to be allocated. The formula for computing the current year's amount is as follows: (Cost − Estimated salvage value) × (Usage in units this period ÷ Estimated total units of capacity)./6

Unrealized (holding) gain/loss The difference between an asset's book value and its fair market value. Under GAAP, unrealized gains/losses generally are not recorded. An exception is that investments in marketable securities accounted for as trading or available-for-sale under *SFAS No. 115* are marked to market at each balance sheet date, and the related unrealized gain/loss is recognized./7

Value chain A sequence of events unique to a firm that creates value and are not easily imitated by competitors./MA

VBO *See* **vested benefit obligation.**/12

Vested benefit obligation In a defined benefit pension plan, the portion of accumulated benefit obligation to which the employee is legally entitled if the employee leaves the organization./12

Vests Indicates when an employee has legally earned the right to a certain benefit, even if the employee leaves the company. The term is used in pension, vacation pay, and sick pay situations./12

Weighted average number of common shares outstanding In an EPS computation, this is the denominator amount used if the capital structure is simple; if the capital structure is complex, it is the denominator used to compute basic EPS./10

With recourse When an account or note receivable is factored or sold by a company, "with recourse" means that the buyer or factor can look to the company if the individual owing the amount defaults (i.e., the buyer or factor has recourse to the company, and the company bears the risk of default)./9

Without recourse When an account or note receivable is factored or sold by a company, "without recourse" means that the buyer or factor cannot look to the company if the individual owing the amount defaults (i.e., the buyer or factor has no recourse to the company, and the buyer or factor bears the risk of default)./9

Working capital Current assets minus current liabilities./1

Working capital ratio Current assets divided by current liabilities./1

Yield (Yield-to-maturity) *See* **effective interest rate.**

Index